DEVELOPMENT ECONOMICS

Following the 2007–2009 financial and economic crises, there has been an unprecedented demand among economics students for an alternative approach, which offers a historical, institutional and multidisciplinary treatment of the discipline. Economic development lends itself ideally to meet this demand, yet most undergraduate textbooks do not reflect this.

This book will fill this gap, presenting all the core material needed to teach development economics in a one semester course, while also addressing the need for a new economics and offering flexibility to instructors. Rather than taking the typical approach of organizing by topic, the book uses theories and debates to guide its structure. This will allow students to see different perspectives on key development questions, and therefore to understand more fully the contested nature of many key areas of development economics.

The book can be used as a standalone textbook on development economics, or to accompany a more traditional text.

Shahrukh Rafi Khan is currently Research Associate at Mount Holyoke College, USA. He formerly served as executive director of the Sustainable Development Policy Institute, Islamabad. He has also formerly taught at the University of Utah and Vassar College and served as Copeland Fellow at Amherst College. He has published extensively in refereed journals and authored and edited numerous books. He has twice won The Akhtar Hameed Khan book prize and engaged in academic consulting for several international organizations.

ROUTLEDGE TEXTBOOKS IN DEVELOPMENT ECONOMICS

For more information about this series, please visit:
https://www.routledge.com/Routledge-Textbooks-in-Development-Economics/book-series/RTDE

DEVELOPMENT ECONOMICS

A Critical Introduction

Shahrukh Rafi Khan

Routledge
Taylor & Francis Group

LONDON AND NEW YORK

First published 2020
by Routledge
2 Park Square, Milton Park, Abingdon, Oxon OX14 4RN

and by Routledge
52 Vanderbilt Avenue, New York, NY 10017

Routledge is an imprint of the Taylor & Francis Group, an informa business

British Library Cataloguing-in-Publication Data
A catalogue record for this book is available from the British Library

Library of Congress Cataloging-in-Publication Data
A catalog record has been requested for this book

ISBN: 978-0-415-78735-2 (hbk)
ISBN: 978-0-415-78736-9 (pbk)
ISBN: 978-1-315-22603-3 (ebk)

Typeset in Times New Roman
by Swales & Willis, Exeter, Devon, UK

MIX
Paper from
responsible sources
FSC
www.fsc.org   FSC™ C013985

Printed in the United Kingdom
by Henry Ling Limited

To the bright, inquisitive and congenial students of Mount Holyoke College

CONTENTS

FIGURES

TABLES

PREFACE

Why another development economics textbook?

I suspect that most professors teaching development economics would like to "do it their own way". Yet being an academic imposes several demands on time so perhaps one settles. Like many, I selected a textbook that came closest to my view of the subject and supplemented it with readings. In my last pre-retirement semester, students in my development economics class asked me what my plans were for my retirement years. I mused that I might write a textbook in development economics among other things. I was surprised that this was met with applause. The thought persisted and so I used research time during the rest of the semester to write a textbook proposal. By the time summer was over, the proposal had been reviewed and accepted and I embarked on my first retirement academic project.

This proposed textbook seeks to address a growing demand among economics students for "new economics", following the 2007–2009 financial and economic crises. More specifically, this demand is for a historical, institutional and multidisciplinary treatment of economics. In addition, The Great Recession is viewed partly as a failure resulting from pursuing just one sterile approach to economics and there is therefore a demand for alternative approaches to enable a broader understanding of issues.

In development economics, these alternative approaches include the developmentalist, structuralist, dependency, neo-Marxist, political economy of development, institutional, neo-classical/neoliberal and new developmentalist approaches among others. The right of center neoclassical/neoliberal approach is referred to as mainstream in this textbook and the others that range from center to left of center as heterodox.

Development economics lends itself ideally to meet this demand for alternative approaches and yet many undergraduate textbooks continue with the old formulaic writing on "topics". As a researcher, student and teacher of development economics since 1973, I have struggled with the hegemony of a dominant approach. As a teacher, I have competed with the hegemony of structure imposed by conventional textbooks. This textbook is thus designed to address the growing demand of discontented students who want a new economics and also of heterodox teachers wanting to expose their students to alternative approaches and key debates in the field.

Most textbooks also do not systematically distinguish between theories of underdevelopment and theories of development. Yet all approaches have a theory of underdevelopment and development associated with them, even if implicit, and so these distinctions are clearly identified as the textbook progresses through the various approaches.

Conventional development economics textbooks are organized by topic, as indicated above. The topical breakdown seems artificial because that is not how thinking in the field has evolved. It also does not do justice to the topic linkages or the important debates on the topics. For example, the debates on foreign aid, foreign direct investment (FDI), agriculture and industry draw from the debates on dependency, structuralism, developmentalism, neo-Marxism and neoliberalism, and hence should emanate from these approaches.

Without an emphasis on alternative approaches the waters are often muddied and impart to students an inaccurate account of the contributions of different approaches. For example, industrial policy is a program for structural transformation proposed by centrist, eclectic and pragmatic new developmentalist scholars as an alternative to a neoliberal program of structural adjustment. They successfully showed using the inductive method (case studies) that the success of many high-performing East Asian economies represented the success of an industrial policy program rather than a market-driven approach that was being proffered as an explanation by neoliberal economists.

Neoliberal economists initially opposed industrial policy based on their non-interventionist ideology. Once the evidence of the success of industrial policy in East Asia became overwhelming, they conceded that it did play a role but nonetheless opposed industrial policy on the more pragmatic grounds that the governance required for effective industrial policy simply did not exist in most low and low middle income countries (L/LMICs).[1] The new developmentalist response was that the structural adjustment program with the vast and complex set of policies that it encapsulates is no less good government intensive. This is an important debate and the reason for providing this brief summary is that documenting such debates and allowing students to clearly see both sides for themselves enhances their understanding of development economics.

Yet most textbooks do not see fit to provide any space to such debates in their topical coverage of the subject. Further, they merge important distinctions. One textbook attributes the authorship of industrial policy to the World Bank. In fact, an ex-Chief Economist of the World Bank actually did try to appropriate industrial policy but suggested that its success is premised on being consistent with comparative advantage. However, industrial policy was designed to oppose the theory of comparative advantage by proposing the concept of dynamic comparative advantage as an alternative and showing how this could be created in industries that countries had reason to believe they should be specializing in e.g. for the technological learning they opted for. Thus the common approach is not only to neglect what is truly important to the subject, such as the important approaches from all political perspectives, but also to muddy the waters and undermine clarity.

This textbook will adopt a historical and history of development economics thought approach with an emphasis on how alternative approaches evolved right up to the current state of the debate.[2] This debating format should be more lively and interesting for students and also more true to the subject.

Conventional development economics addresses a series of topics, as indicated above, but do not get to the essence of what they view development economics to be and who it pertains to. As will be elaborated in Chapter 1, development economics in this textbook is about "catch-up growth". This is defined as the economic process that some L/LMICs undergo to converge to the per capita income levels of high income countries (HICs). Thus this textbook is about L/LMICs. This again distinguishes this textbook from others which often lump together countries as developed or developing. As indicated in Appendix Table 3.1, L/LMICs differ a great deal from middle and upper middle income countries (M/UMICs).

MICs are defined as those who have already gone through some measure of sustained catch-up growth and hence embarked on a convergence toward the per capita income levels of HICs. Attaining MIC status does not ensure a guaranteed path to HIC status. Development economists and other scholars have pointed to a "middle income trap" whereby MICs confront major challenges that can result in the momentum of catch-up growth slowing down or ceasing. These challenges are addressed in a brief chapter devoted to the middle income trap.

However, MICs have attained a level of prosperity whereby they have adequate resources to address the challenges of absolute poverty and inequality as evident from Appendix Table 3.1. It is the persistence of these twin problems in L/LMICs that the various approaches to development economics devote themselves.

Language is important and many use words like neoliberal but are unaware of its lineage or what exactly it stands for and how it differs from other approaches. The word paradigm is loosely used but with a limited understanding of what it is and how it differs from features, approaches, programs, initiatives and mechanisms. Scholars referred to the Post Washington Consensus as a paradigm even though it really represented an approach.

This textbook will start with establishing terminology in Part I that will be used throughout the textbook. For example, paradigms, approaches (perspectives), facets, programs, policies, initiatives, strategies, mechanisms are used by authors, but they mean different things in different contexts. It is important to define such terms based on the most accepted usage and then be consistent in usage throughout the textbook. Similarly, there are at least a dozen ways in which countries in various stages of development can be referred to and after identifying them one (income based) will be selected, justified and then consistently used. Another important introductory task will be mapping the alternative approaches and explaining where they fit into the political spectrum. For each approach the associated theory of development and underdevelopment will be identified as will the initiatives or programs proposed as a theory of development.

This textbook has four parts. Part I provides background, including a chapter on the key twin development problems of poverty and inequality, to set up the review of alternative approaches in Part II. Most importantly, it discusses methodology (Chapter 1) and how this plays into distinguishing the key alternative approaches. Most of the approaches discussed have a macro orientation, but micro poverty alleviation solutions or interventions are discussed in Chapter 4.

Part III explores some of the key topics on which the debates based on alternative approaches play out. These include foreign aid, foreign direct investment, agriculture and industry.[3] Part IV contains the concluding chapter that is based on the synthesis of the first three parts.

Separate chapters are not devoted to gender and the environment. Often this ghettoizes these important topics. Instead, gender issues are addressed as a cross-cutting theme throughout the textbook, with a special focus on it in the chapter on agriculture (Chapter 13).[4] The same is the case for the environment and sustainable development, although there is a special focus on sustainable agriculture and green industry in Chapters 13 and 14. Apart from gender and the environment, another recurring and related theme is social justice, which features prominently in the concluding chapter (Chapter 15). Finally, the difficulty of securing accurate data and consensus on evidence is another recurring theme.

This textbook emerged from teaching and researching this subject for decades. I would like to thank the students of Mount Holyoke College, where I taught for a dozen years, for their interest, inquisitiveness and supportiveness which made teaching them a pleasure and that is why this textbook is dedicated to them. Thanks also to Mount Holyoke College for continuing to provide me with research support in the capacity of a Research Associate. Thanks are due to Routledge for securing excellent comments from two anonymous referees and for keeping me informed throughout the efficient review process. Finally, thanks are due in particular to Emily Kindlysides, Laura Johnson, Natalie Thompson and Lisa Lavelle for their quick, helpful and supportive feedback, and to Kay Hawkins for excellent text editing.

Notes

1 For the 2019 fiscal year (July 1, 2018 to June 30, 2019), the World Bank defines low income economies as those with a Gross National Income (GNI) per capita of $995 or less in 2017; lower middle income economies are those with a GNI per capita between $996 and $3,895; upper middle income economies are those with a GNI per capita between $3,896 and $12,055; and high income economies are those with a GNI per capita of $12,056 or more, https://datahelpdesk.worldbank.org/knowledgebase/articles/906519-world-bank-country-and-lending-groups, consulted 1/15/2019. GNI is equivalent, barring statistical errors, to Gross Domestic Product (GDP). The latter is a measure of market production of goods and services and GNI is the income generated

from that production in a specified time and place. Refer to endnote 4 in Chapter 2 for more details.

2 In this regard it draws on my earlier work on the history of economic thought in development economics when reviewing the work of some pioneering contributors to the field (Khan, 2014).

3 A thriving service sector is built on the foundations of agriculture and industry, the two key sectors in the catch-up growth stage. As economies prosper, the share and nature of the service sector changes as it becomes larger and less informal (or more professionalized), but, even so, it continues to draw on agriculture and industry.

4 Refer to Beneria, Berik and Floro (2016) for a more indepth exposition of gender and development.

References

Benería, L., G. Berik and M. S. Floro 2016. *Gender, Development and Globalization* (New York: Routledge).

Khan, S. R. 2014. *A History of Development Economics Thought: Challenges and Counter-Challenges* (New York: Routledge).

PART I

Background

1

INTRODUCTION

Textbooks generally do not make the distinction between the terms development economics and economic development and, more importantly, between development economics and the much broader term, development. Furthermore, many mainstream economists even doubt the validity and relevance of a field called "development economics". A case is made in this introduction for development economics to be taught as a separate field in economics. This hinges importantly on the validity of an "alternative approaches" perspective adopted for this textbook.[1]

This introduction will start with a definition of development economics, what it is about and how it is distinct from economic development or development. Following that, a case against and for the field is briefly discussed. In making a case for development economics, it becomes necessary to take on additional tasks. It becomes necessary to distinguish paradigm and approaches (the term used in this textbook) and explore method in development economics. The latter task is necessary because doing so is an important way of distinguishing the mainstream neoclassical approach from alternative heterodox approaches.[2] Subsequently, some key terms and concepts that are central to distinguishing alternative approaches are identified.

The subject of study in this textbook is nation states and many terms have been used and are still used in the literature to refer to them. The different ways of referring to nations are reviewed and a case is made for an income-based reference that is neutral and yet still substantive. Having covered the necessary background, the alternative approaches are then introduced. Before the summary and conclusions, a section is devoted to differentiating approaches conceptually and in terms of the method utilized.

What is development economics?

Development economics is a reference to the field and its concern or subject matter is economic development.[3] Development economics is defined for this textbook as the structural transformation of an economy such that it yields economic growth or the *potential* for sustained well-being or prosperity for the society in question (see below). Economic growth is defined as the percentage increase in per capita gross national product (GNP) or gross domestic product (GDP) over a specified time period.[4]

One important classification of countries is based on the level of real per capita GDP attained (see others below).[5] Low and low middle income countries (L/LMICs) are the focus of attention in this textbook. As indicated in the preface, middle income countries (MICs) are viewed as those that have already attained phases of catch-up growth and face a different set of challenges i.e. to sustain growth and not regress. Catch-up happens when income levels of L/LMICs start to converge with HICs (high income countries). This happens if they can sustain per capita GDP growth rates of 7 percent or more for several decades, and countries in this category, such as China and more recently India, are viewed as being part of the convergence club. Most LICs diverge from HICs average income levels and are part of the much larger divergence club.[6]

Catch-up or convergence occurs from high economic growth lasting several decades because it can lead to a several fold doubling of per capita GDP.[7] Compounding and "the rule of 72" explain this. Take the growth of any variable, in this case the per capita gross domestic product (PCGDP) and divide it into 72, and this explains how long it would take the variable to double. Thus, if the per capita GDP is growing at 7 percent, it doubles in about 10 years. If it grows at an average of 10 percent, it takes only about 7 years for the doubling. This is how convergence to the income level of HICs can happen due to catch-up growth in economies that start with a low base. China started as a LIC in the late 1970s and due to several decades of over 10 percent average PCGDP growth rate, it is now ranked comfortably in the middle income category.[8]

Of course, once economies catch up with global leaders, a slow-down, as witnessed in China, is inevitable since the relatively easy part of structural transformation, such as for example organizing and managing the economy to build the requisite infrastructure or for attaining the first phase of industrialization, has been completed.[9] This is why mature economies like the United States are unlikely to clock very high growth rates, and growth rates of up to 4 percent are considered exceptional. Attaining such a growth rate would require widely diffused technological innovations that enhance labor productivity. This is difficult to attain for mature economies that are the technological leaders and on the cutting edge while countries attempting catch-up growth already have a set of "on the shelf" technologies they can get access to.

The word potential was deliberately used and italicized in the definition of economic development above because while with catch-up growth the potential may be there to yield sustained well-being for all, in practice the fruits of economic development may remain concentrated among the wealthy in society who have the political power to appropriate the gains of economic growth. Sensitivity to this aspect of economic development is wide-ranging across the different approaches, but it has been especially highlighted by the political economy of development approach.

Alternative approaches privilege different mechanisms for and different kinds of structural transformation that can yield catch-up growth. The social, political and ecological impacts of economic growth may undermine sustained prosperity even if it is well distributed. In this regard, economic development needs to be distinguished from political, social or human, ecological and other forms of development which contribute to ensuring diffused and sustained well-being. This multi-dimensionality is captured by the terms development or sustainable development.[10] Before turning to a review of key concepts for identifying approaches and the methods they utilize, a case needs to be made for the existence of development economics as a separate field in economics.

Is "development economics" really a field?

Case against

The case against development economics being taught as a separate field from the vantage point of mainstream or neoclassical economics is as follows: The use of the scientific method (see below) generates hypotheses which, if not falsified, apply across the board to all human behavior. Since "economistic" human behavior is viewed by mainstream economists to be universally the same (utility and profit maximization in consumption and production respectively), the same economics should apply across the board. The focus should be on the optimal allocation of resources and hence efficiency as evident from theories of consumer and producer behavior.

Another possible criticism in a similar vein is that development economics is at best a conglomeration of topics that represent the application of insights from different fields in mainstream economics to the problems of L/LMICs, and as such there is no justification for economic development as a separate field i.e. it is not a field like monetary economics or international trade that has coherence and its own internal logic.

Case for: different initial and current conditions in L/LMICs

L/LMICs faced vastly different initial conditions including colonialism. Further, they face very different current conditions. Chapter 3 documents the commonalities across L/LMICs and also key differences. There are also other common structural conditions pertaining to L/LMIC economies that heterodox approaches argue result in the limited relevance of the direct application of the neoclassical or Keynesian models to redress their economic development problems.

Some of these structural commonalities identified in particular by developmentalists and structuralists (see below) are market segmentation and dualism; endemic market failures; missing markets; asymmetrical or missing information; high risk and uncertainty due to missing information paralyzing economic activity; threshold effects (possibilities of multiple equilibrium); bottlenecks resulting from poor infrastructure as a major source of supply rigidities; labor market failures and various kinds of unemployment; and endemic product market failures. These approaches argue that these structural commonalities require a different kind of theorization.

While there may be validity to this contention, mainstream economists may also validly argue that their method and tools are flexible enough to model and theorize for different initial and current conditions. Heterodox scholars however argue that even if this is the case there are nonetheless serious limitations to mainstream economics, and a case for heterodox approaches emerges from the debate on method, discussed next.

Paradigms, approaches and method in development economics

The word approach has been deliberately used since it may come as close as the social sciences get to a paradigm as framed by Kuhn (1962).[11] Using this framework, economists who speak the same language, share common values and beliefs, ask similar research questions, utilize the same tool kit and have a consensus on the body of tested or secure knowledge can be viewed as operating within the same "paradigm". One can think of paradigm broadly as a world view that in economics is driven by ideology.

Socialists have a world view that rejects private ownership of the means of production (like land and capital) because by virtue of private ownership and market transactions, capital, they believe, exploits labor. In principle they support a planned economy to avoid such exploitation and ensure basic needs are met for all. Capitalists have an alternative world view that privileges individual liberty, and in their view private ownership of the means of production and market transactions ensure this and also ensure efficiency.[12]

The use of the term paradigm by Kuhn was used to show how a scientific revolution (paradigm change) can occur within a community of scientists. The scientific method is commonly accepted as the way of shaking the consensus of secure knowledge and the move to a new paradigm. As will be made clear below, the application of this methodological practice in economics is challenged on several grounds. Furthermore, even if that were not an issue, heterodox scholars are not persuaded that the mainstream approach is adequate to capture the multi-dimensional complexity that economic development represents.

Following on from this, as indicated earlier, method encapsulates many ways in which the mainstream approach differs from the heterodox approaches and so it has been elaborated on in some detail. As alluded to earlier, mainstream economists, including mainstream practitioners of development economics, purport to use the scientific or deductive method and practice positive economics (free of value judgments). For example, mainstream practitioners of such positive economics argue that their concern is only with testing hypotheses, such as whether a carbon tax would reduce carbon emissions and by how much, and not with advocating whether or not such a tax per se should be imposed. The latter position they believe to be a normative one and beyond the realm of science.

Thus the scientific method is used for theorizing in mainstream economics. Theorizing involves logically identifying the causal relationship between key economic variables like prices and quantities while abstracting from others not likely to have a bearing on the association. Most fields in mainstream economics, including development economics, utilize various branches of mathematics for this logical reasoning in their theorizing by utilizing economic models.

Since economics is a social science, theorizing by utilizing economic models starts with postulates pertaining to how humans behave. For example, in mainstream economics a key postulate in the theory of consumer behavior is that humans are driven to maximize their utility (broadly well-being) while a parallel postulate in the theory of producer behavior is that business are driven to maximize their profits. Assumptions contextualize the economic model. For example, a model developed to predict internal migration may start by assuming no links with the outside world (closed economy model) but may subsequently relax this assumption. Models that use fewer and less restrictive (more realistic) assumptions to make similar predictions are considered theoretically superior to those making more and more restrictive assumptions.

Following Popper (1992), a central tenant of the scientific method is adding to the body of knowledge within a field by using falsification. The theorizing utilizing economic models gains validity by leading to testable hypotheses or predictions. A theory is only considered one if it leads to testable hypotheses. The non-falsification of the prediction and replication then adds to the body of secure knowledge within a field or to theories that form the core of a field.[13]

An example from introductory microeconomics can be used to elucidate the scientific method.[14] Start with the postulate that individuals are rational (in economics terminology this means individuals are capable of making choices to maximize their own well-being). To contextualize the model, assume average household tastes and income and other relevant variables are held constant for the period in question. Thus whatever conclusion is derived can only hold for the period of time in question, referred to in economics as the short run. Obviously, in the long run, income and tastes cannot be assumed to be constant. This process of "holding other things constant" is referred to as *ceteris paribus*, and it enables a theoretical and quantitative focus on the main association of interest.

Based on rationality and some additional postulates and fairly advanced mathematical techniques, the hypothesis that quantity demanded varies inversely with the price of a product is derived i.e. the prediction is that when prices rise, the quantity demanded will fall. This seems quite self-evident, but microeconomists use mathematics to derive this causal association. This prediction can be tested and if it is not refuted, the postulate of rationality and other associated postulates and the prediction about the inverse association of prices and quantities are not falsified. Rationality and other postulates can only be indirectly tested since only the choices made (such as purchase decisions) can be observed.

To summarize, within an approach, there are many theories such as demand theory in neoclassical microeconomics and product/income determination in macroeconomics. Economic models are utilized to theorize and add to the body of secure knowledge on a particular theory within a particular field. This is the method utilized by mainstream or neoclassical economists, including those working in the development economics field, and their contention is that they practice positive science and in this regard view other approaches as ad hoc or non-scientific.[15]

The common criticisms against the possibility of engaging in positive science are that values and biases creep into the work of social scientists in many ways. First, biases are revealed in the particular choice of subjects chosen by any particular researcher. Second, as indicated, theorizing requires the use of postulates about how humans behave (starting from first principles) and researcher preferences may determine the choice of postulates. Third, theorizing is premised on assumptions and theorists may pick the assumptions to get the predictions they seek. Fourth, economics is a social rather than an exact science, and biases may color research findings. Thus, if findings are consistent with what researchers want to demonstrate, they may stop the research whereas they may continue the scrutiny if that is not the case.[16] Finally, consensus on a theory may develop due to ideology and dominance rather than evidence.

The last point needs elaborating on. What ultimately matters in science as indicated when discussing the scientific method above, is consensus. If there is consensus on a theory then it becomes part of secure knowledge in a field and enters into textbooks at all levels. Thus most economists believe that there is consensus on the theory of comparative advantage in international trade, a theory also important in development economics and hence discussed in several chapters of this textbook.

This theory is taught as established knowledge (that has not been falsified) in introductory, international trade and development economics textbooks across the world with virtually no qualifications. Heterodox economists have challenged this theory based on its assumptions and predictions, but this matters little. Generations of economics students across the world view it as secure knowledge, and if they become professional economists seeking positions in academia they know better than to challenge it. The guardians of mainstream journals and economics departments weed out heretics as students, faculty and scholars.[17] Ultimately, it is ideology that is protecting the "truth" in a social science rather than the scientific method.

Mainstream economists could find a defense against these criticisms should they be willing to engage. Postulates like rationality have even been challenged by behavioral economists, other social scientists, psychologists in particular, but economists can argue that if their predictions hold then that suggests that average human behavior does not suggest a falsification of these postulates. They can argue that over a period of time, via rigorous peer reviewing in the profession, theories improve and the more restrictive assumptions are dropped.[18] This process it could be argued is also a cure for shoddy empirics as the profession moves to more advanced empirical methods and more rigorous criteria to demonstrate the robustness of findings.

Notwithstanding this defense, practitioners of alternative approaches have other grounds on which they challenge the limitations of mainstream economics as applied to studying economic development. In an economic development context, the micro branch of mainstream economics focuses on the efficient allocation of resources. Optimal outcomes (economic growth) result from removing distortions hindering the market mechanisms from inducing such an allocation. In an economic development context, the macro branch views fiscal consolidation (more balanced budgets) and price stability (fighting inflation) of key importance to attaining economic growth.

The new developmentalist approach (see below) challenges the notion that static efficiency and economic stability are necessarily associated with a high growth trajectory. Let us take an extreme example to explain the first aspect of this contention. Suppose a very inefficient economy at time t1 (2020) removes the most egregious distortions by privatizing, deregulating and liberalizing i.e. it follows mainstream economics recommendations and approximately attains marginal conditions identified in introductory and intermediate economics textbooks. Suppose also that even in a second best world this helps.[19] In the best case scenario there would be a one-time boost to output and hence economic growth in the time period relevant for measurement (let us say 2021–2022). However, once efficiency conditions have been attained, they will not add to future economic growth beyond 2022.

New developmentalists argue that economic development is about more than static efficiency conditions that yield a one-time boost to economic growth. Instead they argue that economic development is about structural transformation that unleashes society's productive potential for catch-up growth. The second part of the contention above (i.e. the importance of macroeconomic stability) is challenged using empirical evidence (Chapter 9).

Heterodox approaches to development economics are not necessarily wedded to positive economics and some have no qualms about being normative in terms of their concerns. The left of center approaches are mostly concerned with attaining social justice. They also contend that the theories endorsing the efficient allocation of resources take as a given the existing institutional and social structures. Various heterodox approaches argue that changing institutions and structures is what development economics is really about i.e. they argue that mainstream economics misses out on what really matters.

Heterodox approaches also view mainstream economics to be highly reductionist i.e. everything gets boiled down to seeing the world in terms of economic agents – consumers and producers – or variables like preferences (consumption) and technology (production), and once again this misses out on the essence of economic development. Heterodox approaches therefore include a focus on history, institutions and structures in their treatment of the field.

A large part of development economics is about policy and hence the subject takes intervention for granted. However, intervention is anathema to mainstream purists who believe that the market, if allowed to work, would solve most economic and possibly social problems. Further, even if the market fails to deliver what is needed, governments by their very nature are inefficient and corrupt, and government failure is worse than market failure. Thus, countries are better off with small and non-interventionist governments. This debate, covered in Part II of this textbook, acquires much more urgency for LICs because of the extent of mass poverty they experience.

Heterodox approaches draw much more than any other field of economics on other disciplines – thus their method is multi- and inter-disciplinary. Multi is a reference to the different insights on a particular topic emanating from the different social sciences, while inter is a reference to the insights emerging from the joint work of social scientists of different disciplines on a particular issue. Many societal changes accompany economic development. For example, one could draw on the insights of historians studying post-colonial societies; sociologists and social and cultural anthropologists studying cultural change and social alienation; urban studies experts studying urban blight; ecologists studying environmental degradation; and political scientists studying governance.

The method used by heterodox economists is often inductive (descriptive and historical) and so the focus for the broad story (how nations develop) is on case studies. They generalize from particular case studies that may have broader relevance (particular to the general). For example, scholars may study Japanese or Korean economic development and infer lessons from that for broader application. By contrast, mainstream economists generalize based on the hypothesis testing that emerges from economic models (general to the particular) as explained above. However, many heterodox economists do not rule out the use of the deductive method for garnering evidence in specific contexts (e.g. impact of specific tariffs on specific imports).

By its very nature, mainstream development economics often has a micro focus and students emerging from graduate schools often focus on details. For example, they may address questions such as by how much will treated bed nets reduce the incidence of malaria, or what quantitative impact teacher absenteeism has on student cognitive skills, or what quantitative impact cash transfers have on child stunting. While these are worthy questions and very important in specific contexts, heterodox economists focus on the larger issues such as the exploitive nature of trade and foreign investment that LICs confront.

To summarize, issues in development economics remain unresolved and differences in propositions of alternative approaches on the same issues, such as the benefits from trade, persist. There is little acceptance of the falsification that is done by any of the approaches, the central tenet of the scientific method. Even if scholars utilized the same deductive method, they challenge findings from another approach based on the data, assumptions, or empirical technique utilized. If these pass muster, the interpretation may be questioned. Also, strategies like structural adjustment or industrial policy are multi-faceted and do not easily lend themselves to falsification.[20]

Ultimately, scholars are likely to hold onto their world views driven by their ideology, and hence there is little communication and convincing across the different approaches based on statistical analysis even if it is defensible. The perspective adopted in this textbook is that all the approaches have important insights to contribute and therefore they should all be studied. Before introducing these approaches, some terms and concepts central to the understanding of these approaches are reviewed.

Terms and concepts central to identifying alternative approaches

Structural change and structural transformation

One definition of structural transformation entails putting systems in place for sustained indigenous technological learning and industrialization. These ideas (introduced below) were propagated by the pioneering development economists in the 1940s and 1950s. Structural change and structural transformation are often used interchangeably.[21] Structural change is measurable and the most frequent reference to structural change in development economics pertains to the alteration in the relative size of the various sectors of the economy over time.[22]

Development economists view the economy as composed of three main sectors (primary, secondary and tertiary), and this is one way of sub-dividing GDP (gross domestic product). The defining feature of the primary sector is that it makes direct use of natural resources and so would include agriculture, forestry, fishing and mining. The secondary sector (industry) includes manufacturing as the largest component, but public utilities and construction are also normally considered a part of industry. The tertiary sector produces services and is thus referred to as the service sector (banking and finance, education, entertainment, health, legal and other professions, etc.). One way of defining and measuring structural change then is to estimate how the sector sizes vary as a percentage of GDP over time.

A team of economists led by Chenery et al. (1986) found that such a process was underway in many LICs in the 1960s and 1970s. Chenery and his associates referred to such changes, evident in the data, as "stylized facts". These changes are therefore expected to be autonomous and driven by social and market forces such as rural to urban migration. One such stylized fact is the increasing share of industry as a percentage of GDP as a country prospers and moves from low to middle income status.

However, structural changes could also be policy induced. A policy of deliberately privileging the growth of one sector relative to others can be defined as structural transformation i.e. deliberately induced structural change. For the pioneering development economists, industry was required to be privileged for various reasons, mentioned below. However, if industry could be encouraged using policy mechanisms, then that could also be done for other sectors and so in principle more than one kind of structural transformation is possible.

Another way of viewing economic sectors is based on the extent to which they are formal or informal. Here structural change could be defined as the shrinking of the informal sector of the economy relative to the formal sector. Once again, this could be an autonomous process accompanying economic development or it could be policy induced or both. A component of each sector is marked by informality, and as societies prosper, the extent of informality generally shrinks. Informality refers to the part of each economic sector that is beyond the purview of legislation, regulation or taxation. The reason is simply the inability of an L/LMIC to impose their administrative writ across the board to the millions of self-employed engaged in petty trade and retail. As governance mechanisms and administrative ability improves, another form of structural transformation could be a policy-induced formalization of economic activity.

Institutional and structural change

Definitions of institutions vary, but the one adopted here draws on North (2005). Institutions are understood to mean formal rules or law (constitutions, management procedures, faculty legislation) or informal modes of behavior or constraints (norms, convention, codes of conduct or custom).[23] The formal or informal rules can be embodied in organizations sometimes referred to as the players or implementers. Organizations can be thought of as groups that broadly have the same mission and are governed by specified rules. In this view, a college can be thought of as an organization and the faculty legislation governing it as the institution.

Institutions central to economic development include rules governing ownership patterns and production systems, and norms embodied in culture, religion and other traditions that influence economic activity. Institutional change can lead to structural change and vice versa. For example, privatization (change in ownership rights) represents an institutional change, and if it contributes to greater productivity by giving reign to private incentives, it might lead to an increase in the size of the manufacturing sector and hence structural change. Public sector administrative reforms (rules governing production) that lead to greater productivity could have the same effect.

Another example is land redistribution (change in ownership rights) resulting in structural change if small farm owner cultivation leads to higher labor and land productivity. In this case, the share of agriculture as a percentage of GDP would increase. However, the increase in agricultural output might also boost industry and services as the market size expands, and this indicates the complexity and inter-relatedness that characterizes economics in general and development economics in particular.

Structural change or transformation could also result in institutional change. Pressure points can emerge from structural change that requires institutional change. For example, environmental safeguards may be required as industry expands. China noted the need for sustainable development in the 16th National Congress of the Communist Party.[24] Three and a half decades of catch-up growth that centered on industrial expansion devastated the country environmentally and

China introduced legislation to address the problem. For example, its automobile fuel economy standards introduced in 2004 were the third most stringent in the world (more stringent than the US standards).[25]

The structural change accompanying economic growth can result in institutional change such as a change in family structure, with nuclear families becoming more predominant than extended families as labor mobility to pursue economic opportunities becomes more common. Societal norms and traditions can become more secular, although the social need to seek comfort from the harsh realities of rural-urban migration might reinforce and entrench conservative religious ideologies in some countries. Once again, social responses are complex and context specific.

The context is generally a specific nation, or region within a nation, as nations are often the unit of observation and analysis in development economics.[26]

Since classical political economists implicitly started writing about economic development (Chapter 5), there have been over a dozen ways in which nations have been referred to. Times have changed and with that the terms of reference have also changed. The main ways in which nations have been referred to in development economics is reviewed next and a case made for picking the income-based one that seems most suitable.

Terms of reference to nation states in development economics

Nations have been referred to in terms of the per capita income (LIC/MIC/HIC), as an indicator of the overall level of prosperity attained. This may also reflect their potential to attain a higher level of well-being for most and for low poverty rates, although reversals of prosperity are certainly possible as evident from the cases of Venezuela (2008) and Zimbabwe (2002).[27] The adoption of this variable to classify nations is relatively recent.

The classification used by classical political economists writing in the 19th century was improved / progressive and barbarous / backward. The colonizing nations were improved and likely to attain a progressive state while the other category applied to the rest. When referring to independent nations, at least the most pejorative terms fell out of use. Following World War II, First, Second and Third World came into use. Most of the current HICs constituted the First World, ex-socialist countries the Second World, and many of the current L/LMICs constituted the Third World. After the end of the Cold War, the ex-socialist economies started transitioning toward market economies, (referred to as transitional economies), and this propelled the move away from this post World War II classification.

Prior to the adoption of the per capita income variable to classify nations, several other classifications were used, but most were either pejorative, or incomplete and inaccurate. For example, Poor and Rich is a classification still in use. The classification is one-dimensional and income poor nations could be culturally rich and it ignores the middle category. Developed and underdeveloped, advanced and backward have similar shortcomings.

Developed is a value judgment and economic development might not be accompanied by cultural, social, political and institutional development from some perspectives.[28] Bhutan may not be considered developed but it does well on the Happiness Index that it devised. The use of developing instead of underdeveloped is more politically correct but could be inaccurate since the country in question could be regressing and this is often the case of countries experiencing conflict (conflict economies). Less and more developed is vague since again this makes no reference to what aspect of development the classification refers to.

More recent classifications avoid pitfalls of earlier ones but can still be confusing and inaccurate. North and South (sometimes Global North and Global South though the term global seems redundant) is often used in an international political economy context. However, some have pointed out that geographically the South includes Australia, New Zealand and the Southern cone in Latin America, and all are much more prosperous than most LICs.

Less industrialized and more industrialized economies (sometimes referred to as AIE (advanced industrialized economies) or IMEs (industrialized market economies)) says little about the quality of industrialization i.e. the nature of the technology intensity of the process. Also, many L/LMICs now have a share of industry in GDP higher than high-income economies that have moved on to high value services.[29] Thus the latter are sometimes referred to as post-industrialized economies, which is also inaccurate since a transformed industry is still part of these economies.

Heterodox economists use their own binary classification based on power asymmetry. Due to this uneven power, the more powerful countries are referred to as the core, center and metropolis while the weaker and exploited countries are referred to as the periphery or satellites. Structuralists use the core/center–periphery classification while dependency theorists use the metropolis–satellite classification (Chapter 7).

Most classifications above, including the heterodox ones, leave out the middle category though some classifications only refer to the amorphous middle group. For example, Newly Industrialized Countries (NICs) is one such group. Following on from this, some now refer to "emerging markets", although countries have more to them than just a market. Some in this group have the distinction of being in a phase of catch-up growth and hence converging toward the per capita income levels of the HICs, while the rest are in the divergence group or club.

Another country reference is to failed, failing and fragile states (FFF), or some combination thereof (Reinert, Amaïzo and Kattel, 2011). There is also a reference to post-conflict states. Much of the attention in the literature in this context is to institution building, governance and appropriate use of aid. Countries have the ability to find triggers (Chapter 15) to galvanize a move beyond the status that conflict or other disasters embroil them in, and Ethiopia (2003) and Rwanda (1999) are cases in point.[30] The problems of such states may in general require separate treatment (Carment and Yiagadeesen, 2017).

The per capita income variable has been adopted for country classification in this textbook.[31] The first use of this classification in the development economics literature appears to be Nurkse (1967), a pioneering developmentalist (Chapter 5). It has several advantages not least of which is that it is neutral. Since this textbook focuses on economic development, income is among the most important measurement variables. It also has the advantage of allowing for many gradations such as low, low-middle, middle, high middle and high, and more if necessary and meaningful. Finally, the statistics department of several multilateral organizations collect and report information on this variable.

The data collected and reported by the World Bank Statistics Department in *The World Development Indicators* (online edition) is used in this textbook. These are readily available and annually updated with an adjustment for inflation. The specific thresholds are arbitrary and can be quibbled with, especially for countries near the cut-offs, but they are based on the best judgments of a large team of economists about income levels that reflect a certain level of prosperity for the populations of the countries in question. The World Bank's list of countries classified as LIC and LMIC based on per capita gross national income for 2017 are reported in Table 1.1.

For those not concerned specifically with economic development but with development more broadly, the UNDP (United Nations Development Program) country classifications based on human development are more meaningful. In this case per capita GNP is one of four variables in a composite index (including education and health) that seeks to measure overall well-being (Chapter 3). The common characteristics of country groupings and also the limits to generalization are also discussed in Chapter 3. The alternative approaches to understanding economic development that are covered in Part II, and that drive Parts III and IV, are introduced next.

Alternative approaches

Documentation pertaining to these approaches is deferred to the individual chapters exploring them in Part II. As will become clear from the chapters in Part II, there are overlaps in the various approaches. However, each has a particular focus and hence policy prescriptions that emerge from them. All the approaches introduced below are covered by individual chapters except for the basic human needs / human development and political economy of development approaches. The basic human needs / human development approach is discussed as a poverty alleviation initiative in Chapter 4. The political economy of development approach is viewed as a method of analysis and as such is cross-cutting, as are the gender and environment themes and are referred to in context throughout the textbook.

Neoclassical economics and neoliberalism

Mainstream or neoclassical economics has already been summarized above as the dominant approach, and its manifestation in development economics is often referred to as neoliberalism. The latter is an ideological perspective but draws on

TABLE 1.1 List of low and low middle income countries

Low income ($995 or less)	Low middle income ($996 to $3,895)
Afghanistan	Angola
Benin	Bangladesh
Burkina Faso	Bhutan
Burundi	Bolivia
Central African Republic	Cape Verde
Chad	Cambodia
Comoros	Cameroon
Congo, Democratic Republic	Congo, Republic
Eritrea	Côte d'Ivoire
Ethiopia	Djibouti
Gambia, The	Egypt Arab Republic
Guinea	El Salvador
Guinea-Bissau	Georgia
Haiti	Ghana
Korea, Democratic Peoples Republic	Honduras
Liberia	India
Madagascar	Indonesia
Malawi	Kenya
Mali	Kiribati
Mozambique	Kosovo
Nepal	Kyrgyz Republic
Niger	Lao, PDR
Rwanda	Lesotho
Senegal	Mauritania
Sierra-Leone	Micronesia, Federated States of
Somalia	Moldova
South Sudan	Mongolia
Syrian Arab Republic	Morocco
Tajikistan	Myanmar
Tanzania	Nicaragua
Togo	Nigeria
Uganda	Pakistan
Yemen, Republic	Papua New Guinea
Zimbabwe	Philippines
	Sâo Tomé and Principe
	Solomon Islands

Low income ($995 or less)	Low middle income ($996 to $3,895)
	Sri Lanka
	Sudan
	Swaziland
	Timor-Leste
	Tunisia
	Ukraine
	Uzbekistan
	Vanuatu
	Vietnam
	West Bank and Gaza
	Zambia

Sources: https://datahelpdesk.worldbank.org/knowledgebase/articles/906519-world bank-country-and-lending-groups, consulted 1/15/2019

Notes: The classification in the table is for the 2019 fiscal year (July 1, 2018 to June 30, 2019).

neoclassical economics as its analytical framework and in this regard the focus is on efficiency associated with the optimum allocation of scarce resources and macroeconomic stability. In a nutshell privatization, liberalization and deregulation represent the microeconomic program and liberalization of macro prices (interest and exchange rate); fiscal consolidation (budget cutting for balanced budgets, also referred to as austerity) and monetary restraint (for price stability) represent the macroeconomic program.

Since the 1990s, the World Bank has been expressing sensitivity to the criticisms of heterodox approaches and has extended its programs or paid lip service (according to some civil society critics) to incorporate issues like poverty, gender and the environment. More recently, the IMF seems to have become a "revisionist". Prominent IMF economists expressed qualified reservations concerning capital market liberalizations[32] and suggested support for a fiscal stimulus to overcome the 2007–2008 financial crisis.[33] IMF economists (Ostry, Loungani, and Furceri, 2016) argued that the benefits of elements of neoliberalism (fiscal consolidation and capital market liberalization) have been overplayed and the costs (low growth, unemployment, inequality) understated.

A willingness to accept criticism and change is welcome, even if credit is often not accorded to the critics. However, whether this rethinking has really changed the core World Bank / IMF neoliberal program imposed on countries needing balance of payment or fiscal support is an empirical issue that is explored later in this textbook. Also explored is the issue of whether the program is imposed or home grown as the IMF claims it is.[34]

Developmentalism

Neoclassical economics, with its focus on the optimal allocation of resources and efficiency, was well established after the marginal revolution in the latter part of the 19th century and was the default option for economists' thinking about problems of low income countries newly gaining independence in the 1940s, 1950s and 1960s. However, classical economics, with its focus on production, distribution, economic growth and the wealth of nations, continued to be taught, and it was this tradition that inspired the pioneering development economists as they turned their attention to the economic development of newly formed nation states. The concern with economic development resulted in the reference to this approach as "developmentalism" and its advocates as developmentalists.

During the inception of development economics in the 1940s and 1950s, the pioneering development economists were concerned about economic growth as an outcome of the policies they recommended.[35] Their explorations addressed the question of what would structurally transform societies and produce economic growth. They touched on many issues including those that are now referred to as institutional change (discussed above), better governance and building human capital (education and health). However, industrialization was a central concern.

These economists were students of history and believed that societies that prospered in the past went through an industrial revolution and so such structural transformation would be essential to attain prosperity. More important, they believed that industry was associated with technological learning and so sustained indigenous and endogenous technological learning could be identified as the core to the process of structural transformation for economic development.[36]

Notwithstanding the privileging of industry, the development economics pioneers pointed out that the sectors were complementary and needed to reinforce each other, and therefore an industrial revolution and accompanying technological learning would be held back without accompanying structural transformation in other sectors. Thus, for example, Lewis (Chapter 6), probably the most influential development economist to date, pointed to the importance of a complementary agricultural transformation if industrialization was to succeed. A more productive agriculture, he argued, would release labor for industry, provide a market for industrial goods and provide cheaper food and raw materials, much as Malthus (Chapter 5) had earlier pointed out.

Structuralism

Developmentalists are sometimes referred to as structural economists given their focus on structural transformation based on industrialization. Structural economists share with developmentalists a concern for the domestic constraints regarding a theory of underdevelopment. For both, underdevelopment is attributed to structural factors such as bottlenecks, rigidities and market failures. However, Latin structuralists also focused on external factors to explain underdevelopment. In this regard, underdevelopment was explained by uneven power between core (HICs) and periphery (LICs) nations and this manifested itself in an imbalance of leverage and bargaining power. Trade, investment and capital flows should be mechanisms for mutual benefit, but in relations between the core and periphery they became the mechanisms for transferring surplus from the periphery to the core. The theory of development was again similar to that of the developmentalists in that they advocated for a focus on technology and industrialization for catch-up growth.

Dependency

Dependency theory built on structuralist ideas for their theory of underdevelopment. The approach is more historical in that the roots of underdevelopment are based on the colonial encounters of L/LMICs with HICs. While administrative control ensured the extraction of surplus during colonialism, the mechanisms become more subtle during the post-colonial era. Since, in their view, relations with HICs were doomed to perpetuate underdevelopment in LICs, breaking off links with HICs and embarking on an autonomous industrialization drive was their theory of development.

Neo-Marxists / political economy of development

Dependency scholars were criticized for ignoring class in their analysis. For neo-Marxists, as with Marx, the extraction of surplus is a class phenomenon and so for them class analysis needs to be central even when exploring relations between nations. If HICs manage to extract surplus, how do class alignments in LICs play out to enable this to happen? For neo-Marxists, the theory of development would unfold from social movements that would end social exploitation by changing the rules of the game i.e. establish state control over the means of production.

This approach, like neoliberalism, is overtly rather than implicitly ideological. It is considered the most radical approach and the most extreme version would advocate eliminating class and other forms of exploitation to promote social justice. An extreme agenda would be to promote class equality, but more moderate political economists argue social justice represents the equality of opportunity and not necessarily an equality of outcomes.

The social mechanism, from a Marxian perspective, would include social revolution, including violence if necessary to overthrow the guardians of the existing system who use organized state violence (police, intelligence agencies and the military) to oppress and exploit the working classes. The more moderate radical approaches support social movements to attain a more just society. The specific mechanisms they endorse would be to politically win state power through elections to ensure a fair distribution of assets like land and credit and to ensure fair and equal access to the same quality of education and health and effective safety nets. The problem is not the lack of wealth or the ability to create it but its concentration in a few hands and hence the inability of the masses to attain their productive potential.

The method of analyzing policy within a capitalist market economy in the political economy of development approach is identifying who wins and who loses, and by how much by social group as a result of particular policies. This is often the approach used to show that specific neoliberal policy initiatives such as trade liberalization hurt the poor, women and the environment.

Basic human needs / human development / gender and development

In the 1960s and 1970s, economic growth became a fetish and seemingly the exclusive concern of mainstream economists, much as is still true among many economists and policy makers in HICs. In this regard, the key message of the pioneering development economists was lost. Instead of a focus on the means (i.e. structural transformation), the focus was shifted to the ends (i.e. economic growth). The concern of mainstream economists with economic growth was unapologetic even if the means to attain it were different.

However, among socially concerned scholars studying LICs, this produced a reaction against "growthmanship" or "trickle-down" economics. The ILO and many scholars recognized that economic growth, even if it occurred, was often accompanied by social inequality and marginalization of the poor and hence an intensification of poverty rather than a trickle down of prosperity. The ILO (1977) in its *World Employment Report* made a case for a new approach that would put human needs and the creation of livelihoods central to development. This was a "trickle-up" approach because if human potential is realized by addressing human needs, broad-based labor productivity would be enhanced and economic growth would be an outcome.

Sen (1999) continued in this tradition of broadening the definition of development so that it was inclusive of the well-being and enhancement of freedoms and hence the productive potential of humans more broadly. A subsequent extension broadened the definition to be inclusive of environmental nurturing (sustainable development) for how humans could prosper if the environment they lived in was degrading. A concern with the environment is however in effect a concern for all species.

There were parallel and subsequent extensions of the concept of development to encompass the well-being of women who are generally the most deprived even among the poor and also in society across the whole. Thus human development, gender and development, and sustainable development emerged as sub-fields in the broader field of development.

New-developmentalism[37]

The reaction to developmentalism peaked in the 1970s based on various mainstream theoretical and empirical critiques. Starting in the early 1970s, neoliberalism became the dominant policy approach for L/MICs that has survived to this day, notwithstanding scathing and widespread critiques. However, while in the 1980s it seemed to be "the only game in town", by the 1990s this position of dominance was challenged by new developmentalists. This occurred because of over-reach by neoclassical / neoliberal economists in explaining why economies succeeded. More left of center approaches always challenged the mainstream but had limited adherents.

Economics is referred to as a "dismal science". In fact, as an LIC graduate student specializing in development economics in the 1970s, I felt the label really applied to development economics. This was because, notwithstanding the theoretical optimism of the developmentalists, in practice there seemed little hope of my seeing substantial economic development in my own country, or others like it, in my lifetime. Toward the end of my graduate career, hope had emerged.

Not only had Japan shown the way, but a group of East Asian "tiger" economies, collectively referred to as NICs (Newly Industrialized Countries), had shown that catch-up growth was possible. I followed explanations for why and how this had happened with fascination. Mainstream economists argued that these economies attained catch-up growth by adhering to market principles and macroeconomic stability i.e. via liberalization, privatization and deregulation at the micro level and fiscal and price stability at the macro level.

Starting in the late 1980s and early 1990s, a group of social scientists including economists, both national and foreign, did painstaking case study research challenging the neoliberal story. They showed that the success of economies like Japan, Korea and Taiwan had more to do with the developmentalist story of state-led industrialization and structural transformation than the neoliberal story of liberalizations and economic openness following market principles. While these economists could be referred to as heterodox based on their research method, they did not label themselves as new developmentalists.

However, the label has gained modest traction in the literature.[38] While the differences of developmentalism and new developmentalism will be explored in detail in this textbook, some of the key ideas are presented here. For example, new developmentalists have both strengthened the case for industrialization and expressed reservations about it. A more recent argument in support of the industrial sector is that it lends itself to mass production, economies of scale and increasing returns' activities (Reinert, 2007). This is important because constant return to scale activities, which is how the non-industrial sectors are characterized, yield little surplus for reinvestment once factors are paid by comparison to increasing return activities.

This is why Chang (2011) viewed the above basic human needs / human development characterization of development as missing out on the essence of economic development or as he put it, "Hamlet without the Prince". He argued that development should be about transforming the economy in the sense of moving resources from low to high productivity, increasing returns' activities. Thus, new developmentalists' main focus is developing an indigenous and endogenous technological capacity to diversify the economy and enable it to move up the value chain.

Times change and lessons can be learnt from history. We now know that structural transformation is not without consequences. For example, industrial revolutions had severe environmental consequences that imposed harsh suffering, particularly on the poor who were more exposed to dirty air, water and soil from various forms of emissions. A replay of this story in China between 1978 and today (2019) and in India since the early 1990s has been even more dramatic (Chapter 4, endnote 31). Thus, there is a realization among some scholars that structural transformation advocated by new developmentalists should be based on clean production methods (Chapter 14). The issue of sustainable agriculture and green industrial policy are discussed in Chapters 14 and 15.

Institutional economics

Economists who consider institutions and institutional change as central to understanding the economy are referred to as institutional economists. For example, they view far-reaching institutional changes as vital to initiating economic development rather than say an efficient allocation of resources. Among the most important institutional changes would be the establishment of good government, sometimes referred to as good governance. This would require governance by "the rule of law" rather than arbitrary authority and the establishment of a relatively honest and efficient economic bureaucracy where transparency and accountability are the key features. To attain the latter they advocate civil service among other reforms.

Differentiating approaches

As explained above, the alternative approaches introduced in this chapter are distinct conceptually and also in the method they utilize. Some key distinguishing features are introduced below.

Concepts

Property rights are one of the key touchstones that distinguish schools of thought. For neoliberals, property rights are sacrosanct and this is hence a right of center approach. The more moderate and pragmatic perspectives in the other approaches like basic human needs / human development, gender and development, developmentalism / structuralism and new developmentalism respect property rights for the most part. However, they do not rule out some asset redistribution, such as land redistribution with compensation, to attain a win-win such as social justice and higher productivity.

Another key touchstone for distinguishing alternative approaches is the role of the market and the state.[39] The neoliberal approach relies on the market to deliver efficiency and growth. The implicit presumption of this approach is that if efficiency is attained, economic growth will follow, and once growth is attained, there will be enough resources to address human needs (Chapter 8). Critics charge that neither of the two links necessarily follows from each other i.e. economic growth may not follow from efficiency as explained above, and the satisfaction of human needs may not follow economic growth. Thus the other approaches, except for the extreme Marxist perspective, view the market as a mechanism that could be harnessed for social good, but the state is in the driving seat to institute the social and economic mechanisms that they view as central to economic development or development more broadly.

Finally, the theories of underdevelopment or development in the various approaches emphasize internal or external causal factors, or both, and this represents another way of distinguishing approaches. By way of example, consider how a couple of the approaches fit into this schema. In the neoliberal approach, the theory of underdevelopment suggests that internal factors are the proximate causes i.e. too much inefficient and heavy-handed state intervention resulting in a misallocation of resources. The theory of development is internal in so far as undoing this interventionism and opening up the economy to foreign trade, investment and capital flows is based on internal policy. The driving force in seeking external partners is the state in so far as creating the right conditions would cause a positive external response.

By contrast, the proximate causes in the theory of underdevelopment in the dependency approach are external. Extractive neocolonial forces using the mechanisms of foreign trade, aid and investment perpetuate underdevelopment. The theory of development requires a delinking from such extractive mechanism and instituting instead an internal technology and industrial dynamic for self-sustaining development.

Method

In the method section above, we explained how the alternative approaches arrive at knowledge in different ways. For example, one facet of economic openness, central to the neoliberal approach, is the endorsement of free trade and more specifically import liberalization and export promotion. The relevance and effectiveness of export promotion for example could be gleaned in different ways depending on the approach and hence the method utilized.

An economic model utilizing neoclassical economic tools could first establish the hypothesis that exports are associated with economic growth. The channels or mechanisms through which this happens could be independently modeled and tested. For example, it could be that export orientation results in the adoption of better technology because of the need to compete in international markets, or that competition itself induces greater efficiency, or that lower costs result from economies of scale that result from producing for a larger market, or all of the these in addition to other possible mechanisms. Once the modeling has been completed and the hypotheses are arrived at, they are then tested as part of the falsification process that is part of the scientific method (see above).[40]

Those using the inducted method would focus on the narrative that looks at this issue from the perspective of one successful exporting country. The qualification is made up front that the narrative is context specific and though the method implies generalization, there are limits to such generalization. Those utilizing the descriptive method would look at the story evident in the data.[41]

The political economy of development is explicitly ideological and the focus would be on who wins and who loses, and by how much by income group from an export promotion policy. There is no presumption here that winners will compensate the losers as is the case in mainstream development economics. Since compensation is highly unlikely, political economists privilege development initiatives more likely to yield socially just and more egalitarian outcomes.[42]

Summary and conclusions

This chapter argued that economic development, the subject of development economics, is primarily about structural transformation. It explained that there are different approaches to structural transformation and that development economics is therefore a study of alternative approaches. It made a case for development economics as a valid field. It used the debate on method to make the case that no one approach has a monopoly on providing valuable insights regarding economic development, and that development economics should be about drawing on the insights of all approaches.

If the argument above is correct, what explains the dominance of the mainstream or neoclassical / neoliberal approach? The sustained dominance of this approach will be discussed in Chapter 8 in more detail, but the most important reasons have to do with funds. Any L/MIC country needing assistance has to sign on the dotted line to adopt a neoliberal package, and even HICs like Portugal, Ireland, Greece and Spain were not exempt during and after the 2007–2009 financial and economic crisis. Thus having powerful sponsors (like the United States and Germany) and powerful international organizations (like the International Monetary Fund (IMF) / World Bank Group / World Trade Organization (WTO)) as implementing agencies assures the continuation of this approach even though critics thought they had dealt it a death blow many times. Another sustaining strength of this approach is its ability to take on criticisms, absorb them and then own them, given the immense resources and large research departments of these international organizations.

The other point needing explanation is the centrality of structural transformation to the definition of economic development. Just as one can question the value of economic growth, one can also question the value of economic development as defined above. Many conservationists believe that HICs have attained sufficient prosperity and advocate for a zero-growth society.[43] In their view, with the right political representation, society could redistribute wealth so that all could prosper and further growth would simply add to non-reversible environmental damage. In the same way, structural transformation of the kind that would enable LICs to grow may not result in a shared prosperity and also could lead to non-reversible environmental damage.

However, without structural transformation there is no hope for a shared prosperity or a resource base that is sufficient to deal with social and environmental problems. Clearly it would be foolish to structurally transform society that adds to environmental problems, but not to do so at all may be equally foolish. It is for this reason that some new developmentalists focus on clean production, an issue focused on in Part III of this textbook. In this regard, it is important to sound a word of caution. Suggesting that shared prosperity will result from environmentally sensitive structural transformation is subject to the same charge of "trickle-down economics" that is confronted by neoliberal economists advocating economic growth and then distribution.

By way of summary, approaches can be distinguished based on the sought outcomes, mechanisms instituted and processes set in motion, as alluded to above. The most straight-forward approach in this regard is the neoliberal approach with its focus on enhancing the scope of the market mechanism and economic openness attained with liberalization, deregulation and privatization.

The Marxian perspective in a political economy of development approach would seek social justice by at least eliminating the ability of capital to exploit labor and so the means of production would need to be state owned. A less extreme perspective in this approach would use the agency of the state to attain equality of opportunity and so would seek to unify access to social services of similar quality and livelihood opportunities based on access to assets such as land and credit.

The human development approach focuses on at least a minimum access to education, health and other services such as clean water and nutrition. In this approach, such accesses are the ends to attain human freedom, while there is an acknowledgement that investing in humans would make them more productive and better market players. The UN Sustainable Development Goals (SDG, 2015–2030) have acknowledged the importance of the quality of services that was not explicitly written into the UN Millennium Development Goals (MDG, 2000–2015) and broadened the scope of the goals to acknowledge the role of environmental degradation in enhancing poverty. While indigenous L/LMIC effort to attain these goals is central, the partnership of the international donor community is a facilitating mechanism.

For new developmentalists, these outcomes if attained would indeed characterize countries that are developed. However, like developmentalists, their focus is on how to generate sufficient indigenous resources to attain these objectives in a sustainable manner. In other words, for them human development objectives are endogenous (solved within the system) and not what the initial focus should be on. New developmentalists acknowledge that investing in the education and health of humans would make them more productive, but structural transformation is prioritized.

Chang (2011) views the donor community and multilateral institutions as directing attention at the ends (human development) rather than the means and calls this "false development". He argues that this misdirection of attention is very damaging because it will not enable LICs to attain a sustainable growth trajectory. The improvement of productivity is a collective endeavor and entails much more than a focus on the human development and credit requirements of individuals such as via microcredit. Other scholars like Reinert et al. (2011) are even more critical and refer to the MDGs / SDG as a Band-Aid. This perspective suggests that it might be possible to attain HDI/SDG with donor support but that this is not authentic self-sustaining economic development.

Notwithstanding the sometimes acrimonious debates that are explored in Part III, it bears repeating that all approaches have something important to contribute and their difference is often one of emphasis. In other words, the crux that differentiates approaches is how to initiate economic development. Each approach identifies central concepts from which their main policy prescriptions emerge. Put simply, for neoliberals the emphasis would be on removing distortions, for new developmentalists on structural transformation privileging technology and industry, for institutionalists on rectifying governance, for political economists on social justice, for feminists on gender justice (as central to social justice) and for human developmentalists on meeting basic human needs. Most development economists would concede the importance of the insights from other approaches, but what particular economists consider as the starting point is often driven by their ideological orientations. Thus a particular view of property rights and its impact might incline two different development economists to either a neoliberal or a political economy of development approach.

Questions and exercises

1. Explain the scientific method as applied to development economics.
2. Explain what might be some limitations of extending the use of the scientific method to development economics.
3. Discuss the key features that distinguish alternative approaches.
4. Discuss prescriptions of alternative approaches regarding initiating catch-up growth.
5. Make a case for or against an alternative approaches perspective to development economics.
6. Distinguish structural change from structural transformation.
7. Explain with examples the inter-relationship of structural and institutional change.
8. Explore the debate for and against economic development as a separate field.
9. Pick any country classification of your choice and make a case for it.
10. Pick a hypothesis from your introductory economics course and explain its non-falsification step by step using the scientific method.
11. Pick a hypothesis of your choice and explain how it might be explored using alternative methods.
12. Pick any two alternative approaches and demonstrate how they differ based on key identifying features discussed in the chapter.

Notes

1 For a volume that discusses diverse approaches across time and geographies refer to eds. Reinert, Ghosh and Kettel (2016).
2 As indicated below, there are many heterodox approaches with distinct theories. There is consensus on some of the critiques of mainstream economics, even if from different perspectives. The nuances and details will be discussed in Part II.
3 Schumpeter (1983) popularized the term economic development in *The Theory of Economic Development*, first published in 1934. As with economic growth theory, the focus of this book was on HICs (high income countries). Schumpeter's theory, in a nutshell, was about how businesses in high income capitalist societies innovate, imitate and unleash a process of "creative destruction" which can feed into a business cycle in an HIC market economy. While aspects of this theory and economic growth theory do carry over to development economics, they are not the central aspects of the field.
4 GDP pertains to the production of goods and services, or income (Gross National Income) derived from that, within sovereign territorial limits whereas GNP is the earnings by national factors of production no matter where they are located. The distinction between the two mainly pertains to factor income flows. Thus, the expatriated profits of a Toyota Motors factory in California will count in US GDP but Japanese GNP. The expatriated profits of a GM plant in UK will count in UK GDP but will count in US GNP. Similarly, the wages and salaries of foreign nationals that are remitted from the United States will count in US GDP but not in US GNP. L/LMICs that rely much on foreign companies will have a higher GDP than GNP. Countries that rely on foreign workers sending back remittances will have a higher GNP than GDP. To summarize, GDP measures all domestic production or income generated from that irrespective of whether the factors (labor or capital) are of domestic or foreign origin. Thus GNP = GDP + factor income inflows – factor incomes outflows. The factor income flow results from labor income (remittances) or capital income (interest, dividends, profits). As a welfare measure, GNP is preferable as a first approximation, albeit highly imperfect, because that is what can be counted on as available for enhancing national well-being. GDP is preferable as a predicator of the level of economic activity and its likely impact on other macroeconomic variables such as employment and the price level and hence that is what is used in macroeconomics.
5 Countries are treated differently by international agencies depending on their ranking based on per capita GDP. For example, WTO allows more generous treatment to those in the lowest classification in terms of concessions in multilateral trade rules. Loan terms are also most generous for the lowest income categories and the International Monetary Fund (IMF) and World Bank (WB) have provided debt forgiveness and relief to the lowest income countries.
6 The literature on convergence and convergence and divergence clubs was sparked by Baumol (1986). Also refer to Bradford Delong, www.j-bradford-delong.net/Econ_Articles/Dowrick/conv_club.html, consulted 3/9/2019.
7 The presumption here is that the increase in GDP is based on a fundamental structural transformation of the economy rather than say a lasting commodity boom.
8 Using 1978 as the base, the year generally associated with the initiation of market reforms, China's real per capita GDP in 2010$ has gone up from $307.76 to $6,497.48 in 2015, a twenty-one fold increase. Data are drawn from the online version of the World Bank, World Development Indicators.
9 In China's case, the 8.96 percent per capita GDP growth rate in 2011 (*World Development Indicators*) was probably the turning point. There is controversy on the validity of the reported data, but if the method of data collection is not altered, the trend provides relevant information.
10 The most widely cited definition of sustainable development is from *Our Common Future*, also referred to as the Brundtland Report, after the person who chaired the World Commission on Environment and Development (1987) for which the report was produced. The definition is: "Sustainable development is development that meets the

needs of the present without compromising the ability of future generations to meet their own needs." Hence it brought center stage the needs of future generations and the notion of ecosystem limitations, and this definition shares these concepts with many others that followed.

11 Kuhn's framework has been broadly criticized, and its relevance for the social sciences has also been challenged. Even so, the framework is heuristically useful for explaining the value of an alternative approaches perspective to development economics.

12 The field of comparative economic systems distinguished variations within the "paradigms" such as the experimentation with market socialism in former Yugoslavia within the socialist paradigm, or social democracy in Scandinavian countries within the capitalist paradigm. One could argue that the capitalist countries came much closer to attaining their world view objectives than the socialist countries, and this partly explains the current dominance of the capitalist paradigm and the retreat of socialism.

13 A contrary view that may come closer to method in some heterodox approaches is proposed by Feyerabend (2010).

14 Silberberg's (1978, pp. 6–12) has been drawn on for this explanation.

15 There is irony in economists purporting to adopt the method of natural scientists like physicists while the latter apparently do not follow the top-down axiomatic approach but rather a bottom-up inductive method according to Farmer (2013, p. 3) who was trained as a physicist. He claimed that physicists "humbled by nature" were forced to become more open-minded and so let data and experimentation come first and mathematics and models follow, while economists start with the modeling and the world is expected to fit the preconceived pattern they start with. As a graduate student, I attended a guest lecture by a prominent economist who used several adjoining blackboards for a lengthy proof. It boiled down to something obviously inconsistent with reality and his tongue in cheek comment was "reality needs to change to fit the model".

16 This is referred to as confirmation bias, which may partly explain why replication is difficult in the social sciences. Nosek (2015) led a study in psychology whereby 100 studies published in three top psychology journals in 2008 were reproduced. Findings were statistically significant in only 36 percent of the reproduced studies compared to 97 percent of the original studies, and the magnitude of the impacts were about half that in the original studies. Economists have noted the concern about improved methods and replication in the other social sciences and prominent journals are addressing the issue. Camerer et al. (2016) tried to replicate significance levels for 18 studies published in two of the most highly ranked economics journals published between 2011 and 2014. They found a significant effect in the same direction as in the original study for 11 replications and on average the replicated effect sizes were 66 percent of the original. Christensen and Miguel (2018, pp. 940–942) point out that replication to date has been modest and they report that 11 of 18 experimental economics studies in prominent journals were successfully replicated. In macroeconomics the success rate was lower (26 out of 67). With regards to replication they distinguish between verification that entails getting the same results with the same specification, sample and population (pure replication) and reproduction that entails using a different sample (less stringent).

17 Mainstream economists who establish themselves do at times challenge existing models with technical analysis, but the brainwashing happens across the world in classrooms via textbooks which are not impacted by what happens at the cutting edge and by armies of teachers not exposed to these nuances. For another example, refer to the Cambridge-Cambridge controversy addressed in Chapter 14.

18 This is a deviation from a once commonly held instrumental methodological position introduced by Friedman (1953) that the economic model should be judged by the validity of its predictions and not the assumptions.

19 The reference here is to the "Theory of the Second Best" suggested by Lipsey and Lancaster (1956). In a world, such as the one we all live in, where some distortions cannot be eliminated for political or social reasons, it may not be economically optimal

to remove others in the context of mainstream neoclassical theory. This theorem is an acknowledgement that the world is much too complicated for simple answers.

20 For example, if the effectiveness of the neoliberal program on economic openness were to be tested, it has so many facets such as trade, investment and capital flows that setting up a test of falsification may simply not be possible. Similarly, the new-developmentalist program of industrial policy has many facets such as technology, trade, investment and infrastructure, and may be similarly difficult to test. Even testing a particular facet is not as straightforward as it might seem due to conceptual and data issues. These issues are further explored in the next chapter on data and its uses in development economics and in Chapters 8 and 9.

21 Structural change is also often confused with institutional change, and a distinction is provided below.

22 Other examples include the change in factor intensities (greater use of capital relative to labor) or a change in the composition of trade (more manufactured relative to primary goods).

23 In the Marxian framework, institutions are the superstructure that are determined by and reinforce the economic base. The economic base constitutes the forces (e.g. factors of production) and relations of production (e.g. capitalist labor relations) and an institution such as a legal framework could support and reinforce the economic base and also be shaped by it.

24 www.china.org.cn/english/features/49007.htm, consulted 1/16/2019.

25 www.unep.org/transport/gfei/autotool/case_studies/apacific/china/CHINA%20 CASE%20STUDY.pdf, consulted in 2017 but page no longer exists.

26 John Lennon wrote "imagine there's no countries". Such imagining and efforts to make it real are called for even as we live in the reality of nation states pursuing their own interests. The Paris Agreement on Climate Change signed on April 22, 2016 by 192 nations shows the capacity of nations to come together to solve a global problem and provides hope for imagining a better future.

27 The sharp and sustained declines are evident for 2008 and 2002 for Venezuela and Zimbabwe respectively in the World Bank, World Development Indicators data for PCGDP in constant 2010$s.

28 This in particular applies to the use of the term "least" developed used by the WTO and other international organizations.

29 However, since in absolute terms the value of industrial production in HICs is much greater than in LICs, and the technology intensity of industrial production is much higher and more advanced, there is some salience to this classification. Even so, it would be difficult to address these nuances and also insert a middle category.

30 The sustained increases are evident for 2003 and 1999 for Ethiopia and Rwanda respectively in the World Bank, World Development Indicators data for PCGDP in constant 2010$s.

31 The level of indebtedness is another variable that has been used for country classifications by international organizations. However, the focus here was mainly on Highly Indebted Poor Countries (HIPC) relative to the less indebted, and the classification is mostly relevant for foreign aid and debt relief.

32 The new IMF institutional view takes into account the risks of capital market liberalization such as asset bubbles and financial sector instability that its critics had pointed to (Chapter 8). Refer to www.imf.org/en/News/Articles/2015/09/28/04/53/ sopol120312a, consulted 1/16/2019.

33 www.imf.org/en/News/Articles/2015/09/28/04/53/soint122908a, consulted 1/16/2019.

34 The widely perceived failure of neoliberalism also resulted in soul searching among leading mainstream economists. A prominent dissenter is Serra and Stiglitz (2008) who proposed a post-Washington Consensus (Appendix 8.1). This includes:

> [t]he agreement that a successful development strategy cannot come only from Washington but must include the developing world in a meaningful way;

one-size-fits-all policies are doomed to fail; countries should be given room to experiment, use their own judgment, and explore alternatives; development requires a balanced role between the state and the market and the strengthening of the institutions in each; and finally, success must be measured not only in GDP, but also must account for distribution as well as social and environmental sustainability.

These features also draw on other approaches, as will become evident in Part II. So far there is no consensus in the development economics literature suggesting that the post-Washington Consensus is a distinct approach and it is therefore discussed in an Appendix to Chapter 8 on neoliberalism.

35 A subset of mainstream economists (growth theorists) modeled economic growth, with a focus on HIC (high income countries). Refer to Harrod (1939), Domar (1946), Solow (1956), Lucus (1988) and Romar (1989).

36 Khan (2014) reviewed the history of economic development thought and it is evident that seminal thinkers of all approaches viewed attaining indigenous and endogenous technological capacity as a key determinant of development. It would seem that this is probably the one goal on which there is a consensus in the development economics field. Of course, as is evident from Part III of this textbook, there is no such consensus on how to realize this objective.

37 Detail about what is new in new developmentalism relative to developmentalism is deferred to Chapter 9 when the reader is more familiar with the relevant concepts.

38 A Google search for "new developmentalism" in January 2019 had 29,900 hits, which grew to 41,300 by March 10, 2019. As with structuralism, South American economists have contributed prominently to this school of thought. The work of Luiz Carlos Bresser-Pereira is most prominently associated with this re-thinking of structuralism / developmentalism. Neostructuralism and new development are often used interchangeably in this literature (Chapter 9).

39 The state is the abiding entity while, say, in a democratic dispensation the government at any point in time is the political administration elected to implement its identified electoral agenda subject to constitutional constraints. The key organs of the state include the legislature and judiciary that both aid and limit the ability of a particular administration to exercise its will. Exploring governance mechanisms is where political science interfaces with economics.

40 As indicated in endnote 20, the falsification of a multifaceted strategy or program of a particular approach, such as structural adjustment for neoliberalism or industrial policy for new developmentalism, is far more complicated.

41 Epistemologists would argue that even in this case there is implicitly, if not explicitly, a conceptual framework guiding the use of the data to tell a story.

42 The recognition of what political economists have been saying for decades is finally dawning on some mainstream economists and other pundits who attribute Brexit and the election of Donald Trump to the backlash against free trade among those, mostly low skilled workers, who lost from it. Cheaper consumer goods do little for those without jobs and the magic of the market does not seamlessly guide the displaced to new jobs as assumed. Admittedly many lost out due to technological change but the same argument applies. See Peter S. Goodman, "More Wealth, More Jobs, but Not for Everyone: What Fuels the Backlash on Trade", *New York Times*, September 28, 2016, www.nytimes. com/2016/09/29/business/economy/more-wealth-more-jobs-but-not-for-everyone-what-fuels-the-backlash-on-trade.html?ref=economy, consulted 9/28/2016.

43 The idea of a zero growth society goes back at least to Mill (1904) who suggested that improved nations had already attained adequate prosperity and redistribution could spread that. In his view, humans would be better off avoiding further progress (growth) and instead should preserve nature and solitude. More modern advocates of zero growth like Daly (1992) are explicitly driven by ecological considerations.

References

Baumol, W. J. 1986. "Productivity Growth, Convergence, and Welfare: What the Long-Run Data Show," *American Economic Review*, 76(5), 1072–1085.

Camerer. et al. 2016. "Evaluating Replicability of Laboratory Experiments in Economics," *Science*, 351(6280), 1433–1436.

Carment, D. and S. Yiagadeesen. 2017. "Exiting the Fragility Trap: Rethinking Our Approach to the World's Most Fragile States," World Institute for Development Economic Research (UNU-WIDER), WIDER Working Paper Series, 181, Helsinki.

Chang, H.-J. 2011. "Hamlet without the Prince of Denmark: How Development Has Disappeared from Today's "Development Discourse," in: S. R. Khan and J. Christiansen (eds.), *Market as Means Rather than Master: Towards New Developmentalism* (London: Routledge) 47-58.

Chenery, H., S. Robinson and M. Syrquin. 1986. *Industrialization and Growth: A Comparative Study* (New York: Oxford University Press).

Christensen, G. and E. Miguel. 2018. "Transparency, Reproducibility and the Credibility of Economics Research," *Journal of Economic Literature*, 57(3), 920–981.

Daly, H. E. 1992. *Steady-state Economics* 2nd ed. (London: Earthscan Publications).

Domar, E. 1946. "Capital Expansion, Rate of Growth, and Employment," *Econometrica*, 14(2), 137–147.

Farmer, D. 2013. "Hypotheses Non Fingo: Problems with the Scientific Method in Economics," *Journal of Economic Methodology*, 20(4), 377–385.

Feyerabend, P. 2010. *Against Method* 4th ed. (New York: Verso Books).

Friedman, M. 1953. *Essays in Positive Economics* (Chicago: University of Chicago Press).

Harrod, R. F. 1939. "An Essay in Dynamic Theory," *The Economic Journal*, 49(193), 14–33.

ILO (International Labor Organization). 1977. *Employment, Growth and Basic Needs: A One World Problem* (New York: Praeger).

Khan, S. R. 2014. *A History of Development Economics Thought: Challenges and Counter-Challenges* (New York: Routledge).

Kuhn, T. S. 1962. *The Structure of Scientific Revolutions* (Chicago: University of Chicago Press).

Lipsey, R. G. and K. Lancaster. 1956. "The General Theory of Second Best," *Review of Economic Studies*, 24(1), 11–32.

Lucas, R. E. 1988. "On the Mechanism of Economic Development," *Journal of Monetary Economics*, 22(1), 3–42.

Mill, J. S. 1904. *Principles of Political Economy with Some of Their Applications to Social Philosophy* (New York: Longmans, Green, and Co.).

North, D. C. 2005. *Understanding the Process of Economic Change* (Princeton: Princeton University Press).

Nosek, B. 2015. "Estimating the Reproducibility of Psychological Science," *Science*, 349(6251), 716–718.

Nurkse, R. 1967. *Problems of Capital Formation in Underdeveloped Countries and Patterns of Trade and Development* (New York: Oxford University Press).

Ostry, J. D., P. Loungani and D. Furceri. 2016. "Neoliberalism: Oversold?" *Finance and Development*, 53(2), 38–41.

Popper, K. 1992. *The Logic of Scientific Discovery* (New York: Routledge).

Reinert, E. 2007. *How the Rich Countries Got Rich and Why Poor Countries Stay Poor* (New York: Carroll and Graf).

Reinert, E. S., J. Ghosh and R. Kattel. (eds.). 2016. *Handbook of Alternative Theories of Economic Development*. Northampton: Edward Elgar.

Reinert, E. S., Y. E. Amaïzo and R. Kattel. 2011. "The Economics of Failed, Failing and Fragile States: Productive Structures as the Missing Link," in: S. R. Khan and J. Christiansen (eds.), *Market as Means Rather than Master: Towards New Developmentalism* (London: Routledge) 59-86.

Romer, P. M. 1994. "The Origins of Endogenous Growth," *Journal of Economic Perspectives*, 8(1), 3–22.

Schumpter, J. A. 1983. *The Theory of Economic Development: An Inquiry into Profits, Capital, Credit, Interest, and the Business Cycle* (New Brunswick: Transactions Publishers).

Sen, A. K. 1999. *Development as Freedom* (New York: Anchor Books).

Serra, N. and J. E. Stiglitz. 2008. *The Washington Consensus Reconsidered: Towards a New Global Governance* (New York: Oxford University Press).

Silberberg, E. 1978. *The Structure of Economics: A Mathematical Analysis* (New York: McGraw Hill Co.).

Solow, R. 1956. "A Contribution to the Theory of Economic Growth," *Quarterly Journal of Economics*, 70(1), 65–94.

World Commission for Environment and Development. 1987. *Our Common Future* (New York: Oxford University Press).

2
DATA AND THEIR USE IN DEVELOPMENT ECONOMICS

Introduction

Development economists use data extensively, so it is important to understand how such data are constructed and thereby the limitations of such data when used in empirical work. If the data are faulty, the empirical work cannot be sound no matter how sophisticated the techniques utilized. In other words, the principle of "garbage in–garbage out" applies. The first section of this chapter explores various data collection methods and reflects on how these data might be used in empirical work. In so doing, some of the issues raised in Chapter 1 on the discussion of method utilized by the different approaches are elaborated on. These discussions continue into the second section in which recent macro and micro development economics topics are picked as case studies to elaborate on the use of alternative kinds of data in empirical analysis.

Alternative forms of data collection

There are many kinds of data depending on the form of data collection, and each has its own strengths and weaknesses.

Cross-section (secondary)

The comparative statistics reported in the Appendix Tables in Chapter 3 represent an example of such data. These data are called cross-sectional because all the relevant units for a given variable, such as primary school enrollment rates, are observed at one point in time (in this case some specified year). They are called secondary because the researchers are not collecting the data themselves but are relying on some agency to procure the relevant data. Secondary data are usually collected by national government agencies.

The compilation of primary school enrollment data is based on all schools informing the relevant government statistical department officials of pupils enrolled in a given year in their primary schools. Generally sub-national (say state or provincial) statistical bureaus gather such information forwarded by lower government tiers (say district) and in turn forward these to national agencies (say federal).

Various ministries like health and education collect and compile these data for national use but also pass them on to the various concerned international agencies. Thus education data are passed on to UNESCO (United Nations Educational, Scientific and Cultural Organization) and health data to WHO (World Health Organization). These international agencies in turn compile international comparative statistical compendiums. Thus part of the World Health Statistics reported every year rely on routine reporting from its 194 member states.

The World Development Indicators, compiled by the World Bank, are the largest current source of development statistics. The World Bank relies on credible international organizations such as the WHO. While international organizations have rigorous standards and work with national statistical bureaus to improve the quality of data compiled, they are ultimately dependent on member governments for providing the secondary data. Inaccuracies in the original source carry through the chain of data compilation reported at an international level.

Errors could creep into the national data due to systematic reporting biases. Consider primary school statistics as an example. If school resources at the local level depend on enrollments, there is an incentive to overstate them. Local governments may also want to overstate reported enrollment rates, especially if they are under pressure to enhance school access by the provincial or state governments.

Countries are ranked internationally based on social and economic performance indicators and so there is an incentive at the national level to overstate achievements. Nations also have an eye on domestic constituents when doing this, particularly when the governments are democratic. The press picks up and reports on the lack of comparative social and economic progress and civil society organizations often base their advocacy campaign on such reporting.

Time series (secondary)

If the data reported on above are collected for each year, in the course of time a substantial time series develops. In January 2019, the *World Development Indicators* reported data on 1,600 variables for 264 countries or country groups going back to 1960.[1] For more specialized data such as finance one would consult the International Monetary Fund (IMF) statistics, or for international trade and foreign direct investment (FDI) the United Nations Conference on Trade and Development (UNCTAD), for labor statistics the International Labor Organization (ILO), for industrial statistics the United Nations Industrial Development Organizations (UNIDO), for agricultural statistics the Food and Agricultural Organization (FAO), and as mentioned earlier the WHO for health statistics and UNESCO for education statistics.

In addition to problems pertaining to cross-sectional secondary data the time series in such data could be subject to additional errors. For example, if variable definitions change over time, the data are not comparable (e.g. changes in the definition of literacy) unless the agency concerned revises the earlier reported data, which would be a very time-consuming and expensive endeavor and even then would only represent guesstimates. If definitions become more stringent over time, there would be a systematic understatement of reported progress.

Cross-sectional (primary) quantitative

These data are collected by researchers based on special purpose sample surveys designed with specific research questions or hypotheses testing in mind. Generally the study is designed (probability sampling) so that a relatively small sample can be used to generalize the results to the population of interest. Good probability sampling requires starting with a good sampling frame from which the selection is made, and that is the first challenge.

Errors can creep into the data for various reasons other than a poor sampling frame. Many times, the data collection is based on structured questionnaires produced far away (often in a different country) from the research site. The researcher in this case presupposes that the information they plan to gather exhausts the relevant social information on the issue being researched. If there are limitations to the conceptual understanding of the researcher in terms of their perception of social and economic reality at the site in question, the closed ended questions designed would have limitations.

Even if questionnaire limitations are ruled out, the research design could be faulty. The errors could pertain to coverage or sample design. In this case, the sampling errors may be very large and the information unreliable. It is expensive to increase the sample size to reduce sampling errors. Further, to get reliable data the field interviewers need to be very well trained and highly motivated to withstand the hardships of fieldwork often far removed from the basic amenities (clean eating, living and drinking) that they take for granted. Getting such a team in place for short-term assignments is a difficult task. Without such a team, errors compound in the field. Unless the field team has a very good understanding of the content of the study, their ability to secure the desired information will be wanting.

Even if there is an excellent study and sample design and field team in place, errors are still inevitable. Recall errors are more likely if the sample population is illiterate and do not maintain records. Rough and ready answers might be provided so they can get back to their lives. A badly trained field team might prompt them to give desired answers or the interviewer might glean what the desired answer is and seek approval by responding in a way that they sense is desired. If they have a reason not to provide information that they think might harm them in some way, inaccuracies are inevitable. For example, they may perceive information on income or assets might be passed on to tax authorities or competitors. Even if all this is not a problem, errors can compound during data processing (data entry and cleaning).

Panel (primary – cross-sectional/time series)

Panel data are rare and entail going back to the same households and collecting data over a period of time, sometimes decades. As expected, these are enormously expensive studies (millions of dollars). The most accurate information is possible from these if well conducted. While many additional research questions can be addressed with panel data, they still are sample survey studies and hence subject to the same shortcomings as primary cross-sectional data.

Census

A census by definition means interviewing every household in the population and hence this is enormously expensive and so can only be done periodically.[2] Generally, if the whole nation is the relevant population, they occur every ten years or so if possible.[3] Various questions are sometimes appended to the population survey pertaining to shelter, health and education, but adding more questions adds to the cost across the board.

Even though all the households of a population are supposed to be interviewed, the poorest and richest are the ones most likely to be missed out. The poorest because they may be itinerant and the richest because they live in gated abodes and refuse to concede the time needed for the interviews if present at the time of the survey. Successful surveys require training and managing an army of interviewers and, for example in the United States, the monthly employment rate temporarily ticks up for the duration of the survey. Charges of cooked up responses, sitting far from the survey sites, are mostly likely for poorly trained and poorly resourced government surveys in L/LMICs.

Cross-sectional (primary) qualitative

To avoid the problems of quantitative survey data, social scientists have developed alternative methods to collect and analyze qualitative data. These techniques use quasi-anthropological or ethnographic approaches. This entails staying a few days or weeks at the site rather than a few years as in the case of cultural anthropology.

Apart from the problems alluded to above, proponents of qualitative methods view sample surveys as extractive with researchers taking something to build their careers without giving anything back.[4] The purists who developed this method, like Chambers (1997), view it as a process of metaphorically handing the stick to the poor and empowering them to understand their own reality and change it themselves.

Numerous techniques that have evolved include transect walks for location familiarization, village mapping exercises for ice-breakers, and focus group discussions (FGDs) to hone information via mutual vetting. FGDs are very carefully managed to avoid dominance by the elites or males in mixed FGDs. Often separate FGDs are held to ensure that women, minorities and the poorest have a voice. Even then the coordinator has to ensure that more or less everyone gets a chance to speak. There are some issues that people prefer not to discuss in a group and a household instrument may be better suited for that. In addition, key informant (depending on the subject) interviews are held. The idea is that triangulation (cross-checking) via several sources of information will ensure accuracy.[5]

No data collection method can avoid problems. In participatory research, based on the Heisenberg uncertainty principle, social and economic reality can change in the process of studying it. Response bias might result if a good rapport is established, as required, between the researchers and respondents. The respondents may be more inclined to give the answers they sense the researchers want to hear. Another problem is that, on the one hand, the time spent in the field is not nearly long enough to understand the social and economic dynamics according to cultural anthropologists, the sharpest critics of such qualitative research, but, on the other, it is too much to cover many sites and so by design the findings cannot be generalized.[6] Even so, quantitative and qualitative research methods can be viewed as complementary to enhance triangulation.

Random control trials (primary)

Bannerji and Duflo (2011) have done the most to popularize this method in development economics partly to address a selection bias problem (see next section). Abdul Latif Jameel Poverty Action Lab (J-PAL) was founded by them along with Sendhil Mullainathan in 2005 at the MIT Department of Economics for Policy-Oriented Poverty Research in L/LMICs. It has grown into a network of researchers and, by 2016, included 143 affiliated researchers at 49 universities.

The method is borrowed from epidemiological (medical) research whereby one group of patients gets a treatment and the control group, with the same characteristics, gets a placebo. The theory is that since the two groups are otherwise identical, it is possible to tease out the impact of the treatment. Policy issues explored by RCTs include the impact of microcredit, treated bed nets, de-worming, cash incentives for appropriate behavioral responses and better communications strategies to provide important information.

Illustrating data use

The various kinds of data described above are extensively used in development economics in exploring both macroeconomic and microeconomic topics. To illustrate the use of these data, I have picked premature deindustrialization as a macroeconomic topic that has gained traction since the turn of the 20th century and microcredit as a microeconomic topic that was popularized in the 1980s. For a while the latter was considered an anti-poverty panacea and it is still part of the poverty alleviation tools advocated by development policy organizations like the World Bank.

Recall the concept of structural change in L/LMICs introduced in Chapter 1. One of the "stylized facts" of economic development identified by Chenery and his research associates was the increase in the share of the secondary sector (industry) in GDP and employment and a concomitant decline in the GDP share of the primary sector (mainly agriculture). As catch-up growth continues and countries attain HIC status, the primary sector shares continue to shrink, industry shares also shrink (deindustrialization), and a sophisticated tertiary sector (services) expands.

Since the last decade of the 20th century and into the 21st century, development economists have noticed the setting in of deindustrialization even in most L/LMICs. While the tertiary sector has expanded, this is mostly as a process of informalization of the economy (Chapter 1). Since the deindustrialization has set in at much lower levels of PCGDP than historical trends, as identified by Chenery and his associates, development economists have dubbed this macroeconomic phenomenon premature deindustrialization.

Development economists have empirically and theoretically addressed this puzzle of premature deindustrialization and the findings are discussed in detail in Chapter 9. Here, the various stories[7] that emerged from that body of research are reviewed to illustrate how various kinds of data have and can be utilized to shed light on this puzzle of premature deindustrialization.

The World Bank, IMF, WTO led neoliberal structural reforms (Chapter 8) are one among several stories for premature deindustrialization. While the details are discussed in Chapters 8 and 9, the summary is that these organizations pushed aggressive trade liberalization and that without protective tariffs L/LMIC fledgling industries were decimated.

Again, these organizations aggressively opened up L/LMICs to capital inflows. The FDI of multinational corporations (MNCs) displaced local industries and portfolio investment caused temporarily booming stock and real estate markets that diverted resources from productive investments. Economic instability and recessions were exaggerated from the herd-like disappearance of foreign capital when profit opportunities shrank (for example, the Asian financial crisis of 1997). To sum up, the story here is that induced economic globalization in the form of inter-linkages between HICs and L/LMICs induced premature deindustrialization in the latter.

Another associated story is that neoliberal reforms in L/LMICs resulted in income inequality and that this resulted in premature deindustrialization by inducing consumption pattern changes. High income groups prefer luxury imports they now had access to due to neoliberal enforced trade liberalization. Demand for mass produced manufactured goods among lower income groups accordingly shrank as their income share was squeezed. This was reinforced by rising income inequality in HICs that resulted in less demand for the cheaper labor intensive manufactured imports from L/LMICs.

The obvious question is why L/LMICs would open themselves up to self-harm. The answer is complex and addressing this issue using several different approaches is one of the themes of this textbook. Summary answers are that the organizations identified above have leverage. This leverage increases when L/LMICs need fiscal or balance of payment assistance because they have mismanaged their economies. Loans come with conditions and heterodox economists believe these conditions to be destructive, including to local industry. A political economic explanation is that elites may gain even as the general population loses, and so they have an incentive to accept loans, FDI, portfolio investment and trade policy that is more generally harmful to the population.

Other stories are more technocratic and refer simply to the working of global market mechanisms. One strand in this literature is that global commodity prices rose at the turn of the 20th century for over a dozen years and this resulted in resources being reallocated to the primary sector relative to the secondary sector in many L/LMICs, particularly in Latin America and Sub-Saharan Africa where premature deindustrialization is more acute. Another strand is that higher productivity growth in HICs due to automation resulted in falling prices of manufactured goods and so L/LMICs could not compete. As told, this technocratic story excludes the possibility of market power or predatory pricing focused on by political economists.

Finally, another story pertains to the "China effect". The argument here is that China with its huge labor force and rapid technological progress and productivity growth was able to bring down unit labor costs to levels that most L/LMICs were unable to compete with. Thus, the premature deindustrialization in L/LMICs in the last three decades (starting in the last decade of the 20th century) coincides with China taking over export markets of labor intensive manufactured goods.

The data discussed in the earlier section could be utilized with data analysis techniques to explore these stories and more than one story could be at play at the same time. All data have limitations as explained above and similarly data analysis methods have shortcomings. Here only the broad outlines of these shortcomings will be identified and courses in econometrics are required for more in-depth understanding.

Mainstream economists wedded to the deductive method prefer to use econometrics to test the association between variables for testing hypotheses. For now, consider each of the stories above as a hypothesis, with the structural adjustment story having several sub-hypotheses pertaining to the impact of loans, foreign aid, FDI, portfolio investment and trade policy on premature deindustrialization.

Thus premature deindustrialization is the dependent variable that needs to be explained. One option would be to utilize secondary data for cross-country analysis. In this case, each country is a unit of analysis or observation. If data are available for say 124 countries across all income categories for the dependent variable, and all the independent variables reflecting the different variables, then in principle one can estimate the statistical significance and the magnitude of association of these variables with premature deindustrialization. Engaging in econometric analysis requires being able to adequately define and measure variables. Constructing indices for variables such as for example trade policy are extremely challenging.

One major problem with such cross-country estimations that treat each country as a unit of observation is the implicit assumption that all countries in the sample are structurally similar. But as explained in detail in Chapter 1, if this were so, there would be no need for development economics. There are econometric methods for addressing this shortcoming, but none is entirely satisfactory.

Another problem with such studies is that only countries for which data are available can be in the sample. Studies have shown that the results can dramatically change by adding a few more countries. Also, ruling out countries due to unavailable data limits the sample size and this too can change the estimates.[8] One solution to the shrinking sample size is to pool secondary cross-section and time series data to increase the sample size. However, while the sample size is increased, the other problems remain.

Time series econometrics is another available tool and this utilizes time series data. In principle, such analysis bypasses having to assume structural similarity of countries of very different income levels, and so is preferable. Time series analysis requires an observation for each variable over a specified period of time (hour, day, month, quarter or year). Time series analysis has its own set of demands for the accuracy of estimates, and one of these is that it requires many observations for each variable. Since most country data are annual, this limits the number of observations that can be available. Also, observations on some variables, for example income inequality, are simply not available annually and so this limits the hypotheses that can be tested.

Ioannidis, Stanley and Doucouliagos (2017) explain why much published economics research is false. Most empirical research focuses on the significance of a statistical association between variables. Suppose the null hypothesis to be tested is that treated bed nets reduce the incidence of malaria. In this case, recall from your statistics courses that a type I error would be incorrectly concluding the null is false while type II would be the failure to reject a false null. In this regard, the power of a test of significance identifies the probability of finding an association if it exists. The power of the test can for example be enhanced by the level of significance chosen for the test and the sample size.

Ioannidis, Stanley and Doucouliagos conducted a meta analysis (study of studies) of 159 empirical economics literatures covering 67,076 parameters drawn from 6,700 empirical studies. They found that in half the research areas 90 percent of the studies were under-powered. Further, due to publication and reporting bias, a simple weighted average of results that were adequately powered (80 percent or more), showed that reported effects were exaggerated, typically by a factor of two. In a third of the studies the effects were overstated by a factor of four or more.[9]

Various hypotheses (stories) explaining deindustrialization were presented above without explaining how they were arrived at. The deductive and inductive methods as ways of arriving at hypotheses were discussed in Chapter 1. As practitioners of the deductive method, prospective economists learn the art of economic modeling in graduate school as a mechanism for deriving hypotheses for empirical testing. Economists differ in the amount of skill they acquire in modeling but, across the board, modeling entails a narrow focus to be mathematically tractable.

For example Rodrik (2015) used a two-sector model (manufacturing and non-manufacturing) to explore how demand, technology and trade shape the size of the manufacturing sector in countries across the income spectrum. The modeling is designed to interpret empirical findings regarding premature deindustrialization in L/LMICs. Schweinberger and Suedekum (2015) used a two-sector model (agriculture and manufacturing) to explore how an increase in price of manufactured goods (terms of trade effect) can induce premature deindustrialization in L/LMICs.

Such modeling can be valuable in uncovering important mechanisms but, even when built on defensible assumptions, leave out much that is important.

Heterodox economists do not have a penchant for such modeling and they argue that such modeling leaves out too much that is important. For example, they view premature deindustrialization as a historical phenomenon driven by power asymmetries between HIC and L/LMICs. This power they argue is mediated via international organizations like the World Bank, IMF, WTO and regional multilateral banks to serve the interests of HICs with regards to trade and investment. Thus, for them, analysis needs to holistic and include historical, multi- and inter-disciplinary, institutional and political economic perspectives.[10]

Some heterodox economists are also skeptical of the quality of quantitative data and of the tools used for such data analysis and so shun multivariate or econometric analysis. Some use descriptive methods and compile tables using various kinds of quantitative data in support of their arguments while conceding that their evidence is purely suggestive. Others prefer the inductive method whereby they generalize based on holistic case studies. While they do not avoid quantitative analysis, when they do so, it serves a larger story and is not the story.

All econometric tools used for macroeconomic data analysis can be utilized for microeconomic data analysis and the same shortcomings apply to this analysis. However, while secondary data are used in macroeconomic analysis, primary data are often collected and used in the microeconomic analysis of issues such as the impact of microcredit on household well-being.

The problem in much econometric research that attempts to measure impact is that there might be "unobservables" that cannot be captured by data but which nonetheless affect the nature of the association between the two variables in question. For example, those seeking and getting microcredit may have traits that are more likely to make them succeed. If such individuals are then more likely to show up in the sample of microcredit recipients, their personal success might get reflected as the success of microcredit.

This phenomenon is referred to in the econometrics literature as "selection bias". There are econometric methods that can be utilized to address this selection problem, but a growing group of empirical economists believe that natural experiments,[11] where possible, or RCTs otherwise, are a more "scientific" method ("gold standard") for collecting the relevant data for empirical analysis that avoids the selection problem.

RCTs address the selection problem with the use of a treatment and control group. If the treatment group gets microcredit and the control group, otherwise identical, does not, the selection bias is taken care of since the result does not depend on who is selected for the study. This method of data collection has taken empirical micro development economics by storm and the usual econometrics tools are then used to analyze data that are considered far more superior.

However, RCTs have also been subject to criticism for many methodological shortcomings that Deaton (2010) has explored.[12] They are viewed as technocratic and no overarching conceptual framework appears to be driving the research unless it is individual utility maximization. Critics argue that focusing on individual utility maximization is not what development is about. For them development is more about nation building and adopting the right strategies such as the ones discussed in Part III of this textbook.

Another concern is the ethics of denying a beneficial intervention to the control group that is extended to the treatment group. Behavior of subjects in both the control and treatment group is assumed unaltered by the experiment, but this may not be the case. For example, those in the control group may seek the treatment (say credit) from an alternative source. Finally, treating humans in L/LMICs as guinea pigs for social science experimentation is found objectionable by some observers even if the research might serve a worthy social purpose.[13]

Many prominent economists are not persuaded by the possibility of replicating these studies (so they are not scientific as claimed) and there are even fewer chances of generalizing from these studies given the variability even across adjacent villages or urban localities.[14] Deaton (2010, p. 448) points out that RCTs are neither suited to nor able to explain the underlying mechanisms of why some things work if they do or vice versa and as such are not helpful. Other critics charge that since they have become all the rage, they are therefore more easily funded than other competing research projects which are being crowded out.

Another objection is that a particular technocratic approach to microeconomic development economics is driving the research agenda. If such research projects are more likely to be funded, it creates the incentives to look for topics that can be framed as a natural experiment or an RCT and then decide on a research question. Ideally, the researcher should pursue a research question of interest because it has social relevance and then decide on the best research method to pursue it. Since RCTs are very expensive to set up and execute, the crowding out of other research is very likely an issue.[15]

Summary and conclusion

This chapter pointed out that economists, including development economists, are wedded to the use of numbers and perhaps are not as scrupulous in examining where they come from as they need to be. It pointed out the different ways in which the numbers are generated and that this can be wedded to the analysis techniques that are likely to be utilized for different research topics. For example, mainstream development microeconomics might use quantitative methods or RCTs and utilize primary (survey) data. A very different approach to development microeconomics is based on the use of qualitative research methods. For the purists, data generation is secondary or inconsequential and grassroots empowerment the primary objective. Development macroeconomics is more likely to utilize secondary data, often pooling cross-sectional and time series observations to enlarge the sample size.

Since all the data collection methods have strengths and weaknesses, it is best to be aware of the shortcomings and make the necessary qualifications. Further, when possible, it is best to view them as complementary to get more than one perspective on an issue. Rejecting evidence-based development economics entirely because of flaws in the data and analysis tools is an extreme position. The quality of data and the analytical tools have been improving over time and are likely to continue to do so. However, it is highly unlikely that economics or development economics as a field of the subject will ever legitimately claim to be scientific, as are the natural sciences, the Noble Prize in "economics science" notwithstanding. Economics shares with other social sciences inherent limitations to the understanding of "agents" (e.g. humans, firms, interest groups, classes, governments) that it studies. Thus, while relying on evidence is critical in moving the field along, given inherent limitations of the data, tools and subject, humility in making claims to the addition of knowledge needs to be the hallmark of a development economist.

Questions and exercises

1. Explain the problems associated with the following kinds of data:
   a. Secondary cross-sectional
   b. Panel data.
2. Pick a subject of study and design a primary research project for it. What kinds of issues would you need to be wary off?
3. Pick a subject of study and design a qualitative research study for it. State what you see as potential advantages and disadvantages.
4. Reconstruct Table 9.2 (Chapter 9) for the period 2000–2014 that coincides with the global commodity boom and tell a story of the identified association to premature deindustrialization.
5. Identify a plausible story explaining premature deindustrialization and construct an alternative Table 9.2 to support your story.

More advanced

6. Identify plausible stories to explain premature deindustrialization. Draw on The World Bank, World Development Indicators to construct indices to test your hypotheses using time series analyses for the country of your choice. Identify the shortcomings of your analysis.
7. Identify plausible stories to explain premature deindustrialization. Construct indices to test your hypotheses using cross-sectional analysis by drawing on The World Bank, World Development Indicators. The indices will dictate the countries in your sample. Identify the shortcomings of your analysis.
8. Identify plausible stories to explain premature deindustrialization. Construct indices to test your hypotheses using pooled cross-sectional and time series data for analysis drawing on The World Bank, World Development Indicators. The indices will dictate the countries and time periods in your sample. Identify the shortcomings of your analysis.

9. Explain how an RCT would address the selection problem in a development microeconomics study other than microcredit.

10. Pick a micro development economics topic of your choice. Design an RCT (including sites and sample selection) to conduct an impact analysis. Make a notional budget to identify the possible cost of the study. Identify the shortcomings of this method of data collection.

11. You are an intern in the office of a senior official at the UN and your first assignment is to write a data brief on an L/LMIC country (your choice) that the official will be visiting (three 1.5 spaced (font 12) typed pages excluding tables, footnotes and references).

    a. Start with a brief background for the country you have selected (one paragraph).

    b. The brief should include a comparison of current economic performance with at least one other point in time to indicate change. Feel free to report a time series if showing fluctuations over time is relevant for your selected country.

    c. Construct at least one table from your statistical sources that, apart from providing basic background, highlights the main problems this country confronts and then describe these data.

    d. Your concluding paragraph should contain concise recommendations based on your country analysis.Hints for constructing table(s)

       • Provide context for selected variables e.g. if you report debt statistics, report it as a percentage of GDP rather than in absolute terms.

       • Select variables in constant rather than current prices unless you have a reason to do otherwise.

       • Round out the numbers used to the highest unit possible (billions, millions) and use two decimal places at most (false accuracy is implied by using more decimal places since most of the numbers you will report are probably inaccurate anyway).

       • Only select numbers that you will actually discuss in the text.

       • Provide a caption for the table and report your data source at the bottom.

Notes

1 This is a truly valuable public resource provided by the World Bank.
2 If there is no sampling frame for selection in a primary cross-sectional survey, say for a village or urban neighborhood, the first step would then be to do a village or neighborhood census from which a sample selection can then be made. This obviously adds to the expense of the survey.
3 The same is true for agriculture censuses.
4 While this sensitivity is laudable, one could argue that such research is needed to understand social and economic reality to help improve it via policy.
5 Qualitative methods are more popular in the other social sciences. For details on the use of qualitative methods in economics and development economics, refer to Starr (2014).
6 For a critical perspective refer to Cooke and Kothari (2001).
7 Many economists use the term "story" in recognition of the difficulty of capturing economic reality with their models and empirics due to the problems identified in this chapter and Chapter 1.

8 Economists are now expected to engage in "robustness tests" to show, for example, that the estimates are not sensitive to minor changes in the sample.
9 I plead guilty to not having paid due attention to power issues in my empirical research.
10 An extreme view of economic modeling is that it is pseudo science that obfuscates rather than clarifies.
11 These opportunities can occur fortuitously and are used by scholars for observation and analysis. In this case, researchers do not control and establish the experiment, but it occurs exogenously. For example, if education is a provincial rather than a federal subject, and an educational reform affects schools in all districts of a province, but not in other neighboring districts belonging to a different province, it would be possible to assign children into treatment and control groups for an impact analysis of the reform.
12 Notwithstanding the many methodological, empirical and interpretive problems identified, Deaton does not call for discarding the experimental method but for an alteration of the focus on the scientific method where theory guides the experiment and the experiment aids in the understanding of mechanisms that could have broader applicability.
13 Silicon Valley entrepreneurs have expressed an interest in a Universal Basic Income to offset the employment impacts of automation and funded the long-term RCT trials (funding for 12 years) in Kenyan villages in 2016, www.businessinsider.com/basic-income-study-kenya-redefining-nature-of-work-2018-1, consulted 3/10/2019.
14 For example, refer to Deaton (2010), Rodrik (2010) and Ravillion (2012).
15 Some years ago my research colleague and I received a very welcome response on a research grant we applied for but funding was made contingent on converting the study into an RCT. We withdrew the application since we considered an RCT as wholly inappropriate for the research study in question and informed the granting authority accordingly. Khan and Ansari (2018, appendix 7.1) elaborated on these objections.

References

Bannerji, A. V. and E. Duflo 2011. *Poor Economics: A Radical Rethinking about the Way to Fight Global Poverty* (New York: Public Affairs).
Chambers, R. 1997. *Whose Reality Counts: Putting the Last First* (London: Intermediate Technology Publications).
Cooke, B. and U. Kothari (eds.). 2001. *Participation: The New Tyranny?* (London: Zed Books).
Deaton, A. 2010. "Instruments, Randomization, and Learning about Development," *Journal of Economic Literature*, 48(2), 424–455.
Ioannidis, J. P. A., T. D. Stanley and H. Doucouliagos 2017. "The Power of Bias in Economics Research," *The Economic Journal*, 127(October), F236–F265.
Khan, S. R. and N. Ansari 2018. *A Microcredit Alternative in South Asia: Akhuwat's Experiment* (New York: Routledge).
Ravillion, M. 2012. "Fighting Poverty One Experiment at A Time: A Review of Abhijit Bannerjee and Esther Duflo's Poor Economics: A Radical Rethinking of the Way to Fight Global Poverty," *Journal of Economic Literature*, 50(1), 115–127.
Rodrik, D. 2010. "Diagnostics before Prescription," *Journal of Economic Perspectives*, 24(3), 33–44.
Rodrik, D. 2015. "Premature Deindustrialization," *Journal of Economic Growth*, 21(1), 1–33.
Schweinberger, A. G. and J. Suedekum 2015. "De-industrialization and Entrepreneurship under Monopolistic Competition," *Oxford Economic Papers*, 67(4), 1174–1185.
Starr, M. A. 2014. "Qualitative and Mixed-Methods Research in Economics: Surprising Growth, Promising Future," *Journal of Economic Surveys*, 28(2), 238–264.

3

COMMONALITIES AND DIFFERENCES AMONG LOW AND LOW MIDDLE INCOME COUNTRIES

Introduction

The unit of observation in development economics is often the nation state, as mentioned in Chapter 1. There is also an implicit presumption when claiming there is a field of development economics that it applies to a set of nations that are not "developed". This chapter will start by demonstrating that there is such a set of nations that share common features. It will also be indicated that it is easy to over-generalize and that while L/LMICs share characteristics with others in the same classification, they may also differ in many ways. Since the income variable is used for classification, how it is computed is explained first. In fact, this exercise in and of itself illustrates differences between L/LMICs and HICs.

Classification variable: PCGDP

Per capita gross domestic product (PCGDP) represents a division of GDP by population. As defined in introductory economics textbooks (see Chapter 1, endnote 4), GDP is the sum of final goods and services produced for the market place in a specified time period. Thus to calculate GDP, quantities and prices are needed and for L/LMICs this is not straightforward.

Prices in L/LMICs for similar goods can vary because markets are segmented due to poor infrastructure, lack of information, transportation and communication costs. There may be regional variations because internal movement across administrative entities (districts, provinces, states) is difficult for political reasons or due to poor infrastructure. The lack of storage may mean high seasonal price variations.

Output data may be difficult to procure because illiteracy may result in a lack of systematic record keeping. Producers may have to rely on memory and there can be a great deal of recall error. There is also systematic understatement because tax assessment depends on output. The lack of competent statistical agencies also leads to endemic inaccuracies. This is compounded by a much larger size of the informal sector as a percentage of total production and a much larger proportion of home production than in HICs (La Porta and Shleifer, 2014). Also, a smaller proportion of the economy is monetized (barter is the alternative), so many transactions are beyond the purview of GDP statisticians. For all these reasons, GDP is understated.

To get from GDP to GDP per capita, accurate estimates of population are needed. The problems of getting good data, including census data, were explained in Chapter 2. In addition, conducting a census is fraught due to political tensions. These are exacerbated in countries experiencing regional strife because they might reinforce regional conflict if resources are constitutionally distributed based on regional population sizes. All ethnic groups then have a stake in overstating their own population and understating those of the others, and there are often charges that the census is rigged in favor of the dominant ethnic group.

To make comparisons across countries meaningful (i.e. to have all variables in real terms), inflation needs to be adjusted for. For this an accurate index has to be generated to deflate and convert nominal into real values. Again, the problems of getting accurate price data are greater in L/LMICs for the reasons explained above. This is in addition to the problems resulting from insufficient statistical expertise and the inherent problems of getting good price indices as explained in introductory economics textbooks.

All PCGDPs in real terms are then converted into US$ terms using $ exchange rates for international comparisons.[1] The conversion using the exchange rates is to the US$ since it is currently the global reserve currency.[2] This means, among other things, that it is used by central banks to maintain their reserves in and many key international economic transactions are conducted in $ and key international commodities (like oil and copper) are priced in them. The problem is getting accurate exchange rates since countries may have an incentive to systematically overstate or understate their exchange rate.

Why should LICs have an incentive to maintain an overvalued exchange rate? One reason is that local elite consumption patterns emulate those of HIC elites and are hence based on imported luxury goods, and overvaluation of the exchange rate results in lower local currency prices. This consumption is effectively subsidized by the rest of society, particularly exporters.

Initiating industrialization could be another reason. In local currency terms, the imported capital goods needed are cheaper. Again, local industry is implicitly subsidized by thwarted exporters. The export sector is implicitly taxed since these exports are more expensive in foreign currency terms with an overvalued exchange rate.

Overvaluation overstates GDP per capita in constant $. If there is overvaluation, an active secondary market generally develops. Since secondary market transactions are generally outlawed because they draw away foreign currency from the central bank, there is a risk associated with such transactions. This means the premium over the official exchange rate on the secondary market is likely to overstate the extent of overvaluation.

Countries which are already substantively industrialized and are engaged in catch-up growth may want to encourage their manufactured exports by undervaluing the currency. In this case, exporters are implicitly subsidized by consumers and importers. In some cases, countries have dual or multiple exchange rates for different activities depending on what they want to encourage. For example, foreign travel as a luxury good could be discouraged while studying science subjects abroad could be encouraged.

Such practices are now not common since the IMF is active in most L/LMICs and loan agreements with the IMF make it incumbent on countries to unify the exchange rate and make it flexible or "market driven". The notion of a market-driven flexible exchange rate is a myth since the central bank influences the interest rate as one of the key macro prices influencing the exchange rate. For example, interest rates lower than other countries would result in a higher demand for foreign currency and exert pressure on the local currency to depreciate. Similarly, higher local inflation relative to other countries would reduce exports and again put pressure on the local currency to depreciate. Since the central bank controls the money supply and influences the interest rates, it has a strong influence on the exchange rate. Even if the exchange rate was market driven in this qualified way, the currency could still be undervalued.

Goods that form part of trade (traded goods) determine currency values, but in LICs the proportion of the non-traded sector of the economy is a much higher proportion of total transactions. These would include land, housing/rents, services (restaurant meals, haircuts), transport and utilities.

The larger the ratio of non-traded goods relative to traded goods, and the lower the price of non-traded goods relative to traded goods (due to lower wages), the higher the undervaluation of an exchange rate. One therefore needs to adjust for real purchasing power across countries that conversion of real GDP via the official exchange rate does not capture.

Exchange rates that adjust for purchasing power are referred to as purchasing power parity (PPP) exchange rates. The idea here is to adjust for systematic difference in the cost of living across countries resulting from the higher ratio of non-traded goods and lower real wage rates that figure prominently in prices of non-traded goods in L/LMICs. The method of adjusting exchange rates for cost of living differences requires estimates of prices and expenditures, and international agencies, regional agencies and local statistical offices share responsibilities for this.

The International Comparison Project was initiated in 1968 by the United Nations Statistical Office to adjust for the undervaluation of the official exchange rate in most L/LMICs (Kravis, 1986). A simple way of thinking about the conversion is to use say US prices (much higher) and quantities of a given L/LMIC. Thus, as expected, the result of the conversion would be that PPP adjusted GDP in constant $ is generally much greater for L/LMICs than it is without the PPP adjustment (Appendix Table 3.1).[3]

While GDP adjusted for PPP can be a more accurate representation of comparative purchasing power, it is not a good measure of purchasing power of L/LMICs on the international market for capital, intermediate goods and raw materials. In this regard, GDP per capita in constant $ is a more suitable measure of real LIC economic development prospects.

Commonalities

Appendix Table 3.1 uses data on economic and social variables by income classification to identify commonalities. Appendix Table 3.2 then shows that, notwithstanding commonalities, there are variations across regions. Appendix Table 3.3 picks one region and shows how there are variations even within a region. This theme is explored further in the next section on limits to generalization.

Two caveats are worth repeating here before proceeding. First, it was made clear in Chapter 2 that many errors can creep into all forms of data and so although the Appendix Tables appear to contain facts, this is only so with many qualifications. Second, even if we view what is reported in the Appendix Tables as facts, contrary to the common saying, such facts rarely speak for themselves. Instead, social scientists including economists impose their own narratives or stories on the facts. Some are more plausible than others, but to imagine that social scientists attain the absolute truth or capture social or economic reality is a stretch.

The variable in the first row of Appendix Table 3.1 shows average PCGDP in constant $ terms (adjusted for inflation) in HICs was 58 fold greater than in LICs in 2017. The second row provides PCGDP in PPP terms. As expected, the PPP adjusted gap in average per capita real GDP between HICs and LICs is lower and was 23 fold in the same year.

The next six variables pertain to the structural features of the economy referred to in Chapter 1 i.e. the relative sizes of the various sectors in the economy and sector productivities. The agricultural value added per worker as an indicator of agricultural productivity shows that agricultural productivity in HICs was 70 fold higher than in LICs in 2016. This partly explains the next row, which shows agricultural value added as a percentage of GDP of 1.3 percent in HICs compared to 26.3 percent in LICs. Since agriculture is so immensely productive in HICs relative to LICs and LMICs, labor force employed in the agricultural sector can be a very small percentage of the total labor force. The other reason for the low share of agricultural value added in GDP in HICs is that they are highly diversified, and accordingly the shrinking of the sectoral share of agriculture is one of the "stylized facts" of economic development discussed in Chapter 1.

Industry is also much more productive in HICs relative to the other income groups. However, at 25 fold greater than LICs in 2016, this is much less so the case than in agriculture. The next row explains why it is a misnomer to refer to HICs as industrialized economies to distinguish them from other country groups. The industrial sector in all country groups is larger than in HICs and that is also the case for manufacturing as the largest component of industry for MICs relative to HICs.[4]

The service sector in HICs is almost three-fourths of the whole economy compared to two-fifths for LICs and about a half or slightly more for the MIC groups. However, the bulk of services in HICs are information technology intensive, especially the technical and professional occupations, and this is why the service sector is 27 fold more productive in HICs than in LICs, which is characterized by informality and self-employment (Chapter 1).

One way of assessing the level of prosperity attained is via access to electricity. In 2016, only 30 percent of the rural population in LICs had access to electricity. In urban areas it was much higher at 68 percent, but even then the gap between urban access in LICs and HICs (at 100 percent) was dramatic. A broader gauge of prosperity is energy consumption. Once again, the same linear pattern is evident by country group income classification. Accompanying energy consumption is CO_2 emissions (last row of Appendix Table 3.1) and, as expected, per capita emissions in HICs were 33 fold greater than in LICs in 2014.[5]

For developmentalists, saving and capital accumulation are central to initiating catch-up growth (Chapter 6). In this regard, LICs have low saving rates relative to LMICs and MICs and since LIC investment rates exceed saving rates, the gap is made up by borrowing and aid. LMICs also have a saving/investment gap, but it is much less acute than LICs. Since HIC economies have matured, they do not have the high investment rates of the middle income economies that have experienced or are initiating catch-up growth.

Neoliberal economists privilege the private sector and hence central to the needed structural reforms are those that promote "ease of doing business". A set of indicators reported in Appendix Table 3.1 addresses this issue and across the board there is a negative association of income level and the "cost of business start-up". Here, as elsewhere, heterodox scholars suggest that the causality may well run in the opposite direction and once catch-up growth is underway, management and administration also improve in conjunction i.e. that the ease of doing business emanates from the economy as it improves.

Apart from the saving/investment gap and a fiscal imbalance, LICs and LMICs also suffer from an external imbalance on the goods and services account. Only UMICs and HICs had a balance of trade surplus, though as a percentage of GDP in 2016 it was modest at 1 percent. LICs had a deficit of 18.1 percent while LMICs had a deficit of 3.6 percent.

For new developmentalists, technology is central to catch-up growth and all the indicators point to LICs and LMICs lagging. For example, this is the case with the adoption and use of cell phones and the use of the internet and broadband. Adopting a "glass half full" approach, one could argue that the pace of diffusion of these technologies to L/LMICs has been rapid compared to other technologies in the past as evident from recent time series data (not reported).

While it is difficult to standardize publication in scientific and technical journals by country income groups, LICs and LMICs clearly lag. Information on patents secured by domestic residents is not available for LICs, but LMICs lag behind the other country income groups. While these indicators probably reflect what is true for other variables for which data are not available (e.g. research and development), new developmentalists are also open to the same charge of technological change being endogenous as is true of the heterodox critique of neoliberalism with regards to business conditions. The important question in this debate among alternative approaches is where to focus to initiate the process of catch-up growth and this issue is taken up in the last chapter of this textbook (Chapter 15) after a detailed discussion of alternative approaches in Parts II and III.

For the basic human needs/human development approach, the starting point is ensuring adequate investment in humans to make them productive participants in the economy. The next sets of indicators in Appendix Table 3.1 provide information on social investments and human development. The human development indicators and social investments are at comparatively very low levels in LICs based on expenditures on education and health, access to services like health staff, drinking water, sanitation, life expectancy, mortality rates, literacy rates and enrollments. However, there is also good news in that human development indicators vary positively with country group income levels across the board. Also gender gaps improve by country group income level. For example, the gender literacy gap decreases markedly as country group income increases. Also, within the LIC group, scanning the time series data (not reported) show rapid improvement in human development indicators even over the last five years up to 2017.

Having established the "stylized facts" of what it means to be an LIC, the next two Appendix Tables establish the limits to generalizations. In Appendix Table 3.2, LICs and MICs are bunched into regions and variation by region is demonstrated using economic variables and the human development index. For example, Sub-Saharan Africa (SSA) and South Asia (SA) consistently lag on almost all indicators including the human development indicators.

A scrutiny of Appendix Table 3.2 suggests a possible foreshadowing of the economic emergence of South Asia. Its human development index on average is ten points higher than SSA. Its per capita GDP growth of 5.5 percent, post the 2007–2009 global financial and economic crisis up to 2017, has almost matched the 6.6 percent growth rate of East Asia and the Pacific region. The other three regions have stagnated in this period with a growth rate of almost 1 percent. The high growth rate in SA was accompanied by much higher investment and saving rates compared to SSA and the best business conditions by far across the board in 2018.

However, even here there are limits to generalization, and to demonstrate this Appendix Table 3.3 picks the SA region to demonstrate variation by country within the SA region.[6] Sri Lanka as the only MIC in the region clearly dominates in most economic indicators and its high human development index (.77 compared to .56 for Pakistan). In fact Sri Lanka initially came into notice for its high social investments, high human development indicators, low poverty rates, and then for being the first in the sub-continent to attain MIC status (Gunatilleke, 2000).

Pakistan was viewed as the "development model" to emulate in the 1960s for having initiated impressive catch-up growth (Papanek, 1967).[7] The growth momentum was sustained such that up into the 1980s and 1990s, Pakistan had the second highest per capita GDP growth rate. However, Pakistan lagged in social investments and the associated human development indicators. Experts warned that Pakistan would not be able to sustain its economic growth momentum without concomitant investment in its people, but the latter remained a low priority for Pakistani policy makers, both military and civil. Nonetheless, Pakistan was able to maintain its lead over India in per capita GDP terms until the turn of the century. India overtook Pakistan with a much higher growth trajectory in 2006 (Khan, 2011) and by 2017 Pakistan's per capita GDP was only about three-fifths of India, as indicated in Appendix Table 3.3.[8]

Bangladesh (formerly East Pakistan) declared its independence from West Pakistan in March 1971. As a province, it had a larger population but lagged behind West Pakistan on all economic indicators. Post independence, Henry Kissinger is said to have referred to it as a basket case. Yet all social indicators started to dramatically improve post independence in Bangladesh and the drop in its fertility rate excited the attention of demographers (Cleland et al., 1994; Caldwell et al., 1999).

Subsequently, it invested heavily in the textiles and garment industry in the 1980s, and within a decade became a world beater in garment exports despite growing no cotton (Rhee, 1990). While in 2018 Pakistan ranked fourth in raw cotton exports, in 2017–2018 its total textile exports were $12.5 billion while Bangladesh apparel exports alone in the same period were $30.6 billion. As Appendix Table 3.3 shows, Pakistan still has a higher per capita income, but Bangladesh has a much higher economic growth trajectory (5.3 percent between 2010–2017 compared to 2.0 percent for Pakistan) and is very likely to overtake Pakistan fairly soon.[9]

Pakistan can point to having to cope with the blow back of the Afghan wars and associated terrorism for its poor economic performance. This could have resulted in a poor investment climate and the low domestic investment as shown in Appendix Table 3.3. Alternatively, its stubborn disregard of social investment (lowest human development in SA), pathetically poor saving rates (7 percent compared to 30 percent for Sri Lanka) and lack of structural transformation (12 percent manufacturing as a percent of GDP compared to 17 percent in Bangladesh) are self-inflicted wounds. Of late, it has dramatically improved its business climate compared to other SA countries (6.8 percent of per capita income in terms of cost of business start-ups compared to 21 percent in Bangladesh), but quite clearly this is not a sufficient or even necessary condition for impressive economic performance.[10]

This detour above into SA economies was simply to illustrate the limits of generalization. Ultimately, detailed historical inductive (case) studies are the only way to understand individual economies.[11] Yet, this does not negate the commonalities among L/LMICs that give meaning to the pursuit of development economics and the paragraphs that follow revert to this theme.

To summarize, the stylized facts in Appendix Table 3.1 indicate a large number of commonalities across LICs which represent challenges even as they try to initiate catch-up growth. These include high levels of malnutrition, which is indicative of high poverty rates (Chapter 4). Low levels of literacy and mean education rates in terms of the composition of the labor force suggest a larger proportion of unskilled relative to skilled or professional workers, and these two variables contribute to explaining low levels of labor productivity. Low levels of public investment in health and other social services are associated with high infant mortality and high maternal mortality rates which are indicative of low life expectancy.

The low levels of labor productivity in agriculture, the largest component of rural economic activity, means a large percentage of the population is in the rural sector in L/LMICs. Many LICs export composition is still primary goods intensive (raw material, agricultural or mining based). Some countries like Bangladesh, Cambodia and Vietnam have moved into low-tech labor intensive manufactured goods like textiles or leather goods. As labor costs in China rise further, more opportunities for such specialization in L/LMICs will be created.

Appendix Table 3.1 also points to a number of other challenges. LICs confront high balance of payment deficits and low saving and investment ratios with the latter far exceeding the former. In addition, tax capacity is low and so they also confront fiscal deficits and high debt levels. Structuralists refer to these as the three gaps (i.e. foreign exchange, saving and fiscal) that need to be addressed with the help of foreign aid (Taylor, 1994, chapter 11).

Other challenges include environmental and resource degradation since industrial safeguards are not in place and implementation capacity of existing legislation is weak. In some cases, population pressures could result in resource degradation. To add to the social discontent that may result from high population growth rates, they may face regional and ethnic strife in the competition for limited resources.[12] Three commonalities that deserve special attention are population growth, rural to urban migration and market segmentation.

High population growth rates mean high household population dependency ratios.[13] High population growth rates and a young population can be a plus as an addition to the labor force (demographic dividend). However, to realize the dividend, the state needs to have the resources and capacity to deliver the needed social and physical infrastructure. If opportunities are not available on the demand side, more labor on the supply side means unemployment and social discontent.

Neoclassical economic theory explains the high demand for children among the less well off in LICs premised on using them for chores, care-giving (girls) and for old age security (boys). Due to high infant mortality rates, high birth rates are a strategy to ensure that the numbers of children desired are attained. This is viewed as a demand for children as "investment goods". As household income levels increase, children start being viewed more as "consumption goods" and a quality–quantity trade-off kicks in (Becker and Lewis, 1973). The price of providing quality (schooling, health) is high and so the demand for children drops. Higher female education levels complement this trend if it leads to women entering the labor force. In urban areas this is likely because two paychecks are often needed to maintain a barely middle class lifestyle.[14]

It follows from neoclassical theory that incentives can be used for reducing population growth and this has been tried by a number of countries such as with preference in apartment allocations and school admissions for smaller families.[15] Other mechanisms for influencing fertility rates are enhancing female education levels and population programs that diffuse birth control information and meet the demand for contraception.

An unpleasant demographic story that still plays out in many L/MICs has been referred to by Sen (1990) as the puzzle of the "missing women". The biological sex ratio at birth (M/F) has been estimated to be 1.07. In many L/MICs, particularly India and Pakistan in SA, there has traditionally been a male preference since women were viewed as marrying into other families and therefore an asset to other families and not available for example as old age security to the family they were born into. Sen simulated how many women should be present for the biologically expected ratio to hold and hence his dramatic finding of 100 million missing women. Ultrasound technology is alleged to have made this worse in India.

China put into place a very aggressive "one-child" policy in 1982 and in 1988 extended it to rural areas (with some exemptions). It attained a stationary population growth rate, but not without social repercussions and one of these was the missing women syndrome (Ebenstein, 2010).

In general since rural fertility rates are much higher and living conditions much worse, LICs confront high rates of rural to urban migration. Mainstream economists separately analyze push and pull factors as leading to such migration. Apart from population growth, push factors could include natural disasters, agricultural mechanization, public sector infrastructure projects like dams displacing populations, and predatory landlords. The main urban pull factors include the perception of higher wages and more work opportunities, more security, better living conditions and the glamour of the city.

The term urban bias was coined by Lipton (1977) to describe the asymmetry in investment in social and physical infrastructure in urban relative to rural areas. The reasons could be that the rich and politically powerful live in the cities and also the greater population concentrations in cities compared to the diffused populations in the rural areas are more likely to produce social protest by the poor who are deprived. The high pace of rural urban migration and subsequent high organic population growth rates in the cities far exceed the capacity of urban municipalities to cope and the result is shanty towns and urban blight.

Preston (1979) estimated that the share of urban population in LICs between 1950 and 1975 increased from 17 to about 28 percent. The increase for current HICs between 1875 and 1900 was from 17 to 26 percent. Thus the increase is not unprecedented. However, the rate of internal growth in urban population in LICs between 1950 and 1975 of 188 percent is unprecedented. The corresponding increase between 1875 and 1900 for current HICs was 100 percent. Thus the natural increase in population growth in urban areas now accounts for a greater increase in urban population growth then does rural-urban migration and this contributes to unmanageable megacities in L/LMICs.

Another common characteristic of L/LMICs is the market segmentation and the economic dualism this generates in the product, labor and capital markets.[16] The market, based on a number of assumptions, is viewed in mainstream economics as a homogenizer i.e. price differences across regions should disappear due to the mobility of goods since price differentials for the same goods provide profit opportunities to businesses.[17] Similarly, wage and interest differentials should shrink due to the mobility of labor and capital.

In LICs, price differentials persist and this phenomenon has been referred to as market segmentation which produces dualism. Poor physical infrastructure hinders transportation and communication. Paved roads and rail links have limited coverage, are of poor quality and are not maintained.[18] Poor communications limit information flows (cell phones have redressed this failing to some extent), and the non-existent storage or very high storage costs (warehouse and refrigeration) raise marketing costs. Thus different markets can be physically cut off and one way of inferring the existence of market segmentation and the resulting dualism is from price differences for similar products across region and time.

In both urban and rural areas, two separate interest rates can co-exist. In the formal sector government owned or directed private banks may make loans to large formal sector firms at subsidized interest rates. In the informal sector, capital scarcity could mean very high interest rates. Households have recourse to family and friends, microcredit if available, ROSCAs (Rotating Saving and Credit Associations), or else resort to a money lender.

A similar duality prevails in rural areas. Government-owned or -controlled agricultural development banks provide interest free loans to the so-called "progressive farmers" trying out new agricultural technology. In practice, this often turns out to be the large landholders with "contacts" with the bureaucracy or politicians, even if the loans are intended for the small farmers. Small farmers and other households then have to borrow from moneylenders, shopkeepers, landlords, ROSCAs, or from family and friends. Moneylenders operating in the local environment have access to the relevant local information to assess credit risks and have low or no overheads. The poor infrastructure, lack of information and small size of loans and hence high transaction costs deter private sector banks from opening branches.[19]

Technological dualism drives segmentation in the labor markets in both urban and rural areas. In the formal sector, large industrial firms are likely to use highly capital intensive technology. Various incentives could drive this. For example, wages in the formal sector may be governed by unions and legislation driving up labor costs. As noted above, interest rates might be subsidized, the exchange rate overvalued and various tax incentives (accelerated depreciation or tax holidays) cheapen capital. By contrast, in the informal sector wages are market determined, entry is easy, labor turnover is high and no benefits are provided. There are myriad activities in the informal sector and some examples include crafts, home-based production, petty retail, food stalls, street vending, letter writing, knife sharpening, street entertainment (bear, snake), junk collection, domestic service and day labor.

In rural areas, large farms are highly mechanized and input intensive (i.e. use tractors, harvesters, threshers and also tube-wells, fertilizer and insecticides), use wage labor and often have monopsonistic power. Juxtaposed with this picture are small peasant farmers who work as share croppers and many still use primitive technology. Land is sometimes "rented in" from absentee owners and generally family labor or landless labor is used.

The non-agriculture rural sector is also characterized by informality with a high prevalence of crafts production, trades and services. At least initially, migration keeps rural-urban links intact. Rural migrants generally find entry into the urban informal sector labor but may return during peak agricultural seasons when there is a labor shortage such as during harvesting. There is also the reverse flow of remittances to support family members who stay in the rural areas. However, given the rural-urban migration and incentives for capital intensity in the formal sector, various categories of employment in L/LMICs are characterized by wages exceeding productivity.

Over-staffing in the public sector might result from nepotism or jobs resulting from political connections. Productivity could also be low because of the lack of complementary inputs. Finally, productivity might be low due to low nutrition, education or training (impaired employment). The commonalities pointed to so far pertain to current conditions. Perhaps more important is the common history of colonialism most current L/LMICs faced.

Colonialism and neo-colonialism[20]

There are several theories of imperialism and colonialism and the prominent ones, starting with Marx, are explored in Chapter 5. The debates about the impacts of colonialism are still ongoing. Since there is no counter factual (we cannot replay history without colonialism), this question cannot be directly answered as is the case for so many issues in development economics. Nonetheless, argumentation and clever scholarship attempts to build a case one way or the other.

Prominent development economists such as Rostow (1960, pp. 26–27) and Bauer (1984, p. 58) argued that colonialism paved the path to progress. In their view, it provided poor countries with social and physical infrastructure, bureaucracies and modern attitudes which enabled future progress. The dissenting arguments claim that the legacy of colonialism included demographic devastation, surplus extraction,[21] arrested development (see below), corruption, low tax effort, poor social infrastructure, income inequality, ecological degradation and genocide.

Cypher (2014, chapter 3) reviewed the literature on colonialism and documented by citing various sources the demographic and resource extraction aspects of colonialism. In Latin America, the indigenous population declined from 70–90 million in 1540 to 3.5 million in 1690. The reasons for this were wars, viruses that native populations did not have immunities against, forced labor, deprivation and malnutrition. In Africa, between 1600 and 1900, 12 million were sold into slavery and 36 million died during the walk to the coast or en route. Colonial agents instigated inter-tribal wars that resulted in the enslavement of defeated tribes. Thus, between 1650 and 1850, Africa's share of the world population declined from 18 to 8 percent. In the United States, Canada, Australia and New Zealand, the indigenous populations were virtually exterminated.

Between 1757 and 1812, Great Britain extracted about 5 to 6 percent of Indian GNP annually.[22] Similarly, there was an extraction of 15.6 percent of net national product (GDP − capital depreciation) from Indonesia by the Dutch as late as 1930. The last twenty-four years of Spanish rule resulted in the extraction of 7.2 percent of the annual income from Mexico. The mechanisms of extraction were brute force, including paying only for part of colony exports based on resource extraction from mines or plantations, trade (prices set by colonial administration) and oppressive taxation. Trade, head (per person) and hut taxes raised revenue but also induced forced labor (to pay the taxes) at exploitative wage rates.

Baran (1957, pp 142–149) argued the colonized countries were placed on a lower path to economic development because they arrested productive forces and transferred resources from the colonized to the colonial powers. The needs of the colonizers shaped economic activity in the colonies, and so infrastructural investments served the purpose of connecting hinterlands, plantations, or mines to ports for primary commodity exports. Indigenous development may have required specialization in different kinds of agricultural and manufacturing commodities and regional networks to enhance trade. Even now, many LIC trade networks look to the ex-colonizers rather than to the region they are located in and the old trade patterns of selling primary products and importing luxury goods has continued long after colonialism and into the post-colonial period. Colonial historians point out that the colonial administrations maintained dominance by promoting or exploiting inter-tribal and ethnic tensions (divide, conquer and rule) and that this also deterred the formation of regional trade networks and a sense of nationhood after independence.

Cypher (2014, pp. 97–99) also documents that colonizers were not interested in competition from the colonies and so engaged in a systematic process of instituting deindustrialization. Examples of such deindustrialization include the elimination of sophisticated textile manufacturing in India via brute force, rules and tariffs, and in Egypt via a manipulated war. A tariff of 70 to 80 percent was placed on Indian textile exports to Great Britain while duty free textiles were imported into India. Since cotton could be imported duty free into Great Britain, there was a move away from exporting textiles into exporting the raw material. Gradually the very sophisticated textile industry that was more competitive than any European industry was decimated. Similarly, the attempt by Muhammad Ali of Egypt to build a flourishing cotton textile industry based on indigenous high quality cotton was thwarted by the British.

Another way of exploring arrested development is by examining the impact of colonialism on future development. Alam (1999) demonstrated that the more sovereign a country was in the initial period, the better the growth outcomes between 1900 and 1950. Colonies and quasi-colonies showed the worst performance due to their inability to structure their policies to favor domestic factors because of this lack of sovereignty. Similarly, scholars have shown that economic growth and physical and social infrastructure in the post-colonial period immediately picked up relative to the colonial period and was enhanced multiple folds in a short span of time.[23]

To sum up, it appears based on the information provided above that on balance the colonies had to deal with baggage that negatively impacted their future economic growth trajectory. This information above could be re-cast into institutional and structural factors based on the definitions and distinctions made in Chapter 1. The structural reasons for arrested development included a created dependence on primary commodities for which the terms of trade over time were declining.[24] The exhaustion of natural resources resulted from ecologically unwise commodity specializations forced on L/MICs to fulfill the needs of colonial powers. The distorted infrastructure did not encourage rational development due to distorted trade patterns that served the needs of colonial powers. A quick profit trading mentality was picked up from the mercantile colonial ethos by the elites. Thus, local elites avoided industrialization, which was a higher risk activity. Finally, there was a paucity of social investment (health, sanitation, water supply and education) evident from the comparative progress made in the post-colonial period.

The institutional drawbacks of colonialism that arrested future development included social dualism; with an elite that lived like the colonizers, spoke their language, was often cut off from their own mass culture and did not identify or serve their own country even in the post-colonial period. The concentration of economic and political power based on land grants was and still is detrimental to economic development because it precludes wider economic and political participation (Acemoglu and Robinson, 2012). Another drawback was inheriting an autocratic colonial bureaucracy that had instilled into it a culture of governing rather than serving.

Neocolonialism differs from colonialism in that the political administration is turned over to the colonies after they attain independence, but the power equation is still massively unequal. Scholars like Amsden (2008) argued that even though overt colonialism ended, HICs still politically and hence economically dominate the LICs via various mechanisms. Recall that the mechanism for the transfer of surplus under colonialism was force, manipulating the terms of trade, and taxes. These mechanisms had to be altered since the political administrations were no longer under colonial authority.

One mechanism is loans provided by banks in HICs that create indebtedness and an onerous burden of future interest and principal repayments. While the blame for this rests on LIC elites who misappropriate and badly use funds, future generations and the poor in L/LMICs suffer the collateral damage. Aid often comes in the form of tied loans which reduce the actual value of the loan since the country is not free to get the best price for the best quality of goods. A portion of the loan is a grant in that the interest rate may be below the market rate (LIBOR – London

Interbank Offer Rate is used as a benchmark) and the repayment period may include a grace period and long repayment periods. In the parlance of international giving, soft loans are the ones with a high grant element. Soft loans can be used as a mechanism to cultivate political alliances, influence and secure donor country interests (Chapter 11).

Foreign direct investment is sought by L/LMICs for technology, capital and employment. However, ultimately how well L/LMICs can negotiate the terms determines the benefit-cost nexus. Multinational firms can transfer surplus out of L/LMICs via transfer pricing (over-pricing inputs and under-pricing outputs to siphon profits to low tax locales), excessive royalties, fees, and dividend and profit repatriation. Again, one could ask why political elites would want to bend over backward to attract FDI if its costs exceed its benefits. The political economy of development perspective is that the benefits accrued to the elites (kickbacks/jobs) while the costs are borne by society at large (Chapter 12).

International trade can be another mechanism for the transfer of surplus. Once again, trade has many potential benefits by making markets available and enabling economies of scale, providing access to foreign exchange and technology, inducing higher productivity via competition, providing access to value chains that help in attaining quality control, marketing and managerial knowledge. Once again, the political economy of development perspective is that economic power determines the terms of trade (import and export prices) and this can result in surplus transfer. Monopoly and monopsony power mean high prices for imports and low prices for exports respectively for L/MICs (Chapter 8 and 9).

This approach also views the greater economic power of HICs as leading to greater political power which enables them to reinforce their economic dominance. Thus asymmetrical power in international organizations like the WB/IMF may result in austere conditions for loans that make L/LMICs foreign capital friendly and susceptible to resource transfers. Limited power in the WTO may mean that they see trade rules including tariff structures confronting their exports that are detrimental to L/LMIC economic growth. HICs meanwhile get away with subsidies on their exports (HIC agricultural subsidies have been a big unresolved negotiating issue in the WTO), which were banned by the WTO Uruguay Round (Chapter 8).[25]

With the emergence of the BRICS (Brazil, Russia, India, China and South Africa), a power shift is under way. For example, the Chinese renminbi has been accepted by the IMF as a reserve currency. The IMF board approved more voting rights in the IMF for China, India, Brazil and Russia (now all among the top ten voting powers) in 2010, but the United States resisted approving this measure until 2016.[26] China and the other BRICS countries launched a $100 billion New Development Bank (BRICS Bank) and the China-led Asian Infrastructure Investment Bank. The United States first opposed the BRICS Bank, but once the UK and EU signed up, the World Bank (led by the United States) agreed to work with these BRICS banks. These concessions acknowledged the shifting global economic and political power and the fact that power is acquired and not conceded.[27]

Chang (2002) argued that currently advanced economies utilized policies and tools that global economic rules, such as those embodied in the WTO and policy dictates of the IMF and the World Bank, now routinely deny to L/LMICs. These include protectionism and the tools that engender local technological and industrial capacity development. Moreover, he argued that these are exactly the policies and tools that Japan and other East Asian countries used more recently to structurally transform their economies and attain catch-up growth.

The inspiration for these policies was Alexander Hamilton whose work was a revelation to Friedrich List, a 19th-century German economist, who conceptualized this mode of catch-up growth and coined the term "kicking away the ladder". Both argued that while classical British political economists (Chapter 5) made the case for the US economy to specialize in primary commodities, it made more sense for them to industrialize to attain economic prosperity and that protection would be required to do so. Their view was that Britain was pushing free trade from a position of strength once it had industrialized and that its manufacturing advantage would prevent others from catching up without protection.[28]

Limits to generalization

While it may be possible to sensibly talk about development economics given the commonalities identified above, there are also major and important differences among L/LMICs that have a bearing on the growth strategy they may opt for. Countries vary a great deal by size and this can determine market size, the potential for attaining economies of scale and, consequently, MNC interest. For small countries it becomes more important to have an export-oriented growth strategy to attain economies of scale. While size brings economic advantages, it also brings administration challenges.

Countries can differ by the material resources they begin their development process with and this can have an important bearing on their growth trajectory. Resources can be a curse in that they could direct social energy into the appropriation of resource rents rather than on production. Apart from rent-seeking (corruption), a higher price for the resource on world markets can cause the local currency to appreciate as the higher demand for the resource translates into a higher demand for the local currency. This can hinder the ability of the country to diversify into other exports.[29] Scandinavian countries as well as the United States and Australia are resource rich and thriving, and Norway in particular has used its oil wealth to form a rainy day sovereign wealth fund and hence demonstrated that if well used, resources are a blessing.

Early development economists pointed to cultural traits as militating toward or against nations prospering (Bauer, 1984). This has proved highly controversial as scholars have pointed out that the cause of late industrialization in nations such as Germany and Japan, relative to say Great Britain, was attributed by observers to laziness as a national trait. Of course once these nations prospered, efficiency was attributed to these nations as a cultural trait.[30]

The less homogeneous a country is the more potential there may be of them confronting political instability as a vicious circle. This is particularly the case when a geographic region coincides with an ethnic group, and there are regional development disparities in the nation, since this can promote separatism. The East Asian successes share cultural homogeneity as a commonality, though much else was important in explaining their catch-up growth as will be indicated in Chapter 9. Even so, the lack of ethnic strife is one less factor to worry about when trying to initiate catch-up growth.

Comparative initial conditions

Some of the earlier mainstream development economists suggested that LICs could follow the same economic development trajectory as current HICs.[31] Apart from other analytical problems with this thesis, it ignored that L/LMICs started with a very different set of initial conditions compared to current HICs. The latter did not have to contend with the negative baggage of colonialism. In fact, being colonial countries, they had access to the labor, raw materials and markets of the colonies. They initiated agricultural revolutions that fed into their industrial revolutions. They were comparatively advanced in educational attainment, technological leaders, had political stability, and apart from these achievements had also experienced the socio-cultural and institutional changes complementing an industrial revolution.

These socio-cultural changes included the move to nuclear families and the emphasis on the legitimacy of personal striving and material incentives and rewards, and rational independent calculation which promoted labor mobility. Concomitantly, this reduced the emphasis on clan and ethnic group loyalties and placed more emphasis on efficiency and productivity and loyalty to the nation state. North America and Australia/New Zealand were important outlets for the emigration of those not content for religious or social reasons and also for economic migrants. Thus these lands provided a safety valve and also a resource due to the massive remittances. The movement of South/Southeast Asian labor to the Middle East is an example of this still being possible for LICs, but such opportunities are generally more limited now in that acquiring nationality is not an option.

Earlier development economists set much store by the importance of climate. A harsh hot climate can negatively impact productivity. All currently HIC countries are in the temperate zones. Tropical and sub-tropical climates bring to bear additional challenges of harsh weather and disease vectors.

Current environment

Gerschenkron (1962) pointed out that being a late developer could be an advantage. Perhaps it would be more accurate to characterize attempting catch-up growth in an environment that includes HICs as a mixed blessing. Current LICs have an advantage of having a backlog of technology available for them to choose from. However, this technology is not free and evolved to respond to the very different needs of current HICs in a particular historical juncture. The premature use of labor-saving technology can compound L/LMIC unemployment problems.

Another related issue is that technology can only be viewed as disembodied from the society it evolved in a limited sense. If the social and physical infrastructure that the technology flourished in is different, the diffusion and maintenance of such technology in another context may be limited because of the lack of absorption capacity (Chapter 14).

Even so, at times there are clear advantages of adoption and adaptation. For example, the adoption of cell phones by farmers in Africa to cut out the middle person has been an unqualified benefit. Kenya adapted and used mobile technology for the transfer of funds and overcame the physical insecurity of financial transactions and the lack of banking infrastructure and access – low density of bank branches in the country and access for the poor to these branches. Tanzania is registering births using cell phones since distance and bureaucratic hurdles impede such registrations.

Leapfrogging is also possible and so mobile technology has made cable networks less relevant. Similarly, solar and other alternative energies may make an electrical grid irrelevant. Cheaper water cleaning technologies may make decentralized water supply possible. India adapted and made advances in cheaper medical technologies, like smaller X-Ray machines, that were subsequently imported by the west. China did the same for CT scanners.[32] Rwanda gave approval for the first attempt to parachute medical supplies into remote areas via drones.

Public health technologies often exported with donor support have been a boon for L/LMICs. However, while this has had a beneficial impact on saving lives, it can also lead to a population explosion. Mortality rates declined much before a decline in fertility rates that organically accompanies higher education, incomes and cultural change. This partial demographic transition resulted in high population growth rates with a very high share of young cohorts in the population.[33]

Current conditions also do not easily permit a move to industrialization to attain catch-up growth as in the past. Current HICs dramatically added to the stock of greenhouse gases before knowledge of what they were doing was widely available and continued even after warnings of the consequences became widespread. Now the consequences of global climate change are upon the world and the impacts are being disproportionately felt by LICs whose ability to adapt is most limited. It is no longer possible to industrialize without restraint as a responsible member of the world community. However, clean production technologies have been developed by HICs and present a multi-win opportunity for green agriculture and green industrial development to L/LMICs (Chapters 14 and 15). Learning from the mistakes of current HICs is also a blessing in that some forms of resource degradation are not reversible.

Just as technology is often transplanted rather than an indigenous and organic evolution within L/LMICs, institutions evolved in the west can have side effects when transplanted. Welfare states evolved in response to ideological challenges after western societies had become more prosperous. L/LMICs that were becoming independent in a global environment in which the UN General Assembly had already approved an International Bill of Human Rights (1948) assuring humans of the rights to basic freedoms provided by a welfare state. Health care, education, progressive labor legislation, unions, occupational health and safety are all assured. The basic human needs/human development approach (Chapter 4) views social provision as paying dividends by making humans more productive. However, garnering resources for such provisions is a challenge.

The talented have historically often looked to enhance their skills wherever this may lead them. With more security and fewer restrictions, many of the talented in L/LMICs leave for HICs for higher education. While there is a potential gain, it can represent a loss not only from the productivity foregone but also due to the education subsidy that went into training them if the highly educated do not return. By the late 1980s, Africa had lost a third of its highly skilled labor force. Eighty percent of the highly skilled left Haiti (Khan, 2012).

Eventually the brain drain can be reversed and become a brain gain, such as has happened in China and India in the last decade, resulting in a virtuous circle when LICs eventually get engaged in catch-up growth. Such growth creates job opportunities, draws expatriate talent back home, which further boosts growth.[34] A good example of this is how the growth of the information technology sector in Bangalore and its links with Silicon Valley was mutually reinforced by the flows of talent, information and services.[35]

Perhaps the starkest way in which the catch-up growth environment for current L/LMICs is different from what current HICs faced is the current context of economic globalization. Starting in the 1990s, economic globalization started receiving much attention in the development economics literature as judged by the books and articles published on globalization and economic development. Economic globalization can be thought of as economic interaction among nations, and such interaction, particularly between HICs and L/LMICs, can impact the economic development of the latter. The economic interactions viewed as economic globalization emanate from flows of resources (labor, capital, products and information) between nations. Viewed in this way, there is nothing new about economic globalization although there are time periods during which such flows have been more intense and unimpeded than at other times. As nations became independent, these flows could at least nominally be viewed as resulting from a "national volition" while during colonial times the colonized had little say.

The word nominally is used because national volition is difficult to realize. It would presuppose at least some form of representative government and at a bare minimum the ability to replace political parties representing constituents with elections. Second, it would presuppose the ability of governments to withstand foreign pressure that results from indebtedness or foreign investment and foreign trade dependency. The term neocolonial, as characterized above, represents the lack of independence such that decisions do not serve L/LMIC nationals. The political alliances that are a mechanism for neocolonialism often mean the interests of national elites are concomitantly served with that of foreign governments at the expense of the broader L/LMIC populations (Baran, 1957).

The flows alluded to above include foreign aid and loans (capital), FDI (capital), foreign funds (portfolio or bank loans, capital), foreign trade (products), technology transfer (information) and migration (labor). There are forces opposing economic globalization in all countries based on the perception or reality of adverse consequences. In HICs, labor and environmentalists oppose it and populist politicians capitalize on such resentments. Labor opposes it because of the outsourcing of jobs or because of cheap imports that amount to the same. Environmentalists oppose it because the lack of environmental standards in L/MICs can cause resource degradation, much of it non-reversible, which can have global repercussions such as on climate change from say carbon emissions or deforestation (degradation of a carbon sink). Labor in HICs demands a level playing field so that the L/LMICs products they compete with are subject to the same social and environmental standards. Some in L/LMICs view the imposition of such standards as another form of neocolonialism and argue that current HICs did not confront such standards at similar levels of economic development.[36]

Summary and conclusions

This chapter documents the commonalities among L/LMICs. These include poor social and economic indicators such as low literacy and mean education, high infant mortality, high maternal mortality, low life expectancy, high unemployment rates, high rural to urban migration and urban blight and economic dualism. They suffer from the triple deficits (balance of payments, fiscal and saving), high population dependency ratios, high levels of environmental/resource degradation, and regional and ethnic strife.

While all this is challenging enough, they are also attempting to attain catch-up growth in a global environment that is challenging. Even as they overcome the baggage of colonialism, they confront the challenges of neocolonialism resulting from asymmetric power between HICs and the rest. This power asymmetry results in the global economic rules for trade, capital flows and migration being framed in the interests of HICs and which represent barriers for L/LMICs.

L/LMICs face the additional challenge of attempting catch-up growth at a historical juncture in which the global commons (atmosphere, oceans) have already been severely degraded and have little capacity to sustain more degradation. International agreements that L/LMICs are signatory to require cleaner production standards in L/MICs as do MNC codes of conduct that L/LMIC partners agree to when soliciting FDI. Such pressures may result from buyers or shareholders in HICs pressuring MNCs for corporate responsibility or from international organizations like the WTO or the World Bank. In Chapters 14 and 15 we explore how L/LMICs might be able to own this process to their own advantage.

L/LMICs scholars might be right in pointing out that environmental standards are a domestic and not a trade issue. They might be right in pointing out that current standards in HICs were not the ones prevailing when current HICs were embarked on their catch-up growth. They might be right in pointing out that the lower standards and concomitantly the lower costs are part of their comparative advantage. However, all this is moot given the current state of the global environment. The silver lining of climate change is that it has brought to the fore the notion of global citizenship. While the unit of analysis in this textbook is the nation state, climate change highlights that the world is one entity and all global citizens will survive or sink together.

Social standards imposed on L/LMICs via trade rules and international organizations are not as clear cut. What are referred to as sweatshops in HICs are a source of livelihoods in L/LMICs. The alternative may be unemployment or hazardous occupations in the informal sector including becoming sex-workers or having no livelihood at all.

L/LMICs have rightly pointed to the baggage of colonialism and the challenge of neocolonialism in an economic globalization context. However, they may also need to look to their own managerial failings. The experience of NICs and BRICS suggests that nations have to take their destiny into their own hands. Economic and political power is zero-sum and is not conceded but has to be earned and taken. The BRICS have shown that this is possible but also that MICs should expect push back from HICs.

The challenge for L/LMICs is to attain middle income status so that they can meaningfully function on a global scale, but more importantly, to address internal problems of poverty and inequality based on their own resources. These problems represent the most critical commonality among L/LMICs. The alternative approaches to economic development have different perspectives on attaining catch-up growth to address these problems. Prior to the discussion of alternative approaches in Part II, the issues of poverty and inequality, as key economic development problems, are discussed in the next chapter.

Questions and exercises

1. Explain the distinction between economic growth and economic development.
2. Explain some of the costs of economic growth.
3. Explain economic globalization and its mechanisms from an LIC/MIC perspective.
4. Explain some commonalities across L/MICs.
5. Explain why generalizing across L/LMICs could be problematic.
6. Explain the neoclassical theory of demand for children and how this and an institutional story explain a decline in the population growth rate in LICs.
7. How are current rates of urbanization in LICs different from historical patterns?

8. Explain the significance of the concepts of:
   a. Missing children
   b. Partial demographic transition
   c. Demographic dividend.
9. Explain the concepts and inter-relationships of market segmentation and dualism.
10. Elaborate on the concept of dualism by using conditions in any two markets in LICs as examples.
11. How does dualism interface with rural-urban migration in the LIC context? Identify and explain the main "pull" and "push" factors.
12. Explain rural-urban migration in L/LMICs paying particular attention to private and social costs and benefits.
13. Explain why basing notions of economic development on the experience of current HICs could be problematic.
14. Explain why being "late developers" could be a mixed blessing.
15. Explain the concept of "kicking away the ladder".
16. Explain how the mechanisms of surplus transfer differ under colonialism and neocolonialism.
17. Cite and explain the structural mechanisms by which colonialism is viewed as having resulted in arrested or disarticulated development.
18. Cite and explain the institutional mechanisms by which colonialism is viewed as having resulted in arrested or disarticulated development.
19. Explain how the current global conditions make catch-up economic growth particularly challenging.
20. Use the *World Development Indicators* to construct your own Appendix Table 3.1 by picking different variables.
21. Use the *World Development Indicators* to construct your own Appendix Tables 3.3 by picking a different region.

Notes

1 Since currencies can fluctuate a great deal when flexible, the World Bank uses a three-year moving average (i.e. average of the current and preceding two years) to adjust for such fluctuations.
2 Unless otherwise specified, the reference to $ in this textbook will be to US$.
3 More technically, a PPP ratio between say Kenya and the United States would be a representative basket of commodities weighted by local prices in the numerator for Kenya and denominator for the United States. The problem of course is that since consumption patterns vary, finding a comparable basket of commodities is not straight-forward and neither is finding accurate and relevant prices in an L/LMIC country context. Setting these problems aside, dividing the per capita income converted by the PPP exchange rate with the per capita income converted with the market exchange rate provides an exchange rate deviation index. It measures the extent to which the market exchange rate conversion understates the true purchasing power.
4 As indicated earlier in Chapter 1, endnote 29, since GDP in HICs is much larger than in MICs or LMICs, in absolute terms industry and manufacturing are still much larger in HICs than in MICs or LMICs.

5 This difference and the differential contribution by country income group to the stock of greenhouse gases that trap heat in the atmosphere is why L/LMICs have argued that HICs have a greater responsibility to address global climate change.

6 Data for the more populous South Asian countries are reported in Appendix Table 3.3. The other South Asian countries are Bhutan and the Maldives. Some lists include Afghanistan as part of South Asia while others count it as part of Central Asia.

7 Unlike East Asian countries like South Korea and Taiwan, it was unable to sustain the catch-up momentum and why that was the case should become clear from the Chapter 9 discussion about what the East Asian countries did right compared to Latin American, South Asian and African countries.

8 The debate about what accounted for India's relative success is discussed in Chapter 8.

9 Bangladesh is considered one of the most climate vulnerable countries of the world and it has already experienced sea level rise, salt water intrusion and extreme climate events such as hurricanes. It will need the sustained high growth rates to adapt to climate change.

10 One notable achievement for Pakistan might be containing its poverty rate to 4 percent of the population based on World Bank estimates of poverty headcount ratio at $1.90 a day (2011 PPP). This could result from the computerized safety nets such as the Benazir Income Support Program and the work of rural development NGOs. However, based on the National Poverty Line which is more stringent, its performance in this regard at 24.3 percent is like other comparator South Asian countries.

11 Given local knowledge, all the numbers tell a story. For example, rural electrification at 99 percent in Pakistan even exceeded that of Sri Lanka and is exceptional for an LMIC which has an average of 68.1 percent rural electrification rate (Appendix Table 3.1). Yet, the background story is one that involves Independent Power Producers, generous government contracts and unsustainable fiscal deficits.

12 Recall the "rule of 72" from Chapter 1. A population growth rate of 3 percent would mean a doubling of the population in less than a quarter of a century.

13 Population dependency ratios measure dependent population in a household i.e. those less than 15 or greater than 64 relative to the working population between 16 and 64. This is a crude measure, as is the case for most indicators, since children below 15 work and there is no concept of retirement for the poor so the elderly keep working until they are not able to.

14 This may not be the case for the affluent who have servants for childcare and women do not need to work, particularly in rural areas where working represents a loss of status. Highly educated urban women from affluent backgrounds may choose to work as a lifestyle choice.

15 Singapore experimented with such incentives. Positive monetary and other incentives for having more children are also used in countries (e.g. France, Germany and Hungary) where population growth rates have slowed and are expected to reduce the size of the future labor force.

16 While our focus is on the economic dualism, there is a corresponding social dualism reflected in different qualities of health care, education and social services in general for the rich relative to the poor.

17 These are referred to as arbitrage opportunities where after accounting for transportation and transaction costs, a trader may still earn a profit by buying in the market where the price is low and selling where it is high. The implicit assumptions are that reasonable communication, storage and transportation infrastructures are in place.

18 There is much more money to be made across the board with new projects than in maintenance or the protection of existing social and physical infrastructure. Hence, LICs suffer inordinately from the lack of maintenance.

19 These market failures created the opportunity for the introduction of microcredit (Chapter 4).

20 Cypher (2014) is unique among development economics textbooks for devoting a whole chapter to history including an excellent account of colonialism. Citing sources, he points

out that at its peak in 1914, 84.4 percent of the global land mass had been colonized and only Arabia (some parts), Turkey, Siam (Thailand), Persia (Iran), Mongolia, China, Nepal and Tibet escaped overt colonialism.

21 In the political economy of development approach, societies reproduce themselves economically (think of this as stable GDP). Anything beyond this economic reproduction is surplus.

22 For more recent scholarship of the drain of resources from India, refer to Patnaik (2017).

23 For example, Dreze and Sen (2013, pp. 3–7) document this for India. Recent studies on colonialism are nuanced and rigorously test the impact of various mechanisms on the negative impact of the colonial legacy on future development outcomes. For example, Angeles and Nianidis (2015) document a positive association of the degree or density of European settlement in the colonies and corruption, Bruhn and Gallego (2012) document an inverse association of future development to the nature of colonial activities (good, bad, ugly) and Iyer (2010) relates the negative impact of colonialism on social and physical infrastructure based on whether the rule was direct or indirect.

24 The simple definition of the external terms of trade is the price of exports relative to the price of imports (using price indices). One of the most prominent debates in development economics concerns whether the terms of trade for L/LMICs has been declining over time (Chapter 7).

25 Rounds are periods of negotiations from one treaty to the next. The Doha Development Round started being negotiated in 2001 and is still being negotiated. The Uruguay Round, which was negotiated prior to the Doha Round, took the longest to negotiate up to that point (eight years). One view is that L/LMICs signed away so much against their interests in the Uruguay Round that they became resistant to HIC pressure for more giveaways. In turn, HICs are turning to bi-lateral and regional trade agreements to secure more trade liberalization.

26 http://thebricspost.com/imf-reforms-china-india-brazil-russia-get-greater-say/#. WBXlMS0rK1s, consulted 1/20/2019.

27 However, power is not easily conceded and the United States initiating a trade war against China in 2018 is emblematic of such geo-political tussle.

28 Interestingly Chang, originally from South Korea, pointed out that once South Korea joined the OECD (Organization for Economic Cooperation and Development), the rich country club, it even more aggressively opposed the policies it had used to catch-up than other rich countries.

29 This phenomenon has been referred to as the Dutch Disease, a term coined by *The Economist* magazine. Due to the natural gas finds in Holland in 1959, the Dutch guilder appreciated and set deindustrialization into motion as the price of Dutch manufactured exports rose in world markets.

30 Quotes suggestive of Japanese and later Korean laziness prior to their catch-up growth were documented by Basu (2015, pp. 62–63). The point he was making is that norms can be endogenous and hence can change.

31 The most prominent such thesis was due to Rostow (Chapter 5).

32 Frugal innovation has now become a well-known concept. Refer to http://frugalinnovationhub.com/en/, consulted 1/20/2019.

33 Thus a full demographic transition is when both birth and fertility rates decline in tandem.

34 This phenomenon of virtuous circles (or cycles) has also been referred to by Myrdal (see Chapter 7) as positive cumulative causation or positive path dependency. The obverse i.e. negative cumulative causation or path dependency represents a vicious circle.

35 The timing has to be right for the virtuous circle to come into motion. Even so, countries have sometimes successfully attempted to tap into its expatriate talent. Examples include Taiwan in the 1960s and China in the 1990s. The United Nations Development Program's TOKTEN (Transfer of Knowledge through Expatriate Nationals) is a small initiative for instituting a brain gain after the drain (Khan, 2012).

36 Basu (1999), using the case of child labor, showed how complex such issues are and how policy should depend on context.

APPENDIX TABLE 3.1 Selected defining characteristics by country income group

Country income level	LIC	LMIC	MIC	UMIC	HIC
Economy – structure and indicators					
GDP per capita, constant 2010 US$, **2017**	719.3	2,189.1	4,992.0	8,224.5	41,583.7
GDP per capita, PPP constant 2011, international $, **2017**	1,888.2	6,551.1	11,092.2	16,319.7	43,053.8
Agriculture, forestry and fisheries value added per worker (constant, 2010 US$), **2016**	557.6	2,059.7	3,356.3	6,044.7	39,024.1
Agriculture, forestry and fisheries value added, % of GDP, **2016**	26.3	15.6	8.8	6.8	1.3
Industry, value added (including construction) per worker, **2016**	3,675.1	7,543.5	16,690.8	23,736.1	90,990.1
Industry, value added (including construction), % of GDP, **2016**	29.7	28.0	31.6	32.6	22.9
Manufacturing, value added, % of GDP, **2016**	9.3	15.7	18.9	19.9	14.3
Services, value added, % of GDP, **2016**	39.2	49.3	54.0	55.3	69.6
Services, value added per worker (constant, 2010 US$), **2016**	3,020.8	6,859.2	11,532.2	14,272.7	80,759.4
Access to electricity, % of rural population, **2016**	12.2	68.1	78.3	98.7	99.9
Access to electricity, urban (% of urban population), **2016**	67.6	94.9	97.6	99.8	99.9
Energy use, kg of oil equivalent per capita, **2014**	na	646.3	1,395.8	2,204.2	4,637.5
Gross capital formation (I), % of GDP, **2016**	23.5	26.7	30.6	31.8	21.1
Gross domestic savings (% of GDP), **2016**	9.0	23.7	31.4	33.7	22.4
Cost of business start-up procedures, % of GNI per capita, **2017**	70.1	24.0	22.7	21.6	4.6
Time required to start a business (days), **2017**	23.8	20.9	23.9	26.7	10.7

(Continued)

APPENDIX TABLE 3.1 (Cont.)

Country income level	LIC	LMIC	MIC	UMIC	HIC
External balance on goods and services, % of GDP, 2016	−18.1	−3.6	−0.1	1.2	1.2
Technology indicators					
Mobile cellular subscriptions (per 100 people), 2017	62.1	98.1	104.3	111.5	125.2
Individuals using the internet (% of population), 2016	13.5	29.9	41.8	55.3	81.7
Fixed broadband subscriptions (per 100 people), 2017	0.8	2.4	10.9	20.9	32.3
Scientific and technical journal articles, 2016*	5,439.8	172,760	886,566.6	713,399.1	1,411,362
Patent applications, residents, 2016	na	20,575	1,287,039	1,266,464	841,458
Social investments and human development indicators					
Domestic general government health expenditure (% of GDP), 2015	1.2	1.3	2.8	3.3	7.7
Births attended by skilled health staff, % of total, 2014	58.6	74.5	82.9	97.6	99.0
People using at least basic sanitation services (% of population), 2015	29.1	52.9	66.0	81.0	99.2
People using at least basic drinking water services (% of population), 2015	56.1	85.3	90.2	95.7	99.5
Life expectancy at birth, female, years, 2016	64.7	69.8	73.5	77.6	83.1
Life expectancy at birth, male, years, 2016	61.1	66.1	69.0	73.1	77.8
Fertility rates, births per woman, 2016	4.6	2.8	2.3	1.8	1.7
Maternal mortality ratio, per 100 000 live births, modeled estimate, 2015	479	257	180	41	13
Mortality rate, under-5, female (per 1,000), 2017	64	46	34	13	5
Mortality rate, under-5, male (per 1,000), 2017	74	50	38	15	6
Mortality rate, infant, female, per 1,000 live births, 2017	44	34	26	11	4

Mortality rate, infant, male, per 1,000 live births, **2017**	53	39	30	13	5
Government expenditure on education, total (% of GDP), **2014**	3.8	4.3	4.5	4.5	5.2
Literacy rates, adult female, % for 15 years and above, **2016**	52.8	69.8	81.6	93.4	na
Literacy rates, adult male, % for 15 years and above, **2016**	68.6	82.8	89.6	95.5	na
School enrollment secondary (net), %, **2017**	33.6	59.4	67.4	81.7	92.5
School enrollment tertiary (gross), %, **2017**	8.8	24.4	35.6	52.1	77.1
School enrollment tertiary, gender parity index (female to male ratio), **2017**	0.62	1.01	1.11	1.19	1.25
Pollution					
CO_2 emissions (metric tons per capita), **2014**	0.32	1.47	3.87	6.59	10.71

Sources: World Development Bank development indicators on line, update 1/30/2019.

Notes: The World Bank still reports data for LMIC, MIC and UMIC as reported in the table above. However, its 2017–2018 income classification has merged MIC and UMIC. Author attempts to get the cut-off between MIC and UMIC from the World Bank statistical department were not successful.

LIC = Low income countries (PCPPPUS$ = $995 or less)

LMIC = Lower middle income countries (PCPPPPUS$ = $996 to $4,125)

UMIC = Upper middle Income countries (PCPPPUS$ = $4,126 to $12,745)

HIC = High income countries (PCPPPUS$ = $12,746 or more)

na = Data not available

* = Classified by the Science Citation Index or the Social Science Citation Index

APPENDIX TABLE 3.2 Selected defining characteristics of L/LMICs countries by region

Region	EA&P	LA&C	ME&NA	SA	SSA
GDP per capita, constant 2010 US$, **2017**	6,137.9	8,889.0	4,301.2	1,779.7	1,651.4
GDP per capita growth (annual %), Average **2010–2017**	6.6	1.1	1.0	5.5	1.1
Agriculture, forestry and fisheries value added per worker (constant, 2010 US$), **2016**	4,153.9	5,790.1	5,916.5	1,511.5	1,326.9
Agriculture, forestry and fisheries value added, % of GDP, **2017**	8.7	4.7	9.5	16.0	16.0
Industry, value added (including construction) per worker, **2016**	19,905.1	23,507.2	22,129.5	5,635.6	10,920.0
Industry, value added (including construction), % of GDP, **2017**	39.6	23.3	34.1	25.5	25.2
Manufacturing, value added, % of GDP, **2017**	27.6	12.7	16.6	14.8	10.1
Services, value added per worker (constant, 2010 US$), **2016**	9,918.4	18,062.6	14,822.7	6,772.4	7,629.7
Services, value added, % of GDP, **2016**	51.2	61.6	52.4	49.7	52.2
Access to electricity, % of rural population, **2016**	93.8	94.0	94.7	79.5	24.7
Access to electricity, urban (% of urban population), **2016**	98.8	99.4	99.7	98.1	75.7
Energy use, kg of oil equivalent per capita, **2014**	1,877.4	1,226.0	1,477.1	576.1	686.2
Gross capital formation (I), % of GDP, **2017**	40.3	18.6	29.8	29.4	20.4
Gross domestic savings (% of GDP), **2017**	43.6	18.3	24.8	26.8	18.7
Cost of business start-up procedures, % of GNI per capita, **2018**	21.8	49.5	30.9	11.0	45.1
Time required to start a business (days), **2018**	30.1	34.5	24.6	13.8	23.2
External balance on goods and services, % of GDP, **2016**	1.8	-0.7	-5.3	-4.3	-1.2
Human development index, 2017	.73	.76	.76	.64	.54

Sources: World Development Bank development indicators on line, update 1/30/2019.
For the human development index, UNDP, Human Development Indices and Indicators, 2018 Statistical Update, http://hdr.undp.org/sites/default/files/2018_human_development_statistical_update.pdf, p. 49, consulted, 2/2/2019.

Notes: na = Data not available
EA&P = East Asia and the Pacific
LA&C = Latin America and the Caribbean
ME&NA = Middle East and North Africa
SA = South Asia
SSA = Sub Saharan Africa

APPENDIX TABLE 3.3 Selected defining characteristics of South Asian countries

Countries	Bangladesh	India	Nepal	Pakistan	Sri Lanka
GDP per capita, constant 2010 US$, 2017	1,093.0	1,964.6	732.4	1,222.5	3,849.5
GDP per capita growth (annual %), average 2010–2017	5.3	6.0	3.2	2.0	5.0
Agriculture, forestry and fisheries value added per worker (constant, 2010 US$), 2017	990.7	1,678.8	549.7	1,699.8	2,532.8
Agriculture, forestry and fisheries value added, % of GDP, 2017	13.4	15.5	26.2	22.9	7.7
Industry, value added (including construction) per worker, 2017	4,067.6	6,386.8	2,131.0	2,904.6	10,340.1
Industry, value added (including construction), % of GDP, 2017	27.8	26.3	13.4	17.9	27.4
Manufacturing, value added, % of GDP, 2017	17.3	15.1	5.1	12.0	15.9
Services, value added per worker (constant, 2010 US$), 2017	3,674.5	7,729.8	3,118.3	5,707.9	11,726.3
Services, value added, % of GDP, 2017	53.5	48.7	51.6	53.1	55.7
Access to electricity, % of rural population, 2016	68.8	77.6	85.2	98.8	94.6
Access to electricity, urban (% of urban population), 2016	94.0	98.4	94.5	99.7	100
Energy use, kg of oil equivalent per capita, 2014	222.2	637.4	412.7	484.4	515.7
Gross capital formation (I), % of GDP, 2017	30.5	30.6	45.7	16.0	36.7
Gross domestic savings (% of GDP), 2017	25.3	29.5	11.9	6.8	29.5
Cost of business start-up procedures, % of GNI per capita, 2018	21.2	14.4	22.2	6.8	9.4
Time required to start a business (days), 2018	19.5	16.5	16.5	16.5	9

(Continued)

APPENDIX TABLE 3.3 (Cont.)

Countries	Bangladesh	India	Nepal	Pakistan	Sri Lanka
External balance on goods and services, % of GDP, **2016**	−5.2	−2.9	−33.8	−9.3	−7.8
Poverty headcount ratio at national poverty lines (% of population)	24.3	21.9	25.2	24.3	4.1
	(2016)	(2012)	(2010)	(2015)	(2016)
Poverty headcount ratio at $1.90 a day (2011 PPP) (% of population), World Bank estimate	14.8	21.2	15.0	4.0	0.7
	(2016)	(2012)	(2016)	(2015)	(2016)
Human development index, 2017	.61	.64	.57	.56	.77

Sources: World Development Bank development indicators on line, update 1/30/2019.

Notes: For the human development index, UNDP, Human Development Indices and Indicators, 2018 Statistical Update, http://hdr.undp.org/sites/default/files/2018_human_development_statistical_update.pdf, p. 49, consulted, 2/2/2019.

For poverty estimates, parentheses contain the latest year the data were available.

The data used for each selected variable in all the appendix tables are the latest available in the online World Bank *World Development Indicators*. In Appendix Table 3.1, the income variable is used to classify countries into LICs, LMICs, MICs and HIC to explore commonalities by income classification. The main finding is that economic and social indicators vary positively with income classification. Thus HIC do much better on all indicators than LICs as expected but there is also a linear pattern by income grouping across all variables.

References

Acemoglu, D. and J. A. Robinson. 2012. *The Origins of Power, Prosperity, and Poverty: Why Nations Fail* (New York: Crown Business).

Alam, M. S. 1999. "Does Sovereignty Matter for Economic Growth? An Analysis of Growth Rates between 1870-1950," in: J. Adams and F. Pigliaru (eds.), *Economic Growth and Change* (Cheltenham, UK: Edward Elgar) 46-70.

Amsden, A. H. 2008. *Escape from Empire: The Developing World's Journey through Heaven and Hell* (Cambridge, MA: The MIT Press).

Angeles, L. and K. C. Nianidis. 2015. "The Persistent Effects of Colonialism on Corruption," *Economica*, 82(326), 319–349.

Baran, P. 1957. *The Political Economy of Growth* (New York: Monthly Review Press).

Basu, K. 1999. "Child Labor: Cause, Consequence, and Cure, with Remarks on International Labor Standards," *Journal of Economic Literature*, 37(3), 1083–1119.

Basu, K. 2015. *An Economist in the Real World: The Art of Policy Making in India* (Cambridge, MA: The MIT Press).

Bauer, P. T. 1984. *Reality and Rhetoric: Studies in the Economics of Development* (Cambridge, MA: Harvard University Press).

Becker, G. S. and H. G. Lewis. 1973. "Interaction between Quantity and Quality of Children," *Journal of Political Economy*, 81(2), S279–S288.

Bruhn, M. and F. A. Gallego. 2012. "Good, Bad, and Ugly Colonial Activities: Do They Matter for Economic Development?" *The Review of Economics and Statistics*, 94(2), 433–461.

Caldwell, J. C., Barkat-e-Khuda, B. Caldwell, I. Pieris and P. Caldwell. 1999. "The Bangladesh Fertility Decline," *Population and Development Review*, 25(3), 67–84.

Chang, H.-J. 2002. *Kicking Away the Ladder: Development Strategy in Historical Perspective* (London: Anthem Press).

Cleland, J., J. F. Phillips, S. Amin and G. M. Kamal. 1994. *The Determinants of Reproductive Change in Bangladesh: Success in a Challenging Environment* (Washington, DC: World Bank).

Cypher, J. M. 2014. *The Process of Economic Development* 4th ed. (London: Routledge).

Dreze, J. and A. Sen. 2013. *An Uncertain Glory: India and Its Contradictions* (Princeton, NJ: Princeton University Press).

Ebenstein, A. 2010. "The 'Missing Girls' of China and the Unintended Consequences of the One Child Policy," *Journal of Human Resources*, 45(1), 87–115.

Gerschenkron, A. 1962. *Economic Backwardness in Historical Perspective* (Cambridge, MA: Harvard University Press).

Gunatilleke, G. 2000. "Sri Lanka's Social Achievements and Challenges," in: D. Ghai (ed.), *Social Development and Public Policy: A Study of Some Successful Experiences* (New York: St. Martin's Press/MacMillan Press) 139-189.

Iyer, L. 2010. "Direct Verses Indirect Colonial Rule in India: Long-Term Consequences," *The Review of Economics and Statistics*, 92(4), 693.

Khan, S. R. 2011. "Growth Diagnostics: Explaining Pakistan's Lagging Economic Growth," *Global Economy Journal*, 11(4), 1–17.

Khan, S. R. 2012. "Highly Educated Labor Flows from Low to High Income Countries: Mutual Security," in: K. Khory (ed.), *Global Migration: Challenges in the Twenty-First Century* (New York: Palgrave MacMillan) 87-112.

Kravis, I. B. 1986. "The Three Faces of the International Comparison Project," *The World Bank Research Observer*, 1(1), 3–26.

La Porta, R. and A. Shleifer. 2014. "Informality and Development," *Journal of Economic Perspectives*, 28(3), 109–126.

Lipton, M. 1977. *Why Poor People Stay Poor: Urban Bias in World Development* (Cambridge, MA: Harvard University Press).

Papanek, G. F. 1967. *Pakistan's Development: Social Goals and Private Incentives* (Cambridge, MA: Harvard University Press).

Patnaik, U. 2017. "Revisiting the 'Drain', or Transfer from India to Britain in the Context of Global Diffusion of Capitalism," in: S. Chakrabarti and U. Patnaik (eds.), *Agrarian and Other Histories: Essays for Binay Bhushan Chaudhuri* (New Delhi: Tulika Books) 278-317.

Preston, S. H. 1979. "Urban Growth in Developing Countries: A Demographic Reappraisal," *Population and Development Review*, 5(2), 195–215.

Rhee, Y. W. 1990. "The Catalyst Model of Development: Lessons from Bangladesh's Success with Garment Exports," *World Development*, 18(2), 333–346.

Rostow, W. W. 1960. *The Stages of Economic Growth: A Non-Communist Manifesto*. Cambridge: Cambridge University Press.

Sen, A. K. 1990. "More Than 100 Million Women Are Missing," *New York Review of Books*, December 20.

Taylor, L. 1994. "Gap Models," *Journal of Development Economics*, 45(1), 17–34.

4

POVERTY, INEQUALITY AND SOME PROPOSED SOLUTIONS

Introduction

This chapter addresses the two key problems of L/LMICs that the approaches reviewed in Part II address directly or indirectly. The neoliberal and developmentalist approaches for the most part seek to mitigate these problems by initiating catch-up growth. The political economy and basic human needs/human development approaches differ in directly addressing these problems and hence they get more play in this chapter.

The current state of knowledge on absolute poverty is investigated first. Various definitions of poverty such as income, basic needs, risk and vulnerability poverty are explained. The findings of research that characterize poverty in L/LMICs are presented next, following which inequality is investigated, including policy debates on whether inequality should be addressed. Finally, policy initiatives proffered to address various forms of poverty are discussed and since these are targeted at the poor, social inequality could also be simultaneously addressed by them.

Absolute poverty

National poverty lines

The concept of absolute poverty pertains to how many people in a given geographic entity such as a nation state or regions within a nation state are in a state of poverty. To be able to make such a statement, poverty first needs to be defined. Based on a consensus definition, a national poverty line can then be identified. Following that, everyone that falls below the line could be considered to be in absolute poverty in a particular nation. This is why this way of measuring poverty is also known as headcount poverty since it entails identifying the percentage of the people in a given population who are in a state of poverty based on a given definition of poverty.[1]

The concept of a national poverty line is based on the amount of income needed to meet a minimum caloric intake for a specified period. For example, one estimate for a minimum caloric intake specified by nutritionists for an adult male (greater than 14 years of age) for a given day is 2,250. Nutritional needs of other individuals are determined based on adult equivalents (women 2/3 and children 1/2) of adult male caloric needs.

The next step is to convert a typical basket of commodities that would provide the specified calories using nutritionist conversion chart (food units to calories). The typical basket is then converted to local income equivalents in local currency. Finally, based on survey data, the numbers of people that fall below the income needed for specified calories for a specified time period (say one year) are considered to be in poverty. These estimates are possible for various categories such as region, or urban/rural and gender bifurcations.

Recall the data problems identified in Chapter 2. In addition to those, there are problems specific to constructing national poverty lines. Survey information is usually collected at the household level and then converted to the individual level based on assumptions about intra-household food distribution and adult equivalency. However, because that information on within household inequality is generally not available, estimates of poverty may be underestimated.

Since women often work both within and outside the home, researchers challenge the validity of the sex and adult equivalency assumptions specifying lower requirements for women than men. Beyond that, caloric needs vary greatly based for example on metabolism, body size and activity levels. Thus, averages in poverty research are more likely than usual to mask important variations. Again, at given levels of expenditure, caloric intake could vary significantly due to household consumption patterns. While calories are an important energy measure, critics have pointed out that other nutrient needs such as proteins, minerals, vitamins and micro nutrients also need to be accounted for.

The required information on consumption is collected by asking respondents to recall their consumption over a specified time period. The longer the time period for recall required of respondents, the greater the likely inaccuracy in the data. Poverty research suggests that a one-month recall systematically understated poverty compared to surveys that use a one-week recall.

There may be rural-urban and regional differences not captured by the numbers. For example, there may be a larger component of non-market goods and services in rural transactions that are not captured by survey data and hence rural poverty in this regard could be overstated. This bias could be reinforced by not taking into account that a culture of sharing is more predominant in rural areas.

Headcount poverty estimates per se do not take into account either the duration of poverty or the poverty gap. The duration refers to the time an average household spends below the poverty line. Policy makers have to be concerned about the stability (relative to mobility) below the poverty line. Mobility is desired because it suggests opportunities for movement above the poverty threshold. Such concerns have resulted in distinctions such as transient vs. chronic (long duration) poverty.

The poverty gap is the ratio by which the mean income of the poor falls below the poverty line. The head count index does not take into account how far below the poverty line the mean income of the poor falls. Thus even if policy is successful in ameliorating the condition of the "poorest of the poor" (those in extreme poverty), this may not show up in the poverty statistics if there is a big gap between the poverty line and the mean income of the poorest group. Hence a smaller poverty gap for a specified poverty line is preferable. Statistics are now reported when possible on both duration and the poverty gap.

Appendix Table 4.1 shows the state of poverty in LICs based on the national poverty line and the international poverty lines. The World Bank uses international poverty lines for global estimates of extreme poverty (headcount ratio at $1.90 per day, 2011, PPP, percentage population) and moderate poverty (headcount ratio at $3.20 per day, 2011, PPP, percentage population). Also reported are poverty gaps based on the national and international poverty lines.

As expected, poverty varies a great deal within the LIC group. Even so, 78 percent of the population in Madagascar was in extreme poverty by the World Bank definition. In 20 out of the 29 countries that data were reported for in various years, about a third of the population or more was in extreme poverty by the World Bank definition. Using the National Poverty Lines, in 20 out of the 28 countries that data were reported for in various years about two-fifths or more of the population was in extreme poverty, four-fifths in South Sudan. The average percentage of the population in LICs in extreme poverty using the World Bank and National Poverty Lines were 47.1 and 43 percent respectively. The averages for LICs were much higher than the averages for LMICs at 28 percent and 14.6 percent respectively. Thus moving to higher income status is associated with a decline in average poverty rates.

The average poverty gaps for both the World Bank and National Poverty lines for LICs were 16.2 percent, again much higher than LMIC. The size of these gaps suggests that in most cases a major effort would be required to move populations out of extreme poverty. While these numbers suggest a dire situation, the method of estimating poverty lines, particularly the international poverty lines, are highly controversial, however.[2] For this reason, scholars have turned to other methods to explore the reality of extreme poverty confronted by populations in L/LMICs.

Basic needs poverty

The basic needs approach mentioned in Chapter 1 found income poverty to be grossly inadequate as a measure of the state of deprivation and in keeping with its approach to development advocated a more holistic method of characterizing and measuring poverty. According to this approach, income poverty does not directly take into account other dimensions of well-being such as health, educational attainment and access to shelter and clothing. One way to estimate basic needs poverty is therefore to find the minimum amount of income that would provide for the basic needs of an average household.

The multi-dimensional poverty index proposed by Alkire et al. (2011) quantifies basic human needs poverty. The index measures deprivation by the unit of analysis, say an individual or household, on various sets of indicators of well-being such as education, health and living standards. The indicators are weighted and individuals or households are deemed to be in multi-dimensional poverty if the deprivation scores fall below a cross-dimensional poverty cut-off.

Risk and vulnerability poverty

The critique on data collection methods explored in Chapter 2 applies to measuring poverty and well-being. Recall that sample surveys are an instrument for estimating income poverty and that such data were roundly criticized by those with little faith in survey methods. As critiques developed on the drawbacks of sample surveys, alternative qualitative methods for gathering information emerged as explained. One particular alternative technique was the use of participatory approaches that enabled the poor to define poverty themselves and identify those who by their own criteria were in poverty.

The World Bank Research Department picked up on this initiative, as they often do with innovations emerging from academia. This can add value because, given their ample resources, they can often push such innovations much further than the innovators. In this case, they conducted a large number of participatory poverty appraisals in a number of L/LMICs. Two volumes were published in 1999 (40,000 responses in Vol. 1 and 20,000 in Vol. 2 for 23 countries) with the effort led by Narayan et al. (2000) who edited the responses in volumes titled *Voices of the Poor*.

Some findings that emerged from these studies were that the poor were very preoccupied with their political exclusion and lack of "voice".[3] Further, there was a preoccupation with the risk and vulnerability they confronted in their daily life. Such risk and vulnerability could be associated with for example natural disasters, political violence, feudal oppression and crime. The lack of ability to cope with shocks and covariate risks[4] is another way of viewing risk and vulnerability poverty.

Another finding of this study was that coping mechanisms could perpetuate poverty. The poor sensibly diversify their activities as a form of insurance. However, growing both food and cash crops and engaging in informal sector activities provides insurance but may not maximize income. Cash crops may provide the highest income, but because of possible crop failure, this may also be a high-risk strategy.

When confronting shocks, coping mechanisms might increase long-run poverty. For example, if short-term household survival entails cutting back on education and health expenditure, it perpetuates inter-generational poverty. Another form of coping is loans from within the village (shopkeepers, friends, moneylenders), but shocks often hit the village across the board and so in that case this coping mechanism is nullified.

Environmental degradation poverty

Observation rather than deep research is enough to fathom that the poor are the most vulnerable to environmental depredations. Pedestrians and cyclists are the most exposed to auto-emission and other toxic fumes. Rich motorists can leave behind the smog of inner cities as they drive to relatively clean residential areas or they can roll up the windows and turn on the air-conditioners if caught in traffic jams for some relief.

Again, low-income neighborhoods mushroom around industrial areas as property values fall and because of jobs, and they are hence the most exposed to dirty air, bad odors and effluents. It should thus not be surprising that poor children have a higher incidence of asthma, other respiratory diseases and lead poisoning.[5] Thus those who are the most disadvantaged are made more so. The probability of escaping poverty or enhancing the range of choices for children is thus reduced.

The poor, particularly women, are also more exposed to indoor pollution due to the use of biomass (biological material) for cooking and indoor heating (Ezzati and Kammen, 2005). Again, at work they spend long hours in polluted environments. The poor are also the most exposed to diseases such as diarrhea and dysentery due to the lack of access to clean water and sanitation (Seguin and Nino- Zarazua, 2011). Low nutritional intake also means less resistance to such diseases.

Poor uneducated farmers are more exposed to the detrimental effects of chemical agricultural inputs. Excess use, drifting sprays, leaky applicators and the lack of knowledge of handling equipment and dangerous substances enhances the risk of ill health. Similarly, women and children engaged for example in cotton picking, the cash crop for which pesticide use is the greatest, are exposed to numerous ailments. These include carcinogenic diseases, enzyme imbalances, skin and allergic reactions, lung diseases, sterility, cataracts, memory loss, change in the central nervous system and damage to the immune system(Devine and Furlong, 2007; chapter 13). For all these reasons, a clean environment needs to be viewed as part of an anti-poverty strategy.

Other conceptualizations of poverty

Mullainathan and Shafir (2013) and Mani et al. (2013) originated the concept of bandwidth poverty. Scarcity results in the poor obsessing about what they lack and if this is food, much of their thinking bandwidth is occupied by hunger and food. This negatively impacts cognitive functioning that would enable them to devise strategies to overcome the scarcity, another example of a vicious circle whereby say indebtedness leads to further indebtedness. The authors tested this hypothesis on data collected for sugarcane farmers in India using a natural experiment whereby they were able to compare the cognitive functioning of the same individuals who confronted scarcity and relative plenty. The cognitive functioning of farmers not having to contend with scarcity during harvest periods improved relative to their cognitive functions in times of scarcity.

For mainstream economists, opportunity costs drive decision making for individuals. Very often, hourly wages foregone would be the relevant cost of putting one hour of time toward another activity. This may understate the true opportunity cost of time for the poor relative to those who have adequate income for basic needs. Due to diminishing marginal utility, the marginal utility from income from one hour of work foregone for the poor is much greater than the same amount of income for the more comfortable. This could explain why social organizers find it so difficult to get participation from the poor in poverty alleviation initiatives. For those existing at or near a poverty threshold, the opportunity cost of their time is much higher than those who are more comfortable. This would be true even if the time is not spent in gainful employment but hustling to find ways to make ends meet.

The incidence of poverty

Poverty research in L/LMICs over decades has identified the incidence of poverty and the results are as one might expect. It is disproportionately present in rural areas and the urban bias identified in Chapter 3 has much to do with this. Within urban areas, the bulk of poverty is within shanty towns. Within households, poverty varies positively with the size of household, and females and children are more susceptible than adult men to poverty-related illnesses.

Standard mainstream household economics assumes that the head of the household represents the interests of the whole family in a utility maximization framework (Becker, 1981). Sen (1990) challenged this assumption and argued that there could be both conflict and cooperation within a household. This focus on household decision making revealed that there can be a systematic bias in the allocation of household goods (such as food) and resources (such as health and education expenditures) in favor of males and this is reflected in a higher incidence of female poverty.

Research also shows a higher incidence of poverty in female headed households. On average they are less educated so they get the lowest paying jobs. However, they also suffer from discrimination and so for the same education, skills and experience they get paid less, and this discrimination in L/LMICs is more intense than in HICs. In agriculture in particular, women also have less access to resources like land and capital (Chapter 13). There is also an asymmetry in the introduction of technology and its diffusion since most technology is introduced to ease the burden of the more highly paid male tasks such as tractors for plowing. If the women headed households belong to an ethnic minority the exclusion and intensity of poverty is even greater (Chapter 13).

Inequality

Causes

A great deal of attention is paid to inequality since it may have more to do with social instability than poverty. The idea is that people react more to their deprivation if others are prosperous or living in luxury. Inequality is also viewed as self-reinforcing as the rich parley their economic power to get political power that further consolidates their economic power in an ongoing circle.

Due to the social and political instability, as explained below, it can adversely impact economic growth and hence breed more inequality as the rich are more capable of surviving in difficult circumstances.

Inequality needs to be distinguished from inequity. The latter is suggestive of unfairness as judged by some theory of justice. Inequality may be based on inequity (social exploitation) but it need not be. Also, promoting equality may result in inequity – taking people's due share for redistribution if the initial distribution was just.[6]

Neoclassical economic analysis takes the existing distribution of income as a given and implicitly defends it by defending existing property rights. Heterodox approaches like the political economy of development or neo-Marxist approaches start their analysis by questioning the justness of the existing distribution of income and often advocate for redistribution if the existing distribution represents accumulation based on social injustice perpetrated either by colonialism or predation based on a concentration of political power.

Neoclassical analysis of the distribution of income is based on marginal productivity theory as reviewed in introductory economics. As indicated above, this theory takes the existing distribution of income/assets as a given and then shows it to be just, given certain assumptions including perfect competition or constant returns to scale technology and full employment. Based on these assumptions, factors of production get a share of total income according to their contribution to this income. Sensible employers will hire factors equal to the contribution of these factors on the margin to income.

Assume two factors (labor and capital) to enable graphical representation.[7] W is the market wage determined by the market demand and supply curve for labor in Figure 4.1 below.

In a competitive labor market, each firm has to pay the market determined wage. Given this wage and a downward sloping marginal productivity curve (diminishing returns given capital is fixed) each firm hires labor up to the point where W = MPL (marginal product of labor). The area under the demand for labor curve, up to where labor (L_1) is hired, represents the total product for the firm in Figure 4.1a.[8] Labor gets $W*L_1$ (wage bill) and the rest goes to capital.

The implication of this model is that distribution resulting from free market production is completely fair because all factors get what they contribute to production and the sum of factor contributions exhausts total product (adding

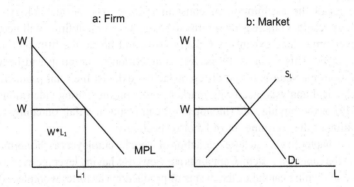

FIGURES 4.1a and b Marginal productivity theory

up theorem). This theory has been critiqued on several grounds by heterodox scholars including by Moseley (2012).

Much else goes into the production process other than the factors of production. For example, companies like Apple that represent the epitome of the success of market capitalism benefitted from a great deal of government support of research. Thus, not only does this theory take the existing distribution of income as a given, it also takes the existing institutional structure as a given and does not acknowledge its contribution to productivity and production.

Consider a student from Nigeria who earns an electronic engineering degree at the Massachusetts Institute of Technology as does her US roommate and friend from San Francisco. Suppose also that her GPA in graduate school is exactly the same as that of her US friend. However, while she returns to Nigeria her friend gets a job in Silicon Valley at a starting salary that is ten times higher than what she is offered.[9] Marginal productivity theory would suggest that the student from the United States is ten times more productive. However, we already know that is not the case and so why the salary differential? The answer is that complementary factors like research facilities, access to university facilities, a critical mass of colleagues and connectivity account greatly for the productivity differential. Thus, productivity is not just inherent to the person but also to the environment in which they work and much of that is provided by the state and the community of the country in question.

Recall that for the theory to hold the markets must be competitive and full employment must hold. If for example, employers have disproportionate labor market power, they can pay workers less than their marginal product and in introductory micro theory this is referred to as monopsony power. If there is unemployment, this would also give firms more leverage.

The theory also assumes that capital (K) and labor (L) are abstract entities and can be sensibly added up for aggregate analysis. Labor is heterogeneous (unskilled, semi-skilled, skilled, professional, technical, managerial) so aggregation is difficult. In fact, much of the social inequality is due to income differences across different categories of labor and so this theory assumes away the problem of inequality. The aggregation of capital is even more problematic and for heterodox scholars, without such aggregation, it is therefore not possible to compute marginal products.[10]

Also recall the assumption of constant returns to scale technology. If the technology results in increasing returns to scale, the efficient firms will necessary grow over time since expansion reduces costs and hence the firm will acquire market power. This violates the perfect competition assumption and hence the presumption that returns to the different factors exhaust the total product. Even in neoclassical analysis, acquiring market power on the selling side (monopoly/oligopoly) or the buying side (monopsony) can result in unfair outcomes i.e. the exploitation of the consumer or of labor respectively.

Marx (Chapter 5) viewed the exploitation of labor by employers as the normal state of play in the capitalist system. Capitalists are viewed as having leverage over workers by virtue of owning capital or the means of production (factories/workplaces). This enables capital to hire workers and set the remuneration below labor's contribution if there is high unemployment.[11] High unemployment was assured by what he called the reserve army of the unemployed and one capitalist strategy was to ensure the refurbishing of this reserve army by moving to ever more capital intensive techniques of production[12] and moving female and child labor into the workforce.

In such labor market conditions (with monopsony power) capital could get away with merely paying a subsistence wage i.e. one considered enough to enable labor to maintain and reproduce labor as a class. The remaining contribution of labor is then appropriated by capital.[13] For example if workers work eight hours (16–18 in Marx's day) and they produce enough to reproduce the household (subsistence wage) with four hours work, capital will hold on to the other four hours. As the unemployment rate falls, capital's leverage over labor declines.[14]

Two other reasons why the adding up theorem may not hold is intermediate products and joint production. The contribution of intermediate product to total output is not accounted for when assuming only factors of production contribute to output and holding intermediate inputs constant to compute the marginal product of a particular factor is not logical. Joint products result when a set of input leads to more than one output due to commercial byproducts such as wood chips in the production of furniture.

Measurement

Measuring inequality within a population requires knowledge of the size distribution of income within that population. This means a frequency distribution of the percentages of population that fit into different income categories. A hypothetical frequency or size distribution is shown in Table 4.1 using a fictitious currency.

Based on the fictitious distribution of income in Table 4.1, it is possible to get a graphical account of the state of income inequality for a particular population. For

TABLE 4.1 Hypothetical discrete size distribution of income

Income category (Galoses (Gs) per month)	Percentage of population in income group
<10,000	0.400
10,001–20,000	0.200
20,001–30,000	0.150
30,001–40,000	0.100
40,001–50,000	0.050
50,001–60,000	0.040
60,001–70,000	0.035
70,001–80,000	0.015
80,001–90,000	0.007
90,001–100,000	0.002
>100,000	0.001

example, we know that 90 percent of the population earns less than 50,000 Gs per month while 10 percent earns greater than 50,000 Gs. Another way to look at it is that only .01 percent of the population earns greater than 100,000 Gs. Either way, the data tell us that there is a high level of income inequality in the population in question. However, it is possible to go further than this in characterizing the nature of inequality in a given country.

The size distribution of income above is called discrete since the population distribution is based on discrete income groups rather than continuous income. Imagine even more granular data so that the income distribution is continuous such that we know exactly what percentage of the income is garnered by each percentage of the population. Such a continuous size distribution of income, admittedly highly demanding of data, can be used to construct measures of income distribution and inequality.

In 1905, the statistician Max O. Lorenz proposed a way to represent inequality in a two-dimensional graph by charting the percentage of population on one axis and the percentage of the variable of interest on the other axis and the distribution that results provides a visual account of the inequality for the variable in question. This tool could be utilized to represent for example inequality in income, wealth or a component of wealth such as land holdings if data are available.

To represent income inequality, we put the percentage of the population on the horizontal axis and the percentage of income on the vertical axis. Perfect equality in a population would be represented by a 45 degree line i.e. 50 percent of the population getting 50 percentage of income as shown in Figure 4.2. Inequality would be present if 50 percent of the population earned less than 50 percent of the total income. The greater the distance below the 45 degree line, the greater the income inequality for every given population point. Joining all such points, the curve that results is named after Lorenz and it is a graphical representation of the extent of income inequality in a population.[15] Thus the way to view inequality visually is to look at the depth of the arc the income line or Lorenz curve makes relative to the 45 degree line or the line of equality. The deeper the arc, the greater is the income inequality in a population being studied, as shown in Figure 4.2.

It is possible to go still further in characterizing inequality. Instead of relying on a visual observation, the Lorenz curve can be used to compute a summary statistic that has been developed as a measure of inequality. Since the arc (A) in Figure 4.2 represents the extent of inequality, that divided by the total area under the triangle (A + B) is a summary statistic representing the extent of income inequality referred to as the Gini coefficient. The Gini coefficient varies from 0 to 1; the coefficient is 0 when there is no arc (perfect equality, A = 0 i.e. 0/B = 0) and 1 when there is perfect inequality (i.e. B is zero; A/A = 1). Perfect inequality means that in the limit one individual gets all the income and everyone else gets none.

The great advantage of the Gini coefficient is that it is conceptually straightforward and can in a simple way represent income and other forms of inequality in a population and also makes possible comparisons across populations. However, if the relevant Lorenz curves intersect in a comparison of two countries

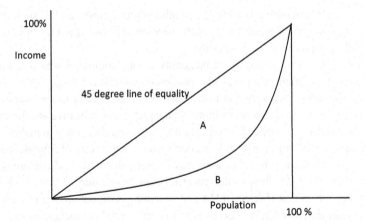

FIGURE 4.2 Lorenz curve

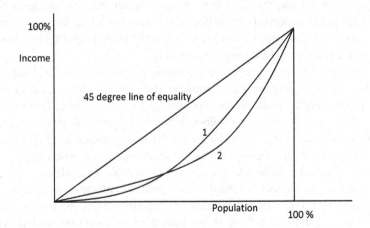

FIGURE 4.3 Intersecting Lorenz curves

or of one country over time, it is then possible to get the same Gini coefficients with very different income distributions, as shown in Figure 4.3.

Figure 4.3 shows two Lorenz curves for country 1 and country 2 (or time periods 1 and 2 within one country). Assume that they yield the same Gini coefficient for two countries. If there is more interest in what is happening to the lower half of the population, then distribution 1 would be preferable even though the Gini for the two distributions are the same. Another related problem is that the Gini coefficient can be scale insensitive. Small changes at the lower end of the distribution may mean much for reducing absolute poverty (push many people close to or above the poverty line), but these changes may not register much of a change in the Gini coefficient.

A more technical problem is that the Gini coefficient cannot be decomposed. Thus the inequality within and between groups should, but does not, add up to the Gini. Several more sophisticated measures such as the Atkinson or Theil index do not have this shortcoming but they have other shortcomings and as such there is no perfect measure. Despite the caveats mentioned above, the Gini remains the most widely used due to its simplicity.

Simpler suggestive measures of inequality can be computed with data on total income by population groupings like deciles or quintiles. For example, one can calculate the ratio of what the top 1 or 10 percent claim relative to the bottom 20 or 40 percent. The ratios chosen are arbitrary, but nonetheless indicative and the specific ratios chosen can vary depending on the point the researcher wants to make.[16]

LICs are for the most part hybrid market systems with a mix of developmentalist interventionism and neoliberal economic philosophy that became dominant starting in the 1980s. The inequality results reported below have emerged from this mix. To provide context, ratios of selected HICs representing different models of capitalism are also reported. Sweden is selected to represent a social democratic model with a focus on social solidarity and hence high marginal tax rates and generous social safety nets. Korea represents East Asian corporate capitalism based on an interventionist state.[17] Notwithstanding the focus on the business sector and economic growth, buy in from the public depended on building such a model on a foundation of equity, as was the case in Japan, which it emulated (Chapter 9). Both these HICs can therefore be expected to have moderate income inequality.

The United States represents the Anglo-Saxon model of market-driven capitalism with think tanks supporting the Republican Party pushing for individual liberty and entrepreneurship based on low tax rates and low regulation. This economic philosophy is also the basis of neoliberalism, which pushes for vibrant economic growth and considers the prosperity created by the capitalists as likely to trickle down to the rest of the population.[18] In this case, one would expect higher social inequality than in the social democrat or corporatist capitalist models.

There is no pure model of capitalism and political pulls and pushes constantly change leanings. For example, Sweden has become notably more conservative, and while the Democratic Party in the United States favors the market system and entrepreneurship, there is much more emphasis on state supported social justice and equity when it is in power. Appendix Table 4.2 reports Gini indices and income share ratios for LICs and for context those of LMICs, Sweden, Korea and the United States.

The average Gini coefficient for LICs of 40 is considered modest and only a couple of countries have a Gini above 50, which is considered to be high inequality. The average of 37 for LMIC is lower but not substantially so. However, the Gini index in LICs is almost twice that of Sweden and 10 points higher than South Korea. As reflected by the Gini index, the average state of income inequality in LICs, which has been under the tutelage of World Bank/IMF-led neo liberalism since the early 1980s, mirrors that of the United States (41.5).

The income share ratio (income share held by top 10 percent to bottom 20 percent) is high at 5.6 but mostly this is pushed up by a few outliers (Benin, Guinea-Bissau, Mozambique and South Sudan). Once again, it is twice that of Sweden and much higher than Korea (3.3) but this time below that of the United

States (6.1). Barring the same outliers, in most cases the income share of the top 10 percent is about the same as that held by the bottom 40 percent.

Given the evidence reported above regarding the high levels of social inequality and some evidence suggesting that this can disrupt economic growth (see below), there is an instrumental economic reason to be concerned assuming that a social philosophy of justice and equity is not enough to drive policy. The policy debates on addressing inequality in development economics are as old as the field itself and ongoing.

Debates on policy to address inequality

National advocacy for policy change can be strengthened using comparative global data. PPP/PCGNP is one component of UNDP's (United Nations Development Program) Human Development Index (HDI – the other two components being education and health). The HDI could be made inequality sensitive by using Gini coefficients as weights for PPP/PCGNP. The way to do this is to subtract the Gini coefficient from 1 and use the residual as a deflator of PPP/PCGNP. The higher the income inequality, the higher the deflation of the PPP/PCGNP and the lower its inequality adjusted ranking. Such a hypothetical exercise is shown in Table 4.2.

As indicated, the higher the Gini (income inequality), the higher the deflation of PCGNP for global ranking. Country 1 dominates country 2 in a straight comparison of PPP/PCGNP, but once inequality is taken into account, the adjusted PPP/PCGNP in Table 4.2 shows country 2 delivering a higher level of well-being to its population.

The size distribution of income can also be used to deconstruct economic growth rates for policy advocacy.[19] The simple hypothetical exercises below show that PCGDP growth is an even worse measure of well-being than commonly assumed. As normally measured, PCGDP implicitly weights the income of the more prosperous by more, simply because the higher income group has a higher income share. Consider the hypothetical example constructed in Table 4.3 for an illustration of this point.

Suppose the upper 20 percent gets 50 percent of the income and the second quintile gets 30 percent. Suppose the income growth rate of the upper quintile is 10 percent and that of the second quintile 3 percent, while it is 0 percent for the remaining three quintiles. The PCGDP growth rate (G1) as usually calculated would be the weighted average $G1 = .10 \times .50 + .03 \times .3 = 5.09$ percent (i.e. growth rates by income group weighted by the income share in the groups). An alternative would be to use population weights based on the justification that each person should have equivalent weight (neutral). In this case each income group would have the same weight of .2 and so the weighted average growth rate would be $G2 = .10 \times .20 + .03 \times .20 = 2.06$ percent. Attaching high normative weights to the poorest quintile would produce a third PCGDP growth rate estimate. Positive high growth is recorded above despite the 0 growth of the bottom 60 percent. If poverty was important as a social objective, one could, for example, have weights as indicated in the last column of Table 4.3. In that case the PCGDP weighted average growth estimate would be $G3 = .10 \times .05 + .03 \times .10 = .08$ percent.

TABLE 4.2 Deflating PPP/PCGNP for inequality

Country	PPP/GNP	Gini	Inequality adjusted PPP/PCGNP
A	4,010	.57	$.43 \times 4,010 = 1,724$
B	3,760	.42	$.58 \times 3,760 = 2,180$

TABLE 4.3 Hypothetical weighted per capita GDP growth rates

Income groups	Growth rates	Income weights	Population weights	Poverty weights
I	0.00	0.02	0.2	0.40
II	0.00	0.05	0.2	0.30
III	0.00	0.13	0.2	0.15
IV	0.03	0.30	0.2	0.10
V	0.10	0.50	0.2	0.05
Weighted growth rate (%)		5.09	2.06	0.08

The "let the market work" perspective of mainstream neoclassical economists is to focus on achieving economic growth, and the presumption is that this will address the poverty and inequality problems as prosperity starts to trickle down with more jobs created by a growing economy. The empirical case for this rested on showing that there is a trade-off between growth and inequality. In other words, if policy makers made addressing inequality a priority, they might jeopardize economic growth in which case such a policy would backfire.

Kuznets, (1955) was the pioneer in exploring the association of economic growth and inequality, although he did so at a time when data were very limited. Based on some simulations and the economic history of the United States, Germany and England, he hypothesized that the relation between growth and inequality was an inverted-U as shown below.

The inverted-U in Figure 4.4 shows that as PCGDP increases due to economic growth on the horizontal axis, inequality represented by the Gini first increases and then decreases as society continues to prosper. Kuznets strongly qualified his findings and conceded in his paper that they were "perhaps 5 percent empirical information and 95 percent speculation, some of it possibly tainted with wishful thinking".

Nonetheless, he suggested as a possible stylized fact of economic development that inequality initially increases with economic growth, but as growth continues inequality eventually declines. Kuznets himself was concerned with identifying a possible empirical regularity based on long-term time series data for the United States, Britain and Germany rather than with establishing a case for trickle down. This was an inference from his findings that other researchers drew; scholars who were much less careful than he was.

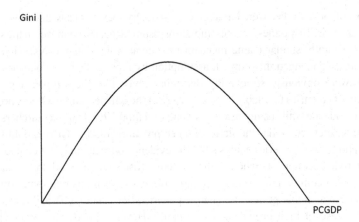

FIGURE 4.4 Kuznets curve

Kuznets proposed a few causal mechanisms for the inverted-U based on market and policy mechanisms. At the beginning of catch-up growth for current HICs, the immigration of workers from low income rural areas to higher income urban ones could initially increase inequality since less prosperous people come into a prosperous area. As such immigration continues, this effect could reverse itself as urban areas prosper and inequality decreases. Further, at the early stage of economic growth, dependency ratios (Chapter 3) are high and rising among the poor and this could contribute to the inequality. With more prosperity, this process reverses itself as the demographic transition kicks in (i.e. as income and education rise and fertility rates decline).

Following neoclassical factor proportions theory, initially migration enhances the return to capital in urban areas because capital is scarce and labor abundant. However, with continuing economic growth the labor force is absorbed and capital becomes relatively abundant and labor relatively scarce. Following the logic of this theory, the returns to capital fall while the productivity and hence remuneration of labor, which has more capital on average to work with, rises. Thus, the economic growth process diffuses prosperity and reduces social inequality.

Policy mechanisms such as the provision of public education reinforce this trend. As the education and skill level of the labor force rises, the consequent higher productivity also results in higher wages. Fertility rates decline with higher education because the opportunity cost of having children increases for women who go into the workforce (Chapter 3). Also, as societies become more prosperous, they can afford to provide subsidies and reduce social inequalities that persist.

Kuznets' findings promoted a spate of research and controversy that is continuing to this day. Using some measure of inequality, like the Gini, as the left-hand side variable, researchers showed that PCGNP had a strong positive association with inequality and that the association followed an inverted-U shape as suggested by Kuznet i.e. that inequality first increased with catch-up growth and then started to decline after some threshold level of per capita GDP was attained.[20]

Most of these studies were based on cross-country regressions with country as the unit of analysis.[21] Thus these studies implicitly assumed that the countries in the sample were structurally similar (same mechanisms operated in similar ways). Heterodox economists challenged this implicit assumption by arguing that the countries in the sample were obviously structurally dissimilar given that the samples included a diversity of countries to establish the existence of the Kuznets curve. Others provided counter evidence while using the cross-country method. Thus many researchers doubt that the Kuznets curve has the status of an empirical regularity. There are now more observations for time series analysis but the evidence once again is not conclusive.

Heterodox economists who use the inductive case study method argue that there really are no commonalities and that case studies can demonstrate many different patterns and also that policy can change patterns. For example, Brazil represented a classic case of high growth-high inequality. However, under the leadership of Luiz Inácio Lula da Silva (2003–2011), through social programs in education, health, nutrition and other welfare programs, Brazil started reversing inequality and brought the income share ratio of the top 10 percent to bottom 20 percent down from to 17.5 when he took office in 2003 to 12.6 in 2011 when he left office and the average economic growth in per capita GDP during this period was 3.3 percent.[22]

Other counter examples include the East Asian Economies (Japan/Korea/Taiwan) all of which demonstrated that high growth and high equality are possible. Land reforms and high wage policies contributed to this. Based on socialist redistributive mechanisms, China is another counter example. In the early 1980s, its social and employment policies ensured high equality even as it started to experience rapid economic growth. A discontinuation of social policies caused inequality to rise with catch-up growth. The Gini in 1981 was 28.8 and subsequently rose to 42.2 in 2012.[23]

Some studies suggested a reverse causality and explored instead the impact of inequality on growth. Thus a cross-country study by Alesina and Perotti (1996) showed more equality could result in more political stability and hence more investment and economic growth.

To sum up, the justification of trickle down in the neoliberal approach is that the rich will save and facilitate capital accumulation and hence redistribution should be avoided. However, the rich in L/MICs do not necessarily save. Luxury imports, foreign travel, real estate investments and capital flight are all possible leakages from savings.

Alternatively, according to the basic human needs/human development approach, investment in education and health of the poor would make them more productive and hence enhance equality and economic growth. Further, since the poor spend more on the local product market this would enhance the market size and enable the attainment of economies of scale.

The upshot is that theory casts doubt on the mainstream trickle-down approach and the data also show many different patterns are evident based on the actual economic experience of different countries. The critical issue is the policy or redistributive mechanisms adopted by the state; something that ironically Kuznets himself recognized as important.[24] Various poverty alleviation policy initiatives are associated with the various definitions of poverty, and solutions proposed by the various approaches are reviewed in the next section.

Poverty alleviation initiatives

The different definitions of poverty have resulted in different policy initiatives associated with the different approaches to be investigated in detail in Part II. In keeping with the Kuznets curve, the mainstream/neoliberal approach is straightforward in that it endorses policy initiatives that it views as economic growth enhancing. While organizations like the World Bank and IMF, which enforce neoliberal prescriptions, have recently been more open to initiatives associated with the other approaches, economic growth is still center stage as the trickle-down mechanism to deliver widespread prosperity. A number of initiatives have been used in the late 20th and 21st centuries to address basic human needs/human development and risk and vulnerability poverty, and these are reviewed below.

The methodology to access the success of these initiatives is not straightforward since while costs are easy to monitor and document, the benefits are more elusive and difficult to quantify. For example, if it is a social investment initiative such as enhanced health or education, mainstream economists may try to quantify the benefits in the form of discounting to the present value the enhanced lifetime earnings. However, most recognize this is difficult to do accurately, particularly when the quality of the intervention is poor and may not enhance productivity, and labor markets are not perfect and much else may explain enhanced earnings. The human freedom approach in any case would place a much higher premium on the intrinsic value of the social investment rather than the instrumental value of higher earnings.

A focus on the intrinsic value provides a resolution to the difficulties in trying to estimate the economic rates of return to social investments. If policy makers choose what the social investment is to be, the cost effectiveness method quantifies the most efficient way of attaining that objective. This is less rigorous than a social benefit cost approach, but also more realistic. Various poverty alleviation initiatives have been devised and implemented over the decades and the important ones are reviewed below.

Basic needs/human development

The basic needs approach, as explained in Chapter 1, was a reaction to trickle-down economics. The argument was that it would take too long if ever for trickle-down economics to deliver well-being to the poor and that, in any case, basic human needs like education, health and water supply must be delivered by the state as a constitutional right. The World Bank under Robert McNamara's leadership adopted this approach. This could well have been motivated by the intense ideological rivalry during the Cold War and the fear that the excluded would be targeted by and be susceptible to radical thought.

Mahbub ul Haq, who served at the World Bank as chief economic advisor to Robert McNamara, championed the basic human needs approach. When this approach fell out of fashion after the Cold War ended it was reconstituted by Haq at the UNDP, with advice from A. K. Sen, as the Human Development approach. This approach gained traction partly due to the annual release of the *Human Development Report* that attempts to measure and rank countries based on the human development attained by its citizens in terms of health, education, sanitation, water supply and other basic human needs. Over time, the definition of development has been broadened to address gender inequality, regional inequality, urban/rural inequality and human freedoms, and metrics accordingly devised.

Another hallmark of the global success of the human development approach was in the framing of the Millennium Development Goals (MDGs) that all 189 member states of the UN signed on to at the turn of the century and hoped to achieve by 2015 with the help of the donor community. The goals included eradicating extreme poverty and hunger, achieving universal primary education, promoting gender equality, reducing child mortality, improving maternal health, combatting HIV/AIDS, malaria and other diseases, ensuring environment sustainability and developing a global partnership for development. Each objective had several targets and critics charged that overall the MDGs became too diffused and cumbersome (Fukuda-Parr, Yamin, and Greenstein, 2015).

The achievements were mixed and the MDGs morphed into Sustainable Development Goals (SDGs) as the objective for the next 15 years until 2030. Environmental sustainability became the central issue and all countries were included in the SDGs rather than just the L/MICs. In the transition from HDGs to SDGs, the need for quality in setting goals, targets (169 in all) and indicators (what is actually measured) was acknowledged.

In practice the rich have better opportunities since for example the best education is accessible to them and the poor are deprived of educational opportunities or attend poor quality government schools. Quality deteriorates when the rich leave public schooling and there is no voice for improvement. Poor public schooling deprives the poor of a key mechanism for social mobility and non-public services (private and NGO) have a very low bar to cross to be better. The same applies to other public services and the result has been the mushrooming of poor quality private sector services as a substitute for public services. This has been encouraged by the World Bank, even with subsidies, as the state readily abandons its key constitutional functions of providing basic human needs. This education and health dualism reflects the broader social dualism in society.

Integrated rural development

Based on the work of development economists like Lewis and Harris and Todaro (Chapter 5), it was acknowledged that the bulk of the labor force in L/LMICs resided in rural areas. Further, the high incidence of rural poverty and that a lack of rural development resulted from urban bias, which in turn led to rural to urban migration with its attendant problems of shanty towns and the associated intensification of crime and urban poverty. A prescription following on from this research in the 1970s was for the provision of a comprehensive package of infrastructure, training, agricultural inputs and credit directed at the rural poor. This was a state-centered and delivered approach and failed for the most part because the landed elite appropriated all the subsidies (elite capture). One notable exception was Korea's Saemaul Undong (cooperative) movement and the success has been attributed to the land reforms that pre-dated the rural development initiative (Park, 2009).

Land concentration leads to a concentration of political and hence economic power and elite capture and exclusion in poverty alleviation initiatives. Thus land distribution in Korea prior to the rural development initiative diffused economic power and negated elite capture. However, as expected, there is a great deal of political resistance to land redistribution and mainstream economists are wedded to property rights and reluctant to push this issue.

Since the 1980s rural development NGOs have inherited the mantle of rural development and generally engage in an overtly non-political fashion. The initiatives, referred to as participatory, for the most part rely on organizing and mobilizing grassroots communities to engage in their own development via collective action with much of the resources provided by the international donor community. This became a way for the latter to bypass the state, which is deemed to be ineffective and corrupt, and in providing service delivery directly to the poor.

Microcredit

One key instrument adopted by rural development NGOs as a poverty alleviation initiative is microcredit. Mohammed Yunus started the Grameen Bank to deliver microcredit on a small scale with his own money in 1983 when he was unable to persuade public sector banks to lend to the poor. Yunus was trained as an economist in the United States and recognized the lack of rural banking serving the poor as a market failure. The nature of the market failure is that rural private or public sector banks confront high information costs (asymmetrical information or lack of knowledge of the poor as credit risks), high transaction costs (too many small loans mean high administrative costs), lack of access (poor rural infrastructure) and no or low collateral that the poor can offer.

The lack of collateral was the most important and Yunus overcame this by relying on peer group pressure/social capital such that in small groups the poor, based on mutual contacts, networks and trust vouched for each other and were willing to incur the penalty of no loans if peers defaulted. The poor therefore became the mechanism to ensure there was a repository of accurate information and reduced transactions costs via self-policing.

The focus soon shifted to women who were the most marginalized and better credit risk, and repayment rates were as high as 98 percent.[25] This basic model has been adopted and adapted by about 60 countries. Some banks turn a profit while most need to be subsidized. However, this subsidy, as a form of public policy to reduce risk and vulnerability poverty, may be well justified if it compares well to the cost of other poverty alleviation initiatives.

There is evidence from numerous earlier impact assessment studies suggesting that microcredit enabled households to engage in consumption smoothing (transfer from surplus to lean periods), engage in high risk–high return options, improve household health and education, and empower women (Pitt, Khandker, and Cartwright, 2006; Khandker and Samad, 2014). Other research based on RCTs was more skeptical and a special issue of the *American Economic Review, Applied Economics* (2015, 7(1), p. 3) contained six randomized evaluations and the summary suggested a "lack of evidence of transformative effects [of microcredit] on average borrowers".

In the 1990s, the World Bank led a shifting of focus from the original poverty alleviation of borrowers to the sustainability of the organization. For-profit, including publicly traded companies, were encouraged to enter this new market. Yunus was so distressed at this trend that he equated it with loan sharking. A spate of suicides in India due to the harsh outstanding loan collection tactics of "for-profit" microcredit led to a Parliamentary inquiry. However, it appears that neoliberalism has won this battle and "for-profit" microfinance persisted. Apart from microcredit, microfinance includes new products including consumer credit, saving accounts, insurance, pensions and remittance services.

While once viewed as a panacea, many critiques of microfinance emerged with the feminist critique as the most telling (Goetz and Gupta, 1996; Parmar, 2003). Feminists critiqued this market-friendly initiative as one that is exploitative of women because the latter are used as a front to secure loans for males and confront abuse from husbands if they fail to secure loans. Moreover, they confront repayment pressure from abusive loan officers and social pressure from peers including interference in their personal life such as with regards to their consumption pattern. Instead of building social capital, such pressure undermines and destroys social capital. Women also confront a higher work burden since husbands do not help with household chores even if women's workload increases due to the credit they receive.

Feminists define social empowerment as real when associated with transformation in the power configuration in gender relations in households and gender equality in society. Instead, advocates of microcredit define female empowerment functionally as greater mobility, access to funds or say in the use of funds. Another feminist critique is that via WB/IMF structural adjustment (Chapter 8), the burden of care has been pushed even more onto individuals with the state abdicating its role. Microcredit is touted as a stand-in for state services and hence implicitly facilitates structural adjustment and hence is very much part of the neoliberal world view and package of reforms (Rankin, 2001, 2002).

Other critics have shown that microcredit programs bypass the poorest of the poor who are not considered bankable by peers and rural banking staff. They criticize the loan treadmill that microcredit puts the poor on (new loans paying for old ones), especially now that the organizations view borrowers as profit units. Due to organizational saturation, there is often loan recycling such that lenders borrow from one organization to pay another.

Critics also argue that the claimed success of microcredit is subject to a "fallacy of composition" in that there is a limit to how many crafts of a particular kind can be sold in a particular market i.e. there is market saturation. Thus what might work for one borrower will not work for all in a community. Thus borrowers are locked in a zero-sum game where the success of one borrower is premised on the failure of another.[26]

For critics like Chang (2011) microcredit and the self-employment it promotes simply cannot provide the needed employment opportunities, the best form of poverty alleviation, or the kind of technological progress industrialization can deliver. Hence they view privileging microcredit as an economically destructive diversion of scarce funds from economic activities with higher social and economic rates of return.

Employment Guarantee Schemes

An Employment Guarantee Scheme (EGS) was initiated as a rural sector poverty alleviation initiative by the Government of Maharashtra in India in the 1970s. The basic idea was "self-revelation". The wage for temporary work was kept a bit below the minimum market wage so that only the poorest would reveal themselves for such jobs. This would limit leakages to those not entitled and reduce the administrative expense of targeting. Also, the EGS projects could help to develop valuable rural infrastructure to raise productivity.

The challenge, as with all public projects, is keeping down administrative costs and limiting corruption. The Congress government in India in 2006 scaled up the EGS to the national level and guaranteed 100 days employment to all the rural poor. There is controversy regarding its effectiveness but early findings in the development economics literature suggests it is a qualified success (Jha et al., 2015; Breitkreuz et al., 2017).

Conditional Cash Transfer[27]

Conditional Cash Transfer (CCT) initiatives started in the 1990s with Bolsa Familia in Brazil and Progresa (now Oportunidades) in Mexico among the most famous of the almost two dozen such initiatives in L/MICs. The idea is to provide cash to households conditioned on the household taking responsibility for enhancing social indicators within the household with the assistance provided. For example, women may need to agree to participate in health care workshops or nutritional assessment programs (child weight and height measurements) or ensure that household children attend school.

Feminist critics charge that CCTs place additional burdens on women's time that is already overloaded with responsibilities. Heterodox scholars view this initiative as yet another in the neoliberal social policy bag of tricks to ameliorate the harsh outcomes of the austerity conditions associated with economic reforms and a forced abdication of state responsibility for its citizens.

Unconditional cash transfers

Some neoclassical economists have suggested that cash without conditions would be a better way to enable the households since relaxing the budget constraint and providing choice enhances utility in a utility maximization framework and that households know what is best for them.

Others argue for unconditional assistance based on a rights-based approach i.e. that basic human needs are a fundamental human right. Unconditional cash transfers (UCT), in the form of a Universal Basic Income, has also garnered the attention of Silicon Valley libertarians on the right and social democrats on the left as a form of a social safety net in response to the threat to unskilled jobs due to automation in HICs (Chapter 14).

Silicon Valley entrepreneurs have funded multi-year (12) RCTs in Kenya to explore if individuals become lazy and less motivated or if instead they make good use of the funds provided. Social democrats are less concerned about incentive effects and more about the right to a decent life. Initial research by Haushofer and Shapiro (2017) suggests a positive impact on psychological well-being and economic outcomes. Finland and Canada have also trialed pilot projects to test outcomes of UCT.

BRAC graduation initiative

This is a multi-dimensional initiative devised by Building Resources Across Communities (BRAC)[28] that views poverty as multi-dimensional and hence draws on other initiatives for a multi-dimensional solution. The concept is to provide a "big push" to the household much as developmentalists argued that nations needed a big push (Chapter 5) to build a momentum that they could subsequently sustain.[29] A multi-dimensional intervention directed at people to get them sustainably out of poverty includes an asset to make a living, such as livestock or an informal sector store, training on how to manage the asset, basic food or cash support to reduce the need to sell the asset in an emergency, frequent (usually weekly) coaching visits to reinforce skills, confidence building and help with handling challenges. In addition, health education or access to healthcare is provided to enable participants to stay healthy and not lose work time and a savings account to help them put away money to invest or use in a future emergency.

Interventions are tailored to the particular circumstances of the L/LMIC in question. Banerjee et al. (2015) conducted an RCT covering Ethiopia, Ghana, Honduras, India, Pakistan and Peru with a large sample including 21,063 adults in 10,495 rural households. The initiative was shown to be cost effective, with positive returns in five of the six countries they studied. The returns ranged from 133 percent in Ghana to 433 percent in India. Thus for every dollar spent on the program in India, the ultra-poor households got $4.33 in long-term benefits.

In terms of specifics, they reported that over a three-year period, there was a 5 percent increase in per capita income, 8 percent increase in food consumption, 15 percent increase in assets and a 96 percent increase in savings. While expensive and personnel intensive, the idea is that the poor can graduate from poverty with this initiative and hence in that regard the intervention is viewed as more cost effective than others that do not provide a sustained pathway out of poverty.

Sustainable development

Human development focuses on extending the range of choices for the poor. This includes sustainable livelihoods to ensure the capacity for making choices and human capital (education and health) to make sound choices over a longer period. The focus on the environment as central to human development has two underpinnings. First, as explained above, a poor environment is associated with negative health impacts to which the poor are most vulnerable. Second, a healthy environment ensures the health of not just current but also future generations.

Initially the concern was with sustainable human development, but this was broadened to sustainable development in recognition that the concern should be for all species. Fortunately, protecting humans by protecting the environment also protects other species, although a special focus is needed on endangered species.

Initially the focus was on the attainment of inter-generational justice. However, a concern with inter-generational justice brought to the fore the importance of intra-generational justice and hence the integration of poverty alleviation into the concept of sustainable development. Sustainable development is an umbrella concept and as such subsumes the initiatives discussed above. Recall that sustainable development has now been adopted by the UN as its key initiative and SDGs replaced MDGs in January 2016. Specific sustainable development initiatives for agriculture and industry are discussed in Chapters 13 and 14.

Cross-cutting mechanisms in poverty alleviation initiatives

Based on the operational experience of the initiatives above a number of cross-cutting mechanisms can be identified. Participation emerged as explained in Chapter 2 from the view that the poor should be empowered via the process of social mobilization, creation of grassroots organizations by tapping social capital and being involved in all stages of projects intended to benefit them (a move away from top-down mechanisms). Rural grassroots organizations of, by and for the poor would also enable them to engage in collective action. This would make use of the information that only the poor have i.e. what would benefit them the most and how best to execute the project to attain those benefits.

It was argued that if the poor are involved in all stages of the project from design to execution, they will be more engaged and likely to contribute to it and maintain it.[30] The big challenge is conceiving such projects in a way that avoids elite capture. Rural grassroots NGOs do the social mobilization, often with donor support, although there are cases of spontaneous evolution of grassroots organizations of the rural poor that engage in collective action (Khan, Kazmi, and Rifaqat, 2007, chapter 2).

The perceived success of this mechanism has also filtered into service delivery by the public sector. One mechanism for this has been public-rural NGO partnerships or the state even contracting out the service delivery to development NGOs. While the ideal is that the development NGOs would merely be catalysts in sparking social organizations of the poor, in practice, like all organizations, they have a stake in survival and do so as long as the funding is available. Some of these organizations remain true to their ideals while others are criticized for putting the organizational agenda, particularly that of the NGO management, center stage, and this is reflected in high salaries and perks, detachment from the grassroots and distrust by those they are supposed to serve.

Targeting is another mechanism for distribution of services to the poorest in rural areas. Recall that the challenge is to avert the power structure to avoid elite capture. In practice, the state administration works closely with the rural elites and so leakages are viewed as inevitable. Even if there were dedicated sections of line department (service delivery) bureaucracy, intent of effective service delivery, resources and administrative capacity are limited.

Evidence shows that targeting women leads to the greatest gains as they are most likely to invest in the nutrition, health and education of children. A study by Rubalcava, Teruel and Thomas (2009) shows that when the balance of power within the household changes in favor of women due to resource transfers, they are more likely than men in a similar situation to invest in the future of the household.

Finally, operational experience with poverty alleviation initiatives shows that there are inter-relationships between different kinds of provisions. For example, better education can ensure the ability to secure job opportunities. It can also ensure better health outcomes because the ability to process information improves and educated mothers ensure better nutrition and health of their children. Healthier children perform better at school and hence ensure the ability to secure livelihood opportunities later on. This could break the vicious circle of poverty.

Better health for adults can make them more productive and also lead to fewer working days lost and less medical expenses. Safety nets, say in the form of an EGS, enable individuals to pursue high risk–high profit options. Political freedom can ensure economic freedom as politicians respond to constituents. Based on these interactions, a holistic approach to service delivery, as for example with the BRAC graduation initiative, suggests the whole is much greater than the sum of the parts.

Summary and conclusions

This chapter reviews the concepts and methods of measuring absolute poverty and inequality. Income poverty, being below a defined poverty line in income terms, is the most common concept, though this has been challenged by broader multi-dimensional poverty concepts. Basic human needs/human development poverty and risk and vulnerability poverty are two such broader concepts reviewed.

There are limitations to the mainstream competitive market approach in examining the issue of inequality. The Marxian or political economy of development approach attributes it to the leverage capital (business) has over workers by virtue of ownership of the means of production and hence of the ability of capital to capture surplus that is rightly due to labor. Neoclassical economics, when not assuming perfect competition and full employment, explains this concept in terms of the monopsony power businesses can exercise over workers.

There have been many initiatives to address basic human needs/human development and risk and vulnerability poverty. These include state provision of basic human needs as a right (rights-based approach), integrated rural development delivered by the state or more recently rural development NGOs, a state-led EGS, state-provided CCTs, Unconditional Cash Transfers and a development NGO-initiated graduation from poverty initiative.

The microcredit initiative, also mostly delivered by development NGOs, is viewed by critics as captured by the IMF/WB market-led development approach. This perspective views microcredit as a Trojan horse that pushes back the role of the state in poverty alleviation and makes the poor responsible for themselves.

More recently, the IMF/WB have recognized that the capital friendly structural adjustment they unleash on borrowing countries intensifies inequality and poverty and have welcomed the poverty alleviation initiatives identified above as safety nets.

These poverty alleviation initiatives can make some difference as a palliative. However, all these approaches are silent about the structural causes of poverty such as the skewed ownership of land and the leverage capital has over labor. In the political economy of development approach, real structural reform, as opposed to neoliberal-led structural adjustment, requires asset distribution, particularly land redistribution, so that the power structure is altered. Other key initiatives are improved tax administration to implement wealth and progressive income taxes and public sector reform to deliver *quality* public sector provision.

Another structural transformation reform would be devolution of service delivery to the local level once the concentration of power has been defused with land redistribution. Institutional changes like devolution could make the implementation of the rule of law more likely and corruption and elite capture less likely. From a political economy of development perspective, without fundamental structural reforms, the various initiatives discussed above may simply be a Band-Aid.

The human development approach captured the imagination of the international donor and development community and they encapsulated it in the MDGs embarked on for a 15-year period, 2000–2015. Recognizing that the poor are the most vulnerable to environmental degradation and therefore of the need for both intra- and inter-generational justice, the UN replaced the MDGs with the SDGs, 2016–2030. As an umbrella approach, the SDGs subsume all the poverty alleviation initiatives discussed in this chapter in addition to addressing the environmental challenges faced by the planet. However, as argued in Chapter 15, a more parsimonious approach to structural transformation that has greening industry and agriculture at the core might be more effective.

APPENDIX TABLE 4.1 Poverty indicators in low income countries

Country	Poverty headcount ratio at national poverty lines (% of population)	Poverty headcount ratio at $1.90 per day (2011, PPP, % population)	Poverty headcount ratio at $3.20 per day (2011, PPP, % population)	Poverty gap at national poverty lines (%)	Poverty gap at $1.90 per day (2011, PPP, %)	Poverty gap at $3.20 per day (2011, PPP, %)
Afghanistan	35.8 (2011)	na	na	8.4 (2011)	na	na
Benin	35.2 (2010)	49.6 (2015)	72.6 (2015)	9.8 (2011)	22.4 (2014)	39.5 (2015)
Burkina Faso	40.1 (2015)	43.7 (2014)	76.4 (2014)	9.7 (2014)	11.1 (2013)	32.2 (2014)
Burundi	64.9 (2014)	71.7 (2013)	89.2 (2013)	25.1 (2014)	30.3 (2013)	51.5 (2013)
Central African Republic	na	na	na	na	na	na
Chad	46.7 (2011)	38.4 (2011)	66.5 (2011)	19.7 (2011)	15.3 (2011)	30.8 (2011)
Comoros	42.0 (2014)	18.1 (2013)	38.1 (2013)	na	6.3 (2013)	15.4 (2013)
Congo, Democratic Republic	63.9 (2012)	77.1 (2012)	91.3 (2012)	na	39.2 (2012)	58 (2012)
Eritrea	na	na	na	na	na	na
Ethiopia	23.5 (2015)	26.7 (2015)	61.4 (2015)	7.8 (2010)	7.7 (2015)	22.7 (2015)
Gambia, The	48.6 (2015)	10.1 (2015)	37.8 (2015)	27.9 (2010)	2.2 (2015)	10.8 (2015)
Guinea	55.2 (2012)	35.3 (2012)	70.3 (2012)	18.4 (2012)	10.3 (2012)	28.4 (2012)
Guinea-Bissau	69.3 (2010)	67.1 (2010)	84.5 (2010)	na	30.5 (2010)	49.6 (2010)
Haiti	58.5 (2012)	23.5 (2012)	48.3 (2012)	24.4 (2012)	7.5 (2012)	19.2 (2012)
Korea, Democratic Peoples Republic	na	na	na	na	na	na
Liberia	50.9 (2015)	38.6 (2014)	73.8 (2014)	na	11.7 (2014)	30.7 (2014)

Madagascar	70.7 (2012)	77.7 (2012)	91.0 (2012)	na	39.0 (2012)	57.9 (2012)
Malawi	51.5 (2016)	71.4 (2010)	88.8 (2010)	18.9 (2010)	33.6 (2010)	53.2 (2010)
Mali	41.1 (2009)	49.7 (2009)	79.4 (2009)	na	15.5 (2009)	36.3 (2009)
Mozambique	46.1 (2014)	62.9 (2014)	81.9 (2014)	na	27.9 (2014)	46.6 (2014)
Nepal	25.2 (2010)	15.0 (2010)	50.8 (2010)	5.4 (2010)	3.1 (2010)	15.8 (2010)
Niger	44.5 (2014)	44.5 (2014)	76.9 (2014)	19.6 (2011)	13.5 (2014)	33.6 (2014)
Rwanda	39.1 (2013)	56.0 (2013)	80.8 (2013)	14.8 (2010)	20.2 (2013)	40.7 (2013)
Senegal	46.7 (2011)	38.0 (2011)	67.5 (2011)	14.5 (2010)	12.8 (2011)	29.6 (2011)
Sierra-Leone	52.9 (2011)	52.2 (2011)	81.3 (2011)	16.1 (2011)	16.7 (2011)	38.0 (2011)
Somalia	na	na	na	na	na	na
South Sudan	82.3 (2016)	42.7 (2009)	64.8 (2009)	23.7 (2009)	18.9 (2009)	33.3 (2009)
Syrian Arab Republic	na	na	na	na	na	na
Tajikistan	31.3 (2015)	4.8 (2015)	20.3 (2015)	na	1.0 (2015)	5.3 (2015)
Tanzania	28.2 (2011)	49.1 (2011)	79.0 (2011)	6.7 (2011)	15.4 (2011)	36.3 (2011)
Togo	55.1 (2015)	42.9 (2015)	73.2 (2015)	24.4 (2011)	19.9 (2015)	37.1 (2015)
Uganda	21.4 (2016)	41.6 (2016)	69.8 (2016)	5.2 (2012)	13.2 (2016)	31.2 (2016)
Yemen, Republic	48.6 (2014)	18.8 (2014)	52.2 (2014)	na	4.5 (2014)	17.3 (2014)
Zimbabwe	na	21.4 (2011)	42.7 (2011)	na	5.2 (2011)	17.3 (2011)
Average LICs	47.1 (14.9)	42.5 (20.6)	66.2 (18.2)	16.2 (7.4)	16.2 (11.0)	32.8 (14.2)
Average LMICs	27.7 (15.8)	14.6 (15.6)	33.8 (24.5)	10.5 (10.2)	4.8 (6.7)	31.9 (23.7)

Sources: For country classifications https://datahelpdesk.worldbank.org/knowledgebase/articles/906519-world bank-country-and-lending-groups, consulted 1/15/2019. For data, World Development Bank development indicators on line update 1/30/2019.

Notes: The classification of LIC is for the 2019 fiscal year (July 1, 2018 to June 30, 2019).Parentheses contain the latest year the data were available for going back ten years.For the averages, the parentheses contain standard deviations.na = Not available

APPENDIX TABLE 4.2 Inequality indicators in LICs and selected HICs

Country	Gini index (World Bank estimate)	Ratio of income share held by the top 10% to bottom 20%	Ratio of income share held by the top 10% to bottom 40%
Afghanistan	na	na	na
Benin (2015)	47.8	11.7	1.6
Burkina Faso (2014)	35.3	3.6	1.0
Burundi (2013)	38.6	4.5	1.1
Central African Republic	na	na	na
Chad (2011)	43.3	6.6	1.2
Comoros (2013)	45.3	7.5	1.3
Congo, Dem. Republic (2012)	42.1	5.8	1.2
Eritrea	na	na	na
Ethiopia (2015)	39.1	4.8	1.2
Gambia, The (2015)	35.9	3.9	1.0
Guinea (2012)	33.7	3.5	0.9
Guinea-Bissau (2010)	50.7	9.3	1.8
Haiti (2012)	41.1	5.7	1.1
Korea, Dem. Peoples Republic	na	na	na
Liberia (2014)	33.2	3.4	0.9
Madagascar (2012)	42.6	5.9	1.3
Malawi (2010)	45.5	6.7	1.4
Mali (2009)	33.0	3.2	0.8
Mozambique (2014)	54.0	10.8	2.1
Nepal (2010)	32.8	3.2	0.9
Niger (2014)	34.3	3.5	0.9
Rwanda (2013)	45.1	6.3	1.5
Senegal (2011)	40.3	5.1	1.1
Sierra-Leone (2011)	34.0	3.4	0.9
Somalia	na	na	na
South Sudan (2009)	46.3	8.5	1.2
Syrian Arab Republic	na	na	na
Tajikistan (2015)	34.0	3.6	0.9
Tanzania (2011)	37.8	4.2	1.1
Togo (2015)	43.1	6.3	1.2

Uganda (2016)	42.8	5.6	1.3
Yemen, Republic (2014)	36.7	4.0	1.0
Zimbabwe (2011)	43.2	5.8	1.3
Average LICs	40.4		
(5.6)	5.6		
(2.2)	1.2		
(0.3)			
Average LMICs	37.2	4.9	1.0
Sweden (2015)	22.9	2.8	0.7
South Korea (2012)	31.6	3.3	0.8
United States (2016)	41.5	6.1	1.1

Sources: For country classifications https://datahelpdesk.worldbank.org/knowledgebase/articles/906519-world-bank-country-and-lending-groups, consulted 1/15/2019. For data, World Development Bank development indicators on line, update 1/30/2019. Columns 2 and 3 are author manipulations.
Notes: The classification of LIC is for the 2019 fiscal year (July 1, 2018 to June 30, 2019).Parentheses contain the latest year the data were available for going back ten years.na = Not available

Appendix 4.1: Environment Kuznets curve

In the 1990s, the Kuznets association was applied to the study of environmental degradation. To illustrate an environment Kuznets curve (EKC), different pollutants could be measured on the vertical axis and once again, PCGDP on the horizontal axis. Some research has shown that the association once again is an inverted-U shape as with the Kuznets curve as shown in Appendix Figure 4.1.[31]

One mechanism in this case is that beyond some threshold level of income, Y_T as shown in Appendix Figure 4.1, the demand for a cleaner environment as a luxury good will increase and this would induce policy to work toward a clean environment. Thus, as with the income Kuznets curve, there is an element of automaticity built into the association suggesting that policy is endogenous and that no premature action is called for. Another mechanism suggested by Grossman and Krueger (1991) is that as nations prosper, the scale of production is polluting but this can be offset by the composition effect (move to cleaner services) and cleaner technology. Before the benign turn of the Kuznets curve, governments may have to confront very angry citizenry as evident from the experiences of China and India.[32] In any case, given the evidence of the rapid increase in the pace of climate change, waiting for benign turns is no longer an option (Chapter 9, endnote 31).

However, for the sake of argument, even if the Kuznets association does hold for some pollutants and for some countries using time series data, ecologists urge caution. They argue that much biodiversity and ecosystem loss is

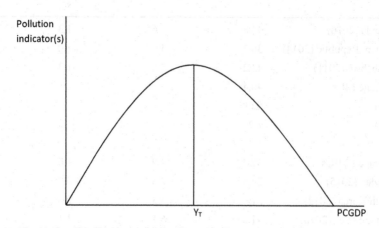

APPENDIX FIGURE 4.1 Environment Kuznets curve

non-reversible and so getting it wrong has a very high cost. Further, knowledge about the non-reversible threshold is limited and these thresholds can change and complex interactions within ecological systems are difficult to fathom. This complexity also suggests that even if the EKC held for one pollutant, it may not do so more generally. Most important, these non-reversibility thresholds may in any case be below the identified income threshold per capita GDP levels Y_T as indicated in Appendix Figure 4.1.

Ecologists therefore urge "the precautionary principle" and suggest preemptive action because the cost of reversing environmental damage is beyond the remit of L/LMICs. As with the income Kuznets curve, there is little faith in automatic improvements in the environment with rising per capita GDPs. They argue that in any case the environment improvements witnessed for HICs are at the expense of L/MICs since they outsource dirty production onto them. Thus, it is important to address the problem globally.

From a development perspective, the poor are disproportionately hurt by environmental degradation as discussed in this chapter and so addressing environment degradation is a key part of poverty alleviation. In a nutshell, instead of moving along the inverted-U, they argued that L/MICs path should be altered and they should be assisted to "burrow through the curve" in a straight line as shown in Appendix Figure 4.2.

The straight line with an arrow indicates a lower level of pollution even at low levels of per capita GDP. This alternative path can ideally come from green industry and agriculture policies as identified in Chapters 13 and 14. Such domestic policies can be facilitated by a grand global bargain in which L/LMICs focus on clean production that is facilitated by technology transfer from HICs. A modest global bargain was struck in the form of the Paris Agreement which went into effect in November 2016 with 195 countries participating.

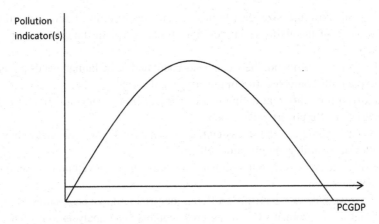

APPENDIX FIGURE 4.2 Burrowing through the environment Kuznets curve

All participating countries pledged to cut emissions to keep global warming to well below 2 degrees centigrade warming compared to pre-industrial levels.[33] HICs pledged to provide L/LMIC with $100 billion per year for clean energy technology starting in 2020.

Questions and exercises

1. Explain how one moves from GNP in current prices to per capita GNP in constant PPP$.
2. Fully explain in Q1 the adjustments and possible problems at each stage in an L/LMIC context.
3. Explain the logic of conversion to PPP$ for comparison of per capita GNIs across countries.
4. Explain why PCGDP in PPP$ may overstate L/LMIC prosperity.
5. Explain how the HDI is computed and adjusted for income, gender or regional inequalities if data are available?
6. Explain the headcount index as a measure of poverty and explain the shortcomings of this approach.
7. Explain the distinction between the functional distribution of income and the size distribution of income.
8. Explain criticisms of the theory underlying the functional distribution of income.
9. Discuss neoclassical and Marx's views on exploitation that call the fairness of the functional distribution of income into question.
10. Explain how the following are conceptually different:
    - Income distribution vs. income redistribution
    - Inequity vs. inequality.

11. Explain how the size distribution of income is utilized for computing a measure of inequality (Gini coefficients) and explain the criticisms of this approach.
12. Explain the distinction between head-count and basic human needs poverty.
13. Explain the characteristics of poverty (incidence).
14. Explain how different definitions of poverty brought about different policy initiatives for poverty alleviation.
15. Discuss some of the cross-cutting mechanisms used to make poverty alleviation policy options more effective.
16. Explain the case for "trickle-down economics" in the development economics literature.
17. What were the mechanisms proffered for "trickle-down economics"?
18. What is the problem with using cross-country data analysis to estimate the Kuznets curve and why do country case studies cast doubt on trickle down?
19. Evaluate the application of the Kuznets curve to the environment.
20. Why is investment in the environment viewed as an investment in the poor?
21. Go to the online World Bank, World Development Indicators and pick an income variable (real PCGDP in constant $). Go to the online UNDP HDI database and pick the HDI for the same group of countries. Review and then correlate the data. Comment in the context of a discussion on growth and development.
22. Go to the online World Bank, World Development Indicators and pick an income (real PCGDP in constant $s) and emission variable for all countries the data are available for. Review and then chart the data. Do you see a pattern? Comment in the context of the EKC.
23. Pick any poverty alleviation initiative for a country of your choice (you can pick one from the list discussed in this chapter).

    a. Identify the conceptual underpinnings of the initiative (e.g. sustainable livelihoods, basic human needs, etc.).
    b. Evaluate the success of the initiatives.
    c. What are your recommendations for improvements in the implementation of the initiative?

Notes

1 The relative poverty threshold is defined as the mean or medium income and the proportion of individuals falling below that are viewed to be in relative poverty (Farina, 2016, p. 126).
2 Refer to the debate between Sanjay Reddy and Thomas Pooge vs. Martin Ravillion on international poverty lines in (eds.) Anand, Segal and Stiglitz (2010).
3 This term was popularized in the development literature by Hirschman (1970).
4 The covariate risk refers to shocks occurring simultaneously such as disease vectors associated with droughts and earthquakes. The cholera outbreak that occurred after the Haiti earthquake in 2016 is an example.
5 The detrimental impact of lead poisoning on children's learning abilities has been widely documented (Aizer et al., 2016).

6 As explained in Chapter 15, catch-up growth can be initiated on a foundation of equity.

7 The result carries over to more than two factors using algebra.

8 For those comfortable with calculus, the total product results from integrating marginal product.

9 Gender discrimination is not being taken into account in this story.

10 For the aggregation problem debate refer to Burmeister (2000) and Cohen and Harcourt (2003).

11 While capital hiring labor is the most common approach to how production is organized, there are alternative production models such as producer cooperatives in which labor hires capital. In this case, labor bears the risk of production and is the claimant of the residual once all other factors are paid. The Mondrogon producer cooperative in Spain is the most famous example of such a producer cooperative. Refer to Campbell (2011) for details.

12 Heterodox economists view such labor displacement by automation as an ongoing issue in capitalist market economies.

13 Marxian theory of exploitation is elaborated on in Chapter 5.

14 For example, the living wage movement gained strength in the United States as unemployment fell after the 2007–2009 financial and economic crises. While recent explanations of growing inequality in HICs eschew Marxian analysis, such as that put forward by Piketty (2014), the crux of the explanation still amounts to capital's ability to garner a higher share of total income relative to labor.

15 The Lorenz curve starts at the origin because zero percentage of the population can only hold 0 percent of total income. Similarly 100 percent of the population holds all of total income, the point at which the curve ends. These therefore are the two points at which the Lorenz curve coincides with the 45 degree line, the starting and end point.

16 The "Occupy Movement" in the United States, which protested Wall Street shenanigans that led to the 2007–2009 financial and economic crisis, used such indices very effectively. It argued that the top 1 percent of the population drew a large part of total income and wealth relative to the other 99 percent. For example, according to a 2014 US Congressional Budget Office Report (Distribution of Household Income and Federal Taxes, table 3), the before tax annual income ratio of the top 1 percent relative to the bottom 20 percent was 59 in 2011.

17 It is also interesting and relevant since it launched itself into HIC status only in the 1990s after three decades of sustained catch-up growth.

18 In the face of evidence to the contrary, or at least the likelihood of long trickle-down lags, the World Bank and IMF now push for social safety nets as part of the reform programs they advocate for L/LMICs that solicit their assistance (Chapter 8).

19 Such exercises were common during the heyday of national centralized planning during the 1960s and 1970s but fell out of favor during the neoliberal era starting in the early 1980s.

20 Following Kuznets' identification of mechanisms, other variables in the regressions included education, urbanization, share of agriculture in GDP, rural workers as a percentage of the total labor force, population growth and various policy interventions.

21 For a brief review of the literature, refer to Kiefer and Khan (2008).

22 Data are drawn from the World Bank, World Development Indicators.

23 The Gini index for 1981 for China was procured from an earlier release of the World Development Indicators and is not reported in the latest release (issued 1/30/2019) at the time of writing.

24 The Kuznets curve has been applied to the environment. Given that the environment is one of the key themes in this textbook, this association is explored in Appendix 4.1.

25 This was shown by Morduch (1999) to be an overstatement based on the accounting methods adopted (historic rather than current portfolio in the denominator), but much better than the 50 percent or so repayment rates for public sector rural banking.

26 Refer to Bateman and Chang (2012) for this view. Khan and Ansari (2018) found that in most competitive informal sector markets in Pakistan, borrowers who had entrepreneurial drive were finding their niche and making repayments based on sales revenue.

27 For a comprehensive review of this social policy refer to (eds.) Adato and Hoddinott (2010). For a comprehensive meta analysis (study of studies), refer to García and Saavedra (2017). They review 94 studies from 47 education-related CCTs across L/LMICs to ascertain how educational outcomes and cost effectiveness are impacted by design features and compare their results to the earlier meta analyses.
28 BRAC was founded in 1972 as Bangladesh Rural Advancement Committee. It is a large development NGO that has diversified and now has a presence in 13 countries across Asia, Africa and Latin America.
29 The analogy often used was that of a gear shift car needing to be pushed until the engine fired up.
30 Newly introduced development initiatives and mechanisms have a tendency to become a fad with a bandwagon effect and this may have been the case with participation as a mechanism. For reservations see da Cunha and Pena (1997).
31 For alternative views, refer to Cole (2003) and Kearsley and Riddel (2010).
32 www.economist.com/china/2017/03/02/chinas-citizens-are-complaining-more-loudly-about-polluted-air, consulted 1/6/2019 and www.livemint.com/Politics/cJeH7pAmyAFnHuFa2ilwYP/Delhi-pollution-fuels-anger-in-citizens-as-toxic-air-burns-e.html, consulted 1/6/2019.
33 Some argue that at this stage even 2 degrees centigrade is too much and would not avert the climate tipping points that would result in more frequent and more severe disasters unfolding. Various populations on the globe have already witnessed a foreshadowing of such events including stronger hurricanes and sea level rises.

References

Adato, M. and J. Hoddinott. (eds.). 2010. *Conditional Cash Transfers in Latin America* (Baltimore: Johns Hopkins University Press).
Aizer, A., J. Currie, P. Simon and P. Vivier. 2016. "Do Low Levels of Blood Lead Reduce Children's Future Test Scores?" National Bureau of Economic Research Working Papers 22558, Boston, MA.
Alesina, A. and R. Perotti. 1996. "Income Distribution, Political Instability, and Investment," *European Economic Review*, 40(6), 1203–1228.
Alkire, S., J. M. Roche, M. E. Santos and S. Seth. 2011. "Multidimensional Poverty Index 2011: Brief Methodological Note," OPHI (Oxford Poverty and Human Development Initiative) Briefing 07, University of Oxford.
Anand, S., P. Segal and J. E. Stiglitz. (eds.), 2010. *Debates on the Measurement of Global Poverty* (New York: Oxford University Press).
Banerjee, A. et al. 2015. "A Multifaceted Program Causes Lasting Progress for the Very Poor: Evidence from Six Countries," *Science*, 348(6236). DOI:10.1126/science.1260799.
Bateman, M. and H.-J. Chang. 2012. "Microfinance and the Illusion of Development: From Hubris to Nemesis in Thirty Years," *World Economic Review*, 1(September 6), 13–36.
Becker, G. 1981. *A Treatise on the Family* (Cambridge, MA: Harvard University Press).
Breitkreuz, R., C. Stanton, N. Brady, J. Pattison-Williams, E. D. King and C. Mishra. 2017. "The Mahatma Gandhi National Rural Employment Guarantee Scheme: A Policy Solution to Rural Poverty in India?," *Development Policy Review*, 35(3), 397–417.
Burmeister, E. 2000. "The Capital Theory Controversy," in: H. D. Kurz. (ed.), *Critical Essays on Piero Sraffa's Legacy in Economics* (Cambridge: Cambridge University Press). 305-314.
Campbell, A. 2011. "The Role of Workers in Management: The Case of Mondragon," *Review of Radical Political Economics*, 43(3), 328–333.

Chang, H.-J. 2011. "Hamlet without the Prince of Denmark: How Development Has Disappeared from Today's 'DEVELOPMENT' Discourse," in: S. R. Khan and J. Christensen. (eds.), *Towards New Developmentalism: Market as Means Rather than Master* (New York: Routledge). 47-58

Cohen, A. J. and G. C. Harcourt. 2003. "Retrospectives: Whatever Happened to the Cambridge Capital Theory Controversy," *The Journal of Economic Perspectives*, 17(1), 199–214.

Cole, M. A. 2003. "Development, Trade and the Environment: How Robust Is the Environment Kuznets Curve?," *Environment and Development Economics*, 8(4), 557–580.

da Cunha, P. V. and M. V. J. Pena. 1997. "The Limits and Merits of Participation," The World Bank, Policy Research Working Paper Series No.1838, Washington, DC.

Devine, G. J. and M. J. Furlong. 2007. "Insecticide Use: Contexts and Ecological Consequences," *Agriculture and Human Values*, 24(3), 281–306.

Ezzati, M. and D. Kammen. 2005. "The Health Impacts of Exposure to Indoor Air Pollution from Solid Fuels in Developing Countries: Knowledge, Gaps, and Data Needs." Resources For the Future, Discussion Paper 02-24, Washington, DC

Farina, F. 2016. "Development Theory and Poverty," in: C. Sunna and G. Davide. (eds.), *Development Economics in the Twenty-First Century* (New York: Routledge). 122-142

Fukuda-Parr, S., A. E. Yamin and J. Greenstein. 2015. "The Power of Numbers: A Critical Review of Millennium Development Goal Targets for Human Development and Human Rights," *Journal of Human Development and Capabilities*, 15(2–3), 105–117.

Goetz, A. and R. S. Gupta. 1996. "Who Takes the Credit?" Gender, Power, and Control over Loan Use in Rural Credit Programs in Bangladesh," *World Development*, 24(1), 45–63.

Grossman, G. M. and A. B. Krueger. 1991 "Environmental Impacts of a North American Free Trade Agreement," National Bureau of Economic Research Working Paper 3914, Cambridge, MA.

Haushofer, J. and J. Shapiro. 2017. "The Short-term Impact of Unconditional Cash Transfers to the Poor: Experimental Evidence from Kenya," *The Quarterly Journal of Economics*, 132(4), 2057–2060.

Hirschman, A. O. 1970. *Exit, Voice, and Loyalty; Responses to Decline in Firms, Organizations, and States* (Cambridge, MA: Harvard University Press).

Jha, R., R. Gaiha, K. Manoj, M. K. Pandeya and S. Shankarb. 2015. "Determinants and Persistence of Benefits from the National Rural Employment Guarantee Scheme – Panel Data Analysis for Rajasthan, India," *European Journal of Development Research*, 27(2), 308–329.

Kearsley, A. and M. Riddel. 2010. "A Further Inquiry into the Pollution Heaven Inquiry and the Environment Kuznets Curve," *Ecological Economics*, 69(4), 905–919.

Khan, S. R. and N. Ansari. 2018. *A Microcredit Alternative in South Asia: Akhuwat's Experiment* (London: Routeledge).

Khan, S. R., S. Kazmi and Z. Rifaqat. 2007. *Harnessing and Guiding Social Capital for Rural Development* (New York: Palgrave/Macmillan).

Khandker, S. R. and H. A. Samad. 2014. "Dynamic Effects of Microcredit in Bangladesh," Policy Research Working Paper No 6821, World Bank Group, Washington, DC.

Kiefer, D. and S. R. Khan. 2008. "Revealed Social Preferences for Equality and Growth," *Journal of Income Distribution*, 17(1), 21–33.

Kuznets, S. 1955. "Economic Growth and Income Inequality," *American Economic Review*, 45(1), 1–28.

Mani, A., S. Mullainathan, E. Shafir and J. Zhao. 2013. "Poverty Impedes Cognitive Function," *Science*, 341(976), 976–980.

Morduch, J. 1999. "The Microfinance Promise," *Journal of Economic Literature*, 37(4), 1569–1614.

Moseley, F. 2012. "A Critique of the Marginal Productivity Theory of the Price of Capital," *Real-World Economics Review*, issue no. 59, www.paecon.net/PAEReview/issue59/Moseley59.pdf, consulted 1/28/2019.

Mullainathan, S. and E. Shafir. 2013. "Scarcity: Why Having Too Little Means so Much," *Science News*, 184(8), 34–35.

Narayan, D., Patel, R, Schafft, K. Rademacher, A. and Koch-Schulte, S. (2000)*Can Anyone Hear Us?: Voices of the Poor* (World Bank, Washington, D. C.).

Park, S. 2009. "Analysis of Saemaul Undong: A Korean Rural Development Programme in the 1970s," *Asia-Pacific Development Journal*, 16(2), 113–140.

Parmar, A. 2003. "Micro-Credit, Empowerment, and Agency: Re-evaluating the Discourse," *Canadian Journal of Development Studies*, 24(3), 461–476.

Piketty, T. 2014. *Capital in the Twenty-First Century* (Cambridge, MA: Belknap Press of Harvard University Press).

Pitt, M., S. R. Khandker and J. Cartwright. 2006. "Empowering Women with Micro Finance: Evidence from Bangladesh," *Economic Development and Cultural Change*, 54(4), 791–831.

Rankin, K. N. 2001. "Governing Development: Neoliberalism, Microcredit, and Rational Economic Woman," *Economy and Society*, 30(1), 8–37.

Rankin, K. N. 2002. "Social Capital, Microfinance, and the Politics of Development," *Feminist Economics*, 8(1), 1–24.

Rubalcava, L., G. Teruel and D. Thomas. 2009. "Symposium: Impacts of the Oportunidades Program: Investments, Time Preferences, and Public Transfers Paid to Women," *Economic Development and Cultural Change*, 57(3), 507–538.

Sandra García, Juan Saavedra. Issued in July 2017. Educational Impacts and Cost-Effectiveness of Conditional Cash Transfer Programs in Developing Countries: A Meta-Analysis, NBER Working Paper No. 23594, NBER Program(s):Development Economics, Economics of Education.

Seguin, M. and M. Nino- Zarazua 2011. "What Do We Know about Non-clinical Interventions for Preventable and Treatable Childhood Diseases in Developing Countries?" World Institute for Development Economic Research (UNU-WIDER) Working Paper WP2013/087, Helsinki.

Sen, A. K. 1990. "Gender and Co-Operative Conflicts," in: I. Tinker. (ed.), *Persistent Inequalities: Women and World Development* (New York: Oxford University Press). 123-149

PART II

Key approaches to economic development and the middle income trap

5

CLASSICAL AND RADICAL ANTECEDENTS OF DEVELOPMENT ECONOMICS

Introduction

Classical political economists focus on the causes of the wealth (income) of nations and the distribution of that wealth across classes. Thus the units of analysis are the collective (economy) and groups or classes. Class is generally not mentioned in mainstream economics textbooks but was introduced as a central unit of analysis by Marx. While Marx is referred to as a classical political economist, he introduced his own conceptual framework and terminology and his writings inspired radical thought in many social science disciplines and fields including development economics.

The transition from classical political economy to economics in the late 19th century shifted the unit of analysis to the individual or the firm and the focus to the efficient allocation of resources.[1] This transition also marked the dropping of the word political and so "principles" (key works) of dominant scholars like Alfred Marshall during the onset of the neoclassical era became principles of economics rather than principles of political economy.

The pioneers of development economics (Chapter 6), trained in both classical and neoclassical economics, recognized that it was the classical political economists who grappled with issues, such as the progress of nations (economic growth), that were more pertinent to newly independent colonies in the 1940s onwards. They also recognized that economic conditions in these newly independent countries were structurally and institutionally different from those in the dominant nations, and their implicit or explicit economic models portrayed this difference and drew on classical assumptions and economics as they saw fit.

In addition to theories of progress, a second theme in development economics pertains to theories of underdevelopment i.e. why do nations not progress? Pertinent to this question are the theories of colonialism and imperialism from which the heterodox strain of development economics emerged. While Marx mostly focused on the critique of capitalism, his writings inspired the radical strain in development economics thought.

The review of Marx in this chapter, like the review of classical political economists in general, is selective. Just as the review of classical political economists focuses on ideas and concepts that inspired the pioneers of development economics, the review of Marx focuses on presenting ideas and views that inspired later thinkers on colonialism and imperialism.

Also, Marx's critique of classical political economy and the capitalist system made class and distribution its centerpiece, and the neo-Marxist and political economy of development approaches in development economics drew on these constructs. This chapter turns to antecedents of the radical strain in development economics after discussing classical political economic thinkers.

Classical political economists

Smith (1908) drew on prior thought but is widely agreed to have been the first to synthesize earlier ideas and present a systematic framework of an economy. The power of a country for Smith was in proportion to the value of its annual produce (GNP) and hence his central focus was on production. He recognized that the wealth of nations was production and welfare generated from the consumption of these products. This may seem obvious now, but it was not so in his time. Mercantilist thinking of his time associated maximizing ownership of specie – gold and silver – with the wealth of nations.[2]

In a nutshell, for Smith the wealth of nations or size of the "fund" (GNP) was principally determined by the skill and dexterity of the workforce and the judgment with which it was applied to production and by the ratio of active and non-active productive labor (participation rate). The prosperity of nations was greater the higher the ratio of productive to unproductive labor (see below). Progress or economic growth was determined principally by capital accumulation and innovations that raised the skill and dexterity or productivity of labor.

His famous observation of a pin factory, with which he started Book I of *The Wealth of Nations*, showed how the division of labor and subsequent specialization unleashed the productive potential of society. Thus, he observed and noted that output increased from a scarce 20 per person per day to 4,800 per person per day with specialization when the job was broken down into 18 tasks. However, machinery (capital accumulation) was necessary for such specialization and division of labor to increase labor productivity, and hence capital accumulation played a primary role. The extent of specialization depended both on the size of the market and the availability of capital. Having an unrestricted exchange economy was thus critical for progress. This was another of his tremendous insights.

Manufacturing lent itself to such division of labor and specialization much more than agriculture and hence its vital role in enhancing the wealth of nations. Because agriculture was by nature limited in the extent to which tasks could be sub-divided, he argued that labor productivity in manufacturing necessarily exceeds that in agriculture. Due to the greater potential for division of labor, and the ingenuity of machine makers whose inventions make tasks "easier and readier" (p. 8), time saving is also more likely in manufacturing.

The savings of the entrepreneur were special because they went into investment and boosting labor productivity whereas landlords frittered away their income.

The hallmark of a more advanced society was one in which the stock of capital per capita was higher and this still has resonance. Given that he assumed only capitalists saved, he regarded a distribution of income in their favor as positive for society.[3] Smith argued that public prodigality can impoverish great nations by eating into the stock that can be used to hire productive labor. By the same token, nations could flourish as a result of the parsimony or frugality of individuals. Frugality is critical for increasing the fund that hires productive labor and it, rather than industry (hard work), is the immediate cause of the increase in capital.

Smith distinguished between two types of labor as mentioned earlier. The [relative] progress of nations is determined by the part of labor that "adds value to the subject it is bestowed on" such as machinery and materials in manufacturing and he considered this component of labor as productive. The other part of labor is not productive and perishes in the moment of performing a service. In this category Smith included the sovereign and associated splendid court services, the ecclesiastic establishments and the military. He criticized "great fleets and armies, who in time of peace produce nothing, and in time of war acquire nothing which can compensate for the expense of maintaining them, even while the war lasts" (p. 254).[4]

Unlike the political economists who succeeded him, Smith was quite optimistic. He envisaged opulence that would raise the general standard of living because of capital accumulation and the increasing division of labor and specialization and skill development that this facilitated. Smith's optimistic evaluation was that in great nations, natural progress is maintained by frugality which offsets public extravagance. He asserted that the driving spirit behind this noble conduct was the "uniform, constant and uninterrupted effort of every man to better his condition" (p. 264). Since these motivations were universal, including in primitive societies, the other supportive conditions such as the collective institutional framework needed to come into play.

These other supporting determinants of prosperity and progress included natural resources such as soil, climate, laws, able administration,[5] stable money (because this facilitated transactions) and navigable rivers (that facilitated transportation and enhanced internal trade and growth).[6] Nations needed tolerable security, otherwise there is an incentive to bury capital for contingencies rather than consume it or employ it for profit. Most current mainstream development economists would probably agree that this list of determinants of economic growth is still very relevant as is the centrality of capital accumulation.[7]

The determinants of prosperity and progress identified above resulted for Smith in "the full complement of riches" which enabled society to be in a progressive state. Eventually, he saw society as moving to a stationary state (growth reproducing society at the level it has attained) but anticipated that this state would not come about for a couple of hundred years for Great Britain.

Smith argued that the great commerce of any civilized nation is carried on between town and country to the mutual benefit of both. Trade within a nation had the advantage of greater control over and security of capital, but the principle of mutual benefit from trade extended across borders. Smith originated modern trade theory, which represents a key complement to development economics.

Smith's trade model suggested countries should specialize and export commodities they had an absolute advantage in producing, and in so doing all countries would be better off by buying from the cheapest source (Appendix 5.1). In so far as foreign trade extends the size of the market, it enables division of labor and specialization and hence enhances productivity. Thus, foreign markets could be a surrogate for limited domestic markets. If an industry in a country has already specialized and it produces a surplus, trade provides a vent or window for that surplus. Thus, trade is principally an avenue for surplus. In serving this purpose it also facilitates the process of capital accumulation. However, Smith insisted that "Those statesmen, who have been disposed to favor it [trade] with encouragements (subsidies), seem to have mistaken the effect and symptoms for the cause" (p. 288).

In his view, colonies did add to the prosperity of nations with empires by opening up new markets and enabling additions to productive employment. However, this was despite the negative aspects of maintaining a monopoly on colonial trade which created distortions in the flow of capital and hence reduced economic diversification. In the case of dissension arising, Smith recommended a graceful exit. He believed that only foolish national pride and the personal interests of those administering the colonies, in conjunction with the interests of merchants, perpetuated an unprofitable course of [military] action.

Just as with colonialism, Smith's theory of the state was progressive and anticipated Marx. He wrote "Civil government, so far as it is instituted for the security of property, is in reality instituted for the defense of the rich against the poor, or of those who have some property against whose whom have none at all" (p. 560).

Classical political economists following Smith quibbled or differed with him but all deferred to his genius in having established the framework and agenda for political economy. Malthus devoted Book II of his *Principles of Political Economy* (1951) to the prosperity and progress of nations and for the most part echoed Smith on the causes of the wealth of nations. He focused his inquiry on "the most immediate and effective stimulants to the continued creation and progress of wealth" (p. 310).

Malthus was concerned with countries that had already reached a certain threshold level of prosperity (i.e. had already attained catch-up growth) rather than with the primary causes of prosperity.[8] As was the case with Smith, Malthus noted that structural change occurred when agriculture was very productive since this enabled a large section of the population to move to towns and into manufacturing.[9] Structural change, along with demand from a growing middle class for "conveniences" and "luxuries", stimulated prosperity (p. 350).

However, his major contribution was to bring the concept of effectual demand (effective demand) centerstage.[10] Classical political economists at this time believed in Say's Law of supply creating its own demand and so the lack of effectual demand was not an issue for them. At most, a lack of demand in one market echoed a surplus in another and so there was only a temporary period of adjustment in which some unemployment was possible.

Malthus viewed this theoretical belief contrary to the reality of the high unemployment he observed. As a strong supporter of the existing social system, he was also highly concerned about the social instability that mass unemployment could trigger. On a theoretical level he recognized that people need not always spend what they had, and argued that this was true of the capitalists who were more concerned with saving and capital accumulation than spending. Hence a shortage of effectual demand was possible contrary to Say's Law and he made theoretical arguments to prove his point (Khan, 2014: p. 5).

He identified the same causes as Smith as crucial for the progress of nations i.e. capital accumulation, labor saving inventions and soil fertility. He added the qualifier that for the positive effects to be realized from these determinants, effectual demand must rise in conjunction. Thus he approached policy analysis through this lens of effectual demand. This included better means of communication as a way to open up internal markets.

He noted that policies to boost effectual demand were needed in particular after wars in which production capacity is created to serve the war effort, but that after the war the demand is missing to balance with the productive capacity. Thus much of this discussion was framed in dealing with the post Napoleonic war problems. He pointed out that recovery must always be premised on policies that assist accumulation from profits. Thus, if production exceeded effectual demand, the policy response must not be to curb production, say by raising taxes, but to boost effectual demand.

As with Smith, the higher the ratio of productive to unproductive labor the greater the annual fund (GNP) would be. Malthus argued that the optimum ratio between the two depended on the productivity of the soil, technological change and differences in propensity to consume among the different social groups in society. He argued that it would not be necessary to encourage the hiring of unproductive labor if capitalists consumed adequately, but that it was not in their nature to do so given that they are accumulators. He noted that part of the unproductive class, such as the military, are supported by taxation, and that while they contributed to effectual demand caution is needed because, like war, taxation is a necessary evil that adversely impacts profits and production. This is also why he did not support simply increasing wages to increase effectual demand.[11]

Malthus also made a case for land distribution, based on his theory that the continued contribution to effectual demand coming from a small number of large proprietors was limited in comparison to the demand generated by a moderate number who would be in "the middle ranks of life" if primogeniture was abolished (p. 374). However, on balance he supported letting things be because he viewed the landed aristocracy to have held despotic monarchy in check and hence contributed to liberty.[12]

Malthus attributed the rapidly growing wealth of the United States to the easy division of and access to land for the industrious and the contribution this made to effectual demand. He reasoned that there must be an optimal land distribution since excessive re-distribution could also hurt the accumulation process by not providing adequate demand for necessaries, conveniences and luxuries emanating from the middle ranks of life.[13]

He also considered debt financing as another possible option in boosting effectual demand, but this too had problems. First, taxation would be needed later on to repay the debt and this would hurt production later. Second, interest payments would represent a burden on the exchequer. Third, there would be an incentive to cheapen the currency to pay off the debt, and this would not just hurt creditors and fixed income groups but if confidence in the currency was eroded, it would also hurt transactions.

Following Smith, he set great store by commerce to boost effectual demand. However, he quoted Smith to indicate that imports can hurt domestic production and therefore they should be cautiously phased in. However, the advantage of trade was not simply in extending the market but also of raising custom revenue to help pay off the war debt.

He also recommended public works as a policy driven method of adding to effectual demand, a recommendation now associated with Keynesianism. The public works would raise the wage bill and add to effectual demand, but the goods created would not directly come to the market to add to productive capacity and hence cancel out the increase in effectual demand. However, they would indirectly boost future productive capacity. This would also be a way of absorbing demobilized sailors and solders.

Malthus is still better known for his contribution to population theory than to political economy. The upshot of his population theory was that for various reasons food production would not keep pace with population growth.[14] One factor he identified as a limit on the growth of food production was diminishing returns from land and this became the basis for Ricardo's very influential theory of rents.

Diminishing returns for Malthus, and Ricardo after him, is not the same concept as in neoclassical economics. In the latter case, diminishing returns to land mean lower returns from additional units of land of the same fertility applied to other factors that are held constant. Thus, the issue is one of factor proportions becoming less favorable for land and hence the diminishing returns.

Malthus assumed that to meet the food needs of the population, it is logical that the most fertile land would be used first and as population and the demand for food increased, less and less fertile land would be brought into cultivation and hence the diminishing returns from the less fertile parcels of land. The rent from the marginal or least fertile parcel or unit of land in cultivation would be zero by definition since that land would not command a scarcity premium and the marginal unit of land represented the base relative to which rent or scarcity value of the more fertile units of land were determined. The rent therefore was due to the "original and indestructible powers of the soil" and accrued to the owners.[15] Competition among the capitalist farmers ensured that this was the case. Ultimately, rents resulted from a scarcity of food relative to the needs of a population.

Ricardo (1933) accepted this definition of rent and, based on it, developed a model to demonstrate factor income distribution and its social consequences and policy implications. As will become evident in the next chapter, a variation of this model developed by Arthur Lewis became the most influential model in development economics. Ricardo was the first to theorize in a formal manner like a modern economist and so had a very far-reaching impact on the discipline. Nonetheless, his concern and analysis made characterizing him as a political economist apt.

There were three agents in his model i.e. landlords, capitalist farmers (who rented in the land) and labor, and he started with the usual assumptions of perfect competition and internal factor mobility. Figure 5.1 shows the base distribution of factor income in his model.

The total agricultural product or income is divided between the landlords (rent, contribution of land), capitalist farmers (profit, return to capital invested) and labor (wage bill). Figure 5.1 shows a demand for land that slopes down due to diminishing returns or diminishing marginal product of the land, as explained above. The total product then is mathematically the area under the marginal product curve determined by the marginal unit of land in cultivation.[16]

The marginal unit in cultivation is shown by the vertical supply curve, intersecting the demand curve, which defines the amount of land in use based on the demand for food. Zero rent is forthcoming on the marginal unit of land where the demand for land (based on the demand for food) intersects the fixed or vertical supply of land. The infra-marginal units of land would get positive rent with the highest rent forthcoming from the most fertile first unit brought into cultivation. Thus the triangle above the horizontal line (starting from the vertical line defining zero rent) and below the demand for land is the total rent (R) that accrues to the landlords.

The amount of labor used for cultivation is also determined by the amount of land in cultivation. Labor is paid a subsistence wage that is horizontal due to

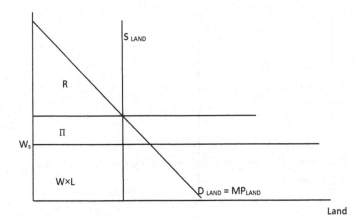

FIGURE 5.1 Factor distribution in Ricardo's model

surplus labor.[17] The wage bill or labor share then is the subsistence wage multiplied by the amount of labor used for cultivation to meet the demand for food (W × L). The share of capital or profit (Π) is then the residual after the wage bill and rent are subtracted from total product. Rent equalizes the rate of profit (r = Π/W) on farms of different fertility because after rent is paid, r is equalized.

Since capital is mobile, the return to capital in agriculture is the same as the return to capital in industry. Thus, if return to capital in agriculture were higher, as in neoclassical economics, funds would flow into agriculture causing the returns to go down and the returns in industry to go up until there was a convergence. Thus, at any given point, the returns are the same in both activities and it is rents that set the returns to capital in both agriculture and industry and hence the centrality of rents in Ricardo's model.

Once Ricardo set up his model, it was possible to explore the impact of various changes just as in modern economics.[18] For example, an increase in population in this model, other things constant, would increase, and demand for corn (food staple) cultivation would move in the direction of the extensive margin of cultivation (shift to the right in S_{LAND}). If this trend continued, the total produce would ultimately be solely divided between wages and rent as shown in Figure 5.2.

As Figure 5.2 shows, due to population growth and diminishing marginal returns to land, rents would absorb all of the profits and hence halt capital accumulation.

Given the equalization of profit rates, profits in manufacturing would be conditioned by the profits on the extensive margin in agriculture. Thus, diminishing returns in agriculture would result in profits across the board converging to zero and the move to the stationary state with no capital accumulation beyond reproduction.[19]

The arrival of the stationary state could be extended in various ways following the logic of Ricardo's model. Recall that Smith's vision for the future was one where the expanded possibilities of the division of labor made possible by technological

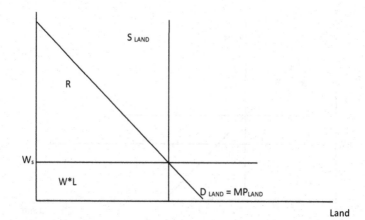

FIGURE 5.2 Stationary state in Ricardo's model

progress would eventually cease when a country attained its "full complement of riches". Thus, there was a natural limit to economic growth based on the division of labor and specialization. Ricardo, having lived some decades later into the industrial revolution, saw more possibilities afforded by technological progress in pushing back the stationary state.

Ricardo considered two kinds of agricultural improvements. If there were better agricultural practices such as crop rotation or better manure that affected all land in the same way, rents would not change. In this case, the return to any improvement on the farm due to capital investments would accrue to capital or capitalist farmers, as indicated in Figure 5.3.

The higher productivity of land due to capital investments can be seen as a shift to the right of marginal productivity of land or the demand for land. The margin of cultivation and the wage bill are shown as unchanged.[20] Thus the higher productivity of land due to the capital investments is captured by the capitalist farmers as higher profits.

However, if better agricultural machinery, such as a plough or a thresher, or economy in the use of horses affects land of different quality in different ways, the outcome would be less determinate. If the least productive land were made more productive, rent would fall and vice versa. In both cases, if cultivation is on the less extensive margin due to higher productivity, total rents would fall.[21]

Another way of pushing back the stationary state would be population control since this would obviate the need to operate on the extensive margin whereby rents increase and profits decrease. Finally, operating on the extensive margin could have been avoided by importing cheap corn into Great Britain from the Continent. The landed gentry had imposed tariffs on the import of corn to protect their rents and these were referred to as the Corn Laws. Repealing the Corn Laws would result in operating on the less extensive margin and hence a reduction of

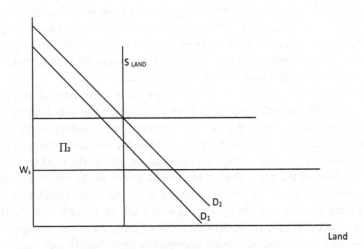

FIGURE 5.3 Capital investments in Ricardo's model

rents and the subsistence wage could also be reduced. The outcome would be an increase in profit share and capital accumulation.

Ricardo's case for the repeal of the Corn Laws was in fact broader than the boost to the capital accumulation this repeal would result in. He made the case for free trade based on an extension of Smith's contribution to trade theory by using the same axiomatic framework (i.e. same assumptions). There was one important difference and that was that unlike in Smith's trade model of absolute advantage, in a two-country context he assumed that one country had an absolute advantage in producing *both* commodities. It would then appear that the country that had an absolute advantage in producing all commodities would have no motivation for trade. It was a remarkable feat of genius for him to demonstrate that even under these circumstances it would be beneficial for both countries to trade and the result could be generalized to the many-country, many-commodity cases (Appendix 5.1).

Ricardo's trade theory is referred to as the theory of comparative advantage and it has remained the core of modern trade theory for decades even if the source of the comparative advantage was defined differently by subsequent trade theorists.[22]

The logic of the theory of comparative advantage is impeccable. In a two-country, two-commodity case, Ricardo showed that even if country A has an absolute advantage in the production of both commodities relative to country B, the two countries could still engage in beneficial trade by specializing in the production of the commodity in which their comparative advantage is greater. For country A, this would mean specializing in the commodity for which its absolute advantage is greater while for country B it would mean specializing in the other commodity for which its absolute disadvantage is lower. Another way of saying this is that B's comparative advantage is in the commodity for which its comparative disadvantage is the least.

Ricardo also argued that the relative gains from trade were determined by the difference or gap between the domestic and world price structure. The greater the difference in domestic and world prices, the more the benefits from trade that could be realized in principle. It followed that there were likely to be more gains from trade for a small country than for a large country.

In general, since a small country's supply is a small part of total world supply, it would not influence world prices much and so the domestic price would diverge from world prices.[23] By contrast, large country supply would be dominant in determining world prices and so the domestic prices in a large country would be closer to that established on the world markets. By this logic, the bulk of the gains from trade would accrue to the smaller countries, which might be more fearful in engaging in world trade (Appendix 5.1).[24] Notwithstanding the seemingly impeccable logic of Ricardo's trade theory and the wide adherence to modern versions of comparative advantage among mainstream economists, heterodox economists have found much fault with it (see for example Chapters 7 and 9).

The heterodox tradition

Ricardo was concerned with factor distribution because of his concern for capital accumulation. He saw the rise in rents as choking off profits and hence capital accumulation and his model showed ways around this. Thus, Ricardo was a champion of the capitalist class and capitalism. He accepted property rights as they existed and therefore had no qualms about the higher welfare accruing to those who had the purchasing power based on existing property rights.

Marx (2011), more than any other scholar, established the heterodox tradition of questioning who had to pay the price for attaining progress and who benefited from it. He did this not only based on a scathing critique of the injustice that in his view was the foundation of the capitalist system but also by developing an alternative conceptual framework with which to analyze this system. While Ricardo's concern was with factor income distribution, Marx was concerned with the distribution of income across classes. Since existing property rights governed the distribution of income, his main challenge was to property rights which he considered to be based on exploitation and which were at the core of the capitalist system.

Classical political economists understood that challenging property rights meant challenging the existing social system. Thus they argued that existing property rights were based on diligence, intelligence and frugality of the capitalist class. Marx viewed property rights as they existed were the result of a historical process (primitive accumulation) based on conquest, enslavement, robbery, pillage and murder.

In Great Britain, this included the alienation of state domains and robbery of the commons (enclosure movement). Enclosing the commons as private property generated accumulation both directly and also indirectly. It did so indirectly by providing labor for the factories (proletariat) as rural workers were displaced by the enclosures. Once the capitalists became established as the ruling class, they used laws, courts and the police to preserve their wealth and further enrich themselves as observed by Smith (see above).

Marx not only considered primitive accumulation as unjust but also the subsequent enrichment of the capitalist class. Once the accumulation process gets underway, it follows its own dynamic or what Marx referred to as the laws of motion of capitalism in reproducing itself on an ever expanding scale based on accumulation. Competition pushed capitalists into ever increasing accumulation and their only option was to accumulate or be accumulated.

Marx argued that capitalism differed from other modes of production because of the nature of circulation of capital. Under primitive modes, the circuit was $C \rightarrow M \rightarrow C$ where C stands for commodities and M for money. In this case, the starting C is the same as the ending C and there is no surplus. In mercantile capitalism, circulation is $M \rightarrow C \rightarrow M'$. In this case surplus value can in principle result ($M' > M$) and be a source of accumulation. However, since like must be traded with like, surplus is only created if someone gains at another's expense. Thus, merchant capital yields a surplus from buying cheap and selling dear. Similarly, in finance capital surplus results from borrowing at low interest rates and lending at high interest rates. For Marx, real surplus could only be derived from production.

Marx delineated the circuit for industrial capital as: $M \rightarrow C \rightarrow P \rightarrow C' \rightarrow M'$. M is money, C are raw materials, intermediate inputs and machinery, P production and C' the finished product. Surplus value can be measured as $M' > M$ or $C' > C$. Marx argued that this surplus value was based on exploitation, and to understand why a small detour into Marxian concepts and terminology is necessary.

Marx argued that all commodities had a common social aspect and this was the labor embodied in them and what gave them exchange value. Only socially necessary labor produces exchange value. Socially necessary is defined as labor required at a particular time based on average skill and intensity of effort given the state of the technology. Unskilled labor is the numeraire or common denominator for measuring all labor and so skilled labor is a multiple of unskilled labor.

Living labor represents that directly involved in transforming nature or its products into commodities. Class is defined with respect to the nature of participation in the production process and not simply with respect to income. The capitalist class is defined as the one engaged in the exploitation of living labor. Living labor is then the precondition for the accumulation of dead labor i.e. capital.

With these concepts and terminology, it becomes possible to explain Marx's concept of exploitation and why he thought that was the basis of capital accumulation. He adopted classical political economy assumptions, including competition, and this made it challenging to show the existence of profits since perfect competition erodes economic profits.

He argued that labor under capitalism sells its labor power to the capitalist as a commodity because that is all she or he possesses to earn a livelihood and the capitalist owns the means of production (capital or machinery) that labor needs to work with. Due to surplus labor, capital is dominant in the relations of labor and capital, and this enables the product of labor to be appropriated by capital.

The use value of labor is the means of subsistence that is needed by the worker and his family to create labor or for labor to reproduce itself as a class. This is based on prevalent customs, habits, needs and skills. The use value of skilled labor would include the labor cost invested in various educational and training programs to upgrade skills. Surplus value arises because it could take say up to 4 hours of labor per day to create the subsistence or use value of labor, but the workers were actually put to work from 14–18 hours a day at the time Marx was writing. The balance was appropriated by capital by virtue of their ownership of the means of production and hence their greater bargaining power.

To sum up, socially necessary labor is the labor time required to produce the means of subsistence and any time put in beyond that generates surplus value. Thus, over a period of time as the working week has been reduced, surplus labor has been converted into leisure with the help of unions and the democratic process.

Applying these Marxian concepts to HICs with their complex production systems, protections and safety nets is now more challenging, but the basic principles can be used. L/LMICs have much less advanced production systems and social protections and the application remains more straightforward.

To continue, the value of the finished good C' comes from raw materials, intermediate goods, capital goods and labor. For Marx, the first three categories were merely embodied labor and their value was transferred to the finished product in the exact amount of the labor value embodied in them. What remained in C' − C or M' − M was surplus value contributed by living labor and that was the source of profits.

Total value was therefore contributed by labor (embodied or living) and therefore profits, interests, rents, were parasitic claims on value created by labor.[25] Marx provided the first serious attempt at digging beneath surface phenomenon to provide an explanation of how profits arise and what the source is.[26] Marx argued that the profit rate varied positively with the exploitation rate.[27] Like Ricardo, he anticipated a secular decline in the profit rate, but he defined profit differently and therefore the reasons were also different.[28]

Capital accumulation is the raison d'être of capitalism for Marx and also the other political economists. Paradoxically, in the Marxian framework this was associated with a decline in the profit rate.[29] In the Marxian framework, it is only from living labor that the capitalist can draw a profit and so a rise in the capital labor ratio (organic composition of capital) resulting from accumulation means a decline in the profit rate.

The solution emerging from Marx's equation is accordingly different from Ricardo's prescriptions (see above) with the primary response of capitalists being that of intensifying the rate of exploitation by speeding up the pace of work, more intense monitoring[30] and raising the length of the working day. An alternative was technological change that enabled the use of female and child labor.

Marx's main focus was critically evaluating the capitalist economy and demonstrating it was not viable. Reviewing that would take us far afield from the subject of catch-up growth. However, Marx viewed colonialism as another strategy in averting the decline in the profit rate. A realization crisis in capitalism resulted from the need to keep wages low to facilitate accumulation. This also meant low purchasing power for workers and hence the inability of capitalists to realize profits. Colonialism could provide markets and also cheaper materials and food to reduce the wage bill and hence raise the profit rate. Capital needed an ever expanding market for inputs and outputs for accumulation and, in this sense, colonialism was inevitable.

It is this strand of Marx's work that other heterodox scholars, following in his wake, drew on. They argued that colonialism represented an exploitative relationship, just as the one between capital and labor. Economies that industrialized first had the power to secure the required markets and materials by advantageous trade treaties or military conquest. The colonies were thus made to focus on the production of raw materials and minerals that were required by the colonizers.

In exploring the colonial question regarding North America and Australia, Marx (1972) perceived the general problem to be a collision in interest between the capitalist regime in the mother country and the self-employed in the colonies. Artisans and peasants enriching themselves were unlikely to be interested in enriching the capitalist needing to exploit wage workers for accumulation. Quoting E. G. Wakefield, Marx agreed the solution was that "dependence must be created by artificial means" (p. 721).

In America and Australia, the problem of creating dependence was exacerbated by the abundance of land, as public property was readily available for conversion to private property by those willing to start their own farms. This reduced the availability of labor and raised wages. The solution was to put an artificial price on land making it relatively prohibitive for wage workers. At the same time, increased revenues from land sales funded the import of "have nothings" from Europe, who became wage workers for the capitalists. This was referred to as "systematic colonization" (p. 723).

Marx used India to elaborate on colonialism in Asiatic society. He viewed Indian agricultural prosperity to have depended on centralized public works in providing irrigation. Urban prosperity resulted mostly from the textile industry dependent on a productive agriculture. The British neglected the first (public works) and destroyed the second (textile industry). While he noted the misery caused by British rapacity, he also viewed this as a potential upheaval that could eventually end the social oppression of the ordinary Indian living in a stagnant Asiatic society.

In the introduction to his edited volume on *Marx on Colonialism and Modernization*, Avineri (1968, p. 6) observed that the absence of private property in the East was the basis of Marx's view that the Asiatic mode of production was stagnant with no internal motive for change.[31] It was subject to despotism with the state or sovereign as the ultimate owner demanding rent in kind. Village communities reproduced themselves (with the same name) as self-sufficient entities if destroyed by natural disasters. Notwithstanding his acknowledgements of the horrors of colonialism, he viewed the destruction of these communities as a step forward since they led an "undignified, stagnatory, and vegetative life" and were oppressed by their own superstition, a caste system, rules and a "brutalizing worship of nature" (pp. 88–89).

Thus, while Marx viewed the English to be driven "by the vilest interests, and stupid in the manner of enforcing them", they were instrumental in initiating a social revolution in stagnant societies (p. 89). By undermining spinning, weaving and other handicrafts in India, British commerce tore apart the "unity of industrial and agricultural production" which Marx referred to in many newspaper essays on India. The English he observed had a similar effect in China when, after wresting five ports by force, they flooded the markets with cheap machine-made goods that wiped out handicrafts.

Marx's assessment of the political economy of imperialism was that it was a mechanism to benefit some British subjects at the tax-payer's expense. As cited by

Avineri, he maintained that the "advantage to Great Britain from her Indian Empire must be limited to the profits and benefits which accrue to individual British subjects. These profits and benefits, it must be confessed are very considerable" (1968, pp. 222–225). He went on in this essay to identify the beneficiaries who included stockholders, recipients of patronage (civil, clerical, medical, military and naval) and pensioners.[32] John Hobson, Rosa Luxemburg and Vladimir Lenin elaborated on Marx's basic insights on imperialism and colonialism.

Hobson (1938, p. 4) distinguished colonialism from imperialism. He viewed colonialism as "migration of part of a nation to vacant and sparsely populated [temperate] lands, the emigrants carrying with them full rights of citizenship in the mother country". In this regard, it was the transplantation of national life abroad where "white colonists carry with them the modes of government, the industrial and other 'arts' (technology) of the civilization of the mother country" (p. 27). Imperialism, by contrast, meant dominating tropical and sub-tropical people and cultures by force for national advantage. The expected advantages included securing foreign markets for export, and facilitating the purchase of food and raw materials that could not be economically produced at home.

Hobson used statistics to argue that trading, investing and discharging surplus population were the real motives for imperial expansion. Echoing Marx, he argued that vested interests such as finance capital, which had much to gain from the imperial project, were able to put their own interests above those of the nation. In terms of the political economy, the principle beneficiaries of imperialism were the investors seeking outlets for surplus capital, along with the owners of the national debt, the military industrial complex (including contractors, arms and shipping manufacturers) and aristocrats seeking careers. Ultimately, these private profits were based on socialized risk since the state would become entangled if the foreign ventures met with obstacles. Yet the press provided a patriotic spin for such ventures because they were owned or controlled by vested interests.

However, for Hobson, this profit seeking was a manifestation rather than the root cause of imperialism. The root cause, as identified by Marx, was the nature of the capitalist system in which capital accumulation and production out-stripped consumption. Growing protectionism in the advanced industrial nations compounded the problem by impoverishing selling nations. He identified the underlying skewed distribution of income as the fundamental challenge to capitalism. Profits, rents and interest secured much of the income for the rich while wages were restrained and not allowed to keep pace with productivity growth. Since the limited consumption of the rich was unable to provide the needed effective demand, capitalism sought alternative solutions.

A supply-side solution was combinations or mergers to limit production and this shut out the less competitive firms, but this was only a partial solution. Demand-side solutions included wasteful advertising, but imperialism was the real solution. Therefore, as he dug deeper, imperialism was ultimately the result of an unequal and unjust distribution of income and the civilized solution was social reform including welfare expenditures to ensure adequate effective demand.

Luxemburg (1951) accepted Marx's argument that capitalism needed non-capitalist social organizations in order to survive. However, she took this concept further by pointing out that to go beyond simple reproduction within the Marxist framework, surplus value needed to be realized outside the sphere of capitalist production. Seeing that relations with the non-capitalist world were inevitable, she predicted that "capital, impelled to appropriate productive forces for purposes of exploitation, ransacks the whole world" (p. 358).

Further, she pointed out that the "industrial reserve army of workers" would prove inadequate because, as Marx was aware, higher wages were not an adequate incentive to balance the propagation of population and labor with the pace of accumulation. Hence, she hypothesized that the "labor for this army is recruited from social reservoirs outside the dominion of capital". In particular, she suggested that "capital needs other races to exploit territories where the white man cannot work" (p. 361).

Since labor power "is in most cases rigidly bound by the traditional pre-capitalist organization of production, it must first be 'set free' in order to be enrolled in the active army of capital" (p. 362). Luxemburg pointed out that capital needed to destroy natural economies that it confronted since they were self-sufficient and had no need to interact with global capitalism. They had no need for capitalist commodities and therefore no need to sell their labor or raw materials. Such natural economies including slave, tribal, communal or feudal social formations therefore had to be destroyed and transformed so that they would need to interact with global capital. Global capital created a market for its surplus commodities and savings by first destroying the natural economies and then creating incentives for the reconstructed economies to sell raw materials and cheap labor in exchange for capitalist products. By imposing a head tax on subjects, wage labor was in turn sought by them to pay the tax. A currency was introduced for monetary transactions and paying the tax.

Marx had maintained that self-sufficiency was anathema to capitalistic and imperialistic goals such as gaining possession of productive forces, coercing labor power into services and separating industry from agriculture by destroying craft production. Luxemburg provided detailed case studies of India, Algeria and China in order to prove this point. She also conducted case studies of Egypt and Turkey to elaborate on the point that finance capitalism was another mechanism for subjugation of colonies because it provided loans for dubious projects that resulted in defaults, which then led to occupation.

Lenin (1948) used statistics to demonstrate that Marx's prediction about the inevitable concentration of industrial capital had been realized in the early 20th century via vertical integration, predatory pricing and other tactics. More important for Lenin was the fact that banking had also undergone a similar monopolization in the form of trusts, syndicates and cartels. Through interlocking directorships and the holding system, banks and finance capital acquired an immense amount of power over industry, commerce, services and every sphere of public life.[33]

Surplus capital was exported to backward countries where capital was scarce and therefore expected to earn higher return based on cheaper prices for land, materials and labor in particular. Inter-imperialist conflict was inevitable in this search for profits as the whole non-capitalist world had been divided into zones of influence by the end of the 19th century and so only a re-division was possible. This conflict was exacerbated due to competition for increasingly scarcer raw materials.

Summary

While they differed in many important ways, all classical economists agreed that capital accumulation was central to the progress of the wealth of nations. Smith can be viewed as the first systematic and pragmatic economist concerned with the progress of nations (development). His prescription to focus on saving, capital accumulation and industry as catalysts for labor productivity growth still has resonance. In identifying human capital as part of fixed capital he preempted later mainstream theorists. He also anticipated Marx in his view of the role of the state. His very functional view of trade as an avenue for surplus and as a symptom rather than a cause of prosperity may also surprise mainstream theorists.

While Smith focused on the supply side and assumed demand would be present, Malthus worried about ensuring adequate effectual (effective) demand in order to maintain prosperity. An efficient agricultural sector was central to progress because it enabled rural urban migration, stimulated industry and also created an urban middle class that sustained effectual demand. While trade could contribute to effectual demand by extending the market, Malthus echoed Smith in arguing that reciprocal trade liberalization should be approached with great caution to avoid hurting domestic industry. He was among the first economists to advocate land redistribution consistent with his broader goal of ensuring adequate effectual demand. He reasoned that a few large proprietors would contribute less to effectual demand than would a much larger number in the "middle ranks of life". However, he refrained from pushing this reform for other class-based reasons.

Ricardo's focus was on potential hindrances and encouragements to capital accumulation and hence economic growth. To explore this issue, he developed a model based on the division of the total produce into rents, wages and profits. Wages were determined by subsistence, and profits were defined as a residual, so that elaborating on the theory of rents was central to his analysis. Any change that enhanced profits would enhance capital accumulation and growth. Profits could be enhanced by cheaper food, either via imports or via improvements in agricultural productivity. Technological change that applied across the board to soils of different fertility or made less productive land more productive could lower wages and rents and raise profits. His theory of comparative advantage made the case for free trade (repeal of the Corn Laws) as being mutually beneficial for nations, but his underlying concern was the need to sustain the accumulation process in Britain.

Marx rigorously formalized theories of profit and exploitation. However, it was his theory of colonialism that was the root of radical development economics. He viewed the self-sufficiency of natural economies, which stemmed from the "unity of industrial and agricultural production", as being on a collision course with the global capitalist system. Since natural economies had no need for the industrial goods of capitalist economies, economic dependence had to be created via artificial means i.e. via the destruction of the natural economies. Hobson, Luxemburg and Lenin elaborated on this basic insight.

Hobson distinguished between colonialism and imperialism. The former he viewed as the settlement of lands with temperate climates by whites who destroyed and displaced native populations and recreated the way of life of the mother countries. Imperialism was the forceful domination of alien peoples and cultures in tropical regions to ensure that imperialist countries had the supply of labor, materials and markets needed for accumulation. The impetus for imperialism was created by wage repression and hence an unequal distribution of income and wealth in the imperialist countries that resulted in a lack of effective demand and hence the search for foreign markets.

Luxemburg argued that the logic of accumulation in industrial countries required the realization of surplus value outside the sphere of capitalist production. She elaborated on the process by which imperialism subordinated natural economies in its drive for capital accumulation, using case studies of several countries including India, China and Egypt.

Lenin used statistics to demonstrate that capital concentration had reached a zenith as a result of recurring crises, thus bearing out Marx's prediction of an ever growing concentration of capital. However, banks had also undergone a process of concentration via the formation of trusts, syndicates and cartels, and had acquired increasing power such that finance capital dominated other sectors of the economy like industry and commerce. Imperialism was a manifestation of the drive for profit by finance capital since the returns to capital in backward capital-scarce nations were likely to be higher than in the capital-abundant industrialized economies.

These theories of imperialism and colonialism come into play in Chapter 7 in various heterodox approaches. Contemporary radical approaches, following in the early heterodox tradition, argue that the legacy of colonialism in hindering catch-up growth is still being combated by LICs which were colonized. Prior to a review of these heterodox approaches, the work of scholars who drew on classical political economy and contributed to what became mainstream development economics for a few decades, is explored next in Chapter 6.

Appendix 5.1: Theories of absolute and comparative advantage

A simple diagrammatic tool that all students with exposure to introductory economics are familiar with is used to illustrate both theories. Smith assumed labor to be homogeneous, non-specialized and freely transferable across industries and therefore the transformation curve or production possibility frontier (PPF) for a two good (X, Y) economy is shown in Appendix Figure 5.1 as linear.[34]

The linear transformation curve or PPF represents constant cost technology.[35] This results from the proposition of labor theory of value whereby goods derive their value from the amount of direct or embodied labor that goes into producing them. The proportions are constant and so the opportunity cost of getting Y in terms of X foregone is constant. Unskilled labor is the numeraire or yardstick with which to measure all forms of labor and so the assumption of homogeneous labor can be relaxed.

While the technology is assumed to be the same across all firms in one industry in one country, it can be different across country. Indeed this difference makes labor more or less productive across countries and this is the basis of advantage and mutually beneficial trade.[36] Thus there is no technological change or economic growth in the model though these changes can be quite easily accommodated.

If the economy is shown to be operating on the PPF (rather than inside it), the implicit assumption is that there is full employment. Internal labor market flexibility and mobility and non-prohibitive economic dislocations are assumed in moving along the PPF. The implicit assumption was that moving from one activity to another means compensating job creation for job loss and so unemployment should not result from such structural changes.[37]

Factor mobility is a substitute for trade since if labor in this model is mobile, production rather than goods would be moving. This would equalize prices and

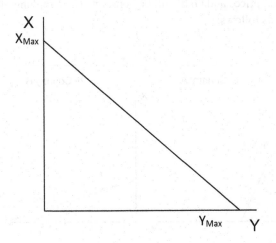

APPENDIX FIGURE 5.1 Linear production possibility frontier

profits and in the limit no trade would be needed and hence factor mobility is ruled out. Trade restrictions were also assumed to be limited since they impact the magnitude and direction of trade as prices with interventions vary from those without interventions.

Perfect competition was assumed with free entry and exit of firms into industries and no market power is exercised by profit-maximizing firms to influence prices. Again, transportation costs are assumed to be low and at least not prohibitive.

Goods are homogenous so one does not need to worry about quality differences and branding. Consumers respond to real prices. Production is national and nationals gain from it, and the model does not address risk and uncertainty which could have quantitative impacts.

For the time of writing, many of the implicit assumptions were reasonable and others easily addressed. Based on them, Smith's contention was that both parties would gain from trade if one country A had an absolute advantage in producing good X and country B in producing Y. Absolute advantage is measured in terms of labor productivity or amount produced per unit (hour) labor. This advantage aggregates into the respective slopes of the PPFs as shown in Appendix Figures 5.2a and b.

The slopes of the respective PPFs for countries A and B show that country A has an absolute advantage in producing good X and country B in producing good Y. In other words, if country A put all its labor toward producing good X, it could produce much more of good X than if country B did the same and vice versa for good Y. To show that both countries gain from trade, we need to show that the slope of the PPFs is the relative price ratios that prevail in the two countries.

The GDP for a two-good economy $= P_x \times Q_x + P_y \times Q_y$. Trade represents a movement along the PPF as the economy produces more of one good and less of the other. As long as the economy is on the PPF, only X and Y in the equation above change and prices and GDP will be constant. Thus, moving along the PPF can be depicted as follows:

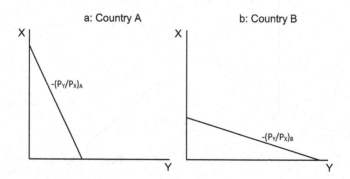

APPENDIX FIGURES 5.2a and b Absolute advantage

$$0 = P_x \times \Delta Q_x + P_y \times \Delta Q_y$$
$$\text{or} - P_x \times \Delta Q_x = P_y \times \Delta Q_y$$
$$\text{or} - \Delta Q_x / \Delta Q_y = P_y / P_x$$

In other words, the slope of the PPF represents the relative price ratio and this holds true for both country A and country B. If the price ratios in the two countries are identical, because there is identical labor productivity in the production of the two goods in both countries, there would be no incentive to trade. If the price ratios differ as shown in Appendix Figures 5.2a and b, the two countries have an incentive to engage in trade. The price ratios shown in Appendix Figures 5.2a and b represent the two extremes of the possible world price ratios.

Appendix Figures 5.2a and b show that country A has an absolute advantage in producing more X while country B has an absolute advantage in producing Y. Clearly, country A will only trade if the world price it confronts is flatter than its domestic price line (it gets more Y for one unit of X foregone) and country B will only trade if it confronts a world price line that is steeper than its domestic price line (it gets more X for one unit of Y foregone). It is logical to presume that the negotiated world price line would be between the two extremes i.e. flatter than A's price line and steeper than B's price line. If this is the outcome, both countries can gain from trade, as shown in Appendix Figures 5.3a and b.

Appendix Figure 5.3a shows that country A can now trade along a flatter world price line $(P_x / P_y)^w$ and this is superior since it now has an option to get more Y for a unit of X foregone. In fact, in a two-country, two-good case, its best option is to specialize completely in producing X and move along the world price line based on that corner solution since that would dominate all others in consumption possibilities. Similarly, country B can now trade along a steeper world price line and again its best option is to specialize completely in producing Y and then trading along the world price line since that dominates all others in consumption possibilities. Smith's conclusion therefore is that both countries are made better off from trade and the prediction of the model is that in a two-good,

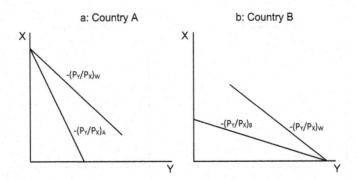

APPENDIX FIGURES 5.3a and b Gains from trade based on absolute advantage

two-commodity world, they would specialize completely in the good they have an absolute advantage in and then trade and be better off.[38]

Another prediction of the model is that the gains from trade depend on how different the domestic price ratio is from the world price ratio. The wider this gap the greater the gains from trade for the respective countries. Thus in Appendix Figures 5.2a and b, the flatter the world price line, the more country A has to gain and the steeper the world price line the more country B has to gain. In this regard, if a large country (in terms of production) was trading with a small country, the world price line would end up being closer to that of the large country since its production has more bearing on the outcome of world market prices. Thus the prediction of the model is that the small country would gain more from the mutual trade. To repeat, since the result is counter intuitive, the small country gains more because its production does not affect world prices as much and so the post-trade world price ratio gap from its domestic price ratio is larger. This result has been referred to in trade theory as the "importance of being unimportant". It follows that if countries are roughly of the same size in terms of production, their populations gain roughly the same amount from trade.

The mechanics and predictions from Ricardo's model are the same except that the starting point is different, as shown in Appendix Figures 5.4a and b.

Appendix Figures 5.4a and b differ from Appendix Figures 5.2a and b since labor in country A is now more productive in producing both goods. Even so, Ricardo's insight was that the world price ratio would still end up being different from country A's price ratio and so it would still be worth its while to specialize and gain from trade. Since B's price domestic price ratio is much steeper, the world price ratio would be steeper than A's ratio (i.e. between the two extremes) and this amounts to A specializing completely in good Y in which it has a greater comparative advantage. By the same token, the world price ratio will be flatter than B's domestic price ratio and it would specialize in good X in which its comparative disadvantage is lower.

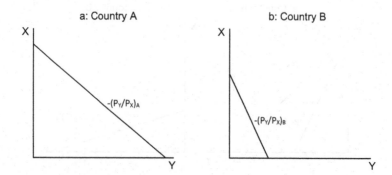

APPENDIX FIGURES 5.4a and b Comparative advantage

Questions

1. Explain what was central to economic growth for Smith.
2. Elaborate on Malthus's signature contribution to political economy.
3. Explain how rents in Ricardo's model deterred capital accumulation.
4. Explain how Smith's and Ricardo's trade models differ and what is a common shortcoming?
5. Explain how the falling rate of profit could be averted in Ricardo's model.
6. Explain Marx's theory of exploitation.
7. Elaborate on the key differences between Ricardo and Marx in a development economics context.
8. Elaborate on the key similarities between Smith and Marx in a development economics context.
9. Explore the distributional impact, in the Ricardian model, of asymmetric technological change that made less fertile parcels of land more fertile.
10. Explore the distributional impact, in the Ricardian model, of asymmetric technological change that made the more fertile parcels land even more fertile.
11. Explain why Hobson considered imperialism and colonialism to be driven by a lack of social justice in colonial countries.
12. Explain why natural economies needed to be destroyed in Rosa Luxemburg's theory of colonialism.
13. What did Lenin add to earlier theories of colonialism?

Notes

1 This is also the shift from classical liberal to neoclassical economics.
2 Of course, the purpose of accumulating species was to have a powerful army and navy that enabled colonial conquest, defense of colonies and accumulation of wealth. Even so, Smith's focus on production was a shift in emphasis.
3 Naturally this insight endeared him to capitalists. This insight was also taken up by development economists in the 1940s and 1950s (see Chapter 6) and is also viewed as the basis of "trickle-down" economics (Chapter 4).
4 This is a salutary lesson yet to be learned by L/LMICs who spend huge sums on military expenditures.
5 Able administration would focus on limited tasks that private initiative would avoid and let private initiative work where it would without undue restraints, regulation or monopolization.
6 Overland transportation by wagons was still slow and expensive.
7 The key determinants of economic growth were modeled to be human capital, knowledge and technology by endogenous growth theorists in the late 1980s and 1990s. Even so, the centrality of capital accumulation to trigger these determinants has persisted and Smith's focus on the skill and dexterity of the workforce captures these determinants in terms of how such skill and dexterity are to be acquired.
8 In this regard, he might be considered of less relevance to development economics. Yet, as will become clear, there are echoes of his thinking not only in modern macroeconomics but also development economics.

9   This process is central to Arthur Lewis's very influential model of rural-urban migration and structural change in development economics, as will be explained in the next chapter.

10 In this regard, he was a precursor to Keynes, who gave him due credit.

11 His contemporary and friend Ricardo tried to undermine the importance of the concept of effectual demand by arguing that Malthus's logic was suggestive of simply increasing wages.

12 Apart from keeping the tyranny of the monarch in check (industrialists were concerned merely with their own accumulation), the landed aristocracy was viewed as contributing to consumption and promoting the arts, and primogeniture induced other than the firstborn sons to serve productively in the professions or military.

13 This awareness of proportions is more broadly the case in his analysis such as in the optimal ratio unproductive to productive labor. He argued that precise determination was "beyond the resources of political economy". His cautionary note was "that the science of political economy bears a nearer resemblance to the science of morals and politics than to the science of mathematics" (p. 434).

14 While some neo-Malthusians and ecologists still see merit in this theory or in variations of it, most consider it to have been falsified by evidence. Among other issues, Malthus did not take into account how technology could improve factor productivity multifold.

15 Ecologists have since pointed out that humans can engage in irreversible damage to the soil.

16 As explained in endnote 8 of Chapter 4, the total product results from integrating marginal product.

17 The labor supply curve can be characterized as infinitely elastic because, due to surplus labor, the subsistence wage would result in as much labor being forthcoming as was needed.

18 Modern economic models are much more mathematical, but the mechanics are similar.

19 At the micro level, think of this as a firm making zero economic profits or just normal profits.

20 In fact the margin of cultivation in the diagrammatic framework could shift to the left, since the least productive land may no longer need to be used, and this would also cause total rents to fall.

21 The concept of Ricardian rents extends to mines, natural resources or whenever there is fixity in supply.

22 For example, the Heckscher–Ohlin theory of international trade located comparative advantage in factor endowments. Refer to Helpman (2011) for a review of the trade theory from classical to modern. Modern trade theory is now firm (MNC) centric incorporating product differentiation, monopolistic competition and firm heterogeneity.

23 Strictly speaking, small and large should here be defined in terms of a share of the commodity in the world market.

24 By this logic, in the current global context the economically weaker L/LMICs stand to gain more from mutual trade than the economically stronger HICs. This could be the logic behind Donald Trump's anti-trade rhetoric, although his reaction pre and post his election was to trade deficits with trading partners.

25 This underlies the concept behind the slogan "labor creates all value" sometimes seen on T-shirts.

26 In mainstream economic theory, profit and exploitation arise due to market power i.e. the exploitation of consumers by monopolies or oligopolies and workers via monopsonies or oligopsonies. Another theory of profit is due to Knight (1921) who attributed profit to the role of the entrepreneur in assuming risk and uncertainty.

27 Marx defined the profit rate $r = S/(C + V)$. S represents the surplus, C is constant capital and V is variable capital including labor (i.e. the denominator included living and embodied or dead labor). This equation can be re-written as $r = (S/V) / (C/V + 1)$ and Marx defined the numerator as the rate of exploitation.

28 Recall that Ricardo defined the profit rate as Π/W (see Figure 5.1).
29 Capital accumulation results in a higher capital labor ratio (C/V) and hence a decline in the profit rate. However, a rise in productivity resulting from capital accumulation that raises C would also raise S and offset the decline in profit rate. Marx therefore assumed that the offsetting effect is of second order of importance in raising the profit rate compared to its fall due to the rise in capital labor ratio.
30 These were later referred to as Taylor principles of scientific management.
31 This view is disputed. For example, Luxemburg (1951, pp. 272–273), whose theory of colonialism is discussed below, takes classical economist, particularly Mill, to task for this view regarding the absence of private property in the East, which she demonstrated to be erroneous.
32 Avineri (1968, p. 170) notes this point but it is contested by South Asian scholars like Alam (2000) who view the outflows from India to far exceed the inflows (also refer to Chapter 3).
33 The ascendency of finance capital and its attempt to garner ever higher returns was noted again a century later by mainstream economists in 2007–2008 as bubbles burst (housing, credit, stock) and a deep and extended economic crisis followed in the wake of the financial crisis in the United States, Europe and other parts of the global economy.
34 This interchangeability of labor in different activities is viewed by heterodox economists (see Reinert, Ghosh and Kattel, 2016: introduction) as a misleading and destructive abstraction (Reinert et al., 2016). For example, for new developmentalists, activities vary in importance in delivering economic development, and manufacturing in this regard has precedence. However, ironically it was classical political economists, particularly Smith, who emphasized this point.
35 Students are likely to be more familiar with the concave production possibility frontier where the concavity results from two factors (labor and capital) and diminishing marginal returns associated with factor proportions theory.
36 Recall from the text that the differences in labor productivity could be based on natural advantages such as climate, soil or mineral wealth or acquired advantages such as the skills and dexterity of the workforce associated with specialization based on capital accumulation, training and technologies. As indicated earlier, more modern trade theories associate the comparative advantage with factor endowments (land, labor, capital) and the associated impacts on productivity based on factor proportions theory.
37 Preliminary assessment of the 2016 presidential elections in the United States suggest that it was this assumption, in addition to labor displacing technological change, that got Donald Trump elected by mobilizing displaced and discontented blue collar white voters.
38 The labor theory of value suggests that prices are purely supply determined i.e. by labor productivity, and that is why the unrealistic complete specialization results in the two-good, two-country case. Mill (1904) addressed this shortcoming by introducing the demand side into the model.

References

Alam, M. S. 2000. *Poverty from the Wealth of Nations* (London: MacMillan).
Avineri, S. (Ed.). 1968. *Karl Marx on Colonialism and Modernization* (New York: Doubleday & Company, Inc.).
Helpman, E. 2011. *Understanding Global Trade* (Cambridge, MA: Harvard University Press).
Hobson, J. A. 1938. *Imperialism: A Study* (London: George Allen & Unwin Ltd.).
Knight, F. H. 1921. *Risk, Uncertainty, and Profit* (Boston, MA: Houghton Mifflin Co.).
Khan, S. R. 2014. *A History of Development Economics Thought: Challenges and Counter-Challenges* (New York: Routledge).

Lenin, V. 1948. *Imperialism, the Highest Stage of Capitalism* (London: Lawrence and Wishart).

Luxemburg, R. 1951. *The Accumulation of Capital.* translated from the German by Agnes Schwarzchild (London: Routledge and Kegan Paul, Ltd.).

Malthus, M. A. 1951. *Principles of Political Economy Considered with a View to Their Practical Application* (New York: Agustus M. Kelley, Inc.).

Marx, K. 1972. *On Colonialism: Articles from the New York Tribune and Other Writings* (New York: International Publishers).

Marx, K. 2011. *Capital, Volume One: A Critique of Political Economy* (New York: Penguin).

Mill, J. S. 1904. *Principles of Political Economy with Some of Their Applications to Social Philosophy* (New York: Longmans, Green, and Co.).

Reinert, E. S., J. Ghosh and R. Kattel. (Eds.). 2016. *Handbook of Alternative Theories of Economic Development* (Northampton, MA: Edward Elgar).

Ricardo, D. 1933. *The Principles of Political Economy and Taxation* (London: J. M. Dent & Sons, Everyman's Library Edition).

Smith, A. 1908. *An Inquiry into the Nature and Causes of the Wealth of Nations* (London: George Routledge & Sons, Ltd.).

6

DEVELOPMENTALISTS AND DEVELOPMENTALISM[1]

Introduction

Among the many other commonalities, developmentalists shared classical economics antecedents reviewed in Chapter 5. Specifically, capital accumulation, the centrality of production (industry in particular) and a focus on the distribution of income were the classical economics antecedents that the developmentalists shared. In this envisaged classical economics scenario, the entrepreneurs were the savers and innovators who would bring about capital accumulation, induce structural transformation and trigger catch-up growth that enabled society to prosper.[2]

While the most successful recent practitioners of developmentalism have been the East Asian economies including Japan, Korea, Taiwan and, more recently, China, Reinert (2010, p. 2) dates developmentalism back to the policies of Henry VII. In Chapter 9, it will become evident how these East Asian economies practiced developmentalism without any self-conscious claim to doing so. However, their practice contributed to the evolution of new developmentalist thinking.

This chapter will first provide an overview of what has come to be viewed as developmentalism in the development economics literature. It will then delve into the unique contribution of the pioneers of developmentalist thought. Drawing on these separate contributions, the next section will summarize the special case for industrialization and also the first attempt to empirically estimate this contribution. The chapter ends with an assessment of developmentalism.

Developmentalism

Developmentalists drew inspiration from Keynes and from his preoccupation with unemployment. However, developmentalism as an economic development strategy was devised for dramatically different institutional and structural conditions than for the excessive unemployment in HICs that Keynes was concerned with during the Great Depression. By contrast, L/LMICs confronted surplus labor as a form of underemployment in rural areas and open unemployment in the urban informal sectors when the rural poor migrated.

The major difference is that in HICs productive structures, including the physical infrastructure, were in place but the market failed in enabling them to be productively employed. Developmentalists were concerned with very different kinds of market failures and with the challenge of putting productive structures in place. Even though writing for very different conditions, Keynes nonetheless laid the groundwork for state intervention and this was something the developmentalists drew inspiration from.

Also, in keeping with the Keynesian inspiration, most of them adopted a macro approach to economic development issues. Thus the concern was with aggregate variables such as saving and investment (animal spirits) and their impact on GDP growth. Again, as with Keynes, the shortfall in aggregate demand was a major concern though far from the whole story.

The developmentalists also drew inspiration from the ability of the Soviet Union to industrialize and seemingly cure its unemployment problem via a planned process over one generation. Thus the state could be used as an agency for development, something that could be attained quite rapidly. Once again, there were dramatic differences. The developmentalists were trained in mainstream classical and neoclassical economics of the day and quite comfortable with the market orientation of this training. All respected the market mechanism and none sought its displacement with wholesale centralized planning. However, in varying degrees, they did view some form of state planning, at least initially in the economic development process, as being a valuable complement to the market mechanism.

The structural conditions in L/LMICs that they theorized about did not conform to the premises of the market paradigm. Endemic missing information, discontinuities, high risk, rigidities (low supply elasticities), bottlenecks (lack of social and physical infrastructure) were some of the market failures they confronted in addition to externalities. The focus on these structural defects is why the group of thinkers reviewed below was referred to by some as structuralists. The structural shortcomings identified above can be viewed as their theory of underdevelopment, and developmentalism, a positive agenda for catch-up growth, was their theory of development.

Developmentalists therefore advocated the need for intervention to cure structural defects. However, as stated earlier, these economists were trained in mainstream economics and were wedded to the market approach. They prescribed a role for intervention within the market framework but not as a substitute for the market. Once sustained growth was attained, the government could step back to a minimalist role such as that of enforcing contracts, ensuring law and order, and ensuring economic stabilization to facilitate the functioning of the market as the classical economists suggested.

A key developmentalist commonality was the emphasis on industrialization since economic history suggested no nation has successfully developed without an industrial revolution. More specifically, the industrial sector needed to be prioritized since it can yield dynamic efficiencies. Dynamic efficiencies can be viewed as including inter-industry and inter-sector linkages with potential for creating technological knowledge and innovation and for diffusing this knowledge. These are referred to as positive spillovers or physical externalities (i.e. they enter the production function as embodied technological change) and pecuniary externalities when production reduces costs for others i.e. producing goods cheaper via economies of scale and lowering costs of production for other industries/sectors. As unit costs decline export potential is enhanced and valuable foreign exchange is earned for the economy.

There are numerous possible mechanisms via which industrialization could have economy-wide benefits. These include skill formation and its transfer; cumulative improvements in technology associated with cost saving via stretching capacity, reducing wastage and minimizing depreciation; altering products to suit local needs and enhancing product sophistication for exports; new uses for waste products; creating pressures to reduce transactions costs for better social, physical and legal infrastructure and utilities; and creating pressure for training and R&D to enhance innovation.

Technological change is both embodied in the machinery and also disembodied in the form of production knowledge of various kinds that enhance the production process. These include marketing, organizational and managerial skills, modern financial and accounting practices, and inculcation of modern work norms that would be diffused to the wider economy. The latter happened because machines control the pace of work and so induce work efficiency or else losses are inevitable. The skills picked up by the labor force are diffused with job mobility.

Living standards were expected to improve with higher labor productivity and falling prices. This would enhance the market size, enable economies of scale and set in motion a virtuous circle of productivity enhancement and higher living standards. Another channel for improved living standards for the lower income groups was the expectation that industrialization would absorb surplus labor and hence cause domestic wages to rise (see below). The dynamic efficiencies identified above and a growing market would be expected to attract foreign direct investment (FDI) that in principle could reinforce such efficiencies, hence setting another virtuous circle in motion.

Like mainstream neoclassical economists, developmentalists did not flesh out a theory of the state.[3] The implicit functional working definition utilized was that the state is the seat of power that enables legislation and administration, but questions of whose interests were served, legitimacy and political change were finessed. This belief in the state's ability to solve economic problems represented the origin of the term developmentalist in the development economics literature; developmentalism refers to the prescriptions of developmentalist scholars for the developmentalist state, as explained below.

Thinkers and theories

Rosenstein-Rodan (1943) could be viewed has having made the first major contribution in the 1940s to what became known as modern development economics.[4] He epitomized the big thinking of the developmentalists. His primary focus was the post-war conditions in Eastern and South-Eastern Europe and the need to address their massive surplus agrarian labor and the consequent underemployment.

His theory of underdevelopment had two aspects. First, poor countries were stuck in a low level equilibrium trap. This low level equilibrium was born of a vicious circle (or cycle) of low income, hence low savings, low investment, low growth and low income. Second, they confronted several market failures that caused the social marginal return to investment to exceed the private return by a large margin and this reinforced the persistence of the low level equilibrium trap.

These market failures included positive externalities or spill-over effects. Private entrepreneurs did not factor in positive externalities (or negative for that matter in the case of pollution) into their profit calculus and hence investment was likely to be less than the socially optimal amount. Since capital markets were imperfect, large projects with a long gestation period would not be funded. Private sector banks were much more likely to fund less risky trading, real estate and financial ventures with quicker returns and lower risk. In any case, private sector entrepreneurs shied away from such high risk projects like power plants even if the potential returns were very high.

Finally, the private sector did not have an incentive to invest in general training because they could not force labor to stay with the firm to recoup the training costs and so once more the social return from this activity exceeded the private return and there was a sub-optimal amount forthcoming.[5] Based on this theory of underdevelopment, Rosenstein-Rodan's theory of development entailed finding a way to address both the capital shortage and the lack of purchasing power. Thus he drew on both classical economics (need for capital accumulation) and Keynesian economics (need for purchasing power).

Rosenstein-Rodan suggested a business proposition between developed and underdeveloped countries to facilitate the movement of capital. Developed countries would finance the formation of a "trust" that would engender technology transfer and industrialization. Structural transformation and progress would result from the application of existing technical knowledge rather than new technical knowledge. The business partnership between the rich and poor nations would ensure the provision of credit, machinery and technical assistance from the rich, but also the willingness to enable the creation of some export industries in the poorer regions and perhaps the consumption of more leisure (shorter working week) in the richer nations to enable the poorer nations to pay back the loans. Since it was preferable not to disrupt the international division of labor, the focus of industrialization would be labor intensive light manufacturing, although complementarities among industries would entail some heavy manufacturing also.

The complementarities among the industries would create the mutual demand without which progress was not possible. This mutuality was one of several externalities that would result, confirming that the social marginal product of the industrialization project was greater than the private marginal product. Much as

Marshallian externalities from the growth of an industry accrued to individual firms, in this case the external economies from the overall industrialization project would accrue to particular industries. Specifically, the mutual assurance of aggregate demand would reduce risk and enhance expected profits. Since individual agents had limited knowledge relative to say a planning agency, the subjective risk of the firm was greater than the objective risk assuming the state-induced industrialization project got underway.

The example Rosenstein-Rodan used was that one shoe factory could not succeed since there was a lack of purchasing power. With loans or aid, the government should set up a range of industries and they would confer dynamic efficiencies (see section on industrialization below) on the production side and also on the consumption side since employment and income created the needed demand. Here he invoked the classical economist Jean-Baptiste Say's well-known law of supply creating its own demand in a low income country context.

Rosenstein-Rodan's theory of development is referred to as The Big Push because capital needed to be applied to a whole range of industries. Such a big push was implicit in the Marshall Plan that was put into place shortly after his theorizing and that was widely viewed as effective in reconstructing war torn Western Europe. But LICs were not war torn Europe and lacked the incipient social and physical infrastructure. The issue here was construction rather than reconstruction and so this would require careful planning in the selection of the appropriate activities for which the social marginal product exceeded the private marginal product.

Apart from facilitating training and skill development, the state would invest in basic industries and public utilities like mines, railways, roads, bridges, canals, ports, dams and hydro-electric power stations. The precise investment would depend on the particular constraints faced. All these activities would encourage private investment and hence is referred to as crowding in.

Rosenstein-Rodan's "Big Push" was conceptualized to get LICs to escape the vicious circle of the low level equilibrium trap and initiate the catch-up growth process i.e. one of a virtuous circle that would sustain an upward growth trend. From a small economic base, the catch-up growth can be very rapid for several decades. However, as the economic base expands, the social and physical infrastructure construction has been completed, and the economy has undergone a structural transformation, the growth rate slows down to less heady numbers.

For example, once China's catch-up growth was initiated around 1978, the average per capita GDP growth rate over 1978 and 2011 was 8.9 percent compared to 2.8 percent between 1961 and 1977. Subsequently, as the economy matured, average economic growth between 2012 and 2017 slowed down to a still high but much more modest 6.7 percent.[6] A similar catch-up growth phenomenon was witnessed in Japan, South Korea and Taiwan at different times in the last century.

Rosenstein-Rodan's theory still has relevance in a LIC context where even the basics are still not available. Businesses often have to run their own generators for reliable electricity supply or buy four wheel drive vehicles when the roads are bad. Similarly there is an under-investment in social infrastructure because the private sector only caters to the rich. This reinforces social dualism and also keeps the current and future generations of labor unproductive because of poor education and health.

As indicated earlier, Rosenstein-Rodan's presumption was that industrialization was not only good for the depressed areas but also for the world economy as a whole via trade creation. If development in backward areas was left to internal capital accumulation, it would entail a tremendous sacrifice of consumption in already poor areas. He noted that either capital needed to migrate to surplus labor regions or surplus labor needed to migrate to capital rich areas. However, capital flow was politically more palatable than migration and would therefore need to represent the bulk of the movement. While he viewed industry as the lead sector, he noted the need to improve agriculture as part of the overall development strategy.

In a retrospective on his own contribution, Rosenstein-Rodan (1984) conceded that some countries might in fact need a soft loan and this was a modification of his original scheme of a business arrangement between HICs and LICs. But he also asserted that his theory of development (The Big Push) could, with adaptations, be relevant to underdeveloped countries in general, more than just to Eastern and South-Eastern European countries.

Nurkse's (1967) prescription was similar to Rosenstein-Rodan's, and he was skeptical of the mainstream prescriptions for economic development including trade, FDI and aid. He challenged the prescription that specialization in labor intensive primary commodities was the best course for LICs because, as suggested by the theory of comparative advantage, they had abundant and cheap labor. He argued that adopting this option was unlikely to move poor countries onto a sustained growth path, a view for which he was dubbed a trade pessimist by mainstream economists.

His pessimism concerning the effectiveness of trade in delivering economic growth was based on several counts, all of which amounted to the terms of trade disadvantaging LICs.[7] He argued that the income elasticity of the demand for primary commodities was low, and hence as incomes rose in rich countries, demand for primary commodities will not rise in proportion. Also, if poor countries were successful in raising the supply of primary commodities, because the price elasticity of demand was low, this would simply result in a decline in price and revenue as shown in Figure 6.1.[8]

Synthetic substitutes discovered by scientific research in rich countries reduced demand for primary commodities like jute and cotton exported by poor countries. The same outcome resulted from agricultural protection in rich countries. Trade also discouraged growth because, without import restraints, there was excessive consumption of high status luxury imports by elites in poor countries to emulate the consumption patterns of elites in rich countries.[9] These imports and luxury travel dissipated the scarce and highly needed foreign exchange that could otherwise be used for developing the industrial base by importing capital and intermediate goods.

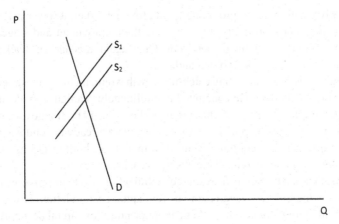

FIGURE 6.1 Inelastic demand causing revenue to fall in L/LMICs as commodity supply increases

He concluded that the small size of the market and poor infrastructure was not likely to attract FDI to produce for the local market. The little FDI that came was directed toward extraction of minerals and production of primary commodities for export back to the home market. Unless the state required it, foreign companies were loath to pass on technical knowledge and managerial skills to poor countries.

Foreign grants and loans were another potential mechanism for advancing capital accumulation, but because capital is fungible, he thought it likely that an inflow of foreign capital, either from grants or as a consequence of improving terms of trade, would simply cause local resources to be diverted to consumption.

Nurkse's theory of underdevelopment based on a low level equilibrium trap was similar though more elaborate than Rosenstein-Rodan's. Nurkse argued that stagnation was perpetuated by vicious circles on both the demand and supply sides. On the supply side, low productivity, resulting partly from low nutrition and ill health, led to low wages, low savings, low investments and low capital labor ratios, which kept labor productivity low. On the demand side, low labor productivity meant low wages, low aggregate demand, a small market size, low expected profits and hence low investment, again resulting in low labor productivity. The question was how to break free of these vicious circles.

Since trade, FDI, aid or endogenous market-based capital accumulation would not work, there was a role for the state in initiating the catch-up growth. Like Rosenstein-Rodan, he favored industrialization and like him believed that simply relying on the market mechanism was unlikely to yield catch-up growth. Nurkse argued that catch-up growth could be achieved by applying the great store of technical knowledge advantageously to industrialization in less developed countries. In addition, to overcome the low level equilibrium trap, capital needed to be systematically applied to a whole range of strategic industries (i.e. as in The Big Push), a process he called Balanced Growth. These industries would be mutually reinforcing by providing inputs for each other at lower prices given dynamic efficiencies on the supply side, and the employment and wages would create mutual markets on the demand side. Once again, this harkens back to Say's Law of supply creating its own demand.

The mechanisms for initiating catch-up growth would include investment based on domestic fiscal effort. He concluded that ultimately "capital is made at home" through the implementation of appropriate policies (p. 141). If a government had the ability to put the right policies in place, they were already beyond needing aid, and if the government had not advanced to that stage, bottlenecks as explained above would in any case reduce the absorptive capacity of aid.

One mechanism for domestic resource mobilization was to improve agricultural productivity, thereby releasing resources for capital accumulation. However, this tactic would merely create a hypothetical opportunity for capital accumulation; it would deliver development only if fiscal policies were put in place to offset the shortage of private savings by mobilizing public savings. He argued that such policies had been needed even in a relatively prosperous country like Japan which used a land tax to mobilize resources. He argued that the population was also "indoctrinated in the virtues of thrift, businesses urged to reinvest and wages kept low" (p. 143).[10]

The state could use existing or created institutions (development banks) to direct resources to private entrepreneurs in selected industries and to stimulate entrepreneurial activity by providing the necessary social overhead capital including education and health. Nurkse argued that once this process was initiated, Schumpeter's (1983) entrepreneurs would deliver and the latter's theory "properly understood is just what the title says it is" (p. 12), i.e. a theory of economic development (Chapter 1, endnote 3). In other words, it was possible to move from the vicious circles creating a low level equilibrium trap to a virtuous circle creating catch-up growth.

Along with domestic resource mobilization, luxury consumption would need to be discouraged with tariffs and this would be another source of revenue to spur catch-up growth. Capital controls could be used to prevent the dissipation of funds in other ways such as financial or real estate investments abroad. Initially, protection from foreign competition would nurture the infant industries until they were able to compete. This policy came to be referred to as ISI or import substitution industrialization.

Thus Nurkse's mechanisms for catch-up growth were different from Rosenstein-Rodan's prescription for centralized planning in the initial phase of industrialization in terms of both funding (domestic) and implementation. As will become evident in Chapter 9, the East Asian economies quite successfully applied this model to become HICs within a generation – thus developmentalist optimism was not misplaced but as will become evident the policies were not easily implementable either.

Like Rosenstein-Rodan, Nurkse recognized that many of the activities needed to get the development process underway had higher social than private returns and hence would not be forthcoming without state intervention. However, he thought the debate between "planners and anti-planners" was moot because, ultimately, national characteristics such as initiative, prudence, ingenuity and foresight were a "surer base of a nation's economic advance than the blueprints of a planning commission". Individual initiative would have to take over as the primary impetus for development once the catch-up growth process was initiated by the state. Both Rosenstein-Rodan and Nurkse were silent about which industries to invest in and this issue was addressed by Hirschman.

Hirschman (1959) supported development planning, but not The Big Push or Balanced Growth. He argued that while the latter policy interventions made sense in theory, in practice it would be difficult to procure the funds available for them via either aid or domestic resource mobilization. Also, if poor countries had the organizational capacity to handle these interventions, they would not be poor countries.

He also did not adhere to the notion fashionable at the time that prerequisites such as investment in human capital, entrepreneurial and managerial capacity, technology and public administration capacity had to be in place before catch-up growth could commence. Hirschman suggested that development had no quantitative prerequisites, but was instead constrained by "dislocations, inequalities and social tensions" (1959, p. 43).

He argued that many of the proximate causes of growth were likely to be endogenous[11] and also that the critical ingredients for progress were similarly already present in underdeveloped countries, so that the economic development process was actually about calling forth "resources and abilities that are hidden, scattered, or badly utilized" rather than finding the optimum use of existing resources as prescribed by mainstream neoclassical economics (p. 5). He was less clear about what would enable this to happen and made reference to "some binding agent" (p. 6) that would get the process underway and bring it all together (Chapter 15).

Like Rosenstein-Rodan and Nurkse, he pointed out that underdeveloped countries had access to a reservoir of technical progress so that inventing and innovating were not the issues to focus on. Neither was saving a constraint; excess savings or frustrated savings showed up as luxury consumption, gifts or leisure. Investment opportunities were also plentiful, but the real issue was the ability to invest. Thus central to his theory of development was a theory of investment particular to underdeveloped countries.

Invariably, some sectors, industries, or activities led the process of development and, invariably, these lead industries were found in the modern sector.[12] The modern sector bred the attitudes, skills and abilities needed for investment. It also had the ability to mobilize the savings of the whole nation and so the classical assumption that only the capitalists saved was not warranted. The ability to invest was the absorptive capacity of the modern sector which grew as long as this ability to invest (v) was less than the potential saving rate (s). A saving constraint only kicked in once v exceeded s, and at that point foreign capital could help more than just in terms of the skills and abilities accompanying it. It is also at this stage that compression of mass consumption could help.

As stated earlier, he argued that balanced growth would require the mustering of managerial and administrative skill at a level that would suggest that the country is not really underdeveloped. Therefore, development would need to rely on an alternative mechanism. In the course of development, uneven advances between sectors and industries were to be expected, and these imbalances, which consist of bottlenecks and constraints, could induce investments. Addressing bottlenecks would create complementarities and thus the objective of development policy must be to give maximum play to addressing these bottlenecks.[13]

In practice only a few key industries could initiate the catch-up growth process. In turn, that could set off a dynamic of imbalanced growth in the private sector that would spur farther growth (virtuous circle). First, bottlenecks would be created in expanding industries because there would be a shortage of key inputs and materials and the subsequent rise in prices would stimulate other industries. Second, the industries that succeeded would reduce prices via dynamic efficiencies and encourage further downstream activity.

Hirschman's theory of development specified which activities LICs should specialize in. He argued that industries have linkages both upstream and downstream called forward (towards final product) and backward (towards primary commodities) linkages. Thus, it would make sense to pick industries with the highest linkages such as steel which would encourage coal and iron upstream and engineering goods, automobiles, bikes and a range of other industries downstream. He argued that these are by their nature capital-intensive industries, but once the linkages were accounted for, their overall contribution to employment would be no less than small-scale labor-intensive alternatives. Activity could be stimulated both by excess capacity as well as shortages, but focusing on the latter was a preferred strategy since excess capacity presents an invitation to invest that may not materialize.

One could operationalize this concept using the input-output model which can be represented as a matrix of the inter-relationships of final, intermediate and primary goods domestically produced and demanded. This matrix enabled a calculation of coefficients that would represent the backward and forward linkages of an industry. Hence, answers to questions such as what the effect would be of a one-unit increase in final demand of a particular industry on outputs upstream and downstream of related industries would be forthcoming.[14]

His theory of development suggested that the provision of social overhead capital should address bottlenecks. He thought that political survival should be enough of an inducement to address these bottlenecks and if not, this reveals that the community was not motivated by economic development.[15] Certainly, if an administration cannot address bottlenecks in an unbalanced development context, they were unlikely to be able to address balanced development either.

Hirschman was not averse to ISI, but thought that imports could also be a mechanism for mapping demand, but this meant that premature protection would result in a loss of important information for development planners. Once demand is identified, however, local production could be encouraged, but he anticipated that moving to local production was not straightforward. Resistance was likely to be provided by importers, foreign suppliers, consumers (at least in the short term) and bankers who prefer to finance short-term risk-free trading activity to industrial projects. Exports could be critical in financing the imports needed for the industrialization project and in this sense the two activities complemented each other.

He conceded in later research (1984) on Latin America that the over-emphasis on industry to the neglect of other sectors such as agriculture created political tensions since the sectors represented different political interests. Thus, if the terms of trade were systematically turned against agriculture, there would be political tensions between the landed aristocracy and industrialists. In L/LMICs the political process might be unable to effectively mediate such conflict. In this regard, he moved toward a political economy of development approach. He also conceded that he had not adequately anticipated Kuznet's (Chapter 4) observed imbalance between growth and inequality or that this could create antagonism and social unrest.

Hirschman was very much in the developmentalist tradition, as the commonalities such as his challenging mainstream economics, optimism, suggested role for the state, focus on social overhead capital and industry make clear. However, within that context he was a critic of The Big Push, Balanced Growth and also Lewis's (1954a) famous model of balanced development.

Lewis's seminal article is probably the most influential and highly cited article in development economics. While his insights may seem obvious now, his article represented a major breakthrough in understanding the process of economic development when published. It spawned a growth industry of articles on two sector models and dualism. The article stood the test of time and for its insight Lewis was awarded a Nobel Prize in economics in 1979. In 2004, a 50-year retrospective was carried by *The Manchester Studies* (Vol. 72, No. 6), the journal that also published the original article, with contributions by the most prominent development economists of the time. The consensus was that this was the most important article in contributing to the emergence of development economics and that the model still had predictive relevance.

Lewis modelled structural change i.e. the rise in the share of industry relative to agriculture in GDP and this process was driven by rural to urban migration.[16] His model is driven by a number of assumptions that can easily be relaxed to yield the same predictions. His model includes two sectors which he referred to as capitalist and non-capitalist sectors.[17] Unlike Marx, Lewis referred to managers of public enterprises or private enterprises as capitalists and his sectoral reference was to manufacturing (capital intensive) and agriculture (labor intensive). Lewis was agnostic on the issue of public vs. private ownership – as a pragmatist he supported whatever worked.

The central assumption and also the central concern of Lewis's model is surplus labor. The unresolved puzzle from the perspective of mainstream economic theory was that the migration from the rural areas was not causing a rise in rural and urban wages. Rural to urban migration should have caused labor scarcity in rural areas, a rise in wages and food prices, and consequently a rise in manufacturing wages because food prices are the largest component of this wage. In turn, this should have reduced manufacturing profits and reduced output and employment in the manufacturing sector and hence curtailed the rural to urban migration as a self-correcting mechanism.[18] But Lewis observed the migration was continuing without these effects coming into play and this is where surplus labor came in.

Using a standard neoclassical microeconomic construct, labor surplus is the difference between the average and marginal product of labor at a given wage as shown in Figure 6.2.

Neoclassical theory suggests that due to the postulate of profit maximization, workers will be hired until the market wage (W) is equal to the marginal product of labor. Labor on a farm is the variable factor and so the MP_L slopes down due to diminishing returns as more and more of the variable factor is combined with fixed factors. At L_1 the wage is equal to the marginal product of labor and that is the employment cut-off since it would make no sense to pay labor more than its marginal product or contribution to production in a maximizing cost benefit framework that characterizes decision making in neoclassical economics.

Lewis realized, however, that the profit maximization postulate did not apply on a family farm in the informal sector and in fact all available labor is utilized and all receive the average product of labor since households share income. In other words, work on the farm continues up to L_2 at which point all receive the average product of labor. From an efficiency perspective, the gap between L_1 and L_2 represents a sub-optimal use of labor, and had other off-farm opportunities existed, this labor would probably have availed of them instead of working on the family farm. Thus the family farm absorbs the surplus labor and, as explained below, this resolves the puzzle alluded to above.[19]

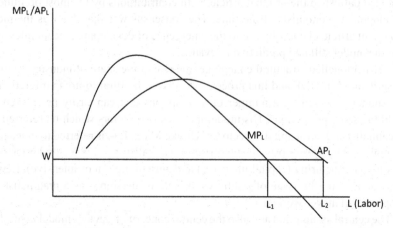

FIGURE 6.2 Surplus labor

Another way of looking at this sub-optimal use of labor as shown in Figure 6.2 is that at the point L_2 where $W=AP_L$, the marginal product of labor is negative (vertical line down from APL at given wage to the MP_L). If due to surplus labor in the agricultural sector, $MP_L = 0$ or close to it, migration would result in no loss in agricultural output and there would be no rise in food prices. In fact, Lewis argued that in some situations MP_L, as shown is Figure 6.2, is negative because of overcrowding on the family farm (too much variable factor relative to land and machinery as the fixed factors) and in this case agricultural output would actually rise due to a more efficient factor mix if the surplus labor migrated. However, the assumption of MP_L being zero or negative is not central to his model and all that is needed to drive rural to urban migration is for wages in the manufacturing sector (W_M) in urban areas to exceed the AP_L (W_A) in rural areas.

Lewis observed that typically W_M was $1.5W_A$ allowing for higher manufacturing productivity, cost of living, standard of living, unions and the psychological cost of moving, and Lewis called this a "conventional wage". In other writings, he asserted that $W_M = APL + 30$ percent. Lewis conceded that the differential he presumed was an arbitrary number based on rough observation, but all that his model needed was some threshold level of wage differential that would encourage migration and for the theory the exact differential need not be specified.

As assumed by classical economists, the source of saving in his model is the profits of capitalists in the modern sector. For Lewis, as for other developmentalists, saving or capital accumulation and industrialization were the key to economic development. In fact, he viewed catch-up growth as occurring when saving consistently reached about 12 to 15 percent of national income compared to 3 to 4 percent of GNP for a backward economy.[20] For this reason, Lewis did not think the Keynesian framework, with its assumptions of scarce labor and surplus saving, was suitable for an analysis of LICs. In the Keynesian framework, there was an abundance of capital and other resources and the issue was putting excess capacity to work by activating the demand side. Lewis also did not view aid as a substitute for domestic saving.

Unlike Nurkse, low savings were not a product of low income but of a small modern sector and some countries were better than others for various reasons, including sociological, in spawning entrepreneurs who responded to opportunities (with political stability as an enabler). Once the process got underway, a virtuous circle continued to expand the modern sector as long as there was surplus labor.

Lewis assumed a closed economy model and then relaxed this assumption (see exercise at the end of the chapter). Like other developmentalists, he assumed the necessary technology for industrialization was freely available and easily diffused. While labor and capital were the two factors in this model, other factors can be added without changing the model's predictions.

Based on these assumptions, Lewis was able to model the process of structural change. Following the assumption of surplus labor in keeping with classical economists, the supply of labor is horizontal at the wage set by convention ($W_M = APL + 30$ percent or $W_M = 1.5 W_M$) at the subsistence level (W_s). To summarize, the classical features in Lewis's model were surplus labor, the concern with capital accumulation, capitalists as a source of saving and its dynamic rather than static nature. The neoclassical feature was the demand for labor which followed neoclassical marginal productivity theory. Thus, as expected from a pragmatic economist, his model was a hybrid based on the economic conditions that he observed. Given these features, the model mechanics can be understood with the help of Figure 6.3.

All firms pay the subsistence wage (W_s) and, given this wage and a downward sloping marginal productivity curve (diminishing returns given capital is fixed), each firm hires labor up to the point where W = MPL (marginal product of labor = D_L). The area under the demand for labor curve, up to where labor (L_1) is hired, represents the total product for the firm in Figure 6.3. Labor gets W × L_1 (wage bill) and the rest (profits = Π) goes to capital or the entrepreneurs in the modern sector.[21] This is where the dynamics come into play. Entrepreneurs invest the profits in the next period and based on the factor proportions theory more capital per worker raises their marginal product and causes the demand for labor curve to shift to the right (D_2). This process of capital accumulation and reinvestment continues until surplus labor is exhausted at L_3, as shown in Figure 6.4.

At L_3 in Figure 6.4, surplus labor is exhausted and therefore the supply curve is no longer flat or infinitely elastic. That was only possible when an unlimited supply of labor was available at W_s, but, once that supply was exhausted, more labor would only be forthcoming at a higher wage (for example via a substitution of work for leisure or more women coming into the work force when the incentive to do so is adequate). At this point, catch-up growth has occurred and Lewis's hybrid model no longer applies. Instead, as long as the labor market is competitive, the standard neoclassical model of a downward sloping demand curve and upward sloping supply curve determine the wage rate and the amount of labor demanded and hired at that wage rate.

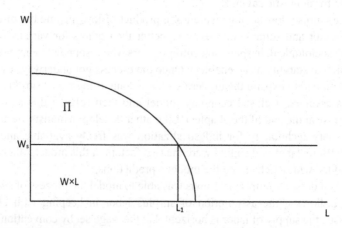

FIGURE 6.3 The Lewis model

This simple model is deceptively powerful in predicting the outcomes of various scenarios that might play out in L/LMICs. Suppose a partial demographic transition causes the population growth to pick up (fertility falls but mortality falls by more due to the introduction of public health technology). The model predicts that there is more surplus labor to draw on thereby extending the process of capital accumulation. Also, catch-up growth could be deterred or delayed because of a rise in food prices due to population growth (more demand for food) and this would raise the subsistence wage and hence reduce profits and the pace of capital accumulation. To continue with this example, suppose the country invests heavily in education and population programs. In this case, fertility may well decline faster than infant mortality declines and an education-driven increase in labor productivity could facilitate capital accumulation.

Technological change also has an indeterminate outcome. On the one hand, capital intensive technology might replace labor and hence extend the catch-up growth process. On the other, higher productivity would shift the demand for labor to the right, facilitate capital accumulation by enhancing profits and hence accelerate the catch-up growth process.

These scenarios suggest that industrialization requires cheap food to contain the subsistence wage and facilitate capital accumulation. In addition, a prosperous agriculture would release more labor for industry, provide cheaper food and raw materials, and also a market for manufactured goods. Lewis discussed this issue with reference to the terms of trade of agricultural vs. industry (P_A/P_I). If agricultural productivity did not keep pace with industrial productivity, the terms of trade would move in favor of agriculture because the growth in demand for food would exceed supply. In turn, this would require a higher subsistence wage and hence hinder capital accumulation and the pace of industrialization.

The economic development prescriptions then followed logically from how various scenarios played out using the Lewis model. He advocated that, in the

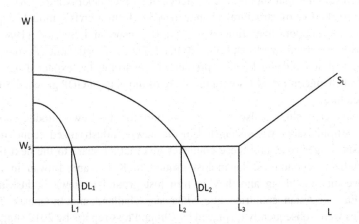

FIGURE 6.4 Capital accumulation in the Lewis model

short run, policy could manipulate the terms of trade to be against agriculture to ensure cheap food for capital accumulation in industry but that this was not sustainable. In the medium to long run, agriculture would have to be developed simultaneously, otherwise food prices and industrial wages would rise and hinder capital accumulation. Thus an agricultural revolution must accompany an industrial revolution.

At equivalent levels of PCGDP, agricultural productivity in current HICs was much higher and LICs needed to redress this shortcoming. In this regard, Lewis's recommendation was for a sectoral balance rather than a balance of aggregate demand and supply as in Nurkse's concept of Balanced Growth.

He also suggested that industrial wages being raised prematurely would stop the catch-up growth process. This prescription caused his model to be criticized as endorsing a trickle-down approach to economic development. The initial inequality implied in the model, by allowing the profit share to rise first for capital accumulation, is consistent with Kuznet's description of the economic growth process in Chapter 4.

Like other developmentalists, Lewis emphasized industry as the key sector in the economy due to dynamic efficiencies. He was willing to advocate protection if necessary in the short run. However, his argument for protection was more nuanced. He argued that since LIC had to pay a wage above the opportunity cost of labor to ensure subsistence, they were at a competitive disadvantage. Thus, he argued that protection was necessary to level the playing field. Like Nurkse, he also saw conspicuous consumption as a problem and so proposed a domestic and import tax to discourage such luxury consumption and secure funds for social and physical infrastructure.

In assessing Lewis's model, both the assumption of surplus labor and the process of structural change this gives rise to need to be examined. Casual empiricism would certainly suggest to those living in many L/LMICs that surplus labor in the urban informal sector is often fed by rural areas. There are some rigorous estimates that support the existence of surplus labor (Chapter 8).

The prediction of structural change derived from Lewis's model acquired considerable support over time. Chenery, Robinson and Syrquin (1986) did extensive empirical work and the stylized facts of economic development they arrived at validated Lewis's predictions regarding the expected nature of structural change in L/LMICs with the share of industry in GDP growing relative to agriculture.

Country case studies also provided support for the Lewis model, showing that, as surplus labor was exhausted in the newly industrialized economies of East Asia, wages rose, and these countries lost market share to the next tier of industrializing economies. Japan lost ground to Korea and Taiwan in labor-intensive manufacturing and they in turn lost ground to newly industrialized South-Eastern Asian countries like Malaysia, Thailand and Indonesia. These countries were subsequently displaced by China. Press reports by 2012 suggested that rising wages in China were enabling economies like Viet Nam, Cambodia and Bangladesh to contest market share in the labor intensive textile and leather industries. Thus in a "flying geese" pattern, as some countries attain catch-up growth and exhaust surplus labor they confront rising labor costs and respond by diversifying and moving up the value chain. In so doing, they create an opportunity for other countries to assume the leadership lower down in the value chain.[22]

Notwithstanding the empirical support, the model did not and does not work universally. The capital accumulation process, if it occurred, was capital intensive and unemployment, and with it poverty and inequality, continued to increase. The bigger problem is that the classical assumption of capitalists saving and investing does not always bear out. The savings can be dissipated via capital flight, luxury consumption and the less risky trading, real estate or financial investment options.

One implicit policy implication of the model is that rural-urban migration is a natural part of the economic development process. If capital accumulation and prosperity is slow or if urban management policies lack foresight, the migration, as was generally the case, was beyond the carrying capacity of municipalities. The result was shanty towns and the crime and exploitation of the vulnerable by predators among other aspects of urban blight that has become associated with rural-urban migration.

While the Lewis model resolved an important puzzle associated with the lack of change in urban wages and food prices by observing and modeling surplus labor, scholars used his basic insight to address other associated puzzles. Fei and Ranis (1964) showed that as long as MPL_A was less than the MPL_I, the process of migration, capital accumulation and growth could continue even if surplus labor had been exhausted and the labor supply curve sloped up as suggested by neoclassical economics. The higher MPL_I could be attributed to the greater capital intensity and other complementary elements like training, labor discipline, and social and physical infrastructure.

Harris and Todaro (1970) addressed two additional puzzles using Lewis's dual sector framework in the context of surplus labor. First, they explained the puzzle of why rural-urban migration persisted despite the high level of urban unemployment. The postulate of rationality governing neoclassical economic theory would suggest that high urban unemployment should discourage rural-urban migration as households revise their plans based on the economic reality they hear about from relatives and friends in the urban informal sector.

Harris and Todaro modeled rural-urban migration in terms of the household (or individual) maximizing the expected net present value from the move. The costs and benefits of migration were discussed in Chapter 3 in terms of push and pull factors. The innovative aspect of the Harris and Todaro model on the pull side was introducing expectations and hence probabilities into their model. Thus, what counts as a pull factor is not only the urban-rural wage differential but also the probability of getting an urban job. A crude probability of getting an urban job can be inferred from the urban unemployment rate. If more job opportunities are created in urban areas, this will decrease urban unemployment or increase the probability of getting an urban job from the perspective of a rural household weighing a migration decision and hence encourage rural-urban migration.

Another innovative feature of the Harris and Todaro model was the distinction between objective and subjective probabilities. They argued that subjective probabilities are what come into play in the migration decision and typically subjective probabilities exceed the objective probabilities. In other words, if each individual considers himself as somehow special in being able to beat the odds suggested by macro phenomenon (unemployment), the rate of migration would be enhanced. This observation about likely human behavior would result in several households migrating for each new urban job opportunity created and hence explain the puzzle of persistent high levels of rural-urban migration despite high levels of urban unemployment.

Second, they addressed the puzzle of the persistence of a rural-urban wage differential despite the high levels of rural to urban migration. Once again, neoclassical theory would suggest that rural-urban migration and high urban unemployment levels as an outcome should cause urban wages to decline and for the wage gap to close via market self-correction. They argued that institutional reasons (labor legislation, minimum wage rate, unions) were part of the reason for the higher urban wage and so the wage differential would persist despite the high urban unemployment.

Recall from Chapter 3 that the neoclassical prescription for urban unemployment is correcting factor price distortions. One recommended solution was wage subsidies to induce more labor-intensive production to address the problem of underpriced capital (due to subsidies) and overpriced labor (due to institutional reasons). This was deemed as a more politically acceptable option than reducing wages or raising the price of capital. However, the Harris and Todaro model suggests that this policy would raise objective and subjective probabilities of getting an urban job and hence increase migration and urban unemployment. An urban jobs program would have the same outcome.

The Harris-Todaro model in this regard was influential in shifting the focus of attention toward developing the rural sector and agriculture if rural-urban migration and urban unemployment was to be avoided. The policy prescriptions that followed included reducing the urban bias (hence reducing the urban pull), integrated rural development (Chapter 4) and avoiding keeping the terms of trade against agriculture. These prescriptions went against the developmentalist prescriptions and agriculture was brought centerstage in the economic development debate.[23]

Lewis's modeling of structural change embodied within it the catch-up growth process that anticipated Rostow (1960). Rostow's theory of economic "take-off" (the earlier term for catch-up growth) was descriptive and complementary to Lewis's model of structural change in that he elaborated on the preconditions for take-off and hence structural change. He became famous for his "stages of growth" description of the historical progression from poor to rich country status.

His theory of history was posited as an alternative to the Marxian theory of historical materialism explaining the progression of societies through various stages such as primitive, slave, feudal, mercantile, capitalism, socialism, and finally to the most advanced stage of communism.

The Marxian theory of historical materialism was based on Hegelian dialectics, and progression from one stage to another was based on the juxtaposition of opposites. In social history this referred to social contradictions and the resolution of the principle contradiction at a historical juncture propelled the onward march of history.

Thus the contradiction between slaves and owners and slave revolts eventually resulted in the overthrow of slavery. Similarly, the contradiction between landlords and peasants resulted in peasant revolts, but the contradiction between commercial and feudal interests was also important in checking feudal power. The contradiction between capitalists and workers is premised on ownership being private and work being social, and the resolution of this antagonistic contradiction would result in the overthrow of the capitalists' order with a social revolution. The contradictions within socialist society were viewed as non-antagonistic, but would nonetheless propel society to the communist order of "from each according to their ability to each according to their *need* [rather than *contribution* as in socialism]". While these stages were linear, Marx himself did not consider that historical movement had to be linear.

Rostow proposed linear historical progression but not based on any underlying conceptual framework or theory. He claimed it to be a theory of history as a descriptive framework based on a study of European history. The early stages were lumped into traditional society and the other stages respectively were pre-conditions for take-off, drive to maturity, and eventually the highest stage of mass consumption societies, which is how current HICs were characterized. The second and third stages are the relevant ones as a description of the catch-up growth process.

Traditional societies were characterized as pre-scientific and subject to feudal control. Accordingly, one of the preconditions for take-off was the need for modern science to shape the production functions in both agriculture and industry for cost reductions. The changes in production structures would need to be accompanied by changes in attitudes toward fundamental and applied science and by new methods of training individuals to operate in disciplined social and industrial organizations.

The preconditions for take-off also required the emergence of financial, political and social institutions that displaced feudal society, and colonialism could be the trigger. Echoing Marx, Rostow thought colonialism "could not avoid" bringing about a transformation in thought, knowledge and institutions. In addition, colonialism supplied social overhead capital such as ports, docks, roads and railways, which moved society along a transitional path (Rostow, 1960, p. 27). In addition, colonialism could provoke "reactive nationalism to colonial humiliation" bringing about the right leadership for society to progress (p. 26).

Institutional development would need to be accompanied by the appropriate social and physical infrastructure, management skills and modern techniques of production. Resources for these social investments would come from rising productivity in extractive and primary commodity production. Like Lewis, he viewed agriculture as key to providing food, materials, revenue, markets and foreign exchange for industrial sector development. Financial development would provide credit to industry and this would contribute to the development of a modern manufacturing base.

Rostow believed that take-off would finally occur once a modern manufacturing base was established and investment exceeded about 10 percent of GDP, signaling that output growth had surpassed population growth.[24] This process would result from a virtuous circle in which social overhead capital would contribute to agricultural and manufacturing growth, exports would increase foreign exchange earnings, and profits/tax revenues would be ploughed back into investments for further growth as in the Lewis model.

Rostow's main contribution was in putting up a broad sweeping framework of the stages of economic development. However, it was not clear how and why the preconditions would emerge, and colonialism has more often been viewed as reinforcing feudalism and arresting the growth process rather than as contributing to it (Chapters 3, 5 and 7). The specified investment threshold could be viewed as the one testable hypothesis he proffered, but with hindsight it is clear that given the high population growth rates confronted by LICs, much higher investment ratios would be needed to absorb the growth in the labor force (Appendix Table 3.1).

The analytical attempt to see similarities between the current HICs and poor countries was also called into question. Recall from Chapter 1 that the initial conditions for current HICs were very different from current LICs. Nonetheless, Rostow was influential as a developmentalist thinker and the terminology he developed gained traction. He successfully identified the important preconditions that needed to accompany capital accumulation and structural change.

Case for industrialization

As is evident from the review of developmentalist thought above, they viewed industry, particularly manufacturing, as playing a central role in economic development.[25] To summarize, this sprang from the belief that industrialization yielded dynamic efficiencies or advantages not available from the production of primary commodities or services.

Developmentalist support for industrialization was conceptual (based on presumed dynamic efficiencies) until Kaldor's (1967) empirical estimation of the unique and dynamic contribution of industry as a driver of catch-up growth. His focus was on HICs which had industrialized and he set about showing how in the process of catch-up growth industrialization played a central role. The primary sector (agriculture, mining) initiated the growth process and as it became more productive, as in the Lewis model, labor was released from agriculture into industry (manufacturing, public utilities, construction). This is the key phase of catch-up growth and Kaldor empirically showed, citing Verdoorn's Law,[26] the dynamic association of higher GDP growth with higher manufacturing sector growth.[27]

After identifying the empirical association, Kaldor went on to provide theoretical explanations for it (pp. 14–29). First, he pointed out that Verdoorn's explanation for this association was premised on labor productivity growth being associated with manufacturing output growth due to increasing aggregate returns to scale. Second, he drew on Young (1928) to point out that increasing returns to scale are a macro phenomenon resulting from industrial expansion. The mechanisms are inter- and intra-industry linkages.[28] Further, a rise in productivity growth in manufacturing resulted in productivity growth in other sectors partly by technological infusions on the supply side and partly by being a source of demand. Young also conditioned increasing returns on an elastic demand for products and this is one of the characteristics of manufacturing sector output.[29] Third, he invoked Arrow's (1962) model of learning-by-doing to explain technical change as more applicable to industry, particularly manufacturing. He ruled out theoretically the possibility that the causal link could run in the opposite direction i.e. from GDP growth to manufacturing sector growth.

Following Young, Kaldor (p. 30) described the process of industrialization (catch-up growth) as a dynamic interaction of demand and supply. Reminiscent of Say's Law, i.e. supply generates demand, but beyond that demand in turn generates supply. This process accelerates once countries start producing their own machine goods. The mark of a mature economy is one where the per capita incomes in all three sectors are roughly equivalent.

While much of this research project was focused on industrialized economies, Kaldor also mused on the great and growing gap between industrialized economies and LICs. While he conceded that solely relying on economics to understand this gap would have limitations, he stated in unequivocal terms that high real per capita incomes are "inconceivable without industrialization" (p. 54). While countries like Australia, New Zealand and Denmark prospered based on agricultural exports, they did this based on a highly productive agriculture that had released labor force for the other sectors.

Thus much as Lewis characterized the economic development process, Kaldor believed the path to an industrial revolution was through an agricultural revolution that kept key industrial and material prices low. However, keeping the terms of trade against agriculture was not the path to industrialization since this would be a disincentive to agricultural progress. Instead, direct taxation of agriculture to finance industry and the elimination of feudal land holdings, policies that Japan pursued for its catch-up growth, could help. He also endorsed temporary protection until a country could compete internationally by attaining dynamic efficiencies of industrialization.

Assessment of developmentalist thought

Developmentalists drew on classical economists for the concepts of surplus labor and subsistence wage, functional distribution of income, capital accumulation and the centrality of industry to catch-up growth. They drew on Keynesian economics regarding the focus on unemployment, notwithstanding its different nature, and the importance of aggregate demand. Again their emphasis was on building production capacity, which can be assumed to be present in Keynesian economics, so the supply side was the key. They immensely enriched the antecedent base of economic thinking in applying it to the particular conditions of L/LMICs at the time they theorized.

A careful reading of the developmentalist pioneers indicates that they were quite aware of what critics charged them with for having missed out on. Their focus on capital accumulation, following on from classical scholars, led critics to accuse them of having neglected other important issues. Much of this criticism is misplaced. For example, they were aware of the need for institutional prerequisites, although Hirschman argued that these were likely to be endogenous to the development process.

One important commonality was the view that industrialization is central to the catch-up growth process because dynamic efficiencies are more likely to be inherent in this sector than others. Notwithstanding this conviction, they were aware of the complementary role that the agricultural sector needed to play. Lewis argued that growth would be constrained unless the industrial revolution was accompanied by an agricultural revolution, and Rosenstein-Rodan and Nurkse also emphasized the importance of agriculture.

While they made a case for ISI, these market economists insisted on competition and efficiency taking centerstage. Kaldor, who provided an empirical and theoretical case for industrialization, viewed protection as relevant until LICs could realize dynamic efficiencies of industrialization and become export competitive. Developmentalist support of ISI thus did not preclude exports or openness; for example, Hirschman viewed exporting and ISI as complementary activities, as did Lewis.

One apparent oversight in developmentalist thinking was not anticipating that industrialization would be unable to absorb the labor surplus in many L/LMICs, although there were exceptions as indicated above. Lewis attributed this to the partial demographic transition and pointed out in retrospect that population growth combined with a rate of rural-urban migration that exceeded the rate of urban job creation exacerbated unemployment. He conceded that, as a result, the race to provide livelihoods for a population may be lost in many cases.

One could charge the developmentalist pioneers with having a trickle-down approach. Capital-intensive industrialization, market concentration and low wages due to surplus labor and unemployment generated inequalities. Economic power led to political power and business elites also got enriched by low taxes, tax evasion and subsidies. Thus the income share of the bottom 40 percent fell and in many cases the drive down the inverted U-shaped Kuznet's curve was not forthcoming. Again, there was an awareness of this as a potential problem; the political instability that such inequalities could generate was viewed as possibly blocking the growth and structural transformation process.

Developmentalists also commonly prescribed a significant role for the state and policy planning because of various market failures. However, once again, Lewis argued "In countries where government is corrupt and inefficient, laissez faire, laissez passer is the best recipe for economic growth" (1954b, p. 83). Similarly Nurkse pointed out that the initiative, prudence and ingenuity of a people trumps the blueprints of planning commissions.

The ideas of the developmentalists were influential and, while their theories were discredited during the heyday of the free-market economics in the 1980s, there has been a reassessment. Indeed, many economists have pointed out that the interventionist period prior to 1980 delivered a higher growth rate in Latin America, Africa and Asia or built a base on which later growth was built. Scholars have pointed out that developmentalist theory explained the East Asian economic growth miracles. However, this may still be a minority view with the mainstream economists preferring non-interventionist free market principles. Even so, the developmentalists have established a prominent place for themselves in the history of macro development economic thought as the pioneers and big thinkers.

Going back and reading the pioneers in development economics is humbling since these scholars seem to have said it all six or seven decades ago. Much of the critique of these pioneers appears to be a caricature. A careful reading of their work reveals that far from being one-dimensional dirigistes (interventionists) as they were dubbed, they were market friendly, aware of the need for a productive agriculture and adopted a nuanced view of ISI.

They were also well aware that what they proposed was no magic bullet. For example, Nurkse put forward the importance of domestic resource mobilization and capital accumulation based on mining agricultural productivity while recognizing that country specificities such as human endowments, social attitudes, historical accidents and political conditions are all critical. Thus he was clear that there can be "no standard recipe of universal applicability" (1967, p. 150). At the same time, it is clear that if everything counts, one is left without a theory. The developmentalists, for their part, managed to put forward theories of underdevelopment and development that still have resonance.

Questions and exercises

1. What were the sources of inspiration for developmentalist scholars?
2. Apart from endorsing industrialization, cite and explain other commonalities in developmentalist thinking.
3. Explain in detail the case they made for industrialization – also referred to as dynamic efficiencies.
4. Explain Rosenstein-Rodan's concept of a low-level equilibrium trap and his proposed prescription for getting out of it.
5. Explain Nurkse's views of why mainstream economic theory did not apply in L/LMICs.

6. What was Nurkse's explanation for "underdevelopment", and what theory of development did he propose?
7. How did Hirschman differ from Rosenstein-Rodan and Nurkse in his analyses and prescriptions?
8. Explain how the association of wage and average product of labor explains surplus labor in the Lewis model and why the assumption of negative marginal product of labor is not necessary for the model.
9. Explain the Lewis model of capital accumulation and structural change, including an explanation of how the accumulation process moves the economy from one that could be characterized by the classical model to one that could more reasonably be characterized by a neoclassical model in terms of the labor market.
10. Explain how Lewis's concept of "balanced development" differed from Nurkse's concept of Balanced Growth.
11. What were the prescriptions and criticisms of the Lewis model?
12. In the Lewis framework, analyze the impact of the following on the capital accumulation process:
    a. Rise in agricultural productivity;
    b. Greater capital intensity of production in industry;
    c. Opening the economy to trade;
    d. Raising the minimum wage in industry;
    e. Population growth;
    f. Higher educational attainment;
    g. Technological change in industry;
    h. Change in food prices.
13. What two puzzles (pertaining to the Lewis model) did the Harris-Todaro model present an answer to?
14. Contrast the policy prescriptions of the Lewis model with the Harris-Todaro model.
15. Explain Rostow's stages of growth model and its criticisms.
16. Elucidate on Kaldor's explanation regarding the centrality of manufacturing to catch-up growth.
17. What constraints did Kaldor identify in the mid-1960s to catch-up growth in L/LMICs and do you think they are still relevant?
18. Make an overall assessment of developmentalist thought.

Notes

1 Wallerstein (2004, p. 1) traces the origin of the word developmentalism to the notion proffered by post-war Latin American writers that ex-colonial countries could develop themselves rather than being developed by the colonial countries for profit. For more on scholars covered in this and the next chapter refer to Sunna and Gualerzi (2016).
2 While the developmentalists did not use the term catch-up growth, it was nonetheless the phenomenon they were concerned with and theorized about. Mainstream growth

theory emerged from and addresses institutional conditions of HICs and is therefore not addressed in this chapter.

3   A theory of the state is central to the analysis of Latin structuralists, dependency theorists, Marxists and radical political economists or the political economy of development approaches (Chapter 7).

4   For earlier contributions refer to Reinert, Ghosh and Kattel (2016).

5   Those who live and observe economic conditions in LICs will still find that Rosenstein-Rodan's theory of underdevelopment has salience.

6   World Bank, World Development Indicators.

7   There is a more detailed discussion of this issue and the associated evidence in Chapter 7.

8   Bhagwati (1958), otherwise an advocate of free trade, showed this result in a two-good, two-country model and called the phenomenon immiserizing growth.

9   This harkened to the conspicuous consumption that Veblin (1953) wrote about.

10 Thus he argued that, contrary to Keynesian concern of a shortfall of aggregate demand due to excess savings leading to recessions in developed countries, thrift, as recommended by Adam Smith (Chapter 5), would serve underdeveloped countries well given the different economic conditions that prevailed there.

11 Emerge concomitantly with and because of the economic development process.

12 There is no theory posited regarding the emergence and size of the modern sector.

13 Hirschman clarified that given the very different economic context of underdeveloped countries, induced investment is very different from the Keynesian concept of investment being induced by an increase in national income.

14 The input-output tables were based on the Leontief or fixed coefficient production functions (Chapter 14) and therefore did not allow for factor substitutions as factor prices change i.e. using more or less labor or capital as the price of labor or capital changes. Nonetheless, they were a good first approximation for computing linkages. Later research allowed for production functions that would accommodate factor substitutions and changes over time.

15 It may be that the leadership, even if civilian, has its own short-term plutocratic agenda and therefore is not responsive to community pressure expressed via the ballot.

16 There is also urban-urban, urban-rural and rural-rural migration in L/LMICs, but rural-urban migration was the path of structural change for current HICs and continues to be in this respect the most significant in L/LMICs.

17 This was not Marxian terminology since Marx defined capitalists as those who have the ability to exploit labor by virtue of the ownership of the means of production (Chapter 5).

18 The rural to urban migration should also have resulted in downward wage pressure in urban areas as an additional self-correction mechanism.

19 Lewis recognized that surplus labor could also emanate from the informal sectors in the urban sector such as from petty trade and services. Other sources included women entering the workforce or urban population growth. Griffin, Khan, and Ickowitz (2002) provide an alternative explanation for surplus labor. They argued that local labor markets in L/LMIC agricultural sectors are often partitioned by natural and social boundaries into "an archipelago of small fragmented labor markets" (p. 287). In such settings, individual employers wield monopsony power such that they pay less and use less labor than a competitive market outcome. The two explanations can be viewed as complementary.

20 With hindsight and better data we now know that catch-up growth is fired by much higher saving and investment rates (Appendix Table 3.1).

21 The similarity to Ricardo's model should be self-evident (refer to Figure 5.1).

22 This pattern of international production restructuring was developed as a descriptive model and referred to as the "flying geese" paradigm by Akamatsu (1962).

23 Schultz (1964) was also instrumental in highlighting the importance of agriculture (Chapter 13).

24 This is the counterpart of Lewis viewing catch-up growth as occurring when domestic savings touched roughly 12–15 percent of GNP.

25 The other sub-sectors include utilities, communications, transportation and mining.
26 P. J. Verdoorn posited and demonstrated a positive association of output growth and labor productivity growth in manufacturing in 1949. The mechanisms for this positive association included increasing returns (scale economies) and learning-by-doing. Kaldor used manufacturing sector growth rather than manufacturing labor productivity in his estimating equations. The identified association is often referred to in the literature as the Verdoorn-Kaldor law.
27 Chapter 9 provides more evidence on the centrality of manufacturing to catch-up growth based on research inspired by Kaldor.
28 The cause of the increasing returns, in industry but not in the other sectors, was the division of labor within *industry as a whole* that resulted from the size of the market. The increasing returns thus resulted from roundabout production of the capitalist market economies whereby derived demand resulted in ancillary production. The relationship of this process with the size of the market was dialectical in that the increasing returns in turn expanded the size of the market. He acknowledged Adam Smith but extended the latter's conceptualization based on the firm-to-sectoral processes.
29 Again, elastic is defined in a special sense of "a small increase in its supply will be attended by an increase in the amount of other commodities which can be had in exchange for it" (p. 534).

References

Akamatsu, K. 1962. "A Historical Pattern of Economic Growth in Developing Countries," *Journal of Developing Economies*, 1(1), 3–25.

Arrow, K.J. 1962. "The Economic Implications of Learning by Doing," *Review of Economic Studies*, 36(3),155-173.

Bhagwati, J. 1958. "Immiserizing Growth: A Geometrical Note," *Review of Economic Studies*, 25(3), 201–205.

Chenery, H., S. Robinson and M. Syrquin. 1986. *Industrialization and Growth: A Comparative Study* (New York: Oxford University Press).

Fei, J. C. H. and G. Ranis. 1964. *Development of the Labor Surplus Economy* (Homewood, IL: Richard Irwin).

Griffin, K., A. R. Khan and A. Ickowitz. 2002. "Poverty and the Distribution of Land," *Journal of Agrarian Change*, 2(3), 279–330.

Harris, J. R. and M. P. Todaro. 1970. "Migration, Unemployment and Development: A Two-Sector Analysis," *The American Economic Review*, 60(1), 126–142.

Hirschman, A. O. 1959. *The Strategy of Economic Development* (New Haven, CT: Yale University Press).

Hirschman, A. O. 1984. "A Dissenter's Confession: 'The Strategy of Economic Development' Revisited," in: G. M. Meier and D. Seers (eds.), *Pioneers in Development* (New York: Oxford University Press).85-112.

Kaldor, N. 1967. *Strategic Factors in Economic Development* (Ithaca: New York State School of Industrial and Labor Relations, Cornell University).

Lewis, W. A. 1954a. "Economic Development with Unlimited Supplies of Labor." *The Manchester School of Economic and Social Studies*. 22 (May),139–153

Lewis, W. A. 1954b. *The Theory of Economic Growth* (Homewood Illinois: Irwin).

Nurkse, R. 1967. *Problems of Capital Formation in Underdeveloped Countries and Patterns of Trade and Development* (New York: Oxford University Press).

Reinert, E. S. J. Ghosh and R. Kattel. (eds.). 2016. *Handbook of Alternative Theories of Economic Development* (Northhampton, MA: Edward Elgar).

Reinert, E. S. 2010. "Developmentalism," Working Papers in Technology, Governance and Economic Dynamics No. 34, The Other Canon Foundation, Norway.

Rosenstein-Rodan, P. N. 1943. "The Problems of Industrialization of Eastern and South-Eastern Europe," *The Economic Journal*, 53(210/211), 202–211.

Rosenstein-Rodan, P. N. 1984. "Natura Facit Saltum: Analysis of Disequilibrium Growth Process," in: G. M. Meier and D. Seers (eds.), *Pioneers in Development* (New York: Oxford University Press) 205-221.

Rostow, W. W. 1960. *The Stages of Economic Growth: A Non-Communist Manifesto* (Cambridge: Cambridge University Press).

Schultz, T. W. 1964. *Transforming Traditional Agriculture* (New Haven, CT: Yale University Press).

Schumpeter, J. A. 1983. *The Theory of Economic Development: An Inquiry into Profits, Capital, Credit, Interest, and the Business Cycle* (New Brunswick: Transactions Publishers).

Sunna, C. and D. Gualerzi. (eds.). 2016. *Development Economics in the Twenty-First Century* (London: Routledge).

Veblen, T. 1953. *The Theory of the Leisure Class: An Economic Study of Institutions* (New York: The Macmillan Company).

Wallerstein, I. 2004. "After Developmentalism and Globalization What?" Keynote address at conference, "Development Challenges for the 21st Century," Cornell University, Oct. 1, Ithica.

Young, A. A. 1928. "Increasing Returns and Economic Progress," *The Economic Journal*, 38(152), 527–542.

7

NEO-MARXISM,[1] STRUCTURALISM AND DEPENDENCY THEORY

Introduction

Structuralism originated in Latin America at the same time (1950s) as developmentalists were theorizing. While the structuralist analysis of the internal causes of underdevelopment was similar to that of the developmentalists (market failures and structural rigidities (Chapter 6)), they differed from the developmentalists in that the theory of underdevelopment also had an external component such as uneven development and therefore asymmetrical global power relations inducing underdevelopment in LICs. Many of the prescriptions in terms of a theory of development were similar in so far as the cause of underdevelopment had internal causes i.e. addressing market failures and structural rigidities and inducing ISI-based industrialization (Chapter 6).

However, beyond endorsing the developmentalists' prescriptions, structuralist authors appealed to developed countries to rectify trade and investment rules and to assist underdeveloped countries in addressing export instability and attaining endogenous technological growth. The combination of these prescriptions was referred to as the New International Economic Order (NIEO), and this was promoted by some L/LMICs in the 1970s. Because the NIEO portrayed the current system of international trade as a zero-sum game, its prescriptions were scathingly criticized by mainstream economists and it did not gain traction in the west (Johnson, 1976).[2]

Partly as a response, a more radical strain of development thinking called dependency theory emerged from Latin America and it focused on exploitative international links between developed and underdeveloped countries as a theory of underdevelopment.

A radical strain in dependency theory attributed underdevelopment to links with developed countries and therefore the theory of development required the severing of these links and then inducing autonomous development. This analysis gained traction and was subsequently used by scholars in other parts of the developing world, particularly the Caribbean and Africa.

For neo-Marxists, as for Marx, class was a central analytical category. Hence the social analysis and the political economy is Marxist. However, the power relations examined go beyond class to examining the unequal power relations and exploitation involved in relations between nation states, specifically those between developed and underdeveloped countries, and how they influence class relations within underdeveloped countries. In this regard, there is a focus on the instruments of exploitation such as foreign trade, FDI/MNCs and foreign aid. The latter paves the way for exploitative trade and investment deals.

Baran's analysis influenced both structuralist and dependency thought and so his seminal contribution is the starting point. Emmanuel used Marxist analysis to elaborate on how international trade is a mechanism for the transfer of surplus from underdeveloped countries to developed countries. This analysis is elaborated on because openness to international trade is a central mainstream economic development prescription. This theme of unequal exchange in trade and FDI carried over into structuralism and dependency theory, which is explored next.

Neo-Marxism

In the *Political Economy of Growth* (1957) Baran put forward the concept of neocolonialism, drawing on earlier theories of colonialism and imperialism (Chapter 5) as well as his observations on the state of the world in the 1940s and 1950s. Neocolonialism posed a major challenge to economic development in newly independent countries, since the need for raw materials and investment outlets in advanced countries meant that they would bitterly oppose the industrialization that was essential for economic development in the newly independent countries.

Baran argued that underdevelopment resulted not simply from the lack of capital but also from outdated political, social and economic institutions, and these could not be taken as a given, as was done in neoclassical economics, since economic development would involve changing these. Such transformation was opposed and resisted by the west, which allied itself with local retrograde elites benefiting from the status quo and also facilitated the presence and profit repatriation of western MNCs.

Baran defined actual economic surplus as the gap between society's actual output and its essential consumption. Potential economic surplus is the gap between potential output and essential consumption in a rationally structured society i.e. when it operates on the production possibility frontier. Essential consumption was defined in terms of meeting what later came to be called basic human needs (Chapter 4).[3]

Colonialism was identified as the cause of backwardness in underdeveloped countries. The forcible shift of colonial production to a focus on export crops destroyed the self-sufficiency of agrarian pre-capitalist societies, while the withering competition from exported manufactured goods from the colonial countries destroyed rural handicrafts in the colonies. Infrastructure in the colonies was established to serve colonial exporting interests. Capital accumulation by locals in the colonies was retarded and surplus was transferred to the colonial countries by manipulating the terms of trade and via direct transfers and taxes.

Explaining British colonialism in India, Baran surmised that land and taxation policy ruined the village economy, while commercial policy ruined the artisan class and generated massive labor surplus. Finally, economic policy ruined incipient industrial development. The local beneficiaries of colonialism included rent seekers like landlords, money lenders, petty merchants and businesses, middlemen and speculators. In his words, "Sharks of all description proliferated whose interests were tied to the British" (p. 149).

Post-colonial societies inherited a system of low productivity peasant agriculture in which landlords appropriated the surplus and engaged in luxury consumption based on imports. Agricultural improvements yielded slow returns and, in any case, imperfect capital markets made loans for such investments prohibitive. Thus money lending was found to be more rewarding than productive investments and the purpose of land acquisition was status rather than production. Surplus was also appropriated by other rentiers, merchants and intermediaries who did not provide a dynamic impetus to the economy.

Baran also documented the evolution of capitalism in HICs from a competitive phase during the era of the classical economists to monopoly capitalism in the mid-20th century. A vast amount of investable surplus was generated in this monopoly capitalistic phase and, with western government backing, the unutilized surplus was invested to secure materials and markets in the underdeveloped countries while they were in their weakened, post-colonial condition. Tied loans and grants and technical assistance, backed by potential military force, became an important mechanism for securing advantage.

Foreign capital investment in materials was highly mechanized and most of the inputs and equipment for extraction were imported. Relative to the profits generated and repatriated, this capital infusion was modest. The "enclave" nature of the operations meant that even many of the consumer goods for local workers were imported. The investments in plantations perpetuated food insecurity relative to what would be forthcoming from a diversified agriculture.

Baran challenged each element of the case for FDI, namely that the surplus transferred was created by FDI, some surplus was locally retained and FDI-induced infrastructure facilitated development. He argued that FDI only exploited the resource that generated the surplus. Also, the mechanics of surplus creation, such as in the case of sugar plantation agriculture in northeast Brazil, was based on exploitation, pauperization and annihilation of large parts of indigenous production.

Rich and fertile land that was abundant in forests and fruit trees was stripped. The subsequent shortages of fruits, greens and vegetables created food insecurity. Much of Latin America, Africa and Asia suffered from such "one-track" exploitation which resulted in depletion and impoverishment (p. 188). Baran argued that in due course local resource extraction would have been possible and the surplus created locally retained had local productive forces not been undermined and hence arrested.

As was true of the colonial infrastructure, much of the FDI-induced infrastructure only served the purpose of exploiting natural resources. In any case, Baran argued that articulated infrastructure did not lead to industrial capitalism but vice versa. Local beneficiaries of FDI were mostly a handful of "comprodores" (local business associates). He argued that the principal effect of MNCs in underdeveloped countries was to strengthen the sway of feudalists, merchants and monopoly capitalists to the exclusion of indigenous industrial capitalists. Competition from the latter would have raised wages and other input costs and hence negatively impacted MNC profits and so such capitalist competition was retarded.

In support of this argument, Baran documented the pronouncements of senior US policy makers, including presidents, who had emphasized the importance of ensuring a hospitable business climate for MNCs. Private foreign capital would be "aided and abetted" by its home government, which would use "all possible means" to obtain concessions that could subsequently be generalized to other US-based MNCs (p. 199). Baran also cited specific comments showing that social services in the post-colonial countries were designed to improve the quality of labor for foreign capital; meanwhile expenditure on these services was externalized to aid programs and local administrations. Vast sums were spent on the maintenance of sprawling bureaucracies and military establishments with western aid money going to prop up friendly regimes and preserve the social order and MNC privileges.

Baran (1952) elaborated on why underdevelopment persisted in underdeveloped countries. He noted that in underdeveloped countries, the middle class attempted to secure privileges by aligning with feudal, monopolistic businesses and obscurantist forces, rather than opposing these groups, as had the middle classes in developed societies. The threat of socialism in the Cold War era reinforced this accommodation. This alliance preserved social stability but also backwardness. The backwardness was reinforced by the class behavior of the ruling elites.

Conspicuous consumption, including foreign travel, by the feudal class matched by that of the monopolistic business class left little surplus for capital accumulation. The incentive for the latter was in any case blunted by the massive wealth and income inequality that curbed effective demand and by the latent political instability threatened by the high degree of social injustice. Because monopolistic businesses with a colonial merchant mentality sought quick returns, these businesses avoided building the industrial base that would improve agriculture by providing the needed utilities, machinery and materials, and would also absorb the surplus labor released as agriculture modernized. Primary exports were an avenue for investment, but this was left to MNCs which possessed the capital for large-scale operations, the ability and willingness to assume the risk entailed in long-term projects and the requisite marketing knowledge.

A possible alternative route to industrialization that Baran considered was the state using progressive taxation and channeling the surplus to productive physical and human investments to crowd in the private sector, as recommended by the developmentalists (Chapter 6). Baran doubted that this could happen. The lack of a competent and honest civil service in underdeveloped countries contributed negligibly to his doubts. The main issue was that the fundamental reforms needed would be opposed by the political and social structure of the government in power. Progressive agrarian reforms, progressive taxation, curbs on capital flight and luxury consumption, and curbing monopolistic practices by extending the industrial base would be opposed by the vested interests of the governing elites.

Emmanuel (1972) extended Marxian analysis to explore international trade.[4] He contended that this task was one that Marx had planned but was unable to get to. Emmanuel launched a comprehensive challenge to Ricardo's theory of comparative advantage by arguing that prices were determined by factor costs rather than by productivity, and that specialization was not premised on natural advantage (Chapter 5).[5]

Most importantly, he showed that international trade between developed and underdeveloped countries represented unequal exchange or exploitation via a transfer of surplus from the latter to the former. As explained below, he did not view this surplus transfer to be dependent on what was produced by underdeveloped countries i.e. primary rather than manufactured commodities.

He argued that, as far as examining the dynamics of trade, the most realistic premise was that capital was mobile and labor was not. Emmanuel reasoned that if capital were mobile, profit rates would be equalized but wages would not. This reversed Ricardo's premise of international trade being based on unequal productivity and profit rates in different activities.

Emmanuel first established the mechanisms via which prices are dependent on wages. Next he established that capital was sufficiently mobile for profit rates to be equalized, but also demonstrated divergence between wages in developed and underdeveloped countries. He argued that wages represented the independent variable and was not determined like other market prices. His third chapter demonstrated that wages were higher in developed countries due to biological (nutrition needs), historical (traditions, habits, custom, morals), social (legislation) and institutional (trade unions) reasons.[6] In underdeveloped countries, labor surplus kept wages at the subsistence level.[7]

Wage inequality led to exploitation or a net transfer of surplus value from underdeveloped to developing countries. Emmanuel showed that, at prices that equalize profits, underdeveloped countries exported products that embodied a larger number of labor hours in return for imported products that embodied far fewer hours of equivalent skill i.e. unequal exchange.[8] This resulted in a vicious circle since poor countries were deprived of the ability to accumulate and continued to stagnate. Wages stayed low while the narrow market created a disincentive to invest.

Structuralism

Structuralists were trained as market economists and were comfortable with the market economy. However, they shared with neo-Marxists the notion of power asymmetry between the developed and underdeveloped countries that led to unequal benefits of trade and foreign investment. However, the analysis was market based and class was not the central feature of the analysis.

Prebish (1950) was one of the earliest and main contributors to this approach. The divergence of the lagging Latin American economies (periphery), particularly Argentina (his country of origin), relative to the advanced economies (center), prompted his inquiry about why the divergence existed. His research led him to conclude that Latin American countries experienced a successful bout of primary exports that contributed to economic growth when Britain was the imperial power. With the ascendancy of the United States to dominance, this ended for several reasons.

The United States had a strong manufacturing base but also an abundance in primary production. The comparative advantage and specialization approach of mainstream economics no longer assured continued prosperity to underdeveloped countries as prescribed by the theory of comparative advantage i.e. specializing in labor-intensive primary goods production and exports for LICs. Not only was less being imported, but the demand was also unstable due to cyclical fluctuations in HIC economies and for other reasons (see below). Worse still, Prebish reported evidence on a systematic decline in the price of primary commodities relative to manufactured goods (see below).

Singer (1950) independently explored similar issues and arrived at similar conclusions. Based on their theorizing and empirical results, they are jointly credited with the Prebish-Singer hypothesis of a secular (over time) decline in the terms of trade of primary commodities that underdeveloped countries (periphery) specialize in. Thus L/LMICs had to export more and more primary commodities in exchange for the same amount of manufactured goods imported from HICs. They concluded that trade was a zero-sum game that enriched HICs at the expense of L/LMICs.

Several reasons were proffered for unequal global relations and the associated declining terms of trade for primary commodities for goods exported by L/LMICs. It was argued that the income elasticity of demand for primary commodities was less than one, as suggested by Engel's Law, while that for manufactured goods was greater than one. Thus, with a rise in world incomes, the demand for manufacturing goods would rise relative to primary commodities.

HICs often found synthetic substitutes for primary commodities such as cotton and jute that lowered the demand and hence price of primary goods L/LMICs export. More recently, bio-tech and material sciences have produced substitutes for vanilla and sugar, genetic research has produced a substitute for cocoa and palm oil, and optic fiber and microwave research for materials like copper. Technological change also enables economizing on the use of primary commodities and once again this means lower demand for primary commodities.

Primary commodities were also alleged to have lower supply elasticities because poor farmers needed to supply for subsistence and so price responsiveness was lower. Another cause for the low supply elasticities was viewed as structural i.e. infrastructure and other bottlenecks that resulted in supply rigidities. Given

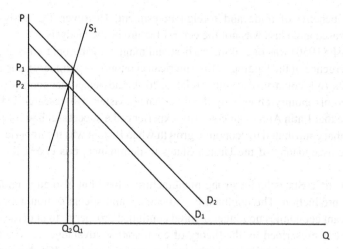

FIGURE 7.1   Price adjustments with low supply elasticity

the lower quantity adjustment, particularly in the short run when resources are committed, the adjustment to falling demand was in lower prices, as shown in Figure 7.1.

As Figure 7.1 shows, the percentage change in quantity transacted suggested in the movement from Q_1 to Q_2, when the demand curve shifts down, is very small relative to the indicated percentage price change in the movement from P_1 to P_2.

Corporations in HICs were viewed as having higher market power and could therefore dictate the price of manufactured goods while primary product producers operated in a competitive market and therefore had less control of prices on the supply side.

Also, on the demand side for primary commodities, L/LMICs confronted monopsonistic buyers who again set the buying prices low. For example less than four companies controlled all the banana trade and four MNCs controlled 85 percent of the soybean market. Holt Giménez and Shattuck (2011) documented that three companies controlled 80 percent of the global wheat trade and two controlled 65 percent of global maize seed trade. Lawrence (2011) documented that the four largest grain traders in the world, Archer Daniels Midland, Bunge, Cargill and Louis Dreyfus, collectively controlled between 75 and 90 percent of the global grain trade. Since MNCs controlled the bulk of world food trade, this inordinate power was used to keep buying prices low.

Again, given the labor surplus in LICs, a productivity gain due to technological change did not result in labor being able to secure higher wages. This, in addition to the high demand inelasticity, means the productivity gain simply results in lower prices that importers benefited from, as shown in Figure 7.2.

In HICs, because of labor scarcity and unionization, the fruits of productivity gain were retained as higher wages. Unit labor costs (ULC) are defined as wages divided by labor productivity. A rise in labor productivity could cause ULC to fall and so lower commodity prices are an option. However, if wages rise to match this rise in labor productivity, the decline in ULC would be offset and so the productivity rise would not result in lower export prices that could benefit buyers in L/LMICs.[9]

Prebish cited evidence showing the terms of trade turned systematically against the periphery from 1876 to 1938 (1950, table 1, p. 9). Compared to the 1860s, only 63 percent of the finished manufacture could be bought in the 1930s with a given amount of primary products (p. 8). This finding sparked a statistical debate that is still ongoing, with empirical studies refuting, or partially or fully supporting the Prebish-Singer hypothesis of a secular decline in the terms of trade of primary commodities.

A review of the literature published in the established journals suggests that, to date, the majority of the evidence is supportive of the hypothesis.[10] This issue of a secular decline in terms of trade for primary commodities remains relevant. For example, UNDP (2016, p. 10) showed that primary commodities still dominate African exports and for 28 of the 38 African countries that they had recent data for, primary commodities made up more than 60 percent of merchandise exports.

Singer and Ansari (1977, pp. 36–37) argued in later work that unequal market power (developed vs. developing country) was an even more significant issue than the nature of the product (manufactured vs. primary) in determining the terms of trade between HICs and L/LMICs.[11] They cited evidence to show that manufactured goods from underdeveloped countries also confronted declining terms of trade.

Even if terms of trade were not declining over time for L/LMICs primary (and manufactured) goods, there was still reason not to be reliant on trade as a growth strategy because it infused instability in the domestic economy. On the demand side, this resulted from the shifts in demand for primary commodities as the

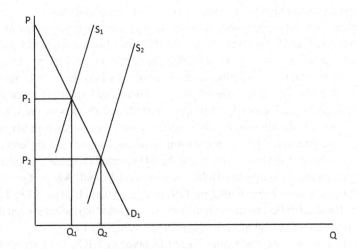

FIGURE 7.2 Lower price resulting from productivity gains

HIC economies went through their usual business cycles. Figure 7.2 shows that inelastic demand and supply curves of L/LMICs could result in big price swings because of a downward shift in the demand curve.

Trade instability was accompanied by a broader economic instability. Since it was not possible to avoid the external shocks to the economic system that resulted from swings in HIC demand based on technological change and the business cycle, L/LMICs could not plan rationally based on a secure foreign exchange base, which was a critical ingredient for catch-up growth.

While structuralists were pessimistic about gains from trade with HICs, like Baran and Nurkse (Chapter 6) they also did not view FDI to be a mechanism for delivering catch-up economic growth. Mines, plantations and other primary agricultural exports operated by MNCs for export had low production linkages with the rest of the economy since they imported their capital and materials. Thus, such investment in net terms adversely impacted the balance of payments.

Latin structuralists were more radical than the pragmatic developmentalists discussed in Chapter 6 and their case for ISI was multi-faceted and included factors other than the problems associated with primary export promotion discussed above. Since labor mobility was not free (i.e. there were immigration restrictions in HICs), they argued there was a parallel case to restrict the flow of goods. The flow of goods amounts indirectly to the flow of people and capital since goods embody factors.

They argued that all new industries need to be nourished with protection initially. They pointed out that all current HICs protected their industries from the industrial leader of the time (Chapter 9). The United States was the most protectionist country in world history until 1945. This is called the infant industry case for protection. In any case, they observed that HIC practice at the time of writing remained protectionist in a systematic way that discouraged industrialization in L/LMICs. Due to tariff escalation (low tariffs on raw material and high tariffs on processed good) the exports of high value goods from L/LMICs were blocked.

Further, even when on paper access was duty free, stringent rules of origin restricted access to HIC markets from L/LMICs, and this was asymmetrically the case. Such practices, and others identified above and in subsequent paragraphs, are argued by heterodox scholars to have continued into the 21st century. For example, the UNDP *Human Development Report 2006* (p. 121) reported that Viet Nam goods paid about $470 million in tariffs on exports to the US worth $4.7 billion while the UK goods paid about the same on exports worth $50 billion.

The most intensive HIC protectionism is on agriculture and differences on this issue between the United States and the EU scuttled progress on multilateral trade agreements including the Doha Development Round. Again, the UNDP's *Human Development Report 2005* (p. 129) estimated that HICs paid $350 billion as agricultural subsidies, most of them going to corporate agriculture, even though such protection was justified in the name of the "small farmer".

Finally, not only are trade rules rigged in favor of HICs, but they also have more resources to take advantage of such rules. Anti-dumping countervailing duties have been widely used by HICs in the WTO. L/LMICs lack the monetary and legal resources for actions and rebuttals on a similar scale in the WTO's dispute settlement process.

To sum up, in relations between HICs and L/LMICs, Singer and Ansari (1977, pp. 74–80) pointed to the adverse impact of market power, export instability, tariff barriers, tariff escalation and non-tariff barriers as trade obstacles poor countries confronted.[12] They calculated that in 1972 the effective rates of protection (Chapter 8) that developed countries imposed against imports from underdeveloped countries were 109 percent higher than on imports from other developed countries.

Structuralists, including Prebish, also introduced an analysis of structural inflation based on the concept of social surplus left over after society reproduces itself in its current form (1984, pp. 185–190). He showed that growth required much of the social surplus to be devoted to investment, and this conflicted with the interests of labor, as well as of those of the elites (wishing to funnel capital toward conspicuous consumption) and the state (needing funds to accommodate surplus manpower and a growing bureaucratic empire). Also, oligopolistic transnational corporations internationalized consumption and siphoned off a disproportionate share of the surplus. Structural inflation resulted when monetary authorities, seeking to ensure social stability, attempted to accommodate these competing claims. Prebish found it ironic that economic liberals recommended wage repression to curb inflation (central also to later structural adjustment programs – Chapter 8) since this entailed curbing political liberalism.

Myrdal's (1957) theory of underdevelopment was based on explaining the causes of uneven development (regional inequality) within countries, but he used the same theory to explain uneven development (global divergence) across countries. He shared with developmentalists the belief in endemic market failures as an explanation of underdevelopment.

Myrdal viewed equilibrium analysis as irrelevant for a sound theory of underdevelopment or development. Vicious or virtuous circles were embedded in his theory of circular cumulative causation and these led away from the initial point such that no countervailing market forces or self-correcting mechanisms pushed back to the initial point. In fact, in the case of regional inequality, Myrdal argued that market forces could exaggerate the trend of divergence from the initial point.

Suppose as a result of historical accident, resource concentration or geographical advantage, a region thrives. Internal and external economies would make this region a magnet for resources as the market mechanism acted to draw in human and financial capital from other regions, exemplifying a virtuous circle. This play of market forces, however, would also set into motion vicious circles in regions from which resources were drawn.

In these regions, the demographics would become unfavorable as the best and brightest leave. Because of the higher fertility rates among the poor, the dependency ratio becomes higher among the depleted working population that became poorer with the out-migration. Higher population intensity could result in resource degradation and hence further poverty and outmigration. Reinforcing this negative cumulative causation would be the shrinking of the market size. Also, handicrafts and industries unable to compete with the nodal centers (growth poles), experiencing increasing returns, would be wiped out.

Myrdal referred to the negative impacts on the deprived regions as "backwash effects". But, these negative effects could be balanced with countervailing market mechanisms that he referred to as "spread effects". He argued that since growth poles would in due course become markets for materials and products from other regions, this would in principle allow self-sustained economic prosperity to spread out into peripheral areas to some extent, but the process is not autonomous.

Myrdal noted that in the more prosperous countries, the state offsets backwash effects and facilitates spread effects by funding social and physical infrastructure. Investing in people's education and health makes them more productive and allows their potential to be realized. This enables prosperity to be generalized and facilitates attaining national integration. In this way, social equality serves as a mechanism for economic growth.

Poorer countries, however, lacked resources to facilitate spread effects and hence regional inequality was the outcome. Rural sector infrastructure was neglected and policy worsened the terms of trade against the agricultural sector. Myrdal believed that this was a colonial legacy and these policies were perpetuated after independence, a process he referred to as negative path dependence. Organizational and institutional formation in the form of banks, finance and shipping were discouraged because the mother country sought to enrich itself by fulfilling these functions. These services remained underdeveloped as part of the negative path dependence.

In other work (1968, 1970) Myrdal argued that negative cumulative causation within underdeveloped countries is associated with the concept of a "soft state" (unlike the developed country hard states) characterized by poor management. Soft states were dominated by self-serving and corrupt elites which acted as though they were above the law and therefore were incapable of inspiring social discipline. These elites served their own interests and so were unlikely to pay the taxes necessary for inculcating spread effects. Land reforms and anti-corruption policies would diffuse the economic power necessary for progressive changes but this begged the question of why the elites would accept such reforms.[13]

The same forces of circular cumulative causation that induced regional inequality within countries enhanced global inequalities. Advanced country manufactured goods wiped out craft and manufacturing products in underdeveloped countries if protection was not provided. As suggested by Prebish and Singer, inelastic demand, price fluctuations and low potential for technological learning were forthcoming from specializing in primary goods, as recommended by rich country economists espousing comparative advantage. Another backwash effect was capital outflows to the richer countries if not constrained. While mainstream economic theory suggests a higher return to capital where it is scarce, Myrdal pointed out that without state support the returns to capital were actually low and insecure in underdeveloped countries.

In the relations between rich and poor nations, there was no global governance and hence no one to impose countervailing spread effects. Based on national interest, the initiatives within the UN to restrain capital outflows and to make global trade rules fairer via price stabilization mechanisms and competition policies to offset international cartels, as called for by the NIEO, were undermined by the developed countries. Similarly, technical assistance was nominal and aid was a mechanism for promoting the national interests of donor countries.[14]

Dependency[15]

Dependency theorists drew inspiration from neo-Marxists like Baran and Latin structuralists like Prebish.[16] They used the historical method to posit neocolonialism as a theory of underdevelopment. Interest in this approach was common to several social sciences and cross-disciplinary studies programs and it peaked in the 1970s. This approach could be broadly bifurcated into a "stagnationist" school that believed in the impossibility of development as long as neocolonial relations with the HICs were extant, and "dependent development" for those who believed that some kind of development was still possible but that it would be distorted by the nature of the association with the center.[17]

Frank (1967) is the most famous representative of the stagnationist view in the English-speaking world. Frank argued that underdevelopment could only be understood by studying the unique social and economic history of each underdeveloped country. Only then would it be possible to formulate an adequate theory of development.

In contrast to Rostow's grand theory (Chapter 6) with its broad brush historical formulations, Frank's approach purported to be country specific. Frank refuted Rostow's presumption that there are significant similarities between currently developed and underdeveloped countries in terms of their respective histories. He conceded that developed countries were at one point *un*developed but that they had never been *under*developed, since the latter condition is an outcome of colonialism which currently developed countries were never subject to.

Frank viewed the non-socialist world to be divided into the metropolitan center (metropolis or core) and periphery, as suggested by Prebish. Trade and foreign investment in primary commodity production were viewed as mechanisms for extracting surplus and the underdevelopment of the periphery was viewed as a precondition for the enrichment of the center. Frank characterized this process as the "development of underdevelopment".

He tried to establish his thesis empirically in a historical context and to show that the closer the ties to the center, the more underdeveloped were countries in the periphery. The same was true for regions within peripheral countries. Thus peripheral countries were mirror images of the exploitative world capitalist system, and regional and federal capital elites (comprador class) enriched themselves as part of a conveyor belt mechanism that extracted surplus from the hinterland and passed it onto the center. While the elites drew some surplus via kick-backs and supply contracts, which they dissipated in luxury consumption, most of the surplus went abroad.

Sunkel (1966) explored in more detail some of the mechanisms of the transfer of surplus from the periphery to the core that resulted from the distorted development conditioned in the periphery due to the association with the core. Monopolistic trade created deficits and these were subsequently financed by "aid" that reinforced the distorted development. The aid was "tied" and financed imports of products that competed with local products and introduced inappropriate technology given the factor endowments in the periphery. The loans or aid were siphoned back partly as royalties for the technology. It was also siphoned back in the high prices of raw materials and capital goods of the MNC-led industrialization that was subsidized by the state and local finance. Ultimately wage exploitation, capital intensity and profit or surplus repatriation limited the size of the domestic market and hence a broad-based indigenous industrial take-off.

Cardoso and Faletto (1978) also wrote about MNC-driven distorted development in the periphery. Plantation enclaves were labor intensive while the mining enclaves were capital intensive, but both resulted in skewing the income distribution. The mining enclave had high worker productivity because of the capital intensity, and hence high worker wages, but nonetheless few links to the domestic economy. The plantation enclaves expanded at the expense of subsistence agriculture.

While the enclaves resulted in no authentic development, there was some possibility of dependent development in industry by relying on MNCs. The latter had a large stock of technological knowledge and highly skilled managerial organizations that could manage large-scale production and quality control. While production was locally managed, capital flows and economic decisions such as profit reinvestment were controlled from abroad.

Local firms were dependent on these MNCs for acquiring the necessary knowledge to compete. Such dependent industrialization was substantially different from enclave economies since a highly diversified output was needed and reinvestment, especially in the capital goods sector, meant low profit repatriation. Further, these economies needed a tertiary sector and a more balanced income distribution to enable a domestic market to absorb output. Some Latin American economies like Brazil and Mexico were able to retain a degree of autonomy with the involvement of the public sector in production.

Cardoso and Faletto foresaw in the mid-1960s the growing space for autonomous development as the world rebalanced due to a diffusion of power (especially the economic strength of Germany and Japan and the emergence of China as a political force) and hence the relative weakening of US hegemony. While MNCs continued to rely on US power to protect their interests, as observed by Baran, they also started making their own accommodations with changing economic realities that they partly ushered in.

A prominent challenge to the branch of dependency theory that suggested the impossibility of economic development in the context of links with global capitalism came from the left. Warren (1973, 1980) mustered evidence to show that East Asian and other developing countries had effectively used global links for catch-up growth.

Prescriptions

Much has been made about the Prebish-Singer hypothesis, but this is a distraction from the real structuralists' concerns. While a secular decline in commodity prices might have suggested not relying on them as a mechanism for development, the real reasons for moving to industrialization were the intrinsic benefits of industrialization as identified by classical economists and developmentalists (Chapters 5 and 6).

The recommendation was to start first with the consumer durables like soft drinks, leather products and apparel. This is also referred to as the "easy phase of ISI" because the technology is simple and available off the shelf and the human skill levels needed are relatively low. Also, the domestic market already exists and it is a question of diverting this demand from imports to domestic production.

The mainstream trade theory of comparative advantage was criticized for being unrealistic, having faulty assumptions, but most importantly for being static. Singer's (p. 172) prescription was for a more fluid international division of labor that would allow for extensive industrialization within underdeveloped countries. He argued that the structure of comparative advantages and countries' relative endowments at a given point in time should not determine the future division of labor (p. 172). Thus he advocated that comparative advantage should be thought of as a dynamic process (dynamic comparative advantage).

Unit costs in LICs are initially high due to a lack of all the skills, complementary inputs (colleagues, libraries, labs, machinery, computers and institutional freedom), entrepreneurship, technological development, managerial and marketing skills, financial development and infrastructure. However, the industrialization process could in principle address these constraints and reduce unit costs. In situations where the domestic market is small because of low population (small country case), low base income or high income inequality, the efficient firms could break into export markets.

Several of the specific structuralist arguments for industrialization were identical to developmentalist thinking (Chapter 6). Since the industrial process involves externalities i.e. benefits go beyond the firm engaged in the investment, there is a case for state intervention because left to the private sector, the forthcoming investment would be less than the socially optimum since they do not include social benefits in their revenue calculation. A higher tax was recommended for luxury imports to save foreign exchange. In fact, given the poor tax administration, import tariffs to induce ISI had the additional advantage of raising revenue.[18]

Their broader case for intervention was also the same as that of the developmentalists. This included various market failures. The financial sector functioned badly, was incomplete and neither deep nor broad and so entrepreneurs with the requisite skills may simply not get the credit. While neoclassical economics starts with the presumption of perfect information, in practice the lack of it deters entrepreneurs. Because investment requires large capital outlays, has a long gestation period, credit is scarce and information is not available, even if the profit opportunities do exist hypothetically, the response from the private sector may not be forthcoming as assumed in neoclassical economics. Agents seek less risky options like trade, real estate and financial investments.

The tools for industrial policy were also the same as prescribed by developmentalists and these included tariffs as shown in Figure 7.3.

A domestic tariff of t on the world price of an import (P_w) enables the domestic price (P_d) to exceed world price in proportion to the tariff ($P_d = P_w (1 + t)$). As intended, this can increase local production along the domestic supply curve (from a to b). Space A represents revenue that accrues to the government that could in principle be used to encourage economic development activities such as providing needed infrastructure.[19] In the initial period, the gap between domestic demand and supply (bd) represents continued imports. If dynamic efficiencies kick in as hoped, the domestic supply curve could shift out over time and displace imports entirely, assuming local production is a reasonable substitute for imports in quality terms.[20]

The same impact could in principle be attained by quotas. Imagine in Figure 7.3 that the gap between domestic supply and demand (cd) is now what is allowed to be imported as a quota. If so, the impact on domestic price (P_d) is exactly the same as when a nominal tariff of t is imposed on the world or import price (P_w).[21] There are some important differences. First, the space A is no longer tariff revenue accruing to the state, but rather rents that accrue to importers who get a license to

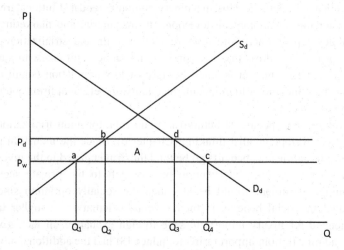

FIGURE 7.3 Encouraging local industry production with tariffs

import. Second, if domestic supply shifts to the right, unless the quota is changed, the domestic price could fall below the world price. Alternatively, if the domestic demand shifts to the right, unless the quota is changed, it would result in a higher domestic price and hence more protection.[22]

It would also be possible to provide the same level of domestic protection and inducement to industrialization in other ways including with various subsidies and incentives to domestic production. However, while tariffs raise revenue, subsidies place a burden on the exchequer. Nonetheless, countries with a solid fiscal effort (tax revenue as a percent of GDP) could subsidize credit, foreign exchange, R&D, training and utilities among other industrial policy initiatives. In addition, exemptions from import taxes and other tax incentives, such as for depreciation and location, could be utilized. Public acquisition to broaden the market has been utilized as an incentive, as has direct production by state-owned enterprises (SOEs), as a short-term measure, when the private sector does not respond to the incentives. Once the activity is initiated and shown as viable, it can be turned over to private enterprise.

Prebish was aware of possible drawbacks that the push to industrialization could produce. Technology is licensed and therefore could be a drain on scarce foreign exchange resources. The capital intensity of the technology would mean fewer employment opportunities for the large numbers coming to cities from the rural areas.

Finally, given the low domestic incomes and inequality, it would be difficult to realize economies of scale without breaking into export markets or forging regional trade associations. On balance he still felt the benefits of industrialization exceeded the costs in the long run and in this regard protectionism could be viewed as an investment.

Other aspects of the structuralist prescriptions were also similar to those endorsed by developmentalists. Like developmentalists, they believed that state expenditures on infrastructure could crowd in private sector activities, but beyond this planning was not a major feature in their program. Like developmentalists, they endorsed a productive agriculture and endorsed land reform as a key to unleashing its productive potential.

On an international level, under Prebish's leadership, the call for the NIEO was initiated in 1974 as a UN declaration. This was a call for restructuring the rules of international transactions to make them fair. This included containing the power of MNCs in international trade and buffer stocks (ICAs or International Commodity Agreements) to stabilize the price of primary commodities, as shown in Figure 7.4.

The idea was to use resources allocated to the ICA, based on HIC contributions, to buy and stock commodities when they were cheap and sell from the stocks when dear to limit price variation to a specified range (P_{ub}, P_{lb}), where P_{ub} and P_{lb} represent upper and lower bounds for the price as shown in Figure 7.4. Suppose at the market clearing price P_{lb} the supply curve shifted to the right to S_2 due to say a good weather induced bumper harvest. This would result in excess supply

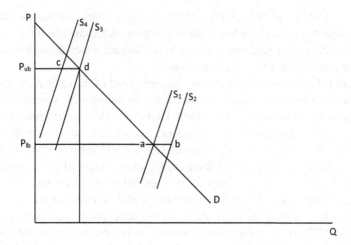

FIGURE 7.4 Price stabilization with International Commodity Agreements

of the amount ab. This amount could be bought and stored using the earmarked ICA funds to restore P_{lb} as the world market price. Now, if at the market clearing price of P_{ub} the supply curve shifted to the left to S_4 due to say a drought, there would be excess demand of the amount cd. This amount could then be released into the market from the stored stock to ensure that the price did not exceed P_{ub}. The problem with an ICA is the incentive created for countries/farmers to cheat or boost supply causing scheme costs to balloon.

In addition to fairer trade rules and ICAs, the NIEO also wanted better terms from MNCs when negotiating FDI contracts, concessionary aid and debt relief, and trade policy concessions by HICs. They also wanted the revamping of international institutions like the World Bank and the IMF to give more influence to L/LMICs.

Myrdal endorsed structuralist and developmentalist prescriptions but cast them in the context of the framework he developed. His theory of development was premised on struggle. He claimed that even in rich countries, rights, privileges and opportunities were hard earned rather than willingly conceded, revealing the limits of a social philosophy with roots in the "enlightenment". Thus, poor countries, too, would need to struggle for greater prosperity, as would the poor within these poor countries. Landlords will not hand over their land to land hungry peasants even if there is an economic productivity case for it and even if shattering the old class structure would enable spread effects. Moreover, because rights in the richer countries are often won at the expense of the poor in poor countries, such as subsidies for cotton farmers, so underdeveloped countries need solidarity in international forums to resist this.

Underdeveloped countries that seek prosperity, regional equality and national integration would need to use state planning to facilitate spread effects. Like other developmentalists and structuralists, then, Myrdal viewed planning primarily as a mechanism to create space for markets by addressing rigidities and bottlenecks, which would in turn facilitate spread effects. In relations with the developed nations, he advocated protection for "infant economies" until they thrived and produced dynamic social gains through the process of positive circular cumulative causation.

The NIEO demands were for the most part brushed aside by HICs, as Myrdal anticipated. The prescription of the more radical dependency approach was to delink from HICs. Since, as explained above, it was the links in the form of foreign trade and investment that produced underdevelopment in L/LMICs, the solution was to break the links and focus on autonomous industrialization.

As neo-Marxists, Baran and Emmanuel could have advocated for a social revolution and the building of socialism. However, both had witnessed the practical attempts to build socialism within the Soviet Union and neither endorsed that model. Instead, both endorsed a socially progressive capitalism. Baran's pessimistic summation was that the "keepers of the past cannot be the builders of the future" (p. 102). His dire warning was that if the capitalist middle classes did not opt to reward the "efficient, able, and industrious" by supporting progressive, competitive capitalism, they would instead face a social revolution leading to authoritarian planning and social collectivism.

Emmanuel discussed a number of ways of breaking out of vicious circles, such as by pursuing regional integration. Trade between countries with similar wage structures would reduce exploitative unequal exchange. Export taxes in underdeveloped countries would also reduce unequal exchange by limiting trade. Regional trade agreements among underdeveloped countries that enabled industrialization and diversification would also help; by reducing dependence on imports from developed countries, underdeveloped countries could reduce unequal exchange and improve their terms of trade.

Emmanuel rightly warned that the measures he proposed would impose adjustment costs on developed countries and would produce ferocious resistance. Indeed, he argued that trade rules are set, monitored and enforced by international financial institutions like the IMF, the World Bank and GATT (later the WTO) to protect developed country interests.

Emmanuel defined underdevelopment as the gap between what the means of production could potentially deliver (being on the production possibility frontier), based on the current state of technology, compared to what was actually produced. He argued that wage increases can precede development. For example, colonies in temperate zones like the United States, Canada, Australia and New Zealand inherited Britain's high wage structure, which proved to be an advantage in creating an internal market, and development followed later.[23] He concluded that the solution for the initial lack of competitiveness in international trade was protectionism, and the United States had shown the way in this regard.

Summary and conclusions

The heterodox approaches considered in this chapter include neo-Marxism, dependency and structuralism. All of them locate their theory of underdevelopment in post-colonial exploitative relations between L/LMICs and HICs. While neo-Marxism and dependency theory framed this in Marxian terms as a transfer of surplus from L/LMICs to HICs, structuralist analysis used the terminology of mainstream economics. However, structuralist economists pointed to the same mechanisms of foreign trade and investment as leading to unfair outcomes.

For neo-Marxists like Baran, class remained important and in this regard the social analysis and the political economy is Marxist. However, the power relations examined go beyond class to examining the unequal power relations and exploitation involved in relations between nation states, specifically those between HIC and L/LMICs. In this regard, there is a focus on the instruments of exploitation such as foreign trade, FDI/MNCs and foreign aid. The latter serves to pave the way for exploitative trade and investment deals. In conventional Marxism the exploitation is class based and results from the ownership of capital by the capitalists (Chapter 5).

However, neo-Marxists, like Baran, believe in the importance of the development of productive forces and in this regard capitalism is viewed as progressive relative to the disarticulated semi-feudal and semi-capitalist social and economic formations that L/LMICs were mired in. Ultimately, a neo-Marxist like Baran would in theory endorse socialism as more socially progressive, though the reality of Soviet socialism was viewed as alarming and a warning to a capitalism that refused to build a progressive social order. Such a social order would be based on progressive taxation, progressive social expenditures, the redistribution of land and fair access to resources like credit i.e. a social democracy might be the preferred goal to aim for as a theory of economic development.

Structuralists were influenced by neo-Marxists and concerned with unequal trade relations between the center and periphery. However, the surplus extraction represented by the declining terms of trade for the periphery was explained using institutional and mainstream economic analysis. Institutions enabled the center to retain the higher surplus generated by higher productivity, while due to surplus labor and institutional conditions, surplus generated by higher productivity in the periphery was passed onto the center. Asymmetrical market and economic power also contributed to unfair prices, trade rules and investment conditions. Structuralists called for a fairer NIEO, a call that was backed by little political clout and summarily ignored by the west.

Discontent with the economic and political power asymmetries between the center and periphery and the unwillingness of the west to address the perceived exploitation of the periphery in a neocolonial world resulted in the popularity of dependency theory in Latin America, the Caribbean and Africa. The dependency theory of underdevelopment was based on the transfer of surplus from L/LMICs to HICs. Since links with the center or metropolis produced underdevelopment in the periphery or satellites, the solution was to delink with the center to avoid the exploitation or outflow of surplus. However, there was no flushed out theory of development beyond recommending autocentric industrialization in a socialist framework.

None of the heterodox alternatives discussed in this chapter proved to have a long shelf life. While neo-Marxists endorsed competitive capitalism and a socially progressive agenda, their inability to endorse socialism meant the lack of a real alternative to capitalism. Structuralists endorsed the developmentalist agenda of industrial policy based on ISI, but in the implementation of this agenda it left itself open to neoliberal criticism, as will be discussed in the next chapter. Even so, the structuralist concern about the heavy dependence of L/LMICs on primary commodities remains relevant, particularly in Africa.

With the heterodox approaches in intellectual disarray or unable to proffer an alternative, the mainstream approach in a neoliberal manifestation was in the ascendency in the 1980s and laid claim to being the only real viable economic development approach. To do so, it needed to intellectually demolish the policy alternatives proffered by developmentalism and structuralism, and this is the subject of Chapter 8.

Questions and exercises

1. Explain the theoretical and empirical underpinnings of export pessimism among Latin structuralists.
2. Explain in detail the case Latin structuralists made for ISI (import substitution industrialization).
3. Explain in detail the case Latin structuralists made for state intervention to promote ISI.
4. Explain the tools Latin structuralists recommended for ISI.
5. Discuss other components (other than ISI) of the Latin structuralist program.
6. Explain cumulative causation as expounded by Myrdal and his proposed solutions.
7. Explain Baran's explanation for underdevelopment and his prescriptions for development.
8. Explain Emmanuel's critique of conventional trade theory and his explanation for unequal exchange.
9. Explain Emmanuel's prescriptions for avoiding unequal exchange.
10. Explain Frank's explanation for underdevelopment and his prescriptions for development.
11. Explain the possibility of dependent development.

Notes

1 Neo-Marxian here refers to extensions of Marxist analysis to post-colonialism.
2 Refer to Bhagwati (1977) for a more serious mainstream attempt to grapple with the issues involved. For a review of the NIEO refer to Dag Hammmarskjöld Foundation (1975).

3   Baran recognized the many definitional difficulties associated with these concepts (p. 30).
4   Nation states rather than class are central to Emmanuel's analysis and he was criticized for this by orthodox Marxists. Emmanuel defended his analysis for being correct and also Marxist, though he conceded he was not orthodox. Furtardo (1964) extended class analysis to the Latin American context, specifically to Brazil.
5   For example, he argued that England possessed neither raw materials nor any weaving experience except in wool prior to establishing its cotton textile industry. Even the woolen industry was artificially implanted with draconian measures including the cutting off of the arms of any person who violated the ban on wool exports (p. 269).
6   Emmanuel (1975) emphasized power relations between social classes in determining wages beyond some vital minimum. The higher the actual wages are relative to this minimum, the lower the ability of unions to deliver increases since they confront greater resistance from employers.
7   In this regard Emmanuel noted that Lewis got it right (Chapter 6).
8   Amin (1977), another prominent neo-Marxist, also showed the existence of unequal exchange. While the nation state was the unit of analysis for Emmanuel so that poor nations were being exploited by rich ones, Amin used a world systems approach whereby the global bourgeois led by rich country capitalists allied with poor country elites to exploit global working classes. While the workers and peasants in underdeveloped countries suffered the brunt of this exploitation, working classes in rich countries were not exempt even if the standard of living was better than the working classes in developed countries.
9   This scenario is less true now than the 1950s. Due to outsourcing, labor intensive imports, migrant labor and a weakening of unions, capital has emerged in a much stronger position in HICs relative to labor. Labor displacing technological change due to automation has reinforced this trend and in Marxian terms added to a reserve army of the unemployed and underemployed. Even so, market power on the selling side may still result in retaining the fruits of technological change and higher productivity than passing it off to buyers in L/LMICs in lower prices.
10 Doubts about the hypothesis were expressed by Ellsworth (1956), Sparos (1980), Michaely (1980) and Ghoshray (2011). More recent and more sophisticated empirical analyses have found contrary results by Cuddington (1992), Newbold, Pfaffenzeller and Rayner (2005) and Balagtas and Holt (2009), mixed results by Kellard and Wohar (2006), Yamada and Yoon (2014), and supportive results by Helg (1991), Ardeni and Wright (1992), Leon and Soto (1999), Lutz (1999), Bloch and Sapsford (2000), Sarkar (2001), Ram (2004), Bunzel and Vogelsang (2005), Harvey et al. (2010), Ocampo (2010), Erten (2011), Alagidede (2012), Erten and Ocampo (2013), Arezki et al. (2014) and Baffes and Etienne (2016).
11 Also refer to Sarkar and Singer (1991).
12 They cited a GATT (General Agreement on Trade and Tariffs) Report that listed 800 non-tariff barriers including quantitative restrictions, procurement procedures, standards and customs regulations (p. 80).
13 Possible ways out of such conundrums are discussed in Chapter 15.
14 Myrdal (1956, p. 124) made a case for international aid to be multilateral to remove the political element from it.
15 It is often referred to as dependency "theory" but approach is more appropriate.
16 As with Emmanuel, dependency focused on asymmetrical power relations between nation states rather than across classes and in this regard the approach is non-Marxist in a classical sense even if inspired by Marx or more specifically a neo-Marxist like Baran.
17 This is a simplified classification and interested readers can refer to Kay (1989) and Palma (1978) for an extensive review of this literature and the many nuances and more elaborate classifications.

18 Imports are a very visible tax base and so easy to tax.
19 The area of the rectangle A is calculated as the net imports after the tariff (Q_2Q_3) multiplied by the tariff rate t.
20 As is the case for all diagrams in economics, this one is purely illustrative. In the real world the determinants on the demand and supply side constantly change causing these heuristic curves or schedules to shift and so the domestic supply gap would not be as shown in the static diagram.
21 Thus the quota price $P_q = P_d = P_w (1 + t)$.
22 This suggests that quotas are more trade restrictive than tariffs and it is for this reason that the Uruguay Round negotiations that led to the birth of the WTO abolished new quotas and required a "tariffication" of existing quotas.
23 Emmanuel did not note that they also inherited Britain's higher labor productivity and institutional framework, which facilitated economic development.

References

Alagidede, P. 2012. "Trends and Cycles in the Net Barter Terms of Trade for Sub-Saharan Africa's Primary Commodity Exporters," *Journal of Developing Areas*, 46(2), 213–229.

Amin, S. 1977. *Imperialism and Unequal Development* (New York: Monthly Review Press).

Ardeni, P. G. and B. Wright. 1992. "The Prebisch-Singer Hypothesis: A Reappraisal Independent of Stationarity Hypotheses," *Economic Journal*, 102(413), 803–812.

Arezki, R., K. Hadri, P. Loungani and Y. Rao. 2014. "Testing the Prebisch-Singer Hypothesis since 1650: Evidence from Panel Techniques that Allow for Multiple Breaks," *Journal of International Money and Finance*, 42(Fall), 208–223.

Baffes, J. and X. L. Etienne. 2016. "Analyzing Food Price Trends in the Context of Engle's Law and the Prebish-Singer Hypothesis," *Oxford Economic Papers*, 68(3), 688–713.

Balagtas, J. V. and M. T. Holt. 2009. "The Commodity Terms of Trade, Unit Roots, Non-Linear Alternatives: A Smooth Transition Approach," *American Journal of Agricultural Economics*, 91(1), 87–105.

Baran, P. 1952. "On the Political Economy of Backwardness," *The Manchester School*, 20(1), 66–84.

Baran, P. 1957. *The Political Economy of Growth* (New York: Monthly Review Press).

Bhagwati, J. (Ed.). 1977. *The New International Economic Order: The North-South Debate* (Cambridge, MA: The MIT Press).

Bloch, H. and D. Sapsford. 2000. "Whither the Terms of Trade? an Elaboration of the Prebisch-Singer Hypothesis," *Cambridge Journal of Economics*, 24(4), 461–481.

Bunzel, H. and T. J. Vogelsang. 2005. "Powerful Trend Function Tests that are Robust to Strong Serial Correlation, with an Application to the Prebisch-Singer Hypothesis," *Journal of Business and Economic Statistics*, 23(4), 381–394.

Cardoso, F. H. and Faletto, E. 1978. Dependency and Development in Latin America, Translated by M. M. Urguidi. Berkeley: University of California Press.

Cuddington, J. 1992. "Long-run Trends in 26 Primary Commodity Prices: A Disaggregated Look at the Prebish-Singer Hypothesis," *Journal of Development Economics*, 39(2), 207–227.

Dag Hammmarskjöld Foundation. 1975. "Towards a New International Order." In: *What Now: Another Development*. Prepared on the Occasion of the Seventh Special Session of the United Nations General Assembly, New York, 1 to 12 September 1975, Uppsala, Sweden.

Ellsworth, P. T. 1956. "The Terms of Trade between Primary Producing and Industrial Countries," *Inter-American Economic Affairs*, 10(1), 47–65.

Emmanuel, A. 1972. *Unequal Exchange: A Study of Imperialism of Trade* (New York: Monthly Review Press).

Emmanuel, A. 1975. "Unequal Exchange Revisited." Institute of Development Studies Discussion Paper No. 77. University of Sussex. Brighton.

Erten, B. 2011. "North-South Terms-of-Trade from 1960 to 2006," *International Review of Applied Economics*, 25(2), 171–184.

Erten, B. and J. A. Ocampo. 2013. "Super-Cycles of Commodity Prices since the Mid-Nineteenth Century," *World Development*, 44(April), 14–30.

Frank, A. G. 1967. *Capitalism and Underdevelopment in Latin America: Historical Studies of Chile and Brazil*. New York: Monthly Review Press.

Furtardo, C. 1964. *Development and Underdevelopment* (Los Angeles: University of California Press).

Ghoshray, A. 2011. "A Reexamination of Trends in Primary Commodity Prices," *Journal of Development Economics*, 95(2), 242–251.

Harvey, D. I., N. M. Kellard, J. B. Madsen and M. E. Wohar. 2010. "The Prebish-Singer Hypothesis: Four Centuries of Evidence," *Review of Economics and Statistics*, 92(2), 367–377.

Helg, R. 1991. "A Note on the Stationarity of the Primary Commodities Relative Price Index," *Economics Letters*, 36(1), 55–60.

Holt Giménez, E. and A. Shattuck. 2011. "Food Crises, Food Regimes and Food Movements: Rumblings of Reform or Tides of Transformation?," *Journal of Peasant Studies*, 38(1), 109–144.

Johnson, G. H. 1976. *"The New International Economic Order,"* Woodwart Court Lecture, University of Chicago, Booth School, Occasional Papers No. 49, Chicago.

Kay, C. 1989. *Latin American Theories of Development and Underdevelopment* (London: Routeledge).

Kellard, N. and M. E. Wohar. 2006. "On the Prevalence of Trends in Commodity Prices," *Journal of Development Economics*, 79(1), 146–167.

Lawrence, F. 2011. "The Global Food Crisis: ABCD of Food – How the Multinationals Dominate Trade," www.guardian.co.uk/global-development/poverty-matters/2011/jun/02/abcdfood-giants-dominate-trade?INTCMP=SRCH, 2/25/2019.

Leon, J. and R. Soto. 1999. *Structural Breaks and Long Run Trends in Commodity Prices*. Policy Research Working Paper Series No. 1406 (Washington, D. C: The World Bank).

Lutz, M. G. 1999. "A General Test of the Prebisch-Singer Hypothesis," *Review of Development Economics*, 3(1), 44–57.

Michaely, M. 1980. *The terms of trade between poor and rich nations*. Volume 162, Institute of International Studies, University of Stockholm..

Myrdal, G. 1956. *An International Economy* (New York: Harper & Brothers Publishers).

Myrdal, G. 1957. *Economic Theory and Under-developed Regions* (London: Gerald Duckworth & Co., Ltd.).

Myrdal, G. 1968. *Asian Drama: An Inquiry into the Poverty of Nations* (New York: Twentieth Century Fund and Pantheon Books).

Myrdal, G. 1970. *The Challenge of World Poverty: A World Anti-Poverty Program in Outline* (New York: Pantheon Books).

Newbold, P., S. Pfaffenzeller and A. Rayner. 2005. "How Well are Long-Run Commodity Price Series Characterized by Trend Components," *Journal of International Development*, 17(4), 479–494.

Ocampo, J. A. 2010. "The Terms of Trade for Commodities since the Mid-19th Century," *Revista De Historia Economica*, 28(1), 11–43.

Palma, G. 1978. "Dependency: A Formal Theory of Underdevelopment or A Methodology for the Analysis of Concrete Situations of Underdevelopment?," *World Development*, 6(7/8), 881–924.

Prebish, R. 1950. *The Economic Development of Latin America and Its Principle Problems* (Lake Success and New York: United Nations Department of Economic Affairs).

Prebish, R. 1984. "Five Stages of My Thinking on Development," in: G. M. Meier and D. Seers (eds.), *Pioneers in Development* (New York: Oxford University Press) 173-191.

Ram, R. 2004. "Trends in Developing Countries' Terms-of-Trade since 1970," *Review of Radical Political Economics*, 36(2), 241–253.

Sarkar, P. and H. W. Singer. 1991. "Manufactured Exports of Developing Countries and Their Terms of Trade since 1965," *World Development*, 19(4), 333–340.

Sarkar, P. 2001. "The North-South Terms of Trade Debate: A Re-examination," *Progress in Development Studies*, 1(4), 309–327.

Singer, H. W. 1950. "The Distribution of Gains between Investing and Borrowing Countries," *The American Economic Review*, 40(2), 473–485.

Singer, H. W. and J. A. Ansari. 1977. *Rich and Poor Countries* (Baltimore: The Johns Hopkins University Press).

Sparos, J. 1980. "The Statistical Debate between Primary Commodities and Manufactures," *Economic Journal*, (90), 107–128.

Sunkel, O. 1966. "The structural background of development problems in Latin America," *Weltwirtschaftliches Archiv*, 97(1), 22–60.

UNDP. 2016. "Primary Commodity Booms and Busts Emerging Lessons from Sub-Saharan Africa," United Nations Development Programme – Regional Bureau for Africa, www.africa.undp.org/content/dam/rba/docs/Reports/undp-rba-primary%20commodities%20boom%20bust%20april%202016.pdf, consulted, 2/20/2019.

Warren, B. 1973. "Imperialism and Capitalist Industrialization," *New Left Review*, 81(September–October), 3–44.

Warren, B. 1980. *Imperialism: Pioneer of Capitalism* (London: Verso).

Yamada, H. and G. Yoon. 2014. "When Grilli and Yang Meet Prebish and Singer: Piecewise Linear Trends in Primary Commodity Prices," *Journal of International Money and Finance*, 42(April), 193–207.

8

NEOLIBERALISM AND ITS CRITICS

Introduction

Neoliberalism is essentially the reemergence of neoclassical or mainstream economic thought in development economics. In broader terms, it is the merging of neoclassical economics with the conservative moral philosophy of Margaret Thatcher and Ronald Regan.[1] It has a strong policy bent which came into its own as L/LMICs sought assistance from the two Bretton Woods institutions (BWI), i.e. the International Monetary Fund (IMF) and the World Bank (WB), following the 1970s debt crisis.[2]

This debt crisis was partly brought on by the aggressive pushing of loans by western banks following the deposits into these banks of petrodollars by oil-rich Middle-Eastern countries after the 1973 oil price hike. L/LMICs needed the financing both for higher oil prices and their economic development needs. Adverse terms of trade and very high interest rates in the United States to confront domestic inflation exacerbated L/LMIC problems.

The debt crisis resulted in L/LMICs seeking IMF/WB bailouts and the neoliberal policy advice accompanied these loans. One set of loans was referred to by the IMF as the Structural Adjustment Facility (SAF), the main facility among several other facilities they extended and one that resulted in the term "structural adjustment". In the heterodox development economics literature, structural adjustment became synonymous with the implementation of neoliberalism by these two organizations.

This chapter will explore the causes of the emergence of neoliberalism, the specifics of the neoliberal policy package, also referred to as The Washington Consensus, conceptual criticisms of this policy package, the evidence regarding its ability to deliver on its objectives, and why it is so resilient despite its conceptual shortcomings and a large body of evidence pointing to its failure.

The rise of neoliberalism

The macro debate

An intellectual battle was waged by monetarists against the Keynesian case for interventionism in the 1970s. Keynes (2007) in 1936 made a case for fiscal and monetary policy during the Great Depression by showing that the market economy in certain circumstances may not self-correct. Classical economists in the 19th century had argued that wages and prices are flexible and this flexibility corrects for surplus and shortages in all markets including the labor market. This remained the received wisdom until challenged by Keynes. One consequence of a lack of self-correction is excess capacity (high unemployment and low capital capacity utilization) of the kind Keynes witnessed during The Great Depression in the 1930s. Using conventional introductory macroeconomics tools, this meant a flat short-run aggregate supply curve of the kind shown in Figure 8.1.

With a short-run aggregate supply curve of the kind shown in Figure 8.1, policy is likely to be very effective since aggregate demand can increase without resulting in a higher price level that could choke off an increase in GDP.[3] Since Keynes was writing for an economy that was operating far below potential GDP (Y_p), inflation was not a concern. Interventionism gained acceptance and in 1971 even President Nixon, a Republican President, was cited as saying, "I am now a Keynesian in economics" with regards to this acceptance of interventionism.

However, circumstances changed in HICs with the oil shocks in the 1970s. The standard textbook Keynesian framework implicitly assumed a horizontal short-run aggregate supply curve and hence demand management (shifting the AD curve) had output and employment effects only. A recession was associated with excess capacity and hence not with inflation. Yet the oil shocks not only induced a recession but also inflation. This simultaneous existence of inflation and unemployment, a phenomenon referred to as stagflation, called into question the validity of the Keynesian analytical framework.

However, as Harcourt (2009) pointed out, this only happened because the standard Keynesian model being taught in textbooks was depression economics (with a

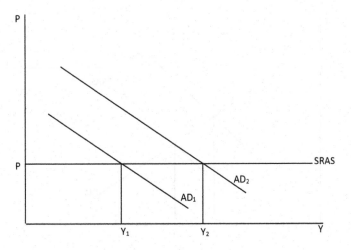

FIGURE 8.1   Keynesian short-run aggregate supply curve

horizontal short-run aggregate supply curve), i.e. a special case of the Keynesian model.[4] The general case is an upward sloping short-run aggregate supply curve with the standard downward aggregate demand curve.[5] In the general case, an increase in unit costs, which higher oil prices represent, results in a shift to the left of the short-run aggregate supply curve as shown in Figure 8.2.

As Figure 8.2 shows, an oil price shock in this modified Keynesian framework explains the simultaneous existence of a recession (decreased output) and inflation (increased price level). However, in the interim period before such clarifications, an opening had been provided to the critics of Keynesian interventionism. The monetarist approach of explaining inflation as a monetary phenomenon (expansive money supply) gained acceptance as did the reaction against interventionism.

Subsequently, new classical macroeconomists proffered a case for policy ineffectiveness. This was premised on markets working well and hence resulting in instantaneous adjustments. With such instantaneous adjustments, the short-run aggregate supply curve is vertical and demand management ineffective, as evident from Figure 8.3. An increase in AD simply results in inflation as implicit in the increase in price level from P_1 to P_2.

The belief in the efficacy of markets goes back to classical economists and hence the term new classical. Just as Malthus had observed, the reality of persistent unemployment and the 2007–2009 financial and economic crises (dubbed The Great Recession) again made evident that unemployment is an economic reality for market economies. Keynesianism regained some ground and the administration in the United States was able to engage in fiscal and monetary stimulus to address The Great Recession. However, the rejection of interventionism has persisted notwithstanding the containment of The Great Recession and preventing it from turning it into a depression based on Keynesian policies. It would seem that the

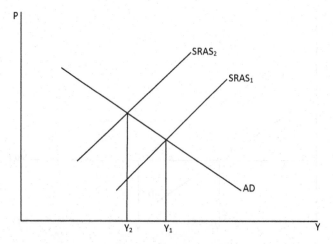

FIGURE 8.2 New Keynesian short-run aggregate supply curve

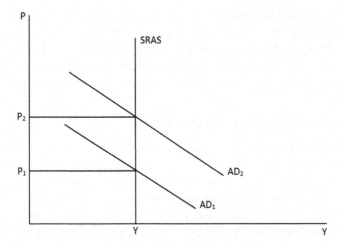

FIGURE 8.3 New classical short-run aggregate supply curve

great macro debate, as with all debates in economics and development economics, is not simply an intellectual debate but one charged with political overtones.

Perceived failure of the radical alternatives and conservative political ascendency

The crisis and later collapse of the socialist bloc and the use by ex-Soviet countries and China of market instruments with varying success discredited Marxist thought and certainly devalued socialism as a viable economic alternative to capitalism. This gave a fillip to market-based economic thinking and discredited the radical political economy of development approach that supported radical structural transformation of LICs to initiate development. It also discredited the Latin American radical dependency school which viewed colonialism and neocolonialism, and the dependency the latter induced, as valid theories of underdevelopment (Chapter 7).

The perceived failure of the left was the larger story. Within this narrative, the macro debate mentioned above paved the way for non-interventionist neoliberalism to take over what, until the 1970s, had become orthodox development economics (Chapter 6). As will be explained later, neoliberalism incorporated monetarism and new classical macroeconomic non-interventionism but is much broader in its policy advocacy. It could be thought of as a political philosophy of small government and free markets married to conservative macroeconomics and neoclassical microeconomics as the analytical frameworks.[6]

The ascendancy of the conservative governments of Margaret Thatcher to power in England (1979–1990), Ronald Regan in the United States (1980–1988) and Helmut Kohl (1982–1998) in Germany created an environment receptive to conservative economic philosophy and powerful sponsors of it. The leadership and orientation of the WB and USAID changed and they became active proponents of the neoliberal doctrine along with the IMF, which until then had drawn heavily on monetary macroeconomics. Most other multilateral and bilateral aid agencies followed suit and promoted this approach and enabled its consolidation.

Conservative critique of developmentalism

The mainstream attack on Keynesian economics had its parallel in development economics. Recall from Chapter 6 that Rosenstein-Rodan made a case for a business proposition of loans from HICs to LICs. LICs would be able to pay back the loans with interest with the additional revenues generated by projects the loans were secured for. Rosenstein-Rodan's case for the loan induced "Big Push" was interpreted to mean a case for aid by conservative economists like Bauer (1972, 1984) who was one of the fiercest critics of aid (Chapter 10).

He argued that aid was ineffective and counter-productive for several reasons including the increased power and patronage of government and how this politicized economic life. In soliciting favors from government, agents were diverted from productive activity as they sought to engage in quick return activities like trading and real estate based on patronage.[7] Aid also created imbalances by strengthening the public sector relative to the private sector and created inequality and urban bias since most of the benefits flowed to the wealthy in urban areas. It was inflationary as it added to purchasing power but not to output due to inefficiency and because it supported wasteful and cost-ineffective prestige projects. Unlike Rosenstein-Rodan's well-functioning business proposition, Bauer foresaw a piling up of the debt burden since the aid generated no revenues. In fact, he saw the rising debt burden as evidence for his position.

He saw in aid all manner of ills even beyond its economic ineffectiveness. For example, he saw it as a promoter of inappropriate western institutions like unions that led to unemployment and universities that contributed nothing. He noted that it was often given to prosperous countries, like the oil rich Middle-Eastern countries or tyrants like Idi Amin of Uganda. This aid to "friendly dictators" was tied, which resulted in more expensive imported inputs and therefore non-competitive exports.

As the debt mounted, calls for debt forgiveness mounted in civil society organizations, but Bauer opposed such calls and argued that debt write-downs would merely create a moral hazard.[8] The crutch that such write-offs and further aid represented would make it more difficult for LICs to learn to stand on their own two feet.

Bauer wondered rhetorically why aid continued if it was so ineffective.[9] His response was that it resulted from a misplaced sense of shame. Even if colonialism did more harm than good, an argument he strongly disputed, current tax-payers who footed the aid bill should not be held responsible for the wrongs their forefathers may have committed. In any case, aid often meant a transfer from the average tax-payers in the west whose per capita incomes were much lower than the corrupt elites that the aid was appropriated by. More importantly, he argued that it continued because it served the interests of political and bureaucratic elites of donor and recipient countries and the overstaffed bilateral and multilateral aid bureaucracies that thrived on aid budgets.

Recall the justification for state intervention by developments in Chapter 6 based on market failures of various kinds, all of which lead to underinvestment because the social profitability of projects exceeds private profitability. Bauer (1972) argued that, despite colonial belief to the contrary, agent (including poor peasants') behavior in LICs conformed to rational profit and welfare maximization. Thus, unleashing private incentives without government restraint was his theory of development.[10]

He challenged Nurkse and structuralist views regarding enclave production and the case against free trade. For evidence, he cited the case of small primary producers in Malaysia and West Africa whom he argued were very successful exporters. In effect, he re-made the case for trickle-down economics based on freely functioning markets and free trade. He also disputed the logic of vicious circles as a theory of underdevelopment since current HICs were not entrapped by them.[11]

Krueger (1974) argued that corruption constituted a theory of underdevelopment and premised her case for non-intervention on this. She coined the term "rent seeking" to represent corrupt activities.[12] The state can create rents by regulations that limit the supply of activities. For example, all activity can be made subject to state licensing, and state functionaries gain leverage based on the ability to dispense permits and licenses. These include import permits, route permits (for buses and vans) and foreign exchange permits. Those who profited from the permits were hence willing to share these rents with those enabling them. Since seeking rents diverted attention from seeking profits from production, neoliberal economists referred to such activities as directly unproductive activities. India became notorious for such regulations in an era (1950s–1980s) that was referred to as the "permit raj" or "license raj".[13] These rents were also used as political instruments in crony capitalist regimes to seek alliances and cement loyalties.

Along with Bauer and Krueger, Lal (1983) synthesized conservative thought to advocate for economic development based on the unhindered market mechanism. He berated the interventionism of the developmentalists and Latin structuralists that he referred to as *dirigisme* (literally "to direct"). Like Bauer, he asserted that there really was nothing institutionally or structurally different about L/LMICs and agents there (households and firms) behaved very much as did agents in more prosperous countries, and so regular neoclassical economics was the relevant economics. He disputed whether there actually was any surplus labor that would make the classical analysis of the labor market more relevant (Lewis in Chapter 6) than neoclassical analysis. Recall from the Lewis model that if there was no surplus labor, trickle down would take place with economic growth and job creation since wages would rise with the increased demand for labor.

He made a case for markets and against intervention by drawing on Hayek (1994), who argued that the decentralized free market system is inherently more efficient because it can automatically process and take advantage of the special local information related to time and place. Finally, he drew on the work of public choice theorists like Buchanan and Tullock (1962) and argued that "government failure" was more prevalent and pernicious than "market failure".

Thus just as Keynesian thought and developmentalism, as a manifestation of interventionist thinking in a development context, emerged by showing there was market failure, the theoretical plank of neoliberalism relied on government failure. Inefficiency, mismanagement and corruption represented the theory of underdevelopment and the WB/IMF prescriptions discussed below a theory of development.

Neoliberal critique of developmentalist prescriptions

Neoclassical economists attacked import substitution industrialization (ISI) on theoretical and empirical grounds in the 1970s. Two sets of work which became particularly noted for these critiques were Little, Scitovsky and Scott (1970) and Krueger (1978, 1983). The former were commissioned by the OECD to explore the outcome of the strategy adopted by the key countries based on developmentalist/structuralist prescriptions. The project was conceived in 1965 and it drew on six volumes representing seven country studies including Argentina (based on existing material) and Brazil, India, Mexico, Pakistan, Philippines and Taiwan (new material). These volumes provided empirical evidence to argue that developmentalist/structuralist prescriptions, particularly those associated with protectionism, led to inefficiency, welfare losses and corruption, and were therefore an economic dead end.

Recall that Figure 7.3 made the developmentalist/structuralist case for protection. Figure 7.3 is reproduced in this chapter as Figure 8.4 to demonstrate the neoliberal critique of protectionism.[14]

As Figure 8.4 shows, protection results in a rise in domestic price from P_w to P_d. This results in the loss of consumer surplus that is the sum of spaces A, B, C and D. Space A is diverted to producers as producer surplus and space C is diverted to the government as tariff revenue. However, spaces B and D are lost to society since no one gets them and thus these are referred to as distortion-induced deadweight losses of protection.[15] Recall that if equal protection was secured with a quota, the quota rent (space C) would accrue to an importer and this might be awarded as patronage or based on a kick-back to bureaucrats. Further, the producer surplus represented by space A would exacerbate income inequality.

Other producers who might want to use this product as an input would now become less competitive since they are buying it at more than the world price and so exports might suffer. Again, as resources move to the now more profitable ISI industries, costs confronted by the export sector competing for those resources would rise.

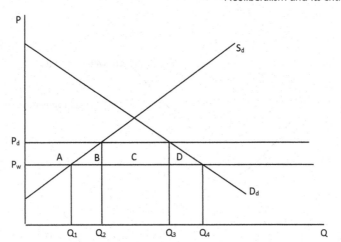

FIGURE 8.4 Welfare losses from protection

If protection is based on an overvalued exchange rate as a protective tool rather than a tariff or quota, this would encourage imports but make exports more expensive. It would also encourage capital flight since exporters would have an incentive to keep their hard currencies abroad rather than turn them over to the Central Bank domestically at a lower rate than is available on the secondary market. All these rational profit-maximizing responses would result in balance of payment problems and possibly a foreign exchange crisis and debt crises if governments have to borrow to meet import needs.

Leibenstein (1966) coined the term X-inefficiency that was said to apply to the outcome of protection. Protection generally enabled domestic industrial concentration and for firms to make a profit even if costs were high. Over time the lack of competition results in the average cost shifting up and that gap between protection-induced average costs and ones that would prevail in a competitive market are the measure of X-inefficiency, as shown in Figure 8.5.

Neoliberal economists coined the concept of effective protection, which estimates net protection after taking into account the protection to the final good and also the inputs. For example, a high tariff on inputs could negate the protective impact of a tariff on the final product. They found that the tariff structure in LICs was often not rational and protection on the input was often greater than to the output, resulting in negative effective protection.

This and other insights can be demonstrated by using the concept of value added (VA). VA is defined as value created by factors of production and this is ascertained by subtracting the value of the intermediate inputs from total revenue (VA = PQ – Intermediate inputs). If there is only protection on the final good, PQ would rise (as P rose) and domestic VA could be higher in principle.

One way of measuring the effective protection rate (EPR) is by estimating the extent to which VA in domestic prices (DVA) is able to exceed VA in world

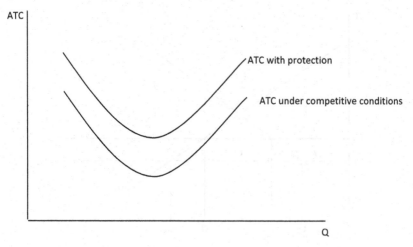

FIGURE 8.5 Protection induced X-inefficiency

prices, world value added (WVA), due to protection, and so EPR is defined as $((DVA - WVA)/WVA) \times 100$. If there is no protection then domestic and world prices should more or less be identical, allowing for transportation cost, and EPR is zero. However, EPR is positive if there is a larger tariff on the final output than on the intermediate inputs. For any given tariff on the final good, the EPR declines for a rise in tariff on the intermediate goods since DVA falls. In fact, a higher tariff on the intermediate good relative to the final good could result in a negative WVA and hence negative EPR. However, neoliberal economists were more concerned with using the concept of EPR to demonstrate inefficiency. DVA and hence EPR could be negative due to inefficiency for example due to the high priced inputs of state-owned enterprises (SOEs).[16]

Another form of inefficiency is allocative and distortions result because EPRs vary by commodity or sector. Thus capital and intermediate goods could be systematically discriminated against relative to final goods and the agricultural sector relative to the manufacturing sector. If tariffs were needed to raise revenue, the neoliberal prescription is for a uniform tariff since that would avoid allocative inefficiency.

Protection could also have unintended consequences. For example, tariffs on luxuries to prevent their import could induce the domestic production of luxury goods and distort the domestic production and consumption patterns. Also, tariffs are normally introduced sequentially starting with consumer goods which are easier to produce domestically. However, this could result in vested interests against domestic production of capital and intermediate goods because producers of consumer goods would rather import the better quality more cheaply from abroad hence making it more difficult to diversify the economy.

Quality and price improve with the time it takes domestic producers to adopt, understand and suitably adapt technology. While protection is justified based on protecting infant industries, neoliberal economists argued that the infants refused to grow up since assured profits are better than facing competition.

Other Little, Skitovsky and Scott's findings were that industrialization had been over-encouraged relative to agriculture, that exports had been discouraged and that inequality had been exacerbated. They contended that there was not enough empirical evidence on positive external economies to justify a special role for industry and in any case the negative environmental externalities were being ignored. Overall they concluded that ISI was harmful since high-cost, inefficient firms, in many cases public enterprises, were being supported with an overvalued exchange rate which was to the detriment of primary exports and agriculture.

The fact that agriculture was neglected with the terms of trade turned against it induced rural to urban migration which defied the carrying capacity of urban municipalities. Mass migration was also induced by administered urban wages that were more than two or three times greater than rural incomes. In addition, higher wages were supplemented by social legislation that improved job security and working conditions. Hence urban population growth rates were more twice the total population growth rates. Unemployment was exacerbated by systematically getting prices wrong. Thus, an overvalued exchange rate, duty free capital goods imports, subsidized credit, tied-aid and accelerated depreciation all created the incentive to utilize capital-intensive techniques.

Balance of payment problems were induced by imports of intermediate and capital goods, but dealing with this deficit created perverse incentives. The practice of allocating scarce foreign exchange based on each firm's existing capacity created the perverse incentive of adding to capacity. This practice resulted in the underutilization of capacity since materials and components could not be procured due to foreign exchange scarcity. As pointed out earlier, another perverse incentive created was inducing domestic luxury goods production since protection enhanced incentives for local production. The most destructive perverse incentive was the rent seeking associated with foreign exchange scarcity and trading since this activity provided higher returns than enterprise; a misallocation of scarce entrepreneurial talent.

Another problem was the scale and range of administrative controls that proliferated in developmentalist states, as discussed above by Krueger. These various interventions included differential taxes, tax holidays, accelerated depreciation, exemptions, rationing, quotas, price controls, licensing, credit guarantees, subsidized credit, duty free imports and multiple exchange rates. The report concluded that such ponderous controls also produced industries encumbered by sub-optimal firms and high costs. Just as Bauer had noted earlier, this scale of public intervention in economic life resulted in inefficiency and corruption. As explained above, for many goods, inefficiency caused the VA calculated in world prices to be negative.

In the OECD country studies led by Anne Krueger and Jagdish Bhagwati, ISI and export promotion (EP) were posited as alternative trade and development strategies. EP was declared as preferable since it was associated with more rapid economic growth, unskilled labor intensity and employment. As also noted by the OECD country studies, ISI resulted in periodic balance of payment crises due to the need to import raw materials, intermediate and capital goods. Many of these economies rapidly proceeded through the easy phase of ISI, achieving economies of scale by producing consumer goods for relatively poor consumers. But after this, they confronted small market sizes. Overall these economies experienced slower growth rates because capital-output ratios increased incrementally and growth decreased. Also controls proliferated and became more complex and harmful. Regulating production through licensing meant that there was no market weeding of the less efficient firms or privileging of the more efficient ones. By contrast, firms in an EP strategy faced no such constraint. Scale could also be easily achieved since they were not confined to the domestic market and efficiency was induced by the need to compete in the global market.

The Washington Consensus as an alternative to developmentalism

This section summarizes the structural adjustment policy package that followed based on the critiques in the section above. Another term used for the policy package was The Washington Consensus and it was coined by Williamson (1990, 2008), who synthesized the various elements of the package.[17] The term was derived from the powerful role of the US Treasury Department in the governance of the IMF/WB, the two organizations based in Washington which implemented this consensus. The United States has about 17 percent of the IMF votes and hence veto power because 85 percent of votes are needed for decisions by the IMF Board. Also, by convention, the President of the WB is a US national.[18] Moving from ISI to export promotion became a key aspect of the Consensus, and structural adjustment is designed to facilitate this and economic openness in general.

Based on the critique of ISI explained above, the case for EP as an alternative trade and industrialization strategy was established as part of a case for economic openness. The argument is that only an open economy with low import restraints can truly be successful. Recall that high import restrictions are a handicap for export success both because inputs for local production are more expensive and because it promotes a culture of non-competitive production.

The case for EP is premised on the theory of comparative advantage. Since countries are concentrating on the goods in which they have a comparative advantage, there is a built-in advantage and so this is not only consistent with economic logic but also common sense. EP induces efficiency, unlike ISI, because in order to succeed, they have to overcome the fierce competition from producers in other L/LMICs.

Several other benefits would accompany EP including the benefits of economies of scale by having access to the world market, and this also solves the problem for small countries with a small domestic market. Since L/LMICs logically have a comparative advantage in goods that are labor intensive, this would create more employment opportunities. Policy transparency would accompany EP because the costs of ISI distortions would be apparent and resisted by exporters with a stake in the new trade regime. EP is also a mechanism for technological learning and upgrading since that is necessary in order to break into export markets. Finally, EP would avoid all the negative effects of ISI identified above.

The structural reforms that are part of the IMF agenda include macro-management/stabilization and this requires addressing inflation and the fiscal and balance of payment deficits (twin deficits). The money supply is expected to be reined in to contain inflation and fiscal stringency (also euphemistically referred to as fiscal consolidation) is expected to result in primary budget surpluses such that government expenditures are less than tax revenue when these are calculated at full employment GDP.

The precise policies include raising taxes and cutting government expenditures including subsidies. The subsidy cuts have often fallen on food, fertilizer, fuel and utilities. The social sector expenditures (health, education) have been the soft targets since there is resistance to cuts in military expenditures and no give on interest payments. The public sector is subject to wage freezes and employment cuts. It is for this reason that these reforms that are conditional on getting loans are referred to as austerity conditions.

Reforms to eliminate the balance of payment deficits include liberalizing the exchange rate, often entailing a large devaluation to encourage exports, and promoting openness. The openness agenda includes cutting tariffs and eliminating quotas and export subsidies. Removing restrictions on capital flows in the context of capital market liberalizations is encouraged.

The WB oversees the structural and sectoral reforms and these are expected to deliver long-term growth. The financial sector is expected to be liberalized and this includes interest rate liberalization in the context of removing factor price distortions. Other capital subsidies are also expected to be removed. Technical advice is provided for institutional reforms including governance broadly and more specifically reforms such as in accounting and prudential regulations for the financial sector.

The labor market is expected to be liberalized and this entails greater flexibility by the removal of institutional protections (referred to as labor market rigidities). Thus, the idea is to make hiring and firing easier and have remuneration based on market conditions. Similarly, the product market is expected to be liberalized by removing price controls and subsidies i.e. getting prices right.

Industry is deregulated to unleash the productive potential of the private sector by getting the government out of the way. Privatization and the enforcement of property rights are encouraged. SOEs are viewed as inefficient and a drain on the budget and so privatization would also help contain the budget deficit, an example of fortuitous cross-conditionality. Opening up to FDI for technology, management and marketing skills by removing unhelpful regulations would also facilitate economic growth.

As earlier mentioned, the WB leads sectoral reforms that apply to education, health, water supply, sanitation and other social sector delivery. The thrust of the reforms is a larger private sector role as the state is rolled back. The WB has for example suggested user charges to recover expenses and gone as far as encouraging subsidies for the private sector (for-profit) schools.

This and the prior section have made a case for neoliberalism and it is one that most economists find persuasive. Even harsh critics like Taylor (1997, p. 7), who rejects the package as a whole, concede there are elements of the package, such as containing the twin deficits, introduction of prudential regulations on financial institutions, containing massive distortions in key macro prices such as the interest and exchange rates, or the terms of trade between industry and agriculture, that the BWIs should get credit for. Others are less persuaded for reasons identified below.

Criticisms of neoliberal concepts and policy package[19]

This section follows the pattern of the last section and starts with a rejoinder to the ideas expressed by conservative development economists. It then turns to the broader criticisms of the various elements of the neoliberal policy package and ends with a review of the evidence.

Bauer's views on agent behavior were shaped by his observations and field research in Malaysia and West Africa. Critics charged that this was a very limited sample and that in any case the terms of trade soon moved against West African primary exports, and the countries that were seemingly on the road to prosperity when he wrote ran into trouble soon after.

His focus in Malaysia was also on plantations. However, critics point out that the real Malaysian development story is one of diversification and moving up the value chain and this represented a very interventionist model of development (Chapter 9) rather than a hands-off free market approach. Ghana had similar initial conditions and a similarly rich resource base, but followed a different model and did much more poorly by comparison (Hill, 1986).

Evidence on corruption is difficult to come by due to the illegal nature of the activity, but there are nonetheless alternative views to Krueger's on corruption as a theory of underdevelopment. For example, Khan and Blankenburg (2009) distinguish between "learning rents" and "redistributive rents" and success in industrial policy (Chapter 9) depends on the specific internal political economy that conditions the state's ability to manage rents to ensure learning and prevent mere acquisition.

Similarly a review of case studies of catch-up growth in Japan, Korea and Taiwan makes evident that local newspapers reported high levels of corruption. Chang (2006) has convincingly documented this point as has Rodrik (1994, pp. 42–47), who pointed out that corruption was a noted problem in all these countries.

In fact, it appears that anti-corruption drives are endogenous in that they succeed rather than precede catch-up growth.

Lal's critics charge that most of his arguments, such as the contention that government failure is worse than market failure, are simply assertions. His evidence on the lack of surplus labor in L/LMICs is contested. For example, Rosenzweig and Foster (2010) estimated surplus labor in Indian agriculture of over 20 percent for farm sizes of 20 acres.

The neoliberal policy package has been critiqued both theoretically and empirically. In some ways, neoliberalism as propounded by the WB and IMF is a moving target since they have accommodated critics over the years, but the core market-driven principles remain unchanged. There has been a rethink on several issues at the IMF and these will be flagged.

Recall that many of the conditionalities identified above target the aggregate demand based on the presumption that inflation is a demand-driven phenomenon. Critics argue that it is possible that at times the inflation is caused by a supply shock (refer to Figure 8.2). In such cases, cuts in aggregate demand when the economy is already headed for a recession if not in one, will only exacerbate the situation.

Combating moderate levels of inflation, as prioritized by the IMF, is empirically contested. For example Barro (1997) and Bruno and Easterly (1998) showed that inflation negatively impacts economic growth beyond a threshold they defined as high as 40 percent. Chang (2006) contends that keeping interest rates low with easy monetary policy can stimulate investment and that inflation rates were fairly high in Korea during their catch-up growth stage.

In any case, critics argue that high inflation could result from structural factors (Chapter 7) which cause the short-run aggregate supply curve to be very steep. In such a situation, investments that would reduce the bottlenecks and rigidities and rotate the short-run aggregate supply curve would be the more appropriate solution, as shown in Figure 8.6b.

Figure 8.6a shows a shift of aggregate demand to the left to contain inflation following neoliberal prescriptions. While theoretically this is likely to be a success, the deflation is accompanied by unemployment. Figure 8.6b shows the short-run aggregate supply curve rotating to the right following structuralist prescriptions, which contains inflation but also boosts GDP (win-win). The investments required to rotate the short-run aggregate supply curve include investments in social and physical infrastructure to remove bottlenecks and raise productivity.

Recall that the structuralists believed that much inflation in L/LMICs results from social group conflict with the state accommodating competing claims. Political solutions that provide a legitimate mechanism for the resolution of such claims are the answer; purely economic solutions are not enough.

The obsession with cutting aggregate demand has been taken to ridiculous extremes according to some critics. During the East Asia contagion of 1997, Thailand had a fiscal surplus and the problem was a shortfall in aggregate demand. Even so, the IMF recommended fiscal austerity and this resulted in an unnecessary recession.

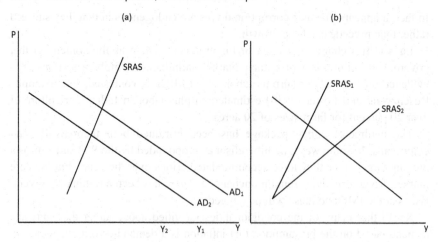

FIGURES 8.6a and b   Neoliberal and structural solutions for inflation

Even if fiscal prudence as suggested by neoliberals is a sensible policy, heterodox economists point out that the emphasis on an annual primary surplus is bad economics. The budget balancing should be over the business cycle, rather than annual, because a deficit may be called for in a downturn to stimulate the economy.

Heterodox critics argue that just as inflation is often misdiagnosed, so too is the balance of payment deficit. If aggregate demand is very import intensive, as is often the case for L/LMICs, a balance of payments crisis will result well before the economy reaches full employment. The IMF's solution is once again to cut aggregate demand, but this would simply increase excess capacity. The real issue in this case is import inelasticity of demand and the need to diversify the economy and change the import structure.

Another IMF prescription to solve the balance of payment problem is to require a devaluation of the currency. The theory is that devaluing will raise exports and restrict imports. However, devaluation results in an increase in the costs of production in local currency terms, particularly if the import intensity of production is high, and so the short-run aggregate supply curve will shift back causing stagflation, as in Figure 8.2

There is also a danger of getting caught in a devaluation-inflation-devaluation spiral, as happened in the 1970s in Latin American economies. This then is one example of the mutual inconsistency of the various elements of the neoliberal reform package i.e. devaluation is at odds with price stability. Also, since the devaluation causes the foreign currency to become more expensive in local currency terms, the foreign debt burden increases in local currency terms and so this is at odds with the conditionality regarding reducing the debt burden.

Whether or not devaluation reduces the trade deficit depends on the price elasticity of exports relative to imports. Exports from L/LMICs depend on a number of factors other than prices. Most important among these factors are income growth in HICs, trade concessions based on political alliances, trade networking via value chains, bilateral trade agreements, quality and competition from rival exporters. Thus exports are likely to be price inelastic. Meanwhile, imports are generally price inelastic because of the inelastic demand for intermediate and capital goods.

While devaluation improving the balance of trade is theoretically questionable, the inflation and unemployment that result from it certainly add to the austerity of the neoliberal package. Consumables get exported due to the changed incentives (export orientation) causing food inflation that disproportionally impacts the poor compared to the rich, since food expenditure is a larger share of their budgets.[20]

Removal of capital controls was another conditionality of the IMF. Prior to the Asian Contagion, it was very aggressively pushing this Wall Street agenda and reports indicate that the IMF Board had come close to agreeing to changes in the IMF Articles of Agreement to formally include capital market liberalization on the IMF agenda.[21] However, even mainstream economists expressed reservations regarding this policy and subsequently internal IMF research expressed only qualified support for capital market liberalizations, as indicated above.

The neoliberal support for capital market liberalization is that allocation of capital by markets is more efficient as funds are drawn to activities with the highest economic returns. Liberalization would also provide additional needed capital and raise productivity and growth via higher investment and access to foreign technology. It would provide funds for government expenditure via the sale of bonds abroad. Finally, it would induce countries to reduce inflation and become more transparent and accountable to draw and retain private capital flows.

Heterodox economists like Grabel (2003) argued that since L/LMIC capital markets are shallow and narrow, they can get overwhelmed and asset bubbles (such as in financial or real estate) can be created with capital inflows. These bubbles then burst with devastating consequences when the funds leave in herd-like movements, as happened during the East Asian Contagion. Large inflows can cause rapid currency appreciation, resulting in balance of payment problems. Speculative financial flows result in mismatches creating financial fragility. There is a maturity mismatch between long-term loans (assets) and short-term borrowing (liabilities). There is also a location mismatch because country liabilities are in foreign currency but earnings are in local currency

Some countries including Chile, Columbia and Brazil have used capital controls with positive outcomes. The specific control measures include registration requirement, financial investment restrictions, local borrowing surcharge, reserve requirements, time limits on retaining locally bought financial assets to reduce speculation, size limits, quantity limits on outflows and exit taxes.

Perhaps the liberalization that the IMF and WB most aggressively promote pertains to trade, and the economic justification for this policy was discussed above. Heterodox economists argue that their insistence on premature trade liberalization has resulted in deindustrialization. It also causes the tax base to shrink since there are fewer industrialists generating income. Lower tariffs mean a lower tax collection and this also violates the fiscal balance conditionality. Taxes on imports are much easier to collect than direct taxes when tax administrations are not mature. Again, this indicates the mutual inconsistency of the neoliberal package.

The export promotion component of the openness agenda could also lead to what Cline (1982) termed "the fallacy of composition". His simulation suggested that if export growth from L/LMICs followed en masse the East Asian model brand of export promotion, the market penetration of the HICs would exceed a critical level and hence promote protectionism. He revisited this issue in (2008) based on 25 years of experience and concluded that L/LMICs' manufactured exports had resulted in an unsustainable US trade deficit and hence the fallacy of composition problem could arise.[22] Other problems are that if merchandise exports are a constant share of the HIC market, L/LMICs are pitted against each other in a zero-sum game. In addition, the market flooded with labor-intensive manufactured exports would hurt the terms of trade of L/LMICs.

Financial sector liberalization includes interest rate liberalization as one of the key components of structural adjustment packages. The economic justification is that low interest rates amount to financial repression and discourage saving. Keynesian theory suggests income as the main determinant of saving and that interest merely determines in part the allocation of that saving among financial assets. The negative aspect of interest rate liberalization is that it promotes a rentier rather than a productive society. It also benefits the upper income groups that can purchase financial assets and hence enhances inequality. Small businesses get marginalized due to the higher cost of capital once again hurting production and tax revenue.

During the 1980s, many L/LMICs experienced ballooning domestic debts which resulted partly due to this interest rate liberalization policy. Instead of borrowing at say 6 percent, governments were told to liberalize the interest rate and then borrow from the open market at close to 20 percent. For many L/LMICs, interest payments on domestic and foreign debt are now the largest part of annual current expenditures. Once again, interest payments on this debt are an important cause of the deficit that the IMF subsequently wants to cut indicating yet again the mutual inconsistency of the neoliberal reform package.

Financial repression was one mechanism to secure income from rich tax-evading savers although admittedly it would be preferable to improve tax administration to tax income and wealth directly. Also, the implicit suggestion undergirding interest rate liberalization is that there is a market interest rate and liberalization would enable the market to find the optimal interest rate. However, this impression is fictitious since Central Banks are a big player in capital markets in all countries and they take macroeconomic and exchange rate considerations into account when influencing the interest rate.

The IMF and WB promote market ideology and hence assume without qualification that privatization of all SOEs and even utilities like municipal water supply would be beneficial. The economic logic is that agents pursuing private incentives will be more efficient than civil servants on a salary and that this will therefore result in a better use of resources and hence also serve the public interest. Heterodox economists view competition and good management as more important than ownership per se. Management, even in private corporations, is divorced from ownership and the issue of making managers (as agents) work in the interests of the principal (owners) rather than themselves therefore applies even in the private sector.

The danger of privatizing sectors like banking, if the market size is small, is that market concentration would increase and that would not be in the public interest. Privatization of social services such as water or sanitation, particularly if it leads to high market concentration, is even more fraught since it might undermine the provision of basic human needs. Finally, even if the case for privatization is established, the privatization process requires able and honest administration or the rich loot assets and become oligarchs, as happened in Russia. Privatization also requires a competent regulatory authority if market concentration is an issue and this too is a tall order in L/LMICs.

Often public sector reforms rather than privatization may be preferable. For example, public enterprises often do not succeed because they are put in an impossible situation such as when the price of the final good is suppressed as a form of indirect public subsidy because it is a wage good. In this case, a direct subsidy to the target population rather than using a blanket subsidy that goes to all income groups, and in the process distorts enterprise incentives, would be called for reform.

Chang and Singh (1993) reviewed the evidence and found privatization per se did not result in higher efficiency. Vickers and Yarrow (1991, pp. 116–117) reviewed the evidence and argued that what ultimately matters in product market privatization is the ability to ensure competition rather than ownership per se i.e. the public sector is not inherently less efficient.[23] For natural monopolies what counts is not ownership per se but the state's ability to regulate and ensure financial discipline. One could argue that privatization might be preferable under circumstances where the ability to ensure competition and to effectively regulate is limited.

In terms of the broader political economy of the neoliberal reform package, heterodox economists argue that wage cuts or freezes, deregulation of product, labor and capital markets, privatization, and capital market and trade liberalizations disproportionately benefit MNCs. The upshot is that local industry is unable to compete and the deindustrialization generates further unemployment beyond that created by the austerity measures. In addition to unemployment, the less well-off are made worse off due to cuts in social sector expenditures and subsidies, food inflation and wage repression. Thus an intensification of poverty and social inequality are the expected outcomes of neoliberal reforms.

The IMF is also charged by developing countries for not being as honest a broker in debt negotiations as it should be. It has been unwilling to talk to debtor countries until commercial banks have been satisfied that there is a serious effort/ intent in meeting arrears and obligations. Argentina wanted bondholders to accept a 75–80 percent debt discount and because it owed over $100 billion, it had clout. However, it desperately needed a new IMF package to remain solvent, but this assistance was made conditional on it settling with private debtors first. The settlement was reached in December 2005 and Argentina agreed to pay 30 cents to a $, a 70 percent discount, less than it was holding out for.[24] The IMF has similarly conditioned loans to L/LMICs on dispute resolution of these countries with MNCs.

The second generation of IMF and WB reforms pertained to "good governance". This included management, accountability and transparency. Critics charged that these institutions do not practice what they preach since there was little transparency in the reforms agreed to in the structural adjustment process. In response to these criticisms, the IMF letter of intent is now posted on the IMF website and the reforms are said to be "home grown". However, an IMF staff member often has an office in The Ministry of Finance of the borrowing country and the reforms that are said to be home grown are viewed as a form of self-policing. These reforms agreed to have little popular support and are normally imposed on the populace after secret negotiations between the IMF and WB teams and a team of local technocrats.

Grabel (2011) has documented that the IMF and WB staff and local technocrats share the same world view.[25] This is because they are often ex-IMF or WB staffers or on leave from these organizations. They have been trained in the same graduate schools and are concerned with networking to secure lucrative consulting contracts or jobs. As suggested by the public choice literature, this is a case where the individual rather than the public interest may be served.

The neoliberal reform packages have produced two major kinds of public responses. On a popular level, riots have occurred in numerous countries following austerity measures including in Egypt, Ecuador, Ghana, Nigeria, Peru, Brazil, Venezuela and numerous other countries. The public response in several L/LMICs like Argentina, Brazil, Nigeria and Pakistan was to retire their IMF obligations and build up foreign currency reserves as a defense mechanism in case of future balance of payment difficulties.

This severely impacted IMF revenues and to regain solvency it had to sell gold reserves and engage in massive staff lay-offs. Morale was so low that a quarter of the staff responded to the voluntary retirement package, about twice the 380 staff member target contemplated by senior management. As mentioned above, the global financial and economic crisis of 2007–2009 gave the IMF a new lease on life as it was drawn on by the G-7/G-20 to play a bigger role in crisis resolution, including in Europe, and allocated the funds so that its portfolio size increased. Better public relations, with first an ex-socialist and then with a woman as Managing Director, and the stated willingness to be more flexible on conditionality like capital controls and inflation, also helped.

Evidence on structural adjustment[26]

The goal when gathering evidence is to get the best possible counter-factual i.e. what would have happened if the neoliberal reform package had not been implemented. There is no perfect counter-factual since history cannot be replayed. Several techniques have been utilized over the years to identify the impact of structural adjustment reforms. One method has been to compare how countries did relative to the targets set for them using time series analysis. One problem is that much could have changed internally and externally that could affect the performance variables like growth, fiscal deficit and balance of payment deficits. Also, time series analysis requires many observations and this condition is so far not satisfied.

An alternative form of times series analysis is using computable general equilibrium models.[27] These are comprehensive models that try to control for initial conditions and build in policy and policy response functions to simulate what policy would have been without the reform program and what the policy impacts would be with and without reforms. These models are very intensive in the information needed and the solutions are very sensitive to assumptions made. Other things are held constant and it is presumed that a new equilibrium will be attained, but it might not be due to system shocks or there might be multiple equilibriums.

Another method is to engage in "with and without" cross-country econometrics. A control group of countries that did not undergo structural adjustment is identified to compare with otherwise similar countries, particularly in terms of initial conditions, that did undergo structural adjustment. The problem is that if the countries did not undertake structural reforms, then by definition they are different from the countries that did in the most important ways. Also cross-country analysis assumes countries as a unit of observation and hence that all countries in the sample are structurally similar, which is clearly not the case.

Heterodox economists prefer the use of in-depth case studies (inductive method) or alternatively the descriptive method (Chapter 1). The latter entails collecting information regarding the state of the economy over the structural adjustment compared to earlier periods. If there is no improvement, or if conditions get worse, they argue that as a minimum structural adjustment did not improve matters or worsened conditions and the burden of proving otherwise is on neoliberal economists. In such circumstances, neoliberal economists have often argued that the reason for conditions not improving or even worsening is that the countries in question did not properly implement the reform package. In other words, they either did not implement all the conditions or did not do so fully or gave up too soon. Another defense, also hard to prove, is that things would have been even worse without the structural adjustment.

In reporting on the evidence in the rest of this section, evidence on the key neoliberal hypothesis of the association of economic openness, particularly trade liberalization, with economic growth is first explored. Following that, the overall impact of structural adjustment on economic growth is explored by drawing on studies that used the descriptive, inductive (case study), deductive (econometric studies) method and also on organizational analysis of the implementing agencies.

Based on deductive methods, trade economists accumulated evidence to suggest that the larger exports are as a share of GDP, the greater is productivity growth and hence economic growth. The neoliberal case for the association of productivity growth and export growth was explained earlier in this chapter. Based on this theoretical framework several authors found support for export promotion as an economic growth strategy in the 1980s and 1990s.[28] However these findings were contested by other economists using the same method and data bases.[29]

The method entailed estimating a production function and including some aggregate trade variable like the ratio of exports as a percent of GDP (X/GDP) as an explanatory variable. Rodriguez and Rodrik (1999) challenged the method arguing that X/GDP did not measure policy, but rather an outcome. They also showed that there was little systematic association between a reduction of tariff and non-tariff barriers (policy variables) in L/LMICs and growth. More recent research has taken into account this critique and the results do not support economic openness per se as a strategy.

Eicher and Kuenzel (2016) constructed measures of export diversity for 85 countries between 1965 and 2009. Along with export diversity they tested a number of other possible determinants of economic growth including economic openness. Their findings showed that the greater the reliance on primary exports, the greater the growth impact there is from export diversification. The impact of such diversification tapers down with country income levels i.e. there are diminishing returns to such diversification.[30] They also found that this positive association of export diversification and economic growth was not mediated via economic openness.

A specific element of a broad approach like structural adjustment can be tested much more easily than a whole approach with its complex mix of elements like openness, deregulation, liberalization and privatization. Nonetheless, it is possible to document what happened over the period economies were subject to structural adjustment. Certainly, this does not constitute causality and matters could have been even worse without the structural adjustment. However, as mentioned earlier, it does lay the burden of proof of the economic benefits of structural adjustment on neoliberal advocates.

Table 8.1 covers three periods for five regional country groupings. The decades of the 1960s and 1970s are often referred to as the ISI period when the policy prescriptions of the developmentalists and structuralists were predominant. By contrast, the following two decades are viewed as the period of global integration and intense structural adjustment.

Kentikelenis, Stubbs and King (2016) argued that prior to the 1980s, consistent with its founding Articles of Agreement, the IMF approach was premised on economic neutrality such that there were no explicit attempts to use policy conditionality to structurally reform L/LMIC economies. However, this changed in the 1980s with the spreading sway of neoliberal economic philosophy in HICs,

TABLE 8.1 Comparing annual average growth rates in the ISI and structural adjustment periods

Region	GDP (Constant 2010 US$)			PCGDP (Constant 2010 US$)		
	1960– 1980	1981– 1999	2000– 2015	1960– 1980	1981– 1999	2000– 2015
South Asia (SA)	3.7	5.4	6.7	1.4	3.2	5.1
Middle East & North Africa (MENA)	5.5	3.6	3.6	2.7	1.0	1.0
Latin America & the Caribbean (LAC)	5.8	2.4	2.9	3.1	0.5	1.6
East Asia & Pacific (EAP)	5.6	7.8	8.5	3.4	6.2	7.7
Sub-Saharan Africa	4.3	1.7	5.1	1.6	−1.1	2.4

Source: World Development Indicators, version updated 6/6/2017.
Note: Selections are identified as IBRD (World Bank) and International Development Agency (IDA) countries in the Database. Data for MENA in the first period starts in 1967 and in the last period ends in 2014.

as explained above, and the conditionality was central to implementing this ideology.

Structural adjustment conditionality of the resuscitated IMF continued in the third period. This period was also marked by a commodity boom and then the aftermath of the 2007–2009 financial and economic crises in HICs, with shock waves that spread out to L/LMICs in an increasingly globalized world. As mentioned above, many L/LMICs built up defensive foreign exchange reserves to prevent an IMF overhaul of their economies that countries started to consider as destructive. Even so, many other L/LMICs succumbed when confronted with foreign exchange crises and subsequently had to accept austerity conditions. Even HICs like Ireland, Portugal, Spain and Greece who were worst impacted by the financial and economic crises were subject to IMF economic supervision and austerity conditions.

The GDP and PCGDP growth rates for the three periods and five regional country groupings are reported in Table 8.1. Data for the LIC category for the first period are not available in the WDI data base and hence there is no reporting of data by income level in Table 8.1. The regional groupings include MICs because several current MICs were likely to be LICs or LMICs in the first period. For the Middle-Eastern and North African Region, Israel and the oil rich Gulf States are excluded. However, this exclusion only marginally altered the averages and

TABLE 8.2 List of countries in the regional country groupings

Regional country grouping	Countries
South Asia	Afghanistan, Bangladesh, Bhutan, India, Maldives, Nepal, Pakistan, Sri Lanka.
Middle East & North Africa	Algeria, Djibouti, Egypt, Iran, Iraq, Jordan, Lebanon, Libya, Morocco, Syria, Tunisia, United Arab Republic, West Bank and Gaza, Yemen.
Latin America & the Caribbean	Argentina, Belize, Bolivia, Brazil, Columbia, Costa Rica, Cuba, Dominica, Dominican Republic, Ecuador, El Salvador, Grenada, Guatemala, Guyana, Haiti, Honduras, Jamaica, Mexico, Nicaragua, Panama, Paraguay, Peru, St. Lucia, St. Vincent and the Grenadines, Suriname, Venezuela.
East Asia and the Pacific	Cambodia, China, Indonesia, Korea, Lao PDR, Malaysia, Mongolia, Myanmar, Pacific Islands, Papua New Guinea, Philippines, Singapore, Timor-Leste, Thailand, Vietnam.
Sub-Saharan Africa	Angola, Benin, Botswana, Burkina Faso, Burundi, Cameroon, Capo Verde, Central African Republic, Chad, Camaros, Cote d'Ivoire, Congo, Republic, Congo, Republic Democratic, Eritrea, Equatorial Guinea, Ethiopia, Gabon, Gambia, Ghana, Guinea, Guinea Bissau, Kenya, Lesotho, Liberia, Madagascar, Malawi, Mali, Mauritania, Mauritius, Mozambique, Namibia, Niger, Nigeria, Rwanda, Sao Tope and Principe, Senegal, Seychelles, Sierra Lone, Somalia, South Africa, South Sudan, Sudan, Swaziland, Tanzania, Togo, Uganda, Zambia, Zimbabwe.

Source: World Development Indicators, version updated 6/6/2017.
Note: As in Table 8.1.

did not alter the trend over time. The various countries included in the regional country groupings are reported in Table 8.2.

The different regions and country groupings represented in Table 8.1 were subject to different levels of structural adjustment discipline and rated differently by the IMF in terms of conditionality implementation. While some broad generalizations are attempted, it is with the caveat that even cursory exploration of country case studies indicates that broad generalizations are extremely difficult to make because of differences even within regions across countries (Chapter 3).

The East Asia and Pacific region has been developmentalist (Chapter 9) and the numbers show an impressive and linear increase in the growth rates over the three periods. The catch-up growth of the Newly Industrialized Countries (NICs) of East Asia including Korea and Singapore dominated the numbers in the first period, that of the South East Asian Countries in the second period and China in the third period.

South Asia shows the same linear trend as the East Asia and Pacific region, though the numbers are not as impressive.[31] South Asia was known for its high level of interventionism in the developmentalist period. In the reform period, Pakistan had several bouts of structural adjustment and was noted for its foot dragging and acrimonious relations with the IMF. The IMF's assistance to Pakistan continued notwithstanding given its strategic importance to the United States. Nepal is an exception as a star pupil of structural reform, but it did not turn in a stellar performance like the other larger South Asian countries such as Bangladesh, India and Sri Lanka.

India, the dominant country in this regional grouping, devised its own set of reforms in the early 1990s in response to a fiscal crisis under the tutelage of an ex-WB finance minister. Many development economists view these to be classic neoliberal reforms and the cause of India's subsequent catch-up growth. However, this issue is contested with some development economists timing the catch-up growth to an earlier period of pro-business (rather than pro-market) developmentalist reforms and arguing that India remains interventionist.[32] Much of Bangladesh's spectacular growth pertains to developmentalist policies that boosted its textile industry and Sri Lanka was a pioneer in experimenting with both developmentalist and liberalization policies but with the state continuing to play a leading role.

The other three country groups, Middle East and North Africa (MENA), Latin America and Caribbean (LAC) and Sub-Saharan Africa (SSA) show a similar trend although it is in the latter two in which the leadership is viewed as having adopted the neoliberal package hook, line and sinker. However, for all three regional country groupings, average growth rates in the structural adjustment period fell dramatically compared to the developmentalist period. The average annual per capita GDP growth rates of MENA and LAC declined from robust levels to 1 percent and 0.5 percent respectively. For SSA, they declined from 1.6 percent to −1.1 percent. Thus the star pupils of structural adjustment appear to have had the worst performance.[33] Economic growth picked up for SSA and LAC in the third period and this has been associated with the commodities boom resulting from demand in emerging countries like China and speculative investments in the first decade of the 21st century. This commodity boom is viewed to have peaked in 2011.

It is impossible to summarize the findings of the numerous country case studies on structural adjustment. We report instead the findings of a few of the most prominent studies which have a broader scope. Mkandawire and Soludo (2004) is probably the most celebrated book on a case study of structural adjustment in Africa. They argued that structural adjustment caused deindustrialization and the pay freezes, nominal salary cuts, retrenchments and inflation seriously undermined civil service capacity and induced a brain drain. At the same time, this was exacerbated by the aid-related requirement of seeking foreign technical expertise. They reported that in a given year, Africa had 100,000 foreign technical staff that cost over $4 billion. In 1985, the foreign expert remuneration amounted to three times the total public sector wage bill. The overall contribution of this expertise has been assessed by scholars to be negative, including in terms of undermining local self-reliance and confidence and inducing demoralization.

Cornia, Jolly and Stewart (1987) sponsored by UNICEF is another landmark study with an accompanying volume of case studies. Keeping the methodological caveats alluded to above in mind, the upshot of their findings was that structural adjustment was associated with a decrease in public outreach, a concomitant reduction in social services, a reduction in public health and a reduction in living standards.

Taylor and Pieper (1996) researched the impacts of structural adjustment reforms based on case studies of countries including Chile, Mexico, Turkey, transition countries of Eastern Europe, and SSA countries. They concluded that these reforms have led to adverse health and educational outcomes, rising unemployment, wage repression, increased poverty and inequality, and a weakening of social protection.[34]

There are numerous econometric studies that have attempted to estimate the impact of structural adjustment on economic growth. Easterly (2005), an ex-WB conservative economist, who looked at data from 1980–1999 for the top 20 recipients, concluded that there was no positive impact of structural adjustment policies on economic growth. He also pointed out that there were many repeat loans (30 for Argentina) making it difficult to claim that the adjustment was achieved or, if so, successful in delivering outcomes.

Hausmann, Pritchett and Rodrik (2005) explored 83 growth accelerations between 1957 and 1992 (defined as a growth increase of greater than or equal to 2.5 percent on a minimum base of at least up to 3.5 percent and sustained for at least eight years). Intense liberalization and structural adjustment were not associated with 82 percent of these episodes. As is the case for most empirical debates in economic development, there is no consensus in the literature on this issue.

The most prominent organizational analysis of the IMF and WB was led by another prominent conservative economist, Alan Meltzer.[35] This was commissioned in 2000 by the US Congress prior to approving funding for these BWIs. The Meltzer Commission assessment of the IMF included a statement that its "response to crises is too slow, advice is often incorrect, and its efforts to influence policy and practice are too intrusive". Another quote is that "IMF programs are unwieldy, highly conflictive, time consuming to negotiate, and often ineffectual".

It judged the WB's mission to reduce poverty "left much room for improvement". It viewed the WB to have mostly pushed loans rather than focus on development or poverty reduction. It pointed out that 70 percent of WB aid flowed to 11 countries that enjoyed substantial access to private resource flows and hence there was a big gap between WB rhetoric and practice. It cited a self-evaluation by the WB on Africa which reported a 73 percent failure rate for its programs. The WB was also criticized for not paying much attention to the sustainability of its program impacts or the evaluation of impacts.

The subsequent focus on poverty at the WB and IMF resulted in The Structural Adjustment facility (SAF) being renamed the Poverty Reduction and Growth

Facility (PRGF) in 2002. A precondition for the approval of a PRGF was the writing of a Poverty Reduction Strategy Paper (PRSP) led by the WB via a "participatory process". Critics were not impressed and viewed the participatory process as mostly a sham, the PRSP in most cases a meaningless wish list, and the conditionalities with bite unchanged. Social critics viewed the PRGF as an oxymoron since they viewed the conditionalities as generating the poverty in the first place for which a safety net then needed to be put in place.

Among the most prominent critics from a feminist perspective is Elson (1992, 1995) who charged that advocates of these programs were unaware of the implicit male biases in structural adjustment programs. In fact the negative impacts on women were reported to be much greater as the fiscal burden on the state was lightened and women had to work with tightening budgets to try to ensure service provision otherwise provided by the state. There was also blindness to women's reproductive role in economic models that treated labor as an abstract entity and also to women's work within and outside the household. The rising unemployment induced by structural adjustment required women to supplement dwindling household income by working outside the home while continuing to bear the burden of household work unassisted by males.

As indicated earlier, critics charged structural adjustment to be associated with poverty and equality and an erosion of social protections.[36] While the IMF and WB responded to its critics by building social protection conditionality into programs, critics still argue that there is much less attention paid to the implementation of these conditions than say to fiscal stringency for which the track record of implementation is much higher. Kentikelenis, Stubbs and King (2016, table 4) provided evidence on conditionality implementation to establish this point.

The broader point is that while there is frequent rethinking in the vast research departments of the BWIs, this does not appear to change what is actually being implemented. Taylor (1997, p. 6) pointed out that the IMF backed off the doctrine that higher interest rates induce more saving, and Ostry et al. (2011) at the IMF argued that capital market liberalization is not an unqualified plus for L/LMICs. During The Great Recession the IMF even endorsed fiscal expansion, at least for HICs, and IMF economists Ostry, Loungani and Furceri (2016) conceded fiscal austerity could lead to growth destructive inequality and therefore endorsed redistribution. For (Rodrik, 2017), it does not appear so far that the rethinking has found its way into reform package implementation.

The second wave of structural adjustment reforms not only ostensibly addressed poverty but also better governance as the diagnoses of what ailed L/LMICs and the associated prescriptions continued to change. Thus the prescriptions of "getting prices right" and "getting policy right" transitioned to the emphasis in the 1990s to "getting institutions right". Poor governance became a key part of the theory of underdevelopment and so better institutions for better governance became an important part of the theory of development.

However, enhanced structural adjustment programs that included institutional and governance reforms also did not deliver the intended results of social and economic development. Heterodox economists like Khan (2012) argued that improved institutions and governance accompanied economic development and so neoliberals once again got the causality wrong by arguing for good governance as a prerequisite. The argument is that just as market efficiency accompanies economic development, good governance and the mitigation of corruption accompanies economic development.

Why does neoliberalism persist?[37]

The first section of this chapter documented the emergence of neoliberal thought in development economics and why it became so influential. The puzzle is why it manages to persist despite its ostensible conceptual shortcomings and the large amount of empirical evidence suggesting that it has been unable to attain its objectives, and that it has worsened living conditions in L/LMICs where the WB and the IMF have been active in implementing the neoliberal agenda.

The answer in large part may be associated with just how influential the BWIs have been and continue to be in the economic development intellectual space. Their very well staffed and richly endowed research departments have been central in continuing to build the intellectual case for neoliberalism, directly via in-house research and indirectly via contract research. Critical economic development scholars risk being shut out from lucrative jobs in these institutions or highly remunerative research contracts. This would disincline young scholars to shift to a world view that undermines their careers.[38] More importantly, being trained in neoclassical economics may in any case incline them to a neoliberal world view in development economics. Universities and college economic departments that expose students to alternative approaches are few and far between.[39]

The in-house training in the IMF and WB and the regional sister development banks like the Asian Development Bank bring on board promising senior bureaucrats from member countries. The trips are a perk including comfortable travel and duration allowance and incline trainees to be well disposed to the organizations. The trainees rub shoulders with top academics from prestigious universities, a heady experience. These trainings are not designed to provide alternative perspectives but represent ideological brainwashing since there is one "truth". The process is one in which these organizations make contacts in high places and the bureaucrats are also keen to network and make a good impression for possible future jobs aboard. Thus this training process may be the most effective ideological force multiplier.

Western aid agencies have actively implemented the proscribed foreign investment and market friendly agenda via engineered policy coherence (Grabel, 2011). While there may appear to have been a greater acceptance and a voluntary turn to neoliberal policies in several countries, Grabel shows that neoliberal influence can be direct via conditional loans or indirect via leadership capture. There is a revolving door between senior economic officials in L/LMIC economic ministries and highly lucrative senior positions (often reserved) in the BWIs.

Private capital has in general followed the lead of these organizations in judging whether or not the countries are capital friendly. Being subject to the discipline of a structural adjustment program has been perceived as a positive signal in this regard. Rating agencies in HICs are also entirely in accord with neoliberal economic philosophy as are consulting firms that produce country risk assessments shaping the movement of FDI. In this regard, the BWIs act as implementing agencies for Wall Street at the behest of the US Treasury Department, which has a major say on the Boards of these organizations.

While the IMF and the WB are also implementing agencies of the WTO's trade liberalization agenda, there has been mutual ideological reinforcement since the formation of the WTO in 1994. Most LICs/LMICs want to join for fear of the cost of exclusion, but joining requires adherence to neoliberal prescriptions.[40]

Much of the influential and well-regarded media is on board with the neoliberal program and hammers away at listeners on the self-evident virtue of these organizations and the success of their programs. Thus most of the BBC and National Public Radio (NPR), US business and economics programs and influential magazines like *The Economist* all pitch in this direction. Newspapers that occasionally or frequently present a heterodox perspective are few and far between, with *The Guardian* being one notable exception.

Summary

Neoliberalism emerged from favorable political conditions receptive to conservative economic philosophy. In the broader discipline, monetarism and new classical economics challenged the dominance of Keynesian thought. In development economics the dominance of interventionist approaches such as structuralism and developmentalism was challenged by neoliberalism. The neoliberal policy package that emerged from the combination of non-interventionist macroeconomics and neoclassical microeconomics was dubbed The Washington Consensus.

The Washington Consensus has been enormously influential because of political support in the major HICs and because countries needing balance of payment support, particularly following the debt crisis of 1980s, have had to turn to the IMF and WB for support. These organizations provided the support conditional on the adoption of the neoliberal reform package of structural adjustment.

These organizations and their policy packages were for a while pushed as "the only game in town". However, a critical literature picked apart this policy package based on theoretical shortcomings and the mutual inconsistency of the various conditionalities that constitute a structural adjustment program. More broadly, critics castigated the increase in poverty and inequality that resulted from the structural adjustment reforms.

Notwithstanding these criticisms, the neoliberal policy package remains influential for several reasons including the enormous resource base of the IMF and WB and their political backing. In the 1990s, new developmentalists demonstrated that neoliberalism was not the only game in town, and Chapter 9 explores this alternative approach.

Appendix 8.1: Post Washington Consensus and its radical critique

Stiglitz (1999) represented an "insider" challenge to The Washington Consensus or neoliberalism based on a much broader view of market failures. These include information asymmetries (some agents have more information than others and can exploit that), imperfect information, missing markets (like insurance or capital), incomplete contracts and transaction costs. He dubbed the neoliberal agenda of liberalization, privatization and deregulation as market fundamentalism and proposed instead a move to a Post Washington Consensus (PWC).

The agenda he proposed was a synthesis of human development (social protection and welfare), institutionalist (good governance), neo-developmentalist (industrial and technology policy, Chapter 9) and mainstream prescriptions (macro stabilization and selective privatization). The goals included environmental conservation and social well-being including poverty alleviation. Interventionism such as competition policy, capital market restraints and financial market regulations, including prudential reforms, in response to market failures were endorsed. In addition, like developmentalists, he supported the provision of physical infrastructure. Overall, he viewed governments as a complement to markets and they needed to catalyze activities, such as technology development and human capital acquisition, when necessary because of market under-provision.

Drawing on institutional economists he suggested that institutional innovations and reforms were needed to make markets work better. These included good governance reforms including judicial and anti-corruption reforms (second generation of neoliberal reforms) and working with civil society organizations that emphasized participation – an approach already adopted by the WB.

Trade liberalization and privatization were welcomed as a means to attain a competitive and efficient marketplace in a framework of competition and regulation as opposed to the ideological gung-ho liberalizations and privatizations pushed by the IMF and WB. He argued that democratization was preferred to authoritarian governments that the WB had a track record of working with and in fact democratic reforms would make markets work better.

The radical critique of the PWC (Fine, 2001, 2002) is that, like neoclassical economics, it continues to be based on methodological individualism (household and firm optimizations) and is hence highly reductionist. Making a case for reform of the social structure based on individual optimization is contradictory and meaningless. The PWC ignores history, path dependency, and internal class and power structure, which are the key ingredients to understanding society in a meaningful way.

Again, like The Washington Consensus, it shields MNCs from host country regulation and emphasizes their importance based on ideology rather than evidence (Chapter 11). The MNCs are part of the international power structure with their interests represented by international financial institutions. MNCs are subject to no international regulation and the WTO pared back domestic regulations constraining them. Thus, the radical political economy perspective sees little to fundamentally distinguish the PWC from The Washington Consensus notwithstanding the more progressive rhetoric.[41]

Probably the greatest weakness of the approach is that it picks and chooses "everything nice" from everywhere and so is diffuse. Is so doing, it has no unique thrust and guidance for L/LMICs seeking an approach to development and perhaps that is why it has gained very limited traction. In this regard, neoliberalism, even if discredited, has a clear set of prescriptions on where to begin. New developmentalism similarly has an alternative set of prescriptions, discussed next in Chapter 9.

Questions and exercises

1. Explain the neoliberal critique of ISI.
2. Elaborate on P. T. Bauer's, Deepak Lal's and Anne Krueger's critiques of interventionism.
3. Outline and explain the main elements of what came to be referred to as The Washington Consensus.
4. Explain the case for export promotion (EP) and review the debate on the evidence.
5. Explain the qualifications associated with the case for EP.
6. Cite and explain the heterodox critique of the misdiagnosis of neoliberal economics – discuss with regards to any three reforms.
7. Cite and explain any three specific structural adjustment conditionalities, the neoliberal case for them and the associated heterodox critique.
8. Cite and explain how any three conditionalities are mutually inconsistent in attaining multiple structural adjustment goals.
9. Cite and explain the shortcomings of the various empirical methods used to gather evidence in the context of the neoliberal/heterodox debate.
10. Review the evidence based on various empirical methods in the context of the neoliberal/heterodox debate.
11. What might have accounted for the persistence of neoliberal economic philosophy despite conceptual shortcomings and operational failures? What is your assessment?
12. Select any country that has entered (is entering) negotiations with the IMF/WB (henceforth referred to as the IMF) to renegotiate its debt or seek a new loan and hence has been made subject to various "conditionalities". The "Letter of Intent" (LOI), which forms the basis of the country contract and contains the conditionalities, is available on the IMF website. [Type your selected country in the search slot].

    a. Select the main conditions that the LIC/LMIC has been asked to satisfy. In *each* case, state the benefits the IMF may expect will result from pursuing the stated condition.

b.   Write a critical appraisal of the country analysis implicit in the IMF prescriptions i.e. do the conditionalities make sense in the specific context of the country you are analyzing?

c.   What would you propose as an alternative structural reform to the neoliberal agenda?

You may select the neoliberal agenda as the appropriate one and argue why that is the case.

Note: There may be many LOIs available on the IMF website for the country you select. For this topic it does not matter which one you select although the earlier ones often contain a clearer statement of the conditions and later ones devote more space to the government's view of progress made on conditions.

13. Pick a reform of your choice such as financial sector reform/interest rate liberalization, devaluation/exchange rate liberalization or privatization.

a.   State the positions in favor of and opposed to this reform.

b.   Assess the experience prior to the reform (use numbers if possible).

c.   What measures have been taken to institute the reform in question?

d.   What have been the effects of these measures to date?

e.   Based on the experience of your country, analyze the political economy or this reform (i.e. who gained and who lost and by how much by class or income group).

f.   What would you propose as an alternative to this reform? Alternatively, indicate why you support this reform.

(For this topic select the earliest LOI that you can find on the IMF website since that gives you more time over which to test your hypothesis. Alternatively, you could go directly to EconLit or another data base and search by country name and type of reform.])

14. Engage in an exercise to assess structural adjustment impacts. There are several possibilities for assessing impacts:

a.   It is possible to assess the impacts on a particular sector of a particular reform such as the impact of trade liberalization on the environment.

b.   The impact of sector-specific policies such as education and health could be explored for impacts on the poor in general, or on narrower disaggregations such as poor female children.

c.   The overall impact of relevant structural adjustment or other reform policies could be explored in terms of impacts on labor, poor, women, environment or food security.

Example

Suppose you chose to write on the impact of structural adjustment or other reform policies on poor women. You could utilize the following outline.

a.   Identify the policies that have had an impact on the economic well-being of poor women.

    b.   Use numbers to demonstrate the nature and magnitude of the impact.

    c.   Assess the policies critically and make recommendations for alternative policies.

    d.   Alternatively, make a case for the structural adjustment policies in terms of their impact on poor women.

    e.   Using this framework, you could study instead the health, environment or poverty impacts of structural adjustment policies.

Notes

1 Neoliberal in this chapter is being addressed in the economic development context. Refer to Harvey (2005) and Srnicek and Williams (2016, chapter 3) for broader reviews. Also refer to Rodrik (2017) on how the approach has assumed different meanings over time. In this chapter and textbook neoliberalism is understood to mean the focus on liberalization, privatization, deregulation and fiscal austerity pushed in the context of structural adjustment programs by the WB and IMF.

2 These organizations are often referred to as the Bretton Woods Institutions named after the place in New Hampshire where the post-World War II conference was held to discuss the shape of the new world economic order. These international organizations were founded based on significant dominance of the United States as the now established world power, to have a major role in financial (IMF's role) and economic development (WB's role) matters. The WB group includes among other organizations the International Bank of Reconstruction and Development (IBRD) and International Development Agency (IDA), which provides development loans on soft terms (Chapter 11), and these two are commonly referred to as the World Bank.

3 The mechanisms for this choking off are higher interest rates, accompanying a higher price level, reducing investment and consumption, and the lower real wealth due to a higher price level reducing consumption. Keynesians argue, with supporting evidence, that without these offsetting mechanisms the fiscal multipliers would be larger.

4 Harcourt pointed out that Tarshis's (1947) textbook contained the correct general version.

5 New Keynesians premised the upward slope of the short-run aggregate supply curve on sticky wages and prices resulting from contracts.

6 Refer to Calclough (1991) and Chang (2002) for expositions on neoliberalism and its association with neoclassical economics.

7 This mirrors Baran's critique of local elite interactions with colonial authorities (Chapter 5).

8 In this case the willingness to abuse the aid because the debt forgiveness would signal they can get away with it.

9 Aid is one of the few topics on which conservative and radical economists seem to agree but not always for the same reasons (Chapter 11).

10 Adam Smith, the inspiration for such views, was more nuanced regarding unleashing private incentives. For example, he was cognizant of the producer tendency toward collusion and restraint of trade.

11 Like Rustow, this implicitly assumes a similar history playing out for L/LMICs as for current HICs.

12 The "new political economy" she contributed to was juxtaposed to radical political economy that focused on the capture of the state by powerful elites to further their interests.

13 *Raj* is the Hindi/Urdu word for rule.

14 The caveat pointed to in endnote 21 of Chapter 7 that the analysis would only hold accurately in a static world applies here also.

15 Thus interventions in the market mechanism that result in such welfare losses are viewed as leading to distortions in neoclassical economics. These triangles are also referred to as Harberger triangles after the economist who attempted to quantify the magnitude of deadweight losses by measuring the spaces they represented. This is not a straightforward empirical exercise, as pointed out by Hines (1999).

16 ERPs at best identify potential rather than actual inefficiency. Fine (2005) explained why even that is a stretch since ERP as an analytical tool is faulty based as it is on unrealistic assumptions.

17 Thus neoliberalism, The Washington Consensus and structural adjustment are used interchangeably. Strictly, neoliberalism can be thought of as the economic philosophy and The Washington Consensus or structural adjustment as the policy mechanisms to attain it.

18 There has been much pressure to change this convention starting in particular with the run up to the appointment of Jim Kim as the 12th president of the World Bank in 2012.

19 The literature on the critique of structural adjustment policies is enormous and the synthesis presented in this section draws on a heterodox consensus. Stiglitz (2002) is a good source for a generalist audience, particularly since he served as the chief economist of the WB. For a more detailed and nuanced analysis of the elements of the neoliberal package than the one provided in this chapter, refer to Taylor (1992). See Bhagwati (2004) for a defense of neoliberalism.

20 Easterly and Fischer (2001) show that the poor are more likely than the rich to mention inflation as being a major priority.

21 The proposal was to abolish Article 6 (Section 3) that enables countries to impose various restrictions based on their economic needs.

22 This prediction proved prescient in view of Donald Trump's call for protectionism before and after being elected US President in 2016.

23 For a vociferous defense of privatization from an economist involved in the process in the UK, see Walters (1989, p. 50). Walters considered the "first and foremost" objective of privatization to be the "reduction of politicization of the economy".

24 While 93 percent of the creditors accepted the deal, the other 7 percent including US-based hedge funds did not. On March 1, 2016, Mauricio Macri agreed to a settlement with the "vulture funds" for $4.6 billion (hedge fund NML capital received $2.28 billion (full value) on its investment of $177 million in buying discounted debt). At this point, a US judge had ruled in favor of the hedge funds, Argentina was under severe financial pressure, and it confronted a rate of interest about twice that of its neighbors. IMF support was contingent on settling with creditors. Refer to www.nytimes.com/2016/04/01/opinion/how-hedge-funds-held-argentina-for-ransom.html, consulted 2/23/2019.

25 World view rather than ideology is deliberately used here since the reference is to variations within the market paradigm – between more or less concern with social justice. Using ideology would suggest a choice between alternative paradigms.

26 See the IMF defence to the criticism of its Enhanced Structural Adjustment Facility posted on its website, www.imf.org/external/pubs/ft/esaf/exr/, consulted 7/23/17.

27 They are general equilibriums in the sense that the mutual interaction of most of the key macro markets is taken into account to solve for equilibrium solutions.

28 Studies suggesting that exports are growth enhancing include Tyler (1981), Feder (1982), Kavossi (1984), Balassa (1985), Chow (1987) and Dollar (1992).

29 Dissenters include Jang and Marshall (1985), Dodaro (1991), Sheehey (1992) and Khan and Bilginsoy (1994). Levine and Renelt (1992) showed that exports were not a robust growth predictor.

30 These results are consistent with the new developmentalist approach, as will be explained in the next chapter.

31 As will be discussed in Chapter 9, South Asia's implementation of developmentalist prescriptions was wanting in several respects when compared to East Asia.

32 Thus, while Panagariya (2004) and Bhagwati and Panagariya (2013) claim that market-driven "pro-entry" (neoliberal) reforms explain the Indian take-off, Rodrik and Subramanian (2004) among others claim this to be based on pro-business and pro-incumbent developmentalist policies.

33 Chile seems to have been the only exception for LAC, but once again there is a debate on just how assiduously Chile adopted structural adjustment prescriptions. As in the case of India and the East Asian countries including China, while neoliberal scholars claim it as a success story of neoliberalism, Pieper and Taylor (1996) argued that while neoliberal adjustment might eventually have delivered some results for Chile, stagnation lasted almost a decade and the state role in an industrial policy including for copper, forestry, fisheries and fruit was prominent in the eventual success. Similarly Joseph Stiglitz, an ex-chief economist of the WB, argued that Chile engaged only in selective privatization, retained capital controls, continued to use SOEs to push exports and extensively used export subsidies for forestry, fisheries and mining (Stiglitz, 2002. "The Chilean Miracle: Combining Markets with Appropriate Reform", Commanding Heights interview). Stiglitz in fact concluded that The Washington Consensus was a failure and proposed the Post Washington Consensus as an alternative. This approach attracted some attention and Appendix 8.1 explores how it differs from The Washington Consensus.

34 In this and other studies on structural adjustment, Taylor is circumspect and noted how much is not known in general and specifically in terms of the mutual interaction of the macroeconomic impacts of structural adjustment and social outcomes.

35 The Report no longer seems to be available online but the report on the hearing before the committee on foreign relations of the US Senate is still accessible, www.gpo.gov/fdsys/pkg/CHRG-106shrg66721/pdf/CHRG-106shrg66721.pdf, consulted 7/23/17. One committee member commented on the use of the IMF as an instrument of US foreign policy, a practice he suggested would need to be discontinued in an increasingly polycentric world.

36 Also see George (2007) as among the prominent critics in this regard. Refer to Lal (2012) for a contrary view. The latter is instructive on how authors cite theoretical arguments and empirical evidence selectively to reinforce prior beliefs. This criticism appears to apply to both sides of the debate.

37 Wade (2011, pp. 39–43) addressed the issue of why neoliberalism won out and Srnicek and Williams (2016, chapter 3) the issue of how the neoliberalism project was conceived, propagated and established.

38 Refer to Chapter 1 on how the hegemony of the mainstream is imposed and sustained.

39 The University of California, Riverside, New School of Social Research, Notre Dame University and the University of Utah had economics departments exposing graduate students to both mainstream and heterodox theory. The past tense is used because departmental politics and hiring can quickly change the complexion of a department as seems to have been the case at The University of Michigan.

40 One critical book refers to these three organizations as The Unholy Trinity (Peet, 2003).

41 Önis and Şenses (2005) similarly argued that PWC ignored power issues at the national (asset distribution) and global levels (decision making power within international organizations and the power of MNCs).

References

Balassa, B. 1985. "Exports, Policy Choices, and Economic Growth in Developing Countries after the 1973 Oil Shock," *Journal of Development Economics*, 18(1), 23–35.

Barro, M. 1997. *Determinants of Economic Growth* (Cambridge, MA: MIT Press).

Bauer, P. T. 1972. *Dissent on Development* (Cambridge, Mass: Harvard University Press).

Bauer, P. T. 1984. *Reality and Rhetoric: Studies in the Economics of Development* (Cambridge, MA: Harvard University Press).

Bhagwati, J. 2004. *In Defense of Globalization* (New York: Oxford University Press).

Bhagwati, J. and A. Panagariya. 2013. *Why Growth Matters: How Economic Growth in India Reduced Poverty and Lessons for Other Countries* (New York: Public Affairs).

Bruno, M. and W. Easterly. 1998. "Inflation Crises and Long-Run Growth," *Journal of Monetary Economics*, 41(1), 3–26.

Buchanan, J. and G. Tullock. 1962. *The Calculus of Consent: Logical Foundations of Constitutional Democracy* (Ann Arbor, MI: University of Michigan Press).

Calclough, C. 1991. "Structuralism vs. Neoliberalism," in: C. Calclough and J. Manor (eds.), *States or Markets? Neoliberalism and the Development Policy Debates* (Oxford: Clarendon Press).1-26.

Chang, H.-J. 2002. "Breaking the Mould: An Institutionalist Political Economy Alternative to the Neoliberal Theory of the Market and the State," *Cambridge Journal of Economics*, 26(5), 539–559.

Chang, H.-J. 2006. *The Third East Asian Development Experience: The Miracle, the Crisis and the Future* (London/Penang: Zed World Network).

Chang, H.-J. and A. Singh. 1993. "Public Enterprises in Developing Countries and Economic Efficiency: A Critical Examination of Analytical, Empirical and Policy Issues," *UNCTAD Review*, 4, 45–82.

Chow, P. C. Y. 1987. "Causality between Export Growth and Industrial Development: Empirical Evidence from NICs," *Journal of Development Economics*, 26(1), 55–63.

Cline, W. R. 1982. "Can the East Asian Model of Development Be Generalized?" *World Development*, 10(2), 81–90.

Cline, W. R.2008. *"Exports of Manufactures and Economic Growth: The Fallacy of Composition Revisited,"* Commission on Growth and Development, Working Paper No. 36, Washing, DC: World Bank.

Cornia, G. A., R. Jolly and F. Stewart (Eds.). 1987. *Adjustment with a Human Face*, Volumes I & 2 (Oxford: Oxford University Press).

Dodaro, S. 1991. "Comparative Advantage, Trade and Growth: Export-Led Growth Revisited," *World Development*, 19(9), 1153–1165.

Dollar, D. 1992. "Outward Oriented Developing Economies Really Do Grow More: Evidence from 95 LDCS, 1996-1985," *Economic Development and Cultural Change*, 40(3), 523–544.

Easterly, W. 2005. "What Did Structural Adjustment Adjust? The Association of Policies and Growth with Repeated IMF and World Bank Adjustment Loans," *Journal of Development Economics*, 76(1), 1–22.

Easterly, W. and S. Fischer. 2001. "Inflation *and the Poor*," *Journal of Money, Credit and Banking*, 33(2), 160–178.

Eicher, T. S. and D. J. Kuenzel. 2016. "The Elusive Effects of Trade on Growth: Export Diversity and Economic Take-off," *Canadian Journal of Development Economics*, 49(1), 264–295.

Elson, D. 1992. "From Survival Strategies to Transformation Strategies: Women's Needs and Structural Adjustment," in: L. Benería and S. Feldman (eds.), *Unequal Burden: Economic Crisis, Persistent Poverty, and Women's Work* (Boulder: Westview Press).46-68.

Elson, D. 1995. *Male Bias in the Development Process* (Manchester: Manchester University Press).

Feder, G. 1982. "On Exports and Economic Growth," *Journal of Development Economics*, 12(1&2), 59–73.

Fine, B. 2001. "Neither the Washington nor the Post-Washington Consensus: An Introduction," in: B. Fine, C. Lapavitsas and J. Pincus (eds.), *Development Policy in the 21st Century: Beyond the post-Washington Consensus* (London: Routledge).1-27.

Fine, B. 2002. "Economics Imperialism and the New Development Economics as Kuhnian Paradigm Shift?" *World Development*, 30(12), 2057–2070.

Fine, B. 2005. "The Development State and Political Economy of Development," in: B. Fine and K. S. Jomo (eds.), *The New Development Economics: Post Washington Consensus Neo-Liberal Thinking* (London: Zed Books).1-20.

George, S. 2007. "Down the Great Financial Drain: How Debt and the Washington Consensus Destroy Development and Create Poverty," *Development*, 50(2), 4–11.

Grabel, I. 2003. "International Private Capital Flows and Developing Countries," in: H.-J. Chang and I. Grabel (eds.), *Re-thinking Development Economics* (London: Anthem Press).106-149.

Grabel, I. 2011. "Cementing Neoliberalism in the Developing World: Ideational and Institutional Constraints on Policy Space," in: S. R. Khan and J. Christensen (eds.), *Towards New Developmentalism: Market as Means Rather than Master* (New York: Routledge).100-118.

Harcourt, G. C. 2009. "The Rise And, Hopefully, Fall of Economic Neoliberalism in Theory and Practice," *Economic and Labour Relations Review*, 20(1), 1–6.

Harvey, D. 2005. *A Brief History of Neoliberalism* (Oxford: Oxford University Press).

Hausmann, R., Pritchett, L. and Rodrik, D. 2005. "Growth Accelerations," *Journal of Economic Growth*, 10(4), 303–329.

Hayek, F. A. 1994. *The Road to Serfdom* (Chicago: University of Chicago Press).

Hill, P. 1986. *Development Economics on Trial: The Anthropologists Case for Prosecution* (New York: Cambridge University Press).

Hines, J. R. 1999. "Three Sides of Harberger Triangles," *Journal of Economic Perspectives*, 13(2), 167–188.

Jang, W. S. and P. S. Marshall. 1985. "Exports, Growth and Causality in Developing Countries," *Journal of Development Economics*, 18(1), 1–12.

Kavossi, R. M. 1984. "Export Expansion and Economic Growth: Further Empirical Evidence," *Journal of Development Economics*, 14(1), 241–250.

Kentikelenis, A. E., T. E. Stubbs and L. P. King. 2016. "IMF Conditionality and Development Policy Space 1985–2014," *Review of International Political Economy*, 23(4), 543–582.

Keynes, J. M. 2007. *The General Theory of Employment, Interest, and Money* (London: Palgrave Macmillan).

Khan, M. 2009. "The Political Economy of Industrial Policy in Asia and Latin America," It is by Mushtaq H. Khan and Stephanie Blankenburg, *Industrial Policy and Development: The Political Economy of Capabilities Accumulation* (Oxford: Oxford University Press).336-377.

Khan, M. H. 2012. "Beyond Good Governance: An Agenda for Developmental Governance," in: Jomo. K. S. and Vos, R. (Eds.) *Is Good Governance Good for Development? United Nations Series on Development* (London and New York: Bloomsbury Academic).151-182.

Khan, S. R. and C. Bilginsoy. 1994. "Industry Externalities Revisited," *Kyklos*, 47(1), 67–80.

Krueger, A. 1974. "The Political Economy of the Rent Seeking Society," *American Economic Review*, 64(3), 291–303.

Krueger, A. 1978. *Foreign Trade Regimes and Economic Development: Liberalization Attempts and Consequences*. Cambridge: Ballenger Press.

Krueger, A. 1983. *Trade and Employment in Developing Countries, Synthesis and Conclusions* (Chicago: University of Chicago Press).

Lal, D. 1983. *The Poverty of Development Economics* (Cambridge, MA: Harvard University Press).

Lal, D. 2012. "Is the Washington Consensus Dead?" *Cato Journal*, 32(3), 493–512.

Leibenstein, H. 1966. "Allocative Efficiency Vs. X-Efficiency," *American Economic Review*, 56(3), 392–415.

Levine, R. and Renelt, D. 1992."Analysis of Cross-Country Growth Regressions," *American Economic Review*,82(4), 92–63.

Little, I., T. Scitovsky and M. Scott. 1970. *Industry and Trade in Some Developing Countries* (Oxford: Oxford University Press for the O.E.C.D. Development Center).

Mkandawire, T. and C. C. Soludo. 2004. *Our Continent, Our Future: African Perspectives on Structural Adjustment* (New Jersey: ICS Press).

Önis, Z. and F. Şenses. 2005. "Rethinking the Emerging Post-Washington Consensus," *Development and Change*, 36(2), 263–290.

Ostry, J. D. et. al. 2011. "Capital Controls: When and Why?" *IMF Economic Review*, 59(3), 562–580.

Ostry, J. D., P. Loungani and D. Furceri. 2016. "Neoliberalism: Oversold?" *Finance and Development*, 53(2), 38–41.

Panagariya, A. 2004. "*India in the 1980s and 1990s: A Triumph of Reforms*," International Monetary Fund Working Paper Series No. 04/43, Washington, DC: International Monetary Fund.

Peet, R. 2003. *The Unholy Trinity: The IMF, World Bank and the WTO* (London: Zed Books).

Pieper, U. and L. Taylor. 1996. "*The Revival of the Liberal Creed–The IMF and the World Bank in a Globalized Economy*," CEPA Working Paper Series I, Working Paper No. 4, New York: Center for Economic Policy Analysis, New School for Social Research.

Rodriguez, F. F. and D. Rodrik. 1999. "*Trade Policy and Economic Growth: A Skeptic's Guide to the Cross-National Evidence*," NBER Working Papers 7081, Cambridge, MA: National Bureau of Economic Research, Inc.

Rodrik, D. 1994. "King Kong Meets Godzilla: The World Bank and the East Asian Miracle," in: A. Fishlow et. al. (ed.), *Miracle or Design? Lessons from the East Asian Experience* (Washington, DC: Overseas Development Council). 13-38.

Rodrik, D. 2017. "Rescuing Economics from Neoliberalism," *Boston Review*, November 6, http://bostonreview.net/class-inequality/dani-rodrik-rescuing-economics-neoliberalism, consulted 2/23/2019,, .

Rodrik, D. and A. Subramanian. 2004. "*From 'hindu Growth' to Productivity Surge: The Mystery of the Indian Growth Transition*," National Bureau Working Paper Series No. 10376, Cambridge, MA: National Bureau of Economic Research.

Rosenzweig, M. and A. D. Foster. 2010. "*Is There Surplus Labor in Rural India?*" Working Paper No 85, New Haven: Yale Growth Center.

Sheehey, E. J. 1992. "Exports and growth: Additional evidence," *Journal of Development Studies*, 28(4), 730–734.

Srnicek, N. and A. Williams. 2016. *Inventing the Future: Postcapitalism and a World without Work* (London: Verso).

Stiglitz, J. E. 1999. "More Instruments and Broader Goals: Moving toward the Post-Washington Consensus," *Revista De Economia Politica*, 19(1), 94–120.

Stiglitz, J. E. 2002. *Globalization and Its Discontents* (New York: Norton).

Tarshis, L. 1947. *The Elements of Economics: An Introduction to the Theory of Price and Employment* (Cambridge, Mass: Houghton Mifflin).

Taylor, L. 1992. "Polonius Lectures Again: The World Development Report, the Washington Consensus, and How Neoliberal Sermons Won't Solve the Economic Problems of the Developing World," *Bangladesh Development Studies*, 20(2–3), 23–53.

Taylor, L. 1997. "The Revival of the Liberal Creed–The IMF and the World Bank in a Globalized Economy," *World Development*, 25(20), 145–152.

Taylor, L. and U. Pieper. 1996. *Reconciling Economic Reform and Sustainable Development: Social Consequences of Neoliberalism* (New York: Office of Development Studies, United Nations Development Programme).

Tyler, W. G. 1981. "Growth and Export Expansion in Developing Countries," *Journal of Development Economics*, 11(1), 121–130.

Vickers, J. and G. Yarrow. 1991. "Economic Perspectives on Privatization," *Journal of Economic Perspectives*, 5(2), 111–132.

Wade, R. 2011. "The Market as a Means Rather than Master: The Crisis of Development and the Future Role of the State," in: S. R. Khan and J. Christensen (eds.), *Towards New Developmentalism: Market as Means Rather than Master* (New York: Routledge).21-46.

Walters, A. S. 1989. "Privatization in Britain: Comment," in: P. W. MacAvoy et. al. (ed.), *Privatization and State Owned Enterprises: Lessons from United States, Great Britain, and Canada* (Boston: Kluwer Academic Publishers).247-257.

Williamson, J. 1990. "What Washington Means by Policy Reform," in: J. Williamson (ed.), *Latin American Adjustment. How Much Has Happened?* (Washington, DC: Institute for International Economics).7-20.

Williamson, J. 2008. "A Short History of the Washington Consensus," in: N. Serra and J. E. Stiglitz (eds.), *The Washington Consensus Reconsidered: Towards a New Global Governance* (New York: Oxford University Press).14-30.

9

NEW DEVELOPMENTALISM

Industrial policy, policy space and premature deindustrialization debates[1]

Introduction

New developmentalism surfaced in the late 1980s and 1990s. Scholars, who could be termed new developmentalists, challenged the neoliberal interpretation of why and how countries like Japan, Korea and Taiwan succeeded in attaining catch-up growth when they did. In so doing, they proffered industrial policy as an alternative policy agenda to structural adjustment. Industry, particularly manufacturing, was viewed by developmentalists as special because unlike other sectors it is subject to dynamic efficiencies including, inter alia, increasing returns, technological learning and skill acquisition that result in productivity increases and higher wages (Chapter 6 and below).

Effective industrial policy thus became a core element of new developmentalism, just as structural adjustment is the core element of neoliberalism (Chapter 8). Also, just as structural adjustment is a broad program, similarly industrial policy entails the implementation of supportive policies addressing trade, R&D and technology, competition, foreign direct investment (FDI), state-owned enterprises (SOEs), finance, exchange rate management, quality control, and standards and equity.

While there were differences among the countries researched, the commonality was their coherent, nuanced and well-implemented industrial and support policies. This observation came as a challenge to the mainstream view that successful development was the result of free market policies. Establishing an alternative explanation was a significant landmark in the economic development literature, one that the World Bank (WB) acknowledged (World Bank, 2005) with qualifications.[2]

This chapter first identifies the key features of new developmentalism including industrial policy. Industrial policy is based on the presumption that industry has a special role in economic development following on from the thinking of developmentalist scholars. We briefly review the post-developmentalist case for industry as the key driver of catch-up growth. Not all are persuaded that an industrial policy is needed for successful economic development and so the debate on industrial policy is reviewed next. Even if the case for industrial policy is successfully made, development pessimists argue that the global scenario L/

LMICs currently face has altered from when developmentalists were making their prescriptions and that the policy space for industrial policy has been closed. Development optimists argue that there still is sufficient leeway for industrial policy. We explore this debate between development pessimists and optimists. Finally, even if developmental optimists are right and there is adequate policy space available for industrial policy, some scholars argue that industrialization is passé. They point to the evidence of premature deindustrialization in L/LMICs and argue that the nature of economic development has changed and that the "stylized facts" of economic development suggesting a larger sector share of industry accompanying the growth in per capita GDP no longer holds. We explore this premature deindustrialization debate i.e. its existence, causes and appropriate responses.

Key features of new developmentalism[3]

This school of thought inherited the mantle of developmentalists (Chapter 6) in advocating an interventionist approach. The approach gained traction by establishing that the success of the East Asian Newly Industrialized Countries (NICs) was not in fact a good example of the success of neoliberalism as was being claimed. New developmentalism relies on the theorizing of the early developmentalists/structuralists but got reestablished by empirically demonstrating what was done by the NICs to attain catch-up growth. The term neostructuralist is the Latin American variant which again emphasizes industry and hence changing the structure of the economy.[1]

In a nutshell, the goal of new developmentalism is to shift resources to high productivity/increasing return activities rather than conform to static comparative advantage. The objective is to diversify the economy and constantly move it to higher value added activities. Diversification has several advantages including a decrease in the volatility of export income which is associated with an excessive dependence on commodity exports. This in turn could lead to a more stable macroeconomic environment and faster economic growth. More diverse economies may be better able to take advantage of export opportunities in global markets as they emerge. Much of trade expansion is viewed to occur through the marketing of new goods rather than enhancing markets for existing products (UNIDO, 2009).

The strategy for attaining this objective of diversification has been distilled from the East Asian experience although advocates acknowledge that the strategy needs to be country specific. Based on commonalities of the East Asian experience the key features are a selective use of the market i.e. utilizing it as an instrument. New developmentalists are willing to draw on neoliberalism when the market is deemed to work well. Thus the approach is eclectic and pragmatic rather than dogmatic or ideological and relies on evidence and common sense reasoning. While they concede government failure and inefficiencies in various cases, the answer is not necessarily less or no government, but rather better government.

The emphasis thus is on "crowding in" due to government activity rather than the crowding out posited by neoliberals.[4]

New developmentalists frame policy recommendations based on "the national interest". The concept of national interest is ambiguous because a nation is rarely a homogeneous entity but generally a mosaic of competing classes, ethnic groups and regions. Thus, does working in the national interest mean working for the particular groups whose interests the state is representing at a point in time? The implicit view taken by new developmentalists is that the state should expand the size of the pie based on a foundation of equity and that virtuous circles set in motion would reinforce equity (Chapter 15). New developmentalism relies on the presence of effective government and identifies its functions but, like neoliberalism, is not able to explain the emergence of effective government.

All NICs extensively used key organizations to provide the lead role for industrialization such as the Ministry of International Trade and Industry in Japan, the Economic Planning Bureau in Korea and the Industrial Development Bureau in Taiwan. These were supra-ministries with sweeping powers of coordination that not only shaped industrial policy but also controlled the financing. When financing of industrial development is controlled by the Finance Ministry, as is normally the case in electoral democracies, the industrialization project can be undermined by other political imperatives such as getting reelected.

The investment to GDP ratio was uniformly raised to construct supporting infrastructure for industry. The funds were often drawn by suppressing capital outflows and suppressing luxury consumption. Chang (1993, p. 139) pointed out that Japan and Korea had far fewer passenger cars per capita than current L/LMICs countries at similar levels of development.

The central feature of new developmentalism is industrial policy. One could argue that industrial policy is for new developmentalists what structural adjustment is for the neoliberals. Any policy that affects industrial development in any way can be termed industrial policy.[5] The Japanese were the path-breakers in this regard and Korea and Taiwan developed it further, and industrial policy now has broad acceptance in L/LMICs. Annual industrial policies are now routinely announced as are for example trade policies.

Industrial policies are not confined to L/LMICs only. In fact, even though it is much maligned by mainstream economists, HICs also routinely utilize them. Examples include support via subsidies for Boeing and Airbus by the United States and the EU respectively. The bailout of General Motors in 2009, support for green energy and for research institutes for innovation are examples of industrial policy engaged in by the Obama administration.[6] The Trump administration's trade protective stance in 2018 was designed to rekindle industrialization in the United States. Of late, even some mainstream economists have been positive about industrial policy based on logical reasoning and evidence and have advocated its use for HICs (Aghion, Boulanger and Cohen, 2011). Others have taken at least a narrow version of it more seriously (Harrison and Rodríguez-Clare, 2010).

The case for industrial policy goes back to the thinking of the developmentalists (Chapter 6). Recall that they argued that some activities will not be forthcoming unless the requisite infrastructure (roads, ports, utilities) is in place, and that the social marginal returns to such infrastructure exceed the private returns and so would be underprovided. Hirschman (Chapter 6) argued that industries have linkages upstream and downstream; forward (toward final product) and backward (toward primary commodities). Thus, it made sense to encourage industries with the highest linkages such as steel (as this would encourage coal and iron upstream and engineering goods, automobiles, bikes and a range of industries downstream). The state role is to provide the necessary infrastructure and facilitate coordination to encourage businesses.

Another key aspect of new developmentalist thinking is that the market is not to be passively relied on to provide the signals concerning what a country is to specialize in based on neoclassical trade theory. Instead, comparative advantage in high value added activities needs to be created (dynamic comparative advantage). The argument is that government is needed to nurture industry since factor availability is not a sufficient basis to be successful in extremely competitive international markets and, left to itself, local industry would get wiped out with free trade.

For example, Korea would not have developed a heavy industry if it relied on comparative advantage (Wade, 2016, p. 34). Korea was repeatedly turned down by the WB in its loan solicitation for a steel industry based on comparative advantage reasoning. It finally secured a loan and joint venture with Japan's Mitsubishi Steel and within ten years broke into export markets. It developed the mini-mill concept and made it impossible for large steel mills in the west to compete and this contributed to the collapse of Bethlehem Steel in Philadelphia.[7]

Thus the argument is that the state should create comparative advantage based on country specificities and potential. The East Asian experience suggests that high dynamic efficiencies such as linkages, complementarities, scale economies, income-elasticity, demand creation and low energy elasticity are among the crucial factors to look for in promoting particular industries.

Again the strategy adopted for industrial policy can vary. Rodrik (2007b) viewed the process as one of public-private partnerships whereby businesses respond to information about opportunities and constraints and the enabling environment is provided by the state. Since the purpose is to encourage diversification of industry, he asserted it should be about promoting new activities. Another approach is for the public sector to follow the lead of the private sector and support and strengthen demonstrated success. This is referred to as followership by Wade (2004), though he argued that leadership (Wade called it "governing the market") is also important and conditions should dictate which approach to use. Amsdem (1989, p.14) called it "getting prices wrong". The idea is to create rents by setting prices to provide incentives for activities that require support.

Operationalizing industrial policy requires open channels of communications between the public and private sectors. Japan institutionalized it in deliberation councils. The function was communication to overcome the coordination problem by having interagency representation at the highest levels. Johnson (1982) documented that MITI had 38 deliberation councils and, in addition, there were formal discussion groups including public and private officials and the exchange of officials between the state and private enterprise. A common understanding and purpose was also cemented by the fact that many ex-bureaucrats became influential politicians, even attaining the top office of prime minister. The purpose of such communication was to generate ideas for investments, push for the needed legislation, put subsidies in place, overcome constraints and transaction costs, and agree on performance criteria (see below).

The legitimate neoliberal concern is that putting protection in place immediately creates vested interests. The social links between politicians, bureaucracy and businesses that are all from the same elite class creates the potential for corruption (bribes for extending protection and for special privileges) and makes it politically difficult to change policy that some gain from even if the public loses.

Evans (1995) discussed effective economic governance in developmentalist states in terms of embedded autonomy – attaining a fine balance such that economic bureaucrats are at sufficient arm's length to avoid rent seeking but embedded enough in networks to be able to facilitate businesses as needed. Some of the mechanisms for attaining this were entertaining pre-investment proposals emerging from a competitive process. In addition, they made the process transparent by publishing minutes of meetings and by ensuring that all support was budgeted and monitored. The schedule for support was pre-announced and deemed as irreversible even if policy makers got the timing somewhat wrong. Policy consistency and sticking to announcements was important for establishing policy credibility. Since vested interests develop fast, having a pre-announced exit policy from incentives is particularly critical.

An exit policy was also needed for firms not deemed to have adequate value. Firms have "specific assets" that are likely to go to waste when they are phased out and so incumbents resist change despite incentives.[8] An important part of industrial policy is to persuade potential losers to allow the structural transformation to happen via orderly capital scrapping arrangements.

The length of protection needed depends on the technological and skill base in the economy and the speed with which transitional inefficiencies are overcome. This partly depends on effective public policy in providing the needed incentives and social and physical infrastructure. The local economic bureaucracy, assuming reasonable competence, should be best able to judge how long to keep protection in place given that it is familiar with local conditions.

A key feature of successful industrial policy is imposing and implementing reciprocal performance criteria i.e. granting incentives in exchange for performance. Amsdem (1989) pointed out that what distinguished the East Asian developmental states from others in Latin America or Asia was not the framing of performance criteria, since most states did this, but in the ability to implement reciprocity. Incentives could be conditioned on profit, productivity/output/

employment, investment rates, local content, financial soundness, improved management practices, or successfully engaging in R&D.

In fact breaking into export markets in a timely manner is a good proxy for ascertaining success in the other goals mentioned above as it implies internationally competitive products so one can be assured that quality is being delivered and standards met with.[9] Breaking into export markets could also indicate a firm is attaining economies of scale and realizing technological learning, and the foreign exchange earnings are certainly welcome for a country embarked on catch-up growth since it is one of the most binding constraints they confront.

These performance criteria or conditionalities, which predate the IMF/WB loan conditionalities, are mainly designed to build indigenous technological capacity. Also, the trade and industrialization strategy that it represents is neither exclusively import substitution industrialization (ISI) or export promotion. ISI nurtures successful export promotion by building a base and export promotion then reinforces further ISI via technological learning, managerial and marketing skills, and relaxing the foreign exchange constraint. As countries diversify and move up the value chain, they simultaneously engage in ISI and export promotion in a mutually complementary manner.

Success is never assured. In the foggy world of economic policy setting, no precision is implied in setting policy or in the ex-ante knowledge of outcomes. Mistakes are expected and inevitable, but overall the East Asian states got it right and showed the way. Rodrik (2008) pointed out that one success pays for many failures and the lack of failure suggests a lack of effort.

While inefficiency and corruption are likely to be present, most bureaucracies have agencies with a good track record and they are the ones to be entrusted with key tasks and therefore the tools for industrial policy are likely to be determined by that. Thus, if the public development banks have a better track record than tax administration, directed credit rather than tax relief may be emphasized. The need for flexibility and pragmatism is paramount in choosing from a whole range of available tools.

The specific tools or incentives that have been used as part of implementing industrial policy include duty free import licenses to exporters for raw materials, parts and capital goods; start-up support; subsidizing credit for equipment; arranging long-term finance and giving investment guarantees to commercial banks if they are reluctant to make loans; undervaluing the exchange rate as an option to promote exports; tax exemptions; investing in quality control/standards; subsidizing inputs and utilities; investing in training and skills development and R&D in partnership with the private sector; developing industry-specific research institutes and universities; using foreign missions for export promotion; and attracting expatriate entrepreneurs with incentives to initiate activities.

The intervention was at times very intensive and unusual. For example, in Korea, President Park on assuming office had some preeminent businessmen arrested for corruption during the tenure of the past regime. He threatened to confiscate the ill-gotten gains but provided the option of rehabilitating these businessmen based on their stated and demonstrated commitment to serving the development imperative (Westphal, 1990, p. 58; Chang, 1993, p. 151).

An export situation room was used to monitor mutually agreed firm level targets relative to achievements on a daily basis. Ministers interceded to facilitate exports as needed and the President chaired a monthly trade promotion conference. Successful exporters were given national awards and positive publicity for national service rendered (Westphal, 1990, pp. 45–46).

Industrial policy was embedded in a whole set of associated policies, including trade, R&D and technology, competition, FDI, SOEs, finance, exchange rate management, quality control, and standards and equity. Initially the focus of R&D was not basic research but to develop the capacity of local industry to import, adapt and absorb state of the art technology under local management and control. Thus, the technology policy was very industry specific. The focus on science and engineering was also product specific (e.g. electronic engineering). Basic research becomes an issue once catch-up growth is attained and China for example has been moving in that direction over the first two decades of the 21st century by establishing a national innovation and research system.[10]

There was public provision of specialized training and compulsory training schemes and worker certification in the larger firms. Employment policies and company unions meant retaining the benefits of the training within the firm.

Competition policy was not as is conventionally understood i.e. putting effective anti-trust institutions and organizations into place. Instead, it was geared to enhancing productivity. Thus, state-facilitated mergers enabled some firms to attain scale economies if there were too many firms in the industry (over-competition). While monopolies were not tolerated, oligopolies were tolerated if it led to joint R&D, export drives, technological upgrading and the greater ability to weather recessions.

Another aspect of competition policy was using the threat of imports to punish local firms as a mechanism for quality control. For example, Taiwan destroyed 20,000 light bulbs due to poor quality and threatened to allow in imports (Wade, 2004). In Korea, the Industrial Development Bank used the approval method for imports in the chemical industry. For example, if domestic chemical firms were not delivering products at a reasonable price and quality, imports would be used as a disciplinary measure (Amsdem, 1989).[11]

While FDI was encouraged, it was carefully managed in different ways in different countries. In Korea, wholly owned MNCs in the 1980s were 5 percent of total FDI compared to 50 percent for Mexico and 60 percent for Brazil at that time (Chang, 1993, p. 144).[12] Also, technical assistance contracts were issued for a short period (three years) so that local firms were forced to internalize the technology. The emphasis was on joint ventures under local ownership with the specific purpose of acquiring the needed technology, and China developed this mechanism into an art form (Linden, 2004).[13]

FDI was viewed as a mechanism for technological acquisition to serve the domestic economic agenda such as attaining high local content. As much as possible, they were directed toward export promotion based on buying local. If allowed to operate in the domestic market, local capital and entrepreneurs were supported to level the playing field. Thus, the idea was to use FDI as a tool to develop local industry rather than over-relying on it to the point of wiping out local industry.

The Taiwanese government often initiated production via SOEs and retained it under state control as a lead firm in the industry until fairly late. Korea often nationalized industries/firms in trouble and then privatized them once they were stabilized. Even in the 1980s, state ownership in banking, oil, steel, coal, gas, electricity and fertilizer (commanding heights of the economy) was greater than 80 percent (Chang, 1993, p. 153). In China, SOEs have been used as the leading edge for technology acquisition and development and as a source of employment.

The financial system was tightly controlled and subordinated to the needs of industrial capital and extensive use was made of directed credit. Most banks were nationalized and even those that were not were subject to state control. In Korea, the state restricted maximum ownership by one individual or group to 8 percent in order to retain control. This control was sustained even after privatization in the 1980s. In fact, policy loans as a percentage of the total increased from 56 percent in 1962–1981 to 68 percent in 1982–1985 (Chang, 1993, p. 152).

Foreign exchange was treated as a very scarce resource and its use prioritized. Stringent capital controls and the exclusion of the use of foreign exchange for luxury goods enabled adequate reserves for vital imports. Violators of exchange controls laws in Korea could face the death penalty (Chang, 1993, p. 152).

While unions were discouraged, higher wages were encouraged as part of a broader framework of equity on which industrial policy was founded. Land reforms created the base for efficient agriculture (Chapters 6 and 14) and provided cheaper food and materials and a larger market for industry. High mean literacy, secondary education, training and sound health policies represented the investments in human development to support industrialization. Thus economic growth was shared and this is also evident from the low level of inequalities compared to comparators. The quintile income share ratios in Table 9.1 are illustrative in this regard.

Much of what has been discussed so far pertaining to industrial policies is at the macro or meso level. However, following logically from them is the

TABLE 9.1 Income share ratios (top to bottom quintile)

Year	Brazil	Mexico	Korea
1984	23.3	13.1	5.7 (1988)
1992	20.4	14.0	na
1999	25.3	13.1	4.6 (1998)
2005	21.9	11.4	5.4

Source: World Development Indicators. Korean data for 1988 and 1998 were drawn from Chang (2006), which made the comparison using less comparable data but nonetheless was able to demonstrate the same point.

micro-level industrial policy of building firm-level capabilities with technology policy, monitoring standards, R&D and the establishment of national innovation systems (Lall, 2013).

As stated earlier, while there were and are commonalities in how developmentalist states pursued catch-up growth, there were important differences Lall (2013, pp. 24–37). For example, Hong Kong, an island economy, was much more market oriented than the others and while it had elements of an industrial policy, openness may also have accounted for a rapid decline in its manufacturing base. While Singapore is also an island economy, it has and continues to use industrial policy extensively. Japan and Korea had differences (e.g. Korea relied on international capital markets while Japan did not), but both used a corporatist model with large industrial conglomerates (*keretsu* or *chaebols*) leading the way under state tutelage. Taiwan relied more on FDI and state-led firms to initiate particular industries and then hand them over to the private sector once established. South East Asian economies and China relied more extensively on FDI for the transfer of technology and, as mentioned above, China with its leverage has been the most successful in this regard.

The global economic environment has changed and current L/LMIC will need to draw on the industrial policy lessons from countries that successfully achieved catch-up growth but will also need to forge their own paths. The fragmentation of production in some industries (where weight to value ratio of products is low) is one such change that they will have to contend with. Large MNCs with complex information technology driven production systems can outsource parts of a product to the most suitable cost-cutting locations. Competing with them on such products may be difficult and in these industries insertion into the value chains might be strategically more sensible in some cases to glean marketing and networking knowledge. Another challenge is the emergence of China and, to a lesser extent, India, that are able to compete across the whole product range. Yet another challenge will be conducting industrial policy in a much less energy intensive manner to meet carbon targets agreed to in global climate agreements (Chapter 14).

The post-developmentalist case for industry

As indicated above, industrial policy has been the central component of the catch-up growth strategy of East Asian, South East Asian states and most recently China. The original case for industry as the key driver of economic development was made by developmentalists and is summarized in Chapter 6. Recall from Chapter 6 that Kaldor provided the empirical support for the developmentalist conviction regarding the importance of industrialization. There has been a fair amount of empirical work since on this issue.

Several authors have utilized Kaldor's framework for testing the centrality of industry to catch-up growth using more recent data. Wells and Thirlwall (2003) find some support for the Kaldor-Verdoorn Laws using a sample of 47 African countries over 1980–1996 (for caveats on cross-country analysis, see Chapter 2). Dasgupta and Singh's (2006) research findings, based again on cross-country analysis, showed industry continues to be a dynamic sector though perhaps not exclusively so (see section on deindustrialization below). This result was replicated by Acevedo, Mold and Perez (2009) for Latin America between 1950 and 2006 who addressed some of the methodological flaws to which pooled cross-sectional studies are subject.[14]

Rodrik (2007b) mustered evidence to argue that economic development is about structural transformation. This entails the diversification of activities (primarily within manufacturing but also new activities such as IT in services or modernized agricultural activities). Thus it is not about comparative advantage and specialization, but rather about learning new things. He cited evidence to show that growth accelerations (of 2 percent or more starting from a base of 3.5 percent and that were sustained for at least eight years) are mostly associated with manufacturing exports.

The evidence cited above showed that policy is as important as, if not more so, factor endowments in what countries specialize in. Policy-based industrial upgrading to enhance product sophistication (moving up the value chain) boosts economic performance. Evidence also showed that L/LMICs that made the effort to produce typically HIC products showed a convergence to the productivity levels of HICs in those products (unconditional convergence).[15] Finally, he cited evidence to show that a country with a broad-based manufacturing sector is more likely to take advantage of new opportunities than one which has specialized in a few primary-based products; yet another reason to industrialize.

United Nations Industrial Development Organization (UNIDO) in its annual *Industrial Development Reports* made a case for industry from various perspectives. For example, UNIDO (2009) pointed out that climate change is likely to directly impact agriculture but not industry and hence industrial development could be part of climate adaptation strategy. Also, while agriculture has natural limitations associated with endowments, this is much less the case for industry. Recall from Chapter 7 that declining terms of trade and low income elasticity of demand pose challenges for the primary sector. Periodic commodity booms with appreciating exchange rates and resource diversions add to these challenges. Unlike services, the large and growing global market provides manufacturing export opportunities for small countries.

UNIDO (2009) pointed out that industrial development is subject to various virtuous circles. For example, productivity growth embodied in manufacturing results in relative price falls (unlike agriculture and service sectors) which result in demand creation, economies of scale, product diversification, further productivity rise and so on.

This broad range of argumentation and supporting evidence endorses the developmentalist conviction that learning, enhancing capabilities and externalities, among other development features, are embodied in industrial expansion (Chapter 6). However, not all scholars are persuaded of the merits of such policy.

The industrial policy debate

Critics argue that industrial policy is about the state "picking winners". They contend that states lack the decentralized knowledge referred to by Hayek (1945) as "particular circumstances of time and place". Further, in a constantly changing world it is difficult to keep abreast of this knowledge. Markets and the price information they generate enable individuals ("man on the spot") to effectively use their special knowledge in response and so non-interventionists argue that states should get out of the way and let this happen for a socially optimum outcome.

A heterodox rejoinder is that markets are a state construct. To function well, markets need complex and sophisticated legislation on property rights and also legal systems for enforcement that only a state could provide. Prices are thus indirectly a state construct. Furthermore, they can also be a state construct directly for example via regulation, micro policies (taxes and subsidies), macro policies (like exchange rates and interest rates) and how institutions and political power dynamics interact with these factors. Thus, there is nothing sacrosanct per se in the prices observed and they constantly change not only in response to market forces but also political, economic and social objectives, as indicated above. To wish for "price purity" via an elimination of policy and regulation is naïve since even market forces are influenced by existing ownership, and the distribution of income and the willingness to accept what exists at a point in time is a value judgment.

New developmentalists also argue that the issue of picking winners is irrelevant since developmentalist states are simply following a track record of success of the countries that successfully industrialized. Thus the issue is not one of picking winners, but rather one of creating them.

Another criticism is that industrial policy requires efficient bureaucracies and while some East Asian economies had them, most L/LMICs do not and so industrial policy is not an option for them. The rejoinder is that neoliberal structural adjustment policies like privatization, liberalization, deregulation and macro stabilization are no less "good government" intensive than industrial policy. Capture and corruption are equally likely with structural adjustment, since winners and losers result from all policies.

As earlier noted, industrial policy advocates argue that there are pockets of efficiency in bureaucracies and these can be used for structural adjustment and can similarly be used for industrial policy (Rodrik, 2004, pp. 23–24). Also, a reasonably efficient bureaucracy, like so many other variables, is endogenous to the development process. In fact, right up to the 1960s, Korea sent its bureaucrats to Pakistan and the Philippines for training so an effective bureaucracy is not an initial condition for industrial policy (Chang, 2015, p. 45).

Factors in cultivating effective bureaucracies include selective hiring, accountability mechanisms and good salaries. Civil servants in developmental states were well paid relative to similar jobs in the private sector (in Korea they got 82 to 99 percent of private sector pay plus the perks, status and privileges of public sector jobs). In Singapore, public sector salaries exceeded the private sector. In contrast, in Argentina, public sector salaries were 20 to 30 percent those of the private sector in a comparative period.

Neoliberal critics who concede that some form of industrial policy might be valuable, nonetheless argue that it should be general (horizontal) rather than specific (vertical) i.e. neutrally facilitate all industries via good infrastructure and R&D policies and after that let the market work to uncover winners. The rejoinder to this point is that while the prescription sounds good, it is not practical. Given limited resources, financial and administrative targeting is both inevitable and desirable.

Critics make much of the most celebrated industrial policy mistakes. For example, the Japanese government discouraged Honda and Sony from entry into the market to avoid over-competition. The rejoinder is that making mistakes is part of industrial policy and the exceptions prove the rule; scratch the surface of most successes and industrial policy will be unearthed and one success pays for many failures. Only a third of US businesses survive into their tenth year so a high failure rate is part of the market system.[16]

Critics also argue that the "initial conditions" with regards to social and physical infrastructure of developmentalist states that successfully pursued industrial policy were very different from most other L/LMICs. Chang (2006) compared initial conditions of Korea, Sub-Saharan Africa (SSA) and Latin America and concluded that there is no basis for this contention. Literacy rates in Korea in the 1950s were 22 percent, way below many SSA countries. However, by 1960 it had increased to 71 percent once catch-up growth was initiated. Secondary and technical education was notably better in Korea, but this was also the case in the Philippines, which is still an LMIC (literacy rate was 72 percent in 1960). Scientists and technicians were roughly equivalent in the 1950s, but again Korea gained and sustained a lead in the 1960s after catch-up growth was initiated.

Physical infrastructure was not much different either as measured by the population intensity of variables like telephones or railroads. The industrial base in Korea was not much better in the 1950s than SSA, and Latin America was way ahead. Many attribute Korean success to a high level of foreign aid from the United States, but Chang showed that foreign aid per capita in the 1960s was not much higher than SSA. Although military expenditures in Korea were much higher, this represented a higher budgetary burden.

Chang also debunks the SSA resource curse myth and argued that most of SSA was not as resource rich as Canada or the Scandinavian countries. He concluded that on most grounds, Korea was similar in the 1940s and 1950s to SSA while Latin America was way ahead. Korea did have lower levels of infant mortality and its life expectancy numbers in the 1950s were better than SSA. The upshot is that with the right developmentalist policies, countries can initiate catch-up growth. However, some critics argue that while this might have been the case in the 1950s and 1960s, the global rules governing economic development have changed and policy choices available then are no longer an option.

The policy space debate

Development pessimists argue that there has been an asymmetrical closure of policy space which has blocked prospects for catch-up growth. The argument is that up until the Uruguay Round (UR) was approved (1993) and the resulting formation of the World Trade Organization (WTO) (1995), countries, including HICs, were able to use performance requirements on MNCs to support local industrialization and enhance local technological capabilities. With the passing of the UR agreements and the formation of the WTO as an implementing organization for trade and investment liberalization, opportunities for such industrialization are now blocked for L/LMICs.

They argue that HICs have more resources to use the Dispute Settlement Mechanism within the WTO to discipline LMICs (Lee, Shin, and Shin, 2014).[17] Apart from trade and investment liberalization enforcement built into the WTO, the IMF/World Bank, which are disproportionately funded by and located in HICs, discipline L/LMICs that require financial assistance.

The view, encouraged by its public relations campaigns, that the IMF no longer imposes onerous conditions curbing policy space and that these conditions are homegrown and tailored to country specificities, has been challenged by Kentikelenis, Stubbs and King (2016). Using extensive archival analysis they show that, notwithstanding the rhetoric to the contrary, the IMF programs have not evolved to allow for more policy space.

Khan (2007) showed that the conditionalities imposed for the financial assistance often resulted in even more aggressive trade liberalizations that the voluntary undertakings L/LMICs subjected themselves to as part of the UR agreements. Again there is asymmetry since HICs are not subject to such conditionalities. Further, WTO agreements are one sided and while HICs lobbied and secured aggressive tariff cutting on non-agriculture, they were able to continue to subsidize their agricultural sectors.

Another source of asymmetrical pressure regarding policy space closure is mediated via MNCs. Pressure from consumers, shareholders and western labor unions have pushed MNCs into requiring their business partners in L/LMIC value chains to abide by "codes of conduct" regarding social, environmental and labor standards. Consumers and shareholders are concerned about production under humane conditions while labor and policy makers are concerned about production occurring on a level playing field that does not undermine production in the west based on lower costs of production due to lower regulatory standards. There is also HIC pressure within the WTO for the adoption of standards, though L/LMICs have balked at this.[18]

The Human Development Report 2005 of the UNDP (2005, pp 133–139) lamented the closing of policy space for economic development. Based on the "single undertaking", post-UR members have had to comply with all agreements as a package. The UNDP (2005) argued that the agreements as a package severely restricted the scope for industrial and technology policy. It pointed out that even as late as the early 1990s, India continued to successfully build its domestic automobile components industry with high tariffs, local content requirements and training clauses that are now ruled out by TRIMs (Trade Related Investment Measures).

The Agreement on Subsidies and Countervailing Measures (SCM) prohibits a wide range of fiscal, export and credit subsidies to support domestic industrialization. Copying and reverse engineering for technology acquisition, standard fare for the early developmentalist states, is blocked by TRIPS (Trade Related Intellectual Property Rights) and TRIPS plus (the more stringent version pushed in regional and bilateral investment agreements).[19] Thus, a path that was open to and followed by the currently high and middle income countries has now been closed.

Wade (2005) argued that the WTO via the UR Agreements has blocked access to technology via TRIPS. It requires countries to protect intellectual property, for example by granting patents and acknowledging copyrights, and blocks off the practice of compulsory licensing in negotiations with MNCs. The cost of knowledge for L/LMIC has become steeper, and Wade (2003, p. 624) cited a World Bank study indicating that post WTO formation, "US companies pocketed an additional net $19 billion a year in royalties from full application of TRIPS".

Wade further pointed out that TRIMs rules out specifying performance requirements (local content, trade balancing (exports to match imports), and export clauses in such negotiations). It also bans requirements on public agencies to procure goods from local suppliers. The General Agreement on Trade in Services (GATS) extends the "most favored nation" clause of the WTO to services which require member countries to provide "like treatment" for foreign firms as given to national firms.

The SDT (Special and Differential Treatment), an enabling feature of GATT (General Agreement on Trade and Tariffs) prior to the UR for L/LMIC, now merely allows more time for compliance, but the date of reckoning inevitably approaches and many requests for extensions have been turned down by the WTO. Gallagher (2007) estimated that, "more than 25 percent of total WTO cases between 1995 and 2005 dealt with dismantling policy space in developing countries". Further, he reported that, "in all cases the final ruling [after appeal] upheld the demand".

However, Gallagher (2008) also argued that there is leeway in UR agreements like TRIMs and TRIPS and so L/LMICs can use exemptions skillfully and continue with the old policies. Even though quotas were ruled out and tariffs reduced by the UR, the balance of payment clause can still be invoked for tariffs and non-essential imports blocked (i.e. there is a safeguard mechanism). The WTO allows countries to define non-essential imports. GATS has a positive list approach so countries can choose what to liberalize (though decisions are not reversible). It is also possible to specify ownership stake and local hiring under this agreement.

While targeted export subsidies are actionable under the SCM Agreement, material damage has to be demonstrated. Below the radar subsidies continue to be possible up until the time a country is ready to export. Mah (2015, 191) pointed out that developing countries can provide subsidies of up to 2 percent of the value of a product, which is substantial. Local content requirements and compulsory licensing are prohibited but not for countries with PCGDP of < $1,000. The latter are exempt from other clauses also.

Amsden (2005) was also more sanguine about policy space than the development pessimists. Echoing some of the points made earlier, she argued that various articles of the WTO still allow for tariffs: Article XVIII to counter balance of payments destabilization; Article XIX to counter import surges; and Article VI to counter unfair trade practices. She asserted (p. 220) that "as a consequence of limited agreement in the area of TRIMs, LICs are able to maintain or even strengthen – various performance requirements including local content, trade balancing and exports".[20] The WTO continues to permit subsidies to promote R&D, regional development and environmentalism. In particular, countries with a per capita income of less than $1,000 are permitted to use export subsidies via science parks and EPZs (Export Processing Zones) based on SDT. Thus, she argued that much scope still existed to support science and technology for industrial policy.[21] For example, tariff rebates and providing production and marketing information are still possible.

While TRIPS has substantially constrained technological learning, Shadlin (2005, p. 9) documented that even while being TRIPS compliant, countries still have considerable freedom to design IPR policies that are development friendly and to create legal environments to promote technology transfer.[22] There is also considerable flexibility in requiring compulsory licensing for domestic production catering to domestic markets with "adequate" (defined locally) compensation for patent holders.

In short, the above measures could be used strategically for industrial policy. Chang in fact argued that many of the tools used by East Asian countries for their catch-up growth are still available.[23] These include credit rationing, tax policies, technical education, public procurement, skills and worker training policies, and administrative guidance and information policy. As Lee, Shin and Shin (2014) pointed out, at least up to 2012, no case based on the practice of LIC industrial policy was brought to the DSM of the WTO by HICs.[24] Correa (2015) pointed out that while TRIPS is a constraint, certain "flexibilities" are still available to L/LMICs. For example, strategic use of compulsory licensing and rigorously defining patentability standards to avoid the granting of unwarranted patent rights can extend policy space for industrialization in this regard.

On balance, L/LMICs still appear to have mechanisms to negotiate or extend policy space and offset its closing. However, the odds against industrialization have increased somewhat. L/LMICs may lack the necessary resources to use subsidies, not have enough leverage when negotiating with MNCs, or lack the knowledge, technical and negotiating skills to take advantage of the leverage they do have. Also, even the existing policy space is threatened by the powerful aid and trade leverage of HICs and the policy leverage mediated through International Financial Institutions (IFIs). Thus while battling the odds is still possible and shown to be done, for most L/LMICs strong determination to industrialize is called for. Ultimately the issue is empirical and if policy space has indeed had a negative impact post the UR, as development pessimists claim, then the numbers should indicate a stall of industrialization or deindustrialization in the post UR period. Table 9.2 addresses this issue.[25]

While industrial policy is the core agenda of new developmentalism, manufacturing has most importance because of its greatest potential for structural transformation, externalities, increasing returns, product diversification and moving up the value chain (elaborated on in Chapter 6 as dynamic efficiencies).

TABLE 9.2 Change in mean size of manufacturing as a percentage of GDP by income classification and region

Country classification and region	1960–1980	1981–1994	1995–2016	% change in mean SOM across the first two periods	% change in mean SOM across the second two periods
LIC	na	na	9.91 (22)	na	na
LMIC	na	17.65 (14)	16.47 (22)	na	−6.69
UMIC	28.43 (15)	28.55 (14)	23.53 (19)	0.42	−17.58
HIC	na	na	16.72 (19)	na	na
EA&P	na	28.87 (14)	23.52 (19)	na	−18.53
LA&C	25.94 (16)	25.36 (19)	16.59 (22)	−2.24	−34.58
SA	16.34 (21)	17.98 (14)	17.35 (22)	10.04	−3.50
SSA	na	13.87 (14)	11.05 (22)	na	−20.33
China	34.79 (15)	34.35 (14)	31.82 (19)	−1.26	−7.37

Source: World Development Indicators.
Notes: Parentheses contain years over which the mean was computed.
No data were available for Middle East and North Africa.
SOM = Manufacturing value added as a % of GDP in nominal local currency units
LIC = Low income countries ($1,025 or less annual per capita gross national income)
LMIC = Lower middle income countries ($1,026 – $4,035)
UMIC = Upper middle income countries ($4,036 – $12,475)
HIC = High income countries (above $12,476)
EE&P = East Asia and the Pacific
E&CA = Europe and Central Asia
LA&C = Latin America and the Caribbean
SA = South Asia
SSA = Sub-Saharan Africa

The rest of the industrial sector complements this role of manufacturing. The state of manufacturing is reviewed drawing on The World Bank's World Development Indicators (WDI) that reported data from 1960 to 2016. Over half a century of data on the size of the manufacturing sector as a percentage of GDP (SOM) has been split into the three periods; 1960–1980, 1981–1994 and 1995–2016.

The post-war period up to 1980 has been referred to by Amsdem (2001, p. 118) as the "golden age" for policy due to benign neglect on the part of the United States, the only force capable of projecting imperial power. The period from 1980s onwards is referred to as the "dark age". This is the structural adjustment era that represented much greater US policy interest in L/LMICs and hence much greater policy constraints on them. This period has been split into 1981–1994 and 1995–2016. The first of these periods represents the onset of the structural adjustment period and therefore one would expect the onset of deindustrialization. The second of these periods may represent the intensification of trade policy restrictions with the conclusion of the UR of trade talks and the formation of the WTO as a trade liberalization implementing agency. Thus, one might expect an intensification of deindustrialization.

In terms of general findings, LICs had by far the lowest SOM showing that industrialization had yet to pick up. As expected, HICs have a low SOM relative to MICs and UMICs and again as expected the latter had the highest SOM. Since data for 1960–1980 are for the most part not available, we are not able to see if there is suggestive evidence for the first hypothesis regarding a decline in manufacturing post 1980 due to structural adjustment. Data are only available for Latin American and the Caribbean and South Asia. For the former there was a modest decline in mean manufacturing (2 percent) while for South Asia there was a sizable increase (10 percent).

The suggestive evidence appears to bear out the second hypothesis regarding the intensification of deindustrialization post-WTO. The deindustrialization post the formation of the WTO as suggested by Table 9.2 is dramatic and across the board. By income classification it was the most notable for UMICs at 17.6 percent. Among regions it was most notable for the Latin American and Caribbean region at 34 percent.

How this deindustrialization played out over these periods for the 62 countries for which data were available can be seen in Appendix Table 9.1.[26] While deindustrialization is the norm, some countries (5 out of 62) showed positive growth in manufacturing activity in both the post 1995 (WTO) periods. Since all of these countries carry a small weight economically, they have been overwhelmed in the regional averages. Some countries (Benin, Democratic Republic of Congo, Guinea and Myanmar) showed very rapid industrialization in the 2009–2016 period, but it was from a very small base.[27]

If it could be conclusively demonstrated that shrinking policy space due to the IMF/WB/WTO policies results in deindustrialization, a case could be made for protecting that policy space. In fact, the literature review above suggests that despite the closing of policy space, there is considerable leeway available for determined countries to pursue industrial policies for catch-up growth. Yet the evidence reported in Table 9.2 and the literature cited below suggests that across the board deindustrialization has set in, perhaps prematurely for L/LMICs, and we turn next to a review of the literature on premature deindustrialization.

Premature deindustrialization

One of the "stylized facts" of economic growth is the process of structural change (Chapters 1 and 6). In this regard, as economies advance, first agriculture and then industry as a percentage of GDP are expected to shrink and a sophisticated service sector to expand as countries attain HIC or at least UMIC status. Yet, the evidence reported in Table 9.2 and elsewhere suggests that L/LMICs are experiencing deindustrialization much before they reach a per capita GDP when the decline in the share of industry should occur based on historical precedents.[28] Thus even L/LMICs are experiencing declines in industry share. This relatively recent phenomenon has been referred to in the development economics literature as "premature deindustrialization".

The relevant questions for L/LMICs addressed in this section are the following: If premature industrialization is occurring, does it matter? What might explain this phenomenon? Are there other engines of growth that L/LMICs could turn to instead for catch-up growth or should policy in L/LMICs try to offset this phenomenon and push harder for an industrial policy?

Recall that economic development for L/LMICs has been defined in this textbook (Chapter 1) in terms of diversifying economic activities and moving up the value chain. Recall also that industry as the engine of growth has so far been central to this process of catch-up growth (above and Chapter 6). Premature deindustrialization suggests that this path is now blocked. Dasgupta and Singh (2005) see the problem as one where labor released from a more efficient agriculture (and surplus population from the rural sectors), as characterized by Lewis in Chapter 6, moves to informal industry and services and stays mired there. This represents a loss of hope for L/LMICs in attaining catch-up growth.

Similarly, Rodrik (2015) argued that for those without a strong comparative advantage in manufacturing, some Asian economies became net importers of manufacturing, reversing a long process of import substitution. Thus he concluded that the industrialization driver for catch-up growth had closed.

Dasgupta and Singh (2005, 2006) appear to be the first to conceptually tackle the phenomenon of premature deindustrialization based on shrinking employment share of manufacturing.[29] Their empirical estimates showed premature deindustrialization (in employment rather than output terms) in India and more broadly. They speculated that one cause of the premature deindustrialization is the IMF/World Bank-led structural adjustment which caused the adoption of laissez faire policies and the virtual abandonment of industrial policies.

Structural adjustment policies include enforced trade, investment and capital market liberalizations in the context of financialization (Chapter 8 and Tan, 2014).

Trade and investment liberalizations can contribute to deindustrialization by aggressively enforcing the dropping of tariff barriers (Khan, 2007). This pushes L/LMICs to prematurely compete domestically against much more established exporters and domestically based foreign companies.

FDI is increasingly moving into L/LMICs in the context of fragmented production whereby L/LMICs are expected to insert themselves into global value chains. MNCs retain control of technological innovations and IT-enabled governance of the chains (Gereffi, Humphrey and Sturgeon, 2005; Baldwin, 2011). MNCs enhance their profits by outsourcing labor-intensive activities in the context of this production fragmentation to the cheapest source. This is contrary to the organic manufacturing experienced by the East Asian countries during their catch-up growth stage, as documented above, whereby they controlled the whole manufacturing process and enabled its rapid expansion. L/LMICs industrialists vie for being part of a global value chain, but this happens at the expense of producing the whole product themselves. MNCs' outsourcing strategies make them far more competitive in producing the final product.

Financialization (growth in financial sector relative to non-finance), including capital market liberalization, privileges portfolio investments so that returns on financial investment increase. In L/LMICs, this results in a reallocation of resources toward speculative and away from real investments. Thus, as the financial sector grows, it is at the expense of industry.

Financialization and other structural adjustment policies are also collectively associated with income inequality (Chapter 8) and this is another channel via which neoliberal structural adjustment policies might have promoted premature deindustrialization. Grabowski (2017) focused on the demand side rather than the supply side (factors hindering production) and argued that rising income inequality in L/LMICs reduced the demand for mass-produced labor-intensive goods and privileged imported luxury consumption. This was reinforced by growing inequality in HICs, which also caused a reduction in demand for labor-intensive manufactured goods consumed more by the lower income groups. He provided suggestive evidence for this hypothesis.

Rodrik (2015) suggested the deindustrialization was based on a trade channel such that the falling relative prices of manufacturing goods resulting from manufacturing productivity growth in HICs, made it difficult for price-taking developing economies to compete. Hence he associated premature deindustrialization with economic globalization and market outcomes rather than political economy or power asymmetry outcomes, as suggested above. However, following this market logic, MNCs from HICs are price makers and so they may well engage in predatory pricing to induce premature deindustrialization.

The rise in commodity prices is another market channel through which premature deindustrialization could have been mediated. The commodity boom is dated for the period 2000–2014 and this overlaps with the last two of the four periods for which mean manufacturing shares are reported in Table 9.2. Latin America and SSA were the most likely to have gained from this commodity boom and this is consistent with among the greatest percentage mean deindustrialization evident in these regions for this period. Resources may have been reallocated away from manufacturing to take advantage of the higher commodity prices. Concomitantly, the classic Dutch disease could have been operational whereby the rise in commodity prices resulted in currency appreciation and impeded manufactured exports.

Another possible cause of the premature deindustrialization in many L/LMICs is the "China story" (see for example, Gallagher and Shafaeddin, 2011). The story is that manufacturing efficiency in China and the scale of its operations has turned it into the global factory and this has displaced production in other L/LMICs and even MICs. The numbers in Table 9.2 show that even China's manufacturing output share has declined. However, since its economy has grown rapidly, in absolute terms its manufacturing could still be having a massive displacement effect.

Some scholars view the premature deindustrialization in L/LMICs as suggestive of the need to find alternative drivers for take-off growth. Dasgupta and Singh (2005) showed that the service sector reveals some of the dynamism that the developmentalists attributed to industry and so services, particular IT, could serve as an additional engine of growth.

They speculated that an IT-driven service sector might play a complementary role of an economic development engine, since its spillover effects might be even stronger than manufacturing and because it generates products and processes that are tradable.[30] However, it is possible that IT is more of an enabler for productivity growth across the board. Further, it requires an R&D infrastructure associated with more advanced development than L/LMICs possess, barring the possible exception of India. Notwithstanding their endorsement of the service sector as a possible alternative economic growth driver, their broader recommendation nonetheless was that L/LMICs should restore "energetic and creative" industrial policies with the necessary supportive institutions. Acevedo, Mold and Perez (2009) explored growth engines or drivers in Kaldor's framework and found evidence that subsectors of the service sector like finance, commerce and transport can also act as economic growth drivers.

However, as explained above, advocates of industrial policy are concerned with dynamic comparative advantage and so this argument citing comparative advantage would not carry weight with them. Based on the evidence supporting industry as a driver of catch-up growth and the lack of convincing evidence for an alternative driver, it would follow that industrial policy advocates would suggest doubling down on crafting intelligent and well-governed industrial policies.

Summing up the response to the questions raised at the beginning of this section, there is evidence of premature deindustrialization. There is a difference of opinion on the causes of this phenomenon with mainstream scholars emphasizing market outcome (price responses) and heterodox scholars emphasizing political economy factors like the deindustrialization impact of various components of structural adjustment. The evidence shows that the manufacturing sector continues to be an important driver for catch-up growth and this provides a case for doubling down on industrial policies rather than abandoning them in response to structural adjustment pressures. There is some support for services but not for agriculture as a possible alternative driver for catch-up growth. However, while the mechanisms via which manufacturing can act as a catch-up growth driver have been fleshed out (Chapter 6, and this chapter), that is not the case for services.

While across the board premature deindustrialization could be viewed as a problem from a catch-up growth perspective, ecologists may welcome it. Climate change has changed the world dramatically since the catch-up growth of East and South East Asian countries.[31] L/LMICs will need to voluntarily move to or be pushed toward clean production methods and industrialization without consideration of local or global externalities is likely to become increasingly difficult. All countries (the United States plans to withdraw in November 2020) endorsed the Paris Agreement of November 2016 and have therefore voluntarily undertaken to limit carbon emissions. While no enforcement mechanisms were agreed to, at a minimum, countries violating voluntary undertakings will be subject to international pressure. This issue of sustainable industrial development is addressed in Chapter 13.

Summary

This chapter reviews key features of new developmentalist thinking. It argues that industrial policy is the central feature of new developmentalism just as structural adjustment is the key feature of neoliberalism. After a review of new developmentalism, it explores the post-developmentalist case for industry. Following this, there is a review of industrial policy and the debate revolving around industrial policy.

Even if industrial policy were an important reason for the attainment of catch-up growth in East Asian developmentalist states, development pessimists view the policy space for industrial and associated policies to have closed since the approval of the UR (1993) and the establishment of the WTO (1995). We explore this debate between development pessimists and development optimists who believe that there remains sufficient leeway to conduct industrial policy.

If development pessimists are correct, L/LMIC should be experiencing deindustrialization since the onset of policy space closure. We review the evidence in this regard and find that L/LMICs have indeed experienced deindustrialization post the formation of the WTO. We explore the literature on premature deindustrialization to identify the causes. Despite the closure of policy space and the reality of deindustrialization, the fact remains that to date no country has attained catch-up without successful industrialization. In this era, this process will need to be based on clean production and that is an issue addressed in Chapter 13.

The essence of new developmentalism is to create the market and non-market conditions to premit continued learning, innovation, diversification to enable countries to keep moving up the value chain. As Alice Amsden pointed out, the developmentalist model of late industrialization is based on "learning".

An important precondition of this approach to development is reasonably good managerial ability to facilitate the learning for catch-up growth. However, once the catch-up has occurred, countries like Japan, Taiwan and Korea faced a new set of much steeper challenges as they moved beyond simply learning to begin innovating and inventing. Some scholars have argued that the inability to transcend this new challenge results in many LICs, who successfully initiated catch-up growth to attain MIC status, getting trapped in the middle income range. This phenomenon is referred to as the "middle income trap" and we turn to this issue in the next chapter.

Questions

1. Review the key debate that accounts for the emergence of new developmentalism as a heterodox alternative.
2. Elaborate on the post-developmentalist case for industrialization and identify what you view as new compared to the developmentalist case (Chapter 6).
3. Review the critique of industrial policy by neoliberals and the heterodox defense.
4. Explore the method and key tools for implementing industrial policy.
5. Apart from industrial policy, what other key policies do new developmentalists advocate?
6. How do Hirschman's ideas fit in with industrial policy? (Chapter 6)
7. What is the implicit new developmentalist theory of the state and what are some policies associated with "embedded autonomy"?
8. Review the debate on the closing of policy space for pursuing a heterodox approach.
9. Identify the various explanations for premature deindustrialization. Which do you find most plausible and why?
10. It appears that premature deindustrialization has set in. What would you recommend as an alternative option for catch-up growth?
11. What are the parallels between what structural adjustment represents for neoliberalism and what industrial policy represents for new developmentalism?

Notes

1 The term new developmentalism has been used by Bresser-Pereira (2006) who also drew inspiration from East Asian economies, and so there is considerable overlap between the nationalist development program he proposed for middle income Latin American economies as an alternative to neoliberalism and the new developmentalist program proposed in this chapter. Bresser-Pereira (2006, p. 9) pointed out that his collaborator Yoshiaki Nakano suggested the term new developmentalism in 2003 for the program they were working on. Bresser-Pereira (2016, p. 9) is a more recent statement of his understanding of new developmentalism and represents a macroeconomic policy framework that complements the meso policies identified in this chapter. The industrial

policy and anti-poverty mix developed by independent Latin American scholars (Sunkel, 1993) and ECLAC in the 1990s as a heterodox alternative to neoliberalism is referred to as neostructuralism. This program with its emphasis on changing production patterns and technology is similar to new developmentalism and Bielschowsky (2009) reviews and compares neostructuralism to structuralism. The emphasis on social inclusion and environmental conservation in neostructuralism differs from the silence on these issues in new developmentalism.

2   It would be a fair question to ask why the World Bank's endorsement matters. The answer is that the World Bank has been the most active producer and diffuser of economic development literature for several decades (Chapter 8). Not all are impressed with the quality of the research or with the systematic ideological leaning of the policy advocacy it is used for (refer, for example, to Banerjee et al. 2006 and Bayliss, Fine and Waeyenberge, 2011).

3   This and the following sections draw on the contributions of many authors, particularly Alice Amsden, Ha-Joon Chang, Chalmers Johnson, Dani Rodrik and Robert Wade, and some of their key works pertaining to the topics addressed are listed in the references. For an application of a hybrid version of this program to Brazil in the first decade of the 21st century, refer to Ban (2013). Ban refers to the program as a hybrid by arguing that it mixed features of neoliberalism with new developmentalism.

4   The crowding out mechanism in macroeconomics is via the higher interest rate resulting from government borrowing which limits private sector access to capital.

5   For other definitions refer to UNCTAD (2006, p. 196, fn. 2). For supportive expositions, refer to Amsdem (2001), Wade (2004) and Chang (2006). For a critique of industrial policy, refer to Pack and Saggi (2006) and Baumol, Litan and Schramm (2007, chapter 6). The latter concede that state-guided capitalism may be effective during the catch-up growth stage when low income countries borrow, adapt and absorb technology ("imitate"), but that they ultimately need to move beyond this to innovate, the ultimate driver of economic growth.

6   The US Department of Commerce actively promotes small business exports at subsidized rates using the network of commercial councilors posted at embassies around the world (Podcast, Public Radio International, "The underfunded government program that got drill bits from rural North Dakota to Zimbabwe", July 25, 2017).

7   The Trump administration's inclination to support domestic steel is based on the same instinct even if it is ironic. If global trade rules were fair and gave all an equal opportunity, nurturing domestic industries would be unfair. But given that global trade rules were framed with disproportionate input from the more powerful nations, the catch-up growth imperative requires state support.

8   The implication is that fixed costs do matter to entrepreneurs in the real world.

9   Export success could be purely incentive driven. Thus care has to be taken, as was done in Korea, to tailor and change incentives to ensure that exports become privately profitable in the medium term (Westphal, 1990, p. 54).

10 Technology adoption and adaptation obviously does not rule out that some firms or even industries might start operating at the technological frontier based on local resources and needs. Perez-Aleman and Alves's (2017) argue for a broader reconceptualization of industrial policy for emerging economies from this vantage point using the case of Brazil.

11 Without such competitive discipline, ISI can degenerate into crony capitalism as was the case in many L/LMICs.

12 Shapiro (2007, p. 9) reported on the continued dominance of MNCs in manufacturing in Latin America well into the 1990s.

13 This practice resulted in an outraged Trump administration threatening tariffs against China in 2018. Current administrations do not look back to practices the United States engaged in when it was embarked on catch-up growth. The more advanced countries complained bitterly about US protectionism and intellectual property theft when

the latter was single-mindedly engaged in catch-up (Chang, 2005). Current western administrations, batting for their companies, take the right of these companies to be in China and to reap profits for granted and consider it outrageous that China should require joint ventures to acquire technology in exchange. One can imagine that the Chinese view such requirements as a quid pro quo.

14 Using different methods, Khan, Bilginsoy and Alam (1997), Pieper (2000), UNIDO (2009, pp. 4–6) and Gurbez (2011) also find empirical support for the centrality of manufacturing or industrialization to catch-up growth.

15 Conditional convergence requires the requisite structural characteristics like physical, social and financial infrastructure to be in place.

16 www.usatoday.com/story/money/business/small-business-central/2017/05/21/what-percentage-of-businesses-fail-in-their-first-year/101260716/, consulted 2/24/2019. Silicon Valley is viewed as having a culture whereby failure is viewed as a "feather in the cap" of serial entrepreneurs rather than having a stigma associated with it.

17 Lee, Shin, and Shin (2014) showed that LICs are as of yet not deemed to be a sufficient threat and no case was brought against them in the DSM between 1995 and 2012.

18 Standards have a positive ring to them but are complicated. First, should standards in LICs be based on current standards in HICs or based on standards prevailing in HICs when their income levels were equivalent to current income levels in L/LMICs? Second, should standards be viewed as a domestic issue or an FDI and trade issue? L/LMIC representatives argue that lower standards and lower costs are part of their comparative advantage and current HICs did not have to confront the high standards they are now pushing on them when they were industrializing. Further, so-called sweatshops provide jobs and the alternative may be hazardous occupations in the informal sector, becoming sex workers, or no livelihood. Child prostitution in Bangladesh rose when donors pushed against child labor i.e. it is important to think about unintended consequences when framing global policy. For a balanced view on standards, refer to Basu (1999).

19 TRIPS now forces local authorities to grant patents to MNCs in a uniform manner whereas in the past they had more discretion and could deny, delay, defer, limit, or even condition the granting of patents on technology transfer (Shadlin, 2005, pp. 8–9).

20 Wade (2003, p. 628) pointed out that HICs attempted to rule out joint venture, technology transfer, and R&D conditionality from TRIMs, but this was resisted in the Doha Development Round by L/MICs. Nonetheless, HICs press for the most restrictive interpretation when the language is ambiguous and given their leverage via aid, trade and other mechanisms, their MNCs are not challenged.

21 Chang and Grabel (2004, p. 69), Chang (2006), UNCTAD (United Nations Conference on Trade and Development) (2006), Rodrik (2007b) and Cimoli, Dosi and Stiglitz (2009) are other scholars who have argued that there is still room for creative industrial policy. Wade (2016, p. 36) also seems to have had a change of heart and suggested that it is cumbersome to take L/LMIC to the WTO DSM and that in principle all the tools for industrial policy identified in the text can still be used if countries are committed to doing so.

22 This and other freedoms are curbed in bilateral or regional agreements and so L/LMICs need to be extremely wary in entering such agreements where power is extremely asymmetrical and strength in numbers as a countervailing force is not an option.

23 Natsuda and Thoburn (2014) show how WTO rules impinged on the use of conventional tools for supporting automobile industries in Malaysia and Thailand and how alternative tools like fiscal policy and subsidies (actionable) were used instead.

24 Of course this could be because their quantitative impact on HIC trade disruption as competitors is nominal and because HICs have other mechanisms, such as the imposition of structural adjustment, to discipline them.

25 Refer to Rodrik (2015) for a very comprehensive compilation of data starting in the mid-1940s and extending to the early 2010s for 42 countries across the income spectrum and quantitative cross-country estimations of industrial and deindustrialization trends. He

supplemented this data base for robustness checks and further analysis with another one with a larger group of countries but a shorter time span (starting in the early 1970s).

26 Countries with populations of less than 5 million are viewed as special cases from the perspective of realizing dynamic efficiencies and are not included in the sample. Also, the third period was split into 1995–2007 and 2006–2009 to avoid the high impact of the Great Recession of 2008–2009 on the averages of some countries.

27 As indicated in the notes to Table 9.2, the ratio variable used (SOM) was manufacturing value added as a percentage of GDP in nominal local currency units. As Rodrik (2015, p. 6) pointed out, using nominal values conflates movements in prices and quantities and hence does not effectively uncover real structural changes such as deindustrialization. Unfortunately, data to construct this ratio variable in constant prices was not accessible. As such, the numbers reported in Table 9.2 are suggestive. In contrast to output deindustrialization reported in Table 9.2, another definition of deindustrialization is based on a decline in employment share (as a percentage of the total labor force) in the manufacturing sector (employment deindustrialization). Since manufacturing technology has historically shown a tendency to become more capital intensive over time, one would expect employment share in manufacturing to decline in L/LMICs to the extent that they borrow technology from HICs (Chapter 14). Thus, employment deindustrialization may not coincide with output deindustrialization since more capital intensity is likely to be associated with higher productivity and therefore a higher output share of manufacturing. However, computing employment deindustrialization was not an option since the numbers available in the WDI were ILO (International Labor Organization) estimates derived from a model rather than actuals, and the series started in 1991 so there was a limited opportunity to do the period analysis reported in Table 9.2.

28 Dasgupta and Singh (2006, p. 5) cited cross-country evidence drawing on various sources which suggested that the historical turning point occurred at a per capita of almost US$10,000 in current prices and declined by the turn of the century to levels of income as low as US$3,000 in some countries. Subramanian reported that in 1988 the global peak share of manufacturing was 30 percent and attained at a per capita GDP level of $21,700. By 2010, the peak share of manufacturing was 21 percent and attained at a level of $12,200 (www.cgdev.org/blog/premature-de-industrialization, consulted 2/24/2019). Also refer to Rodrik (2015) for changing turning points.

29 In the academic literature, Wong (1996) mentioned premature deindustrialization in the context of Singapore's changing development strategy. Wong's concern was that rising land prices in Singapore might cause an outflow of FDI, central to Singapore's industrialization drive, and hence to premature deindustrialization.

30 The reshoring of production back to HICs due to additive manufacturing and automation will impact both IT and manufacturing in L/LMICS and could be another source of premature deindustrialization. Information on this trend is currently too limited to be able to gauge macro and sectoral impacts. Rough estimates suggest that between 2004 and 2015, the rate of offshoring from the United States ranged from 150,000 to 300,000 jobs per annum. The reshoring for 2014 for the United States was estimated to be 10,000 jobs. Even if we take the lower estimate for offshoring, the ratio of reshoring to offshoring of jobs was 7 percent in the middle of the second decade of the 21st century (refer to https://en.wikipedia.org/wiki/Offshoring, consulted 2/24/2019 and https://en.wikipedia.org/wiki/Reshoring, consulted 2/24/2019).

31 Some 97 percent or more of actively publishing climate scientists agree that climate warming is underway, significant and humanly induced. See, for example, https://climate.nasa.gov/scientific-consensus/, consulted 2/24/2019. The Intergovernmental Panel on Climate Change released a Special Report on October 8, 2018 on the impact of an increase of global temperatures of 1.5°C. The gist of this new report is that going past this threshold will threaten the planet's liveability in many respects and the impacts will be felt as early as 2030, a dozen years from when the report was released. The summary version for policy makers is available at https://ipcc.ch/news_and_events/pr_181008_P48_spm.shtml, consulted 10/9/2018.

APPENDIX TABLE 9.1 Average size of manufacturing value added (SOM) as a percentage of GDP over time for low and middle income countries

	1960–1980	1981–1994	1995–2007	2009–2016	% change in SOM across first two periods	% change in SOM across second two periods	% change in SOM across third two periods
Algeria	13.25 (16)	12.82 (14)	7.78 (13)	na	-3.25	-39.31	na
Angola	na	6.91 (10)	4.04 (13)	na	na	-41.35	na
Argentina	35.94 (16)	26.83 (14)	20.33 (13)	17.95 (8)	-25.34	-24.23	-11.71
Bangladesh	na	13.88 (14)	16.02 (13)	17.25 (8)	na	15.42	7.68
Benin	10.45 (10)	7.94 (14)	8.48 (11)	14.87 (7)	-24.02	6.80	75.35
Bolivia	13.44 (11)	17.03 (14)	15.71 (13)	13.48 (8)	26.71	-7.75	-14.19
Brazil	29.29 (21)	30.18 (14)	17.43 (13)	13.02 (8)	3.04	-42.25	-25.30
Burkina Faso	15.57 (21)	14.88 (14)	14.77 (12)	7.16 (8)	-4.43	-0.74	-51.52
Burundi	8.96 (11)	10.27 (14)	8.32 (11)	9.80 (8)	14.62	-18.99	17.79
Cameroon	9.67 (16)	14.17 (14)	19.69 (13)	14.92 (7)	46.53	38.96	-31.97
Chad	9.84 (19)	11.52 (12)	8.67 (13)	2.20 (8)	17.07	-24.74	-74.62

(Continued)

Appendix Table 9.1 (Cont.)

	1960–1980	1981–1994	1995–2007	2009–2016	% change in SOM across first two periods	% change in SOM across second two periods	% change in SOM across third two periods
Chile	23.88 (21)	19.62 (14)	17.89 (13)	12.07 (8)	-17.84	-8.82	-32.53
Columbia	21.78 (16)	21.11 (14)	16.00 (13)	13.20 (8)	-3.08	-24.20	-17.5
Congo, Dem. Rep. of	na	10.63 (12)	6.05 (12)	18.48 (8)	na	-43.09	205.45
Côte d'Ivoire	9.91 (16)	16.69 (14)	19.08 (13)	14.77 (4)	68.42	14.32	-22.59
Dominican Republic	18.13 (16)	16.33 (14)	16.07 (13)	15.79 (8)	-9.93	-1.59	-1.74
Egypt, Arab Rep. of	15.24 (7)	15.47 (14)	18.03 (13)	16.50 (8)	1.51	16.55	-8.49
Ethiopia	na	4.41 (14)	5.21 (13)	4.20 (8)	na	18.14	-19.39
Ghana	10.97 (16)	8.49 (14)	8.83 (13)	6.11 (8)	-22.61	4.00	-30.80
Guatemala	15.69 (16)	15.35 (14)	16.40 (13)	19.29 (8)	-2.17	6.84	17.62
Guinea	na	4.52 (7)	3.90 (13)	6.93 (8)	na	-13.72	77.69
Honduras	13.95 (21)	15.65 (14)	20.17 (13)	18.58 (8)	12.19	28.88	-7.88

India	15.08 (21)	16.42 (14)	15.97 (13)	16.98 (8)	8.89	-2.74	6.32
Indonesia	9.87 (21)	17.86 (14)	27.28 (13)	21.90 (8)	80.95	52.74	-19.72
Iran, Islamic Rep. of	8.43 (16)	9.46 (14)	12.15 (13)	12.03 (7)	12.22	28.44	-0.99
Jordan	11.38 (16)	13.06 (14)	16.50 (130)	19.07 (8)	14.76	26.34	15.58
Kenya	11.31 (21)	11.58 (14)	11.54 (13)	11.82 (8)	2.39	-0.35	2.42
Kyrgyz Republic	na	27.67 (5)	14.22 (13)	11.57 (8)	na	-48.61	-18.63
Lao PDR	na	11.85 (6)	18.16 (13)	8.75 (8)	na	53.25	-34.75
Madagascar	na	10.78 (11)	12.39 (13)	na	na	14.94	na
Malawi	12.98 (6)	16.26 (14)	13.47 (13)	10.51 (8)	25.27	-17.16	-21.97
Malaysia	13.55 (21)	22.20 (14)	29.17 (13)	22.79 (8)	63.84	31.40	-21.87
Mali	6.89 (14)	7.66 (14)	4.14 (13)	na	11.18	-45.95	na
Mexico	21.90 (16)	21.99 (14)	19.82 (130)	17.72 (8)	0.41	-9.87	-10.60

(Continued)

Appendix Table 9.1 (Cont.)

	1960–1980	1981–1994	1995–2007	2009–2016	% change in SOM across first two periods	% change in SOM across second two periods	% change in SOM across third two periods
Morocco	na	18.25 (14)	17.02 (13)	17.48 (8)	na	-6.74	2.70
Myanmar	9.56 (21)	8.28 (14)	6.90 (6)	19.75 (7)	-13.40	-16.67	186.23
Nepal	3.95 (16)	6.30 (14)	8.90 (13)	6.48 (8)	59.50	41.27	-27.19
Nicaragua	na	na	15.31 (14)	15.61 (14)	na	na	1.96
Niger	4.70 (12)	6.17 (14)	6.54 (9)	na	31.28	6.00	na
Pakistan	15.13 (21)	16.34 (14)	16.55 (13)	13.79 (8)	8.00	1.29	-16.68
Papua New Guinea	7.90 (11)	10.37 (14)	7.68 (13)	na	31.27	-25.94	na
Paraguay	16.25 (21)	15.19 (14)	15.01 (13)	12.11 (8)	-6.52	-1.18	-19.32
Peru	19.70 (20)	21.69 (9)	16.07 (13)	16.11 (7)	10.10	-25.91	0.25
Philippines	24.99 (21)	24.70 (14)	22.63 (13)	20.63 (8)	-1.16	-8.38	-8.84
Rwanda	7.33 (16)	13.93 (14)	8.29 (13)	6.43 (8)	90.04	-40.49	-22.44

Senegal	na	14.64 (14)	15.95 (13)	14.02 (6)	na	8.95	−12.10
Sierra Leone	5.84 (16)	6.35 (12)	4.80 (9)	2.01 (8)	8.73	−24.41	−58.12
Somalia	5.61 (21)	4.96 (10)	na	na	−11.59	na	na
South Africa	21.75 (21)	22.66 (14)	19.27 (13)	13.60 (8)	4.18	−14.96	−29.42
Sri Lanka	17.33 (21)	15.12 (140)	17.47 (13)	18.91 (8)	−12.75	15.54	8.24
Sudan	6.63 (21)	7.56 (14)	7.62 (13)	6.09 (3)	14.03	0.79	−20.01
Tajikistan	na	28.19 (10)	25.66 (13)	12.46 (5)	na	−8.97	−51.44
Thailand	16.80 (21)	25.82 (14)	32.92 (13)	28.57	71.55	21.57	−13.21
Togo	8.28 (21)	8.38 (14)	8.74 (11)	6.55 (8)	−1.21	4.30	−25.06
Tunisia	9.48 (16)	15.56 (14)	18.06 (13)	17.33 (7)	64.14	16.07	−4.04
Uganda	7.37 (21)	5.79 (14)	8.01 (13)	9.40 (8)	−21.44	38.34	17.35
Venezuela R. B. de	16.00 (12)	16.61 (14)	18.18 (11)	13.13 (5)	3.81	8.64	−27.78

(Continued)

Appendix Table 9.1 (Cont.)

	1960–1980	1981–1994	1995–2007	2009–2016	% change in SOM across first two periods	% change in SOM across second two periods	% change in SOM across third two periods
Ukraine	na	37.48 (3)	24.99 (14)	14.50 (8)	na	-33.32	-41.98
Vietnam	na	16.93 (10)	18.81 (13)	15.03 (8)	na	11.10	-20.10
Yemen	na	20.01 (5)	8.45 (14)	10.52 (8)	na	-57.77	24.50
Zambia	14.03 (16)	27.30 (14)	11.84 (13)	11.55 (8)	94.58	-56.63	-2.45
Zimbabwe	18.79 (16)	22.99 (14)	15.39 (10)	na	22.35	-33.06	na

Source: World Development Indicators na = Not available

Notes: Parentheses contain years over which the mean was computed.

Country income classifications were revised July 1, 2016 and based on 2015 incomes (https://blogs.worldbank.org/opendata/new-country-classifications-2016).

No data were available for Middle East and North Africa.

SOM = Manufacturing value added as a % of GDP in nominal local currency units

LIC = Low income countries ($1,025 or less annual per capita gross national income)

LMIC = Lower middle income countries ($1,026–$4,035)

UMIC = Upper middle income countries ($4,036–$12,475)

HIC = High income countries (above $12,476)

EE&P = East Asia and the Pacific

E&CA = Europe and Central Asia

LA&C = Latin America and the Caribbean

ME&NA = Middle East and North Africa

SA = South Asia

SSA = Sub-Saharan Africa

References

Acevedo, A., A. Mold and E. Perez 2009. "The Sectoral Drivers of Economic Growth: A Long-term View of Latin American, Economic Performance," *Cuadernos Econmicos De I. C. E.*, 78(December), 117–142.

Aghion, P., J. Boulanger and E. Cohen. 2011. "Rethinking Industrial Policy," Bruegel Policy Brief, No. 4.

Amsdem, A. H. 1989. *Asia's Next Giant* (New York: Oxford University Press).

Amsdem, A. H. 2001. *The Rise of "The Rest": Challenges to the West from Late-Industrializing Economies* (Oxford: Oxford University Press).

Amsden, A. H. 2005. "Promoting Industry under WTO Law," in: K. P. Gallagher (ed.), *Putting Development First: The Importance of Policy Space in the WTO and Financial Institutions* (London: Zed Book) 216-232.

Baldwin, R. 2011. "Trade and Industrialization after Globalization's 2nd Unbundling: How Building and Joining a Supply Chain are Different and Why It Matters," Working Paper No. 17716, National Bureau of Economic Research, Cambridge, Massachusetts.

Ban, C. 2013. "Brazil's Liberal Neo-developmentalism: New Paradigm or Edited Orthodoxy?" *Review of International Political Economy*, 20(20), 298–331.

Banerjee, A., A. Deaton, N. Lustig, K. Rogoff and E. Hsu. 2006. "An Evaluation of World Bank Research, 1998 – 2005," http://siteresources.worldbank.org/DEC/Resou rces/84797-1109362238001/726454-1164121166494/RESEARCH-EVALUATION-2006-Main-Report.pdf, consulted 10/26, 2017.

Basu, K. 1999. "Child Labor: Cause, Consequence, and Cure, with Remarks on International Labor Standards," *Journal of Economic Literature*, 37(3), 1083–1119.

Baumol, W. J., R. E. Litan and C. J. Schramm 2007. *Good Capitalism, Bad Capitalism and the Economics of Growth and Prosperity* (New Haven: Yale University Press).

Bayliss, K., B. Fine and E. V. Waeyenberge Eds. 2011. *The Political Economy of Development: The World Bank, Neoliberalism and Development Research* (New York: Pluto Press).

Bielschowsky, R. 2009. "Sixty Years of ECLAC: Structuralism and Neo-structuralism," *Cepal Review*, 97(April), 171–194.

Bresser-Pereira, L. C. 2006. "The New Developmentalism and Conventional Orthodoxy," *Economie Appliquee*, 59(3), 95–126.

Bresser-Pereira, L. C. 2016. "Reflecting on New Developmentalism and Classical Developmentalism," *Review of Keynesian Economics*, 4(3), 331–352.

Chang, H.-J. 1993. "Political Economy of Industrial Policy in Korea," *Cambridge Journal of Economics*, 17(2), 131–157.

Chang, H.-J. 2005. "Kicking Away the Ladder: Good Policies and Good Institutions in Historical Perspective," in: K. P. Gallagher (ed.), *Putting Development First: The Importance of Policy Space in the WTO and Financial Institutions* (London: Zed Books) 102-125.

Chang, H.-J. 2006. *The East Asian Development Experience: The Miracle, the Crisis and the Future* (London: Zed Books).

Chang, H.-J. 2015. "Is Industrial Policy Necessary and Feasible in Africa? Theoretical and Historical Considerations and Historical Lessons," in: A. Noman and J. E. Stiglitz (eds.), *Industrial Policy and Economic Transformation in Africa* (New York: Columbia University Press) 30-52.

Chang, H.-J. and I. Grabel 2004. *Reclaiming Development: An Alternative Economic Policy Manual* (London: Zed Books).

Cimoli, M., G. Dosi and J. E. Stiglitz 2009. "The Political Economy of Capabilities Accumulation: The Past and Future of Policies for Industrial Development," in: M.

Cimoli, G. Dosi and J. E. Stiglitz (eds.), *Industrial Policy and Development: The Political Economy of Capabilities Accumulation* (Oxford: Oxford University Press) (2-14).

Correa, C. M. 2015. "Intellectual Property: How Much Room Is Left for Industrial Policy?" United Nations Conference on Trade and Development (UNCTAD), Discussion Paper No. 223, Geneva.

Dasgupta, S. and A. Singh 2005. "Will Services Be the New Engine of Indian Economic Growth?" *Development and Change*, 36(6), 1035–1057.

Dasgupta, S. and A. Singh. 2006. "Manufacturing, Services and Premature Deindustrialization in Developing Countries," United Nations University - World Institute for Development Economics Research (UNU-WIDER) Research Paper No. 2006/49, Helsinki, Finland.

Evans, P. 1995. *Embedded Autonomy: States and Industrial Transformation* (Princeton, New Jersey: Princeton University Press).

Gallagher, K. P. 2007. "Measuring the Cost of Lost Policy Space in the WTO," IRC Americas Program Policy Brief, Washington, D. C.

Gallagher, K. P. 2008. "Understanding Developing Country Resistance to the Doha Round," *Review of International Political Economy*, 15(1), 62–85.

Gallagher, K. P. and M. Shafaeddin 2011. "Government Reform and Industrial Development in China and Mexico," in: S. R. Khan and J. Christiansen (eds.), *Market as Means Rather than Master: Towards New Developmentalism* (London: Routledge) **177-202**.

Gereffi, G., J. Humphrey and T. Sturgeon 2005. "The Governance of Global Value Chains," *Review of International Political Economy*, 12(1), 78–104.

Grabowski, R. 2017. "Premature Deindustrialization and Inequality," *International Journal of Social Economics*, 44(2), 154–168.

Gurbez, A. A. 2011. "Comparing Trajectories of Structural Change," *Cambridge Journal of Economics*, 35(6), 1061–1085.

Harrison, A. and A. Rodríguez-Clare 2010. "Trade, Foreign Investment, and Industrial Policy for Developing Countries," in: D. Rodrik and M. Rosenzweig (eds.), *Handbook of Development Economics, Vol. 5* (The Netherlands: North-Holland) 4039-4214.

Hayek, F. A. 1945. "The Use of Knowledge in Society," *American Economic Review*, 75(4), 519–530.

Johnson, C. 1982. *MITI and the Japanese Miracle: The Growth of Industrial Policy, 1925-1975* (Stanford: Stanford University Press).

Kentikelenis, A. E., T. E. Stubbs and L. P. King 2016. "IMF Conditionality and Development Policy Space 1985–2014," *Review of International Political Economy*, 23(4), 543–582.

Khan, S. R. 2007. "WTO, IMF and the Closing of Development Policy Space for Low-income Countries: A Case for Neo-developmentalism," *Third World Quarterly*, 28(6), 1073–1090.

Khan, S. R., C. Bilginsoy and M. S. Alam 1997. "Dynamic Efficiencies of Industrialization and Economic Growth," *Economia Internazionale*, 50(1), 85–98.

Lall, S. 2013. "Reinventing Industry Strategy: The Role of Government Policy in Building Industrial Competitiveness," *Annals of Economics and Finance*, 14(2B), 767–811.

Lee, K., W. Shin and H. Shin 2014. "How Large or Small Is the Policy Space? WTO Regime and Industrial Policy," *Seoul Journal of Economics*, 27(3), 307–348.

Linden, G. 2004. "A Study in Strategic Industrial Policy," *Business and Politics*, 6(3), Article 4, (Berkeley Electronic Press) 1-26.

Mah, J. S. 2015. "R&D Promotion Policies of Developing Countries and Fairness in International Trade Relations," *Journal of Economic Issues*, 49(1), 179–196.

Natsuda, K. and J. Thoburn 2014. "How Much Policy Space Still Exists under the WTO? A Comparative Study of the Automotive Industry in Thailand and Malaysia," *Review of International Political Economy*, 21(6), 1346–1377.

Pack, H. and K. Saggi 2006. "Is There A Case for Industrial Policy? A Critical Survey," *The World Bank Research Observer*, 21(2), 267–297.

Perez-Alemana, P. and F. C. Alves 2017. "Reinventing Industrial Policy at the Frontier: Catalyzing Learning and Innovation in Brazil," *Cambridge Journal of Regions, Economy and Society*, 10(1), 151–171.

Pieper, U. 2000. "Deindustrialization and the Social and Economic Sustainability Nexus in Developing Countries: Cross-country Evidence on Productivity and Employment," *Journal of Development Studies*, 36(4), 66–99.

Rodrik, D. 2004. "Industrial Policy for the Twenty-first Century," file:///C:/Users/shahrukh/Downloads/-RodrikUNIDOSep%20(1).pdf, consulted 12/ 12/2017.

Rodrik, D. 2007a. *One Economics Many Recipes: Globalization, Institutions, and Economic Growth* (Princeton: Princeton University Press).

Rodrik, D. 2007b. *Industrial Development: Some Stylized Facts and Policy Directions* (New York: UN-Department of Economic and Social Analysis).

Rodrik, D. 2009. "Industrial Policy: Don't Ask Why, Ask How," *Middle East Development Journal*, 1(1), 1–29.

Rodrik, D. 2015. "Premature Deindustrialization," *Journal of Econ Growth*, 21(1), 1–33.

Shadlin, K. C. 2005. 'Reforming and Reinforcing the Revolution: The Post-TRIPS Politics of Patents in Latin America', GDAE Working Papers, Tufts University, http://www.ase.tufts.edu/gdae/Pubs/wp/09-02PostTRIPSApril09.pdf, downloaded, 8/22/2019.

Shapiro, H. 2007. "Industrial Policy and Growth," UN-Department of Economic and Social Analysis Working Paper No. 53, New York.

Sunkel, O. Ed. 1993. *Development from Within: Toward a Neo-structuralist Approach for Latin America* (Boulder and London: Rienner).

Tan, J. 2014. "Running Out of Steam? Manufacturing in Malaysia," *Cambridge Journal of Economics*, 38(1), 153–180.

UNCTAD (United Nations Conference on Trade and Development). 2006. *Trade and Development Report* (New York: United Nations).

UNDP (United Nation Development Program). 2005. International Cooperation at a Crossroads: Aid, Trade and Security in an Unequal World, *Human Development Report 2005* (New York: Oxford University Press).

UNIDO (United Nations Industrial Development Organization). 2009. *Industrial Development Report 2009, Breaking in and Moving Up: New Industrial Challenges for the Bottom Billion and the Middle-Income Countries* (Vienna: United Nations).

Wade, R. 2004. *Governing the Market: Economic Theory and the Role of Government in East Asian Industrialization* (Princeton, New Jersey: Princeton University Press).

Wade R. H. 2005. "What Strategies Are Viable for Developing Countries Today? The World Trade Organization and the Shrinking of "Development Space"", in Gallagher, K. P. (ed), *Putting Development First: The Importance of Policy Space in the WTO and Financial Institutions* (London: Zed Book),80–101.

Wade, R. H. 2016. "The Role of the State in Escaping the Middle-income Trap: The Case for Smart Industrial Policy," *METU Studies in Development*, 43(1), 21–42.

Wells, H. and A. P. Thirlwall 2003. "Testing Kaldor's Growth Laws across the Countries of Africa," *African Development Review*, 15(2), 89–126.

Westphal, L. E. 1990. "Industrial Policy in an Export-Propelled Economy: Lessons from South Korea's Experience," *Journal of Economic Perspectives*, 4(3), 41–59.

Wong, T. 1996. "Information Technology and Its Spatial Impact on Singapore," *Review of Urban and Regional Development Studies*, 8(1), 33–45.

World Bank. 2005. *Economic Growth in the 1990s: Learning from a Decade of Reform.* (Washington, D. C.: World Bank).

10

IS THERE A MIDDLE INCOME TRAP?[1]

Introduction

While the focus of this textbook has so far been on L/LMICs and how they could initiate catch-up growth, it is interesting to explore what their likely economic future is depending on the path they adopt and the historical experience of other countries who have reached upper middle income status. Many development economists have argued and cited evidence to show that the transition from the middle income to high income status is fraught and many countries are unable to make this transition and get locked into a middle income trap.

Bulman, Eden and Nguyen (2017) point out that all HICs in 1960 remained high income in 2009 and the majority of MICs remained middle income. Out of 110 countries ranked as middle income in 1960, only 13 transitioned to high income status by 2009. These include Greece, Hong Kong, Ireland, Japan, Republic of Korea, Puerto Rico, Singapore, Spain, Seychelles and Taiwan. To this list can be added the MICs like Poland and Hungary that joined the EU and prospered.[2]

Numerous countries in the Baltic States, Central and Eastern Europe, Latin America, Middle East, South-East Asia along with South Africa have been mentioned in the context of the middle income trap. In fact, since 1960, only the East Asian economies of South Korea, Taiwan and Singapore, which started their catch-up growth much later than say the Latin American economies, have proceeded smoothly from low to high income status. These are also the only non-western economies that have done so. Now that China has attained upper middle income status, there has been a spate of papers on how China might be impacted by a middle income trap and how it could go about avoiding it (Woo, 2014; Zhang, 2014; Islam, 2015).

On the one hand, the fact that not all countries have stalled suggests that this is not a universal phenomenon and so the exceptions question the theoretical validity of this phenomenon. On the other, the paltry list of countries who have graduated from middle to high income status in and of itself is suggestive of reasons for persistence in the middle income category whether or not one refers to sluggish growth in middle income as a trap.

This chapter explores the debate on this phenomenon referred to as "the middle income trap". The theory is reviewed first to explain why countries may get trapped. This is followed by evidence to evaluate the empirical relevance of this phenomenon. Finally, assuming the existence of a middle income trap, what policy solutions or economic strategies might enable countries to exit from it.

Theory

In questioning the validity of a middle income trap on theoretical and empirical grounds, *The Economist* (February 13, 2017) dubbed the phenomenon "the middle-income claptrap". Even so, a case could be made on theoretical grounds that countries embarked on catch-up growth are likely to confront discontinuities. To sustain the momentum of catch-up growth from middle to upper income levels, transitions are inevitable. In the early phases of economic growth, countries are starting from a small base and double digit growth rates are relatively easy to clock, but this is a purely arithmetic.

More substantively, one mechanism for rapid growth is the huge requirements of social and physical infrastructure to establish the base for economic growth and this itself contributes to the economic growth. Once this need has been met, the social investment for routine maintenance has to overtake the social investment for expansion and this certainly is a transition all countries embarked on catch-up growth are likely to face.

The technological transition is likely to be even more challenging. In the early phases of catch-up growth, the returns to capital accumulation are high but diminishing returns set in as middle income status is reached. Off-the-shelf technology is readily available for L/LMICs and the challenge is to adopt and adapt. This learning process stimulates economic growth, but at some point countries also exhaust this low hanging fruit and confront intellectual property rights fees for more cutting edge technology or have to establish their own national innovation systems to operate on the technological frontier. In a nutshell, countries need to transition from capital accumulation to enhancing factor productivity via technological progress.

Another transition is that countries exhaust surplus labor (Chapter 6) and are no longer able to compete based on cheap labor. The migration-based gains of labor moving from low productivity rural/agricultural activities to relatively higher productivity industrial activities is exhausted. In order to keep unit labor costs low, productivity has to be enhanced and this again requires national investments in training and higher education.

Lee, Shin and Shin (2014) pointed to another challenging transition. Their research suggests that HICs focus on MICs for the enforcement of their intellectual property rights. L/LMICs are clearly not a threat, but as countries attain middle income status, the global economic environment for technology acquisition becomes much more hostile.[3] Thus the bulk of the cases referred to the Dispute Settlement Mechanism of the WTO in the context of enforcing the provisions of Trade Related Intellectual Property Rights (TRIPS) pertain to MIC violations.

Another potential hurdle is that the strategy adopted to engage in catch-up growth may actually set the trap. For example, South-East Asian countries like Malaysia, Thailand, Indonesia and the Philippines that have relied heavily on FDI have found themselves locked into various rungs of a value chain that they are unable to withdraw from and which MNCs, who profit from the status quo, have no incentive to change. This limits the ability of such countries to move up the value chain and diversify their economies.

Financing development with aid and loans could similarly set a future trap. The temptation to seek aid is strong particularly for countries with weak tax administrations or those unable to make hard political decisions. As the debt burden mounts, countries become subject to IMF/WB conditionalities that are antithetical to sustained economic growth (Chapter 8).

Demographics are another factor that can accentuate a middle income trap. A fear expressed by Chinese scholars is that it could become old before it becomes rich. In this scenario, a high dependency rate becomes a drag on economic growth and the country lacks the resources to put safety nets into place to care for an aging population.

As the economy becomes more complex, there is an expectation that the regulatory authority and economic bureaucracy concomitantly increase in sophistication. If such institutional capacity lags, it could be a constraint on the economic growth momentum.

Finally, leadership with a vision and the political authority to make difficult choices is needed. Each phase of economic growth creates winners, and therefore vested interests, and potential losers. To pivot or transition to an alternative strategy requires confronting vested interests, which have become politically powerful based on the entrenched economic growth strategy, that are likely to lose from needed strategy changes.

In short, theory suggests that the transition is difficult and qualitative leaps are necessary to bring it about. Nonetheless the good news is that the evidence suggests that the transition has been made by a few countries and it may be possible to learn from their experience.

Evidence

The phenomenon of a middle income trap is viewed as plausible to most of the many scholars who have written about it since the term was popularized in the development economics literature by Gill and Kharas (2007).[4] Various related methods have been used in the literature to empirically show that countries are locked into a middle income trap. There are many contested definitional issues pertaining to these methods such as the specification of the income groups (i.e. low and upper middle income) and specifying the "normal" time period to transit from one income group to another relative to which one can assess if a country is trapped.

One method utilized to determine which countries are trapped follows from these definitional issues i.e. specifying income ranges to identify country income status and specifying a criterion in terms of years in a given range to determine which countries are in a middle income trap. Felipe, Abdon and Kumar (2017) have engaged in such a country classification exercise.

Another method is showing that MICs have a greater proclivity to exhibit economic growth slowdowns which would then partly explain the persistence in the middle income range. Aiyar et al. (2013) conducted such an exercise and followed it with estimating the determinants of such growth slowdowns. They pointed to variables such as the lack of infrastructure, regulation and lack of trade integration as determinants of slowdowns.

Eichengreen, Park and Shin (2014) estimated the income ranges at which growth slowdowns have occurred and identified their correlates. They suggested that quality education and technological learning reduced the probability of such slowdowns while an undervalued exchange rate (along with cheap labor exporting strategy), high investment rates (diminishing returns) and old age dependency rates increased the probability of slowdowns.

Pritchett and Summers (2014) empirically demonstrated that past economic growth rates were not a good predictor of future growth rates, and "regression to the mean is perhaps the single most robust and empirical relevant fact about cross-national growth rates". This suggests slowdowns following growth accelerations are likely. The explanation proffered was the conditions that induced the growth acceleration start yielding diminishing returns unless accompanied by improved policy environment and governance.

A third method follows from the first two and is based on showing the lack of convergence to HIC status, another way of thinking about the middle income trap. If countries are trapped for various reasons in a productivity and growth slowdown in a middle income range, they will not be converging to the HIC income threshold. There is an implicit conceptual distinction in the income range trap and convergence studies because instead of thinking in terms of an absolute income range in which the middle income countries may be trapped, convergence or the lack of it views income in a relative sense.

Not all scholars are persuaded that there is a middle income trap. Bulman, Eden and Nguyen (2017) suggested based on their empirical work that there is no systematic slowdown when middle income status is attained. Im and Rosenblatt (2013) conceded that the concept of a middle income trap might be useful for policy discussions, but their empirical results suggested that MICs showed no uniform growth patterns and, in terms of transitions, were no different from countries in the other income groups.

Escaping the trap

All the usual suspects such as investment in quality education, training, R&D, to build indigenous technological capabilities at the micro level (firms), higher savings and investments including on infrastructure, domestic resource mobilization, export diversification, regional trade agreements, income redistribution to boost aggregate demand and buy-in from the population, macroeconomic stability, institution building and better governance are mentioned in the literature on how to escape the middle income trap. This sounds like a prescription for doing everything right and is therefore not very helpful. Perhaps more promising is looking at this issue in terms of approaches, as has been done throughout this textbook.

In terms of approaches, the debate between neoliberal and heterodox scholars is playing out on this vital issue also. WB and IMF scholars and those sympathetic to the neoliberal approach advocate more and better implementation of neoliberal reforms (Chapter 8). Heterodox scholars like Wade (2016) argue for a more extensive and better implementation of industrial policy (Chapter 9). The latter approach has become more influential and even many of the WB and IMF working papers concede the importance of building firm level capabilities.

Conclusion

The existence of a middle income trap is empirically contested. Recent economic history shows that not all countries experienced such a trap, but some moved relatively smoothly from middle to upper income status. Thus, it cannot be viewed as a universal phenomenon. The review of theory suggests that there are substantial transitional challenges in moving from middle to upper income status.

Empirical evidence, however, suggests that some countries were able to adapt and overcome these challenges, belying the notion of a trap. A trap is suggestive of something designed to catch and retain or something that allows entry but not exit. The closest one comes to this in reality is that countries may trap themselves by not doing the needful. There is nothing holding back countries but themselves. During colonialism and early post-colonialism, externalizing the blame was possible but, given examples of successful catch-up growth, externalizing the blame for slow progress is no longer convincing. Discussing slow middle income country transitions to high income status makes sense, but talking about traps is suggestive of some external force that simply is not there.[5]

Since all the non-western economies that did not fall into a so-called middle income trap are East Asian, perhaps learning from their economic approach would provide the greatest insights. The effective use of industrial policy is central to the arsenal of tools they used. Adopting these approaches is no guarantee of success since successful implementation is complex and much, including good leadership, needs to fall into place (Chapter 15). Nonetheless, studying the approach of those that did successfully transition into HIC status is a good place to start.

As mentioned earlier, this chapter echoes the debates explored in Part II in this textbook between the neoliberal approach and the heterodox approaches to economic development. These debates also play out in Part III of this textbook but in the context of specific topics.

Questions and exercise

1. Explain why the transition from lower middle to upper middle income and beyond might be difficult.
2. Explain the different methods to conceptualize and estimate the middle income trap phenomenon and what their inter-relationships are.
3. Do you think the middle income trap is a useful conceptual construct? Explain.
4. Explain why it might be better to think of escaping the middle income trap in terms of approaches rather than specific policy measures?
5. Pick any regional country group (e.g. Latin America) and pick a base year (e.g. 1960). Rank all countries in the base year by income status and determine how many in the terminal year (for which most recent data are available in the World Development Indicators) remained in the middle income status and how many graduated to the upper income status. Engage in a comparative exercise and propose policies for those still in middle income status to graduate to the upper income level.

Notes

1 Appendix Table 10.1 lists the upper middle income countries as classified by the World Bank. This is the most relevant income group category for this chapter. The World Bank no longer distinguishes between lower middle income and middle income in their income group classification.
2 Gill and Kharas (2015, p. 19) point out that the self-discipline imposed by countries seeking to join the EU has provided a path to HIC status for half the middle income countries which have attained HIC status. These include Croatia, Cyprus, the Czech Republic, Estonia, Hungary, Latvia, Malta, Poland, Portugal, the Slovak Republic and Slovenia. However, this is not an opportunity other MICs can avail themselves of and this does highlight the importance of geography as one determining factor for economic opportunities.
3 The hostility China has faced from the Trump administration on intellectual property rights as it developed its indigenous technological capacity is a case in point.
4 Gill and Kharas (2015, p. 5) attribute the first reference to this phenomenon to Garret (2004).
5 One could argue that this distinction is all about splitting hairs or semantics, but it is more than that. It is about having the right perspective and accordingly the right policies.

APPENDIX TABLE 10.1 World Bank list of upper middle income economies (> $3,896 and < $12,055) as of June 2017

Albania	Jamaica
Algeria	Kazakhstan
American Samoa	Lebanon
Argentina	Macedonia
Aruba High income	Malaysia
Azerbaijan	Marshall Islands
Belarus	Mauritius
Belize	Mexico
Bosnia and Herzegovina	Montenegro
Botswana	Namibia
Brazil	Nauru
Bulgaria	Panama
China	Paraguay
Colombia	Peru
Costa Rica	Romania
Croatia	Russian Federation
Cuba	Samoa
Dominica	South Africa
Dominican Republic	St. Lucia
Ecuador	St. Vincent and the Grenadines
Equatorial Guinea	Suriname
Fiji	Thailand
Gabon	Tonga
Grenada	Turkey
Guyana	Turkmenistan
Iran, Islamic Rep.	Tuvalu
Iraq	Venezuela, RB

References

Aiyar, S., R. Duval, D. Puy, Y. Wu, and L. Zhang. 2013. "Growth Slowdowns and the Middle-Income Trap," IMF Working Paper WP/13/71, Washington, DC.

Bulman, D., M. Eden, and H. Nguyen. 2017. "Transitioning from Low-income to High-come Growth: Is There a Middle-income Trap?" Asian Development Bank Institute (ADBI) Working Paper Series No. 646, Manila, Philippines.

Eichengreen, B., D. Park, and K. Shin 2014. "Growth Slowdowns Redux," *Japan and the World Economy* 32(C), 65–84.

Felipe, J., A. Abdon, and U. Kumar 2017. "Middle-income Transitions: Trap or Myth?," *Journal of the Asia Pacific Economy* 22(3), 429–453.

Garret, G. 2004. "Globalization's Missing Middle," *Foreign Affairs* 83(6), 84–96.

Gill, I. S. and H. Kharas 2007. *An East Asian Renaissance* (Washington, DC: World Bank).

Gill, I. S. and H. Kharas. 2015. "The Middle-Income Trap Turns Ten," Policy Research Working Paper 7403, World Bank, Washington, DC.

Im, F. G. and D. Rosenblatt. 2013. "Middle-Income Traps A Conceptual and Empirical Survey," Policy Research Working Paper 6594, World Bank, Washington, DC.

Islam, S. N. 2015. "Will Inequality Lead China to the Middle Income Trap?" UN Department of Economic and Social Affairs (DESA) Working Paper No. 142, New York.

Lee, K., W. Shin, and H. Shin 2014. "How Large or Small Is the Policy Space? WTO Regime and Industrial Policy," *Seoul Journal of Economics* 27(3), 307–348.

Pritchett, L. and Summers, L. H. 2014. "Asiaphoria Meets Regression to the Mean", National Bureau of Economic Research Working Paper No. 20573, https://www.nber.org/papers/w20573,downloaded 8/23/2019.

Wade, R. H. 2016. "The Role of the State in Escaping the Middle-income Trap: The Case for Smart Industrial Policy," *METU Studies in Development* 43(1), 21–42.

Woo, W. T. 2014. "The Major Types of Middle-income Trap that Threaten China," in: W. T. Woo et al. (ed.) *A New Economic Growth Engine for China: Escaping the Middle-Income Trap by Not Doing More of the Same* (London: Imperial College Press) 3-39.

Zhang, D. 2014. "The Mechanism of the Middle Income Trap and the Potential Factors Influencing China's Economic Growth," *Frontiers of Economics in China* 9(3), 499–528.

PART III

How key approaches play into some key debates

11

DEBATES ON FOREIGN AID

Introduction

Foreign aid (referred to hereafter as aid) along with foreign direct investment (FDI – Chapter 12) are probably the two topics in development economics on which alternative approaches come most into play. The chapter starts by defining what constitutes aid and indicating what the various kinds of aid are. Next, it identifies who the main donors and recipients are and how this has changed over time. The various theoretical rationales for aid are explained next followed by sections on the early and more recent debates on aid. The conflicting evidence is reviewed following these sections and finally debt, one consequence of foreign aid, is briefly explored

Definition and kinds of foreign aid

There is considerable misunderstanding about what exactly aid is, and that is clarified first in this section. Following that, various kinds of aid are discussed. This chapter focuses mainly on economic aid and to a lesser extent on social or human development aid, which can directly or indirectly assist catch-up growth by building physical and social infrastructure. A portion of this aid could be geo-politically motivated and that might reduce its effectiveness in enhancing catch-up growth (Minoiu and Reddy, 2007). As opposed to economic or human development aid, humanitarian aid is provided for disaster relief or in post-conflict situations and these forms of aid or how to make them more effective are not explored. Thus the reference to aid in this chapter is to economic or human development aid.

Aid can be in the form of physical or monetary resources or technical assistance (knowledge). Also, it can take the form of projects or programs or both and this bifurcation has been referred to in the literature as project vs. program aid. Another bifurcation is between bilateral aid (country to country or donor to recipient) and multilateral (aid channeled via international agencies like those of the UN).[1] The perception of "government failure" in the 1980s started a trend toward channeling aid via NGOs. International NGOs often work in partnership with domestic NGOs which have often grown quite large by drawing on several funding sources. A prominent example is BRAC (Building Resources Across Communities) in Bangladesh.[2]

Not all that is termed aid is actually so. It might be an outright grant, which is unusual, and in that case all funds made available to a recipient country by a donor country count as aid. Alternatively it might be a loan and in that case only the grant element of the loan counts as aid. A hard loan from say an international bank is at market rates and hence contains no concession or grant element. A soft loan has a concession built into it and the extent of the concession or grant element counts as aid. The method of identifying the extent of the concession is therefore to compute the grant element.

The grant element in a soft loan results from the easier terms of the soft loans compared to hard loans. For example, a commercial loan may require repayments starting within a short period of time, say one year. A soft loan might allow for a grace period before repayment begins. The grant element of a loan varies positively with the length of the grace period. This follows from the simple maxim that funds available now are worth more than the same amount available later since interest can be earned on funds available now. This is how the grace period essentially makes a grant available. It specifies that the funds are available "for free" to the borrower for a specified period of time. Since the recipient can in principle put the funds to good use in that specified period without making any repayments, they are in effect getting a grant.

The period over which the loan has to be paid back in a soft loan is longer than a commercial loan. So once again, the grant element in a loan varies positively with the length of the repayment period relative to a commercial loan. Again, the later the loan comes due, the less the amount is worth in say current dollars. Finally, the most important element in the terms of the loan is the interest rate. The commercial bank rate is often anchored to the Intercontinental Exchange London Interbank Offered Rate (ICE LIBOR).[3] The grant element varies inversely with the extent to which a soft loan rate falls below a commercial loan rate.

By comparing the grace period, repayment period and interest rate on soft loans relative to commercial or hard loans, it is possible to quantify the grant element of a loan. Intuitively it would entail computing what a recipient has to pay in present value terms on a soft loan relative to a hard loan with the same face value.

However, other elements in the terms of a loan can reduce the grant element. The donor might impose certain conditions (ties) that could directly reduce the monetary value and hence the grant element in the concessionary loan. Such loans have been referred to as "tied aid" and for example if a donor requires that the funds provided need to be spent by the recipient in the donor country for specified products, this could reduce the monetary value by constraining choice. If the recipient was able to purchase say the same machinery of roughly equivalent value elsewhere on the international market, then accordingly the tie reduces the grant element of the concessionary loan.

The Organization of Economic Cooperation Development (OECD) estimated that ties increase project costs by as much as 15 to 30 percent. The OECD donors forming the Development Assistant Committee (DAC) reported that tied aid as a percentage of the total increased from 46 percent in 1991–2001 to 82 percent in 2008.[4] Ties may also shape priorities or political decisions and, if so, ties become difficult to monetize.

Bilateral aid was initially mostly project aid based on the perception that projects are easier to assess based on a cost-benefit or project analysis and also easier to monitor. A small stake in a large number of projects could also enhance the leverage of the donor country. It could in principle attain donor goodwill by using identifying markers on prominent projects for public information in the recipient country. For this reason, there has been a bias toward the new projects rather than on maintenance, even though the latter might often be a better investment.

In practice, project appraisal and monitoring turned out to be much more difficult than economists had anticipated. The information needed for project appraisal to assess benefits and costs were difficult to procure and calculations were often based on assumptions. Projects also turned out to be slow and cumbersome to execute with a very long gestation period between the various stages of identification to project completion. Hence there was a bias toward large projects since it was less challenging administratively to handle a few large projects rather than several small ones. Recipients prefer program aid (budget support) because it entails quicker disbursement of funds, and because it is not tied to specific projects it can provide more freedom in determining recipient national priorities.

Biscaye, Reynolds and Anderson (2017, p. 1425) point out that most aid (about 70 percent) is still bilateral (country to country or to multilateral agencies with restrictions). Unrestricted multilateral aid (the remaining 30 percent or so) is channeled via various UN agencies including various specialized agencies like the World Health Organization (WHO) or the United Nations Children Fund (UNICEF) and numerous others, but also via the UN Bretton Woods agencies (World Bank and IMF) and regional development banks including the Asian Development Bank (ADB), African Development Bank (AfDB) and the Inter-American Development Bank (IDB).

Multilateral aid is viewed as more disinterested since it is free from ties pertaining to any specific donor country and less susceptible to capture by domestic vested interests.[5] However, as indicated in Chapter 8, multilateral aid via the World Bank and IMF and the regional development banks comes with conditions. From a donor perspective, multilateral agencies are helpful partly because they facilitate the coordination of programs and the harmonizing of conditionality with bilateral aid agencies such as, for example, for the implementation of the neoliberal agenda.

With the launching of the World Trade Organization (WTO) Doha Development Round in 2001, a trade for aid proposal was floated by several scholars to win support for this multilateral trade agreement.[6] It was meant to be a "development" round, but it soon became evident from the associated agreements being discussed (such as Non-Agricultural Market Access, NAMA) that L/LMICs were likely to be the net losers from signing on. Since the bulk of the gains were expected to accrue to HICs (Gallagher, 2008), redistribution via aid could make the agreement a win-win.

This trade for aid proposal is consistent with the developmentalist strategy outlined in Chapter 9. As Stiglitz and Charlton (2006) proposed it, aid could be used to help overcome internal barriers (structural supply constraints, Chapter 7) to exporting and hence to help diversify the economy. This would include support for public investments in infrastructure and institutions to facilitate production (roads, communications, customs, ports, energy, finance), which is the conventional aid endorsed by the developmentalists (Chapter 6).

The novel aspect of this proposal is that it recommends technical assistance to meet product standards in order to successfully export. This includes sanitary, environmental and technical standards and support for the requisite certification that has to be met in order to export successfully. Such support would also enable L/LMICs to address their balance of trade deficits that resulted from the Uruguay Round trade liberalization and any additional liberalization that might result from future rounds such as the Doha Round currently underway.

HICs were interested in extending globalization by bringing L/LMICs more intensively into the global market orbit, but there had been very limited bilateral or multilateral resources committed to this agenda. Stiglitz and Charlton (pp. 9–10) proposed a Global Trade Facility (GTF) to be administered through UNCTAD because it has a history of being a "champion" for L/LMICs. The proposed board was to be diversified to represent all interests, unlike the World Bank and IMF where the Board disproportionately represents the interests of HICs. The proposal was for diverting part of the total aid commitment to GTF to facilitate trade through the trade-specific measures indicated above. As with other proposals proffered to further the interests of L/LMICs (like the NIEO, Chapter 7), this aid for trade proposal has not received much traction. However, over the decades since World War II donors have made several aid commitments in several agreements, and how they measured up is reviewed in the section below.

Donors and recipients

Most donors are members of OECD, also referred to as the rich country club. DAC of the OECD started referring to aid as Official Development Assistance (ODA) and started tracking who gave how much to whom in the late 1960s. The DAC defined ODA as funds provided by state agencies (hence official) to promote economic development and welfare. Loans were included in ODA if they had a grant element of at least 25 percent.[7] Table 11.1 provides an overview of net (after principal but not interest[8] payments) ODA flows as a percentage of Gross National Income (GNI) over time by country income classification and region. To account for fluctuations, the numbers are averaged over decades.

TABLE 11.1 Mean net ODA received by income classification, region and decades as a percentage of GNI

Country classification and region	1968–1980	1981–1990	1991–2000	2001–2010	2011–2016
LIC	na	9.1	11.99	13.09	9.57
LMIC	2.67	2.32	2.15	1.34	0.86
UMIC	0.21	0.25	0.26	0.21	0.07
EA&P	0.33	0.19	0.13	0.08	0.04
LA&C	0.41	0.44	0.33	0.25	0.19
ME&NA	na	na	0.87	0.82	0.68
SA	1.96	1.62	1.24	0.85	0.60
SSA	2.36	4.32	5.22	4.68	2.99

Source: World Development Indicators.
Notes: LIC = Low income countries (PCPPPUS$ = $995 or less)
LMIC = Lower middle income countries (PCPPPPUS$ = $996 to $4,125)
UMIC = Upper middle Income countries (PCPPPUS$ = $4,126 to $12,745)
HIC = High income countries (PCPPPUS$ = $12,746 or more)
ODA = Overseas Development Assistance
GNI = Gross National Income
EE&P = East Asia and the Pacific
E&CA = Europe and Central Asia
LA&C = Latin America and the Caribbean
ME&NA = Middle East and North Africa.
SA = South Asia
SSA = Sub-Saharan Africa

The popular media has been reporting on "aid fatigue" for several decades, but it appears that if this is a real phenomenon it did not set in until the 2010s.[9] For middle income countries, aid progressively declined right from the inception of data collection in the late 1960s. This is again contrary to perceptions that aid is mostly given to allies and not necessarily to the poorest. These trends by income classification are mirrored by the regional trends that showed the highest and increasing aid (until the turn of the 21st century) directed toward SSA. Aid started from a much lower base in the other regions and progressively declined.

Of course since LICs in general and SSA in particular had a much lower GNI, it is possible that aid, which was a much higher percentage of GNI of this income group and region, was much lower in absolute terms in constant $. Data are not available to explore this issue in depth. However, average aid between 1990 and 2004 received by LMICs and UMICs in constant 2015$ was $607 million and $303 million respectively. This indicates that the more prosperous countries did not receive more in absolute terms over the specified period.

Two related issues with regards to who gets aid are notable. Since aid is generally directed at countries rather than populations, aid per capita is lower in the larger countries (Alesina and Dollar, 2000, p. 36). This is important because of the changing geography of global poverty as pointed out by Kanbur and

TABLE 11.2 Net ODA provided by country and time as a percentage of GNI

Country	1968–1980	1981–1990	1991–2000	2001–2010	2011–2016
Australia	0.54	0.44	0.31	0.28	0.32
Canada	0.44	0.46	0.37	0.29	0.28
Denmark	0.51	0.84	1.01	0.87	0.83
France	0.48	0.58	0.52	0.42	0.41
Germany	0.37	0.44	0.31	0.33	0.46
Italy	0.12	0.30	0.22	0.19	0.20
Japan	0.24	0.30	0.27	0.21	0.20
Netherlands	0.69	0.98	0.82	0.80	0.69
Norway	0.59	1.06	0.94	0.93	1.02
Sweden	0.63	0.88	0.84	0.91	1.07
Switzerland	0.17	0.29	0.33	0.38	0.49
United Kingdom	0.41	0.33	0.29	0.42	0.70
United States	0.28	0.22	0.13	0.17	0.19

Source: World Development Indicators.
Notes: ODA = Overseas Development Assistance; GNI = Gross National Income

Sumner (2012). Populous countries like China, India, Indonesia, Nigeria and Pakistan have been reclassified as MICs and therefore less likely to qualify for assistance. However, just these five countries continue to house the bulk of the global population classified as income poor. Even as the countries on average have prospered, due to inequality, masses of the populations remained mired in poverty. Donors may decide that since in principle these countries have more resources, they should be responsible for their own poor. In fact, China and India are now global aid donors. A contrary view would be that international aid should be directed at the poorest no matter where they reside.

Aid is generally not as significant in the budgets of western donors as popularly imagined. The elevated sense of giving among donor country populations may be based partly on the rhetoric of ill-informed or populist politicians. Table 11.2 provides a percentage and absolute distribution of aid provided by the major donor countries for which data were available.

Table 11.2 provides another perspective on donor fatigue in that about half the countries provided less aid on average in 2010–2016 than in 1968–1980. However, the other half more than made up for this at least in percentage terms by enhancing their aid effort. Again, since some economies are much larger than others, contributing a smaller percentage of GNI can nonetheless lead to a larger absolute amount, as indicated in Table 11.3.

Overall, in absolute terms, the picture is more positive with steadily rising aid contributions almost across the board. While the United States contributes the smallest amount as a percentage of its GNI, it provides the largest amount of aid in absolute terms. The size of its absolute contribution has been used as a justification by the United States for not increasing its percentage contribution.

TABLE 11.3 Absolute amount of net ODA provided by country and time in constant 2015$ (billions)

Country	1968–1980	1981–1990	1991–2000	2001–2010	2011–2016
Australia	1.54	1.84	1.86	2.47	3.63
Canada	2.27	3.34	3.22	3.64	4.16
Denmark	0.71	1.42	2.17	2.37	2.46
France	4.76	7.87	8.66	9.09	9.73
Germany	5.02	7.53	7.76	9.67	15.46
Italy	1.07	3.85	3.27	3.34	3.56
Japan	3.82	7.79	9.42	8.46	8.54
Netherland	1.95	3.45	3.90	5.05	4.99
Norway	0.68	1.77	2.22	3.07	3.94
Sweden	1.21	2.03	2.23	3.55	5.14
Switzerland	0.53	1.10	1.56	2.16	3.22
United Kingdom	4.46	4.25	4.72	9.69	17.05
United States	15.42	16.72	13.83	25.58	32.60

Source: World Development Indicators.
Notes: ODA = Overseas Development Assistance
GNI = Gross National Income

A Commission for International Development convened by the World Bank in 1968 and headed by a former Prime Minister of Canada, Lester Pearson, recommended a number of goals. Among these was an aid target for HICs of 0.7 percent of GNP to be attained by 1975 but no later than 1980.[10] This goal was reaffirmed at a UN Summit at Monterrey, Mexico in 2002 and HICs agreed to reach this goal by 2015. In September 2005, prior to the UN Summit of World Leaders, the United States insisted on removing references to attaining the Millennium Development Goals (MDGs – Chapter 4) and the 0.7 donor target.[11] As a compromise measure, the language on MDGs and the target was retained, but the United States made clear that it has no intention of meeting the target.

As evident from Table 11.2, the Scandinavian countries and the Netherlands, with their social democratic focus on social solidarity, were already meeting the Pearson Commission target in 1980–1990. By 2011–2016, the UK had joined their ranks and while in 2017 its economy was about a seventh the size of the US economy, it provided about half as much aid as the United States in absolute terms.

Some perspective on the aggregate ODA provided comes from comparing it to other numbers relevant to L/LMICs. In 2017, the OECD reported the total ODA provided amounted to $146 billion, which was less than a third of the $466 billion in migrant remittances in 2017 into L/LMICs.

One important change is the non-DAC aid from countries that have attained catch-up growth and MIC status. China, Arab countries, India and Turkey are among countries who have relatively recently become donors. The United Arab Emirates and Turkey ranked respectively 8th and 11th among donors in absolute amounts in 2015.[12] These countries, some of whom are recent aid recipients, understand the recipient perspective and are more flexible. China in particular has focused on infrastructure, not a high priority among traditional DAC donors. As more such donors enter the donor club, the leverage of recipient governments regarding conditionality they are willing to accept will increase.

Rationale for aid

The Cold War and the political/ideological competition to win allies was an important motivator for aid. Alesina and Dollar (2000) found evidence that the pattern of aid giving, barring the Nordic countries, was dictated by political strategic considerations including alliances and colonial links. Also, democratization, which meant adopting western political philosophy, was rewarded with increases in aid flows of up to 50 percent.

The west also wanted to create capitalist economies with aid, whereby prosperity trickled down via job creation. This was viewed as a defense against the susceptibility to communism likely to be found among impoverished populations. The additional advantage was creating market economies in the image of the prosperous capitalist economics, which would be receptive to FDI and trade. Thus the developmentalist proponents of aid found a receptive audience and the necessary political will in the 1940s and 1950s.

Recall from Chapter 6 that the developmentalists followed the classical economists in viewing capital accumulation as central to the progress of nations. All recognized capital scarcity in L/LMICs was at least a temporary constraint, but aid was no panacea for the developmentalist pioneers. Recall Rosenstein-Rodan initially suggested capital flows from HICs to LICs as a business proposition, though he later became a champion of aid. Lewis, Nurkse and Hirschman were concerned with domestic resource mobilization. Nonetheless, the 1950s and 1960s, when developmentalist thinking dominated development economics, were also decades in which aid-based development planning was in vogue and so the justification for economic aid was macro based.

In the simplest models, economic growth was assumed to be a function of capital accumulation or investment. Thus the macroeconomic objective was to identify an economic growth target and thereby identify the investment rate consistent with what would follow from the standard aggregate production function. The planning process would come up with an aggregate investment target based on disaggregated sectoral targets. The gap between the domestic resource mobilization and the required investment would in turn identify the needed aid.

More sophisticated models recognized that there was more than one gap relevant for industrialization and economic growth (Chenery and Strout, 1966). The simple Keynesian accounting equation could be used to identify the gaps.

$$C + S + T + IM = C + I + G + EX \tag{1}$$

C = Consumption
S = Saving
T = Taxes

IM = Imports
I   = Investment
G   = Government expenditure
EX = Exports

By manipulating equation (1) above, the relevant gaps are identified in equation (2) below.

$$(G - T) + (I - S) = (IM - EX) \qquad (2)$$

In L/LMICs, G is generally > T (fiscal deficit due to weak tax administration) and I > S (low saving), and therefore IM > EX i.e. a balance of trade deficit.[13] It was acknowledged that the shortage of hard currency for the imports of capital and intermediate goods was a separate constraint from the local resource mobilization constraint. Aid could address these gaps until the catch-up growth momentum picked up.

The macroeconomic approach above was consistent with economic planning and program aid. The disenchantment with economic planning based on alleged government failure (inefficiency and corruption) resulted in program aid morphing into the neoliberal structural adjustment programs discussed in Chapter 8 in the late 1970s and 1980s.[14]

The microeconomic approach of project aid also continued but was to be made more efficient based on project appraisal or evaluation. The landmark competing studies supported by United Nations Industrial Development Organization (UNIDO) and OECD respectively suggested alternative methods to doing such evaluations (Sen, Dasgupta and Marglin, 1972 and Little and Mirrlees, 1969). Project appraisal required performing social cost-benefit analyses for each project whereby the costs and benefits to society, accounting for market failures and social objectives, were expected to be computed.

While the early popularity of these approaches faded, they endured and environmental and gender impacts were incorporated as additional key components in analyzing the feasibility of projects as donor priorities evolved. As discussed in Chapter 4, various microeconomic and meso economic initiatives were subsequently proposed as more effective vehicles for aid delivery starting in the 1980s. These include microcredit, conditional and unconditional cash transfers, and other direct micro interventions to alleviate poverty and enhance well-being. Randomized control trials (RCTs – Chapter 2) are the favored method to evaluate aid effectiveness.

There are other rationales for aid that are proffered outside of the development economics literature. Global inequality and poverty and disease within LICs are highlighted to make this case.[15] Some still point to the injustices of colonialism to justify aid as a form of restitution (Chapter 3). Yet another argument is that providing aid is in the enlightened self-interest of donors since mass poverty threatens collective prosperity via various mechanisms including possibly terrorism. Also, making the poor nations better off will make all nations better off as their catch-up growth will enhance global markets and trade.

The early debates

Foreign aid is one topic in development economics on which critics from the right and left seemed to agree although mostly for different reasons. The radical political economists thought that political criteria rather than poverty or need determined the allocation of ODA (recall Baran's critique from Chapter 5). They considered it a vehicle for HICs to secure markets to promote their exports and create a favorable climate for their FDI. Unlike mainstream economists, radical political economists did not view trade and FDI as a win-win, but rather as mechanisms for the extraction and siphoning of surplus back to HICs.

They also viewed aid as accentuating or creating imbalances in L/LMICs. Thus, for example, the focus of aid on industrial sectors resulted in an urban bias and hence worsened regional inequalities. The social sectors were ignored but insofar as they got resources, the focus was on tertiary rather than primary education, curative rather than preventive medicine, and urban showcase hospitals rather than rural clinics. Infrastructure development was imbalanced in that the purpose was not articulated and integrated development but the facilitation of MNCs.

Aid was also perceived as creating economics imbalances. Much of aid was tied and this hurt the balance of payments. The ties were often in the form of imports of capital goods from donor countries, which resulted in capital intensity in labor surplus economies. Foreign imports financed by aid also competed with domestic production. To get rid of agricultural surplus in HICs, food aid was provided, but this lowered domestic prices and hurt agricultural self-sufficiency in recipient countries.

Radical political economists also viewed aid as propping up tyrannical regimes that represented the opposite of values HICs championed domestically. On this point, the radical political economists and right wing conservative critics of aid such as Peter Thomas Bauer and Deepak Lal, whose positions were discussed in Chapter 8, agreed. But overall, the conservative critique attacked aid from a different perspective.

They considered aid to be pushed by bleeding heart liberals with a sense of guilt. This guilt was in their view misplaced since they viewed countries to be better off in direct proportion to the intensity of their colonial experience. Aid was viewed as an alliance of convenience between misguided "do-gooders" with bureaucrats for whom bilateral aid meant jobs and status. This was also the case for multilateral donor agencies that liked to maximize the volume and scope of their activity ("empire building").[16] This was a likely outcome since staff incentives (evaluations and promotions) were tied to disbursements. At times, the incentive to disburse rapidly was driven by trying to avoid a likely recipient country default.

The right wing critique included many examples of prestige aid projects that were ill conceived and had not worked (e.g. factories with snow roofs in tropical countries). They argued that if the projects had good prospects and met the market test they would get funded anyway and so aid was not needed. Besides funds are fungible and so aid monies would be used for purposes that would otherwise have been accomplished with domestic resources.

They argued that aid was in any case mostly captured by elites and benefited individuals who were richer than median income tax payers in HICs that bore the burden of the aid and such a redistribution of income was regressive. Conservatives also argued that aid relieved the pressure on L/LMIC governments to mobilize resources domestically. As a consequence, they became answerable to donors rather than their own constituents, as would happen if the government was funded by local taxes, and this in turn eroded the quality of governance.

Apart from being institutionally destructive, it was also economically destructive since it expanded the public sector and crowded out the private sector. It politicized economic life and by giving the state resources for rent seeking, adversely impacted productivity. The aid-related capital inflows resulted in an overvaluation of the currency, as in the Dutch disease, and this again undermined self-sufficiency by hurting exports. Overvaluation also enhanced capital intensity and hence resulted in the wrong choice of technology for labor surplus economies. Finally, the capital inflows reduced domestic interest rates and saving and promoted capital flight seeking better financial opportunities abroad.

Moderate supporters of aid claimed that these critiques were not based on evidence. They provided evidence to indicate that much of aid-provided infrastructure complemented rather than displaced private sector activity. Further, contrary to conservative assertions, the size of the public sector in L/LMICs was no larger than that in HICs. They claimed that the critique did not address the counter-factual on whether many L/LMICs would be even worse off without the aid. Finally they pointed out that the assertion that sound projects would get funded anyway was not empirically verified. L/LMICs had weak tax administrations and could not raise the resources domestically and foreign capital shied away from risky projects with long gestation periods.

More recent debates

Research on assessing aid led by David Dollar (summarized in World Bank, 1998) of the World Bank Development Research Group reignited the debate. In a simulation in one of many papers with co-authors, Dollar showed that aid lifted 30 million people out of poverty per annum and if a poverty efficient allocation could be achieved, 80 million could be lifted out of poverty per annum. Poverty efficient would mean aid targeted at countries with severe poverty but good policies (i.e. structural adjustment policies) and sound institutions (good governance) to implement them.

This sparked a controversy because of how influential the findings became in the donor community after the press picked them up. It provided a justification for structural adjustment policies and good governance reforms promoted by the World Bank and IMF. More importantly, it made a case for directing aid to countries that adopted such policies and reforms, a case that donors found persuasive.

Several scholars challenged these findings on theoretical and /or empirical grounds.[17] The debate also raged on the pages of the leading mainstream economic journal, the *American Economic Review*. Burnside and Dollar (2000) published their extended findings on aid mentioned above. Easterly, Levine and Roodman (2004) replicated Burnside and Dollar's method, extended the data to run to 1997, instead of 1993, and extended the sample to include additional countries and found the Burnside and Dollar results were not robust.[18] Dollar and Burnside responded that the reason for the change in results was the inclusion of six countries that had good policies but poor growth. But there is no end to this game because one could then dig up the original data and find six countries with good policies and good growth and remove them from the sample and clearly the results would change.

One of the three critics of David Dollar and associates' research, William Easterly, is an ex-World Bank staffer who moved to academia. He followed in the tradition of Peter T. Bauer and Depak Lal (Chapter 8) in being critical of aid. In *White Man's Burden* Easterly (2006) complained that the press and aid agencies publicized studies that indicated a positive aid impact and ignored those that show no impact or were critical of positive findings. He showed there was no empirical support for developmentalist "big push" and "poverty trap" theories that justified aid (see Chapter 6).

He argued that UN and other multilateral and bilateral agencies did not have the capacity to deliver aid. Other problems included a lack of accountability. If plans based on aid were announced and not achieved, there were no repercussions. Since many agencies pursued the same objective, the blame shifting becomes easier. Echoing the radical political economic critique narrated earlier, he used the AIDS epidemic as a case to demonstrate how donors refused to fund prevention. Instead, they supported expensive cures that had a very high opportunity cost in terms of lives not saved e.g. up to 1,000 lives could have been saved for the amount spent on saving one HIV/AIDS patient.

In his next book, *The Tyranny of Experts* (2013), Easterly adopted a libertarian perspective and in the tradition of Friedrich Hayek (Chapter 1) suggested that democracy and human freedom enables decentralized market and civil society initiatives (by searchers rather than planners) based on local knowledge. He argued that it is the sum of these initiatives that ultimately makes a substantive difference and hence are worth facilitating. Easterly viewed aid givers, including the World Bank and IMF, as top-down planners self-interestedly aligned with authoritarianism and as organizations that have the arrogance to assume they have the answers.[19]

Jeffrey Sachs, an ex-neoliberal development practitioner,[20] contested Easterly's position in *The End of Poverty* (2006) to make a case for aid. Sachs suggested that knowing what to do in improving the well-being of millions in poverty is not rocket science and the problem is the lack of resources rather that the ill-advised use of aid. Sachs is among influential advisors who galvanized the global aid effort around the MDGs (2000–2015) and subsequently the UN SDGs (2015–2030) (Chapter 4).

Evidence

While ultimately the debates and the various hypotheses implicit therein can only be settled by evidence, for various reasons pointed out below and in Chapters 1 and 2 this is easier said than done. Leaving aside the limitations of data and empirical methods (Chapters 2 and 8),[21] as with most topics in development economics, one can find almost as much empirical support for hypotheses as against them. In this case, there are conflicting empirical findings on the impact of aid on several variables of interest such as economic growth or well-being. Also, any given finding is easily challenged as evident above in the David Dollar and Craig Burnside vs William Easterly, Ross Levine and David Roodman debate on the impact of aid on economic growth.

Apart from results changing when the sample size, time period or variables change in the estimation, it is difficult to identify the specific mechanism (see below) via which aid impacts various macroeconomic variables including economic growth even if the data and method pass muster. In some cases, researchers have not separated humanitarian and development aid. The former by definition goes to countries suffering from low growth due to disasters and so finding a negative aid-growth association is inevitable.

There are literally hundreds of empirical multi-country studies and many times more individual country studies exploring just the aid-growth association.[22] Others include an exploration of mechanisms that might account for a positive or negative aid-growth association such as via more or less saving or investment, or better or worse governance. One of the earliest empirical debates was on the issue of whether foreign aid encouraged consumption and reduced domestic saving via various mechanisms.[23] If it displaced domestic saving, aid was inherently ineffective.

Hristos Doucouliagos and Martin Paldam have conducted a series of meta-studies (quantitative aggregation of results of cross-country studies) to explore the association of aid with a number of relevant variables. Doucouliagos and Paldam (2006) revisited the early 1970s debate on the impact of aid on saving and investment.[24] The aggregate result of 43 of 97 studies conducted until 2004 suggested that about 25 percent of the aid increased investment while most of the remaining 75 percent was crowded out by a fall in saving mainly due to a rise in public consumption. In a companion meta-study (2008) drawing on 68 papers that yielded 543 estimates of the aid-growth association, they detected a small positive association of aid and economic growth, but it was not statistically significant. In an update, Doucouliagos and Paldam (2011) added 32 studies and drew on an additional 678 estimates for their meta-analysis and concluded that their aid-ineffectiveness result was reinforced.[25]

Since many studies have found a negative aid-growth association,[26] it is worth speculating on the causes since it seems self-evident that more resources for more uses should be beneficial and boost economic growth. Thus on the face of it, the negative aid-growth association seems to lead to the facile interpretation that countries would be better off with less funds, which defies common sense. The more sophisticated interpretation is that aid comes with baggage that could produce a negative outcome. Ties and consulting contracts siphon funds back to the donor country. Aid has been shown to worsen the quality of governance by facilitating patronage, crony capitalism, inefficiencies, misappropriation, leakages and rent seeking (see conservative critique above and Knack, 2001). Also, the state's ability to draw resources facilitated by aid has a high opportunity cost. Alternatively, if aid is given to pursue strategic donor interests,[27] it should not be surprising that it does not promote economic growth. However, these reasons may negate aid effectiveness but in and of themselves would not explain a negative sign in the aid-economic growth association.

To explain a negative sign, various authors have identified mechanisms via which the negative impact comes into play. The early literature (see above) showed that aid resulted in a reduction of domestic saving. They also showed that aid resulted in a "foreign exchange drag" such that aid caused freestanding foreign exchange to leave due to capital outflows because aid caused the domestic interest rate to fall. To the extent that critics of structural adjustment conditionality are right (Chapter 8), conditioned multilateral aid can have negative economic growth impacts.

Following Karnoi's (1986) logic, as applied to public sector enterprises, unconditioned aid could be viewed as a "soft budget constraint" that undermines management and efficiency.[28] Rajan and Subramanian (2005) showed a negative long-run aid-growth association resulting from an over-valuation of the exchange rate and the subsequent decline in manufactured exports due to a loss in competitiveness (Dutch disease).[29] Finally, the "aid curse" has been shown to have undermined the rule of law and worsened bureaucratic quality via rent seeking.[30]

The evidence on the success of disaggregate program and project aid is also contested. For example, the aid and MNC-driven Green Revolution program to boost agricultural productivity of traditional agriculture is viewed as a massive success. A founder of the movement, Norman Borlaug, received the Nobel Peace Prize in 1970. While there is little doubt that traditional agriculture received a major boost, chemical fertilizers, insecticides and high yielding varieties of seeds have been criticized for negative environmental impacts and a rise in social inequality (Chapter 13).

Most concede that countries that had the absorption capacity, like Korea and Taiwan, made very good use of aid. In other countries technical assistance did much to promote universities, technical institutes and training establishments, although recall that even this was criticized for being misdirected and for creating educational imbalances. Support for population programs may have helped reduce fertility rates, though the reigning wisdom now is that female education and gender equality do far more in this regard.

Much less contested are the benefit of immunization campaigns to eradicate diseases like smallpox, polio and diphtheria and support for cures of diseases like river blindness, trachoma, leprosy and guinea worms. Sachs (2006) argued that with more funds such as from ODA and donors like the Gates Foundation, more headway can be made against malaria, HIV/AIDS and other diseases. While virtually no one contests the worthiness of these objectives, Easterly (2013) doubts that such programs can be effectively executed.

Project aid has been controversial but much of the evidence (some anecdotal) is mixed. While there are certainly examples of bad projects which aid opponents harp on about, by the same token there are at least as many examples of well-executed and sustained projects that would not have been possible without aid. Thus the evidence on the effectiveness of aid at a micro level is also mixed, but scholars have provided suggestions for making it more effective.

Making aid effective

Much of the focus of attention of the UN is now on the SDGs with the UNDP spearheading the initiative. The thinking is that aid does not achieve concrete outcomes because it is managed by too many agencies (80) and heads in too many directions. Thus the idea was to have the donor community focus on a limited number of concrete goals to make headway. The eight goals for 2000–2015 MDGs were agreed to in 2000 by 189 world leaders and approved in the UN (Chapter 4). This consensus was a major achievement and was attained when support for international aid was at an all-time low.

One of the main criticisms of the MDGs was a limited focus on the environment. The two associated targets were concerned with sustainable access to safe drinking water and improvement in the lives of 100 million slum dwellers. The third was amorphous and required integrating the principles of sustainable development in country policies and programs and hence reversing the loss of environment resources. Another criticism was that the MDGs with 18 targets and 48 indicators were too broad.

The SDGs (2015–2030) brought climate change and environmental issues centerstage and sustainable features in 12 of the 17 goals. This was unavoidable given the rapid reality of climate change as pointed out by the fifth assessment report of the UN's inter-governmental panel on climate change.[31] There was a hope of narrowing the focus of the SDGs, but this proved impossible given the inter-governmental and civil society inclusive participatory process pursued for arriving at the goals. The SDGs have 169 targets and 230 indicators associated with them.

There are some sensible suggestions for improving aid effectiveness. One suggestion is that donors should impose the same transparency on themselves that they require from recipients and be open about how much of their aid is tied. The estimates vary from 20 to 40 percent on average, but scholars making the estimates concede that they have very faulty data to work with to make the estimates. For the United States, 72 percent was estimated to be tied in 1996, the latest year for which numbers were reported.

Since food aid and technical assistance have negative outcomes for domestic production and capacity building, another suggestion is to limit these forms of aid. Estimates suggest that these amount to 7 percent and 43 percent respectively for the United States and an average of 4 percent and 24 percent respectively for other donors.

Multiple donors and individual reporting requirements are viewed as imposing high costs on local agencies. The finance minister of Afghanistan (Ashraf Ghani, 2002–2004) stated that reporting and meeting donors took up 60 percent of his time. If donors can coordinate on objectives such as SDGs, then they can coordinate on the reporting. The advantage of aligning behind objectives like the SDGs are that they represent long-term commitments and local capacity building can be engaged in for attaining them.

Donors express an interest in local capacity building but often undermine it. They often raid local capacity to enrich their own programs and projects. The World Bank and UN are guilty of this by raiding the best for local offices at very high pay. The staff is then deskilled because the advanced training of local hires is underutilized (e.g. PhDs handing out air-tickets to less trained personnel of foreign missions).

Oxfam estimated that only 20 percent of the aid actually goes to the poorest countries and only 50 percent of that was linked to MDGs. Most of the rest went to strategic allies and pet projects. For example, much of US aid went to Afghanistan, Iraq, Israel, Egypt and Pakistan. There was little left after that.

In Chapter 2, RCTs were discussed as a possible data collection method and their use as a tool for impact assessment of microcredit was reviewed as an application and to demonstrate the various shortcomings of this method. RCTs have also been proposed as a tool to evaluate aid effectiveness of project aid at a micro level. The contention is that evidence-based policy action will allocate resources to what works. However, the shortcomings pointed to in the case of microcredit also apply in the case of micro aid-effectiveness RCTs.

Debt

Indebtedness is one downside of aid even when it comes with a high grant element. If the funds are not used wisely to pay back the loans with the surplus thereby generated, the debt starts to accumulate and paralyze indebted countries. This is because the principal and interest payments absorb so much of the fiscal revenues or export earnings generated that there is little left for development expenditures and critical imports. The options are to accept anemic growth (politically unpopular) or extend the begging bowl for more aid to push back the day of reckoning i.e. let some other political regime deal with it in the future. Table 11.4 shows how the debt situation has played out over the past half century or so of aid.

As evident from Table 11.4, L/LMICs confronted a debt crisis in the 1980s decade following the two oil price shocks at the beginning and end of the 1970s. Debt service absorbed between a fifth and a quarter of income generated by exports

TABLE 11.4 Debt service by income classification, region and decades as a percentage of exports of goods, services and primary income

Country classification and region	1968–1980	1981–1990	1991–2000	2001–2010	2011–2016
LIC	9.31@	26.20#	10.77*	4.76^	4.27
LMIC	10.40&	22.13	17.89	8.75	5.21
UMIC	10.80&	20.26	12.67	6.86	3.08
EA&P	na	na	na	na	na
LA&C	13.72	26.51	21.16	13.70	7.34
ME&NA	na	na	na	na	na
SA	15.67+	22.07	21.90	8.60	3.95
SSA	na	na	9.88!	5.91	4.24

Source: World Development Indicators.
Notes: LIC = Low income countries ($995 or less annual per capita gross national income).
LMIC   = Lower middle income countries ($996 – $4,035)
UMIC   = Upper middle income countries ($4,036 – $12,475)
HIC   = High income countries (above $12,476)
EE&P   = East Asia and the Pacific
E&CA   = Europe and Central Asia
LA&C   = Latin America and the Caribbean
ME&NA = Middle East and North Africa.
SA   = South Asia
SSA   = Sub-Saharan Africa
@   = 1971–1978
#   = 1986–1989
*   = 1995–2000
^   = 2005–2010
&   = 1974–1980
+   = 1974–1980
!   = 1994–2000
na   = Not available

and other financial flows. Debt relief for the LICs resulted in a stabilization of this crisis by the 1990s whereas the other countries, left to their own devices, managed to stabilize this crisis by the turn of the century.

Boyce and Ndikumana (2002) refer to the debt of non-democratic countries as *odious* because the benefits are privately appropriated (via embezzlement, kickbacks on contracts, revenue misappropriation) while the liabilities are social. They pointed out that the 34 SSA countries (classified as Highly Indebted Poor Countries by the World Bank) had borrowed $11.4 billion but paid $14.5 billion in principal and interest payments by 2001. They were spending 3.8 percent of GDP in 2000 on debt servicing while allocating 2.4 percent of GDP to health. George (2007) estimated that in 1980, the debt stock of L/LMICs was $540 billion and this increased by 2004 to $2,600 billion. However, between 1980 and 2004, the flows of debt repayments from the South to the North were $5,300 billion.

Summary and conclusion

The debates on foreign aid reflect the broader development debate based on alternative approaches. This is however one topic on which the right and left perspectives, both opposing aid, converge even if for different reasons. The left critique has been valuable in that it did influence bilateral and multilateral aid priorities over time. However, whether or not aid is effective has been the subject of empirical debate since the 1950s and the issue remains unresolved.

The ability to econometrically address the reverse causality problem (i.e. that poor growth may be drawing more aid) and the many other problematic issues such as country heterogeneity discussed in this chapter has resulted in even mainstream economists concluding that cross-country econometrics may have nothing of value to contribute to this discussion. Time series analysis addresses the heterogeneity issue but is associated with another set of problems. RCTs, as discussed in Chapter 2, could identify effective micro initiatives, but this method has also been found problematic. At a macro level, Edwards (2015) proposed the detailed historical / descriptive case study method (Chapter 2) because aid policies change over time and econometrics (cross-sectional or time series) is unable to capture nuances and complexities.

More traditional methods of project appraisal are built on many assumptions but can at a broad level identify success. Few question the success of many medical and humanitarian interventions. Several scholars noted early on that project and even program aid cannot succeed if the recipients do not have the absorption capacity, and aid has been redirected to building absorption capacity such as by strengthening institutions and also tax administration to offset the finding that aid inflows can weaken fiscal effort.

In some ways, foreign aid is a red herring since even remittances make more funds available for many L/LMICs and capital inflows via portfolio investment and FDI are alternatives. The real issue, the recurring theme in this textbook, is catch-up growth based on developing local strategies and effectively implementing them. Beyond that, one could argue that aid represents an opportunity that could be put to good use (for example as in the case of Korea and Taiwan) or dissipated as has been more frequently the case.

Questions

1. Explain the different kinds of aid and why this matters.
2. Why might aid be systematically overstated?
3. Does the evidence suggest that aid fatigue has set in?
4. What was the traditional rationale for aid and what is the modern rationale for aid?
5. Explain the radical political economy perspective on aid.
6. Explain the conservative perspective on aid.
7. Is there a convergence of views between left and right wing scholars? Explain.

8. How has the empirical debate on aid evolved over time?
9. What has almost seven decades of empirical investigation revealed about aid effectiveness and why?
10. Is it plausible to imagine that foreign aid can have a negative impact on L/LMIC economies? Explain your response.
11. How do you think aid could be made more effective?
12. Could one reasonably argue that aid is a side-show when it comes to economic development?

Notes

1 Gulrajani (2016) pointed out that bilateral aid includes aid channeled via the public sector, NGOs and public-private partnerships. Recipients prefer multilateral aid and consider multilateral institutions as possessing more policy and technical expertise and as being more flexible, responsive and reliable.
2 It was founded in 1972 and has retained its acronym but has gone through two name changes.
3 At the onset of the global financial crisis in 2007, large multinational banks were suspected of manipulating LIBOR. After investigations, these banks were found guilty and fines started being imposed by the UK and US financial authorities in 2012. LIBOR is set to be replaced by 2021, although no alternative has yet been worked out (*New York Times*, 7/20/2018).
4 www.oecd.org/dac/financing-sustainable-development/development-finance-standards/untied-aid.htm, consulted 7/26/2018.
5 However, since individual donors have votes on the boards of multilateral institutions based on their contributions, they can exert influence on the allocations of multilateral institutions. Biscaye, Reynolds and Anderson (2017) reviewed 45 papers and concluded that there is no evidence that bilateral or multilateral aid is more effective overall.
6 The successful completion of the Doha Round which started in 2001 is in doubt. The L/LMICs balked at any further non-agricultural sector liberalization and the Trump administration seemed set against multilateralism, arguing that the United States could get better deals via bilateral negotiations. In June 2018, President Trump questioned why the United States was still in the WTO but later denied it had any intentions to withdraw (www.aei.org/publication/the-weekly-trade-kerfuffle-trump-wants-to-withdraw-from-the-wto/), consulted 2/28/2019.
7 www.oecd.org   dac/stats/officialdevelopmentassistancedefinitionandcoverage.htm, consulted 2/28/2019.
8 Engel (2014, p. 1378) cited this definition of *net* which overstates aid. She also cited a study by World Bank economists who estimated that the average grant element for the mid-1990s was overstated by 100 percent. She cited Homi Kharas who showed that once administrative cost, refugee and resettlement costs, technical assistance, food aid and debt relief are excluded, 37 percent of aid is left for country programmable aid.
9 The decline could have resulted from scholarly and popular literature on the ineffectiveness of aid (see below), populist politics in HICs, or because across the board improvements in human development in LICs reduced the necessity for aid. Also, many countries graduated to LMIC status and no longer qualified for ODA directed at least developed countries.
10 http://unesdoc.unesco.org/images/0005/000567/056743eo.pdf, consulted 2/28/2019.
11 The United States suggested that the targeted amount specified was arbitrary.
12 https://en.wikipedia.org/wiki/Official_development_assistance, consulted 2/28/2019. Since DAC does not collect and report information on non-DAC countries, comparative data (of the kind reported in Tables 11.1 to 11.3) are not available.

13 Refer to Taylor (1991, p. 10) for a more elaborate version of public sector borrowing needs than G-T.

14 Ranis (2013, p. 5), recognized as a very moderate and erudite development economist, stated that "the evidence suggests that the World Bank and IMF have usually followed USA strategic priorities since the latter is the largest shareholder of both institutions".

15 Oxfam researchers of late have been publishing the most striking statistics in this regard. For example, its 2018 report pointed out that the richest 1 percent acquired 82 percent of all wealth created in 2017 while the poorest half of humanity got none of this wealth creation www.oxfam.org/en/pressroom/pressreleases/2018-01-22/richest-1-percent-bagged-82-percent-wealth-created-last-year, consulted 3/1/2019.

16 This is consistent with the public choice theory economic critique discussed in Chapter 8.

17 For example, Lensink and White (2000, pp. 403–404) challenged the presumption that the only channel of poverty reduction via aid is economic growth. They argued, as others had, that redistribution policies such as human development investments and asset reallocation supported by aid could benefit both growth and poverty reduction. Dalgaard and Hansen (2001) challenged the empirical growth model specification on theoretical grounds and also showed that the results were empirically sensitive to outliers. Also, if there are diminishing returns to aid, as might be expected, a quadratic term should be included in the specification and this was not done. Hansen and Tarp (2001) showed the key policy findings of the World Bank report disappeared once a quadratic term was introduced into the specification. Ram (2004) disaggregated aid into bilateral and multilateral and showed that when this is done then the finding of aid-effectiveness being conditioned by "good policy" disappears.

18 Several other scholars including Murphy and Tresp (2006) supported Easterly et al.'s conclusions.

19 Since the IMF and World Bank are among the organizations that have done the most in promoting privatization, deregulation and liberalization, this position is puzzling. However, Easterly empirically showed that structural adjustment policies enforced by these organizations have been unmitigated failures.

20 Sachs is also famous for being an advisor on structural adjustment reforms in Bolivia and Russia.

21 Deaton (2010) presents a convincing critique of the shortcomings of quantitative research (econometric and RCTs) as applied to macro and micro aid-effectiveness studies and more generally.

22 The literature search strategy for this chapter was based on drawing on multi-country studies (rather than country or regional studies) published in the highly ranked peer reviewed journals or by well-known economists. While country case studies are often methodologically preferable, they are difficult to generalize.

23 For example, Griffin and Enos (1970), Weisskopf (1972) and Griffin (1973) provided the radical political economic perspective on aid ineffectiveness while Papanek (1972) provided evidence for the orthodox view supportive of aid.

24 Meta studies are not less suspect methodologically than individual studies and in fact have additional problems resulting from the aggregation methodology. However, they have been cited here as a short cut with reference to the findings of the bulk of the voluminous research in the field.

25 These meta-studies, while comprehensive, were unlikely to settle the debate once and for all. Indeed Mekasha and Tarp (2013) challenged the results of this meta-analysis and Doucouliagos and Paldam's (2013) rejoinder suggested they were not persuaded. The debate is likely to continue although scholars have claimed in the past and more recently that the positive aid-growth association is settled. For example, McGillivray et al. (2006) surveyed the cross-country studies literature from 1950–1996 and concluded that a positive aid-growth association had been established while the nature of the association could be influenced by aid volatility, policy, political stability, external and climactic factors, and institutions. Minoiu and Reddy (2007) argued that a positive development

aid-growth association was evident once development aid is separated from geo-political aid in cross-country studies. Rajan and Subramanian's (2008) suggested a weak or zero aid-growth association in cross-country analysis once they tried to econometrically resolve for the possibility of reverse causality i.e. that poor growth draws more aid. Clemens et al. (2012) argued that when the appropriate lag structure is used (aid does not contemporaneously impact economic growth), a modest positive aid-growth association is found on average using modified specifications of even skeptical studies like that of Rajan and Subramanian. Arndt, Jones and Tarp (2015) reported evidence of positive long-term aid-growth association using time series analysis, which in principle addresses the country heterogeneity problem of cross-country studies. Roger (2015) identified problems with the data used in time series analysis. In addition, his analysis showed that the results were sensitive to individual country model respecification.

26 For example, refer to Osborne (2002), Brumm (2003), Ovaska (2003), and Kimura, Mori and Sawada (2012). The first three of the articles in the list above were published by the right wing Cato Institute Journal, which holds an ideological anti-international aid position.

27 See, for example, Alesina and Dollar (2000), Osborne (2002) and Leeson (2008).

28 A hard budget constraint is what the private sector operates under and the options are to be efficient or fail. A soft budget constraint facilitated by aid means the absence of this hard edge that private businesses operate under and so is a lack of incentive for efficient management.

29 They did not find that remittance inflows had the same kind of negative effect that aid inflows did.

30 See, for example, (Svensson (2000), Easterly, 2006, pp. 136–137), and Djankov, Montalvo and Reynal-Querol (2008).

31 www.ipcc.ch/report/ar5/, consulted 3/1/2019.

References

Alesina, A. and D. Dollar. 2000. "Who Gives Foreign Aid to Whom and Why?" *Journal of Economic Growth*, 5(1), 33–63.

Arndt, C., S. Jones and F. Tarp. 2015. "Assessing Foreign Aid's Long-Run Contribution to Growth and Development," *World Development*, 69(5), 6–18.

Biscaye, P. E., C. W. Reynolds and T. L. Anderson. 2017. "Relative Effectiveness of Bilateral and Multilateral Aid on Development Outcomes," *Review of Development Studies*, 21(4), 1425–1447.

Boyce, J. K. and L. Ndikumana. 2002. "Africa's Debt: Who Owes Whom?" Political Economy Research Institute (PERI), University of Massachusetts, Amherst, Working Paper Series Number 48.

Brumm, H. J. 2003. "Aid, Policies, and Growth: Bauer Was Right," *Cato Journal*, 23(2), 167–174.

Burnside, C. and D. Dollar. 2000. "Aid, Policies and Growth," *American Economic Review*, 90(4), 847–868.

Chenery, H. B. and A. M. Strout. 1966. "Foreign Assistance and Economic Development," *The American Economic Review*, 56(4), 679–733.

Clemens, M. A., S. Radelet, R. R. Bhavnani and S. Bazzi. 2012. "Counting Chickens When They Hatch: Timing and the Effects of Aid on Growth," *The Economic Journal*, 122(561), 590–617.

Dalgaard, C. and H. Hansen. 2001. "On Aid, Growth and Good Policies," *Journal of Development Studies*, 37(6), 17–41.

Deaton, A. 2010. "Instruments, Randomization, and Learning about Development," *Journal of Economic Literature*, 48(2), 424–455.

Djankov, J., G. Montalvo and M. Reynal-Querol. 2008. "The Curse of Aid," *Journal of Economic Growth*, 13(3), 169–194.

Doucouliagos, H. and M. Paldam. 2006. "Aid Effectiveness on Accumulation: A Meta Study," *Kyklos*, 59(2), 227–254.

Doucouliagos, H. and M. Paldam. 2011. "The Ineffectiveness of Development Aid on Growth: An Update," *European Journal of Political Economy*, 27(2), 399–404.

Doucouliagos, H. and M. Paldam. 2013. "The Robust Result in Meta-analysis of Aid Effectiveness: A Response to Mekasha and Tarp," *Journal of Development Studies*, 49(4), 584–587.

Easterly, W. 2006. *The White Man's Burden: Why the Wests Efforts to Aid the Rest Have Done so Much Ill and so Little Good* (London: Penguin Press).

Easterly, W. 2013. *The Tyranny of Experts: Economists, Dictators, and the Forgotten Rights of the Poor* (New York: Perseus Books).

Easterly, W., R. Levine and D. Roodman. 2004. "Aid, Policies, and Growth: Comment," *American Economic Review*, 94(3), 774–780.

Edwards, S. 2015. "Economic Development and the Effectiveness of Foreign Aid: A Historical Perspective," *Kyklos*, 68(3), 277–316.

Engel, S. 2014. "The Not-so-great Aid Debate," *Third World Quarterly*, 35(8), 1374–1389.

Gallagher, K. P. 2008. "Understanding Developing Country Resistance to the Doha Round," *Review of International Political Economy*, 15(1), 62–85.

George, S. 2007. "Down the Great Financial Drain: How Debt and the Washington Consensus Destroy Development and Create Poverty," *Development*, 50(2), 4–11.

Griffin, K. B. 1973. "The Effect of Aid and Other Resource Transfers on Savings and Growth in Less-Developed Countries: A Comment," *The Economic Journal*, 83(331), 863–866.

Griffin, K. B. and J. L. Enos. 1970. "Foreign Assistance: Objectives and Consequences," *Economic Development and Cultural Change*, 18(3), 313–327.

Gulrajani, N. 2016. "Bilateral Vs. Multilateral Aid Channels: Strategic Choices for Donors," Overseas Development Institute Report, London, www.odi.org/sites/odi.org.uk/files/resource-documents/10492.pdf, consulted 7/26/2018.

Hansen, H. and F. Tarp. 2001. "Aid and Growth Regressions," *Journal of Development Economics*, 64(2), 547–570.

Kanbur, R. and A. Sumner. 2012. "Poor Countries or Poor People? Development Assistance and the New Geography of Global Poverty," *Journal of International Development*, 24(6), 686–695.

Kimura, H., Y. Mori and Y. Sawada. 2012. "Aid Proliferation and Economic Growth: A Cross-Country Analysis," *World Development*, 40(1), 1–10.

Knack, S. 2001. "Aid Dependence and the Quality of Governance: Cross-Country Empirical Tests," *Southern Economic Journal*, 68(2), 310–329.

Kornai, J. 1986. "Soft Budget Constraint," *Kyklos*, 39(1), 3–30.

Leeson, P. T. 2008. "Escaping Poverty: Foreign Aid, Private Property, and Economic Development," *The Journal of Private Enterprise*, 23(2), 39–64.

Lensink, R. and H. White. 2000. "Aid Allocation, Poverty Reduction and the Assessing Aid Report," *Journal of International Development*, 12(3), 399–412.

Little, I. M. D. and J. A. Mirrlees. 1969. *Manual of Industrial Project Analysis in Developing Countries* (Paris: OECD).

McGillivray, M., S. Feeny, N. Hermes and R. Lensink. 2006. "Controversies over the Impact of Development Aid: It Works; It Doesn't; It Can, but that Depends," *Journal of International Development*, 18(7), 1031–1050.

Mekasha, T. J. and F. Tarp. 2013. "Aid and Growth: What Meta-Analysis Reveals," *Journal of Development Studies*, 49(4), 564–583.

Minoiu, C. and S. Reddy. 2007. "Aid Does Matter, after All: Revisiting the Relationship between Aid and Growth," *Challenge*, 50(2), 39–58.

Murphy, R and Tresp, N. 2006. "Government Policy and the Effectiveness of Foreign Aid," Boston College Department of Economics, Boston College Working Papers in Economics: 647, http://fmwww.bc.edu/EC-P/WP647.pdf, downloaded 8/23/2019.

Osborne, E. 2002. "*Rethinking Foreign Aid*," *Cato Journal*, 22(2), 297–316.

Ovaska, T. 2003. "The Failure of Development Aid," *Cato Journal*, 23(2), 175–188.

Papanek, G. F. 1972. "The Effect of Aid and Other Resource Transfers on Savings and Growth in Less-Developed Countries," *Economic Journal*, 82(327), 934–950.

Rajan, R. G. and A. Subramanian 2005. "What Undermines Aid's Impact on Growth?" IMF Working Paper WP/05/126, Washington, DC.

Rajan, R. G. and A. Subramanian. 2008. "Aid and Growth: What Does the Cross-Country Evidence Really Show?" *The Review of Economics and Statistics*, 90(4), 643–665.

Ram, R. 2004. "Recipient Country's 'policies' and the Effect of Foreign Aid on Economic Growth in Developing Countries: Additional Evidence," *Journal of International Development*, 16(2), 201–211.

Ranis, G. 2013. "Another Look at Foreign Aid," WIDER Working Paper No. 2013/119, Helsinki.

Roger, L. 2015. "Foreign Aid, Poor Data, and the Fragility of Macroeconomic Inference," Centre for Research in Economic Development and International Trade (CREDIT) Research paper No. 15/06, University of Nottingham.

Sachs, J. 2006. *The End of Poverty: Economic Possibilities for Our Time* (New York: The Penguin Press).

Sen, A. K., P. Dasgupta and S. A. Marglin. 1972. *Guidelines for Project Evaluation* (New York: UNIDO).

Stiglitz, J. and A. Charlton. 2006. "Aid for Trade," *Aussenwirtschaft*, 61(2), 143–156.

Svensson, J. 2000. "Foreign Aid and Rent-Seeking," *Journal of International Economics*, 51(2), 437–461.

Taylor, L. 1991. "Foreign Resource Flows and Developing Country Growth," World Research Institute of Development Economics Research, United Nations University, https://pdfs.semanticscholar.org/4a79/98f31eee7b266b178609100d6c948e75ce17.pdf, consulted 3/1/2019.

Weisskopf, T. E. 1972. "The Impact of Foreign Capital Inflow on Domestic Savings in Underdeveloped Countries," *The Journal of International Economics*, 2(1), 25–38.

World Bank. 1998. *Assessing Aid: What Works, What Doesn't and Why?* (Oxford: Oxford University Press).

12

DEBATES ON FOREIGN DIRECT INVESTMENT

Introduction

Foreign direct investment (FDI) demands attention given its immense scope and the global impact of multinational corporations (MNCs), the vehicles of FDI. By 2008, they accounted for 27 percent of world value added, 66 percent of world trade and 60 percent of world R&D.[1] (UNCTAD, 2018) reported that FDI flows to developing economies amounted to $671 billion in 2017, about 4.5 times ODA in 2017.

Like foreign aid, FDI is the subject of much controversy. Radical political economists eye it very suspiciously as being super exploitative while neoliberals push it as the salvation for L/LMICs. This chapter first reviews the type of capital flows and pinpoints FDI as the subject of study in this chapter. Next a brief overview of the sources and destination of FDI is provided followed by the mainstream theoretical rationale for it. This is followed by a radical political economy critique of FDI. Notwithstanding this critique, most L/LMICs welcome FDI. The possible benefits are reviewed as well as possible bargaining issues when soliciting FDI. The macro evidence regarding the benefits of FDI to L/LMICs is reviewed next. One mechanism for soliciting FDI is by engaging in bilateral investment treaties (BIT) with MNCs. The last section of this chapter reviews the BIT literature.

Types of foreign investment and associated issues

Portfolio investments seek returns on financial assets wherever they are to be had by balancing the trade-off between risk and returns. L/LMICs offer the prospect of higher returns but the volatility of the economies and institutional weaknesses, including less established property rights, mean much higher risk. One way in which FDI differs from portfolio investment is that in principle it adds to the stock of physical capital in L/LMICs.

FDI is viewed as brownfield when funds flow into L/LMICs for investment in domestic firms or for outright purchase of plants, often to repurpose an alternative productive activity. This saves a foreign company from taking on the risk of building a new plant. Existing foreign subsidiaries could be expanded via reinvestment of profits earned in L/LMICs and this would be considered foreign investment. Finally, the most coveted form of FDI is the setting up of a new plant in a foreign country by an MNC and this is referred to as a greenfield investment.[2]

L/LMICs can also license technology for a fee or solicit technical training. A good example of this is the licensing of technical training in garment manufacturing by the Bangladeshi firm Desh from Daewoo Korea (Rhee, 1990). Bangladeshi trainees were flown to a Daewoo plant in Korea for a specified time period to undergo the training before returning to operate the Desh plant in Bangladesh. An MNC might do this if the domestic market they plan to operate in is small and therefore the fixed costs of operation are perceived as too large. These fixed costs include market assessment, dealing with a foreign bureaucracy, coordinating with the parent firm and dealing with poor communications and infrastructure.

Alternatively, an MNC might engage in a joint venture with a local firm. This entails pooling skills and strengths for the short or long term to initiate a new activity for the local and/or foreign market. Local firms know the domestic market and how to interface with the local government, while the foreign partner may bring technology, managerial and marketing skills to the partnership. An example of such a partnership producing cars initially for the Indian market is Maruti, India and Suzuki, Japan.[3]

Sometimes governments may require joint ventures to ensure the retention of some of the earnings but more to facilitate the transfer to technology, marketing and management information. China, with its large and attractive market, very successfully engaged in such practice. However, this precondition resulted in complaints by US and other MNCs and drew the ire of the Trump administration in the United States. China agreed to loosen such conditions in 2018 as one concession in the US-declared trade war on China.

FDI is increasingly part of global value chains that integrate global production (Gereffi, 2000). Global value chain activity peaked in 2010–2012 but even in 2017 UNCTAD (2018) reported that it accounted for 30 percent of global trade. Global value chains are facilitated by IT-enabled governance by the lead firm and thereby a fall in communication and transportation costs. Production is fragmented and offshored or outsourced to where it can be most economically produced. L/LMICs seek to insert themselves into such chains to earn foreign exchange and in the hopes of acquiring technology, managerial and marketing skills.

A value or product chain is defined as activities required to bring a product from its conception to the final consumer. Thus, all the firms in this chain are connected. There is a distinction between production and retail chains (branded / non-branded) with the apex firm located in HICs and engaged in the high value activity. For example, General Motors heads a production chain and all the supply firms are part of the supply chain operations. Much of the work of the chain might be outsourced to L/LMICs such as the upholstery but with rigid specifications and technical input to ensure quality control.

Gap or Nike are examples of branded retail chains. The high value added activities of the chain such as marketing R&D, data processing and distribution are retained in the home base. Walmart is an example of a non-branded retail chain which simply places the orders via its network of suppliers.

FDI could be single plant or part of an MNC multi-plant operation. The global assets of large multi-plant MNCs are often larger than the GDP of even large host countries. For example, the assets of General Electric ($647 billion) exceeded the GNP of India of $568 in 2003. Apple and Amazon stock valuations in August / September 2018 exceeded $1 trillion, which exceeded the GDPs of most L/ LMICs. However, such comparisons are misleading because GDP represents value added. Thus, it would make more sense to compare MNC profits with GDP. Despite the conceptual error in this often made comparison of MNC assets and a host country's GDP, the assets, valuation, revenue or sales of a large MNC do represent economic power. This matters when large MNCs negotiate on the terms of investment contracts with L/LMICs.

Country risk was one reason why MNCs would insist on generous terms with many protections. The most dreaded risk from an MNC perspective is having its assets nationalized by L/LMICs. Such nationalizations had become very rare until 2006 when Venezuela, Russia, Ecuador and Bolivia all increased state control of oil resources or warned that they would. Prior to this, 76 percent of all nationalizations had occurred during 1966–1976 when radical thought in L/LMICs had more play. As indicated above, L/LMICs now actively solicit FDI, and nationalizations for the most part appear to have become a thing of the past.

MNCs were traditionally drawn to primary activities like mining but moved onto retailing and manufacturing – standalone or as part of global value chains. Their objectives were to maximize the profit of the whole company (not that of a subsidiary which might be of more interest to L/LMICs).

It is difficult to assess the impact of new technology on FDI. For example, on the one hand, AI-driven robotics can reduce unit costs and reshore production back to HICs. On the other, technological change enables production fragmentation and outsourcing moves production to lower unit cost L/LMICs (Chapter 9, endnote 30).

Destination and sources

As Table 12.1 shows, there are inflows and outflows of FDI to and from all regions and income classifications. Since numbers vary from year to year, a six-year average from 2010 to 2016 is reported. As a starting year, 2010 is viewed as appropriate since the numbers during the 2007–2009 financial and economic crisis were likely to have been skewed and 2016 was the latest year for which numbers were available at the time of writing. As a percentage of GDP, inflows into Latin America and the Caribbean followed by Sub-Saharan Africa were the highest. While it was not possible to explore the nature of the inflows, it is likely that the bulk of these were into the primary sector.[4]

As a percentage of GDP (not in absolute amounts), LICs drew the most FDI and it is likely that apart from the primary sector, the bulk of it went into the

TABLE 12.1 Net FDI inflows and outflows by income classification, regions and countries as a percentage of GDP (2010–2016)

Country classification and region	Inflows	Outflows
LIC	4.30	0.44*
LMIC	2.07	0.53
UMIC	2.74	1.23
EA&P	2.71	2.18
LA&C	3.42	0.94
ME&NA	1.95	1.09
SA	1.59	0.40
SSA	2.53	0.71
China	2.81	1.11
India	1.74	0.48
EU	3.82	3.97
Japan	0.24	2.53
US	1.91	2.17

Source: World Development Indicators.
Notes: LIC = Low income countries ($995 or less annual per capita gross national income).
LMIC = Lower middle income countries ($9,966–$4,035)
UMIC = Upper middle income countries ($4,036–$12,475)
HIC = High income countries (above $12,476)
EE&P = East Asia and the Pacific
E&CA = Europe and Central Asia
LA&C = Latin America and the Caribbean
ME&NA = Middle East and North Africa.
SA = South Asia
SSA = Sub-Saharan Africa
* = 2010–2014

assembly of labor-intensive manufacturing goods. The largest outflows of FDI as a percentage of GDP were from the EU, about double that of US companies.

While flows yield important insights into current MNC investment patterns, positive flows accumulate into stocks, and these are reported in Table 12.2.

Rationale for FDI

The neoclassical analysis in Figure 12.1 explains factor movement in general and the analysis applies to both capital and labor moving across country income classifications. As it applies to capital, the expectation is that capital is abundant in HICs and scarce in L/LMICs. Thus, other things remaining constant, due to diminishing marginal productivity of capital, the returns to capital will be lower in HICs and higher in L/LMICs. Further, neoclassical theory predicts that, if there are no impediments, capital will flow from where the returns to capital are

TABLE 12.2 FDI inward stocks by country classification, regions and years (billion $)

Country group / region / country	2010	2017
Developed economies	13,480.30	20,331.17
Developing economies	6,123.09	10,353.18
North Africa	201.11	275.10
Central Africa	39.23	87.82
LA&C	37.86	82.60
Southern Africa	220.10	235.03
East Asia	1,875.96	3,828.19
SSA	1,144.32	2,162.29
South Asia	268.96	506.93
West Asia	591.92	765.53
Latin America & the Caribbean	1,629.25	2,194.40
China	587.82	1,490.93
India	205.58	337.68

Source: Constructed from UNCTAD (2018), Annex Table 2.

lower to where they are higher. Thus capital should flow to L/LMICs where many opportunities for capital use have not been exhausted as in HICs and the low hanging fruit is still there for the picking. The theory suggests that capital flows will continue until eventually there will be equality to factor returns across all country income classifications, much as water finds its own level as shown in Figure 12.1.

Neoclassical theory is embedded in Figure 12.1. Assume for simplicity that the world contains only HICs and L/LMICs. BCF (before capital flows) represents the allocation of world capital between the two groups of countries. HICs have a much higher share of world capital and according to the theory it therefore has a lower MPK. The reverse is the case for L/LMICs. The ACF (after capital flows) line shows the equalization of the returns to capital as capital flows from HICs to L/LMICs. The theory therefore predicts that over a period of time the returns to capital should be equalized across the world.

While there is a kernel of truth to this theory, the basic prediction of the theory is not borne out by economic reality. As Table 12.1 shows, there are high levels of inflows into HICs in both relative and absolute terms. For example, the EU has roughly the same amount of inflows as outflows. More FDI therefore is intra HIC than a flow from HICs to L/LMICs. This suggests that profit opportunities are not exhausted as countries reach MIC and HIC status.

New or endogenous growth theory sheds some light on this issue by highlighting the importance of elements in HICs that are complementary to capital (or labor)

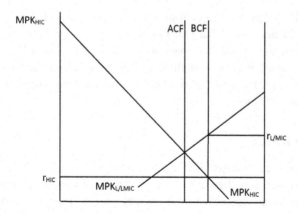

FIGURE 12.1   Neoclassical theory of capital flows

such as research; social, legal and physical infrastructure; information; facilities; quality services; and supportive institutions. All these complementary elements explain higher productivity and sustained higher returns to factors in HICs relative to L/LMICs.

In a production function framework, the mechanism for FDI to impact short-term economic growth is via capital accumulation as posited by neoclassical growth theory. Once a new steady state is reached and capital labor ratios across countries converge, this source of economic growth fizzles out. The mechanism of FDI in endogenous growth theory is via technology enhancement, knowledge diffusion and productivity growth, and hence the impact is on long-term economic growth.

Evidence (Table 12.1) suggests that FDI does flow into L/LMICs and so the question is what might induce such flows. The main draw for MNCs is expected profits and there are several determinants including political stability.[5] MNCs invest a great deal in purchasing risk analysis results from consultants or do risk analysis research in-house. Expected profits are likely to vary positively with a large market that affords economies of scale and sound physical and social infrastructure. Expected profits also vary positively with disciplined, educated and cheap labor (i.e. low unit costs).

Repressive regimes in the past were motivated to suppress unions and engage in wage repression to encourage FDI. The terrain has changed somewhat with HIC union protest (self-interested) in combination with civil society concern (humanitarian), and MNCs are under pressure to certify that they do business with partners that meet social and environmental standards as part of their corporate social responsibility.[6]

High transportation costs of raw material would be more likely to result in processing in L/LMICs. Again, if it is a high value product such that transportation cost is a small part of total value, there may be an incentive to produce in L/LMICs and ship to other markets. FDI might also be strategic in that by being the first mover, an MNC may want to control a major input supply to get a competitive edge. The evidence shows that FDI inflow has much more to do with expected profits and strategic calculations than the concessions L/LMICs are able to make to draw FDI, which may be a small part of the total calculus and ends up being a "free lunch" for MNCs that were likely to invest anyway based on the above-mentioned considerations.

Critique of MNCs

Radical political economists cited many reasons to be wary of MNCs. To begin with, they warned that they are likely to displace local labor-intensive small-scale manufacturing and hence raise unemployment. They also drive out local competition with their access to better technology, risk-taking capacity and scale economies and hence attain market power to the detriment of local consumers. Even if they do not completely drive domestic producers out of the market, they force them to produce at a higher point on their average cost curves by capturing market share. FDI is also associated with a rise in inequality since it is mostly elites that benefit via patronage jobs and kickbacks.[7]

MNC products are often inappropriate for the local market; the most notorious example was Nestlés milk formula. Women dressed like nurses, and hence as authority figures, in advertisements and touted the benefits of formula. The problem is that formula requires sterilized bottles in villages where getting potable water is a major chore. Often mother's milk would dry up after the free samples were used up and ill-prepared formula with dirty unboiled water did more harm than good. Meanwhile, the infant was deprived of the immunities that come with the mother's milk.[8]

Perhaps the most pernicious practice is transfer pricing. This is a form of tax evasion that results from buying inputs from a subsidiary in another country at inflated prices and selling the final output at a low price to show low profits in the host country. Internal accounting can thus show profits where it suits the MNC, generally in tax havens such as the Bahamas or Panama. Since an increasing amount of world trade is inter-MNC, reference prices are not easily available to tax authorities to offset these practices even if they had the capacity to do so. Since MNCs internally source most of their inputs, they have limited linkages with the rest of the economy. A local brain-drain also results from their ability to offer better salaries and career prospects.

Overall, critics argue that high royalties, high interest on loans, licensing fees, transfer of dividends and profits mean a massive resource outflow. MNCs jealously guard their technology and are not interested in building local R&D capacity. So, for all the resource outflows, they get back little in exchange. In fact, with their higher credit ratings, instead of bringing in funds they tap the local credit market and crowd out local firms.

Studwell (2013) argued that South East Asian countries like Malaysia, Thailand, Indonesia and the Philippines engaged extensively with MNCs but were not quite as successful as South Korea, which was very selective. Instead, they got locked into assembly and hence stayed stuck on the lower rungs of the value chain. MNCs have no interest in engineering L/LMIC catch-up growth since the fewer competitors the better.

As indicated above, most MNCs have revenues that dwarf host country GDP and this gives them bargaining power with both the host and home countries. For example, they are able to influence home country aid allocations to suit their purposes such as for selective infrastructure development. Size also enables MNCs to engage in questionable political activities to protect their interests. One of the most notorious cases was that of International Telephone and Telegraph (ITT) Corporation funding a political campaign against candidate Allende's socialist party in Chile and then funding activities and soliciting US government support to destabilize and overthrow the successful socialist government once it won office via democratic elections.[9]

L/LMIC motivation and bargaining

Notwithstanding the critique above, L/LMICs actively solicit FDI. A cynical view is that political elites gain through kickbacks and jobs for themselves and their offspring while society loses. It is nonetheless possible that political elites are accountable, even if only through the imperfect mechanisms of elections or social discontent that constrains them to act at least partially for the social good. A more charitable view is that they are well intentioned and there is much to gain by soliciting FDI.

They might solicit FDI to benefit from the transfer of technology, marketing knowledge, managerial skills including quality control procedures, funds inflow, exports (to stabilize the balance of payments), tax revenues and employment. The critique above however suggests that for various reasons none of these objectives is likely to be achieved.

Developmentalist scholars argue that L/LMICs need to create absorption capacity while engaging with MNCs (Lall and Narula, 2004). Sound institutions and governance, infrastructure and financial development create absorption capacity and that is what makes the difference with regards to benefitting from FDI. MNCs build on host country strengths because this is what determines their profitability.

Industrial policy in conjunction with investment, technology, competition and trade policies can help in building these capacities. They argue that the hands-off neoliberal approach is meaningless. Linkages and spillover effects in the non-natural resource sectors (backward, horizontal, forward) cannot be taken for granted if host country capacity is not there.[10] In fact, in this case FDI can be detrimental because there can be crowding out of domestic investment. L/LMICs can insert themselves into value chains and this can help with industrialization so long as they view such insertion as a stepping-stone to building full production capacity and going on to own brand manufacturing.

Bargaining issues include ownership, local hiring, participation in decision making (e.g. representation on the board), market concentration and pricing policy, profit tax and input tariffs, profit repatriation and reinvestment, royalties, transfer pricing, legislative provisions such on labor and the environment, infrastructure provision, training for labor and management, facility provision (e.g. housing), export clauses, inputs subsidies (e.g. credit and utilities) and local R&D provisions.

L/LMICs need to cultivate skills to bargain effectively since they deal with highly skilled professionals sitting on the other side of the table. For example, Central American governments were falsely persuaded by MNC negotiators that a $1 export tax per box of bananas would kill the market. Wald (2018) documented how the Saudi Finance Minister realized that the Saudi government was not getting a good deal from Aramco. The Saudis hired DeGolyer & MacNaughton, a well-known petroleum consultant firm, to negotiate on their behalf sitting alongside Saudi oil bureaucrats. Much to the chagrin of Aramco executives, whom they were acquainted with, the consultants secured a good deal for the Saudis who prior to that were being hoodwinked.

Recall also that there is a danger of over-conceding. If MNCs are willing to come to the table, it means they have already spotted a profit opportunity. Concessions if deemed necessary should be timed and phased out once profitability is established. Some concessions simply do not need to be made. For example, based on double-taxation treaties, low taxation on MNCs would simply mean a tax subsidy to the MNC's home country from the host country.

L/LMICs may enhance their leverage by negotiating collectively (or having a common negotiating stance) regionally to avoid giving away too much. Thus regional trading blocs like the Association for South East Asian Nations (ASEAN), the East African Community (EAC), Economic Community of West African States (ECOWAS), the South Asian Regional Cooperation (SARC), the South American trade bloc (MERCASOR) and other regional trading blocs could have a common internal policy for negotiations.

L/LMICs must ensure that the FDI is complementary rather than competitive and that that there are linkages with the rest of the economy. China had a lot of leverage because of the market size on offer and bargained for joint ventures and a transfer of core technologies, reinvestment of a specified portion of the revenue and meeting 50 percent of the development costs for eligible software products (UNDP, 2006, p. 121). While these concessions from MNCs evoked a negative reaction in the United States, being hardnosed about protecting national interests is an important lesson for other L/LMICs.

If L/LMICs know what they are seeking from FDI, it may be possible to divest profitable aspects of the FDI package if the whole comes at too high a price. For example, it is possible to contract with management, marketing, or engineering consultants. It is therefore important to be clear on what the objectives are in soliciting FDI.

As shareholders and boards become sensitive to public opinion in home countries, they pressure companies to behave responsibly. A good example of successful bargaining is a 60-year contract between Madagascar and QMM, a subsidiary of Rio Tinto.[11] The latter earned a bad reputation when mining in West Borneo and sought to redeem itself via socially and environmentally responsible mining in Madagascar. It won over some hardcore environmentalists that agreed to come onto the payroll as advisors or serve on independent review boards.

A large part of the land won as a concession for mining exploration is being kept as a natural park. Rio Tinto views this as an investment because a good reputation means successful future bids. Also, given the long-term nature of the contract, they consider themselves as having a vested interest in the health and education of the population they will draw on. L/LMICs can strategically use local and international NGOs for successful leverage to get better social and environmental deals.

Ultimately L/LMICs need to do a hard-headed social cost-benefit analysis to assess each FDI project. If the social rate of return is greater than the return from the next best alternative, after building in all the concessions as a cost, then there is a reason to grant a contract to an MNC for the FDI.

Evidence

As in the case of foreign aid, the quantitative research has methodological problems and the results are not conclusive.[12] Cipollina et al. (2012) arrived at this conclusion from a review of empirical studies using cross-country, panel-, sector-, firm- and plant-level data. Also, as in the case of foreign aid, the literature dates back far enough for several authors to attempt meta-analyses and we report the results of the two most comprehensive ones.

Iamsiraroj and Ulubaşoğlu (2015) reviewed the literature which included 108 empirical studies from around the globe that reported 880 regression estimates of the impact of FDI on economic growth. Of these, 43 percent reported positive and statistically significant results and 17 percent negative and statistically significant results; the rest were not statistically significant.

Bruno, Campos and Estrin (2017) based their meta-analysis on 1,100 estimates over the period 1940 to 2008 collected from 175 studies conducted on Eastern European, Asian, Latin American and African data. They combined country and firm effects and found 44 percent of interfirm estimates were positive and statistically significant and 12 percent were negative and significant; the rest were insignificant. Some 50 percent of the macro (economy wide) estimates were positive and significant, 11 percent were negative and significant while the rest were insignificant. They also found macro impacts to be six times larger than firm-to-firm effects, which were not very large in magnitude. It follows that firm-level studies are unable to capture all the spillover and externality benefits captured at the macro level. They also argued that the positive FDI impacts were not conditional on attaining a threshold level of say human capital, or institutional, financial or infrastructure development.

The macro investigation focuses on the overarching economic growth / FDI association, but there are several other issues discussed in the literature that are addressed using different kinds of data mentioned above which are not reviewed here. These issues include the determinants of FDI such as political stability, governance, infrastructure and absorption capacity; impacts on domestic investment (is there crowding out), technology transfer, R&D, productivity growth, human capital, spillovers and externalities, industrialization, environment and income inequality; association with exchange rate management, financial development, economic openness, tax regime, domestic wages and foreign aid.

Recall, as with foreign aid, some studies identified the lack of a positive or even a negative economic growth / FDI association[13] and as with foreign aid the mechanisms for such a negative association need to be explained. After all, even with some crowding out of local investment, it still represents an addition to the capital stock. Radical political economists provide many reasons for the negative association (see above). In addition, they posit that the opportunity cost of the concessions L/LMICs make to solicit FDI exceed the benefits, thereby resulting in a negative macro outcome for the economy.

A mainstream view is that resources are used inefficiently in producing for the protected domestic market (Moran, 2005, p. 291).[14] Again, there are at least as many empirical studies showing a positive FDI/GDP association in both cross-country and time series studies as those showing a negative association.[15]

While the macro economic growth / FDI association may provide some information, with qualifications, it might be more valuable, as with foreign aid, to focus on individual investments. Understanding which ones worked better and under what conditions might yield much more useful information for policy planning.

In this regard, the overarching aggregate macroeconomic economic growth / FDI association has shortcomings typical to aggregate analysis. For example, it does not take into account the nature of the FDI (brownfield or greenfield), the type (asset privatization, local market or export), sector (resource, manufacturing, agriculture) or nature of investments within sectors (e.g. electronic, chemical, textiles within manufacturing). Thus, there is a great deal of heterogeneity across countries that cross-country analyses do not address, but there is also a great deal of heterogeneity within country that can be better captured by country case studies.

Some of the other issues raised earlier are also not addressed by aggregate analysis. For example, while evidence on transfer pricing is sketchy, it suggests that host country fears in this regard are well founded. Similarly, the fears regarding market power, at least in the resource sector, are well founded. Less than four companies controlled all the banana trade, six controlled 70 percent of the cocoa market, six controlled 85–95 percent of the leaf tobacco market, and six roasters accounted for 50 percent of world coffee trade. This market power results in low returns for sellers. For example, Arabic coffee fetched about 1 cent for coffee farmers in Tanzania for every $1 worth sold in HICs.[16]

Supermarkets have become the gatekeepers for imports and compliance costs of specified standards are so high that only the very large farmers can qualify as suppliers to the value chain. Notwithstanding the possible downsides of FDI, the conventional wisdom at the moment is that it should be solicited.

Bilateral Investment Agreements (BITs) are encouraged by international financial organizations and investing countries as a mechanism to signal that L/LMICs are responsible and serious parties to FDI contracts and their willingness to respect property rights and the rule of law.

Bilateral investment agreements (BITs)[17]

Neoliberal economists are convinced that FDI is an unmitigated win-win and make various recommendations on how to solicit it. Based on their research, they argue that FDI is mediated via several supportive conditions such as institutional development (e.g. good governance protecting property rights), removing market distortions, deregulation, financial development, macroeconomic stability and openness including trade liberalization. Apart from embarking on neoliberal reforms, L/LMICs can also reassure MNCs that they are well intentioned by signing BITs. In fact, L/LMICs are engaged in a competitive process of signing up to BITs to attract FDI. Demir and Duan (2018, p. 235) report that 3,140 BITs had been signed by 2015.

Van Harten (2011) pointed out L/LMICs face a serious loss of policy space and a regulatory chill because of BITs they sign up to. A clause in many BITs enables foreign investors to sue if domestic regulation or policy negatively impacts their business and hence from their perspective amounts to expropriation. This could for example result from environmental regulation or macro policy that impacts say the exchange rate. Although it impacts domestic and foreign investors in the same way, since the latter have the right to sue they have a privileged position relative to domestic investment and this violates the principle of "equal treatment".

Van Harten notes several other points of concern. First, BITs require capital-importing states to consent to mandatory arbitration of disputes with any foreign investor (MNC) whose assets are subject to regulation by the state. Second, they assign to foreign investors the triggering authority for the arbitration mechanism. Third, they create a structural bias in favor of foreign investors by delegating to private arbitrators, rather than judges, the authority to determine the legality of regulatory acts of the state and the state's obligation to pay public funds to foreign investors. Fourth, to discipline states, they rely on broadly framed standards that are subject to wide discretion in their interpretation by arbitrators. Fifth, they utilize the remedy of state liability and permit enforcement of damages awards against the unsuccessful state's assets abroad.

Because of a lack of legal capacity recipient states bind themselves to treaties that are framed ambiguously, and they are often ignorant of what they are binding themselves to. The terms are asymmetric; vastly in favor of investors. Moreover, the incentives of the arbitrators are aligned with the investors to generate more business for the arbitration industry.[18] Thus, it is not surprising that the arbitrators often adopt an expansive reading of standards like "national treatment", "like treatment", "most favored nation" or "fair and equitable treatment". Standards of investor protection are applied to L/LMICs that would not be applied to HICs.

Other aspects of BITs also disadvantage the host country. Many investment treaties contain an "umbrella clause" that obligates the state to observe or respect their "obligations" to foreign investors, beyond the obligations contained in the treaty itself. Performance requirements on FDI, used very successfully by East Asian economies, are ruled out. Finally, a liberal approach to forum-shopping (location where arbitration will occur), furthered in the treaties themselves, enables investors to design their corporate structure (ensure holding companies in suitable locations) so as to maximize opportunities to bring treaty claims on the most favorable terms against a state in which they own assets.

The view above has been challenged by Franck (2007) whose empirical research on actual cases suggested that investors won roughly only half the cases, and when they did win, they did not win big. There was a big discrepancy between claims and awards, and based on these findings she claimed that the arbitration system is not biased against L/LMICs and seems to be working well overall, though it could be improved with some tweaks.

Gallagher and Shrestha (2011) challenge Franck's conclusions on several grounds. First, the data set is too limited in terms of size (102 awards (82 cases) pared down to a sample size of 49 for empirical analysis) and composition to draw any strong conclusions. Second, Franck's analysis is unable to capture the policy and regulatory chill and the subsequent harm to public welfare that the threats or fear of being taken to arbitration results in.[19] Third, the cases brought against L/LMICs are disproportionately higher than their share in global FDI. Fourth, the fines in terms of per capita incomes or as a percentage of the government's budget of L/LMICs are substantial when compared to such fines borne by HICs.[20]

Since L/LMICs sign away so much in BIT contracts, the question that follows is: Do they at least secure more FDI by signing BITs than they would have otherwise? More importantly, do these treaties represent a net social gain for L/LMICs? Not surprisingly the evidence on these questions, as is the case for most if not all empirical issues in development economics, is mixed.

Bellak (2015) conducted a meta-analysis using 1,000 estimates and did not find an empirical association of BITs on FDI after correcting for publication selection bias. Pohl (2018) documented conceptual problems that in any case call into question the validity of econometric studies. Based on a comprehensive study, he argued that the complexity of the issues involved and limited empirical evidence precluded a definitive assessment of social benefits and costs of BITs.

Summary and conclusions

While much can be gained from FDI, this is only possible if L/LMICs know exactly what their objectives are, build the requisite absorption capacity and invest in the technical expertise to successfully bargain with MNC professionals. The same care and investment in legal expertise is called for before signing up to bilateral investment agreements to secure FDI.

When soliciting FDI, L/LMICs need to heed the warnings of the radical political economists and engage in a case-by-case social cost-benefit analysis to ensure society as a whole gains relative to the next best option that could be approved. It may be possible to selectively seek what is required via consulting contracts rather than solicit the whole package that may drain resources from L/LMICs rather than infuse it with net social benefits.

When contracts are well negotiated, the social benefits of FDI could offset the costs. South Korea selectively used FDI, including with short-term contracts, to secure what was required to meet its economic objectives. Other countries like Singapore, Taiwan and more recently China have benefited from a much more extensive engagement with MNCs. Other countries like Malaysia, Thailand and Indonesia got locked into assembly and hence stayed stuck on the lower rungs of the value chain.

The challenge for L/LMICs is to build their absorption capacity and engage with MNCs to acquire the needed technology to diversify their economies. However, they need to do so without getting trapped in the MNC agenda of using them as money-generating outposts with no real indigenous and endogenous technological capacity building. This is a difficult task as is the case for catch-up growth more generally.

Questions and exercises

1. Critically evaluate the mainstream economics rationale for FDI.
2. Does endogenous growth theory shed more light on the flow of FDI? Explain.
3. Critically evaluate the political economy critique of FDI.
4. What does the evidence to date suggest about the value of FDI for L/LMICs? Explain.
5. Imagine that you are across the table from a team of MNC negotiators representing an L/LMIC in an FDI contract. What are some of the issues you would press hard on? Explain.
6. Imagine that you are across the table from a team of MNC negotiators representing a L/LMIC in a BIT contract. What are some of the issues you would simply refuse to budge on? Explain.

Notes

1 Kozul-Wright (2003) reported that only 500 HIC MNCs accounted for this two-thirds of world trade.
2 Lall and Narula (2004, p. 453) argued that linkages and spillovers might be greater in the case of mergers and acquisitions, while using panel data for 100 developing countries for the period 2003 to 2011 Ashraf and Herzer (2014) found that mergers and acquisitions have no impact on domestic investment, but greenfields have a large negative impact on domestic investment due to crowding out of domestic investment.
3 Maruti Suzuki now exports various models to 125 countries and is now India's top exporter of passenger cars. https://auto.ndtv.com/news/maruti-suzuki-becomes-indias-no-1-exporter-of-passenger-vehicles-1765843, consulted 4/20/2019.

4 Demir and Duan (2018, p. 236) explored the distribution of global greenfield FDI flows to the South and reported that most went to the service and primary sectors, jointly accounting for 54 percent of the total during 2004–2013, while manufacturing received the remaining 46 percent.
5 Williams (2017) found that political instability manifested as protest significantly reduced FDI inflows.
6 The collapse of the ready-made garment producing Rana Plaza in Bangladesh in April 2013 led to the deaths of 1,134 and injuries to about 2,500 workers. This incident reinforced pressure from civil society for MNC corporate social responsibility, www. theguardian.com/global-development/2018/apr/24/bangladeshi-police-target-garment-workers-union-rana-plaza-five-years-on, consulted 3/17/2019.
7 Herzer, Hühne and Nunnenkamp (2014) show using panel data that inequality is positively associated with inflows of FDI in Latin American economies, most likely by enhancing skilled labor wages.
8 www.businessinsider.com/nestles-infant-formula-scandal-2012-6#hospitals-were-also-accused-of-pushing-mothers-to-use-formula-7, consulted 3/17/2019.
9 www.nytimes.com/1972/07/03/archives/papers-show-itt-urged-us-to-help-oust-allende-suggestions-for.html, consulted 3/17/2019.
10 Few linkages and spillovers are expected in the natural resource sectors.
11 www.riotinto.com/energyandminerals/qit-madagascar-minerals-4645.aspx, consulted 9/6/2018.
12 Apart from the problems specific to cross-section and panel analysis (see critique by Herzer, Klasen and Nowak-Lehmann, 2008 in the FDI context), as with foreign aid, causality may run in both directions and there is the tricky heterogeneity issue among others. Several studies have attempted to econometrically address the heterogeneity issue and some of these have been cited in endnotes 13 and 15. The same literature search strategy was followed as for foreign aid (Chapter 11, endnote 22).
13 Notably, Herzer, Klasen and Nowak-Lehmann (2008) used time series analysis and showed there was no FDI growth association for a sample of 28 countries for which they viewed the time series as reasonably long (at least 25 years). In a later study, Herzer (2012) conducted time series analysis for 44 countries over a 35-year time span (1970–2005) and found a negative long-run economic growth / FDI association for two-thirds of the countries in the sample. However, a positive outcome was expected from reducing government regulatory interventions and distortions, enhancing economic and political stability (hence FDI volatility) and diversifying the economy. Demir and Duan (2018) used bilateral FDI flow data (to eliminate aggregation bias resulting from heterogeneous investments) from 108 host and 240 home countries over 1990–2012 and found no significant effect of these flows on either host country productivity growth or on the productivity gap between the host and the home (productivity frontier) country. Herzer and Donaubauer (2018) found that on average FDI has a negative long-run effect on total factor productivity in developing countries. The relationship could be positive and significant for countries with higher levels of human capital, financial development and trade openness.
14 Using the case study method, Moran (2005) sought to establish that host countries fared much better if they did not insist on joint ventures and local content requirements. Allowing the MNC full ownership, such that the firm made the subsidiary part of its international production and exporting network, yielded efficiencies including economies of scale, local sourcing and spillovers.
15 For example Nair-Reichert (2001) found a positive association of economic growth and FDI. Duttaray, Dutt and Mukhopadhyay (2008) conducted time series studies for 66 countries and found a positive causal association of FDI with economic growth for 29 (44 percent) of the countries either directly or via an export or productivity channel, but the reverse causality from growth to FDI was evident in 30 of the countries. Toulaboe, Terry and Johansen (2009) found a positive association of FDI and economic growth and the

impact varied positively with absorptive capacity, which was higher in the more advanced L/LMICs. Batten (2009) found that this association is enhanced the higher the level of educational attainment, institutional and stock market development, openness to trade and lower levels of population growth and country risk. Driffield and Jones (2013) found the positive association of economic growth and FDI was enhanced by better institutions.

16 Refer to Chapter 7 for other statistics and documentation.

17 Free Trade Agreements (FTAs) that L/LMICs sign up to with HICs often contain chapters with BIT-like provisions.

18 While the "respondent country" (in this case an L/LMIC) has the right to select one of the three arbitrators, the MNC selects the other one and arbitration body selects the presiding arbitrator with the critical overseeing role and in cases of differences likely to be the ultimate decision maker.

19 In the data Franck (2007, p. 83) collected, arbitration disputes arose in only 49 out of 1,700 active treaties collected, which may suggest that threats might be adequate in securing desired outcomes. It also suggests that meaningful quantitative research on this topic is very difficult.

20 For example, Gallagher and Shrestha (2011, p. 9) document that of the total US wins, the average award amount has been around $47 million, a substantial amount for L/LMICs.

References

Ashraf, A. and D. Herzer. 2014. "The Effects of Greenfield Investment and M&As on Domestic Investment in Developing Countries," *Applied Economics Letters*, 21(14), 997–1000.

Batten, J. A. 2009. "An Analysis of the Relationship between Foreign Direct Investment and Economic Growth," *Applied Economics*, 41(13-15), 1621–1641.

Bellak, C. 2015. "Economic Impact of Investment Agreements", Vienna University of Economics and Business, Department of Economics Working Paper No. 200, http://epub.wu.ac.at/4625/1/wp200.pdf,downloaded 8/23/2019.

Bruno, R., N. F. Campos and S. Estrin. 2017. "The Benefits from Foreign Direct Investment in A Cross-Country Context: A Meta-Analysis," Centre for Economic Policy Research, Discussion paper series 11959, London.

Cipollina, M., G. Giovannetti, F. Pietrovito and A. F. Pozzolo. 2012. "FDI and Growth: What Cross-country Industry Data Say," *The World Economy*, 35(11), 1599–1629.

Demir, F. and Y. Duan. 2018. "Bilateral FDI Flows, Productivity Growth, and Convergence: The North Vs. The South," *World Development*, 101(1), 235–249.

Driffield, N. and C. Jones. 2013. "Impact of FDI, ODA and Migrant Remittances on Economic Growth in Developing Countries: A Systems Approach," *European Journal of Development Research*, 25(2), 173–196.

Duttaray, M., A. K. Dutt and K. Mukhopadhyay. 2008. "Foreign Direct Investment and Economic Growth in Less Developed Countries: An Empirical Study of Causality and Mechanisms," *Applied Economics*, 40(15), 1927–1939.

Franck, S. D. 2007. "Empirically Evaluating Claims about Investment Treaty Arbitration," *North Carolina Law Review*, 86(1), 1–89.

Gallagher, K. P. and E. Shrestha. 2011. "Investment Treaty Arbitration and Developing Countries: A Re-Appraisal," Global Development and Environment Institute Working Paper No. 11-01, Tufts University, Boston.

Gereffi, G. 2000. "Beyond the Producer-Driven / Buyer – Driven Dichotomy: An Expanded Typology of Global Value Chains, with Special Reference to the Internet," Duke University, www.ids.ac.uk/ids/global/pdfs/gereffi3.pdf (consulted, 8/11/2018).

Herzer, D. 2012. "How Does Foreign Direct Investment Really Affect Developing Countries' Growth?" *Review of International Economics*, 20(2), 396–414.

Herzer, D. and J. Donaubauer. 2018. "The Long-run Effect of Foreign Direct Investment on Total Factor Productivity in Developing Countries: A Panel Co-integration Analysis," *Empirical Economics*, 54(2), 309–342.

Herzer, D., P. Hühne and P. Nunnenkamp. 2014. "FDI and Income Inequality—Evidence from Latin American Economies," *Review of Development Economics*, 18(4), 778–793.

Herzer, D., S. Klasen and D. F. Nowak-Lehmann. 2008. "In Search of FDI-led Growth in Developing Countries: The Way Forward," *Economic Modelling*, 25(5), 793–810.

Iamsiraroj, S. and M. A. Ulubaşoğlu. 2015. "Foreign Direct Investment and Economic Growth: A Real Relationship or Wishful Thinking?" *Economic Modelling*, 51(December), 200–213.

Kozul-Wright, R. 2003. "The End of Global Laissez-faire?" Lecture delivered at the Royal Society for the Encouragement of Arts, Manufactures and Commerce (RSA), London, April 30.

Lall, S. and R. Narula. 2004. "Foreign Direct Investment and Its Role in Economic Development: Do We Need a New Agenda?" *The European Journal of Development Research*, 16(3), 447–464.

Moran, T. H. 2005. "How Does FDI Affect Host Country Development? Using Industry Case Studies to Make Reliable Generalizations," in: Center for Global Development *Does Foreign Direct Investment Promote Development?* (Washington, DC: Institute for International Economics). 281–313.

Nair-Reichert, U. 2001. "Causality Tests for Cross-Country Panels: A New Look at FDI and Economic Growth in Developing Countries," *Oxford Bulletin of Economics and Statistics*, 63(2), 153–171.

Pohl, J. 2018. "Societal Benefits and Costs of International Investment Agreements : A Critical Review of Aspects and Available Empirical Evidence," *OECD Working Papers on International Investment*, 2018/01, OECD Publishing, Paris, 10.1787/e5f85c3d-en consulted 3/2/2019.

Rhee, Y. W. 1990. "The Catalyst Model of Development: Lessons from Bangladesh's Success with Garment Exports," *World Development*, 18(2), 333–346.

Studwell, J. 2013. *How Asia Works: Success and Failure in the World's Most Dynamic Region* (New York: Grove).

Toulaboe, D., R. Terry and T. Johansen. 2009. "Foreign Direct Investment and Economic Growth in Developing Countries," *Southwestern Economic Review*, 36(1), 155–170.

UNCTAD. 2018. *World Investment Report 2018: Investment and New Industrial Policies* (Geneva: United Nations Publications).

UNDP. 2006. *Human Development Report* (New York: Palgrave Macmillan).

Van Harten, G. 2011. "Investment Treaties as a Constraining Framework," in: S. R. Khan and J. Christiansen. (eds.), *Market as Means Rather than Master: Towards New Developmentalism* (London: Routledge) 154-174.

Wald, E. R. 2018. *Saudi, Inc.: The Arabian Kingdom's Pursuit of Power and Profit* (New York: Pegasus Books).

Williams, K. 2017. "Foreign Direct Investment, Economic Growth and Political Instability," *Journal of Development Economics*, 42(2), 17–37.

13

DEBATES ON AGRICULTURE/ SUSTAINABLE AGRICULTURE

Introduction

As theorized by classical economists and later by developmentalists, catch-up growth is not possible unless an agricultural revolution precedes or at least accompanies an industrial revolution. This chapter explores various debates pertaining to L/LMIC agricultures after exploring background issues.

Background issues include highlighting the size of the agricultural productivity gap between HIC and L/LMIC agricultures. After that, some regional commonalities and differences in L/LMIC agricultures are reviewed. In this context, the dominant agricultural tenure relations are explored and also how farms are managed. Tenure relations include renting and share cropping, but apart from these, farm management includes wage labor and small farm owner cultivation or peasant agriculture. Since small farm peasant agriculture is still dominant in many L/LMICs, its key characteristics are explored.

Following this, the debates on agriculture, and implicitly on how to close the agricultural productivity gap, are reviewed based on the positions adopted by the alternative approaches to economic development reviewed in Part II of this textbook. The neoclassical challenge to the developmentalist perspective on agriculture is reviewed. This challenge pertained to the nature of peasant agriculture, the magnitude of supply elasticities in agriculture (and the associated policy implications) and the appropriate role of agriculture in developing economies.

The appropriate role of agriculture and modernizing it led into the debate, going back to the 1960s, about the effectiveness of the "Green Revolution" (GR). While some viewed the GR as humanity's savior, political economists and ecologists viewed it as a mixed blessing at best. More recently (1990s), a similar debate was initiated with the introduction of biotechnology into agriculture.

There are two other related debates on improving agricultural productivity. One pertains to the neoliberal prescription of turning over large tracts of land to MNCs and this FDI-based technological infusion is viewed as a solution to closing the productivity gap between HICs and L/LMIC agricultures. Opponents view this phenomenon in the context of a "land grab". They propose instead agrarian and land reforms to support smallholder agriculture, which they view as inherently more productive.

Such reforms can also be used to address two other key problems pertaining to the agricultural sector including environmental degradation and gender discrimination. Critics of biotechnology have proposed sustainable agriculture as an alternative and we explore various proposed sustainable agricultural practices that can be second nature to smallholder agriculture. Women play a pivotal role in agriculture, which is both under-appreciated and under-supported, and they have also been the repositories of sustainable agricultural practices. This role can be reinforced by social justice reforms that grant or reinforce women's property rights to the land they cultivate.

The agricultural productivity gap

Agriculture is the dominant activity in rural areas in L/LMICs in which the rural population as a percentage of the total is still large. As indicated in Chapter 1, two related key structural changes as countries prosper are that the rural population as a percentage of the total and agriculture's contribution to GDP shrinks. The latter is quite evident from Table 13.1.

As Table 13.1 shows, agriculture's contribution to GDP in LICs was about one-sixth; 16.7 percent in South Asia and 16.2 percent in Sub-Saharan Africa respectively. In HICs, it was only 1.3 percent.

What makes a low rural population in HICs possible in relative terms is the phenomenal agricultural labor productivity in HICs relative to L/LMICs, so that in absolute terms agriculture's contribution is very high even if it is low in relative terms. In HICs, per capita value added in agriculture was $39,035 in 2016, which was 26 times higher than South Asia and 30 times higher than Sub-Saharan Africa respectively. These are the two regions with the lowest labor productivity in agriculture and they have much catching up to do.

Regional commonalities and differences in L/LMIC agricultures

The norm in L/LMICs is for high land concentration and this is particularly true in South America. Asia is known for a very high population to land ratio or very high population density. Even so, economic forces militate toward increasing land concentration. As rural areas become monetized, the influence of money-lenders increases. Adverse weather conditions can drive individual farmers into debt, and their land gets mortgaged and appropriated. Inheritance and piecemeal selling results in land fragmentation that constrains land productivity and smallholders sell out to larger landlords and migrate to earn a living in urban and semi-urban areas.

In Africa, land was in plentiful supply and shifting agriculture a common practice. As the population exploded in the 1980s due to the partial demographic transition, this practice was no longer possible in high population density areas. There is a donor-MNC push for a GR as occurred in the 1960s in Asia (see below).

To sum up, the key broad commonalities in L/LMICs' agricultures are land concentration, subsistence cultivation and an urban bias (Chapter 3). Agriculture

TABLE 13.1 Background rural/agricultural statistics by country classification and region

Country classification and region	Value added per capita in agriculture, forestry and fishing (constant 2010$) (2016)	Value added in agriculture, forestry and fishing as a % of GDP (2016)
LIC	557.6	26.3
LMIC	2,059.7	15.6
UMIC	6,044.8	6.8
HIC	39,034.5	1.3
EA&P	4,574.2	5.1
LA&C	6,861.1	5.0
ME&NA	6,679.1	5.4
SA	1,511.5	16.7
SSA	1,316.7	16.2

Source: World Development Indicators.

Notes: LIC = Low income countries ($995 or less annual per capita gross national income).

LMIC   = Lower middle income countries ($996–$4,035)

UMIC   = Upper middle income countries ($4,036–$12,475)

HIC   = High income countries (above $12,476)

EE&P   = East Asia and the Pacific

E&CA   = Europe and Central Asia

LA&C   = Latin America and the Caribbean

ME&NA = Middle East and North Africa.

SA   = South Asia

SSA   = Sub-Saharan Africa

has been systematically discriminated against in terms of rural social and physical infrastructure. This partly accounts for the low productivity in agriculture as documented in Table 13.1.

Land renting based on absentee ownership is the main form of tenure. The absentee landlords generally reside in a metropolitan center and lease out the land for a fixed rent in cash and/or kind. Often the landlord maintains some family on the farm to represent the family's interest. Share cropping is an alternative land tenure system whereby the owner agrees to take a proportion of the gross output. The contracts vary a great deal even across regions within a country, but they normally specify what portion of the agricultural inputs the two parties will provide and how the gross output will be shared.

Risk and uncertainty[1] in the rental contract is borne by the tenant while it is shared under share cropping. The incentive to work harder may be assumed to be greater under renting as long as there is security of tenure.[2] In the latter case, the tenants have the incentive to improve the land since income above the pre-specified rent is retained by the tenant. A long-term contract helps in this regard since the landlord may otherwise revise the rent upward if the peasant is doing well. However, despite long-term contracts, tenants may not be willing to engage in farm improvements on land not owned by them unless the landlords share the burden.

Enforcement costs are higher under share cropping since gross output needs to be monitored, while such monitoring is not necessary under land renting since the amount due to the landlord is pre-specified. Much research on agriculture in development economics has been focused on the relative efficiency of these two contracts and some research indicates that they have the same impact in terms of work effort and efficiency.

Given the uncertain outcomes under share cropping and difficulties in actually getting tenants to pay the rent, landlords often decide to assume the risk and also appropriate the higher returns via self-management. The solution then is to hire a manager who runs the farm with casual labor. Even in this case the enforcement costs are high since managers may develop their own agendas. Thus, landlords often designate a family member, living on or near the farm, to be a manager, but efficient supervision is still not guaranteed.

The most common form of cultivation in African and Asian agricultures is the small family-run peasant farms. One key characteristic of peasant agriculture is that production and consumption are integrated. Output is shared by the household so the implicit wage, as in the Lewis model (Chapter 6), is the average product of labor. The objective function being maximized is survival and the replication of the household rather than profit.

Land holdings are too small and fragmented to be assured subsistence so the family is likely to seek alternatives to complement farm income by working as wage labor (depending on the agricultural season), hiring land on a contractual basis when possible, maintaining farm animals to supplement diet and income, and growing vegetables.

Since production is for subsistence, households are risk averse and resist the adoption of new technologies. Adoption is likely when the mean minus the standard deviation of output from the new practice is above the mean output from the old practice. Risk aversion is inversely associated with food production as a proportion of the total income and general incidence of food production in the area. Both these factors suggest access to food may be easier for subsistence. Risk aversion is also inversely associated with the availability of other employment opportunities in the area, which reduces the likelihood of not meeting subsistence needs. Finally, the availability of credit and information provided by extension agents on for example the variability of yields on alternative crops and production practices reduce risk.

As Lewis recognized, there is a hidden surplus in subsistence peasant agriculture. If no other options are available, and since no profit or rent is imputed, a family household can continue to produce long after a commercial operation would cease production.

The obstacles faced by subsistence peasant farms in converting to commercial farming include the urban bias that results in poor infrastructure, a lack of access to credit, inputs and extension service. They generally own poor marginal land

and engage in intensive farming without the ability to recharge the soil by leaving it fallow. Thus, they can get locked into a vicious circle of soil erosion and declining output. If circumstances force the household to borrow from money lenders, they have to sell during harvest when prices are at the lowest because they lack storage capacity. These background conditions are broad brush and, as true in all such generalizations, do not cover important variations. However, the debates on agriculture covered below apply across the board.

Debates on agriculture [3]

Developmentalist perspective

Recall from Chapter 6 that developmentalists viewed industry as the source of dynamic efficiencies and hence the key sector for catch-up growth. While they recognized the importance of a productive agriculture, this was so it could better serve industry. Thus a dynamic agriculture ideally was a source of capital (by keeping terms of trade in favor of industry), cheaper food (to keep wages low), raw materials and a market for manufactured goods.

The relegation of agriculture to secondary status was based on the view, going back to Adam Smith, that agriculture represented a constant return to scale activity and hence was not a source of ongoing surplus for reinvestment. Further, supply elasticities in response to price changes in the agricultural sector were considered low.

In any case, higher food prices to incentivize agriculture would predominantly hurt the lower income groups in the urban areas and result in squeezing reinvestable surplus for industry due to lower profits. The beneficiaries of higher prices would be large landlords given to "skimming the cream" rather than utilizing land resources efficiently. This was because feudal lords viewed land as a source of status and power rather than strictly as an economic asset. If holdings were very large, extensive farming would generate adequate returns for a very luxurious lifestyle and that is all large landlords sought. This view of the farm sector resulted in developmentalists, and Latin structuralists in particular, calling for "land to the tiller" land reforms (see below).

Supply responsiveness in peasant agriculture

These views on peasant farming and low price elasticity on the supply side were contested by neoclassical economists. Recall that the colonial view, adopted by developmentalists, of peasant farmers as backward, lazy and unresponsive to economic opportunity was challenged by Bauer (Chapter 8). He viewed peasant farmers as rational agents who demonstrated maximizing behavior that was universal among economic agents. As evidence, he provided case studies of Malaysian and West African plantation farmers engaged in primary export production.

Bauer's views were reinforced by four other economists in particular and this contributed to changing the view of agriculture in mainstream development economics. The empirical work conducted by Schultz (1964) also showed peasants as responding to incentives and engaging in rational maximization as postulated by neoclassical economic theory. Further, peasants allocated their existing resources well to get the most from what they had. Enhancing peasant farm production would therefore require extending the range of what was available to them in terms of inputs taking due account of their risk taking capabilities as explained above. The most efficient way of conveying information to farmers would be to invest in human capital (education) so that a new generation of peasant farmers would have access to printed materials. The award of a Nobel Prize to Schultz gave his research more credibility.

The hypothesis of low price elasticity of output in the agricultural sector was shown to be flawed for two reasons. It was argued that the empirical studies supporting this hypothesis did not allow for long-run responses and that once that is done the supply elasticities are actually much higher. This body of research made the case for the importance of using the right incentives to boost food production in agriculture.

Depressing food prices would result in a substitution of resources away from growing food and into livestock, vegetables and fruits and this would primarily benefit rich consumers in the urban areas. In addition, there would be food scarcity and rationing in the urban areas. If food had to be imported, the balance of payments would be adversely impacted. The implicit subsidies to industrialists (via low wage goods) that depressed food prices were viewed as indiscriminate. This is because on the consumption side in addition to the needy they benefited the well-off who had no reason to be subsidized. The solution then was targeted subsidies for the poor and this would also address fiscal deficit problems.

Three other economists contributed to putting the role of agriculture in development economics centerstage. Mellor (1966) headed the International Food Policy Research Institute (IFPRI), which is part of 15 international research organizations (CGIAR – Consultative Group of International Agricultural Research). As such, Mellor's advocacy based on his research had a force multiplier. He advocated for agricultural extension and building rural infrastructure, both designed to improve the supply response.

The other important contributors to changing the status of the rural sector more broadly were Harris and Todaro (1970). Recall from Chapter 6 that they showed that creating more jobs in the urban sector by privileging industry accelerated rural to urban migration. Thus they made a case for rural development as a mechanism for limiting rural to urban migration. This view gained much strength when the World Bank adopted it as part of its policy advocacy.

Scholars criticized both Bauer and Schultz for the paucity of the evidence (a few case studies) they relied on for their theorizing. Further, they showed that peasant agriculture was riven by market failures in the land, credit, product and labor markets so optimization was not likely and therefore the subsistence view of peasant agriculture made more sense. Ball and Pounder (1996) pointed out that this missed the key point that Schultz (also Bauer) was trying to get across i.e. that peasant agriculture is characterized by a supply response to incentives when opportunities are available.

Mellor's advocacy of modernized agriculture provided support for the GR based on a friendly climate for investments by MNCs. As noted earlier, this was central to the neoliberal prescription for L/LMIC agriculture although the GR predated the ascendancy of neoliberal development economic philosophy in the 1980s.

The green revolution (GR)

The GR was seen as an alternative to the "red revolution". The appeal of the latter was viewed as inevitable in the Cold War context as inequality accelerated and the rural masses in L/LMICs sank deeper into poverty. The GR introduced two packages of inputs. The mechanical package included machinery such as tractors, threshers, winnowers, harvesters, sprayers, driers and pumps. While this was expected to raise land and labor productivity, it was recognized as being potentially labor displacing. However, the biological package was expected to offset this labor displacement effect.

The biological package included the high yielding variety (HYV) of seeds that were the outcome of research and development funded by The Ford Foundation and The Rockefeller Foundation.[4] These seeds were intended to raise land productivity and thereby increase food security by increasing output and concomitantly the demand for labor.

One key to the higher yield was a short stalk (hence the term dwarf-variety hybrids) that would raise the yield by a factor of 3 to 8 fold without being knocked down by the wind (lodging). Dwarf varieties were also more responsive to nitrogen fertilizer. Another key factor was that with applications of chemical fertilizers the maturation period shortened and multiple cropping (3 possibly 4) became possible. In addition to the chemical fertilizers, these seeds also required heavy doses of insecticide and herbicides since the new varieties were susceptible to pests and weeds. Yield stability improved once seed varieties were developed that were more resistant to disease and pests (e.g. rust in wheat and plant hoppers in rice). Finally, the hybrid seeds initially did best with heavy doses of water though ongoing research later produced modern varieties for arid and semi-arid conditions.[5]

Advocates of the GR argued that complementary public policies were vital for its success. These included the correct pricing policy to ensure that farmers, whether large capital intensive farmers or small owner cultivators, had the right incentives to respond to. In addition, the urban bias had to be overcome to provide the necessary hard infrastructure for irrigation, feeder roads, warehouses and electrification. Also, the soft infrastructure like marketing networks and extension service for the dissemination of information through demonstration farms and training to encourage adoption needed to be put into place. Finally, there needed to be an adequate and fair distribution of rural credit and other inputs. Since the administrative costs of disbursing small loans is high, grassroots credit coops were founded for credit disbursement. Thus the GR combined elements of developmentalist (soft and hard infrastructure) and what later became central to neoliberal prescriptions (incentives, openness to FDI).

There were several benefits associated with the GR according to its advocates and supporters. Lipton (2007) pointed out that over two and half decades, the GR more than doubled food supply with an increase of only 4 percent in net cropped area. Given that staples are a much higher proportion of the consumption pattern of the poor, they gained in relative terms more than the rich and poverty was reduced sharply in GR areas between 1970 and 1990. In non-GR areas within a country, small farmers lost out, unless they were net buyers of grain, as grain prices fell causing them to change cropping patterns.

Evidence suggested that higher labor requirements for weeding, transplanting and harvesting offset the impact of mechanization and in net terms increased the demand for labor and wages.[6] Rural service and repair and maintenance of machinery encouraged small-scale rural industry (Child and Kaneda, 1975). Higher production-related trade, transportation and construction activity also increased employment opportunities. The fall in food prices benefited poor consumers and contained industrial labor wages. The risk associated with HYV was smaller because the yield variability was lower than conventional seeds and this encouraged even the smaller farmers to adopt them. Small farmers also created a rental market for the mechanical package and engaged in water-expense sharing. With these innovations indivisible inputs were made divisible (Johnston and Kilby, 1975).

Advocates argued that the GR not only enhanced production and food security on the supply side, it also boosted employment and wages and hence also promoted food security from the demand side. Thus advocates of the GR argued that up to a billion people were saved from starvation.

Radical political economists and ecological economists focused on its darker side. Due to the high costs of inputs and access to water (for water intensive crops), the large farmers had capacity to shoulder the risk and adopted the new technology first. This had a negative impact on land tenure relations since the mechanical package enabled them to attain scale economies and dispense with renting and share cropping, and hired casual wage labor as needed instead. While the old feudal relations were viewed as exploitative, they nonetheless were viewed as having a paternal element such that share croppers and renters had a security umbrella. However, these tenure arrangements also conveyed land rights to labor and large landlords were quick to take advantage of the new technology to avoid extending any form of land rights to labor farming their land.

Griffen (1974) in a landmark study argued that the GR enhanced rural inequality and poverty because of the scale of labor displacement due to the mechanical package.[7] The evidence he cited suggested that employment and wages declined. With subsidized irrigation or with diesel and electric pumps, large farmers secured water for multiple cropping. As the water table dropped, small farmers had to dig wells deeper to access water and often the cost was prohibitive.[8]

Cooperatives formed to distribute state-subsidized credit and inputs to small farmers proved ineffective because the larger land-owning members of the coops often captured what was on offer with impunity leaving little or no credit and inputs for the small farmers. Notwithstanding these negative political economic and social impacts, critics argued that MNCs gained from sales of hybrid seeds,[9] machinery, fertilizer, pesticides and herbicides. In fact the packaging and hard-sell of the GR is viewed as having been driven by MNCs.

While a consensus is difficult to arrive at on any debate in development economics, as in Chapters 11 and 12, a meta-study is relied on to indicate the conclusions of the bulk of the empirical research. Freebairn (1995) reviewed 307 studies on the GR published over a 20-year period (1970–1989) and found that about four-fifths of the studies that addressed distributional effects of the new technology found that inter-farm and inter-regional inequality increased. There was however a similar overwhelming majority that noted an increase in farm productivity and production.

Critics emphasizing ecological downsides argued that the dominance of HYV varieties resulted in losses in biodiversity as indigenous genetic material was phased out. They argued that farmers had innovated for millennia and all that genetic material was jeopardized due to excessive reliance on a few dominant varieties. Food security was also threatened if the few varieties relied on were subject to pest or other diseases. They argued that HYVs are high in carbohydrates and low in protein content relative to indigenous varieties. Also, government incentives for adoption resulted in a change in cropping pattern so that there was a displacement of pulses and soybeans that are high in protein (Alauddin and Tisdell, 1991).

Ecologists also argue that chemical pesticides, insecticides, herbicides are extremely harmful.[10] These poisons got into the food chain directly and via run-offs into water bodies (underground aquifers and streams, rivers and lakes) and the destructive health impacts are ongoing (Sandhu, 1993).[11] The ecosystem and wildlife are similarly threatened. Brainerd and Menon (2014) found that the poor are the most vulnerable, particularly infants and children.[12]

The lack of education makes matters worse; farmers do not use protective gear as they are unaware of the dangers. Weir and Schapiro (1981) documented that pesticide poisoning in L/LMICs was about 13 times worse than in the United States despite the latter's highly chemically intensive agriculture. Leaky applicators and the lack of knowledge about handling these dangerous substances enhance health hazards. Rich farmers use air spraying that result in chemical drifting, making matters worse for the rural population. Chemical fertilizers are high in nitrogen or phosphorous and that results in eutrophication or algae blooms which kill life in water bodies (dead zones).

Aggressive marketing by MNC-hired agents got farmers into preventive spraying, but pests built up immunities. Thus farmers got on a "pesticide treadmill".

This means more and more spraying to get the same level of protection. Similarly, there are diminishing returns from the use of chemical fertilizers and so more and more needs to be used to yield the same incremental output (Sanders, 2006, p. 205). This meant many small farmers became indebted and lost their land. Chemical inputs into agriculture are fossil fuel based and therefore not sustainable fiscally (when oil prices rise) or ecologically (due to the carbon footprint).

As indicated in Chapter 4, women and children engaged in cotton picking, the cash crop for which pesticide use is the greatest, are exposed to numerous ailments. The negative impact on the fetus has also been documented (Colburn, Dumanoski and Myers, 1996).

The success of the GR in at least raising food production in the short and medium term in Asia and Latin America was premised on an industrial policy for agriculture with the developmental state being heavily involved in providing the needed physical and research infrastructure, price support and protection. MNCs piggy-backed on this effort to provide inputs and the three-way partnership of state, private capital and farmers was the key to its success.

Holt-Gemenez (2008) argued that neoliberal structural adjustment policies rolled back state support and undermined the possible success of the GR in Africa. He argued that the initiative to launch support for a renewed GR ("doubly green" – productive and sustainable) in Africa via the Alliance for Green Revolution in Africa (AGRA) faces the same challenge. AGRA has western political support and the backing of bilateral and multilateral aid agencies, philanthropies (prominently The Gates Foundation) and MNCs. His concern was that this initiative suffers from the same ideological anti-developmentalist neoliberal blinkers that resulted in the failure of the first attempt to diffuse a GR in Africa.[13]

Biotechnology

As the focus of attention of MNCs and corporate "industrial" agriculture shifted to biotechnology in the 1990s, the academic debate likewise shifted from the GR to the role of biotechnology in agriculture. While genetic modification (GM) is part of nature and hence not new, genetically engineered (GE) or transgenics as a patented corporate product were commercially introduced into agriculture in the 1970s in the United States.[14] Genes that produce insecticidal proteins such as bacillus thuringiensis (*Bt*) were engineered into crops including corn, cotton, canola, soybeans, sugar beets and alfalfa. In this regard, this process could be viewed as an extension of the GR, sometimes referred to as the "gene revolution".

The techniques so far utilized entail using plants, animals and microbes to produce useful substances. These techniques range from basic tissue culture to advanced genetic and molecular manipulation of biological material.[15] The latter includes the use of genetic engineering to identify and transfer single genes for desired traits into certain plants, thereby offering biotechnological alternatives to chemicals for the control of insects and weeds. Thus the concept is to genetically engineer seeds, for example, to produce pest resistance so that less pesticide is needed. With pest attacks cost-effectively contained, higher yields are subsequently attained.

Other biological endeavors include seeds with enhanced or enriched nutrition (e.g. vitamin A enriched rice) and seeds resistant to drought, acidity, salinity and disease. In some cases, the seeds are engineered to be resistant to a corresponding (possibly benign) herbicide that is then sold as a combination with the seed. These techniques can be more precise in attaining desired traits in seeds (germ plasms more broadly) and in principle are much quicker and cheaper than conventional plant breeding.

GE crops have been aggressively pushed by MNCs like Monsanto and Du Pont, rather than foundations, with the help of the US Department of Agriculture. This is predominantly a private sector led initiative, unlike the GR, making profits even more central to the enterprise. Nonetheless, supporters claim that this seed plus weed management combination simplifies matters for the farmer even as it enhances profits for the MNCs.

The indicated benefits (Pray and Naseem, 2007; Shelton, 2007) are lower environmental degradation resulting from conditioning plants to respond to lower doses of less toxic herbicide, less need for pesticides since plants are conditioned to be pest resistant as indicated earlier,[16] land-saving due to productivity enhancement, complementing sustainable practices such as conservation tillage,[17] and biodiversity via the proliferation of plant varieties. Less pesticide use reduces harm to non-target organisms and benign insects, reduces health hazards (and health care costs) and so enhances labor productivity. In addition, food security is enhanced due to higher and stable yields. Finally, there is less pressure on marginal lands, food prices are lowered, labor costs are lowered (less weeding and fewer applications of pesticides) and more employment opportunities are created which can alleviate poverty. Barrows, Sexton and Zilberman (2014) using a simulation model estimated that the higher yields from GE seeds "averted emissions that are equivalent to roughly one-eighth of the annual emissions from automobiles in the USA".

Critics however refer to GE products as Franken-foods, due to the untested properties of the food,[18] and also as terminator technology.[19] The seeds can be doctored to lose potency, so retaining them after harvest, which is conventional farmer practice, would be futile. Since the seeds are expensive, once farmers adopt them they are hostage to monopolistic price increases and this creates a vicious circle of debt and poverty.[20]

This became a big concern in India where increasing numbers of farmer suicides (often by ingesting insecticide) were blamed by critics on price gouging and predatory practices by MNCs and the failure of GM wheat and cotton seeds. Thomas and De Tavernier (2017) mentioned 300,000 farmer suicides over the past two decades, subsequent to seed commercialization by Monsanto in partnership with a local firm Mahyco.

Thomas and De Tavernier (2017) evaluated both sides of the debate in India (for and against GE seeds) and concluded that "there is a definite association between economic factors associated with Bt. cotton farming and farmer-suicide". These economic factors included the use of market power to charge higher prices and create dependence among farmers with limited management skills. They also concluded that saving and reusing BT seeds by farmers is problematic since hybrid seeds "produce off-spring with irregular phenotypes" even if they are not sterile. Finally, perhaps due to lack of farmer knowledge, they concluded that pesticide use actually increased due to over use and the outbreaks of secondary pests. The water-intensive nature of GM seeds added to costs and the crisis of farmer indebtedness. Ultimately they blamed the neoliberal model for pushing liberalization without putting into place extension services and the necessary protections, and the government for holding victims culpable for failure.

As with the HYV seeds, critics view GE seeds as resulting in a loss of biodiversity since farmers select seeds that at a point in time are successful. Other concerns include the patenting and legal ownership (claiming of intellectual property rights) for discoveries involving living organisms. There are also bio-safety concerns in that genes may have implications for public health (potentially toxic or allergy impacts), non-target organisms and environmental safety (via pollen, soil leaching or flows into other plants). The lack of indigenous research capacity in L/LMICs adds to these concerns. Finally, biotechnology has also rekindled the structuralist concern (see Chapter 7) about the development of synthetic substances (e.g. sugar and vanilla substitutes) that will displace L/LMIC exports.[21]

The claims of delivering higher productivity of GE seeds have also been contested.[22] If even higher productivity is not forthcoming and there are serious bio-safety and ecological downsides, there is cause for caution. Further, evidence shows that pests develop resistance to the plant-produced pesticide and sometimes even to the related organic variant. Resistance to the weedicide has sometimes produced out of control super weeds.[23] Since short-term benefits are visible to farmers and some of these side effects take time to emerge, it is not surprising that there has been rapid uptake of GE crops even in LMICs like India.

Rao, Pray and Herring (2015) pointed out that the first generation of GE seeds with "input traits" (e.g. pesticide and herbicide resistance) had been fairly successful and cropped area grew at 6.6 percent annually to reach 181.5 million hectares across 28 countries in 2014 from 1.7 million hectares in 1996 in 13 crops, including maize, soybean, cotton, canola (mustard), sugar beet, alfalfa, papaya, squash, tomato, poplar, sweet pepper, potato and eggplant. About 93 percent of adopters were small farmers and about 53 percent of the cropped area was in L/LMICs.[24]

To date, the bulk of the agricultural biotechnology research has been done by a handful of private sector firms in HICs and therefore it is not surprising that the focus is on the needs of HIC agriculture that can generate profits for these firms. Changes in laws that allowed the patenting of biotechnology tools (processes) and products (including living organisms) incentivized this private sector research, although public sector research was keeping pace in the early 2000s (Pray and

Naseem, 2007). A few large MICs countries, such as China, Brazil, Egypt, India and South Africa, have developed biotechnology research capacity and perhaps this may drive at least some public sector research that will address the needs of poor farmers in L/LMICs. Poor farmers need protection when dealing with complex new technology but also from another relatively new phenomenon threatening their property rights.

Global corporate "land grabs"[25]

Land acquisitions, or "grabs" as referred to by critics, were partly accelerated by the rise in food and commodity prices in 2007–2008. A 2011 issue of the journal *Development*, 54(1), carried several articles about the "alarming" land deals in LICs giving control of large tracts of lands to foreign investors.[26] These articles contend that the deals were enabled by neoliberal structural adjustment policies with their emphasis on privatization, individualizing property rights with land titling to create land markets and inducing the creation of a friendly climate for FDI.[27]

The buyers are sovereign wealth and private equity funds, agricultural producers, agri-business MNCs and wealthy individuals. These acquisitions serve various purposes including food security for the investing countries (that are rich but land, labor or water poor), mining, tourism (or ecotourism), forestry, ranching, retirement migrations by westerners into gated communities, special economic zones, forest clearing for export crops like palm oil, finance capital-driven speculative investments and bio-fuel cultivation or forest plantations to meet climate targets in the investing countries.

The neoliberal view, one which many L/LMIC governments appear to have owned, is that FDI-driven technological change should be encouraged to boost agriculture. Others do not share this sanguine view of land deals with MNCs and the articles in *Development* raised several concerns that echo the criticisms of the GR (see above). First, the land deals signed by the government with foreign governments or MNCs displaced local smallholders and their access to communal land and water rights. Second, biodiversity was negatively impacted as modern varieties displaced local varieties. Third, hybrid seeds, such as the Chinese hybrid rice seed introduced into Mali, require large doses of fertilizer and hence were out of reach of small farmers. Also, chemical fertilizers and herbicides had devastating environmental impacts. Those that adopted the modern varieties found they could not save part of the crop at harvest as seed for the next planting season but had to purchase new seed each year. Finally, displaced families moved to more marginal lands and risked conflict with existing residents or became part of the expanding urban shanty towns.

Academics subsequently took note of large-scale land acquisitions as well and several articles and country case studies have since been published in development economic journals. Bujko et al. (2015) found that over the 2000 and 2011 period, corruption was associated with the occurrence and size of land deals. Similarly, Arezki, Deininger and Selod (2011) found that poor governance and poor protection of land rights attracted land-related FDI. Krieger and Meierrieks (2016) used data for 133 countries over the 2000 to 2012 period and showed large-scale land acquisitions to be positively associated with ethnic tension risk. Further, they showed that countries with strongly democratic institutions are better able to withstand the fallout of such tension.

Other scholars like Akram-Lodhi (2012) and Wolford et al. (2013) proposed examining "land deals" in the context of the political economy of global capitalism rather than as investments. In this framework, global capital drives the land acquisitions for profits via cheaper food (to keep wages down and profits up), and also via export-driven profits. Their contention therefore is that the issue is about more than simply improving governance for getting the right kind of deal. However, it seems that the focus on how to make land deals more palatable diverts attention from more important related issues in agriculture such as land and agrarian reforms, sustainable agriculture, and gender and agriculture.

Land and agrarian reforms

Some scholars argued that the GR was not to blame for social and economic ills but rather that the socioeconomic system into which it was introduced shaped its impacts. Due to uneven economic and political power, upper income groups inevitably appropriate the benefit of any innovation. Hence they argue that the real issue in agriculture is to redistribute land from absentee owners extracting rent to the tillers as part of a package of agrarian reforms to change the economic power configuration.[28]

The economic case for land reforms is premised on the farm size productivity association. Those advocating for land redistribution or "land to the tiller" policies argue that small farms are inherently more productive and therefore there is an inverse size productivity association. Others worry that land distribution following land reforms, to establish owner cultivation, will result in smaller farm sizes and the concern is that these small holdings would not benefit from economies of scale and therefore might be less productive than mechanized "industrial" agriculture based on large holdings. There is an ongoing debate on this issue that dates back several decades and appears to have picked up steam once again. As on so many other development economic issues, the evidence is not conclusive though it appears at the moment to weigh in favor of small farm sizes.[29]

If small family farms are indeed more efficient, the question is why? Boyce (2004) documented and cited evidence regarding a number of possible reasons. Small farmers engage in higher cropping intensity (more crops per unit of land per time period), higher intensity of labor effort (possible driven by poverty),[30] leave much less land unutilized, cultivate more high value crops (such as vegetables) that are labor intensive, employ locally available inputs such as manure and use local knowledge accumulated over generations. In addition, family supervision of household labor means less transactions and supervision costs.

Paradoxically, hard work on one's own farm as a labor of love could mean lower labor productivity if more time is allocated to a task because the opportunity cost of labor is low.[31] However, what counts more is the higher land productivity due to the reasons mentioned above. Beyond economic efficiency there are other economic advantages claimed for small family-owned farms. For example, the consumption pattern may be less import intensive and hence entail more domestic inter-linkages of the agricultural and manufacturing sectors.

In the current global climate dominated by neoliberal economic philosophy, few states even discuss land reform let alone consider appropriating private property.[32] Thus, even if there is to be land redistribution to tillers, it would have to be with compensation. There are several possible compensation mechanisms, and providing land owners with a combination of cash and state bonds is one possibility. Another is neoliberal supported market-based negotiated reforms whereby small farmers or the landless are given the cash to negotiate purchase.

There are several historical examples of land redistribution as a political mechanism to thwart radical ideology and gain political support for the ruling regime. The Shah of Iran's (Mohammad Reza Pahlavi) "White Revolution" (to avert a "red" revolution) was pushed by the US administration. It included the 1962–1971 land redistribution. Making a case for the success of Iran's land reforms, Majd (1987) documented that land was redistributed to all of Iran's peasant share croppers such that the reform benefited 74 percent of all farmers and 67 percent of all rural households.

Araghi (1989) conceded that the identified scale of the redistribution was correct, but the reforms failed for several reasons. The amount received by the overwhelming majority of beneficiaries was in fragmented parcels difficult to manage and totaling to an amount that was below the household's subsistence needs. There was limited investment in irrigation infrastructure that would benefit the small peasants and credit was virtually unavailable except from money lenders at exorbitant rates. The prices of food staples were kept low based on administered prices and food imports. Thus many of the small peasants sold their land and migrated to urban areas.

Majd (1989) however strongly disputed Araghi's thesis arguing that it was not supported by data and provided evidence to show that the land reforms ushered in an unprecedented increase in rural prosperity based on an increase in farm productivity. The issue of the lack of state support was not addressed, however.

The examples of successful land redistribution to tillers that stand out for their long-lasting impacts are those of South Korea and Taiwan. In South Korea, Japanese colonial rule concentrated land ownership among Japanese owners and Korean collaborators. Dorner and Thiesenhusen (1990) pointed out that 3 percent of the owners held about three-fifths of the land in the mid-1940s and high rent extraction by absentee owners created peasant unrest. The South Korean land redistribution with compensation was conducted by the US Occupation and South Korean authorities over the 1946 to 1950 period such that the dispossession first impacted the Japanese owners (without compensation) and then the absentee Korean landlords (with compensation). The two phases of the land reform essentially turned South Korea into a country of smallholders.

Pak (1955) documented how small farmers lacked state support in terms of agricultural inputs and infrastructure and were constrained to sell to the government at below market prices. This lack of support and incentives produced poor productivity outcomes even though the land redistribution did break the back of feudalism and allayed peasant unrest. However, land consolidation and the rise of tenancy reemerged as smallholders failed to effectively subsist.

Between 1970 and 1991, output in Korea agriculture increased fivefold or 500 percent.[33] In Korea, the earlier land distribution in conjunction with the Saemaul Undong (village) movement launched on April 22, 1970, resulted in a highly productive Korean agriculture. It included providing small farmers with support for investment in rural infrastructure including electrification, link roads (farm to market), storage facilities, input subsidies, credit, support for mechanization and research and development, and extension support. Thus agriculture was treated as an industry and in this regard part of Korea's broader industrial policy.

Another positive outcome was that powerful agricultural interests were not there to hinder the industrial development effort as was the case in Latin America. Korea is among the few countries where rural conditions have not worsened over time. As food prices increased, most in the rural areas gained. Thus getting prices right only made sense in the context of fundamental asset redistribution and state support for smallholders.

In Taiwan, The Sino-American Joint Commission on Rural Reconstruction (the JCRR) engaged in a phased rent control, land to the tiller (with compensation) and rural support policies over the 1949 to 1954 period. As in Korea, warding off peasant unrest and susceptibility to socialist doctrine, due to exploitative rents drawn by absentee landlords, was a motivating factor (Dorner and Thiesenhusen, 1990). Subsequent to the reforms, agriculture production increased and farmer prosperity improved substantially despite the internal terms of trade being against agriculture. Agriculture was able to build on the strengths in infrastructure, agricultural research and farmers' associations inherited from the Japanese.

Under current conditions, due to the dominance of neoliberal thought[34] and domestic political power realities, the emphasis may need to be on agrarian reforms. Where the politics permit, land redistribution could be one element of that. If not, agrarian reforms could substitute for land redistribution and include for example a change in tenure rights to provide cultivators with more security of tenure in the rental and share cropping contracts. They may require rent ceilings and a greater contribution of inputs by the landowner in share cropping as well as long-term contracts with protections against eviction.

The lessons from the successful reforms in South Korea and Taiwan are that land redistribution needs to be seen as part of a package of broader agrarian reforms that include extension, input and infrastructure support. Without such support, cultivator gains can be reversed as happened in Iran and even in South Korea in the decade after the land reforms.

Another lesson is that a tradeoff between equity and efficiency is not inevitable. The agrarian reforms in South Korea ended feudalism, awarded land to the tiller, but also created a basis for prosperity in the rest of society by boosting agricultural productivity and provided the other sectors with resources and a market. As always, changes in aggregates (rural peasant conditions) mask important distinctions such as how women fare even when conditions improve. Land redistribution to women can contribute to both gender equity and sustainable agriculture, and these two topics are addressed next.

Gender and agriculture

Women engage in much of the fieldwork in crop agriculture (about two-fifths in Africa), partly because men often migrate to earn non-farm income to remit back to the household (Doss, 2018). Despite this, women have problems in getting legal title to land and in protecting their access to communal land.[35] Lacking collateral, they are resultantly denied credit and men get the preponderance of agricultural loans. Similarly, they have less access to other inputs like water, fertilizer and farm machinery. For cultural and other reasons women have difficulty in accessing markets and are ignored by governmental extension agencies and female farmers receive far fewer visits other things constant. Men generally move onto the cash crops (or crops where the profit opportunity is higher) and leave growing and processing food to women. Most of the technological innovations that eased work burdens are applied to the work done by men and such technological changes can enhance women's work burden for example due to greater weeding and processing needs.[36]

Boserup (1986) made seminal contributions in the gender and development fields more broadly and also to gender and agriculture. Her focus was on the sex pattern of productive work emerging from the modernization of agriculture and rural-urban migration. In this process, she saw work becoming more hierarchical. Women were systematically denied education and perceived as inferior; as a consequence they were confined to unskilled, routine and low productivity work utilizing primitive equipment. Agricultural modernization, which might have militated to their advantage by reducing the premium on physical strength, actually bypassed women because men monopolized the more efficient equipment operated with animal or mechanical power. Thus, women continued with traditional activities and methods. Extension service was exclusively for males, cash crops remained a male preserve and land reform privileged males.

Sen and Grown (1987) pointed out that women as the collectors of food, fuel and water, and also as food workers and processors, needed to be recognized as central to resolving the triple crises of food, water and fuel which plagued L/LMICs. They argued that the austerity imposed by structural adjustment resulted in women having to make do with less and their work burden rose. Instead of this austerity, they suggested that women needed to be accorded equal status during and after productivity enhancing land reforms and provided with access to credit, technology and markets to address the triple crises.

Agarwal (1988) cited available evidence from India to demonstrate that poor rural women often worked longer than men and that, despite getting paid less for the same agricultural tasks, women's gross contribution, including "invisible" non-market work in the households, which men did not acknowledge, was greater. Even so, women's and girls' access to crucial needs like food and health, based on intra-household distribution, was less than that of men's and boys', accounting for systematic gender differentials in malnutrition, morbidity and mortality. Such differentials intensified in lean periods. Labor force participation rates and marriage costs (dowry or bride price) were among the factors that accounted for such differences and these in turn were shaped by factors such as history, culture and geography.

Agarwal (1994) made a multi-pronged case for extending both land ownership and control (since the latter does not follow automatically from the former) to women.[37] The most compelling elements in this case included the need for social security if women are deserted, divorced or widowed. Land provides more assurance of shelter and livelihood than any other support mechanism. It strengthens women's "fallback position" and hence strengthens their leverage and bargaining position within the household. She pointed out that for the land distribution to women to be effective, even more so the case than for land reform in general, technical (access to extension services) and institutional support (access to input and product markets) would need to be provided.

Lastarria-Cornheil (1997) pointed out that in Africa women lost access and cultivation land that they possessed during western colonial and post-colonial donor influenced privatizations based on land titling and registration. Private ownership by male household heads and community leaders displaced customary land tenure systems. Women traditionally had cultivation rights (even if through men), but as land became scarcer and cash crops more common, land became more desired for its cash rather than subsistence value and as a result women's cultivation rights were ignored. Ideological biases and capital and labor market imperfections make it difficult for women to acquire land.

Deere and Leon (1998) documented how the agrarian reforms in Latin America in the 1960s and 1970s mostly bypassed women in land distribution (and associated water, pasture and tree rights). In the structural adjustment period of the 1980s and 1990s reforms focused on privatization of collectives or communal land, restitution of land to former owners and land titling. Notwithstanding the neoliberal focus on efficiency rather than social equity, the international feminist movement with support from UN agencies resulted in progressive changes in Latin America. In five countries, land rights are no longer exclusively vested in household heads, which usually means males. Four of the countries studied moved to joint land titling rather than exclusively giving titles to males. These are significant but still small steps in the direction of de jure and de facto gender equity in agriculture.

Agarwal (2011) cited several studies showing that given the same inputs and services, women are more efficient farmers while Doss's (2018) review of the literature suggested that under these circumstances they were about as productive.[38] This is despite the multiple burdens they already shoulder. These burdens come from being care givers (child/elders/handicapped), doing household chores, engaging in home-based work when available and now increasingly also being the main food producers. In addition, they are paid less for the same work as casual labor. While the feminist movement and consequently donors are now addressing the neglect of women in their role as agricultural producers, doing so effectively is not straightforward.[39]

The focus in this chapter is on crop production. Apart from agriculture more broadly, the primary sector includes forestry, fisheries and livestock, and the role of gender analysis in each case is critical. For example, Agarwal (2009) demonstrated how enabling women to have a greater say in decision making in community forestry institutions (CFI) enhances sustainability and livelihoods. Her estimates based on an analysis of 135 CFI (65 in Gujarat and 70 in Nepal) showed that greater representation of women on executive committees of CFI resulted in a 75 percent higher probability that the forest canopy would be thick rather than thin.

It is possible to speculate on the mechanisms for these findings. Women charged with ensuring food security in the household have much more knowledge of non-timber forest products such as fuel, fodder, grasses, wild vegetables and herbs. Since women rely on forests for survival, they have a greater incentive to ensure sustainable use. Thus the rule formation is drawn from better local knowledge of forest ecology and better collective implementation given the incentives. Degraded resources like forests or water mean longer distances and travel time for collection. Thus if sustainability is the goal, this can be attained more effectively by understanding the role women play in agriculture (or the primary sector) and enabling it to become more effective. This is particularly because, as indicated above, women play a large and growing role in L/LMIC agricultures and they are the repository of much of the local knowledge leading to effective biodiversity and sustainability.

Sustainable agriculture

The potential hazards of chemical use in agriculture were discussed above. Pretty (1995, p. 1248) pointed out that the definition of the term sustainable, and hence sustainable agriculture, is contested. He pointed out that even by the mid-1990s there were over 100 definitions of sustainable. One of the earliest and most well known of these definitions was cited in Chapter 1 (endnote 10) and most definitions have in common with this one a concern for future generations and ecosystem impacts.[40]

Pretty pointed out that in the last century chemical intensive agricultural yields were boosted by substituting external inputs for internal or organic ones. Chemical fertilizers replaced livestock manure, nitrogen fixing crops (like legumes) and composts; pesticides and herbicides replaced biological methods based on local knowledge for containing pests, weeds and diseases; and fossil fuel intensive machinery replaced labor.

The case for the GR chemical farming was premised on boosting farm productivity and thus in addressing hunger and starvation in the L/LMIC context. Critics argued that addressing hunger is more a distributional than a production issue. Further, that higher production (than alternatives), if forthcoming, comes at the cost of ecosystem degradation and the associated human and wildlife damage. Finally, that the boost in food productivity was not sustainable in any case and could be matched by low chemical or chemical-free agricultural practices.[41] The debate on the relative profitability and productive efficiency of various agricultural practices is ongoing (see below). Nonetheless, the need to eliminate or limit the use of environmentally destructive external inputs while maintaining yields at high levels has been widely acknowledged.

It is in this context that advocates of biotechnology view it to be part of the sustainability movement (see above). They argue that not only is it a solution for poverty by boosting land productivity, but it is also green since in principle it can reduce the use of synthetic chemical inputs like herbicides and pesticides. Moreover, it promises in the future to deliver seeds that can thrive in drought, water-logged, cold and other extreme conditions. Finally, by boosting productivity, it reduces the amount of land that needs cultivation and this contributes to reducing greenhouse gases.

Those concerned about the hazards of conventional agriculture are not persuaded and endorse alternative practices. The terms used to characterize these alternatives include integrated pest management (IPM), organic and sustainable.[42] IPM evolved in the late 1950s from entomologists' realization that increasing doses of pesticides, as the pests developed resistance, were also killing predator and parasites (beneficial insects) and, hence, compounding the problem. Inadvertently killing beneficial insects can then produce secondary pest outbreaks. By the early 1970s this discovery was formalized in the practice of IPM that integrated biological and chemical control of pests.

IPM also strives to maintain soil fertility with much more limited use of chemical inputs. Some chemicals are still used but in combination with other practices such as crop rotation, traditional farming methods to contain soil erosion, nitrogen fixing via planting legumes, using natural predators of pests and using pheromones to trap pests and organic fertilizers/manures.

There is evidence suggesting that it is possible to reduce destructive chemical use while sustaining output if not in enhancing it. van Veen et al. (1998, p. 249) documented that via IPM Cuba reduced pesticide use by four-fifths in the 1980s, Brazil reduced pesticide use by four-fifths in soybean cultivation over a seven-year period and Indonesia by three-fifths in rice cultivation. There are numerous such case studies in the literature about the successful use of IPM.

Dasgupta, Meisner and Wheeler (2007) conducted one such case study for Bangladesh. Chemical use in Bangladeshi agriculture (three-fourths is rice) doubled since 1992 into the turn of the century. State subsidies and extension services encouraged this to combat pests and weeds that accounted for losses of up to 10–15 percent of the total crop. Massive ecological and health damage heighted interest in sustainable agricultural practices, however. The comparative farm surveys showed that IPM resulted in a 52 percent increase in output, 67 percent less pesticide use (hence higher profits per acre) and 70 percent of the farmers reported improvements in soil, water and air and in wildlife (birds, fish and soil organisms such as earthworms).

IPM is not as stringent as zero synthetic chemical use organic agriculture. For products to be classified as organic, they need to be certified to have not used any synthetics and to have engaged in long-term soil management to enhance natural biological activity.[43] Organic agriculture also includes engaging in activities that enhance biological diversity, recycling, using local renewable resources (as substitutes for external inputs) and minimizing pollution associated with agricultural practices.[44]

Sanders (2006) reviewed the initially modest but persistent effort to encourage production of organics in China.[45] For farmers that had been practicing conventional chemical intensive agriculture, it can take up to three years to eradicate traces of chemicals that persist due to the past practice of chemical intensive agriculture.[46] Farmers therefore need up-front funding, credit support, technical assistance and assured markets (mediated by the state or enterprises) to assume the risk of making the conversion, since certification is not assured.[47] The move to production of organics is challenging even in a MIC like China with a relatively high level of managerial and administrative ability at all levels of government. China is likely to continue to make progress in this regard since with persistent effort it has managed to establish an internationally recognized body to certify for organic products.

Pretty (1998) documented evidence regarding sustainable agricultural practices in L/LMICs and inferred that it is possible to reduce soil destroying external inputs while sustaining output if not enhancing it. While the evidence cited above is positive regarding sustainable agricultural practices, authors usually cite words of caution. Dasgupta, Meisner and Wheeler (2007) pointed out that since there are externalities involved, giving up pesticides needs to be collectively done or a lone adopter will be overwhelmed by surrounding farms that do not adopt.

Pretty (1998, p. 43) noted that projects that engage L/LMIC farmers to adopt sustainable practices need painstaking development practitioner engagement so that small farmer participation drives each stage of the evolving and learning process. The returns to having farmers centerstage and driving the process is much higher than inducing temporary adoption with subsidies since the practices are discontinued when the incentives dry up.

The case for land redistribution and small farm agriculture (see above) has been made on equity and efficiency grounds. Boyce (2004) made this case based on the preservation of biodiversity. The premise is that crop biodiversity is like an insurance policy that monoculture dispenses with. Vigorous seeds that evolve with experimentation are better suited to slightly altered conditions within the same locality but also to withstanding problems like diseases, pests, weeds and drought. In principle, biodiversity can then also reduce the need for chemical inputs that can be environmentally destructive.

While subsidized monoculture of corporate agriculture is promoted by legislatures who are influenced if not controlled by landlords, the hard work of preserving the crop genetic biodiversity falls to the small farmer. Boyce pointed out that experimentation and adaptation to local conditions resulted in small farmers in the Bengal delta growing about 10,000 varieties of rice. Similarly, while in the early 2000s small farmers in Mexico grew 5,000 varieties of maize, US corporate agriculture confined itself to about half a dozen interbred lines on about 70 percent of the maize-growing acreage. This is a risky strategy since pests and diseases are constantly adapting to attack modern seed varieties. Small farms are more suited to biodiversity preservation, which is inherently a local knowledge and labor-intensive process and in this regard provides a public good not acknowledged by a market driven by short-term profit maximization.

Boyce, Rosset and Stanton (2005, p. 11) pointed out that sustainable agricultural practices like IPM and organic farming (see above) are inherently more labor intensive (for example weeding, manure management) and so small farmers have a comparative advantage in adopting them if they are not already using them based on local knowledge. Moreover, many practices they have used for generations based on this knowledge such as crop rotation, inter-planting, recycling and soil maintenance are already eco-friendly.

The economic incentive of small owner-occupied farmers is naturally to preserve the soil their livelihood depends on and this is not the case for land renters or share croppers farming for absentee owners. They also have an incentive to protect themselves and their families from toxins which also destroy their land. Small farmers also have a comparative advantage in the labor-intensive maintenance of agricultural infrastructure like water courses, terraces, bunds and drains that biodiverse agriculture depends on.

Summary and conclusions

The topic of agriculture in L/LMICs is characterized by several debates. This chapter explores the neoclassical challenge to the neglect of agriculture in economic development. It subsequently explores the debates associated with the GR, biotechnology, land grabs, land and agrarian reforms, gender and agriculture, and sustainable development. Each of the policy debates is important in that it may address the tremendous productivity gap between L/LMIC agricultures and HIC agricultures in a sustainable way.

The colonial attitude to traditional agriculture was that peasants were ignorant, lazy and lacked the qualities of frugality and drive that could improve agricultural practices. While developmentalists did not necessarily accept this view, for them the real action was in the industrial sector, and while an agricultural revolution was perceived as important, this was because it could better serve industrial development.

The view of peasants being poor because they were backward and lazy was challenged by neoclassical economists like Bauer and Schultz. They established, albeit with limited evidence, that peasants responded to incentives when presented with the necessary opportunities. The case for the importance of the rural sector more broadly was made by Harris and Todaro and of the agricultural sector in particular by Mellor who advocated for its modernization. One important initiative to modernize agriculture and unleash its productive potential was the GR of the 1960s.

The GR proved very controversial though its impact on boosting land productivity has been widely acknowledged. However, the social, political, economic and ecological impacts of the GR were believed by heterodox economists to be very negative. The more recently introduced biotechnology applications to agriculture are also contested in terms of the ecological impacts. While some claim the "gene revolution" to be doubly green due to its possible positive productivity and sustainability impacts, others view it as a continuation of corporate or industrial agriculture primarily enriching MNCs with threatening consequences for the ecosystem. The more recent attempt to acquire land for modernized agriculture as part of attracting FDI is also negatively viewed by critics as part of the toxic neoliberal economic ideology. This is partly because of the nature of the corporate "industrial" agriculture being promoted but also because the land acquisitions (grabs for critics) displace smallholder agriculture.

Critics of corporate agriculture propose small owner agriculture as one alternative. The economic case for this, and hence the "land to the tiller" policy, is premised on evidence of an inverse association of farm size and land productivity. Notwithstanding this greater efficiency, small owner operated farms are threatened by low prices induced by doubly subsidized HIC agricultures. HIC corporate farms benefit from direct subsidies and also indirect subsidies because they are not required to internalize negative externalities. Thus, at a minimum, critics of corporate agriculture argue that the playing field needs to be leveled.

The ecological case for small farmers is that based on millennia of practice they contribute to biodiversity and more sustainable farm practices. Since women are often the repository of such practices and significant in crop production, backstopping the growing role of women by extending land property rights to them would encourage sustainability.

Not all are persuaded that the move to chemical-free agriculture is called for. However, while the scientific debate on the hazards of chemical use in agriculture is ongoing, alternative practices of low or no chemical use can be encouraged by policy makers based on either the evidence regarding the negative externalities of chemical intensive farming or based on the "precautionary principle" of avoiding possible harm.

Sustainable as identified in this chapter is a broad term and even low-input or zero synthetic chemical agriculture like IPM or organic farming may produce potentially climate-altering greenhouse emissions that can therefore have ecosystem impacts. For example, farm machinery use fossil fuels, manure emits nitrogen and livestock emits methane. That notwithstanding, pragmatist policy would call for sequentially dealing with impacts as better and economically viable options such as clean energy become available.

In a development context, sustainable agriculture is a promising though not a politically easy objective to attain. Based on the evidence cited in this chapter, encouraging small farm agriculture with a prominent female role should result in more equity, efficiency and sustainability (win-win-win). In addition, small organic farmers have the opportunity to sell their products at a premium both locally and abroad as markets develop and certification is established – again, not an easy task. Finally, organic agriculture has been noted to be an effective part of adaptation and mitigation in addressing climate change.[48]

However, notwithstanding the potential multiple wins, the transition to sustainable agricultural practices is not straightforward even if the evidence suggests that it is more profitable and that the original output level can be regained and sustained if not exceeded. Large landlords are influential in both democratic and autocratic governments. Also small farmers are risk averse and having once been sold on chemical agriculture, they can be expected to be reluctant to change course. This is especially so since chemicals promise a hassle-free way of dealing with problems like pests and weeds while the transition to chemical-free agriculture is labor intensive and tedious even if profitable, individually and socially, in the long run.

Complicating matters further is that the transition to sustainable agricultural practices is more effective via collective action both due to economies of scale in external support and because individual farmers' efforts can be overwhelmed by the inaction of neighbors. The transition to sustainable industry may be even more complicated if the multiple wins, as in sustainable agriculture, are not forthcoming. This is an issue explored in the next chapter.

Questions and exercises

1. Evaluate alternative tenure arrangements in agriculture.
2. Discuss the characteristics of peasant agriculture.
3. Compare the neoliberal, developmentalist/structuralist and new developmentalist perspectives on agriculture.
4. Explain the institutionalist perspective on agriculture.
5. On what grounds was the neglect of agriculture challenged by mainstream development economists?
6. How has the role of women in agriculture been neglected and thwarted?
7. In what way does sustainable agriculture represent a multiple win and why might sustainability nonetheless be difficult to attain?
8. Make the case for land distribution to women along with property rights enforcement.
9. Make the case for and against "land to the tiller" land reform. Where do you stand on the issue and why?
10. Make the case for and against the Green Revolution in L/LMICs. Where do you stand on the issue and why?
11. The impact of interventions depends on the social and economic environment it is introduced into. Discuss with regard to the impacts of the Green Revolution.

12. Make the case for and against the role of biotechnology in L/LMIC agriculture. Where do you stand on the issue and why?
13. Make the case for and against FDI-led agriculture (including land contracts). Where do you stand on the issue and why?

Notes

1 Following Knight (1921), uncertainty is characterized by the lack of knowledge of a probability distribution of outcomes. Risk is characterized by a large variation in outcomes but with known probabilities.

2 The rental contract is viewed as a lump sum tax while share cropping is a proportional tax. Thus, it would seem that the rental contract would be preferable from the viewpoint of the tenant since it provides more incentives for work effort and innovation and also by the landlords since they can set the rent for optimum revenue extraction. One would therefore expect the rental contract would drive out share cropping. Economists are puzzled that this has not happened and sometimes even adjoining farms have alternative contracts. Chaudhuri and Maitra (1997) addressed this puzzle and also the determinants of contract selection.

3 Refer to Buckland (2006) for a likeminded review of debates on agriculture in development economics.

4 Norman Borlaug received the Nobel Peace Prize in 1970 for developing high yielding hybrid seeds. IRRI (International Rice Research Institute, Philippines) took forward the rice hybrid and CIMMYT (International Maize and Wheat Improvement Center, Mexico) the wheat hybrid. HYVs have been developed for other crops like corn, millet and sorghum.

5 Byerlee (1996, p. 699) reviewed the large-scale adoption of modern variety (MV) seeds, even to rain-fed areas (classified as arid or semi-arid) as plant-breeding research progressed. By 1990, between 60 to 70 percent of the combined planted area of maize, rice and wheat (57 percent of calories consumed in L/LMICs) used MVs as opposed to traditional varieties.

6 For example Johl (1975) and Blyn (1983) provided evidence from India and showed that both employment and wages increased during the GR period and that the income gains were across the board. Johl found larger gains for larger farms (ten-fold) since they had a larger marketable surplus, but Blyn suggested the inverse. Chaudhry (1982) provided similar evidence for Pakistan but also argued that income inequality between classes and regions during the GR period under study decreased with larger gains accruing to smaller farmers. Also see Ruttan (2002) for a retrospective on the benefits of the GR that provided broader empirical support for the evidence cited above.

7 Critics conceded that mechanization had more to do with capital subsidies than the GR per se.

8 He conceded however that in the irrigated areas suited to hybrid seeds there was a boost in production. However, given the social and economic dislocations accompanying the GR, the boost in productivity came with a high price tag.

9 Replanting hybrid seeds produced inferior results.

10 Other chemicals, particularly in HIC agriculture, include fumigants, miticides (to kill mites), desiccants (drying agents), defoliants and growth regulators.

11 Sandhu cited an FAO study claiming that only 5 percent of the insecticide fell on targeted plants while the rest polluted the environment.

12 One of their findings was that a 10 percent increase in the average level of fertilizer chemicals in water (in the month of conception) increases the likelihood of infant mortality by about 4.6 percent. The Indian Punjab was very prominent in the Green Revolution and is now referred to as the cancer capital of India attributed to the chemical agriculture the Green Revolution ushered in (www.npr.org/templates/story/story.

php?storyId=103569390, consulted 12/5/2018). In the three years prior to 2016, cancer in Kerala grew 10 percent faster than the rest of India and state authorities decided to shift entirely to organic agriculture by 2020. Experts urged caution to prevent farmer losses and recommended a partial move as in IPM (see below), www.loe.org/shows/segments.html?programID=18-P13-00018&segmentID=5, consulted 1/5/2019.

13 Nin-Pratt and McBride (2014) and Frankema (2014) provided other explanations of why the GR bypassed Africa. These include the agro-ecology, cash crops less suited to available GR technologies, water scarcity, low population density (hence labor scarcity), biological vectors (such as mosquito and the tsetse fly, which also threatened livestock), ambiguous land ownership rights, currency overvaluations (cheaper food imports) and the lack of state capacity. The resulting agriculture (such as shifting cultivation and crop choices) did not result in adequate incentives for farmers to adopt these technologies. Nin-Pratt and McBride (2014) challenged the contention that changing conditions including rapid population growth, land and food scarcity now make these technologies suitable and an Asian style GR in Africa more likely. They provided evidence using the case of Ghana, which is a resource rich and therefore high labor cost country, to sound a cautionary note. For a more optimistic view based on new seed varieties, transport, information and communication infrastructure reducing physical distances, demographic pressure and relative macroeconomic stability, refer to Frankema (2014).

14 The argument is that the transgenics that occur in nature over millennia now occur over years with biotechnology. In this regard, supporters of this technology argue that everyone has been consuming genetically modified (GM) food (Johnson, 2002).

15 Refer to Rao, Pray and Herring (2015) for details.

16 Shelton (2007, p. 894) reported evidence concerning the dramatic reduction of insecticide sprays needed on Bt cotton (up to 15 million fewer insecticide sprays in the United States in 1999). Another reported benefit is the reduction of ear rot disease in corn, which is toxic for mammals and carcinogenic for humans.

17 The Conservation Technology Information Center (CTIC) in the United States defines conservation tillage as any tillage and planting system that leaves at least 30 percent of the soil surface covered by residue after planting and this limits soil erosion. It also enhances carbon storage.

18 The EU has subjected GE products to highly stringent regulations and there is evidence of health hazards (allergens and toxins) associated with GE foods. Refer to Altieri and Rosset for references (1999). This is contested and Rao, Pray and Herring (2015) documented that the EU has concluded, based on a review of extensive research over a 25-year period, that GE crops like maize products and soybeans are no more risky than conventional crops.

19 These are also referred to as genetic use restriction technologies (GURTs) or suicide seeds.

20 (Herring, 2007) pointed out that the terminator or suicide seed was banned by the Government of India in 1998 (Monsanto owns the patent to this technology and in 2012 promised not to use it). He also provided a narrative of farmers' stealth experimentation and local dealer sales of hybrid indigenized Bt (*Bacillus thuringiensis*) transgenic cotton varieties. One estimate showed that "on an all-India basis, about 34 percent of (packaged) the cotton seed packets sold are transgenic, of which 9 percent are legal and 25 percent stealth" (p. 135).

21 For a critique of biotechnology from a development perspective, refer to Altieri and Rosset (1999) and references they cite. For a review of the debate in the Indian context, refer to Herring (2015) and in the Zambian context, Bowman (2015). For endorsements, refer to Byerlee (1996), references in Byerlee and Fischer (2002), Johnson (2002), Davies and Newton (2006), Lipton (2007), Pray and Naseem (2007), Shelton (2007), Zilberman, Ameden and Qaim (2007), Barrows, Sexton and Zilberman (2014) and Rao, Pray and Herring (2015). Supportive studies appear to outnumber the critics in the

scholarly literature and several supportive authors are often vituperative and scathing of critics, particularly about international NGO advocacy and the EU's cautious regulatory approach.

22 See for example, Altieri and Rosset (1999). Studies need to be careful to compare like with like since several cultivars exist for seeds depending on the agro-ecological conditions. Herring (2007, p. 137) cited a study of Bt cotton suggesting less pesticide use against cotton bollworm and higher land productivity, particularly in conjunction with integrated pest management (IPM – see below).

23 Refer to Altieri and Rosset (1999) for references.

24 "Output traits" such as food fortification that could directly benefit the consumer and address abiotic stresses (e.g. drought, salinity, acidity, water inundation) involve multiple gene insertion and are therefore more complex. These traits are the subject of current and future research.

25 A working definition of land grabs based on the Tirana Declaration is provided by the International Land Coalition www.landcoalition.org/sites/default/files/documents/resources/tiranadeclaration.pdf, consulted 11/18/2018). Land grabs are:

(i) in violation of human rights, particularly the equal rights of women; (ii) not based on free, prior and informed consent of the affected land-users; (iii) not based on a thorough assessment, or are in disregard of social, economic and environmental impacts, including the way they are gendered; (iv) not based on transparent contracts that specify clear and binding commitments about activities, employment and benefits sharing; and (v) not based on effective democratic planning, independent oversight and meaningful participation.

To this can be added that a grab is a sizable (by local standards) land acquisition, involves a foreign government/company but one that entails payoffs to local elites, and/or has a sizable uncompensated impact on local livelihoods including that of small farmers. Development economists supporting FDI are more likely to refer to this phenomenon as acquisitions, investments, deals and transactions. While the focus here is on global corporate land grabs, these could also emanate domestically or regionally (Borras et al., 2012).

26 See for example, articles by GRAIN (2011, pp. 31–34), Land Research Action Network (2011, pp. 5–11), Zoomers (2011, pp. 12–20) and Chu (2011, pp. 35–39), all published in *Development*, 54(1), on the gender inequalities accentuated by these land acquisitions. Other studies exploring a gender perspective of land acquisitions include Doss, Summerfield and Tsikata (2014) and Verma (2014). For the scope of these land grabs, refer to Akram-Lodhi (2012, p. 126), Land Matrix Global Observatory, https://landmatrix.org/en/about/, consulted 11/18/2018, and "Seized! The 2008 land grabbers for food and financial security, GRAIN Briefing Annex", www.grain.org/media/BAhbBlsHOgZmSSI3MjAxMS8wNi8zMC8xNl8wMV8z NF80MTNfbGFuZGdyYWJfMjAwOF9lbl9hbm5leC5wZGYGOgZFVA /landgrab-2008-en-annex.pdf, consulted, 11/14/2018. The Land Matrix states upfront that the data are inherently unreliable. Arezki, Deininger and Selod (2011, p. 12) provide context with their calculation that between 2004 and 2009 confirmed land acquisitions in Sudan, Mozambique and Ethiopia amounted to respectively 8.6 percent, 16.6 percent and 25.4 percent of the total suitable non-forested non-protected area, while Doss, Summerfield and Tsikata (2014, p. 6), citing Michal Kugelman, noted that Cambodia had leased more than half its arable land.

27 While the World Bank in partnership with other international organizations including the UN FAO (Food and Agricultural Organization), IFAD (International Fund for Agricultural Development) and UNCTAD (United Nations Conference for Trade and Development) subsequently came up with guidelines for responsible land investments, critics argue that the damage had already been ushered in. Also, these guidelines in

effect endorse corporate agriculture relative to smallholder agriculture and sustainable alternatives discussed later in this chapter.

28 There are numerous examples of land reforms from across the world (over 40). Given space limitations, only a few will be discussed to illustrate key points.

29 Empirical support for the inverse association of land size and productivity has been provided among others by Kagin, Taylor and Edward (2016), Ali and Deininger (2015), Gaurav and Mishra (2015), Carletto, Savastano and Zezza (2013), Verschelde et al. (2013), Banerjee (2000), Heltberg (1998), Faruqee and Carey (1997), Prosterman and Riedinger (1987), Johnston and Tomich (1985), Berry and Cline (1979), Dorner (1972), Dorner and Kanel (1971) and Ruttan (1969). Several of these authors argue that equitable provision of research and extension services and inputs across farm size is a prerequisite for small farms to show greater technical efficiency. Deininger et al. (2018) show a weakening of the farm size–productivity association between 1982 and 2008 in India due to better functioning of the labor market. Studies that have questioned this inverse association, or have found a positive association, include Dorward (1999) and Wang et al. (2015) for China, and Desiere and Jolliffe (2018). Foster and Rosenzweig (2017) estimated an inverted U-shaped farm size productivity association for India and explained large farm (beyond some threshold) to be as productive as small farms due to lower labor transaction costs and also scale economies in the use of agricultural machinery.

30 Large farms are inclined to underuse labor because of monitoring costs. In addition, recall from Chapter 6 (endnote 19) that the fragmented and hence monopsonistic local labor market structure results in an incentive for large farms to use less labor.

31 Johnston and Le Roux (2007) challenged the presumption of household labor being more efficient based on a common goal (sharing of residual profit) and hence higher labor effort with less supervision. They argued that this presumes intra-household harmony whereas alternative modeling of intra-household associations indicate the possibilities of conflict, coercion and exploitation of women and junior household members. Thus the presumption of greater productivity of household labor needs empirical verification.

32 If the existing distribution is unjust based on a theory of justice for which there is broad philosophical support, redistribution can be considered just. For example, if colonial distribution that favored collaborators is viewed as unjust, there is a philosophical case for appropriation. In Zimbabwe, land redistribution (first with and then without compensation) was justified on the grounds that the colonial administration favored white settlers and deprived the native population. South Africa in 2018 changed its constitution to follow Zimbabwe's precedence of appropriation and distribution without compensation. It hopes to avoid Zimbabwe's disastrous results by distributing land not to regime cronies but to small but productive native farmers.

33 Refer to Jeon and Kim (2000) for estimates of production increase due to the end of tenancy in South Korea. Iscan (2018) showed only a marginal production increase due to land redistribution in Japan, South Korea and Taiwan, but argued that it contributed to the structural change that boosted industrialization and catch-up growth in all three countries.

34 This dominance persists notwithstanding the claims of heterodox economists that the economic philosophy has been shown to be moribund on conceptual and empirical grounds (Chapter 9).

35 For example, FAO statistics for 2007, as reported by the World Bank (2009, p. 523), show that fewer than 10 percent of women farmers in India, Nepal and Thailand owned land and this deprivation is fairly typical. Meanwhile they produced 80 percent of all food in Sub-Saharan Africa, while in five African country credit schemes they received one-tenth of the credit men received and only 15 percent of worldwide extension agents were women.

36 For accounts of gender discrimination in agriculture and policy prescriptions to facilitate women's increasing role in agriculture, refer to Doss (2001), Quisumbing

and Pandolfelli (2010), Agarwal (2011), Croppenstedt, Goldstein and Rosas (2013) and Doss (2018).

37 A similar distinction between ownership and control has been made in the context of microcredit loans ostensibly given to females but used by male household members (Parmar, 2003).

38 Doss (2018) indicated how methodological difficulties (such as conceptualizing women's productivity in agriculture relative to that of men) make the empirics even more problematic than usual.

39 Reviewing 25 years of research, Doss (2001) pointed out that simple and static categorizations, such as male and female crops, in a heterogeneous, complex and dynamic agriculture are not possible. Policy interventions to enhance women's well-being need to address complexities, such as varying women's roles and responsibilities, to avoid unintended consequences. For example, technological adoption that makes land more productive might cause women to lose access to it. Thus, security of tenure reform may need to precede technological change. Agarwal (2011) made a case for female group farming because the collective has leverage in securing inputs, diffusing information, providing protection and changing oppressive cultural norms.

40 The broader debate on sustainability based on alternative approaches is explored in the context of industry in Chapter 14.

41 On the one hand, productivity is less relevant relative to profitability and sustainability. The point about low or no synthetic chemical agriculture is that the low input cost boosts profitability even if the output is lower and the higher profit is attained with much less ecosystem damage. On the other, productivity per unit land is important in that less land is needed to feed more people.

42 Hall et al. (1989) reviewed the scientific debate on the hazards of chemical use in agriculture and the definitions of alternative agricultural practices in the US context.

43 A more detailed definition is provided by the FAO/WHO Codex Alimentarius as cited by Muller (2009, p. 2), who discussed organic agricultural practices in detail.

44 The International Federation of Organic Agriculture Movements (IFOAM) has even broader standard-setting principles of organic agriculture www.ifoam.bio/sites/default/files/poa_english_web.pdf, consulted 12/5/2018.

45 In China only 0.03 percent of total agricultural area in the early 2000s was devoted to organic agriculture. For state and civil society support for organic agriculture in India, refer to Puttaswamaiah, Manns and Shah (2006).

46 Organic farming can be problematic even in HICs. If residues show any positive traces of chemical use, farms can lose their certification and their niche markets in which they command premium prices. The problem is that neighboring non-organic farms could be the cause of chemical residues via aerial drifts and water run-offs.

47 Sanders points out that there are economies of scale in providing financial, technical and marketing support to farmer associations relative to working with individual small farmers.

48 Refer to Muller (2009) who extensively reviewed and cited the literature on this issue.

References

Agarwal, B. 1988. "Neither Sustenance nor Sustainability: Agricultural Strategies, Ecological Degradation and Indian Women in Poverty," in: B. Agarwal. (ed.), *Structures of Patriarchy: The State, the Community and the Household* (London: Zed Books) 83-120.

Agarwal, B. 1994. *A Field of One's Own* (Cambridge: Cambridge University Press).

Agarwal, B. 2009. "Gender and Forest Conservation: The Impact of Women's Participation in Community Forest Governance," *Ecological Economics*, 68(11), 2785–2799.

Agarwal, B. 2011. "Food Crises and Gender Inequality," DESA (UN Department of Economic and Social Affairs) Working Paper No. 107, New York.

Akram-Lodhi, H. 2012. "Contextualising Land Grabbing: Contemporary Land Deals, the Global Subsistence Crisis and the World Food System," *Canadian Journal of Development Studies*, 33(2), 119–142.

Alauddin, M. and C. Tisdell. 1991. "Welfare Consequences of Green Revolution Technology: Changes in Bangladeshi Food Production," *Development and Change*, 22(3), 497–517.

Ali, D. A. and K. Deininger. 2015. "Is There a Farm Size-Productivity Relationship in African Agriculture? Evidence from Rwanda," *Land Economics*, 91(2), 317–343.

Altieri, M. A. and P. Rosset. 1999. "Ten Reasons Why Biotechnology Will Not Ensure Food Security, Protect the Environment and Reduce Poverty in the Developing World," *AgBioForum*, 2(3 & 4), 155–162.

Araghi, F. A. 1989. "Land Reform Policies in Iran: Comment," *American Journal of Agricultural Economics*, 71(4), 1046–1049.

Arezki, R., K. Deininger and H. Selod 2011. What Drives the Global Land Rush? IMF Working Paper WP/11/251, Washington, DC.

Ball, R. and L. Pounder. 1996. "Efficient but Poor" Revisited," *Economic Development and Cultural Change*, 44(4), 735–760.

Banerjee, A. V. 2000. "Prospects and Strategies for Land Reforms," in *Annual World Bank Conference on Development Economics, 1999* (World Bank: Washington, DC).

Barrows, G., S. Sexton and D. Zilberman. 2014. "The Impact of Agricultural Biotechnology on Supply and Land-use," *Environment and Development Economics*, 19(6), 676–703.

Berry, R. A. and W. R. Cline. 1979. *Agrarian Structure and Productivity in Developing Countries* (Cambridge: Cambridge University Press).

Blyn, G. 1983. "The Green Revolution Revisited," *Economic Development and Cultural Change*, 31(4), 705–725.

Borras, S., Jr., M. C. Kay, S. Gómez and J. Wilkinson. 2012. "Land Grabbing and Global Capitalist Accumulation: Key Features in Latin America," *Canadian Journal of Development Studies*, 33(4), 402–416.

Boserup, E. 1986. *Women's Role in Economic Development* (Aldershot: Hants: Gower).

Bowman, A. 2015. "Sovereignty, Risk and Biotechnology: Zambia's 2002 GM Controversy in Retrospect," *Development and Change*, 46(6), 1369–1391.

Boyce, J. K. 2004. "A Future for Small Farms? Biodiversity and Sustainable Agriculture," University of Massachusetts, Political Economic Research Institute, Working Paper Series No 86, Amherst, MA.

Boyce, J. K., P. Rosset and E. A. Stanton 2005. Political Economic Research Institute, Working Paper Series No 98, Amherst, MA.

Brainerd, E. and N. Menon. 2014. "Seasonal Effects of Water Quality: The Hidden Costs of the Green Revolution to Infant and Child Health in India," *Journal of Development Economics*, 107(March), 49–64.

Buckland, J. 2006. "International Obstacles to Rural Development: How Neoliberal Policies Constrain Competitive Markets and Sustainable Agriculture," *Canadian Journal of Development Studies*, 27(1), 9–24.

Bujko, M., C. Fischer, T. Krieger and D. Meierrieks. 2015. "How Institutions Shape Land Deals: The Role of Corruption," CESifo Working Paper Series: 5178, Munich.

Byerlee, D. 1996. "Modem Varieties, Productivity, and Sustainability: Recent Experience and Emerging Challenges," *World Development*, 24(4), 697–718.

Byerlee, D. and K. Fischer. 2002. "Accessing Modern Science: Policy and Institutional Options for Agricultural Biotechnology in Developing Countries," *World Development*, 30(6), 931–948.

Carletto, C., S. Savastano and A. Zezza. 2013. "Fact or Artefact: The Impact of Measurement Errors on the Farm Size-Productivity Relationship," *Journal of Development Economics*, 103(July), 254–261.

Chaudhry, M. G. 1982. "Green Revolution and Redistribution of Rural Incomes: Pakistan's Experience," *The Pakistan Development Review*, 21(3), 173–205.

Chaudhuri, A. and P. Maitra. 1997. "Determinants of Land Tenure Contracts; Theory and Evidence from Rural India," Working Paper, No. 1997-10, Department of Economics, Rutgers University, New Brunswick, NJ.

Child, F. C. and H. Kaneda. 1975. "Links to the Green Revolution: A Study of Small-Scale, Agriculturally Related Industry in the Pakistan Punjab," *Economic Development and Cultural Change*, 23(2), 249–275.

Colburn, T., D. Dumanoski and J. P. Myers. 1996. *Our Stolen Future, Are We Threatening Our Fertility, Intelligence and Survival? A Scientific Detective Story* (New York: Plume).

Croppenstedt, A., M. Goldstein and N. Rosas. 2013. "Gender and Agriculture: Inefficiencies, Segregation, and Low Productivity Traps," *World Bank Research Observer*, 28(1), 79–109.

Dasgupta, S., C. Meisner and D. Wheeler. 2007. "Is Environmentally Friendly Agriculture Less Profitable for Farmers? Evidence on Integrated Pest Management in Bangladesh," *Review of Agricultural Economics*, 29(1), 103–118.

Davies, W. P. and D. J. Newton. 2006. "Agricultural Innovation and Biotechnology Development Towards Sustainable Goals: Can We Make It More Pro-poor," *World Review of Science, Technology and Sustainable Development*, 3(2), 99–122.

Deere, C. D. and M. Leon. 1998. "Gender, Land, and Water: From Reform to Counter-reform in Latin America," *Agriculture and Human Values*, 15(4), 375–386.

Deininger, K., S. Jin, Y. Liu and S. K. Singh. 2018. "Can Labor-Market Imperfections Explain Changes in the Inverse Farm Size–Productivity Relationship?: Longitudinal Evidence from Rural India," *Land Economics*, 94(2), 239–258.

Desiere, S. and D. Jolliffe. 2018. "Land Productivity and Plot Size: Is Measurement Error Driving the Inverse Relationship?" *Journal of Development Economics*, 130(January), 84–98.

Dorner, P. 1972. *Land Reforms and Economic Development* (Harmondsworth: Penguin Books).

Dorner, P. and D. Karnel. 1971. "The Economic Case for Land Reform: Employment, Income Distribution and Productivity," University of Wisconsin Land Tenure Center Reprint 74, Madison, WI.

Dorner, P. and W. C. Thiesenhusen. 1990. "Selected Land Reforms in East and Southeast Asia: Their Origins and Impacts," *Asian-Pacific Economic Literature*, 4(1), 65-.

Dorward, A. 1999. "Farm Size and Productivity in Malawian Smallholder Agriculture," *Journal of Development Studies*, 35(5), 141–161.

Doss, C., G. Summerfield and D. Tsikata. 2014. "Land, Gender, and Food Security," *Feminist Economics*, 20(1), 1–23.

Doss, C. R. 2001. "Designing Agricultural Technology for African Women Farmers: Lessons from 25 Years of Experience," *World Development*, 29(12), 2075–2092.

Doss, C. R. 2018. "Women and Agricultural Productivity: Reframing the Issues," *Development Policy Review*, 36(1), 35–50.

Faruqee, R. and K. Carey. 1997. "Land Markets in South Asia: What Have We Learned," World Bank Research Paper No. 1754, Washington D.C.

Foster, A. D. and M. R. Rosenzweig. 2017. "Are There Too Many Farms in the World? Labor Market Transaction Costs, Machine Capacities," and Optimal Farm Size," National Bureau of Economic Research Working Paper 23909, Cambridge, MA.

Frankema, E. 2014. "Africa and the Green Revolution A Global Historical Perspective," *NJAS – Wageningen Journal of Life Sciences*, 70–71(December), 17–24.

Freebairn, D. K. 1995. "Did the Green Revolution Concentrate Incomes? A Quantitative Study of Research Reports," *World Development*, 23(2), 265–279.

Gaurav, S. and S. Mishra. 2015. "Farm Size and Returns to Cultivation in India: Revisiting an Old Debate," *Oxford Development Studies*, 43(2), 165–193.

GRAIN. 2011. "Rice Land Grabs Undermine Food Sovereignty in Africa," *Development*, 54(1), 31–34.

Griffen, K. 1974. *The Political Economy of Agrarian Change: An Essay on the Green Revolution* (New York: Palgrave Macmillan).

Hall, D. C., B. P. Baker, J. Franco and D. A. Jolly. 1989. "Organic Food and Sustainable Agriculture," *Contemporary Economic Policy*, 7(4), 47–72.

Harris, J. R. and M. P. Todaro. 1970. "Migration, Unemployment and Development: A Two-Sector Analysis," *The American Economic Review*, 60(1), 126–142.

Heltberg, R. 1998. "Rural Market Imperfections and the Farm Size-Productivity Relationship: Evidence from Pakistan," *World Development*, 26(10), 1807–1826.

Herring, R. J. 2007. "Stealth Seeds: Bioproperty, Biosafety, Biopolitics," *Journal of Development Studies*, 43(1), 130–157.

Herring, R. J. 2015. "Politics of Biotechnology: Ideas, Risk, and Interest in Cases from India," *AgBioForum*, 18(2), 142–155.

Holt-Gemenez, E. 2008. "Out of AGRA: The Green Revolution Returns to Africa," *Development*, 51(4), 464–471.

Iscan, T. B. 2018. "Redistributive Land Reform and Structural Change in Japan, South Korea, and Taiwan," *American Journal of Agricultural Economics*, 100(3), 732–761.

Jeon, Y.-D. and Y.-Y. Kim. 2000. "Land Reform, Income Redistribution, and Agricultural Production in Korea," *Economic Development and Cultural Change*, 48(2), 253–268.

Johl, S. S. 1975. "Gains of the Green Revolution: How They Have Been Shared in Punjab," *Journal of Development Studies*, 11(3), 178–189.

Johnson, D. G. 2002. "Biotechnology Issues for Developing Economies," *Economic Development and Cultural Change*, 51(1), 1–4.

Johnston, B. and T. P. Tomich. 1985. "Agricultural Strategies and Agrarian Structure," *Asian Development Review*, 13(2), 1–37.

Johnston, B. F. and P. Kilby. 1975. *Agriculture and Structural Economic Strategies in Late-Developing Countries* (New York: Oxford University Press).

Johnston, D. and H. Le Roux. 2007. "Leaving the Household Out of Family Labour? the Implications for the Size-Efficiency Debate," *European Journal of Development Research*, 19(3), 355–371.

Kagin, J., J. Taylor and Y. A. Edward. 2016. "Inverse Productivity or Inverse Efficiency? Evidence from Mexico," *Journal of Development Studies*, 52(3), 396–411.

Knight, F. H. 1921. *Risk, Uncertainty, and Profit* (Boston, MA: Houghton Mifflin Company).

Krieger, T. and D. Meierrieks. 2016. "Land Grabbing and Ethnic Conflict," *Homo Oecon*, 33(3), 243–260.

Lastarria-Cornheil, S. 1997. "Impact of Privatization on Gender and Property Rights in Africa," *World Development*, 25(8), 1317–1333.

Lipton, M. 2007. "Plant Breeding and Poverty: Can Transgenic Seeds Replicate the Green Revolution' as a Source of Gains for the Poor?" *Journal of Development Studies*, 43(1), 31–62.

Majd, M. G. 1987. "Land Reform Policies in Iran," *American Journal of Agricultural Economics,"*, 69(4), 843–848.

Majd, M. G. 1989. "Land Reform Policies in Iran: Reply," *American Journal of Agricultural Economics*, 71(4), 1050–1053.

Mellor, J. W. 1966. *The Economics of Agricultural Development* (Ithaca, NY: Cornell University Press).

Muller, A. 2009. "Benefits of Organic Agriculture as a Climate Change Adaptation and Mitigation Strategy for Developing Countries," Environment for Development Discussion Paper Series, EfD DP 09-09, School of Business Economics and Law, University of Gothenburg, Gothenburg.

Nin-Pratt, A. and L. McBride. 2014. "Agricultural Intensification in Ghana: Evaluating the Optimist's Case for a Green Revolution," *Food Policy*, 48(October), 153–167.

Pak, H. K. 1955. "Pak Outcome of Land Reform in the Republic of Korea," *Journal of Farm Economics*, 38(4), 1015–1023.

Parmar, A., 2003. "Micro-Credit, Empowerment, and Agency: Re-evaluating the Discourse," *Canadian Journal of Development Studies*, 24(3), 461–476.

Pray, C. E. and A. Naseem. 2007. "Supplying Crop Biotechnology to the Poor: Opportunities and Constraints," *Journal of Development Studies*, 43(1), 192–217.

Pretty, J. N. 1995. "Participatory Learning for Sustainable Agriculture," *World Development*, 23(8), 1247–1263.

Pretty, J. N. 1998. "Toward More Conducive Policies for Sustainable Agriculture," in: E. Lutz. (ed.), *Agriculture and the Environment: Perspectives on Sustainable Rural Development* (Washington, DC: The World Bank) 35-49.

Prosterman, R. L. and J. M. Riedinger. 1987. *Land Reforms and Democratic Development* (Baltimore, MD: Johns Hopkins University Press).

Puttaswamaiah, S., I. Manns and A. Shah. 2006. "Promoting Sustainable Agriculture: Experiences from India and Canada," *Journal of Economic and Social Development*, 8(2), 147–176.

Quisumbing, A. R. and L. Pandolfelli. 2010. "Promising Approaches to Address the Needs of Poor Female Farmers: Resources, Constraints, and Interventions," *World Development*, 38(4), 581–592.

Rao, N. C., C. E. Pray and R. J. Herring. 2015. "Biotechnology for a Second Green Revolution in India: Socioeconomic, Political, and Public Policy Issues," *AgBioForum*, 18(2), 126–141.

Ruttan, V. W. 1969. "Equity and Productivity Issues in Modern Agrarian Reform Legislation," in: U. Papi and C. Nunn. (eds.), *Economic Problems of Agriculture in Industrial Societies* (New York: St. Martin's Press) 501-685.

Ruttan, V. W. 2002. "Controversy about Agricultural Technology: Lessons from the Green Revolution," Department of Applied Economics, College of Agricultural, Food and Environmental Sciences Staff Paper P02-15, Minneapolis, MN.

Sanders, R. 2006. "A Market Road to Sustainable Agriculture? Ecological Agriculture, Green Food and Organic Agriculture in China," *Development and Change*, 37(1), 201–226.

Sandhu, G. R. 1993. "Sustainable Agriculture," A Pakistan National Conservation Strategy Sector Paper, International Union for the Conservation of Nature and Environment and Urban Affairs Division, Karachi.

Schultz, T. W. 1964. *Transforming Traditional Agriculture* (New Haven, CT: Yale University Press).

Sen, G. and C. Grown. 1987. *Development, Crises, and Alternative Visions* (New York: Monthly Review Press).

Shelton, A. M. 2007. "Considerations on the Use of Transgenic Crops for Insect Control," *Journal of Development Studies*, 43(5), 890–900.

Thomas, G. and J. De Tavernier. 2017. "Farmer-suicide in India: Debating the Role of Biotechnology," *Life Sciences, Society and Policy*, 13(8), online edition, www.ncbi.nlm.nih.gov/pmc/articles/PMC5427059/, consulted 12/9/2018 .

van Veen, T. W. S., W. Forno, S. Joffe, D. L. Umali-Deininger and S. Cooke. 1998. "Integrated Pest Management; Strategies and Policies for Effective Implementation," in: E. Lutz. (ed.), *Agriculture and the Environment: Perspectives on Sustainable Rural Development* (Washington, DC: World Bank) 242-253.

Verma, R. 2014. "Land Grabs, Power, and Gender in East and Southern Africa: So, What's New?" *Feminist Economics*, 20(1), 52–75.

Verschelde, M., M. D'Haese, G. Rayp and E. Vandamme. 2013. "Challenging Small-Scale Farming: A Non-parametric Analysis of the (inverse) Relationship between Farm Productivity and Farm Size in Burundi," *Journal of Agricultural Economics*, 64(2), 319–342.

Wang, J., K. Z. Chen, S. Das Gupta and Z. Huang. 2015. "Is Small Still Beautiful? A Comparative Study of Rice Farm Size and Productivity in China and India," *China Agricultural Economic Review*, 7(3), 484–509.

Weir, D. and M. Schapiro. 1981. *Circle of Poison* (San Francisco, CA: Institute of Food and Development Policy).

Wolford, W., S. M. Borras, J. R. Hall, I. Scoones and B. White. 2013. "Governing Global Land Deals: The Role of the State in the Rush for Land," *Development and Change*, 44(2), 189–210.

World Bank, Food and Agricultural Organization, International Fund for Agricultural Development. 2009. *Gender in Agriculture: Source Book* (Washington, DC: World Bank).

Zilberman, D., H. Ameden and M. Qaim. 2007. "The Impact of Agricultural Biotechnology on Yields, Risks, and Biodiversity in Low-income Countries," *Journal of Development Studies*, 43(1), 63–78.

14

DEBATES ON TECHNOLOGY AND ADDRESSING ENVIRONMENTAL PROBLEMS/GREEN INDUSTRIAL POLICY

Introduction

Just as in agriculture, closing the gap between L/LMICs and HICs industrial value added per worker is a key concern of policy makers in L/LMICs.[1] The role of technology is central to attaining this objective even more so than in agriculture. However, as in agriculture, closing the productivity gap now needs to be done in a sustainable way as the reality of global climate change looms ever larger. All countries are on notice that their inaction regarding the climate problem is being observed and all should therefore confront global pressures.

On December 12, 2015, at the Conference of Parties (COP) 21 meetings in Paris, which included virtually all countries of the world, the United Nations Framework Convention on Climate Change (UNFCCC) reached a landmark agreement (Paris Agreement) to combat climate change and "to accelerate and intensify the actions and investments needed for a sustainable low carbon future".[2] The Paris Agreement requires all Parties to put forward their best efforts through "nationally determined contributions" and to strengthen these efforts in the years ahead.[3]

The main aim of the Paris Agreement is to strengthen the global response to the threat of climate change by keeping a global temperature rise in the 21st century well below 2 degrees Celsius above pre-industrial levels and to pursue efforts to limit the temperature increase even further to 1.5 degrees Celsius. It agreed to assist L/LMICs to deal with the impacts of climate change via the appropriate provision of financial resources, technology and enhanced capacity-building based on their "nationally determined contributions" to the global climate challenge. The Agreement also provided for an enhanced transparency framework for action and support and an important step in this regard was taken by the COP 24 meetings in Katowice, Poland.

An important outcome of the December 15, 2018 Katowice Agreement was that all countries would agree to a common format or transparent reporting of what has been attained with regards to the nationally determined targets. After the Katowice Agreement, going forward the world was expected to watch what all countries were doing to address the global climate problem.[4] This Agreement imposed a voluntary binding constraint on the policy framework L/LMICs adopt for all sectors and subsectors, but particularly the primary sectors (including agriculture as a key subsector) and industry.

As noted in Chapter 13, the acknowledgement of a symbiotic relation of industry and agriculture was acknowledged by developmentalists. There is also acknowledgement that for some HICs like Denmark and New Zealand, agriculture has and continues to play a key role in generating exports. Nonetheless, as explained in Chapter 9, new developmentalists still view industry as crucial to catch-up growth because many more industrial sector activities yield increasing returns. Further, they argue that industrialization is the path to diversifying the economy and moving up the value chain. This path is now constrained by meeting climate goals and so the issue of what technology to adopt is crucial. The new developmentalist advocacy of industrial policy discussed in Chapter 9, while still a relevant perspective, now needs to be conditioned by climate commitments undertaken in international agreements.

As for agriculture in Chapter 13, this chapter first identifies the size of the labor productivity gap between HICs and L/LMICs in industry. It next reviews the key development economics debates on technology in industry. These still have salience but less so due to the climate constraint. While an overwhelming agreement on the part of the scientific community and mounting evidence resulted in economists acknowledging the importance of addressing environmental issues, perspectives on how to do so vary, and these perspectives apply also to technology adoption in industry and so this debate on sustainability is reviewed.

In development economics, green industrial policy was advocated after the turn of the century and the associated literature is reviewed to identify if multiple wins are possible as in sustainable or green agriculture. Finally, apart from the climate challenge, automation is another key challenge likely to impact the future of industry in L/LMICs. While much of this literature focuses on HICs, automation is likely to have some bearing on industrialization in L/LMICs as well and so this potential challenge is explored.

Productivity gap

Recall from Chapter 13 that the labor productivity gap in agriculture between LICs and HICs is 26-fold and this labor productivity gap in industry at 25-fold is very similar, as evident from Table 14.1.

Data on the size of the manufacturing base are also included in the table since developmentalists (also new developmentalists) viewed manufacturing as the source of economic dynamism (Chapters 6 and 9). South Asia and Sub-Saharan Africa have the lowest manufacturing base at close to single digits.

The data confirm the process of structural change introduced in Chapter 1. Thus, as expected, the manufacturing base increases with income category and declines subsequently when HIC status has been attained. UMICs have the

TABLE 14.1 Background industrial and manufacturing statistics by country classification and region

Country classification and region	Industry value added per worker (constant 2010, US$) (2016)	Industry value added as a % of GDP (2016)	Manufacturing value added as a % of GDP (2016)
LIC	3,675.3	29.7	9.3
LMIC	7,543.5	28.0	15.7
UMIC	23,736.1	32.6	19.9
HIC	90,990.1	22.9	14.3
EA&P	27,253.5	33.6	23.2
LA&C	24,500.2	23.9	13.0
ME&NA	43,441.2	37.2	11.1
SA	5,635.6	25.7	15.0
SSA	9,776.2	22.5	10.0
China	22,107.0	28.8	39.9

Source: World Development Indicators.
Notes: Industry includes construction
LIC   = Low income countries ($995 or less annual per capita gross national income).
LMIC   = Lower middle income countries ($996–$4,035)
UMIC   = Upper middle income countries ($4,036–$12,475)
HIC   = High income countries (above $12,476)
EE&P   = East Asia and the Pacific
E&CA = Europe and Central Asia
LA&C = Latin America and the Caribbean
ME&NA = Middle East and North Africa.
SA   = South Asia
SSA   = Sub-Saharan Africa

largest manufacturing base, which is about twice as large as LICs. Middle Eastern and North African countries have an impressive industrial base but much of it represents mining and petroleum. Its manufacturing base is more akin to that of LICs. Similarly, the Latin American region has a much smaller manufacturing base compared to industry.

Data for China are included in the table since it represents the transition from LIC status in the 1970s to UMIC status currently (2019) and its trajectory represents a path many L/LMICs aspire to. In this regard they have a long way to go since China's manufacturing base, past its peak of 32.5 attained in 2006, is still about three times higher than LICs.[5]

In the earlier development economics literature, technology was expected to play a central role in closing the productivity gap in industry between L/LMICs and HICs and the next section reviews the relevant debates on technology.

Historic debates on technology[6]

The debates on technology associated with industrialization pertain to causes and scale of industrial employment and unemployment. Static neoclassical analysis of technology in the L/LMIC context focuses on the efficient allocation of resources. Figure 14.1 shows unemployment in L/LMICs resulting from factor market distortions.

Figure 14.1 shows a convex isoquant and a straight line isocost in labor (L) and capital (K) space. The isoquant represents the available technology to produce a commodity and as such represents a menu of choices to produce a given level of output. Iso thus stands for the "same" output with different combinations of capital and labor and each combination representing a technique. Thus the right technique to draw from the available technology to produce a particular product is governed by factor prices, as represented by the isocost line.

Iso in the case of an isocost line means that the cost is identical for different factor use at given factor prices. In this simple two-factor model, cost is represented by $w \times L + r \times K$ where w stands for the wage rate and r the cost of capital.[7] Thus as one moves along the isocost line the cost does not change and so change can be represented by $w \times \Delta L + r \times \Delta K = 0$. Following on from this, the slope of the isocost line is $\Delta K / \Delta L = -(w/r)$. This line rotates if factor prices change and the tangency of the isocost with the isoquant would be at a different point and thus represent a different choice of technique. Thus if wages rise, the factor price ratio would become steeper as it rotates from $-(w_1/r_1)$ to $-(w_2/r_1)$ and this would cause a move away from a relatively labor-intensive technique A to a more capital-intensive technique B. The gap between labor hired due to a change in technique (L_2) and the available labor force (L_F) represents higher unemployment resulting from the inappropriate choice of technique, as shown in Figure 14.1.

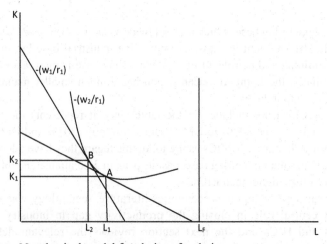

FIGURE 14.1 Neoclassical model for choice of technique

Neoliberal economists adopted this analysis and argued that higher capital intensity in L/LMICs results from policies that under-price capital and over-price labor. The under-pricing of capital could result from overvalued exchange rates, interest rate subsidies and tax incentives for capital use such as accelerated depreciation. Labor could be over-priced due to labor legislation such as minimum wages and mandatory benefits and also from unions representing labor to secure higher wages.

Thus the universal neoliberal prescription for adopting the right techniques is to get factor prices right. The various options implicit in this prescription and ones frequently found in structural adjustment conditionalities (Chapter 8) are wage repression, interest rate liberalization, devaluing the exchange rate and removing capital subsidies.

Neoliberal economists believe that the elasticity of factor substitution, the responsiveness of the factor use ratio to factor prices, is relatively high. If the isoquant curve in Figure 14.1 is flat then substitution is not easily forthcoming, but if it is deep, substitution possibilities are more easily forthcoming. This is so because it would take a large change in factor prices to attain a limited change in factor use if the isoquant is flat and vice versa. Elasticity optimists assume a deep isoquant while elasticity pessimists assume a flat one, as shown in Figure 14.2.

Ultimately, if the model is realistic, the validity of the policy prescriptions depend on the evidence regarding how flat or deep the isoquant is or on the responsiveness of factor use to factor prices (see below). The elasticity optimists argue that the analysis needs to be disaggregated rather than conducted at say an industry level (e.g. textiles) since substitution possibility at finer levels of disaggregation also need to be explored (e.g. yarn, linen, garments). Further, they argued that substitution possibilities are also available within processes at finer levels of disaggregation and so while it may make sense to adopt a capital-intensive container system for handling cargo, adopting forklifts when labor is cheap may not.

The logic of this neoclassical model for prescribing the optimal technique is criticized by other schools of thought. Recall from Chapter 4 the theoretical

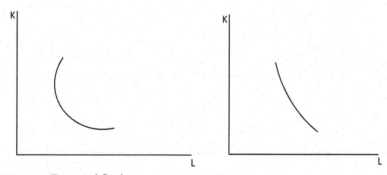

FIGURE 14.2   Deep and flat isoquants

critique by heterodox economists who claim that it is not possible to aggregate factors of production, particularly capital. Another theoretical critique, among others, is that it is not possible to uniquely identify factor prices with factor use.[8] These theoretical critiques call into question the validity of using the neoclassical model to identify optimal techniques.

Structuralists called into question the existence of smooth continuous isoquants as shown in Figure 14.1. They argued instead that at best a few techniques constitute the technological options available to an industry. In the limit, if there is just one technique available, then there would be no substitution possibilities because the isoquant would be L-shaped, referred to in the literature as emanating from the Leontief fixed coefficients production function.[9] While the general form of a two-factor neoclassical production function can be written as $Y = F(K,L)$ (i.e. output Y as a function of variable labor and capital), the Leontief production function is written as $Y = \min(aK,bL)$. Thus the minimum of the two factors defines the output forthcoming. The factor use is defined as $K = Y/a$, and $L = Y/b$ respectively. These coefficients determine how much L and K are simultaneously needed to get a given Y. Given L, more K will not raise Y and vice versa. This implies zero substitution of factor inputs as factor prices change, as shown in Figure 14.3.

Figure 14.3 shows two isocost lines tangential to the L-shaped isoquant. This implies that as factor prices change, factor use remains unchanged. For developmentalists this means that investment is an all or nothing proposition (i.e. subject to discontinuity and thresholds) and because of high risk and high capital requirements, the state may initially need to make such investments until private businesses gain confidence from state activity and move into the industry.

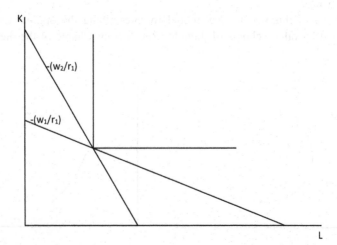

FIGURE 14.3 Leontief production function

If technology for an industry constitutes three or four techniques, factor substitution in response to factor price change would hold but in ranges as shown in Figure 14.4a. A good way of contrasting the outcome of this assumption with the neoclassical model is that the demand for any factor (say K) based on the choice of a technique would be a step function rather than a smooth and continuous downward sloping linear curve, as shown in Figure 14.4b (Stewart, 1972).

The isoquant in Figure 14.4a is based on the assumption of three techniques constituting the available technology in a given industry. The isoquant is segmented such that two segments converge to a technique i.e. A, B or C representing more to less capital intensity. For a range of factor prices, technique C will be used corresponding to the use of K_1 capital. As the price of capital continues to fall (steeper isocost line), there will be a tipping point such that there will be a jump to a more capital-intensive technique B. If the price of capital continues to fall, technique C will be opted for.

The corresponding demand for capital shown in Figure 14.4b is downward sloping but segmented. For a range of the price of capital (r_1 to r_2), capital use will be K_1 corresponding to technique C. Once the tipping point is reached and the price of capital drops below r_2, the demand for capital increases to K_2 corresponding to technique B and so on. In this altered structuralist model, factor prices still impact factor use but not in the smooth continuous way suggested by the neoclassical model. Again, this may vary by industry and ultimately the choice of model would need to be determined by the evidence.

Recall from introductory microeconomics, cost minimization is the flip side of profit maximization. Institutional economists (more recently behavioral economists) have challenged the underlying postulates and assumptions of neoclassical economics (rationality, profit maximizaton, perfect competition). For example, Nobel Prize winning scholar, Herbert A. Simon, argued that firms engage in "satisficing" rather than maximizing or optimizing behavior and this would be reflected in the choice of technique opted for.

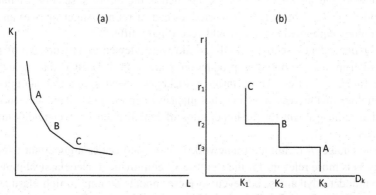

FIGURES 14.4a and b Segmented isoquant and corresponding factor demand curve

Even if the logic of the neoclassical model does not hold but capital intensity is nonetheless an empirical reality in L/LMICs, alternative explanations for this phenomenon need to be explored. In a HIC context, neoclassical economists argue that the evolution of technology is neutral and a "natural" outcome of the market mechanism. Thus labour scarcity has induced the search for capital-intensive technology and more lately for automation.[10]

Rifkin (1995) pointed out that the opening salvo on the non-neutrality of technology was that of Marx. Capitalists fund the development of labor-displacing technology to enhance profits but also to add to the reserve army of the unemployed to better control labor and reduce the wage bill to enhance profits. Machines directly facilitate control as machine-paced operations make oversight easier and they can also eliminate labor management conflict by displacing "troublesome" labor.[11] While this debate was conducted in an HIC context, the desire on the part of industrialists to weaken labor bargaining power and undermine unions also applies to L/LMICs.

Structuralists (Chapter 7) argued that high capital intensity resulted from impaired employment or low worker productivity. The causes for this included low nutrition, health and education, and this would give employers an incentive to opt for more capital intensive technology because these deficiencies would result in marginal productivity being below a subsistence wage.

Another reason for capital intensity was the lack of competition due to crony capitalism or the market power of MNCs which enabled the use of capital-intensive technology even if labor-intensive technologies were more economical despite the incentives for capital use. The lack of competition meant cost minimization was not an imperative and they had other reasons for preferring capital intensity as explained above.

For institutional economists technology is embodied in the product and the consumption pattern determines what will be produced. Given high levels of income inequality in L/LMICs (based on existing distribution of income and property rights), the production pattern in the modern sector caters to the tastes of the rich and such products are inherently capital intensive.[12] In a dual economy framework the substitute products consumed in the informal sectors (Chapter 3) would differ (e.g. brown sugar or rice instead of refined sugar or rice) and the technology embodied in them would accordingly differ.[13]

For dependency scholars, FDI and aid were viewed as instruments of post-colonialism that imposed a production pattern in L/LMICs that suited the ex-colonial countries. Thus, through kickbacks MNCs induced adoption of technology that increased their capital-intensive exports and tied aid was similarly used as an instrument for the importation of capital-intensive technology into L/LMICs.

The choice of technique framework is static and critics argued that dynamic analysis is more relevant for the analyses of employment. Neoclassical tools can accommodate dynamics, but even so these models assume a high elasticity of factor substitution.[14]

For heterodox economists, the concept of elasticity of factor substitution is meaningless, as explained above. However, if one accepts the model in principle and the structuralist economists are right, this elasticity of factor substitution should be low or close to zero. However, if the neoclassical economists are right, the elasticity should be quite high. Technology varies by industry and the evidence suggests that the elasticity varies between .5 and 1.[15]

In dynamic models the elasticity of factor substitution is only one of the variables that impact factor use in a given sector. For the modern sector, using Lewis's framework (Chapter 6), another key variable is the growth in the demand for labor. This in turn depends on the size of the modern sector and the growth of the modern sector itself. Thus even if the elasticity is on the higher end of the range reported above, its impact on factor use on the demand side is limited and the prescription of "getting factor prices right" can only have a limited impact.

Another major contributor to the debate on technology was Schumacher (1974), who also eschewed the neoclassical model. Schumacher was among the first development economists to give voice to the growing ecological concerns being expressed in the early 1970s, and he is notable for his advocacy of holistic development. His main concern was that modern production technology was on a collision course with nature and the ecological system. This collision was even more likely due to the aspirations of poor countries to engage in catch-up growth.

He viewed western technology as a villain of the modern world because it caused environmental degradation, exhaustion of non-renewable resources and, echoing Marx, imposed a rigid and alienating way of life on individuals. Schumacher made several prescient contributions to the development economics literature, but his enduring legacy was the coining of the term "intermediate technology" and the movement this initiated.[16]

Such technology, he argued, fit between primitive and advanced capital-intensive modern technology to address the rural and urban informal sector unemployment problem. Schumacher turned the economic problem on its head. Instead of maximizing production and consumption (profits and utility), he proposed organizing the economy around maximizing meaningful jobs. For LICs, this would mean using intermediate technology that was eco-sensitive, inexpensive, easily accessible, small scale, labor intensive, indigenously developed and maintained and compatible with the human need for creativity. The "work places" created with such technology would conserve on capital, foreign exchange (use local materials), skills, finance and marketing, organization and supervision.

He argued that employment is the precondition of everything else in a market economy and so a market would be assured.[17] Those willing to develop intermediate technology would find applications in water and power, crop storage, food processing, health and transport. Thus, a new agro-industrial culture could be created.

While Schumacher viewed mainstream economists as wrong-headed, they in turn saw him as a pariah. Even heterodox economists opposed his ideas and a prominent early critic was Emmanuel (1976) who viewed appropriate or intermediate technology as anti-development since it would relegate underdeveloped countries to backwardness. Developmentalists and new developmentalists view dynamic efficiencies of industrialization to be forthcoming from large-scale industry (Chapters 6 and 9) and hence are not supportive of redirecting resources to small-scale initiatives like microcredit (self-employment) or even small-scale industry (Chang, 2011).

Even if the advocacy of intermediate technology did not persuade many development scholars, the evidence on climate change has vindicated Schumacher. As mentioned, in a development context his concern in the early 1970s was with how inappropriate technology could devastate the local environment in L/LMICs. While his concern as such was not directly with the impacts of global climate change, heeding his advice would have addressed the climate problem since the emissions that degrade the local environment also impact the global climate. Starting in the later decades of the 20th century, economists started to address environmental concerns, but perspectives on how to do so vary.

Debates on analyzing and addressing environmental problems[18]

Natural resource economics and environmental economics represent neoclassical fields and draw on its analytical tools as in the case of "choice of techniques". Natural resource economics focuses on the optimal flow into production of raw materials derived from the land and water bodies (e.g. mines, forests, oceans). There are tradeoffs regarding extraction rates based on current and expected interest rates and output and input prices. Sustainability enters the picture when future generations are taken into consideration i.e. to leave them no worse off in terms of access.

Because of fixed supply, non-renewable resources yield scarcity rents and in principle these could be used to compensate losers from the pollution and environmental degradation associated with resource extraction. Examples include sovereign wealth funds established first by Norway and then many other resource-rich countries for the well-being of future generations. Alaska has established a Permanent Fund, which makes annual payments to residents. The amount varies and the largest dividend ever paid was in 2000 and amounted to $2,844 in 2017 dollars per person.[19] The state also uses the Fund to build infrastructure such as roads, telecommunications and a better education system that will benefit future generations.

Environmental economics focuses on impacts of resource use and policies to minimize impacts and redress problems. More production is acknowledged to generate harm in the form of pollution of the air, water and soil and cause deforestation. These negative effects are called externalities and represent social costs imposed on society and are as such acknowledged to be a market failure. Historically producers in HICs did not have to pay for the costs they imposed on society and this continues to be the case in L/LMICs due to low enforcement capacity even if environmental regulations exist.

The profit motive is not the sole cause of environmental degradation. The Soviet Union and China operated without a profit motive as such and had an even worse environmental record than high income market economies. Thus the lack of restraints is a key issue and regulations or taxes could ensure that firms internalize social costs within the market framework. This is referred to as the "polluter pay principle". Without polluters paying for the costs they impose on society, they produce too much from a social viewpoint. If marginal costs are raised by say well-tailored taxes so that marginal revenue is brought into equality with the marginal private plus social costs, this would result in better social outcomes in so far as lower production is associated with lower pollution.

Environmental economists argue for an optimal amount of pollution and do not view zero pollution as realistic or desirable. They propose a decision-making framework whereby the pollution abatement cost is equated with environmental damage on the margin. This framework is shown in Figure 14.5.

The horizontal axis on Figure 14.5 indicates environmental damage (ED) while the vertical axis shows the marginal damage curve (MD) and the marginal abatement cost (MAC). Both the latter curves are nonlinear suggesting exponentially rising environmental damage and the abatement cost of addressing it. The origin represents zero environmental damage and so the MAC becomes exponentially higher the closer the curve gets to the vertical axis. Optimal ED on the horizontal axis (ED*) in this framework corresponds to where the two curves intersect such that at the margin the cost of abatement is equal to environmental damage. As technology improves, the MAC curve is expected to shift down resulting in a lower optimal ED.[20]

Environmental economists argue that attaining environmental objectives can best be attained by giving producers a choice rather than by prescribing a specific method for attaining a particular outcome. Thus, if policy makers set emission targets, this can result in a superior economic outcome since it gives producers an incentive to develop the technologically lowest cost method to meet targets (lower MAC in Figure 14.5).

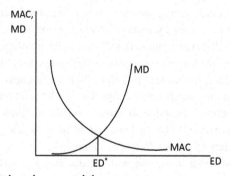

FIGURE 14.5 Optimal environmental damage

The question of how much to restrain production is determined in individual projects though environmental impact analyses. In exploring project impacts, the decision making embedded in social cost-benefit analysis relies on the neoclassical analytical framework. In this framework, the social benefits are to be balanced on the margin with the social costs of production. If mitigation is called for via regulation, the social benefits for example are better health, productivity, more working days from lower morbidity and higher life expectancy, and a better environment for animals and plants (i.e. benefits resulting from curtailing the direct costs of pollution).[21]

These benefits can be quantified based on the average salaries of those impacted and are expected to be subject to diminishing returns from pollution abatement. Apart from direct abatement or mitigation costs, since the externalities are a byproduct of producing goods that society desires, fewer goods represent benefits foregone or a social cost of abatement. In an unregulated world, consumers receive an implicit subsidy in the form of lower prices. Since consumers will have to bear part of the costs in the form of higher prices or lower consumer surplus, this loss is also part of the social cost-benefit calculus.[22]

While negative externalities are the most commonly acknowledged market failure by neoclassical economists, others resulting from ill-defined property rights and public goods are acknowledged to exacerbate the problem of attaining solutions to environmental problems. The "tragedy of the commons" is a term coined by Hardin (1968) pertaining to "open access" resources such as the air and oceans. The degradation of marine fisheries is an example of such a tragedy and economists believe this happens due to the lack of defined property rights. Fisherfolk do not have an incentive to conserve because, in their view, doing so only means others will benefit from their conservation. In situations like this, no market outcome is possible. The same applies to the atmosphere; no nation has an incentive to leave it clean for others to pollute and hence greenhouse gases like carbon dioxide, nitrous oxide and methane are difficult to contain at a global level without global treaties with some enforcement mechanism.

Another related market failure that can complicate attaining a solution to environmental problems is referred to as a "free rider" problem that results from public goods. Such goods are non-rivalrous in consumption (consumption by one does not preclude consumption by others e.g. biodiversity; although the capacity to enjoy it may vary by income level) and non-excludable. Thus, if the air is cleaned, all will benefit and this makes a market solution difficult in that individuals have an incentive to understate the benefit they derive from policy action such as cleaning the air and therefore their willingness to pay for it. Free riding is involved in this case because those who work for a solution, via activism or otherwise, will confer benefits on those who do nothing. Self-interest is a postulate regarding average human behavior in neoclassical economics and in these cases such behavior proves to be problematic.

Institutional economists took issue with Hardin. Based on empirical work from around the world, scholars showed that there is much more collective action than the self-interest postulate governing neoclassical theory may suggest. Ostrom (1990, 1997), a political scientist and also the first woman to receive a Nobel Prize in Economics, accumulated a body of work demonstrating such collective action. She argued that cooperative behavior results from traditions and norms for protecting community resources such as forests and pasturelands. Household have rights to the "commons" such as pasturelands and forests even though these do not constitute individual property rights. Collective action could still be argued to be self-interested behavior as is "free riding" on the other end of the spectrum of human behavior. Part of collective action is minimizing free riding via community sanctions to prevent collective action from breaking down. While institutional economists have shown that communities can self-police for conservation where some property rights exist, such rights do not exist for "open access" resources, and conservation as suggested above would require national regulations or international treaties.

Ecological economists adopt a "strong sustainability" perspective, which is one whereby the environment should not erode at all. Thus they do not accept the neoclassical environmental economics "weak sustainability" tradeoff whereby more human and physical capital can be traded off with some (optimal) degradation of environmental capital so long as total capital remains unchanged for future generations. Strong sustainability is derived from the need to ensure inter-generational justice i.e. future generations should receive a planet that is at least in its current form if not better.

Ecological economists are also very concerned with the innate value of species and also their value to humanity as genetic materials, medicines, natural pesticides and for other uses. Scientists had described about 8.7 million species (plant and animal) by 2011 (plus or minus one million) although the vast majority had not yet been documented at that point and cataloging all of them it was estimated would take another 1,000 years.[23] However, the rate of species loss is so rapid that many are expected to become extinct even before they are described. Thus preserving species and biological diversity rank high on ecological economist agendas.

Their focus is on ecosystems which provide beneficial services including water purification (water absorbs and breaks down toxins up to a limit), nutrient recycling (silt accompanies floods), waste processing (by water bodies), soil stabilization (by trees), pest and disease control (via genetic materials of plant species), disaster mitigation (via coral reefs and mangroves which can limit wave erosion of beaches and provide protection from hurricanes), and culture and recreation. In addition ecosystems yield resources such as food, water, fiber, timber and non-timber forest resources, and marine resources including fisheries.

Ecological economists emphasize the complexity of ecosystems and also how little humans still understand of their internal interactions. Ecosystem stresses like greenhouse gases can lead to catastrophic change and so, given this ignorance, they invoke the precautionary principle of not tampering with them. This principle is also invoked because they believe ecosystem services to be unique and the damage to ecosystems to be irreversible. Ecological economists also regard the assumptions underlying cost-benefit analyses that prescribe tradeoffs of natural for other forms of capital to be heroic and attempts at quantification often baseless. Thus while environmental economists are technology optimists and believe that the market responds to price signals and yields solutions, ecological economists are more pessimistic based on the observation of irreversible damage.

Ecological economists argue that the same economic decision-making logic that applies to individuals, firms and projects should also apply to national economies and the global economy. Growth provides benefits (i.e. greater prosperity for some citizens) but also imposes social costs. If the harm exceeds the benefits, the net value of growth is negative. They argue that growth that the planet can sustain has already been exceeded. They suggest that the existing population, consumption and hence resource use is beyond the earth's carrying capacity.[24] Earth provides *sources* (natural resources) for use and *sinks* (air, water, land) to absorb waste. Resources are becoming exhausted beyond replenishment from overuse, natural capital has degraded and sinks are becoming ineffective from saturation. Among other problems, they point to alarming losses in fresh water, habitat, species, tropical forests, biodiversity, fisheries, top soil (desertification) and forests. Ocean acidification and their saturation with plastics, ozone depletion, nitrogen-induced algae growth in water bodies and aquifer destruction are also serious problems.[25] In view of this global perspective and the reality of global imbalances, they are willing to entertain growth in L/LMICs to address poverty alleviation only if it is counter-balanced by reduced growth in HICs.

Like other heterodox economists, ecological economists recognize that insights from all disciplines are needed, including the social sciences, natural sciences and the humanities, for effective conservation (see Chapter 1 on method). For example, natural sciences come into play to understand climate change, but to understand impacts and adaption and to find solutions the social sciences and humanities are also central.

While ecological economists agree that distribution is important, it plays a central role in the analyses of the political economy of development practitioners. From their perspective, the key questions to ask in terms of any action or inaction are as follows: Who wins and who loses and by how much? Further, how are the gains and losses distributed by class or income group?

These questions and concerns distinguish the political economy of the development perspective from mainstream environmental economists who are willing to concede that there are winners and losers but see them as a homogeneous mass. As long as the winners are able in theory to compensate the losers, the social efficiency criterion (Pareto optimality) is satisfied and action or inaction justified. The problem of course is that the compensation is hypothetical and actual redistribution is left to policy makers and rarely happens.

For the political economist, the world is made up of heterogeneous individuals and they often act as groups or classes. In this regard, the rich are more economically powerful and therefore politically powerful. They also have more influence with the media and policy makers, if they do not directly control them, and therefore have the ability to limit or spin information. In such a world, decisions do not satisfy the Pareto optimality criteria.

This section broadly addressed alternative perspectives on tackling sustainability issues. The development economics literature on the issue of green industrial policy is relatively recent and picked up pace at the turn of the century as climate change started being taken seriously beyond just the scientific community. The prescriptions fit in best with the developmentalist approach discussed in Chapter 9, and the tools of industrial policy discussed there could be tailored to implement a green industrial policy.[26]

Green industrial policy[27]

Green industrial policy uses regulations and taxes in addition to the tools of conventional industrial policy such as subsidies and other incentives discussed in Chapter 9. In addition to diversifying the economy and moving up the value chain, the objectives now also include reducing the use of material inputs and the associated pollution. This is a big ask and one that could be forthcoming from using the appropriate processes and technologies.

Since such technologies are expected to generate positive externalities, there is in principle a case to subsidize their development and use. This is particularly so since the positive externalities in the climate change context accrue globally. In fact, this is why the Paris Agreement agreed in principle to a Green Climate Fund to assist the adoption and adaptation of green technologies in L/LMICs.[28]

Two critiques of industrial policy are often mentioned in the development economics literature (Chapter 9). First, that the state is incapable of "picking winners". Second, that the state lacks managerial ability to implement industrial policy, and this would also apply to green industrial policy. Both critiques were addressed in detail in Chapter 9 and those arguments will not be revisited here. However, the first critique is less relevant in the global climate change context since the winners are preselected as those that meet the objectives of green industrial policy specified above.

However, the question of why any particular L/LMIC government should sign up to a green industrial policy agenda needs to be answered. It is unlikely that their share from the Green Climate Fund after 2020, if forthcoming, will be a significant inducement in and of itself.[29] As signatories to the Paris Agreement, they may be subject to global peer pressure. However, this could be easily overruled by domestic politics due to resource scarcity and pressing short-term objectives.

The answer as to why governments should sign up to green industrial policy is similar to the case for green agriculture i.e. because in principle multiple wins are possible.[30] The evidence of a positive association of pollution of the air, water and soil with ill health is overwhelming. The World Bank (1999) estimated using data from China that the cost of saving a life is $300 using available abatement methods. Since then, one can safely assume that abatement or green technology has improved considerably as HICs have engaged in the race to be the first movers to develop green technologies for economic advantage (Janicke, 2012). Adding the benefits to health and productivity into this social cost-benefit calculus makes developing and adopting green technology in industry a "no brainer" from a policy perspective.[31] Reinforcing this is the evidence that prevention (green industry) is much cheaper than cure (clean up). L/LMICs do not have the resources to put in place programs like the Super Fund in the United States.[32] As industrialization picks up pace with catch-up growth, LMICs like China and India, which did not have adequate safeguards in place, have had to confront very angry citizenry demanding clean-ups and restraints (Chapter 4, endnote 32).

Of course even with industrial policy tools inducing adoption of clean technology and regulations requiring it, some businesses may be reluctant to adopt based on their knowledge of limited enforcement capacity. One policy option is the environmental protection agency imposing pollution charges on emissions (World Bank, 1999). The high social return justifies high charges and the logic is that this would incentivize businesses to opt for abatement technology. Where monitoring capacity is not highly developed, random audits, much as conducted by tax authorities, could be utilized.[33] These pollution charges not only cut emissions but generate public revenue as well, which could be directed to facilitating green industrial policy.

Another win from various green technologies results from their ability to green and conserve energy (using natural light and renewables), raw materials (realize economies, reduce chemical use, reuse and joint use) and water. Other economies can result from industrial symbiosis or circular production, whereby unwanted output or byproducts (such as steam and even carbon) are used elsewhere, integrated waste management and recycling. By providing cleaner and safer work environments, worker productivity is enhanced. All this can add up to significant cost savings and, for businesses, adopting the right kinds of green technology and practices is about generating economies rather than "doing good".[34]

Sultan (2013) documents a case study from Mauritius that relies heavily on the textile and clothing industry to generate jobs and foreign exchange. By adopting clean technology and practices, leading firms were able to generate substantial cost savings and reduce their carbon footprint by up to a third. As in the case of green agriculture, standard setting in HIC means that greening industry can win export markets.[35]

A key aspect of green industrial policy is making businesses aware of the multiple wins via extension services and incentivizing with subsidies and capital for the transition period. The multiple wins enhance the probability of securing a transition to green industry though the task is challenging. Unfortunately, addressing the oncoming automation challenge may be even more difficult for L/LMICs.

Automation[36] and industrialization in L/LMICs[37]

Much has been written about how the future of work is likely to be impacted in HICs due to automation.[38] More specifically, the worst case scenario is that automation may create mass unemployment in HICs. Since HICs are at the forefront of automation, not surprisingly there has been little attention to how automation might impact industrialization in L/LMICs. However, some studies have explored this and the findings are disquieting.

Oxford Martin School and Citi (2016, p. 18) indicated that 85 percent of the jobs in Ethiopia, 77 percent in China, 72 percent in Thailand, 69 percent in India, 67 percent in South Africa and 65 percent in Argentina and Nigeria are at risk of being replaced by automation. Chang and Huynh (2016) led an ILO study on the five largest Association of Southeast Asian Nations (ASEAN) countries. With some caveats, they found that 56 percent of all jobs were at risk of technological displacement over the next two decades or so. Further, they found that women, less-educated workers and lower-wage occupations were most at risk of displacement. World Bank (2016) reported that two-thirds of all jobs in developing countries could be automated in the coming decades. While estimates vary, there appears to be a consensus that the challenge that automation poses for L/LMICs could be large.

Automation could also be a force for de-globalization. Ford (2015) pointed out that between 2010 and 2012, US textile exports increased by 37 percent to $23 billion based on automation. For perspective, garment exports from Bangladesh were $21.5 billion in 2013 and represented 80 percent of the country's total exports while textile exports represented about 1 percent of total US exports in 2013.[39] Thus while the decline in the textile sector could be devastating for Bangladesh, it would only represent a marginal change for the US economy.[40] Ford observed that what is most remarkable about the US textile factories is a virtually empty shop floor due to automation.

Oxford Martin School and Citi (2016, p. 21) provided evidence of a reversal of product fragmentation that undergird value chain production and offshoring. Instead, the trend is of global reshoring of production to HICs of jobs that can be codified and hence routine and subject to automation. This is an impending threat to industrialization in L/LMICs.[41] L/LMICs have a limited amount of time to prepare for the challenge and education, training and skill development, to complement technological change, is the universal recommendation.

Summary and conclusions

The historic debates in development economics on technology are reviewed in this chapter. Following that, sustainability perspectives emerging from different schools of development economic thought are reviewed. These debates play into the core section that follows on green industrial policy.

Chapter 13 ended on an optimistic note. While politically difficult, attaining sustainable agriculture represents a multiple win scenario and therefore is potentially attractive for policy makers. The questioned framed at the end of Chapter 13 was whether multiple wins were also possible for industry. The research on this issue suggests that the answer is in the affirmative. The key conclusion emerging from this chapter is that it is still possible for L/LMICs to industrially diversify their economies and move up the value chain even as they constrain themselves to meet the Paris Agreement self-declared targets. As in agriculture, the push for sustainability is likely to be facilitated by the global pressure to meet voluntarily agreed to targets.

Correctly framing sustainability is important. For example, the narrative of winning export markets by greening industrial policy is framing the issue as a zero-sum game. One helpful narrative is that green industrial policy could be seen as a solution for premature deindustrialization or breaking out of the middle income trap (Chapter 10). The multi-win narrative, if supported by evidence as it appears to be, is also helpful since the framing is that of a global solution for a global problem.

Rapid automation in HICs in the wake of the information and digital revolution represents a threat to the industrialization project in L/LMICs. Jobs that were once taken for granted due to low wages may be resourced back to HICs and this threatens impoverishment to those already in low income status. Thus L/LMICs are in a race against time to transition to green agriculture and industry. How they might go about attaining this has been the subject of this textbook and is synthesized in the concluding chapter that follows.

Questions

1. Consider the debate on technology. Which approach do you consider most persuasive and why?
2. Capital intensity in LICs is viewed as one of the main causes of unemployment. Explain how perspectives on the causes of capital intensity differ and therefore how the proposed solutions for unemployment differ.
3. Explain a perspective on technology that would make the concept of the elasticity of factor substitution irrelevant.
4. Explain how the dynamic extension of neoclassical theory implies limits to factor substitution as a possible solution for unemployment. Discuss alternate solutions to the unemployment problem that pertain to raising the elasticity of employment with respect to output.
5. Explain the concept of appropriate technology, its overlap with the concept of sustainable development and its limitations.
6. Consider the debate on sustainability. Which approach do you consider most persuasive and why?
7. Do you consider the developmentalist approach to economic development (recall from Chapter 9) relevant for catch-up growth in the 21st century? Explain your answer.
8. Explain how green industrial policy could yield multiple wins.
9. Compare and contrast conventional industrial policy with green industrial policy.

10. Cite and explain the problems L/LMICs may confront in executing a green industrial policy.
11. What dilemma does automation pose for L/LMICs industrialization and why? How might they address this dilemma?

Notes

1   Recall that productivity is critical in determining the ability to export products from all sectors, something of crucial importance for L/LMICs. One measure of competitiveness is unit labor cost defined as average cost of labor per unit of output, or wage per hour over output (productivity) per hour.
2   https://unfccc.int/process-and-meetings/the-paris-agreement/what-is-the-paris-agreement, consulted 12/16/2018. By December, 2018, 184 of the 197 parties had ratified the Paris Agreement. The parties represent 193 countries that are UN members, two with UN observer status (Holy See and Palestine) and Taiwan and Kosovo.
3   Domestic politics in the United States influenced the terminology. Thus it was an "agreement" rather than say a "treaty" and voluntary "nationally determined contributions" rather than legally "binding commitments".
4   www.bbc.com/news/science-environment-46582025, consulted 12/16/2018.
5   The series on manufacturing value added as a percentage of GDP for China extended from 2004 to 2016.
6   Technology was traditionally understood to mean the application of scientific knowledge for practical purposes. Industry was much of the focus of attention of such applications. Since the onset of the "information revolution" technology is often understood to mean hardware, software or associated applications. Sections on technology in prestigious newspapers like the *New York Times* or influential podcasts, like the BBC's *Tech talk*, reinforce such a view. Alphabet, Facebook and Uber are accordingly referred to as technology firms. This new understanding has justification since IT enables most other businesses and this is very evident in the case of Tesla Inc. as it incorporates IT-enabled production, based on the application of scientific knowledge for practical purposes, in all sectors particularly industry.
7   Intermediate inputs are not directly represented in this model.
8   This result was demonstrated by Sraffa (1960). This debate about capital was conducted between economists based in Cambridge, Massachusetts and the critics based in Cambridge, United Kingdom in the 1950s and 1960s and it was therefore referred to as the "Cambridge Cambridge" or "Cambridge capital controversy" among other similar terms. Economists at Cambridge, Massachusetts were fully engaged and even conceded on theoretical points. For the most part, current generations of mainstream neoclassical economists are not exposed to and are therefore not aware of these theoretical issues. Even those who might be aware of them do not appear to regard them to be of much significance.
9   The production function was named after the Nobel Prize winning economist Wassily Leontief who proposed this production function.
10 However, since automation pressed on through the Great Depression (Bix, 2000), and more recently the Great Recession (Khan, 2018), this claim is not supported by the evidence.
11 Bix (2000) pointed out that "science is under the effective jurisdiction of business management" and not of labour and hence the neutrality of technology argument defies common sense. Refer to Hanlin and Kaplinski (2016) on a broader view of the various forces that induce innovations and technologies. These include market forces like factor prices and demand but also infrastructure, firm-level factors and regulations.
12 This is exacerbated by the fascination with the latest technology available from HICs which is capital intensive, a phenomenon referred to as the "engineering bias".

13 Since each product is uniquely mapped to a particular technology / technique, this is represented by a dot in the capital / labor space, rather than a continuous or segmented isoquant, and hence approximates the fixed coefficient production function.

14 Joseph Schumpeter's (referred to in Chapter 6) view of invention, innovation and creative destruction in capitalism is an alternative way of viewing the dynamics of technological change in HIC economics.

15 Since estimation approaches, factor inputs, production functions, sectors and time periods vary, it is difficult to get comparable estimates for even one country, so to get estimates that approximately apply across the board for L/LMICs is virtually impossible. For an example of the complexities involved, refer to Su et al. (2012) who estimated capital / labor substitution elasticities for China during the 1979–2006 "market period" to be less than one (.77).

16 Schumacher inspired many with his approach to poverty alleviation and the Intermediate Technology Development Group he co-founded in 1964 is still active, among other groups, in trying to realize a mission statement derived from his work. Refer to https:// practicalaction.org/history, consulted 12/22/2018. Intermediate technology has also been referred to as "appropriate technology", but the latter term is more flexible and suggests that what is appropriate depends on circumstances.

17 Here Say's Law of supply creating its own demand is implicitly invoked.

18 For textbook treatment, refer to Field and Field (2017) for environmental economics, Daly and Farley (2011) for ecological economics and Boyce (2002) for the political economy perspectives respectively.

19 www.adn.com/opinions/editorials/2018/10/02/5-things-you-might-not-know-about-the-alaska-permanent-fund-dividend/, consulted 12/29/2018.

20 Figure 14.4 is an analytical framework. In practice, much scientific and technological knowledge would be embedded in the MD and MAC curves respectively. Also, as in Figure 14.4a, the MAC may be segmented, representing a few available techniques, rather than smooth and continuous. Refer to Khan (2013) for an example of the policy relevance of a segmented MAC.

21 If the medical costs are borne by the persons who become ill, as is likely in LICs, they also bear the indirect cost. In HICs, medicine is often socialized so citizens bear the indirect costs as taxpayers. Even where private insurance is relied upon, premiums may go up and so the indirect costs are once again passed on more broadly.

22 Firms with market power would of course appropriate most of the benefit of being unregulated.

23 www.bbc.com/news/science-environment-14616161, consulted 12/27/2018.

24 The concern with population has resulted in critics referring to ecologists as neo-Malthusians. Paul Ehrlich and John Holdren developed the IPAT equation (Impact = Pop*Affluence*Technology) as an analytical tool for thinking about environmental damage. Impact (I) depends on Population (P), Affluence (A) (consumption) and Technology (T). Since population and consumption are mostly individual choices, technology would need to save the earth, http://theconversation.com/population-is-only-part-of-the-environmental-impact-equation-4009, consulted 12/29/2018. Since this equation was not theoretically derived, mainstream economists consider it arbitrary.

25 https://ocean.si.edu/ocean-life/invertebrates/ocean-acidification and www.whoi.edu/ science/B/people/kamaral/plasticsarticle.html, consulted 12/27/2018.

26 While many mainstream economists remain critical of industrial policies, some are more accepting of green industrial policy including, with qualifications, staff members of the World Bank. Refer to Hallegatte, Fay and Vogt-Schilb (2013).

27 Green industrial policies are often embedded in "green growth" strategies. Mathews (2012) reviews such strategies for South Korea and China. The subsectors and processes that green industrial policies have focused on to date include energy production and conservation, transportation, waste management, water conservation and temperature control.

28 The non-binding transfers from developed countries to developing countries are mentioned to amount to $100 billion per annum from 2020 to 2025 (Padilla, 2017, p. 32). Various articles of the agreement mention such support, particularly Article 9, https://unfccc.int/resource/docs/2015/cop21/eng/10a01.pdf, consulted 1/7/2019.

29 Other funds to tap into are the Clean Development Mechanisms, https://cdm.unfccc. int/, consulted 1/7/2019, and the Global Environment Facility, www.thegef.org/, consulted 1/7/2019. Even if what is on offer to a particular LIC is modest, it would make sense for them to compete for the funds to facilitate their green industrial policy.

30 Refer to Padilla (2017) for arguments and evidence regarding multiple wins from more broadly greening the economy.

31 Unfortunately that does not mean that the transition is straightforward. For obstacles such as the lock in of old technologies, lack of information, incentives and finance, even in HICs, refer to Kemp and Never (2017). Cosbey et al. (2017) point to problems of entrenched interests in dirty industries resisting subsidy cuts and pollution charges and of ensuring the vulnerable are protected when they are faced with job losses or subsidy cuts as dirty industries are phased out. Another problem has emerged from L/LMICs wanting to develop indigenous green technological capacity and requiring local content was a traditional mechanism for doing this until barred by the Trade Related Investment Measures Agreement (TRIMs) agreed to as part of the Uruguay Round of trade talks. Here the Paris Agreement comes into conflict with WTO rules (Mathews, 2017). Matthews proposed a GATT Article XX exemption for indigenous development of green technology on the grounds of public good (climate change mitigation) provision. Also refer to Cosbey (2017) on how WTO trade and investment law can constrain green industrial policy. For the most part, LICs can operate under the radar without being noticed as long as they do not become market beaters in an industry, as for example Bangladesh did with their textile and clothing industry.

32 www.epa.gov/superfund, consulted 1/6/2019.

33 Another possibility is to gradually institute self-reporting.

34 Even in HICs corporate social responsibility is mostly public relations (green-washing) and this practice, for what it is worth, is not widely in use in L/LMICs.

35 For examples of dividends from green industrial production from around the world, refer to Leuenberger and Mehdi (2017) and Altenberg and Assmann (2017). Singapore is also notable for its green industrial policy achievements framed as public private partnerships with the state in the driving seat (Chinying, 2005).

36 Automation refers to all forms of technological displacement of labor including with IT and digitization-induced machine learning or AI, robots and computerization (including with algorithms, software or machine-to-machine communications).

37 This forward-looking and hence speculative section draws on Khan (2018).

38 Contributors to this debate include Autor (2015), Brynjolfsson and Mcafee (2014), Ford (2015), Frey and Osborne (2017) and Susskind and Susskind (2015).

39 Bureau of Economic Analysis, United States, www.bea.gov/iTable/iTable. cfm?reqid=19&step=2#reqid=19&step=2&isuri=1&1921=survey, consulted 3/4/2019. Use interactive National Income and Product Account tables to explore international transactions.

40 Textiles to date were considered a highly labor-intensive industry and therefore among those that countries embarking on catch-up growth started with.

41 L/LMICs have embraced IT, as evident from the spread of cell phones (smart or otherwise). World Bank (2016) provided a detailed account of digital adoption in L/LMICs. About 70 percent of the lower 20 percent of the income quintile in developing countries owned a cell phone, more than had access to electricity or improved sanitation, and 40 percent of developing countries had broadband access with governments going increasing digital (financial, customs and income tax management). Digital identity cards that enable service provision and applications for business, marketing and finance (M-Pesa – digital payment system developed in Kenya) were spreading. Uber faced

local competition in China, India, Nigeria and Pakistan. The uptake of back office business process outsourcing to India, Philippines and more recently Kenya and other countries also reflects a diffusion of IT in the service sector. Spillover effects to other sectors are likely as the comfort level with IT in L/LMICs grows.

References

Altenberg, T. and C. Assmann. (eds.). 2017. *Green Industrial Policies, Concept, Policies and Country Experiences* (Nairobi / Bonn: United Nations Environment Program / German Development Institute (DIE))).

Autor, D. H. 2015. "Why are There Still so Many Jobs? the History and Future of Workplace Automation," *Journal of Economic Perspectives*, 29(3), 3–30.

Bix, A. S. 2000. *Inventing Ourselves Out of Jobs? America's Debate over Technological Unemployment, 1929-1981* (Baltimore: The John Hopkins University Press).

Boyce, J. K. 2002. *The Political Economy of the Environment* (Northhampton, MA: Edward Elgar).

Brynjolfsson, E. and E. Mcafee 2014. *The Second Machine Age: Work, Progress and Prosperity in a Time of Brilliant Technologies* (New York: W. W. Norton and Co.).

Chang, H.-J. 2011. "Hamlet without the Prince of Denmark: How Development Has Disappeared from Today's 'development' Discourse," in: S. R. Khan and J. Christensen (eds.), *Towards New Developmentalism: Market as Means Rather than Master* (New York: Routledge) 47-58.

Chang, J. and P. Huynh. 2016. "ASEAN in Transformation: The Future of Jobs at Risk of Automation," Bureau for Employers' Activities, Working Paper No 9 International Labour Office, Geneva.

Chinying, L. J. 2005. "Zero Landfill, Zero Waste: The Greening of Industry in Singapore," *International Journal of Environment and Sustainable Development*, 4(3), 331–351.

Cosbey, A. 2017. "Trade and Investment Law and Green Industrial Policy," in: T. Altenberg and C. Assmann (eds.), *Green Industrial Policies, Concept, Policies and Country Experiences* (Nairobi / Bonn: United Nations Environment Program / German Development Institute (DIE))) 134-149.

Cosbey, A., P. Wooders, R. Bridle and C. Casier 2017. "In with the Good, Out with the Bad: Phasing Out Polluting Sectors as Green Industrial Policy," in: T. Altenberg and C. Assmann (eds.), *Green Industrial Policies, Concept, Policies and Country Experiences* (Nairobi / Bonn: United Nations Environment Program / German Development Institute (DIE)) 69-86.

Daly, H. E. and J. Farley 2011. *Ecological Economics: Principles and Applications* 2nd ed. (Washington: Island Press).

Emmanuel, A. 1976. "The Multinational Corporation and Inequality of Development," *International Social Science Journal*, 38(4), 754–772.

Field, B. C. and M. K. Field 2017. *Environmental Economics: An Introduction* 7th ed. (Boston: McGraw Hill Irwin).

Ford, M. 2015. *Rise of the Robots: Technology and the Threat of a Jobless Future* (New York: Basic Books).

Frey, C. B. and M. A. Osborne 2017. "The Future of Employment: How Susceptible are Jobs to Computerisation?" *Technological Forecasting and Social Change*, 114(1), 254–280.

Hallegatte, S., M. Fay and A. Vogt-Schilb. 2013. Green Industrial Policies: When and How," Policy Research Working Paper No. WPS 6677, World Bank, Washington, DC.

Hanlin, R. and R. Kaplinski 2016. "South-South Trade in Capital Goods –The Market-Driven Diffusion," of Appropriate Technology," *European Journal of Development Research*, 28(3), 361–378.

Hardin, G. 1968. "The Tragedy of the Commons," *Science*, 162(3859), 1243–1248.

Janicke, M. 2012. "Green Growth: From a Growing Eco-industry to Economic Sustainability," *Energy Policy*, 48(1), 13–21.

Kemp, R. and B. Never 2017. "Green Transition, Industrial Policy, and Economic Development," *Oxford Review of Economic Policy*, 33(1), 66–84.

Khan, S. R. 2013. "Discontinuous Functions and Environmental Regulation," *International Journal of Ecology and Development"*, 26(3), 84–88.

Khan, S. R. 2018. "Reinventing Capitalism to Address Automation: Sharing Work to Secure Employment and Income," *Competition & Change*, 22(4), 343–362.

Leuenberger, H. and H. Mehdi 2017. "Sustainable Production: Can Industry Go Truly Green?" *Development*, 58(4), 492–499.

Mathews, J. A. 2012. "Green Growth strategies—Korean Initiatives," *Futures*, 44(8), 761–769.

Mathews, J. A. 2017. "Global Trade and Promotion of Cleantech Industry: A post-Paris Agenda," *Climate Policy*, 17(1), 102–110.

Ostrom, E. 1990. *Governing the Commons: The Evolution of Institutions for Collective Action* (Cambridge: Cambridge University Press).

Ostrum, E. 1997. "Investing in Capital, Institutions, and Incentives," in: C. Clague (ed.), *Institutions and Development: Growth and Governance in Less-Developed and Post-Socialist Countries* (Baltimore: Johns Hopkins University Press) 153-181.

Oxford Martin School, University of Oxford and Citi, "Technology at Work" v. 2.0, 2016, www.oxfordmartin.ox.ac.uk/downloads/reports/Citi_GPS_Technology_Work_2.pdf, consulted, 1/31, 2016.

Padilla, E. 2017. "What Can Developing Countries Gain from a Green Transformation?," in: T. Altenberg and C. Assmann (eds.), *Green Industrial Policies, Concept, Policies and Country Experiences* (Nairobi / Bonn: United Nations Environment Program / German Development Institute (DIE)) 22-37.

Rifkin, J. 1995. *The End of Work: The Decline of the Global Labor Force and the Dawn of the Post-Machine Era* (New York: G. P. Putnam's Sons).

Schumacher, E. F. 1974. *Small Is Beautiful: A Study of Economics as if People Mattered* (London: ABACUS).

Sraffa, P. 1960. *Production of Commodities by Means of Commodities: Prelude to a Critique of Economic Theory* (Cambridge: Cambridge University Press).

Stewart, F. 1972. "Choice of Technique in Developing Countries," *Journal of Developing Studies*, 9(1), 99–121.

Su, X., W. Zhou, K. Nakagami, H. Ren and H. Mu 2012. "Capital Stock-Labor-Energy Substitution and Production Efficiency Study for China," *Energy Economics*, 34(4), 1208–1213.

Sultan, R. M. 2013. "A Green Industry for Sustainable Trade Strategies: The Case of the Manufacturing Sector in Mauritius," *International Journal of Green Economics*, 7(2), 162–180.

Susskind, R. and D. Susskind 2015. *The Future of Professions: How Technology Will Transform the Work of Humans* (Oxford: Oxford University Press).

World Bank. 1999. *Greening Industry: New Roles for Communities, Markets, and Governments* (Oxford: Oxford University Press).

World Bank. 2016. *World Development Report 2016: Digital Dividends* (Washington, DC: World Bank).

PART IV
Conclusion

15

CATCH-UP GROWTH

Finding a trigger[1]

Introduction

I have taken the liberty of beginning this last chapter of this textbook on a personal note. I was born in a LIC and have lived much of my life in one. Thus it is not surprising that most of my professional life and thinking has been devoted to the issue of how nations may catch up with those that have progressed.[2] I got my first job as a research economist at the Pakistan Institute of Development Economics in 1973 and so this has been a long preoccupation. This issue of how nations might engage in catch-up growth is what I turn to in this chapter (also see Chapter 10). More precisely, to what might be possible triggers for sustained catch-up growth.

This chapter is different from the other chapters in this textbook in which I have drawn on widely accepted knowledge or documented debates. Instead, this chapter represents a synthesis of my understanding of those I consider leading thinkers in development economics. The focus is on a broad vision but not one likely to lend itself to persuasive modeling. While there is a suggestion at the end of the chapter on how one might engage in the associated empirics, the data and tools seem inadequate to engage in such exercises at such an aggregate level. Nonetheless, the classical economists and early developmentalists, who partly assumed the classical mantle, taught us that logical reasoning can go a long way in attaining understanding.

Catch-up growth is the economic process that L/LMICs undergo to reach the per capita income levels of M/HICs. Based on "the rule of 72" this happens if these countries can sustain per capita gross domestic product (PCGDP) growth rates of 7 percent or more for several decades. A 7 percent growth rate causes PCGDP to double in about ten years. As mentioned in Chapters 1 and 9, China has doubled and re-doubled its PCGDP several times since the late 1970s when its catch-up growth began, and it is now comfortably a UMIC. The focus in this chapter is on the many L/LMICs that have not sustained high enough economic growth rates to catch up in a meaningful way and hence are not considered part of the convergence club.[3]

This chapter starts by defining effective government since that is needed for policy implementation whatever the economic development approach adopted for catch-up growth. Assuming effective government, a hypothetical catch-up growth process is delineated next. While there are excellent case studies documenting the catch-up growth process, there is little attention given to triggers that might bring it about; addressing this issue is intended to be one contribution of this chapter.[4]

Effective government needs to rely on galvanized citizens willing to be part of the catch-up process, especially since short-term costs and tradeoffs are likely to be involved. The association between effective government and willing citizenry is dialectical and mutually reinforcing. However, there is a chicken and egg dilemma of which comes first and this chapter addresses the issue of breaking the Gordian knot to create a willing citizenry.

After explaining a process of catch-up growth, a case for effective government rather than "good government" is presented and it is argued that corruption is not necessarily a valid theory of underdevelopment. Next, by briefly summarizing the various approaches to economic development discussed in Part II of this textbook potential triggers for social galvanization or a willing citizenry for effective government are considered.

Examining past catch-up growth episodes in East Asia, it is argued that they may be explained by a synthesis of the basic human needs (equity/Chapter 4) and new developmentalist/neostructural approaches (Chapter 9). What is new in new developmentalism is briefly reviewed and how a broader view of equity can play into it discussed.[5]

To sum up, this chapter draws on the development economics literature covered in this textbook to synthesize contributions by way of a summary and conclusions for this textbook. It presents a conceptual synthesis describing the catch-up process, highlights the importance of identifying a trigger mechanism for catch-up growth, suggests a possible trigger and suggests that the emphasis on good governance is overrated and that a focus on effective government is a better avenue for implementation.

Defining effective government and describing a hypothetical catch-up growth process

Effective government is defined in this chapter as one in which the leadership is willing and able to deliver catch-up growth in conjunction with businesses and civil society. Thus effective government is not necessarily "good" government (see below) but one that can induce citizens to play their crucial part in a national project of catch-up growth.

While catch-up growth has mechanically been defined above in terms of GDP growth rates, the underlying process cannot be captured by a summary statistic. In the East Asian experience, the essence of the process was improving the quality of goods and services delivered by the public and private sectors. Pride of performance results in good public service, good social and physical infrastructure, and lower transactions costs, and these mechanisms in turn facilitate businesses.

Individual motivations are complex, but that notwithstanding, the catch-up growth process demonstrates that individual functioning in civil society, bureaucracies and businesses is allied with the national project of delivering quality. By delivering reasonably honestly on contracts and terms of service, individuals on average serve the broader purpose.

The profit motive is harnessed by government to have businesses deliver innovations and improved product quality to break into export markets. As explained in Chapter 9 and summarized below, in the East Asian episodes of catch-up growth (Japan, Korea, Taiwan), this profit motive was harnessed by the economic bureaucracy in a partnership with business for a broader purpose. The market mechanism was not deemed adequate, but rather used as a tool.

Since catch-up growth entails harnessing millions of public and private decisions for a common national purpose, it is an immensely complex and messy process. If the public at large is willing to trust the leadership's purpose, hurdles can be overcome along the way and mistakes rectified. Since initial conditions and political systems vary, one should expect different paths. However, the commonality so far is the dominant state role in guiding the catch-up growth process.

Predation as a barrier to catch-up growth

Lay persons are often convinced that corruption is *the* theory of underdevelopment. In addition, influential development economists also suggest predatory and corrupt leadership is to blame for underdevelopment. Acemoglu and Robinson (2012) offer perhaps the most influential narrative in the development economics literature on predation as a theory of underdevelopment.[6] They view elites as prone to predation and self-enrichment. However, economic development is premised on harnessing the productive potential of the bulk of the nation's population and hence requires inclusive political and economic institutions. Inclusive political institutions evolve historically via different mechanisms and processes in different countries. At critical junctures, small differences, possibly due to luck, can have lasting impacts due to cumulative causation (Myrdal, Chapter 7) and the onset of vicious and virtuous circles.

One can take issue with this thesis for four reasons. First, the evidence suggests that predation need not block catch-up growth (see below). Second, the evidence also suggests that institutions are often endogenous and therefore not a precondition for catch-up growth. Third, nations, like individuals, often create their own luck and need not await the long span of history. Fourth, predatory leadership has self-interest in promoting catch-up growth and need not necessarily be engaged in a zero-sum game as implied in the Acemoglu and Robinson thesis. However, consider for the moment how predation may block catch-up growth.

The notion is that predatory leadership will perceive their interests at odds with those of the governed and act accordingly in a rapacious fashion. In these circumstances, one would expect the governed to focus on surviving and getting ahead as best as they can. If catch-up growth is viewed as collective action in the broadest sense of the term, predatory leadership would clearly undermine it.

However, this scenario need not be the only one that plays out even when institutions are weak and the rule of law not widely prevalent. Currently, both the Chinese and Indian governments are making much of corruption. However, China has already attained the key phase of its catch-up growth, and corruption seems not to have been a constraint in its doing so. India has been clocking high economic growth rates for close to three decades. If it manages to sustain these, it will be yet another example of sustained catch-up growth. Like China, India's catch-up growth was initiated well before its anti-corruption drive.

A review of case studies of catch-up growth in Japan, Korea and Taiwan shows that local newspapers reported high levels of corruption. Chang (2006) has convincingly documented this point as has Rodrik (1994, pp. 42–47), who disputed that the East Asian economies conformed to "good governance" as identified by the World Bank (see below). Rodrik argued that all the good governance criteria were violated and that corruption was a noted problem in all these countries.

Even if the leadership is predatory, it has reasons for wanting catch-up growth. The motivation might be national pride or avoiding a loss of face from seeing others in the region prosper. It might be the legitimacy and political survival that delivering economic development brings. It might be the association of economic development with military strength for those in rough neighborhoods. Catch-up growth certainly enhances the global power and prestige of the leadership. Also, the leadership may be smart enough to realize that the larger the pie, the larger its slice even if it is predatory.

A leadership that is driven to make catch-up happen is among the key ingredients for a catch-up growth process, and the leadership's motivation for catch-up growth can be thought of as the source of "political will". While political will is often seen as a requirement for economic development, there is little consideration of how it is likely to emerge.

Some possible triggers

It is possible to draw on various approaches to economic development (Part II) to identify possible triggers. For example, economists have recently emphasized "good" governance, the flipside of the coin from predation. This has been most associated with North (2003, 2005), though it has been adopted by the World Bank and other organizations as the second wave of neoliberal reforms on good governance including protecting property rights, enforcing the rule of law, effectively implementing anti-corruption policies and achieving government accountability and transparency (Chapter 8).

Another key associated neoliberal recommendation is to get the business conditions right and the market will take care of the rest. This has been made operational by the World Bank by ranking countries on various indicators measuring how business friendly they are.

Basic human needs/human development are alternative approaches privileging different preconditions. The Basic Human Needs (BHN) approach (Chapter 4) was proposed by ILO (1977) and it was reincarnated in the early 1990s by Mahbub ul Haq with advice from Amartya Sen as the Sustainable Human Development approach (Anand and Sen, 1994). With the organizational backing of UNDP, the approach gained traction and the UNDP annually ranks countries based on Human Development Indicators. The BHN approach is broader since it includes asset redistribution.

Sen (1999) extended this approach conceptually and suggested that "expansion of freedom is both the primary end and principal means of development" (p. 11). Various rights, opportunities and entitlements expand freedoms, which have both an intrinsic and instrumental value. Several multi-dimensional indicators have been developed to measure the enhancement of capabilities (Alkire et al., 2011).

Chambers (1983) popularized grassroots participation as a method that complements the human development approach with participation making service delivery more effective (Chapter 4). Acemoglu and Robinson (2012) extended the concept of participation to the political realm and hence suggest political inclusion as a starting point. The Human Freedom Index is often used in empirical work pertaining to this issue.

Scholars have argued that the triggers identified above are endogenous to or byproducts of the development process such that as societies prosper, institutions strengthen, human development is enhanced, business conditions improve and political participation increases.

Chang (2011) made this argument for the human development approach. Khan (2012) provided evidence to suggest that "good governance", as defined by the World Bank, was not necessarily effective in triggering and sustaining economic growth and that the causality could run in the opposite direction. Yeung (2017) argued that East Asian political history demonstrated that political inclusion followed rather than preceded catch-up growth.

The extent to which any potential trigger is endogenous is a question of degree. Evidence from East Asia cited below suggests that equity has been effective as a trigger to initiate catch-up growth episodes and virtuous circles (equity as an initial condition reinforcing effective government and so on). Proposing equity as a possible trigger does not preclude others in different contexts: there is absolutely no reason why there needs to be a search for a unique trigger since more than one could operate at any given time to initiate catch-up growth.

Equity principles could be distilled from some theory of justice. Since inequality has received much attention, especially after the publication of Piketty (2014), inequality needs to be distinguished from inequity as explained in Chapter 4. Inequity is suggestive of unfairness as judged by some concept of justice. Inequality may be based on inequity (social exploitation) but it need not be. Also, promoting equality may result in inequity – taking people's due share for redistribution if the initial distribution was just. Further, in the context of catch-up growth it may blunt incentives. Based on the East Asian experience, equity here can be summarized as meeting basic human needs as an initial condition and this includes human development along with land reform.

To demonstrate that equity might be an effective trigger, we need to adopt a particular approach to economic development among several proffered in the literature. Of the various economic development approaches discussed in Part II, two are currently competing for attention.[7] One is the mainstream neoclassical approach that is focused on a set of neoliberal market-oriented structural adjustment reforms (Chapter 8). In a nutshell, the strategy can be summarized as fiscal austerity (euphemistically referred to as fiscal consolidation),[8] privatization, deregulation and liberalization. The alternative is the new developmentalist approach with industrial policy at the core (Chapter 9). In a nutshell, the strategy is to promote technological learning and movement up the value chain by diversifying the economy.

Implementing either set of reforms requires strong and competent leadership and a fully committed bureaucracy. This is so because there are winners and losers from reforms and foot dragging is inevitable. The success of neoliberal reforms is contested, partly because they accentuate social inequality.[9] It is proposed that the success of the East Asian growth episodes represents a synthesis of the basic human needs approach with new developmentalism, a distillation of the economic development lessons learnt from their catch-up growth episodes.

What is new about new developmentalism and how does equity play into it?

As discussed in Chapter 9, the conceptual underpinnings for new developmentalism are market failures and an important component of the policy agenda is industrial policy. Industrial policy is defined as the ability of the state to strategically influence targeted industries that exhibit increasing returns. More broadly, effective industrial policy requires supportive trade, technology, employment, financial, infrastructure, competition and institutional policies, and this is a core element of the new developmentalism approach just as structural adjustment was, and arguably still is, the core element of the neoliberal approach.

The trade theory underpinnings for this approach is that of dynamic comparative advantage of selected industries resulting *inter alia* from high potential for technological development, learning by doing, training, labor productivity, income elasticity, economies of scale, energy efficiency and externalities (including diffusing managerial and marketing skills). These features justify product selection and specialization even if static comparative advantage does not point in that direction (Chapter 9).

New developmentalism scholars have established the important role of the state, premised on a reasonably efficient economic bureaucracy, and this came as an important challenge to the neoliberal agenda of rolling back the state based on "government failure" (Chapter 8). They also pointed out that implementing the neoliberal program of structural adjustment is actually no less "government" intensive than implementing the industrial policy program. However, that notwithstanding, the commonality among new developmentalism scholars is that they are eclectic, pragmatic and supportive of institutional development with the market harnessed as a means.[10]

So far, one could argue that little has been said that really distinguishes developmentalism from new developmentalism. It would be difficult to make the case that the pioneering developmentalists were not pragmatic and eclectic. Indeed, Arthur Lewis (Chapter 6) was agnostic about whether industrialization should be engineered by public or private enterprises. In this regard, the vision of the developmentalists and new developmentalism is likely to be the same. Both argue for sustained economic development and believe that industrialization based on developing an indigenous technological capacity is likely to deliver that.

The vision underlying the developmentalist import substitution industrialization (ISI) program became conflated with the tools used by governments and hence dismissed. Thus, developmentalism in this critique is not associated with a vision but with heavy-handed intervention, centralized planning and corrupt and inefficient bureaucracy.

The body of scholarship referred to as new developmentalist represents a careful and painstaking empirical demonstration that the developmentalist vision has resulted in catch-up growth. While there were differences among countries, the commonality was coherent and nuanced and well-implemented industrial and support policies. This came as a challenge to the mainstream view espousing East Asian economic development success to free market policies. Establishing the alternative explanation has been a phenomenal breakthrough in the economic development literature. Even the World Bank, a bastion of neoliberalism, acknowledged this view of the success of high performing East and South East Asian countries, although it added undermining qualifications and did not acknowledge key authors responsible for the breakthrough.[11]

There are many additions and conceptual refinements that can be added to developmentalist thinking based on case studies of East and South East Asian countries that experienced catch-up growth. Drawing on the essence of the writings of the many scholars cited above, several notable additions stand out. First, incentives to businesses were premised on delivery and performance criteria were used to access success. Thus, for the incentives to be continued, firms had to show productivity growth, local content use, profit growth or all of the above by breaking into export markets. Further, if needed, the state had the ability to sanction non-delivery.

Second, the government ensured the discipline of internal market competition, even as firms were protected from premature external competition, by determining an optimal number of players in an industry (enough for competition but not so many that economies of scale would be diluted). Without such competitive discipline, import-substitution industrialization can degenerate into crony capitalism, as happened in many L/LMICs.

Third, to create the rents necessary to induce some activity, the state needed to systematically get the incentives right, which was not the same as getting the prices right. Finally, ISI and export promotion (EP) had a symbiotic association and were not alternative trade and industrialization strategies. Thus, different industries may have been going through different phases and so while some might have been in an ISI phase, others may have graduated to EP. ISI here was viewed as necessary to build the base for EP and in turn the latter provided resources, particularly foreign exchange, to further ISI in other industries, propelling the economy to move up the value chain and diversify.

New developmentalism represents as much a theory of effective government as of economic development policy. Since it has been distilled from what worked in terms of embodying eclectic and pragmatic industrial policies in a coordinated set of support policies, it would have been difficult for the early developmentalists to have conceived it.[12] Perhaps the early developmentalists should also not be faulted for the lack of environmental consciousness that is now much more widespread, but the onus of ensuring sustainable industrial development falls on new developmentalists (Chapter 14).

Finally, distinguishing new developmentalism from developmentalism distances it from what developmentalism has become associated with, as indicated earlier: the use of heavy-handed and incompetent bureaucracies, misguided policies that backfired, rent seeking, inefficiency and ineffectual support policies by planning agencies.

Also as explained above, the new developmentalist policies and practices identified above are meaningless if citizens are not motivated to strive for catch-up such that their individual and collective decisions sustain the process. For citizens to identify with a national project of catch-up growth, equity, more broadly defined, needs to play into the process.

If individuals feel that it is not simply their class position that ensures social mobility then hard work is more likely. If they feel that there is reasonable delivery of credit and quality social services, they are more likely to be willing and able to participate in a national project such as catch-up growth. If farmers own the land they cultivate, they work harder and are better shepherds of the resource (Chapter 13, endnote 29).

To harness bureaucratic will, which is crucial to initiating developmentalist catch-up growth, bureaucrats need to feel that merit counts in delivering for the public. If incentives are so structured and applied across the board, all bureaucracies (civic, economic, police, legal, military) are likely to work much harder for the public interest.

If businesses know that cultivating economic bureaucrats is not the path to quick rents, it is more likely that they will want to become the engine of catch-up growth. If they know that the performance criteria (in exchange for incentives) are fairly implemented, they are more likely to be willing to deliver on them. If they know that taxes are justly paid at the highest political levels in a transparent way, they are more likely to contribute to the fiscal effort to implement industrial policy. Again, harnessing business will is about equity.

If there is a fairer distribution of national resources, ethnicities and regions will be more willing to subsume their ethnic and regional consciousness into a national consciousness and make the nation more governable. Sectarian and communal conflicts are challenging, but they are likely to abate or be less intense in societies that provide more opportunities and where individuals are therefore less easy to manipulate.[13] Once catch-up growth delivers prosperity, history suggests that such conflicts continue to recede in importance as a byproduct of the prosperity.

Also, once the catch-up growth process is underway, equity reforms of the kind described above can sustain it in a virtuous circle. It is in this context that the Chinese and Indian governments' current concern with corruption and social safety nets is eminently sensible. Equity reforms are likely to be popular and therefore the political economy more straight-forward.

Evidence for equity as a trigger in the new developmentalist approach

Certainly, a democratic political regime may find equity reforms more consistent with its polity, but the evidence suggests that the more autocratic East Asian countries laid a very strong foundation of equity with land redistribution, social sector delivery and rapid wage growth. Johnson (1982, p. 11) referred to the "three sacred treasures" as fundamental to Japanese catch-up growth. These were traditional enterprise unions, seniority-based wages and lifetime employment, which created labor-capital harmony, innovation (including labor saving ones), a focus on quality control and product development timed to market demand.

Amsden (1989, p. 146, 189) pointed out that although unionization was repressed in Korea during its catch-up growth, worker's wages rose rapidly from a low base due to government pressure. This was done to attain a number of objectives including sharing wealth with labor for social stability, a larger market, inducing productivity and technology acquisition and an incentive/reward for workers to learn to operate this technology.

Wade (2004, p. 138) documented that Taiwanese catch-up growth was accompanied by an unusually equal distribution of income. Real earnings increased by 18 percent between 1960 and 1980, even while unionization was repressed. Also during roughly this period (1968 to 1982), unemployment was halved from the 4 percent at the beginning of the period. He also pointed out that in Taiwan, as in Korea, land reforms ended absentee ownership and transferred land to local smallholders (Chapter 13).

Post World War II, the "mainlanders" (from mainland China) instituted another round of land reforms, invested in irrigation and rural infrastructure, and provided smallholders with inputs at subsidized rates (Chapter 13). This enabled the state to turn the internal terms of trade against agriculture and also draw off the agricultural surplus with taxation (25 percent) for industrialization-based catch-up growth. The state also blocked other means of wealth accumulation such as land speculation (via the land reform) or financial activity that enhanced social inequality while undermining industrialization.

In challenging the World Bank's (1993) neoliberal view on what accounted for the growth of high-performing East Asian economies (HPEA), Rodrik (1994) argued it was the much greater equity in land ownership, income and access to education and human capital, as part of the initial conditions, which explain the superior economic growth performance of these countries.

While the focus in this chapter is on equity as a trigger mechanism, not surprisingly HPEA that demonstrated catch-up growth also had a high level of social equality by initially focusing on equity as evident from the case studies cited above. Social equality could facilitate political stability and hence sustain the catch-up growth process.[14]

While observers are struck by the institutional reforms China initiated in the late 1970s onward that are associated with catch-up growth, they neglect the foundation of equity that was laid earlier with investments in gender, social and human development.[15] Similarly India's democratic polity has been concerned with social safety nets including employment guarantees (Chapter 4), public food distribution and public health even while an LMIC.

While this emphasis on initiating catch-up growth and building it on a foundation of equity may seem like common sense, policy naturally needs to be based on evidence, notwithstanding the difficulty in accurately gathering it and attaining consensus.[16] As cited above, there is much evidence, based on the inductive method, to associate the initiation of catch-up growth with equity. Orthodox economists however prefer evidence to be based on the deductive method.

Cross-country econometrics often used to identify significant determinants in growth equations is problematic for several reasons but particularly because of the straitjacket of structural similarity imposed on countries when treated as a unit of observation. This is meaningless if the point of the exercise is to identify differences. Another problem is that the number of catch-up growth episodes post World War II are limited. There is no easy way to get control groups because countries can differ in so many ways and certainly randomization is not possible. Time series analysis is somewhat more promising as demonstrated by Rodrik (1994) but finding enough observations for effective time series analysis is challenging.

While the qualifications above need to be borne in mind, the *poverty and equity* data set of the World Bank may be a good place to start in constructing an equity index. Other indices that could be mined for this exercise include the Physical Quality of Life Index, Measurement of Economic Welfare Index, Human Development Index and Happiness Index.

Conclusion

While there are many excellent case studies of individual episodes of catch-up growth, the focus in this chapter is on identifying a trigger that initiates the process by creating a virtuous circle. It argues that the evidence contradicts the notion that corruption and predation are a valid theory of underdevelopment. By the same token, it argues that evidence does not support good governance, as conventionally defined, as either a critical trigger or implementing mechanism for economic development. It argues that the focus needs to be on effective government, rather than on good government, as a policy implementing mechanism.

The evidence also suggests that good government and other possible triggers like better business conditions and political inclusion are more likely to be endogenous to economic growth rather than factors that will initiate the catch-up process. Finally, the evidence suggests equity (human development with asset distribution) as an alternative trigger and though it too can be viewed as endogenous, this chapter argues that case studies and limited econometric evidence suggest it has been an effective trigger.

This chapter heuristically explains the East Asian catch-up growth process as a synthesis of the basic human needs (equity) and new developmentalist approaches. It explains what is new about new developmentalism and how equity can more broadly play into it. Finally, this chapter points to possible empirical problems in testing the hypothesis of equity as an effective trigger using the deductive method but nonetheless proposes the construction of an equity index to explore this issue further.

This chapter suggests that addressing equity rather than inequality should be the priority. This is easier said than done even if the political economy works in favor of a reforming government (winners far outnumber the losers). One problem is that policy advice, such as that forthcoming from donors or even the sustainable development goals (SDGs, Chapter 4), requires addressing an overwhelming number of objectives and lacks an overarching vision of economic development.

Instead, based on equity, prioritizing a few policies might yield catch-up growth. Based on material covered in this textbook, the policy recommendations are to prioritize green agriculture (accompanying land reform, Chapter 13), green industry (Chapter 14)[17] (since pollution makes competing difficult for poor children), quality education (access is not enough for equity) and quality health (with a focus on clean water) with gender equity as a cross-cutting issue. The overarching vision driving the structural reforms in this case would be diversifying the economy and moving up the value chain.

Questions and exercises

1. Explore why "good governance" as conventionally defined may not be a prerequisite for catch-up growth.
2. Cite and discuss some other possible triggers for catch-up growth and make a case for one that you think is most compelling.
3. Pick a trigger of your choice and an economic approach of your choice. Elaborate heuristically on how the trigger might induce catch-up growth.

Notes

1 The synthesis represented in this chapter was published as a research note in *The Pakistan Journal of Applied Economics*, 29(1), Summer 2019. It was presented in Fall 2017 in talks at the Lahore University of Management Sciences (LUMS) and the Sustainable Development Policy Institute, Islamabad (SDPI). Thanks are due to Sanval Naseem for inviting me to give the talks and to him and Kamran Asdar Ali of LUMS for facilitating the funding for the talks via the American Institute of Pakistan Studies. Many thanks are also due to Tariq Banuri, who was the discussant of the talk presented at the SDPI, for engaging with me at the seminar and afterwards.

2 Attempts to understand the progress of nations began with the classical economists like Adam Smith (Chapter 5).

3 The literature on convergence, and convergence and divergence clubs was sparked by Baumol (1986).

4 For the classics on catch-up growth, refer to Amsden (1989), Johnson (1982) and Wade (2004).

5 A narrower technique to what is proposed in this chapter is growth diagnostics (Hausmann and Rodrik, 2005; Hausmann, Klinger and Wagner, 2008).

6 Evans (1995) and Kohli (2004) present useful theories of the state relevant to catch-up growth and discuss the concept of a predatory state.

7 Also refer to Khan (2014) for a detailed exposition of alternative approaches to economic development.

8 Fiscal consolidation sounds less onerous than fiscal austerity or budget cutting that often targets social expenditures.

9 Refer to Chapter 8 for a critique of neoliberal reforms.

10 Wade (2004) captures this well with his term "governing the market".

11 For example, while discussing industrial policy, World Bank (2005) makes no reference to the relevant works of Alice Amsden, Ha-Joon Chang or Robert Wade.

12 Reinert (2007) and Chang (2002), however, argue that this lesson is self-evident from historical analysis of how the west industrialized.

13 Getting past deep-seated communal hatreds is one of the major challenges confronting India in its bid for sustained catch-up growth.

14 Alesina and Rodrik (1994) and Persson and Tabellini (1994) suggest that one channel through which social inequality might lead to lower growth is the demand for redistribution which may in turn negatively impact investment.

15 In fact a review of the early *Human Development Reports* show that all ex-socialist countries, including China, are notable in starting their transition to some form of a market economy with very high life expectancy, mean education and gender parity indicators relative to their per capita GDP in purchasing power parity $. Thus while equity is not a sufficient condition for take-off growth, since not all transition economies have prospered like China, it may be necessary for countries consciously embarking on a national catch-up growth project as described above.

16 This has been one of this textbook's recurrent theme.

17 The sectoral share of the service sector increases as countries prosper, but if the productive sectors are greened, this is reflected in the service sector to the extent that it draws on the productive sectors.

References

Acemoglu, D. and J. A. Robinson. 2012. *The Origins of Power, Prosperity, and Poverty: Why Nations Fail* (New York: Crown Business).

Alesina, A. and D. Rodrik. 1994. "Distributive Politics and Economic Growth," *Quarterly Journal of Economics*, 109(2), 465–490.

Alkire, S., J. M. Roche, M. E. Santos, and S. Seth. 2011. "Multidimensional poverty index 2011: Brief methodological note'. OPHI (Oxford Poverty and Human Development Initiative) Briefing 07, University of Oxford.

Amsden, A. H. 1989. *Asia's Next Giant* (New York: Oxford University Press).

Anand, S. and A. K. Sen. 1994. "Sustainable human development: Concepts and priorities," http://hdr.undp.org/en/content/sustainable-human-development-concepts-and-priorities, consulted 3/4/2019.

Baumol, W. J. 1986. "Productivity Growth, Convergence, and Welfare: What the Long-run Data Show," *American Economic Review*, 76(5), 1072–1085.

Chambers, R. 1983. *Rural Development: Putting the Last First* (Essex: Longman Scientific and Technical).

Chang, H-J. 2002. *Kicking Away the Ladder: Development Strategy in Historical Perspective.* (London: Anthem Press).

Chang, H.-J. 2006. *The East Asian Development Experience: The Miracle, the Crisis and the Future* (London/Penang: Zed Books/Third World Network).

Chang, H.-J. 2011. "Hamlet without the Prince of Denmark: How Development Has Disappeared from Today's "development Discourse," in: S. R. Khan and J. Christiansen. (eds.), *Market as Means Rather than Master: Towards New Developmentalism* (London: Routledge).

Evans, P. 1995. *Embedded Autonomy: States and Industrial Transformation* (Princeton, NJ: Princeton University Press).

Hausmann, R., B. Klinger, and R. Wagner, 2008, "Doing growth diagnostics in practice: A 'MINDBOOK'," Center for International Development Working Paper No. 177, Harvard University.

Hausmann, R. and D. Rodrik. 2005. "Self-discovery in a Development Strategy in El Salvador," *Journal of Latin America and Caribbean Economic Association*, 6(1), 43–101.

ILO (International Labor Organization). 1977. *Employment, Growth and Basic Needs: A One World Problem* (New York: Praeger).

Johnson, C. 1982. *MITI and the Japanese Miracle* (Stanford, CA: Stanford University Press).

Khan, M. H. 2012. "Beyond Good Governance: An Agenda for Developmental Governance," in: Jomo, K. S. and A. Chawdhury eds. *Is Good Governance Good for Development?* United Nations Series on Development (London and New York: Bloomsbury Academic). 151–182.

Khan, S. R. 2014. *A History of Development Economics Thought: Challenges and Counter-Challenges* (New York: Routledge).

Kohli, A. 2004. *State-Directed Development: Political Power and Industrialization in the Global Periphery* (Cambridge: Cambridge University Press).

North, D. C. 2003. The Role of institutions in Economic Development. Gunnar myrdal lecture. Occasional Paper No. 1. New York and Geneva: Economic Commission for Europe. United Nations.

North, D. C. 2005. *Understanding the Process of Economic Change* (Princeton, NJ: Princeton University Press).

Persson, T. and G. Tabellini. 1994. "Is Inequality Harmful for Growth?" *American Economic Review*, 84(3), 600–621.

Piketty, T. 2014. *Capital in the Twenty-First Century* (Cambridge, MA: Belknap Press of Harvard University Press).

Reinert, E. 2007. *How the Rich Countries Got Rich and Why Poor Countries Stay Poor.* (New York: Carroll and Graf).

Rodrik, D. 1994. ""King Kong Meets Godzilla: The World Bank and the East Asian Miracle," in: A. Fishlow. et al. (ed.), *Miracle or Design? Lessons from the East Asian Experience* (Washington, DC: Overseas Development Council) 13-33.

Sen, A. K. 1999. *Development as Freedom* (New York: Anchor Books).

Wade, R. 2004. *Governing the Market: Economic Theory and the Role of Government in East Asian Industrialization* (Princeton: New Jersey: Princeton University Press).

World Bank. 1993. *The East Asian Miracle*. (Oxford: Oxford University Press).

World Bank. 2005. *Economic Growth in the 1990s: Learning from a Decade of Reform* (Washington, DC: World Bank).

Yeung, H. W. 2017. "State-Led Development Reconsidered: The Political Economy of State Transformation in East Asia since the 1990s," *Cambridge Journal of Regions, Economy and Society*, 10(1), 83–98.

INDEX